Encyclopedia of
Women and Crime

Nicole Hahn Rafter, Editor-in-Chief

Oryx Press
2000

The rare Arabian Oryx is believed to have inspired the myth of the unicorn. This desert antelope became virtually extinct in the early 1960s. At that time, several groups of international conservationists arranged to have nine animals sent to the Phoenix Zoo to be the nucleus of a captive breeding herd. Today, the Oryx population is over 1,000, and over 500 have been returned to the Middle East.

© 2000 by Nicole Hahn Rafter
Published by The Oryx Press
4041 North Central at Indian School Road
Phoenix, Arizona 85012-3397
www.oryxpress.com

Published simultaneously in Canada
Printed and bound in the United States of America

∞ The paper used in this publication meets the minimum requirements of American National Standard for Information Science—Permanence of Paper for Printed Library Materials, ANSI Z39.48, 1984.

Library of Congress Cataloging-in-Publication Data

Encyclopedia of women and crime / Nicole Hahn Rafter, editor-in-chief.
    p. cm.
  Includes bibliographical references and index.
  ISBN 1-57356-214-9 (alk. paper)
    1. Female offenders—Dictionaries. 2. Women, Crimes against—Dictionaries. I. Rafter, Nicole Hahn, 1939–
  HV6046.E56 2000
  364'.082—dc21

                                                              00-033625

CONTENTS

CONTRIBUTORS

Elaine S. Abelson is an associate professor of history at the New School for Social Research in New York City.
SHOPLIFTING AND KLEPTOMANIA

Freda Adler is a professor of criminal justice at Rutgers University, Newark, New Jersey.
LIBERATION EXPLANATION OF CRIME

Celesta A. Albonetti is an associate professor at the University of Iowa.
CHARGING AND PLEA-BARGAINING

Christine M. Alder is an associate professor in the criminology department of the University of Melbourne, Australia.
FEMINIST CRIMINOLOGY, AUSTRALIA

Kristen Weede Alexander is a doctoral student in the department of human and community development at the University of California, Davis.
CHILD WITNESSES

Teresa Allen, a veteran newspaper journalist, now teaches crime reporting in the department of journalism at Boston University.
GRAHAM, BARBARA

Julie A. Allison is an associate professor of psychology at Pittsburg State University in Pittsburg, Kansas.
DATE RAPE

Geoffrey P. Alpert is a professor in the College of Criminal Justice at the University of South Carolina, in Columbia.
POLICE ASSIGNMENTS AND SPECIALIZATIONS

Alexander Alvarez is an associate professor of criminal justice at Northern Arizona University, in Flagstaff.
HOMICIDE VICTIMS

Tammy L. Anderson is a visiting assistant research professor at the Great Cities Institute and school of public health, University of Illinois at Chicago.
PROPERTY CRIME

Arlene Bowers Andrews is an associate professor of social work and director of the division of family policy, Institute for Families in Society, at the University of South Carolina, in Columbia.
VICTIM ADVOCACY

Joanne Ardovini-Brooker is an assistant professor at Sam Houston State University in Texas.
TERRORISM

Ronet D. Bachman is an associate professor in the department of sociology and criminal justice at the University of Delaware.
DOMESTIC VIOLENCE AGAINST WOMEN, EPIDEMIOLOGY OF

Eileen Baldry is a lecturer in the school of social work, University of New South Wales, Sydney, Australia.
WOMEN IN PRISON, AUSTRALIA

Anne M. Bartol is an associate professor of criminal justice at Castleton State College, in Castleton, Vermont.
WHITE-COLLAR CRIME

Larissa Behrendt has taught law at the University of New South Wales and is now a postdoctoral fellow at the Research School of Social Sciences, Australian National University.
ABORIGINAL WOMEN AND CRIME, AUSTRALIA

Joanne Belknap is an associate professor at the University of Colorado at Boulder.
COMMUNITY POLICING; GENDER DISCRIMINATION AND STATUS OFFENSES

Contributors

Raquel Kennedy Bergen is an assistant professor of sociology at St. Joseph's University, Philadelphia, Pennsylvania.
RAPE LAWS AND SPOUSAL EXEMPTIONS

Frances P. Bernat is an associate professor in administration of justice at Arizona State University West, in Phoenix.
VICTIM IMPACT STATEMENTS

Barbara E. Bloom is an assistant professor of administration of justice at San Jose State University.
PRISONER CHARACTERISTICS

William R. Blount is chair and a professor in the department of criminology, University of South Florida.
CHRONIC OFFENDERS

Rebecca L. Bordt is an assistant professor in the department of sociology at the University of Notre Dame.
GENDER DISCRIMINATION AND SENTENCING

Christine Boyle, LL.B., LL.M., is a professor in the faculty of law, University of British Columbia, Canada.
PRIVACY OF RECORDS IN SEXUAL ASSAULT TRIALS, CANADA

Tim Brennan teaches in the psychology department of the University of Colorado at Boulder.
PRISONER CLASSIFICATION

Dana M. Britton is an assistant professor in the sociology department at Kansas State University.
CORRECTIONS OFFICERS, HISTORY OF

Laure Weber Brooks is an instructor in the department of criminology and criminal justice at the University of Maryland.
POLICE RECRUITMENT AND SELECTION

Henry H. Brownstein is a professor and director of the graduate program in criminal justice at the University of Baltimore.
HOMICIDE, USA

Hoan N. Bui holds a law degree from the University of Saigon and is a doctoral student in criminal justice at Michigan State University.
PRISONER SUBCULTURES

Jane Caputi is a professor of women's studies at Florida Atlantic University in Boca Raton.
CALL GIRLS

Susan Caringella-MacDonald is a professor in the department of sociology and the women's studies program, Western Michigan University, in Kalamazoo.
RAPE LAW REFORM

Kerry Lynn Carrington is an associate professor and head of the critical social sciences/criminology department in the faculty of social inquiry, University of Western Sydney (Hawkesbury), Australia.
VICTIMIZATION AND MANLY RITUALS, AUSTRALIA

Taj C. Carson is an assistant professor of criminal justice at Northern Arizona University, in Flagstaff.
ORGANIZED CRIME (THE MAFIA)

Gray Cavender is a professor of justice studies at Arizona State University, in Tempe.
POLICEWOMEN ON TELEVISION

Meda Chesney-Lind is a professor of women's studies at the University of Hawaii at Manoa.
WOMEN IN PRISON, USA

Dorothy E. Chunn is a professor in the school of criminology and director of the Feminist Institute for Studies on Law and Society at Simon Fraser University, Burnaby, British Columbia.
FEMALE CRIME, CANADA; VICTIMIZATION PATTERNS, CANADA

Elizabeth Comack teaches feminist criminology and the sociology of law in the department of sociology at the University of Manitoba, Canada.
BATTERED WOMEN AND SELF-DEFENSE, CANADA

Sandy E. Cook is a senior lecturer in the school of law and legal studies at La Trobe University, Bundoora, Australia.
PROSTITUTION, FORCED

Barbara J. Costello is an assistant professor of sociology at Mississippi State University.
STRAIN EXPLANATION OF CRIME

Kimberly Coxe is a graduate student in dental medicine at the Medical University of South Carolina.
POLICE ASSIGNMENTS AND SPECIALIZATIONS

Susan Crimmins is director of the Institute on Trauma and Violence of National Development and Research Institutes, Inc., in New York City.
VIOLENT CRIME

Chris Cunneen is an associate professor at the Institute of Criminology, University of Sydney, Australia.
HOMICIDE, FILIPINO WOMEN IN AUSTRALIA AS VICTIMS OF

Richard Curtis is an associate professor of anthropology at the John Jay College of Criminal Justice in New York City.
DRUG DEALERS

Kathleen Daly is an associate professor in the school of criminology and criminal justice, Griffith University, Brisbane, Queensland, Australia.
RESTORATIVE JUSTICE

Mona J. E. Danner is an assistant professor of sociology and criminal justice at Old Dominion University, Norfolk, Virginia.
SEXISM AND RACISM IN CRIMINAL JUSTICE POLICY

Robert C. Davis is a senior research associate at the Vera Institute of Justice in New York City.
VICTIM SERVICES

William DeJong is director of the U.S. Department of Education's Higher Education Center for Alcohol and Other Drug Prevention.
MOTHERS AGAINST DRUNK DRIVING

Shari S. Diamond is a professor of law and psychology at Northwestern University.
JURY SELECTION

Jo Dixon is an associate professor in the department of sociology and Institute for Law and Society at New York University.
LEGAL PROFESSION, WOMEN'S CURRENT PARTICIPATION IN

R. Emerson Dobash is a professor in the department of social policy and social work and co-director of the Violence Research Centre, University of Manchester, England.
VICTIMIZATION, FEMINIST PERSPECTIVES ON

Russell P. Dobash is a professor in the department of social policy and social work and co-director of the Violence Research Centre at the University of Manchester, England.
VICTIMIZATION, FEMINIST PERSPECTIVES ON

L. Mara Dodge, a historian, teaches at Westfield State College in Westfield, Massachusetts.
REFORMATORY MOVEMENT

R. Gregory Dunaway is associate professor of sociology and director of the crime and justice research unit of the Social Science Research Center at Mississippi State University.
STRAIN EXPLANATION OF CRIME

Mary Eaton is vice-principal at St. Mary's College, Strawberry Hill, Twickenham, England.
FRY, ELIZABETH; WOMEN IN PRISON, ENGLAND AND WALES

Robert Elias is Davies Professor and chair of the politics department at the University of San Francisco.
VICTIMS, HISTORICAL TREATMENT OF

Lori A. Elis is an assistant professor of criminal justice at Florida Atlantic University at Boca Raton.
MEDICAL EXPLANATIONS OF DELINQUENCY; PSYCHOLOGICAL EXPLANATIONS OF DELINQUENCY

Liz M. Elliott is a lecturer in the school of criminology, Simon Fraser University, Burnaby, British Columbia.
PRISON REFORM, CANADA

Leslie Ellis is a graduate student and research assistant at the University of Illinois at Chicago and the American Bar Foundation.
JURY SELECTION

Sandra L. Enos is an assistant professor of sociology at Rhode Island College.
INCARCERATED MOTHERS

Edna Erez is professor and chairperson of the criminal justice studies department at Kent State University, Kent, Ohio.
VICTIMS IN COURT

Carol A. Facella is a professor in the department of criminal justice at Salem State College, Salem, Massachusetts.
AMERICAN SOCIETY OF CRIMINOLOGY; MADONNA/WHORE DICHOTOMY

Kenneth L. Faiver is the president and chief executive officer of Correctional Health Resources, Inc., Lansing, Michigan, and a former associate director of health care for the Michigan Department of Corrections.
PRISONS, HEALTH CARE IN

Amy S. Farrell is a doctoral candidate in Northeastern University's Law, Policy, and Society Program, in Boston.
POLICE ADMINISTRATORS AND SUPERVISORS; PRISONER RIGHTS

Kathleen J. Ferraro is an associate professor and associate director of the women's studies program at Arizona State University, in Tempe.
DOMESTIC VIOLENCE CASE PROCESSING

Marianne Fisher-Giorlando is a professor of criminal justice at Grambling State University, Grambling, Louisiana.
GENDER DISPARITIES IN PRISONS; IMPRISONMENT IN THE SOUTH, PRE–CIVIL WAR

Contributors

Gail Flint is chair of the department of criminal justice at West Virginia State College.
STALKING

Edith E. Flynn is a professor of criminal justice at Northeastern University, in Boston.
SOCIAL CONTROL OF WOMEN

Lisa Frohmann is an associate professor at the University of Illinois at Chicago.
RAPE VICTIMS, DISCREDITING OF

Patricia Gagné is an associate professor in the department of sociology at the University of Louisville, Kentucky.
SHELTER MOVEMENT

Shelley A. M. Gavigan, a lawyer and criminologist, is a member of the faculty of Osgoode Hall Law School and the graduate programme in women's studies at York University, Toronto, Canada.
CRIMINALIZATION OF PREGNANCY, CANADA

Loraine R. Gelsthorpe is university lecturer in criminology and director of the Ph.D. programme in criminology at the Institute of Criminology, University of Cambridge, England.
FEMALE CRIME, BRITAIN

Amanda George is a lawyer at the Brimbank Community Centre in Melbourne, Australia.
PRIVATE PRISONS, AUSTRALIA

Mary S. Gibson is professor of history at John Jay College of Criminal Justice and the graduate school of the City University of New York.
LOMBROSO, CESARE

Evelyn Gilbert holds a Ph.D. in criminology from Florida State University and is a criminal justice consultant in Daytona Beach, Florida.
ELDERLY VICTIMS; POLICE OFFICERS, WOMEN OF COLOR AS

Peggy C. Giordano is a professor in the department of sociology, Bowling Green State University, Bowling Green, Ohio.
DESISTANCE FROM CRIME

Gail S. Goodman is a professor in the psychology department, University of California, Davis.
CHILD WITNESSES

Lynne I. Goodstein is a professor in the crime, law and justice program and in women's studies at Pennsylvania State University.
CHIVALRY EXPLANATION OF FEMALE CRIME RATES

Nanette Graham has taught criminal justice at several universities and published in that area, and she is currently a medical student.
JUVENILE DELINQUENCY AND FAMILY CONFLICT

Judy Greenspan is chairperson of the HIV in Prison Committee of the group California Prison Focus, in San Francisco.
COMPASSIONATE RELEASE FROM PRISON

Carol Gregory is an adjunct instructor in criminal justice studies at Kent State University, Kent, Ohio.
VICTIMS IN COURT

Marie L. Griffin is an assistant professor at Arizona State University West, in Phoenix.
PRISON VIOLENCE

Randall P. Grometstein, a lawyer and teacher, is a doctoral student in Northeastern University's Law, Policy, and Society Program, Boston.
BORDEN, LIZZIE; PRISON TREATMENT PROGRAMS, LEGAL ISSUES IN

John R. Gruhl is a professor of political science at the University of Nebraska at Lincoln.
GENDER AND JUDICIAL DECISION-MAKING

Robin N. Haarr is an assistant professor at Arizona State University West, in Phoenix.
POLICE WORK AND STRESS

John Hagan is university professor in the faculty of law, University of Toronto.
POWER-CONTROL EXPLANATION OF CRIME

Donna C. Hale is a professor of criminal justice at Shippensburg University of Pennsylvania.
INTERNATIONAL ASSOCIATION OF WOMEN POLICE; KELLOR, FRANCES A.

Valerie P. Hans is a professor in the department of sociology and criminal justice at the University of Delaware.
LEGAL TRAINING

Mary Q. Hawkes is professor emerita of sociology, Rhode Island College.
MAHAN, EDNA

Esther Heffernan is a professor of sociology at Edgewood College, in Madison, Wisconsin.
ALDERSON PRISON; COFFIN, RHODA

Frances Heidensohn is professor of social policy at Goldsmiths College, University of London.
DEVIANCE AND REFORM, HISTORICAL OVERVIEW OF, BRITAIN; FEMINIST CRIMINOLOGY, BRITAIN; POLICE WORK, HISTORY OF WOMEN IN, BRITAIN

Denise C. Herz is an assistant professor in the department of criminal justice, University of Nebraska at Omaha.
GENDER DISCRIMINATION AND JUVENILE JUSTICE; JUVENILE DELINQUENCY AND RACE; STATUS OFFENSES

Cheryl D. Hicks is a Chancellor's Minority Postdoctoral Fellow in the Afro-American studies and research programs at the University of Illinois, Urbana-Champaign.
BEDFORD HILLS REFORMATORY

Kristi Holsinger is an assistant professor at the University of Missouri, Kansas City.
GENDER DISCRIMINATION AND STATUS OFFENSES

Julie Horney is Kayser Professor, University of Nebraska at Omaha.
PREMENSTRUAL SYNDROME

Kathy M. Howlett is an associate professor of English and co-director of cinema studies at Northeastern University, in Boston.
FICTIONAL CRIME VICTIMS

Jennifer C. Hunt is an associate professor of sociology at Montclair State University, New Jersey.
POLICE SUBCULTURE AND GENDER

Mic Hunter is a family therapist and an adjunct associate professor at St. Mary's University, Minneapolis.
SEXUAL ABUSE OF CHILDREN

Russ Immarigeon is a freelance writer and editor who specializes in prisons.
PRIVATE PRISONS, USA

G. Roger Jarjoura is an associate professor in the school of public and environmental affairs, Indiana University, Indianapolis.
JUVENILE DELINQUENCY AND SCHOOL INFLUENCES

Robert W. Jensen is an associate professor in the department of journalism, University of Texas at Austin.
PORNOGRAPHY

Jeffrie F. Jinian is a graduate student in public administration at the Florida Gulf Coast University, in Ft. Myers.
FEMALE CRIME, PATTERNS AND TRENDS IN, USA

John M. Johnson is a professor of justice studies and women's studies at Arizona State University, in Tempe.
PROTECTION ORDERS

W. T. Jordan is an assistant professor at Florida Gulf Coast University, in Ft. Myers.
BARKER, "MA"; FEMALE CRIME, PATTERNS AND TRENDS IN, USA

Nancy C. Jurik is a professor of justice studies at Arizona State University, in Tempe.
POLICEWOMEN ON TELEVISION

Renee Goldsmith Kasinsky is a professor in the department of criminal justice, University of Massachusetts, Lowell.
CHILD-SAVERS MOVEMENT

Glenda Kaufman Kantor, a sociologist and criminologist, works at the Family Violence Center, University of New Hampshire.
VICTIM-BLAMING AND VICTIM-PRECIPITATION, CONCEPT OF

Kathleen A. Kendall-Tackett is a research associate at the Family Violence Research Laboratory, University of New Hampshire.
INCEST VICTIMS

Wayne A. Kerstetter is an associate professor in the department of criminal justice, University of Illinois at Chicago.
SEXUAL ASSAULT CASE PROCESSING

Dorie Klein is a research scientist at the Public Health Institute in Berkeley, California.
FEMINIST CRIMINOLOGY, USA

Lloyd Klein is an adjunct associate professor at Medgar Evers College, City University of New York.
VICTIM NOTIFICATION

Barbara A. Koons teaches in the college of criminal justice, University of South Carolina.
PREJEAN, SISTER HELEN

Mary P. Koss is a professor of public health, family and community medicine, and psychiatry and psychology at the University of Arizona College of Medicine.
RAPE RATES, USA

Shirley Koster is a senior lecturer in sociology at Buckinghamshire Chilterns University College, England.
GREENHAM COMMON WOMEN'S PEACE CAMP

Jeremy Raymond Krum is enrolled in a joint master's degree and law program in the Department of Criminology and Criminal Justice at the University of Maryland.
POLICE RECRUITMENT AND SELECTION

Susan T. Krumholz is coordinator of the criminal justice option at the University of Massachusetts, Dartmouth.
DOMESTIC VIOLENCE, POLICE RESPONSES TO

Contributors

Kristen J. Kuehnle is an assistant professor in the department of criminal justice at Salem State College, Salem, Massachusetts.
CRIME FICTION WRITERS; POVERTY AND CRIME

Dany Lacombe is an associate professor in the department of sociology and anthropology and the school of criminology, Simon Fraser University, Burnaby, British Columbia.
FEMINIST CRIMINOLOGY, ORIGINS OF, IN CANADA

Kathy Laster is a senior lecturer in the school of law and legal studies, La Trobe University, Australia.
PUNISHMENT, AUSTRALIA

Kenneth E. Leonard is a senior scientist at the Research Institute on Addictions in Buffalo, New York.
VICTIM-FACILITATION THEORY

Renee S. Levant, a scholar and activist, has been an advocate for inner-city youth and worked in anti-racist and anti-imperialist movements.
DAVIS, ANGELA Y.

Walter E. Lippincott teaches in the department of criminology and criminal justice at Central Connecticut State University.
JUVENILE INSTITUTIONS

Joan Luxenburg is professor and chair, department of sociology and criminal justice, University of Central Oklahoma.
PROSTITUTION

Doris Layton MacKenzie is director of the Evaluation Research Group and professor in the department of criminology and criminal justice at the University of Maryland.
BOOT CAMPS

Esther I. Madriz teaches in the sociology department, University of San Francisco.
FEAR OF CRIME

Sue G. Mahan is an associate professor and criminal justice coordinator at the University of Central Florida, Daytona Beach.
CO-CORRECTIONAL PRISONS

Lisa Maher is a senior lecturer in the school of medical education, University of New South Wales, Sydney, Australia.
GANGS: CABRA GIRLS (AUSTRALIA)

Peter K. Manning is a professor of sociology and criminal justice at Michigan State University.
POLICING, MODELS OF

Susan E. Martin is program director at the National Institute on Alcohol Abuse and Alcoholism, National Institutes of Health.
POLICE FOUNDATION, THE; WOMEN PROFESSIONALS IN THE JUSTICE WORKPLACE

Karen J. Maschke holds a Ph.D. in political science from Johns Hopkins University and is currently completing a master's degree at the Center for Biomedical Ethics, Case Western Reserve University.
CRIMINALIZATION OF PREGNANCY, USA

Paul Mazerolle is an assistant professor in the division of criminal justice, University of Cincinnati.
JUVENILE DELINQUENCY, USA

Dorothy S. McClellan is a professor of criminal justice at Texas A&M University, Corpus Christi.
PRISON DISCIPLINE

Jill A. McCorkel is an assistant professor in the department of sociology, Northern Illinois University.
POLICE ATTITUDES TOWARD POLICE WORK

Candace McCoy is an associate professor of criminal justice at Rutgers University, Newark, New Jersey.
CHIVALRY EXPLANATION OF COURT OUTCOMES

M. Dyan McGuire, a lawyer, is currently pursuing a Ph.D. in criminology from the University of Missouri–St. Louis, where she is also an instructor.
JUDGES

Michelle L. Meloy is a doctoral student in the department of sociology and criminal justice, University of Delaware.
POLICE ORGANIZATIONS, MUNICIPAL AND STATE

Carrie J. Menkel-Meadow is a professor of law at Georgetown University.
LAWYERS AND GENDER DIFFERENCES

Robert Menzies is a professor in the school of criminology, Simon Fraser University, Burnaby, British Columbia.
FORENSIC PSYCHIATRY AND GENDER, CANADA

Alida V. Merlo is a professor in the criminology department at Indiana University of Pennsylvania and in 2000 was president of the Academy of Criminal Justice Sciences.
HIV AND AIDS IN PRISON

Sylvia I. Mignon is an assistant professor of criminal justice at University of Massachusetts, Boston.
DOMESTIC VIOLENCE BY WOMEN

Amy C. Miller is a graduate student at the department of sociology, University of Minnesota, Minneapolis.
PRISON REFORM, USA

Brenda Miller, professor and director of the Center for Urban Social Work Practices, University of Buffalo, worked on this encyclopedia as an associate editor.

Michelle Hughes Miller is an assistant professor in the department of criminal justice, University of Nebraska at Omaha.
CRIME VICTIMS AND DEFINITIONS OF JUSTICE

Susan L. Miller is an associate professor in the department of sociology and criminal justice, University of Delaware.
GENDER AND POLICING; POLICE OFFICERS, LESBIAN

Merry Morash is director and professor, school of criminal justice, Michigan State University.
PUNISHING WOMEN OFFENDERS; WOMEN'S PRISON ADMINISTRATION, CONTEMPORARY

Phoebe A. Morgan is an assistant professor of criminal justice at Northern Arizona University, in Flagstaff.
SEXUAL HARASSMENT

Joann B. Morton is an associate professor at the college of criminal justice, University of South Carolina.
FARNHAM, ELIZA W.

Martha A. Myers is a professor of sociology at the University of Georgia.
FEMALE CRIME, HISTORY OF, EUROPE

Carolyn Uihlein Nilles is an instructor in the sociology department of Marshall University, in West Virginia.
MASCULINITY EXPLANATION OF CRIME

Maureen A. Norton-Hawk is an assistant professor at Suffolk University, Boston.
FRAMINGHAM EIGHT

Dana M. Nurge is an assistant professor in the college of criminal justice at Northeastern University, in Boston.
JUVENILE DELINQUENCY AND GANGS, USA

Robbin S. Ogle is an assistant professor at the University of Nebraska at Omaha.
BATTERED WOMEN AND SELF-DEFENSE, USA

Barbara Owen is a professor of criminology at California State University–Fresno.
PRISON SECURITY; PRISON TREATMENT PROGRAMS, RATIONALES FOR AND PROBLEMS WITH; RACE RELATIONS IN PRISON

Robert Nash Parker is director of the Presley Center for Crime and Justice Studies and professor of sociology at the University of California, Riverside.
LIFESTYLE AND VICTIMIZATION

Kim Pate is executive director of the Canadian Association of Elizabeth Fry Societies, in Ottawa, Ontario.
WOMEN IN PRISON, CANADA

April Pattavina received her doctoral degree from Northeastern University's Law, Policy, and Society Program, in Boston, and worked on this encyclopedia as an associate editor.

Susan E. Pease is chair of the department of criminology and criminal justice at Central Connecticut State University.
DRUG AND ALCOHOL TREATMENT FOR PRISONERS; DRUG OFFENSES

Barbara Perry is an assistant professor in the department of criminal justice, Northern Arizona University, in Flagstaff.
PARKER, BONNIE

Rebecca D. Petersen is an assistant professor of criminal justice at the University of Texas–San Antonio.
PRISONS, TREATMENT PROGRAMS IN

Carolyn Petrosino is an assistant professor of criminal justice, University of Massachusetts at Lowell.
PROBATION AND PAROLE

Oliver Charles Phillips is a lecturer in the department of law, Keele University.
HINDLEY, MYRA

Sharon Pickering is a lecturer in justice studies at Charles Sturt University, New South Wales, Australia.
FEMALE CRIME, AUSTRALIA

Jennifer L. Pierce is an associate professor of American studies and sociology at the University of Minnesota.
PARALEGALS

Diane L. Pike is a professor of sociology at Augsburg College, in Minneapolis.
POLICE ACADEMY TRAINING

Nicole Leeper Piquero is a doctoral student in the department of criminology and criminal justice at the University of Maryland.
SOCIAL PROCESS EXPLANATIONS OF DELINQUENCY; SOCIAL STRUCTURAL EXPLANATIONS OF DELINQUENCY

Contributors

Deborah Marie Plechner is a doctoral student in the department of sociology, University of California, Riverside.
LIFESTYLE AND VICTIMIZATION

Kenneth Polk is a professor in the department of criminology, University of Melbourne, Australia.
HOMICIDE VICTIMS AND OFFENDERS, AUSTRALIA; VIOLENT CRIME VICTIMIZATIONS, AUSTRALIA

Joycelyn M. Pollock is a professor of criminal justice at Southwest Texas State University.
LEGAL PROFESSION, HISTORY OF WOMEN IN

Barbara Raffel Price is professor emerita, John Jay College of Criminal Justice, City University of New York.
OFFENDERS

Martin E. Price is director of the Victim-Offender Reconciliation Program Information and Resource Center in Camas, Washington.
MEDIATION PROGRAMS

Nicole Hahn Rafter, the editor in chief of this encyclopedia, is a professor in Northeastern University's Law, Policy, and Society Program.

Elizabeth Rapaport is a professor of law at the University of New Mexico School of Law.
DEATH PENALTY

Christine E. Rasche teaches criminology and directs the graduate program in criminal justice and sociology at the University of North Florida.
WOMEN'S PRISON ADMINISTRATION, HISTORICAL

Brian A. Reaves is chief of the law enforcement statistics unit at the Bureau of Justice Statistics, U.S. Department of Justice.
POLICE ORGANIZATIONS, FEDERAL, STATISTICS ON

Marge Reitsma-Street teaches in the multidisciplinary masters program in policy and practice at the University of Victoria, Canada.
JUVENILE DELINQUENCY, CANADA

Claire M. Renzetti is a professor and chair of the department of sociology, St. Joseph's University, Philadelphia.
LESBIAN PARTNER BATTERING; VICTIMIZATION PATTERNS, USA

Aviva M. Rich-Shea is a doctoral student at Northeastern University's Law, Policy, and Society Program, in Boston.
LEKKERKERKER, EUGENIA; ROSENBERG, ETHEL

Amanda L. Robinson is a doctoral student in the interdisciplinary social science degree program at Michigan State University.
POLICING, MODELS OF

Paul Rock is professor of social institutions at the London School of Economics.
HOLLOWAY PRISON

Rita Rupal is a policy advisor on women's issues to local governments in the London area.
SOUTHALL BLACK SISTERS

Roxann Ryan is assistant attorney general in the Iowa Department of Justice.
O'CONNOR, SANDRA DAY; RENO, JANET

Judith Anne Ryder is senior project director at the Institute on Trauma and Violence in New York City and a doctoral student in criminal justice at John Jay College, City University of New York.
WOMEN'S PRISONS, HISTORY OF

Inger Sagatun-Edwards is professor and chair, administration of justice department, San Jose State University.
ABORTION

Susan Kiss Sarnoff is an assistant professor in the department of social work, Ohio University, in Athens, Ohio.
VICTIM COMPENSATION

Kathryn E. Scarborough is an associate professor in the department of police studies at Eastern Kentucky University.
POLICE WORK AND CIVIL RIGHTS LAWS

Lynn Hecht Schafran is director of the National Judicial Education Program to Promote Equality for Women and Men in the Courts, in New York City.
GENDER BIAS TASK FORCES

Frederika E. Schmitt is an assistant professor of sociology/anthropology at Millersville University, Millersville, Pennsylvania.
LEGAL TRAINING

Sharon Schnelle is a doctoral student in criminal justice at the University of Cincinnati.
JUVENILE DELINQUENCY AND AGE

Pamela J. Schram is an assistant professor at California State University, San Bernardino.
SEXUAL ABUSE OF PRISONERS

Dorothy Moses Schulz is an associate professor at John Jay College of Criminal Justice, City University of New York.
POLICE WORK, HISTORY OF WOMEN IN, USA

Miriam D. Sealock is an assistant professor of criminal justice at Xavier University in Cincinnati, Ohio.
JUVENILE DELINQUENCY AND DRUG AND ALCOHOL ABUSE; JUVENILE DELINQUENCY AND PEER INFLUENCES

Patricia Searles is a professor of sociology and women's studies at the University of Wisconsin–Whitewater.
RAPE SHIELD LAWS, USA

Dale K. Sechrest is a professor in the criminal justice department of California State University, San Bernardino.
PRISON ACCREDITATION

Susan F. Sharp is an assistant professor in the department of sociology, University of Oklahoma.
ALCOHOL ABUSE AND ALCOHOLISM

Elizabeth A. Sheehy teaches on the faculty of law, University of Ottawa.
RAPE SHIELD LAWS, CANADA

Randall G. Shelden is a professor of criminal justice at the University of Nevada–Las Vegas.
JUVENILE INSTITUTIONS, HISTORY OF

Ira J. Silverman is a professor in the department of criminology, University of South Florida.
CHRONIC OFFENDERS

Marisa Silvestri is a lecturer in criminology at Buckinghamshire Chilterns University College, England.
SUFFRAGETTES

Candace A. Skrapec is a psychologist and criminologist on the faculty at California State University, Fresno.
SERIAL KILLERS

Beverly A. Smith is a professor in the department of criminal justice sciences, Illinois State University, in Normal, Illinois.
FEMALE CRIME, HISTORY OF, USA

Jinney S. Smith is a Ph.D. candidate in the department of political science, Northwestern University.
GLUECK, ELEANOR

Sherri Smith, an assistant professor at Florida Gulf Coast University, served as an associate editor for this encyclopedia.

Cassia C. Spohn is a professor in the department of criminal justice, University of Nebraska at Omaha.
CASE PROCESSING AND GENDER; SENTENCING, DRUG OFFENDERS

Elizabeth A. Stanko is professor of criminology, department of social and political science, Royal Holloway, University of London, and director of the Economic and Social Research Council's Programme on Violence.
VICTIMIZATION PATTERNS, BRITAIN

Debra L. Stanley is an associate professor in the department of sociology and criminal justice at Central Connecticut State University.
CRIME VICTIMIZATION

Catherine Stayton is a research associate at the Vera Institute of Justice in New York City.
VICTIM SERVICES

Mary K. Stohr is an associate professor in the department of criminal justice at Boise State University.
JAILS, ISSUES FOR WOMEN IN; JAILS, WOMEN IN

Sandra S. Stone is an assistant professor in the department of sociology, anthropology, and criminology at the State University of West Georgia.
CHILD ABUSE BY WOMEN

Victor L. Streib is dean of the college of law at Ohio Northern University, Ada, Ohio.
DEATH ROW

Julie Stubbs is an associate professor at the Institute of Criminology, University of Sydney, Australia.
BATTERED WOMEN AND SELF-DEFENSE, AUSTRALIA; HOMICIDE, FILIPINO WOMEN IN AUSTRALIA AS VICTIMS OF

Anne Sullivan is an assistant professor of criminal justice at Salem State College, Salem, Massachusetts.
CONTROL EXPLANATIONS OF CRIME; FEMALE CRIME, EXPLANATIONS OF

Becky L. Tatum is an assistant professor of criminal justice at Southern University, at New Orleans.
HARRIS, JEAN

Renee Taylor, a member of the Namgis First Nation (Kwakwak'wakw) at Alert Bay, British Columbia, is supervisor of the University of British Columbia faculty of law's First Nations Clinical Law Program.
ABORIGINAL WOMEN AND CRIME, CANADA

Stephen G. Tibbetts is an assistant professor in the department of criminal justice and criminology, East Tennessee State University, Johnson City, Tennessee.
JUVENILE DELINQUENCY AND INTELLIGENCE

Contributors

Anthony P. Travisono is executive director emeritus of the American Correctional Association.
<small>AMERICAN CORRECTIONAL ASSOCIATION</small>

Ruth Ann Triplett is an associate professor in the department of sociology and criminal justice, Old Dominion University, Norfolk, Virginia.
<small>JUVENILE DELINQUENCY AND SOCIAL CLASS; LABELING EXPLANATIONS OF FEMALE CRIME</small>

Austin T. Turk is a professor of sociology at University of California, Riverside.
<small>POLITICAL OFFENDERS</small>

Marjorie M. Van Ochten, J.D., is an administrator in the Michigan Department of Corrections.
<small>PRISONER LITIGATION</small>

Anthony Walsh is a professor at Boise State University.
<small>RACISM IN RAPE CASE OUTCOMES</small>

Neil Websdale is an associate professor of criminal justice at Northern Arizona University, in Flagstaff.
<small>SERIAL KILLERS, VICTIMS OF</small>

Michael Welch is an associate professor at Rutgers University, in Hoboken.
<small>ADULTERY</small>

Janine I. White is a senior research specialist at the University of Arizona College of Medicine.
<small>RAPE RATES, USA</small>

Cathy Spatz Widom is a professor of criminal justice and psychology at the State University of New York at Albany.
<small>VICTIMIZATION, REPEAT</small>

Ania Wilczynski is a research consultant at Keys Young, in Sydney, Australia.
<small>INFANTICIDE</small>

Nanci Koser Wilson is a professor of criminology in the department of criminology at Indiana University of Pennsylvania.
<small>WITCHES</small>

Nancy A. Wonders is an associate professor of criminal justice at Northern Arizona University, in Flagstaff.
<small>SENTENCING GUIDELINES</small>

Joy Wundersitz is director of Office of Crime Statistics, South Australian Attorney General's Department.
<small>JUVENILE DELINQUENCY, AUSTRALIA</small>

Mary Ann Zager is an assistant professor in the division of criminal justice, Florida Gulf Coast University.
<small>GENDER AND CRIME</small>

Linda L. Zupan is a professor of criminal justice at Northern Michigan University, in Marquette.
<small>WOMEN CORRECTIONS OFFICERS IN MEN'S PRISONS</small>

ALPHABETICAL LIST OF ENTRIES

Entry titles preceded by bullets (•) are overview essays written by the editors. Titles preceded by asterisks (∗) are cross-references to related entries.

Alphabetical List of Entries

TOPIC FINDER

Entry titles preceded by bullets (•) are overview essays written by the editors.

International entries appear twice, first in the criminological category to which they belong and second in their national grouping.

Crime: Offenders, Offenses, and Theories of Offending

•Gender and Crime

Crimes by Women

Abortion
Adultery
Alcohol Abuse and Alcoholism
Child Abuse by Women
Domestic Violence by Women
Drug Offenses
Female Crime, Australia
Female Crime, Britain
Female Crime, Canada
Female Crime, History of, Europe
Female Crime, History of, USA
Female Crime, Patterns and Trends in, USA
Greenham Common Women's Peace Camp
Homicide, USA
Homicide Victims and Offenders, Australia
Infanticide
Organized Crime (The Mafia)
Property Crime
Prostitution
Shoplifting and Kleptomania
Terrorism
Violent Crime
White Collar Crime

Theorists and Theories of Adult Female Crime

American Society of Criminology
Chivalry Explanation of Female Crime Rates
Control Explanations of Crime
Crime Fiction Writers
•Female Crime, Explanations of
Feminist Criminology, Australia
Feminist Criminology, Britain
Feminist Criminology, Origins of, in Canada
Feminist Criminology, USA
Glueck, Eleanor T.
Kellor, Frances A.
Labeling Explanations of Female Crime
Liberation Explanation of Crime
Lombroso, Cesare
Madonna/Whore Dichotomy
Masculinity Explanation of Crime
Poverty and Crime
Power-Control Explanation of Crime
Premenstrual Syndrome
Strain Explanation of Crime

Juvenile Delinquents and Delinquency

Desistance from Crime
Gangs: Cabra Girls (Australia)
Juvenile Delinquency and Age
Juvenile Delinquency and Drug and Alcohol Abuse
Juvenile Delinquency and Family Conflict
Juvenile Delinquency and Gangs, USA

LIST OF FIGURES AND TABLES

List of Figures and Tables

PREFACE

The *Encyclopedia of Women and Crime* is the first comprehensive reference book on the topic of women and crime. Covering women as offenders, victims, criminologists, criminal lawyers, reformers, and workers in the criminal justice system, it brings together—in one volume—information developed in widely separated places and published in diverse sources since the late 1960s.

The *Encyclopedia* consists of 240 alphabetically arranged entries from more than 200 contributors—including the field's best-known representatives, as well as the younger activists and scholars who are turning work on women and crime in new directions. Tables, graphs, and pictorial illustrations appear throughout to augment the text. Each entry is accompanied by recommendations for further reading, and an extensive resources list at the end of the volume points the way to a wealth of additional information.

Three decades ago, it would have been difficult even to conceive of a book like this. For most of the twentieth century, criminology was an androcentric field, focused almost exclusively on the crimes and punishments of male offenders. This focus was inevitable, given that the majority of offenders were male, that females formed only small proportions of jail and prison populations, and that the overwhelming majority of criminologists, too, were male. But about 30 years ago, three feminist criminologists (Marie-Andrée Bertrand, Frances Heidensohn, and Dorie Klein), working independently in three different countries (Canada, Britain, and the United States, respectively), began to question criminology's androcentrism, arguing that because gender plays such a large role in determining rates of offending, criminologists should include females in studies of crime causation and punishment (Bertrand 1967; Heidensohn 1968; Klein 1973). Researchers around the globe heeded this argument, and since the early 1970s, the field of women and crime has grown exponentially.

The study of women and crime was brought to maturity by an international conference titled Women, Law, and Social Control, which was held in Québec in 1991 (Bertrand, Daly, and Klein 1992). This conference brought together scholars and activists from around the world, cross-fertilizing and globalizing the study of women and crime. The conference organizers—Kathleen Daly and Dorie Klein of the United States and Marie-Andrée Bertrand of Canada—deliberately sited the conference outside of the United States to signal their commitment to multiculturalism and their determination to prevent U.S. voices from dominating discussions. Since 1991, work on women and crime has been furthered by other conferences; by the journal *Women and Criminal Justice;* and by research reports, policy statements, and hundreds of scholarly books and articles.

While there has been a great deal of publishing activity in the subject area—including monographs, textbooks, anthologies, and articles in leading criminology, history, law, psychology, and sociology journals—until this *Encyclopedia*, no one had pulled the material together and made it available to general readers. The central goal of the *Encyclopedia of Women and Crime* is to gather these research findings into one place and to present them alongside information gained from the grassroots activists who have also contributed strongly to our understanding of women and crime. By using straightforward, jargon-free prose, the *Encyclopedia* makes the wealth of material on women, gender, and crime accessible to a broad audience, including agency personnel, criminal justice officials, college and university students and teachers, high school and public library users, legal researchers, and policymakers.

The Scope of "Women and Crime"

The conceptual territory covered by the term "women and crime" has steadily expanded. Contemporary studies in this area began modestly in the 1960s, with suggestions that we might learn more about the causes of crime if we looked at groups with low rates of offending (such as women), as well as at high-rate groups (such as men). But it was not long before the study of women and crime assumed validity in its own right, particularly in the work of women criminologists who believed that female defendants, judges, and prisoners were just as worthy of attention as men in these categories.

From the start, feminist criminologists such as Dorie Klein (1973) also closely examined what male criminologists had to say about female offenders and victims, demonstrating that these texts were often more informed by prejudice against women than by the objectivity called for by social science. Even when male criminologists and penologists totally ignored women, their silence seemed to women colleagues to perpetuate inequalities and to distort the realities of crime and punishment. Such silence—as well as outright victim-blaming and misstatements based on male-only samples—became part of the material analyzed in studies of women and crime.

Moreover, what had begun, in part, as a study of gender differences in offending flowed into the study of ways in which gender influences every aspect of criminal justice—not only crime rates and the types of crime in which men and women specialize, but also the ways judges react to male and female defendants and even to male and female attorneys. Scholars are still struggling to define and differentiate "sex" and "gender" (Daly 1997; Hawkesworth 1997), a fact which some critics cite in an effort to discredit the whole enterprise. The study of gender is relatively new, however; research that purports to ignore it actually reinforces inequalities by assuming that everyone who counts is male. Thus it seems wise to keep definitions of sex and gender open until more is known about how they structure our worlds and shape our thinking. In any case, users of this *Encyclopedia* will find that it deals with not only women and crime but also with ways in which gender permeates criminal justice, raising profound issues about the meaning of "justice" itself.

Subject Themes

The *Encyclopedia of Women and Crime* was developed around four themes, each encompassing a particular body of information on women and crime and related issues:

- crime: offenders, offenses, and theories of offending
- victims and victimology
- policing, courts, and case processing
- punishment and treatment

Because the alphabetical arrangement of the *Encyclopedia* disperses conceptually related entries throughout the book, a Topic Finder is provided on pages xix–xxii to show the entries included in each of the four thematic groups.

Crime: Offenders, Offenses, and Theories of Offending

The first of the *Encyclopedia*'s themes is crime itself, including types of crime committed by women and girls, such as drug offenses, infanticide, prostitution, and serial killing. It also includes the major theories that have been put forth over time to explain female offending. Other entries on this theme deal with facets of juvenile delinquency and with well-known offenders who have made an imprint on popular culture, such as "Ma" Barker, Lizzie Borden, and Bonnie Parker.

Victims and Victimology

A second theme encompasses crime victims, explanations of victimization, and fear of crime. Entries discuss crimes that tend to have female victims, including domestic violence, rape, and stalking, as well as the effects on females of more general offenses such as homicide. Some entries outline the theories that have been used over time to explain victimization. Others deal with specific categories of victims and victim-events, such as elderly victims and lesbian partner battering; with attempts to curtail victimization such as protection orders and victim notification rules; and with efforts to help victims such as mediation programs and the shelter movement.

Policing, Courts, and Case Processing

The third major theme is policing, the courts, and criminal case processing, insofar as these relate to gender and criminal justice. Community policing, police responses to domestic violence, police work and stress, and the history of women in policing are among the topics included. Entries also deal with specific case-processing issues, such as racism in rape case outcomes and gender discrimination in the juvenile justice system, and with theoretical issues such as the "chivalry" explanation of court outcomes. In sum, this thematic group involves women as defendants and professionals in the arenas of policing and the courts.

Punishment and Treatment

The fourth theme is concerned with the consequences for women of violating the criminal law, and with the work of women who administer punishment and treatment. Entries deal with prisons, particularly well-known prisoners and prison administrators, and problems such as HIV and AIDS that appear with special intensity in penal institutions. Other prison-related entries discuss the history of juvenile and adult institutions for females, alternatives to prison such as boot camps and probation, and the death penalty. This thematic grouping also includes entries on various efforts to care for and rehabilitate female offenders, from drug and alcohol programs to prison health care.

International Dimensions and Issues

The study of women and crime has been international from the start. To reflect and advance this international thrust, this *Encyclopedia* includes material from four geographical regions:

- Australia
- Britain
- Canada
- The United States

When the contemporary study of women and crime began in the late 1960s, it developed in three different countries—Britain, Canada, and the United States. Although the majority of research on women and crime is conducted in the United States, due to its size, wealth, and flexible university system, the field remains international in character and politics.

Various additional reasons mandated the inclusion of Australia, Britain, and Canada in the *Encyclopedia*. Because they are predominantly English-speaking areas of the world, entries from them could easily be incorporated into an encyclopedia produced in the United States, although spelling and diction have been regularized so as to avoid confusing readers with linguistic variations that are irrelevant to the topic of women and crime. Moreover, in those countries, the study of women and crime is relatively advanced.

Nonetheless, their inclusion meant that other countries with their own distinctive approaches to the topic had to be excluded. Space constraints also made it impossible to cover Australia, Britain, and Canada in as much depth as the United States, or as systematically. However, some U.S. entries reflect the experiences and practices of other nations as well. (Feminist perspectives on victimization, for example, are similar across English-speaking countries.) Moreover, the international editors (see the chart on page xxix) were asked to use their entries to touch upon issues of special concern or unique scholarship in their countries. Thus we have entries on victimization and manly rituals in Australia, on the Southall Black Sisters in Britain, and on Aboriginal women and crime in Canada.

Australia, Britain, and Canada, then, are specifically represented by entries that do not necessarily parallel U.S. entries but rather reflect their own unique histories, concerns, and scholarship. Entries pertaining specifically to these three countries are so labeled in the entry titles.

Types of Entries and Criteria for Inclusion

Almost 20 percent of the *Encyclopedia*'s entries deal with people or groups of people. These entries cover individuals as diverse as U.S. Supreme Court Justice Sandra Day O'Connor and England's infamous "moor murderer," Myra Hindley. Entries on groups of people cover types of offenders, reform organizations such as Mothers against Drunk Driving, and various types of workers in the criminal justice system. Roughly another 20 percent of the entries are devoted to aspects of the criminal justice process, such as the death penalty and prison discipline. About 15 percent of the entries deal with concepts and theories of female crime, while about 10 percent cover forms of, and patterns in, female offending. Another 10 percent of the entries focus on legal processes, issues, and trends, with an additional 10 percent covering victimization phenomena. Smaller proportions

of the entries focus on historical matters (e.g., the child-savers movement), on institutions (e.g., Alderson Prison), and on organizations (e.g., the International Association of Women Police). In terms of time span, the great majority of entries deal with contemporary issues, offenses, institutions, and criminal processes.

A number of criteria helped determine a topic's inclusion in the *Encyclopedia*, in particular, its relevance to issues of women and crime and its overall significance. To judge significance, a topic's historical consequences were sometimes considered—thus, for example, an entry has been included on Cesare Lombroso, the author of the first book on female offenders, even though his work has long been discredited. Biographical entries on living criminologists are not included, however, although the work of a number of active scholars is discussed. Overall, comprehensive coverage of the four thematic areas of offending, victimization, processing, and punishment was sought. This approach meant including entries on such topics as compassionate release from prison, about which little is as yet known in terms of gender differences. A final criterion was timeliness—information was included, for instance, on newly emerging issues such as the criminalization of pregnancy in cases of drug-abusing women.

The *Encyclopedia's* Origins and Development

When Henry Rasof, senior acquisitions editor at the Oryx Press, invited me to put together a proposal for a volume on women and crime, I wrote for advice to Frances Heidensohn, a professor of social policy at Goldsmiths College, University of London, and my co-editor on a 1995 collection of essays on women and crime (Rafter and Heidensohn 1995a). Daunted by such a mammoth project, I was inclined to respond negatively to the invitation; but Frances, ever intrepid, immediately faxed me a list of 20 possible headwords, and the *Encyclopedia* was off and running.

My next step was to assemble an editorial team: four section editors (Mary Ann Zager, Debra L. Stanley, Susan E. Martin, and Edith E. Flynn) and four international editors (Christine M. Alder, Frances Heidensohn, Marisa Silvestri, and Dorothy E. Chunn). These editors and I drew up preliminary lists of entry titles that we then circulated for critique. This process, whereby all of us searched the lists for gaps and discussed the balance in coverage, contributed greatly to the strength and inclusiveness of the final list of entries. I am especially grateful to Susan E. Martin for her astute suggestions for additions. After the list of entries was completed, the section editors invited other scholars to join our team as associate editors. Each associate editor was responsible for a subdivision within one of the four thematic areas of the book. With regard to the editorial team as a whole, I am particularly proud of the way it includes a range of younger and well-seasoned scholars.

While there were no hard-and-fast divisions of labor—this *Encyclopedia* has been a collaborative effort from the start—the associate editors and international editors were primarily responsible for contacting authors to write individual entries. This process began in May 1998, with entries due in January 1999. Thereafter, the various editors reviewed the articles and forwarded them to the next person up the line, with everything reaching my desk in May 1999. Working closely with Henry Rasof, I completed the first draft in August 1999. At that point, the manuscript went out for review and was returned to me for revision. Working with authors and editors, I finished revising the manuscript in February 2000.

In most cases, the editors also wrote entries that provide an overview of the subject for which they were primarily responsible. Thus, for example, Paul Mazerolle, the associate editor for material on juvenile delinquency, wrote an entry titled *Juvenile Delinquency, USA*. Cassia C. Spohn, the associate editor responsible for entries on courts, wrote an overview entry titled *Case Processing and Gender*. In the Alphabetical

List of Entries (pages xv–xvii) and in the Topic Finder (pages xix–xxii), the titles of the editors' essays are preceded by bullets (•). Thus, readers who want to begin with an overview of a topic can easily spot the general essay covering it.

Readers will find considerable variety among the entries. Entries differ, for instance, in the degree to which they focus on women and gender issues, with some authors dealing solely with females, others comparing and contrasting the treatment of men and women, and still others placing the issues of both men and women in a larger context. Entries also differ in approach: some are historical, others statistical, some analytical, others sociological. Even two entries on closely related topics may vary in their emphasis and approach.

These variations flow partly from the way the project was organized and coordinated. The international editors, in particular, had considerable latitude in deciding how to allocate their total word allowances among the authors they chose. The section editors and associate editors, with their relatively large numbers of entries and word allotments, sometimes spread coverage of a single topic over several related entries.

Variety among the entries further stems from the fact that we sought out authors with disparate backgrounds and asked them to write on topics that have received very different degrees of attention. While most of the authors are academics, others work in public or private agencies. Some are lawyers, others psychologists, still others sociologists. Some were asked to write on subjects that have been studied in-depth for decades; others were assigned topics that have just begun to be explored.

Diversity among the entries, then, reflects the organization of the project, its international character, the different backgrounds of the authors, and unevenness in the development of women-and-crime studies. This diversity is, to some degree, inevitable at this point in time—it is also a sign of the ferment in research on women and crime and of the diversity among women themselves.

Acknowledgments

Literally hundreds of people were involved in the making of this encyclopedia. I owe my biggest debt of thanks to members of my editorial team and to the contributors. Also helpful were Barbara Brenzel, Meda Chesney-Lind, Suman Kakar, Kimberley Mitchell, Ira Schwartz, Martin Schwartz, John Schrader and Robert Hahn of Johnson (Vermont) State College. I am also grateful to my acquisition editor, Henry Rasof, who never failed to respond to my questions with wisdom and humor; to my main Oryx Press editor, Elizabeth Welsh, who spent months preparing the manuscript for publication; and to my final Oryx Press editor, Mary Swistara, who shepherded the *Encyclopedia* through its final stages.

Nicole Rafter, Editor-in-Chief
February 2000

A

Aboriginal Women and Crime, Australia

Aboriginal (or indigenous) women are over-represented as both offenders and victims in the Australian criminal justice system, a fact that reflects their history of colonization by the British. Many traditional Aboriginal societies were matrilineal, with Aboriginal women holding power within their communities. These societies had gendered roles and gendered ceremonies, and they forbade the sharing of certain laws, lore, and practices with the opposite sex. Women were in charge of making sure that women's rules were followed, and they were responsible for the punishment of women who broke those gendered laws. This separation within communal life was devoid of subjugation. In decision-making matters, women had as much influence as men, their power deriving from experience and age, not gender. But when the British colonized Australia, disrupted traditional cultural practices, and imposed Anglo/European sexism, many Aboriginal women lost status within their communities.

The *Royal Commission into Aboriginal Deaths in Custody* (E. Johnston 1991) reported on an extensive investigation of the institutional and historical racism against Aboriginal people in Australian society. It found that despite their small number within the overall population, in Queensland, Western Australia, South Australia, and the Northern Territory, there were more Aboriginal women in police custody than non-Aboriginal women. Since 1993, the prison rate for Aboriginal women has increased by 97 percent.

Aboriginal women are detained mostly on "good order" or "street" offenses, that is, public disturbance charges such as drunkenness or use of offensive language. The disproportionate representation of indigenous women in these statistics reveals their vulnerability to police discretionary powers. Eighty percent of Aboriginal women do not drink. However, in the towns and fringe communities, where the number of women drinking—and drinking heavily—is disproportionately high, Aboriginal women appear to be especially targeted by policing practices.

Sixteen percent of all homicide victims are Aboriginal women. In some Queensland communities, one in three Aboriginal women dies because of injuries inflicted by domestic violence. The majority of assaults, in which alcohol consumption by the offender is often a factor, are not reported. Few men who commit violent assaults against Aboriginal women are made accountable for their actions in the criminal justice system. Aboriginal women have protested against the minimal sentences imposed for violence against them, noting that drunk driving often carries harsher penalties.

Judicial attitudes perpetuate the devaluing of Aboriginal women within Australian society. In *Lane* (unreported, N.T. Sup. Ct.,

May 29, 1980), three indigenous men pled guilty to the rape of an indigenous woman. The judge stated:

> there is evidence before me, which I accept, that a rape is not considered as seriously in Aboriginal communities as it is in the white community, except in certain circumstances which do not apply here, and indeed the chastity of women is not as importantly regarded as in white communities. Apparently the violation of an Aboriginal woman's integrity is not nearly as significant as it is in the white community.

Here, the judge reinforced the devaluation of Aboriginal women.

Another disturbing trend that minimizes punishment for violence against Aboriginal women is the increasing use of a "customary law" defense by men accused of physical or sexual assault. Claims that maltreatment of Aboriginal women is "customary" do not in fact reflect traditional laws, but rather reflect a tolerance of violence against women, especially indigenous women. Further, these claims reflect racism within the legal system, in the legal profession, and in the tactics of defense lawyers. Aboriginal and Torres Strait Islander women have referred to these "customary law" claims as "bullshit law." They argue that the tolerant treatment of offenders who commit violent crimes against Aboriginal women distorts traditional culture.

In an alternative, more acceptable, approach in *R. v. Dennis Narjic* (unreported, N.T. Sup. Ct., 1988 at 24–26), the "customary law" defense was used against charges of the rape of two young girls. When the defense indicated that customary elements would be surveyed in the pre-sentencing report, the judge asked that the views of indigenous women be included.

Aboriginal women are disproportionately victims of violent crimes. The level of violence against them is a reflection of their vulnerable and low socioeconomic status within Australian society. In 1994, Aboriginal women made up just over 1 percent of the total Australia population. Ninety percent of them were over the age of 15 but lacking post-school qualifications; 34 percent were unemployed.

Many Aboriginal women are deprived of access to mainstream services and economic resources. They lack support when they become the victims of violent crime. Many Aboriginal Legal Services (staffed predominantly by men) will not take cases where both parties are indigenous. This has left indigenous women without legal recourse unless they go to mainstream legal services, which many will not do because of feelings of discomfort, the cost, and their social, linguistic, and cultural isolation.

In 1994, the Australian Law Reform Commission recommended that advocacy centers for Aboriginal and Torres Strait Islander women be established. This was achieved, after opposition from the Aboriginal Legal Services, primarily through the determination and work of Aboriginal women themselves. In some communities, refuges for battered women have been set up and run with very little outside assistance. Indigenous women are seeking to return women to the power, respect, and roles they enjoyed before colonization. Aboriginal women academics, such as Judy Atkinson of the University of Northern Queensland, have been investigating alternatives to the criminal justice system that offer holistic, community-based healing and that encompass both traditional methods and contemporary understandings. *See also* BATTERED WOMEN AND SELF-DEFENSE, AUSTRALIA; FEMALE CRIME, AUSTRALIA; JUVENILE DELINQUENCY, AUSTRALIA; WOMEN IN PRISON, AUSTRALIA.

Further Reading: Cunneen and Libesman 1995, *Indigenous People and the Law*; E. Johnston 1991, *Royal Commission into Aboriginal Deaths in Custody*; Nettheim, McRae, and Beacroft 1991, *Aboriginal Legal Issues*.

Larissa Behrendt

Aboriginal Women and Crime, Canada

Comparative data on Aboriginal and non-Aboriginal women in the Canadian criminal justice system consistently demonstrate that the former are seriously overrepresented relative to the latter. Research also suggests that the severe deprivation and abuse experienced by many Aboriginal women are directly implicated in their criminalization and, often, imprisonment. Two strategies for change have been promoted in the current context of emergent Aboriginal self-government in Canada: the development of an autonomous Aboriginal justice system and the implementation of equality for Aboriginal people within the existing criminal justice system.

A unique initiative aimed at fostering both strategies is the University of British Columbia Faculty of Law's Clinical Program in Aboriginal Law. "The Clinic" opened in January 1995 with a mandate to represent Aboriginal clients who cannot qualify for publicly funded legal aid or afford to hire a private lawyer. It is located in the Downtown Eastside of Vancouver, British Columbia, frequently described as the poorest neighborhood in Canada, where Aboriginal people constitute 20 percent of the approximately 12,000 residents. Most clients live in the area, but the Clinic also serves Aboriginal people living in an adjacent neighborhood, as well as some from nearby reserves and from First Nations in rural British Columbia.

Although involved in developing Aboriginal justice systems, the Clinic focuses primarily on equality issues within the Canadian justice system. To that end, the Clinic concentrates on training Aboriginal law students as litigators who will assertively pursue their clients' interests and empower clients to tell their stories in their own way. Aboriginal women are clients in approximately one-third of the criminal and two-thirds of the civil cases handled by the Clinic. Virtually all of the women are financially dependent on welfare assistance.

Criminal cases typically involve such charges as soliciting, petty theft, minor assaults, and breach of probation. Many of these offenses are "crimes of poverty." Mothers work as prostitutes or steal food to support their children in between welfare checks that are inadequate to feed and shelter a family for an entire month. Civil cases also are pov-erty-related in many instances, as in the instance of appeals to the Ministry of Social Services tribunals for income assistance.

The Clinic's strategy for helping clients charged with criminal offenses is to provide access to legal and nonlegal assistance that will lead to rapport with, and empowerment of, the person. The legal emphasis is on out-of-court case resolution. After hearing a client's story, a Clinic lawyer may approach Crown Counsel to drop criminal charges and/or to discuss a guilty plea and sentencing recommendations that take account of the accused's circumstances. If mediation fails, diversion is a possibility for first-time offenders, although breach of a diversion contract could lead to reinstatement of the criminal charge. When cases go to court, Clinic lawyers work to obtain the best-case scenario— acquittal if the accused has a "meritous defense" such as self-defense, and mitigation of sentence if a client pleads or is found guilty.

What differentiates the Clinic from other legal aid clinics is that, throughout the legal process, Clinic lawyers try to present the client's story to justice officials in a way that enables them to see "the whole person standing there" and to understand "the particular historical circumstances of Aboriginal people" (Culhane and Taylor 2000). Similarly, the Clinic's efforts to connect clients with non-legal support services such as counseling also are aimed at helping Aboriginal people to deal with issues behind their immediate legal problems and to move beyond the often ingrained idea that they are "inferior individuals of an inferior people" (Culhane and Taylor 2000).

Through the provision of legal and non-legal assistance to Aboriginal people, the Clinic achieves small victories when lawyers win individual cases in the lower courts, but these positive outcomes can also make a difference on a broader scale. Clearly, they can influence future legal decisions, but, more important, they can help change the way that judges and Crown Counsel see Aboriginal women (and men) and the way that Aboriginal people view themselves and the justice system. *See also* FEMALE CRIME, CANADA;

PRISON REFORM, CANADA; WOMEN IN PRISON, CANADA.

Further Reading: Monture-Angus 1995, *A Mohawk Woman Speaks;* Wiebe and Johnson 1998, *The Journey of a Cree Woman.*

Renee Taylor

Abortion

Over time in the United States, laws forbidding abortion have been one of governments' main means of criminalizing female behaviors—those of the women who seek abortions, those of the women (and men) who perform them, and those of the friends who aid and abet abortion-seekers. Moreover, abortion laws have also formed an important site for struggles over women's right to control their own bodies and reproduction. Protests for and against abortion laws and abortions themselves have led to arrests, prosecutions, imprisonment, and deaths. Today, a new development connected with abortion is enactment of laws enabling criminal prosecution of pregnant women who ingest illegal substances or otherwise harm a fetus.

Historically, the debate on abortion has centered on the right of women to make their own reproductive decisions versus the states' rights to intervene. Prior to the 1970s, most U.S. states had criminalized abortion. However, in 1973, the United States Supreme Court ruled in *Roe v. Wade* that the Fourteenth Amendment to the U.S. Constitution provides a fundamental privacy right for women to obtain abortions, and that this right cannot be abridged in the first trimester of pregnancy (i.e., prior to viability, which is the point at which the fetus can survive outside the womb). Since abortion is a fundamental right, according to *Roe*, any state laws regulating abortion must meet the "strict scrutiny" standard and show a "compelling interest" in order to comply with the *Roe* decision.

Prior to *Roe,* the legality of abortion in the United States rested in state legislatures; after *Roe,* whether abortion was considered legal or not depended on Supreme Court decisions specifying the scope of *Roe*. With two more decisions, *Webster v. Reproductive Health Services* in 1989 and *Planned Parenthood v. Casey* in 1992, the Supreme Court expanded the rights of states to regulate abortion. In *Webster*, the Court let stand a Missouri statute which held that human life begins at conception, barring the use of state property for abortions, and requiring viability tests for advanced pregnancies. In *Casey*, the Court upheld a 24-hour waiting period, an informed consent requirement, a parental consent requirement for minors, and a record-keeping requirement, while striking down a spousal notice requirement. Although it upheld a woman's fundamental right to abortion, the Court overturned *Roe*'s trimester framework and its strict scrutiny standard of review, instead instituting a new "undue burden" standard (implementation of the law should not place an undue burden on any party). The Court also created a floating viability line: Whereas the earlier *Roe* decision had set viability at three months, the Court now recognized that new technologies could move viability to an earlier point in time. The *Casey* decision replaced *Roe v. Wade* as the dominant precedent on abortion and represents the closest the Court has come to overturning the rights established in *Roe*. Subsequent attempts by abortion rights advocates to reinstate *Roe*'s strict scrutiny standard through congressional action have failed.

State legislatures have moved toward increasing states' rights to control women's reproductive behavior, limiting access to abortion where possible. In recent years, pro-life (anti-abortion) advocates have been successful in limiting the right to late-term abortions necessary for a woman's physical or mental health through several state laws banning "partial birth" (late-term) abortions. The Supreme Court has not followed this trend. A similar federal bill, the Partial Birth Abortion Ban Act, was not successful, while The Freedom of Access to Clinic Entrances Act, which provides criminal and civil sanctions for obstructing or limiting a woman's access to abortion facilities, was passed by Congress.

Prosecutions of women for ingesting illegal substances during pregnancy have important implications for abortion law. In *Whitner v. State* (1997), the Supreme Court of South Carolina held that a viable fetus is a "person" for the purposes of the state's child neglect statute and upheld a pregnant woman's conviction for criminal child neglect. The U.S. Supreme Court declined a hearing. This case and similar state legislation raise important issues regarding the states' interests in reproductive choices that result in abortion and maternal acts (such as drug abuse) that may harm a fetus carried to term.

These new laws criminalizing the behaviors of some pregnant women are merely the latest act in the long conflict between those who believe that pregnant women should have complete autonomy over their own bodies and those who advocate the criminalization of harm to fetuses. *See also* CRIMINALIZATION OF PREGNANCY, CANADA; CRIMINALIZATION OF PREGNANCY, USA; PRISONER RIGHTS.

Further Reading: *Planned Parenthood v. Casey,* 1992; *Roe v. Wade,* 1973; *Webster v. Reproductive Health Services,* 1989; *Whitner v. State,* 1997.

Inger Sagatun-Edwards

Adultery

Adultery, or voluntary sexual intercourse by a married person with someone other than his or her spouse, is a transgression that has been shaped historically by cultural, religious, and legal factors. In ancient Israel, adultery reflected the imperatives of a staunchly patriarchal society, and violators (both men and women) customarily were stoned to death. In most countries, women were more likely to be punished than men for adultery, largely because wives were considered the property of their husbands. Indeed, adultery by a married woman was likened to sexual theft from her husband's estate. Other legal disparities demonstrate further the double standard of adultery, including an 1857 British divorce law that permitted a husband to divorce his wife for adultery alone but required a wife to prove additional grounds in order to obtain a divorce. Similarly, a former Texas law permitted a man who caught his spouse and her lover in adultery to kill the lover with impu-

nity; however, a woman was not granted the corresponding right.

Currently, social scientists avoid the term "adultery" due to its moral connotations, preferring to describe such activity as "extramarital relationships." Although adultery is still used as a grounds for divorce, its stigma has waned with the secularization of morality. Nonetheless, adultery remains a serious charge in many circumstances, and gender bias in its punishment persists. In the U.S. military in the 1990s, several female officers were court-martialled for adultery while their male counterparts were spared comparable punishments. In a 1998 divorce case, a Virginia man seeking child custody and ownership of the family's home filed adultery charges against his wife for having a lesbian affair. The judge rejected the charge, stating that adultery requires sexual intercourse, an act that can occur only between persons of the opposite sex. However, the judge suggested that the husband argue that his wife violated a Virginia state law making extramarital sodomy grounds for divorce. Clearly, cultural and legal factors continue to influence definitions of adultery and its consequences for women's lives.

Further Reading: Lawson 1988, *Adultery;* Shrage 1994, *Moral Dilemmas of Feminism.*

Michael Welch

Aggression. *See* CHILD ABUSE BY WOMEN; DOMESTIC VIOLENCE BY WOMEN; HOMICIDE, USA; HOMICIDE VICTIMS AND OFFENDERS, AUSTRALIA; MASCULINITY EXPLANATION OF CRIME; PRISON VIOLENCE; VIOLENT CRIME.

Alcohol Abuse and Alcoholism

Alcohol abuse, a harmful pattern of ongoing alcohol use with negative physiological, psychological, and/or social consequences, is often distinguished from alcoholism, meaning chronic and compulsive alcohol dependence. However, both of these maladaptive patterns in alcohol use are linked in a number of ways to female crime and victimization.

In the United States, the crimes most commonly linked to alcohol use and abuse are public-order offenses including public intoxication, driving while intoxicated, and vice offenses. Nearly two-thirds of the women convicted of public-order offenses were drinking at the time of their offense (Bureau of Justice Statistics 1998a). Alcohol abuse and alcoholism are also associated with violent behavior: Over one-fourth of female probationers and over one-third of female inmates incarcerated in local jails for violent offenses were using alcohol at the time of their offenses.

Alcohol abuse has also been linked to higher levels of victimization of women in the United States, including spousal abuse and sexual assaults. Almost two-thirds of those reporting violence by an intimate partner indicated that alcohol was a factor (Bureau of Justice Statistics 1998a). Sexual assault victimization, too, is associated with alcohol abuse: On the average, 183,000 rapes annually involve an offender who has been drinking. According to offender reports, approximately 11 percent of rape victims were drinking at the time of the assault. Early childhood victimization seems to lead to high levels of drinking, with more alcoholic than nonalcoholic women reporting being victims of sexual or physical abuse before the age of 18. Many women apparently experience a sequence from childhood abuse to alcoholism to criminal activity.

More than one-third of all offenders supervised by the various corrections departments in the United States were drinking at the time of their offense (Bureau of Justice Statistics 1998a). While the percentage of women inmates who were drinking alcohol is lower than that of men, alcohol was nonetheless involved in one-quarter of the female cases. Furthermore, among probationers who were drinking at the time of their offenses, the blood-alcohol levels of females were higher than those of men. Other postconviction data, too, indicate that problematic drinking is associated with female crime. For instance, a 1991 survey indicated that 35.8 percent of female state prison inmates used alcohol at least once a week during the year before the offense leading to their incarceration, with approximately 20 percent reporting daily use (Bureau of Justice Statistics 1994c).

Female alcoholics and alcohol abusers face limited treatment options. There are fewer treatment facilities available for women than men, women often have more limited economic resources for treatment, and their roles as primary caretakers of children may interfere with their ability to obtain treatment. Alcoholic women face potential loss of custody of their children, a factor that often deters them from seeking help. Alcoholism in women tends to develop at a later age but to progress more rapidly than in men. Finally, because alcohol-dependent women are likely to report a constellation of problems, including hopelessness, family stresses, and economic hardship, they often have difficulty identifying alcohol use as their primary problem. *See also* FEMALE CRIME, HISTORY OF, USA; JUVENILE DELINQUENCY AND DRUG AND ALCOHOL ABUSE; POVERTY AND CRIME; PROSTITUTION; VICTIM-FACILITATION THEORY; VICTIMIZATION, REPEAT.

Further Reading: Center for Substance Abuse Treatment 1994, *Practical Approaches in the Treatment of Women;* Kinney 2000, *A Handbook of Alcohol Information;* National Institute on Alcohol Abuse and Alcoholism 1990, *Alcohol and Women.*

Susan F. Sharp

Alderson Prison

Alderson Prison, originally named the Federal Industrial Reformatory and Industrial Farm for Women, opened in 1927 on 200 donated acres at Alderson, West Virginia. It was immediately hailed as a showcase of the women's reformatory movement. The first federal prison for women in the United States, Alderson owed its establishment to a combination of factors: an increasing number of women convicted under new federal prostitution, drug, and prohibition laws; a heightened awareness of prison conditions by white, politically active, middle-class women arrested during suffrage protests; and the 1921

Alderson Prison. Courtesy of Federal Prison Camp, Alderson, West Virginia.

appointment as U.S. assistant attorney general of Mabel Walker Willebrandt, who steered the legislation through Congress.

Partially built with prison labor at a cost of $2.5 million, Alderson had 14 cottages (including a nursery cottage) with kitchens. Each cottage had room for 30 women and a warder, and each was staffed and administered by women. Mary Belle Harris, Alderson's first superintendent, ran the institution for 16 years.

Harris was one of a network of early-twentieth-century women's prison reformers. Under her leadership, women officers supervised the farm and the power sewing room while introducing a range of educational, inmate-led programs. From the beginning, Harris struggled with the Federal Bureau of Prisons' male administrators for autonomy and recognition of Alderson as a model prison.

While Alderson had women superintendents until 1976, changes in administrative policy gradually centralized the kitchens and eliminated the Georgian-style cottages and live-in warders. Alderson's history—from its inception as a model reformatory administered by and for women to its present position as an institution interchangeable with others under a centralized federal prison administration—illustrates the wider society's shifting attitudes toward incarcerated women. *See also* Prison Reform, USA; Reformatory Movement; Women's Prison Administration, Historical; Women's Prisons, History of.

Further Reading: Heffernan 1994, "Banners, Brothels, and a 'Ladies' Seminary"; Schweber 1982, "The Government's Unique Experiment."

Esther Heffernan

American Correctional Association

The American Correctional Association (ACA), the largest organization of corrections professionals and volunteers in the world, has, since its inception in 1870, included a cadre of women activists concerned with the issues of incarcerated women.

The ACA was born out of circumstances following the Civil War. At that time, one of the most vexing problems for governors and state legislatures was the return to society of thousands of jobless war veterans and freed slaves, many of whom were forced to forage and steal in order to survive. Crime became an increasingly serious public issue, and the use of prisons became widespread. At the same time, reformers formerly involved in the struggle to abolish slavery were seeking new causes, which some found in the reform of men's prisons and the establishment of separate prisons for women.

From October 11–20, 1870, prison officials and reformers met in Cincinnati, Ohio, to form the National Prison Association (NPA), as the ACA was originally known. They chose the governor of Ohio, Rutherford B. Hayes, to be the organization's first president. Hayes later became the nineteenth president of the United States, and at the end of his term, he again became NPA president, from 1883 to 1893. The NPA became the voice of corrections throughout the United States and parts of Europe. Renamed the American Correctional Association in 1954, the organization today has more than 20,000 members.

Since the ACA's founding, women have played a role in its development. Well represented at the initial 1870 meeting, women have always taken the lead in suggesting ways to tailor the prison system to meet the needs of women (and men) prisoners. In 1912, the association established a women's committee. Twenty-four years later, in 1936, Blanch LaDu became the first woman president of the ACA. Between 1936 and 2000, four women were elected ACA president. *See also* COFFIN, RHODA; MAHAN, EDNA; PRISON ACCREDITATION.

Further Reading: Freedman 1981, *Their Sisters' Keepers;* Keve 1991, *Prisons and the American Conscience;* Travisono and Hawkes 1995, *Building a Voice.*

Anthony P. Travisono

American Society of Criminology

The professional organization known since 1958 as the American Society of Criminology (ASC) originated in 1941, when August Vollmer and a group of eight male colleagues assembled in Berkeley, California, to advance the field of criminology. Throughout the 1940s and 1950s, the organization and its membership grew; its name, scope, and policies changed; but one feature remained constant—it was an all-male group.

In the 1960s, a few pioneering women began to appear on the membership rolls, and by the early 1970s, two women, Christine Schultz and Barbara Price, had held the position of secretary. The number of females in the organization was small, however, constituting only 11 percent of the membership in 1972. Female membership grew to 15 percent by the mid-1970s, and women began to participate in annual meetings, presenting papers and chairing panels. The first panel specifically on the topic of women and crime was scheduled in Toronto, Canada, in 1975 and was chaired by Freda Adler.

As women's involvement in the ASC increased, so did their desire to share intellectual interests, provide a forum for discussion of gender issues, and offer support and encouragement for scholarship by and about women. In 1976, those involved in the subject of women and crime began informal discussions at the ASC's annual meeting in Atlanta, Georgia. Subsequently, they formed a special Women's Caucus to share their interest in the study of women as victims, offenders, and professionals in the criminal justice system. These early discussions also revealed, however, that the female members of ASC shared feelings of isolation, insecurity, discontent with, and exclusion from this male-dominated organization.

By the early 1980s, some women recognized the necessity to formally organize and structure their group. Thus they proposed to the ASC the establishment of the Division on Women and Crime (DWC) as a constituent unit of the organization. The DWC's constitution states its purposes: to discuss issues related to females in their roles as victims, offenders, or professionals in the criminal justice system; to encourage the development of theories and research on women; to advance courses on gender and crime; to act as a liaison and facilitate interaction among criminal justice academics, researchers, practitioners, and policymakers; to examine problems and offer resolutions for women involved in the criminal justice system; to plan conference panels and presentations; to heighten ASC's awareness of gender issues and crime; and to draw attention to the accomplishments of female criminologists.

The DWC's constitution was approved by the ASC executive board in 1982 and ratified the following year. Elections were held, with Phyllis Jo Baunach becoming the first chairperson in 1984. Women who figured prominently in the establishment and growth of the division in its early years include Meda Chesney-Lind, Nicole Hahn Rafter, Christine Rasche, Elizabeth Stanko, and Nanci Koser Wilson. According to the DWC's records, the first, 1982, meeting was attended by only 25 people, but by 1995 the group had 300 members, including some men. The DWC has helped its members in a variety of ways, particularly by providing women a voice in a male-dominated profession and by emphasizing the importance of including gender in the study of crime and criminal justice.

The visibility of women in the ASC has increased not only in membership and paper presentations, but also through awards and election to office. At the beginning of the twenty-first century, women constituted 7 percent of the Fellows and had received 16 percent of all ASC awards, including the prestigious Sutherland (5 percent), Vollmer (13 percent), Sellin-Glueck (17 percent), and Bloch (29 percent) awards. Women had also held elected offices within the parent organization, with Joan McCord becoming the first female president in 1988, followed by Joan Petersilia (1989). Other women were subsequently elected, totaling 5 percent of all ASC presidents. Women have also served as vice-president, beginning with Barbara Price (1981) and Marguerite Q. Warren (1982), and followed by others for a total of 12 percent. Other positions held by women include executive counselor, with Freda Adler (1971 and 1974) first serving in this capacity, followed by Edith Flynn (1975).

The role of women in the American Society of Criminology attests to their determination and commitment to the discipline of criminology. *See also* AMERICAN CORRECTIONAL ASSOCIATION; FEMINIST CRIMINOLOGY, USA; WOMEN PROFESSIONALS IN THE JUSTICE WORKPLACE.

Further Reading: Adler 1997, "The ASC and Women"; Morris 1975, "The American Society of Criminology."

Carol A. Facella

B

Barker, "Ma" (ca. 1872–1935)

"Ma" Barker has become part of American popular mythology as the female criminal mastermind behind the notorious Barker-Karpis gang. Although her actual role in the gang is a matter of dispute, it is most likely that she was little more than a tag-along and not a planner or prime mover.

The legendary Ma Barker was first immortalized by J. Edgar Hoover's FBI media machine after Ma was killed, along with her son Freddie, during a shootout with the FBI near Oklawaha, Florida, in early 1935. Prior to her death, she was unknown to the public, and barely known to the FBI.

Ma (also known as Arrie and Kate) was born Arizona Donnie Clark in approximately 1872 in the Missouri Ozarks. Married to George Barker, she had four sons who were involved in increasingly serious crimes from a young age. Ma is believed to have been an overprotective (if not paranoid) mother who thought her sons were persecuted by the community and the police. All of her sons were imprisoned for an assortment of crimes, and all met their deaths in violent ways. Her oldest son committed suicide after being wounded in a shootout with the police. Another son was killed by his own wife. Yet another son was killed while trying to escape from Alcatraz, while her fourth and youngest son, Freddie, was killed by the FBI at the same time as his mother. Some suspect that Freddie himself killed Ma.

Ma Barker was never arrested, and had she been captured, it is unlikely that she would have faced charges of any greater severity than harboring her sons and their fugitive friends. There is no evidence that she participated in any of the burglaries, robberies, kidnappings, or murders credited to the Barker-Karpis gang. Members of the gang who outlived Ma indicated that she traveled with her sons for no other reason than that they were family. They stated that she was not particularly bright and that the only role that she played within the gang was as a form of cover.

The only official notices taken of Ma prior to her death were a small reward offered for her in 1931 (after Freddie Barker and Alvin Karpis killed a police officer), and in 1934 when a dying gangster alerted the FBI to the existence of the gang. In both cases, the sole accusation against Ma was that she traveled with her criminal sons. When Ma Barker was killed in the 1935 FBI raid, the media were quick to depict her as a criminal mastermind of mythological cunning, a portrayal taken directly from the FBI propaganda machine guided by J. Edgar Hoover. The manufactured legend of Ma Barker has been kept alive by numerous publications (including current publications about the FBI and general encyclopedias), as well as by at least four motion pictures. Most sensationally, Ma Baker was the likely inspiration for the character of the overly loving mother of gangster James Cagney in the 1949 classic, *White Heat*.

Further Reading: Hamilton 1989, *America's Most Wanted;* Encyclopædia Britannica Online <http://www.britannica.com/>, "Barker, 'Ma,'" accessed 24 March 2000.

W. T. Jordan

Battered Women and Self-Defense, Australia

Until recently in Australia, battered women who killed abusive partners had little success establishing self-defense. The law does not explicitly exclude such cases, but gender bias in the development and interpretation of legal concepts has disadvantaged women. Historically, most homicide offenders and victims have been men, and thus the law of self-defense developed to reflect men's experiences. However, men and women kill in very different circumstances. Of the few women who kill, the majority do so in response to domestic violence that has occurred over long periods of time.

Australian law on self-defense varies by state, but in general it requires that the defendant believed that the defensive action was necessary, and that this belief was reasonable within the circumstances as she believed them to be. However, lawyers, judges, and juries have not always understood why a woman who has been abused might find it necessary to kill an abusive partner, and why such behavior might be reasonable in defense of herself and her children. Concepts such as "reasonable" have been interpreted in gender-biased ways, using the "reasonable man" as a model.

Feminist work to ensure that self-defense also reflects women's experiences has important consequences for individuals (a person found to have acted in self-defense is legally entitled to be acquitted of a charge of murder) and is crucial to securing fair and equal treatment for men and women.

Battered woman syndrome (BWS) is one strategy used in courts to offer evidence about domestic violence and its effects. BWS describes common patterns in abusive relationships and the consequences that abuse may have for women, including a psychological state called "learned helplessness" (L. Walker

1984). It is not a special defense for battered women. Expert evidence concerning BWS is offered in support of other defenses. Since 1991, courts in all Australian states and territories have accepted evidence of BWS. It has not been limited to cases of homicide or self-defense; for example, it was used in the trial of a woman charged with company fraud committed under threat of further violence by her abusive partner. BWS has also been used by a man who had killed his abusive male partner.

In Australia, the use of BWS evidence is controversial. Critics claim that BWS places too much emphasis on whether the abused woman has psychological characteristics consistent with the syndrome, rather than on the coercion and abuse she experienced. Critics also object that BWS, in emphasizing the psychological impact of the abuse (and particularly learned helplessness), undermines the defendant's claim to have acted reasonably. They further object that BWS obscures other relevant factors such as a woman's lack of access to social, economic, or legal resources that could have assisted her; that it is based on flawed research; that it represents a new stereotype against which a battered woman's behavior is judged; and that BWS encourages a reliance on professional discourses (psychiatry or psychology) rather than on the woman's own account. An important focus of Australian research has been the concern that BWS is based on a white, middle-class understanding of battered women, which disadvantages Aboriginal women and other minorities.

Recent decisions suggest that courts have begun to respond more sympathetically to some battered women who kill, but BWS has not been associated consistently with positive outcomes. Australian jurisprudence has focused narrowly on the merits of BWS, interpreted to mean the perceptions of the battered woman, with insufficient attention to other forms of evidence that might assist the courts in understanding domestic violence. Canada and the United States have recognized that BWS is a limited construct. A broader range of information about domestic violence than is conventionally understood by BWS, so-called "social context information," is relevant and necessary in the determination of whether an accused person acted in self-defense. Such information might include the nature and history of the abuse; the economic, social, and other resources available to the woman dealing with the violence; and the responses of police or other agencies. This is yet to be acknowledged by Australian courts. *See also* BATTERED WOMEN AND SELF-DEFENSE, CANADA; BATTERED WOMEN AND SELF-DEFENSE, USA; HOMICIDE, FILIPINO WOMEN IN AUSTRALIA AS VICTIMS OF; HOMICIDE VICTIMS; HOMICIDE VICTIMS AND OFFENDERS, AUSTRALIA.

Further Reading: Leader-Elliot 1993, "Battered but Not Beaten"; Stubbs and Tolmie 1995, "Race, Gender and the Battered Woman Syndrome"; Tolmie 1997, "Pacific-Asian Immigrant and Refugee Women."

Julie Stubbs

Battered Women and Self-Defense, Canada

Prior to the 1990 Supreme Court of Canada decision in *R. v. Lavallee*, battered women who killed their abusive partners had little recourse under the law on self-defense. Under Canadian law, a successful claim of self-defense required that the accused had a reasonable fear of death or grievous bodily harm and that the force he or she used to dispel this harm was necessary and reasonable. In deciding what was reasonable, the courts adopted the objective standard of what the "ordinary man" would do under the circumstances. To ensure that the use of deadly force was necessary, the courts applied the "imminence rule," which stipulated that the threat of force must be immediate. The paradigmatic case of the one-time barroom brawl between two men of equal size and strength was used to illustrate this rule. The courts ignored the patterns of abuse that women encounter in battering relationships, the psychological effects of an abusive relationship on a woman's perception of "reasonableness," and the size and strength differentials between men and women. In so doing, the courts imposed significant barriers to the availability of self-defense for women charged with killing their abusers.

The *Lavallee* decision marked the legal recognition of battered woman syndrome (BWS) in cases involving women who kill their batterers. Angelique Lavallee was charged in 1987 with second-degree murder in the shooting death of her common-law partner. Her lawyer led a self-defense argument that included expert testimony on BWS. A psychiatrist testified that Lavallee had been terrorized by her partner to the point of feeling "trapped, vulnerable, worthless, and unable to escape the relationship despite the violence" (*R. v. Lavallee* 1990:103). The jury found Lavallee not guilty. The decision was appealed by the Crown and subsequently heard by the Supreme Court, which affirmed the acquittal. Much of the Court's decision focussed on the admissibility of expert testimony on the BWS and its relevance to elements of self-defense.

Written by Madame Justice Bertha Wilson, the first woman to be appointed (1982) to the Supreme Court of Canada, the decision was applauded by many feminists for acknowledging the male bias in the law on self-defense. On the issue of the objective standard of reasonableness, the Court noted:

> If it strains credulity to imagine what the "ordinary man" would do in the position of a battered spouse, it is probably because men do not typically find themselves in that situation. (*R. v. Lavallee* 1990:114)

With regard to the imminence rule, the Court rejected the requirement that a physical assault must actually be in progress before self-defense can apply, as such a requirement would be tantamount to sentencing a woman to "murder by installment" (*R. v. Lavallee* 1990:120). The Court rejected the paradigmatic case of the barroom brawl, noting that expert testimony on BWS had established the cyclical pattern of such abuse, which "allows for a degree of predictability to the violence which is absent in an isolated encounter between two strangers" (*R. v. Lavallee* 1990:119). On the question of alternatives to self-help, the Court held that testimony on BWS can assist in explaining a woman's psychological inability to leave the relationship.

Critics have noted several limitations encountered in using expert testimony on BWS. By locating the source of the problem in a woman's psychological state, BWS fails to adequately locate the violence in terms of the behavior of violent men and the social, economic, and political conditions that promote the violence. Rather than focusing on the reasonableness of a woman's actions, expert testimony explains why a woman acted unreasonably due to her condition of "learned helplessness." Moreover, in setting out a new legal standard for interpreting the actions of battered women, BWS may disadvantage those women whose behavior does not conform to the syndrome.

While *Lavallee* held the promise of making the doctrine of self-defense more accessible to battered women, developments since then have been less than encouraging. In her review of 35 cases decided after *Lavallee*, Shaffer (1997) found that successful self-defense claims had not significantly increased, and that a stereotype of the "authentic" battered woman was being used by the courts, making it difficult for women who did not fit the criteria to argue self-defense. Similarly, a 1997 *en bloc* review of 98 cases of women convicted of murder or manslaughter (all but one of which had occurred before *Lavallee*) resulted in conditional pardons or reduced parole for only four women and the referral of a fifth to an appeal court. *See also* BATTERED WOMEN AND SELF-DEFENSE, AUSTRALIA; BATTERED WOMEN AND SELF-DEFENSE, USA; DOMESTIC VIOLENCE BY WOMEN; WOMEN IN PRISON, CANADA.

Further Reading: Comack 1993, *The Feminist Engagement with the Law;* Martinson, MacCrimmon, Grant, and Boyle 1991, "A Forum on *Lavallee v. R.";* Shaffer 1997, "The Battered Woman Syndrome Revisited."

Elizabeth Comack

Battered Women and Self-Defense, USA

In the United States, battering has historically been a legal activity, often understood as a necessary evil—albeit sometimes excessive—and part of the Judeo-Christian tradition in which men are the head of the household and are responsible for the control and discipline or punishment of all family members. Most U.S. law evolved through the experience of men and to serve the interests of men. Consequently, common law developments in the area of battering were primarily directed at regulating the amount of damage that the male head of household was allow to inflict without drawing a response from the state.

Battering was not recognized as a social problem or deemed illegal until the second half of the twentieth century, following extended efforts by the women's rights movement. By the 1970s, cities and states had begun to develop laws prohibiting—rather than regulating—battering, recognizing battering as a primary source of injury to women. However, these legal developments have met with enforcement difficulty and less than enthusiastic social support. Part of the difficulty may be a result of our concentration of efforts on socially assisting the victims of battering to take responsibility for ending their victimization, rather than on a more aggressive and direct approach of removing batterers from the situation and treating the problem behavior, so that victims can be safe and free to move on with their lives with minimal disruption. Some battered women still find themselves in a "kill or be killed" situation when the efforts of the criminal justice system and social agencies have failed.

Contrary to popular belief, there is no battered woman's defense in the United States. During the 1980s and early 1990s, most women who went to trial for killing their abusers utilized either a self-defense or insanity defense, supplemented by expert testimony on battered woman syndrome (BWS). Although BWS has been widely accepted in U.S. courts, it has not been particularly successful, for several reasons:

- It relies solely on psychology to explain behavior, ignoring all of the social, structural, and cultural variables that influence the battered woman's perspective and behavior.
- It creates a stereotype of the battered woman as a person with a psychological problem, acting unreasonably, which disadvantages women who act reasonable and assertively in their own defense.
- It does not address the issues of reasonableness and imminence in the self-defense law, but rather provides a psychological excuse for what is seen under self-defense law as unreasonable behavior (i.e., use of lethal force against nonlethal force).

Recognition of these problems led scholars to debate other approaches to the use of self-defense.

The elements of self-defense that have been most problematic for battered women who kill their abusers are the requirements that the person reasonably perceive herself to be in imminent danger of serious injury or death and that the force used to repel that danger is proportional to the threat. There have been many debates over the correct interpretation of imminence (e.g., immediate, close in time, inevitable). However, most courts still interpret this element as immediacy. The second major problem has to do with the interpretation of reasonableness. Historically, the standard for reasonableness has been that of the "prudent man" and the level of force he might need to protect himself. This standard ignores the greater strength and social power of men. That interpretation of self-defense arose out of the "barroom brawl" scenario of confrontation between men, and it assumes that there are two approximately equal combatants with limited knowledge of each other in a one-time, short-term confrontation. Battering is, unfortunately, not this type of confrontation. It involves two unequal combatants with intimate knowledge of one another developed over time in a long-term, ongoing confrontation. Consequently, in order to understand battering within the context of self-defense law, it is essential that the finder of fact be presented with a view of the battering as a long-term confrontation in which the victim, regardless of the immediacy of the attack, knows it is coming and reasonably perceives the danger presented by a physically stronger adversary against whom she will need assistance to successfully defend herself.

There have been many debates among U.S. scholars concerning the best approach to providing this perspective on self-defense. Some have called for a subjective standard of reasonableness such as a "battered woman's perspective." Others believe imminence should be redefined from immediacy to "close in time" or "inevitable." However, at present, most of these ideas have been rejected. In the late 1990s, a new approach began to emerge based on the belief by battered women and their advocates that the lethal actions of battered women who kill their abusers are "reasonable" responses of victims facing long-term and escalating abuse.

Today, courts are beginning to admit more testimony from both expert and lay witnesses about the social contexts in which homicides occur. Such testimony is intended to explain in detail the long-term interaction process of the battering in a particular relationship, so that the finder of fact can understand why the victim believed the danger was lethal and inevitable, as well as why the victim felt that neither the criminal justice system nor other social resources could protect her, thus leaving her no choice but to end the violence through lethal self-defense. Although this movement is still in its infancy in the United States, it seems to hold great promise for a fairer and more realistic approach to self-defense for battered women who kill. At present, there is no theoretical framework available for this sociological approach to understanding battering, although such work is underway. Its completion may provide the theoretical groundwork for a broader acceptance of social-context testimony in U.S. courts. *See also* BATTERED WOMEN AND SELF-DEFENSE, AUSTRALIA; BATTERED WOMEN AND SELF-DEFENSE, CANADA; CRIME VICTIMIZATION;

FRAMINGHAM EIGHT; HOMICIDE VICTIMS; VICTIMIZATION, FEMINIST PERSPECTIVES ON.

Further Reading: Dutton 1993, "Understanding Women's Responses"; Maguigan 1991, "Battered Women and Self-Defense"; National Clearinghouse for the Defense of Battered Women 1996, *When Battered Women Are Charged;* Ogle and Jacobs forthcoming, *Battered Women Who Kill;* Yllo and Bograd 1988, *Feminist Perspectives on Wife Abuse.*

Robbin S. Ogle

Battered Women. *See* DOMESTIC VIOLENCE AGAINST WOMEN, EPIDEMIOLOGY OF; DOMESTIC VIOLENCE CASE PROCESSING; DOMESTIC VIOLENCE, POLICE RESPONSES TO; HOMICIDE VICTIMS.

Battered Woman Syndrome. *See* BATTERED WOMEN AND SELF-DEFENSE, AUSTRALIA; BATTERED WOMEN AND SELF-DEFENSE, CANADA; BATTERED WOMEN AND SELF-DEFENSE, USA; FRAMINGHAM EIGHT; VICTIMIZATION, FEMINIST PERSPECTIVES ON.

Bedford Hills Reformatory

In the early twentieth century, the New York State Reformatory for Women at Bedford Hills emerged as the model U.S. institution for rehabilitating young female offenders. After New York state had established two other women's reformatories, the Houses of Refuge at Hudson (1887) and Albion (1893) in upstate New York, leading penal reformers Josephine Shaw Lowell and Abigail Hopper Gibbons successfully lobbied the state legislature for a third women's reformatory. In May of 1901, Bedford Hills (as the institution was informally known) admitted its first prisoners. At first the prisoners were primarily working-class women who reflected the diversity of New York City in race and ethnicity; some were native and foreign-born whites, while others were black. Women received automatic three-year sentences, mainly for minor offenses such as vagrancy, prostitution, drunkenness, petty larceny, and incorrigibility; in some cases, the institution also accepted felons who were first-time offenders. Like many women's reformatories,

Bedford Hills embodied in administration and practice the three basic principles of the women's reformatory movement: that fallen women could be rehabilitated; that attempts to reform them should occur in separate, all-female institutions; and that these institutions should be staffed entirely by other women.

Bedford Hills' program and management stemmed from the premise that wayward women between the ages of 16 and 30 could be taught domesticity and morality within a family-style cottage system located in the countryside. Instead of living in a prison cell, an inmate was assigned, on the basis of behavioral assessment, to an individual room within a cottage that included a kitchen, dining area, and small laundry and was supervised by a matron. Inmates' training included domestic chores such as washing, cooking, and gardening, along with required attendance at the institution's school and religious services (Protestant, Catholic, and Jewish).

During her 13-year tenure (1901–14), Bedford Hills' first superintendent, Katharine Bement Davis, became a national spokesperson on female reform and criminality. Her impressive background, which included an undergraduate degree from Vassar College and a Ph.D. from the University of Chicago, as well as settlement house work in Philadelphia, distinguished her from the evangelical prison reformers of the nineteenth century. Furthermore, her social science approach and the research conducted under her leadership at Bedford Hills strongly suggested that female criminality stemmed from mental deficiency, a theory quickly adopted by the nascent eugenics movement. When, not long after Bedford Hills opened, the newly instituted sentence of probation began siphoning off the most redeemable offenders, the institution had to deal with a growing population of probation violators and more serious offenders. Davis argued that large numbers of these women were feebleminded or psychopathic, and thus lacking the capacity for rehabilitation. For such prisoners, Davis recommended lifelong eugenic segregation.

This medical approach to female criminality, which Davis used to explain Bedford Hills' growing disciplinary problems, was soon adopted by many other penal institutions, male and female. After Davis left the institution in 1914, the inability of Bedford Hills' administrators to handle problematic inmates prompted several investigations and public inquiries. As a result, a series of female superintendents resigned, and in 1920, Amos T. Baker became the reformatory's first male superintendent. The final blow to the ideal of reform for women by women came in 1933, when state officials transferred female felons from the New York State Prison for Women at Auburn to Bedford's campus. Thereafter, Bedford Hills lost its identity as a reformatory and became a more traditional type of prison. *See also* ALDERSON PRISON; HARRIS, JEAN; MEDICAL EXPLANATIONS OF DELINQUENCY; PSYCHOLOGICAL EXPLANATIONS OF DELINQUENCY; REFORMATORY MOVEMENT; WOMEN'S PRISONS, HISTORY OF.

Further Reading: R. M. Alexander 1995, *The "Girl Problem";* Freedman 1981, *Their Sisters' Keepers;* Rafter 1990a, *Partial Justice;* Rafter 1997, *Creating Born Criminals.*

Cheryl D. Hicks

Boot Camps

Correctional boot camps for women are short-term penal institutions, alternatives to prison that require inmates to participate in a rigid daily schedule of physical exercise, hard labor, drill, and ceremony. The programs are modeled after military basic training. Inmates are required to follow a strict daily schedule. They are told when to eat, when to sleep, and when to get up. They march to meals and to training. Orders must be obeyed instantly and personal liberty is almost nonexistent. Those who complete the program may be rewarded with a reduced prison sentence. Some programs also include therapeutic programming, drug and alcohol treatment, academic education, and vocational training.

The first correctional boot camps opened in Oklahoma and Georgia in 1983. The idea spread rapidly throughout the United States. Ten years later, 25 states and the Federal Bureau of Prisons had boot camp programs for adult felons, and additional programs were being opened for local jail populations and for juvenile delinquents. Research has found that the programs have some positive effects on offenders while they are enrolled. However, there is no evidence that the programs significantly reduce recidivism, the post-release return to crime.

The earliest camps were designed as alternative correctional programs for young, nonviolent, first-time male offenders. However, in the interest of parity, many departments of corrections opened the male boot camps to female offenders or opened separate boot camps for female inmates. By 1992, 13 states had women in boot camp programs, with women making up 6.1 percent of the entire boot camp population.

Correctional boot camps are controversial. Some scholars argue that such an environment is not conducive to therapy and positive change. There is particular concern about how appropriate boot camps are for female offenders because the programs were designed for male offenders. Because the characteristics, past histories, and needs of female offenders are very different from those of males, such programs are of questionable benefit for women.

Further Reading: Lutze 1998, "Do Boot Camp Prisons Possess a More Rehabilitative Environment?"; MacKenzie and Donaldson 1996, "Boot Camps for Women Offenders."

Doris Layton MacKenzie

Borden, Lizzie (1860–1927)

Lizzie Borden, tried and acquitted for the hatchet murders of her father and stepmother in the most celebrated American trial of the late nineteenth century, is known today through a street rhyme:

> Lizzie Borden took an axe,
> And gave her mother forty whacks.
> When she saw what she had done,
> She gave her father forty-one.

Formally acquitted in 1893, Lizzie has been judged guilty in the court of public opinion, in large measure due to the true-crime books of author Edmund Pearson.

On August 4, 1892, Andrew and Abby Borden were found hacked to death in their home in Fall River, Massachusetts. Andrew was a businessman who had amassed a fortune through hard work and sharp business deals; Abby, his second wife and stepmother to his two daughters, was a quiet homemaker. The only persons known to be at home that day were Andrew's 32-year-old daughter, Lizzie, and the servant, Bridget Sullivan. The medical examiner estimated that Abby had been killed an hour and a half before Andrew.

Reasoning that the time gap between the murders made it unlikely that an intruder had committed the crimes, the police quickly identified Lizzie as the prime suspect, even though witnesses reported seeing more than one strange man in the vicinity of the house that morning, no one had seen blood on Lizzie's person, and there was some doubt that the murder weapon (a broken-handled hatchet found in the cellar) had been correctly identified.

The legal process that followed was thorough, including an inquest, a preliminary hearing, a grand jury proceeding, and a trial. Lizzie testified only at the inquest. At trial, the defense disputed the prosecution's case, pointing out the circumstantial nature of the evidence and presenting character witnesses on Lizzie's behalf. The jury quickly returned a verdict of acquittal, and the press and public rejoiced. Lizzie inherited her share of her father's substantial estate and lived out her days quietly and in comfort in Fall River. She died at the age of 67, leaving most of her fortune to the Animal Rescue League.

In 1924, while Lizzie was still alive, true-crime writer Edmund Pearson revived interest in the story by proposing that Lizzie was guilty. Pearson theorized that women were more able than men to get away with murder (E. Pearson 1924). His view was not contested until 1961 when author Edward Radin asserted both Lizzie's innocence and Pearson's selective presentation of the evidence against her. The case has since inspired dozens of retellings, both serious and fictional. Many of these accounts are based on

Lizzie Borden. *Collection of the Fall River Historical Society.*

Pearson's books, because until the 1980s, most of the primary source material was not readily available. Additional sources of secondary information are the first- or second-hand accounts of the case given by Fall River residents in interviews with writers. Thus has developed the legend of Lizzie Borden.

Popular works on Lizzie Borden have tended to focus on solving the killings. Scholarly works usually assume Lizzie's guilt and seek to place the case in a larger context. Since there is still unpublished material that may appear (for example, materials compiled by Andrew Jennings and George Robinson, two of Lizzie's lawyers), the case against Lizzie Borden seems not to be closed. Until more information and records surface, a definitive case cannot be made for her guilt or innocence.

Further Reading: A. Brown 1991, *Lizzie Borden;* E. Pearson 1937, *Trial of Lizzie Borden;* Ryckebusch 1993, *Proceedings, Lizzie Borden Conference.*

Randall P. Grometstein

C

Call Girls

Call girls are a class of prostitutes so named because originally they worked in brothels or call houses. However, by the 1930s, "call girl" colloquially referred to a prostitute who did not solicit clients on the street or work in a brothel but rather made appointments with clients via telephone, acquiring clients through an informal network of referrals. Clients might be seen in their homes, hotels, or at the call girl's residence. Traditionally, call girls worked independently, with a list or "book" of clients.

In the 1980s, a new type of call girl was created by the development of a system of escort services that connected clients with prostitutes. Call girls today also sometimes take out advertisements in the personal sections of weekly newspapers and specialized magazines, offering services as models or escorts. Appointments are made by phone. It is extremely difficult to estimate the number of practicing call girls or their proportion among all prostitutes, although it is clear that call girls are generally seen as the aristocrats of prostitution.

Call girls, particularly those most distant from associations with the police and/or the criminal underworld, are less vulnerable to police actions, harassment, and violence than street prostitutes; they are also almost always free of pimps, although some use a madam as a middle person. Call girls generally serve a more affluent clientele and command higher fees than other prostitutes. Call girls are expected to be better dressed, more educated, and more professional in their erotic artistry. Reflecting race and class social inequities, most call girls are white and middle class. According to some observers, they are the most independent of prostitutes and most in control of their lives on and off the job.

Though most call girls cater to men, some take women as clients. Lesbian brothel prostitution has existed historically, and some form of lesbian call girl prostitution has also undoubtedly existed. In the 1990s, lesbian prostitution is more overt. A number of gay and lesbian publications carry ads in their personal sections offering female masseurs and female escorts. There also are lesbian call girls who make appointments through informal networks and others who stay exclusively with one client for an extended period before moving on.

A number of prostitute rights organizations exist, though often with radically differing perspectives. The membership is usually former and current sex workers, as well as non-prostitute activists. COYOTE (Call Off Your Old Tired Ethics), founded in 1973 by former sex worker Margo St. James, is generally perceived as the organization that is most representative of call girls. COYOTE leaders, however, stress the importance of solidarity and support among all types of sex workers. Another group, WHISPER (Women Hurt in Systems of Prostitution Engaged in

Revolt), was founded by ex-prostitute Sarah Wynter in 1985. Citing women's general economic disadvantages, the abuse of girls in their homes, the control of prostitutes by pimps, and drug addiction among sex workers, Wynter (1987) rejects the argument that prostitution is chosen or is a viable career choice. She also repudiates what she terms the false hierarchy between call girls and street workers, arguing that the only material distinction between them is that call girls are abused in private while street workers are abused in public.

Although the social structure of prostitution is still debated, call girls seem to be at the top of this hierarchy. *See also* PROSTITUTION.

Further Reading: Chapkis 1997, *Live Sex Acts;* Delacoste and Alexander 1987, *Sex Work;* Diana 1985, *The Prostitute and Her Clients.*

Jane Caputi

Case Processing and Gender

There is compelling evidence that gender affects case-processing decisions in criminal court. Researchers have investigated the treatment of women who appear in court either as victims of crime or as criminal defendants. Studies of the treatment of female victims of crime, most of which focus on sexual assault or domestic violence cases, reveal that legally irrelevant victim characteristics, such as the relationship between the victim and the offender or risky behavior by the victim at the time of the assault, affect case outcomes. Studies comparing the treatment of male and female offenders generally reveal that female offenders are treated more leniently than male offenders; however, the explanations for this more lenient treatment vary.

Research examining sexual assault case-processing decisions, and particularly research conducted prior to the 1990s, demonstrates that criminal justice officials use legally irrelevant assessments of a victim's character, behavior, and relationship with the defendant in making decisions regarding the processing and disposition of sexual assault cases. Studies reveal that sexual assault case

outcomes are affected by the victim's age, occupation, and education; by evidence of "risk-taking" behavior such as hitchhiking, drinking, or using drugs; by the victim's behavior during and after the assault; and by the victim's character and reputation. The relationship between the victim and the offender, and the racial makeup of the offender-victim dyad, also affect decision-making in these types of cases. Sexual assaults involving strangers are considered more serious and result in harsher treatment than sexual assaults involving someone the victim knows. Sexual assaults involving black men and white women are more likely than intraracial assaults to be successfully prosecuted. Black-on-white sexual assaults also result in harsher sentences than either black-on-black or white-on-white assaults.

These results suggest that the response of the criminal justice system is predicated on stereotypes about rape and rape victims, and that the most serious dispositions are reserved for "real rapes" involving "genuine victims." Estrich (1987:28), for example, argues that the law distinguishes between the "aggravated, jump-from-the-bushes stranger rapes and the simple cases of unarmed rape by friends, neighbors, and acquaintances." LaFree (1989) similarly concludes that nontraditional women, black women assaulted by black men, and women who were engaged in risky behavior at the time of the attack are less likely to be viewed as genuine victims who deserve protection under the law.

Concerns about the processing of sexual assault cases and the treatment of sexual assault victims in court eventually led to changes in rape law. Beginning in the mid-1970s, women's groups, led by the National Organization for Women's (NOW) Task Force on Rape, lobbied state legislatures to revise common-law definitions of rape that excluded males and spouses as victims and that excluded acts other than sexual intercourse. They also called on legislatures to repeal rules of evidence that required the victim to physically resist her attacker, required corroboration of the victim's testimony, and allowed evidence of the victim's past sexual conduct to be admitted at trial. As a result of these efforts, by the mid-1980s, most states had enacted rape law reforms designed to remove legal barriers to effective prosecution and to make arrest, prosecution, and conviction for rape more likely.

Studies evaluating the impact of these reforms reveal that they did not produce the dramatic instrumental changes envisioned by reformers. Although the reforms did result in more enlightened attitudes toward the crime of sexual assault and in more humane treatment of sexual assault victims, they did not affect the number of sexual assaults reported to the police or produce significant increases in either the prosecution or conviction rate for sexual assault.

Victim characteristics also have been shown to affect decision-making in domestic violence cases. Although most of the research on domestic violence case outcomes focuses on the decision to arrest or not, there are a few studies that examine charging and sentencing decisions. These studies reveal that, until fairly recently, most domestic violence arrests did not result in the filing of charges and that those cases that were prosecuted rarely resulted in lengthy jail or prison sentences.

The high dismissal rate in cases of domestic violence is attributed to a variety of factors: the "nonserious" nature of the offense; the victim's reluctance to proceed with prosecution or to testify if the case goes to trial; questions about the adequacy of evidence; and concerns about the credibility of the victim's testimony. A study of screening decisions in misdemeanor domestic violence cases in Milwaukee (Schmidt and Steury 1989), for example, found that prosecutors were more likely to file charges if the victim was seriously injured, if a weapon was used during the assault, and if the defendant failed to appear at the charging conference. Prosecutors were less likely to file charges if the victim and defendant were sexually intimate or living together at the time of the assault.

Reforms implemented in response to concerns about attrition in domestic violence cases include the creation of specialized domestic violence prosecution units and the development of "no-drop" policies for domestic violence cases. A number of states also adopted batterer programs that permit or require judges to impose some form of counseling as a condition of probation. Despite these changes, domestic violence continues to be treated less seriously than other forms of assault.

As for defendants, there is a substantial body of research examining the treatment of women who appear in court as criminal defendants rather than as victims of crime. Many studies conclude that female defendants are treated more leniently than male defendants, even after legally relevant factors such as the seriousness of the offense or the defendant's prior criminal history are taken into consideration. This pattern of results characterizes studies conducted in the 1970s and 1980s, as well as more recent research. Studies reveal that women are more likely than men to be released (on their own recognizance or on bail) prior to trial and to have their cases dismissed prior to trial. They also are less likely than men to be sentenced to prison, and those who are incarcerated receive shorter sentences. Other studies conclude that females are treated no differently than males, particularly with respect to the decisions to prosecute, to plea-bargain, or to convict.

Despite these contradictory findings, the bulk of the evidence points toward more lenient treatment of female defendants, especially at the sentencing stage of the criminal justice process. Most researchers conclude that this preferential treatment reflects paternalism or, alternatively, chivalry. According to this view, criminal justice officials treat women more leniently than men because they presume that women are physically weaker than men and thus must be protected from the harshness of the criminal justice system, or because they believe that women are less culpable, less dangerous, or less likely to recidivate than men and thus deserve less punitive treatment.

Other researchers contend that the explanation is more complex. They suggest that the more lenient treatment of female defendants might reflect more *practical* concerns about the childcare responsibilities. Judges may refuse to sentence female offenders to prison, in other words, not because of paternalistic or chivalrous attitudes toward women, but because they assume that many female defendants have young children and believe that sending these defendants to prison would both disrupt family life and place the burden of caring for the children on society.

Concerns about sentencing disparities based on legally irrelevant factors such as gender or race/ethnicity prompted Congress and many state legislatures to enact reforms, including sentencing guidelines and mandatory minimum sentences, that reduced judges' discretion at sentencing. The push for reform began in the late 1970s; by 1990, the federal government and most states had implemented one or more sentencing reforms. The results of studies conducted during the post-reform period indicate that these reforms have not eliminated gender discrimination in sentencing. Studies of sentences imposed under federal and state sentencing guidelines reveal that female offenders are sentenced more leniently than similarly situated male offenders. Female offenders sentenced under the Pennsylvania sentencing guidelines, for example, were less likely than male offenders to be incarcerated, and those who were incarcerated received sentences that averaged 5.3 months less than those imposed on their male counterparts. Female offenders also were more likely than male offenders to receive a dispositional departure—that is, the appropriate sentence according to the guidelines was incarceration, but the judge imposed probation or some other alternative to incarceration. Despite substantial changes in sentencing laws and practices, in other words, female offenders continue to receive more lenient sentences than male offenders.

In sum, there is convincing evidence that gender affects case-processing decisions. The character, behavior, and credibility of women who appear in court as victims of sexual assault or domestic violence may be called into question. This, in turn, may affect the likelihood of successful prosecution of these types of cases. Women who appear in court as offenders may be viewed as physically weaker, less culpable, or less dangerous than male offenders; they also may be presumed to be responsible for the care of young children. As a result, female offenders may be treated more leniently than similarly situated male offenders. *See also* CHARGING AND PLEA-BARGAINING; CHIVALRY EXPLANATION OF COURT OUTCOMES; DOMESTIC VIOLENCE CASE PROCESSING; GENDER DISCRIMINATION AND SENTENCING; SEXUAL ASSAULT CASE PROCESSING.

Further Reading: Buzawa and Buzawa 1996, *Domestic Violence;* Daly 1994, *Gender, Crime and Punishment;* LaFree 1989, *Rape and Criminal Justice.*

Cassia C. Spohn

Charging and Plea-Bargaining

Charging and plea-bargaining are stages in the U.S. criminal justice system in which the suspect's gender may affect the prosecutor's decisions. Due to the informal and low-visibility nature of charging decisions and the frequent interplay between charging and plea-bargaining, relatively few studies have focused explicitly on the role the suspect's gender may play in these two important stages of criminal adjudication. Moreover, these studies are inconclusive in their findings about whether gender affects charging and plea-bargaining outcomes.

The chivalry/paternalism thesis (Pollak 1961) hypothesizes that female defendants are treated more leniently than male defendants because court officials perceive females to be dependent persons who are in need of protection. Several early descriptive studies of charging and plea-bargaining reported findings consistent with this thesis. However, other studies produced contradictory evidence. One (I. Nagel, Cardascia, and Ross 1980) found that gender did not significantly affect prosecutors' decisions to charge. Consistent with the "evil woman" thesis, Daly's (1987) research indicated that women were *less* likely than men to have charges dismissed. Daly's study also indicated that males with dependents were more likely to have charges dismissed than either males with no dependents or females with dependents. These latter two studies used multivariate procedures to examine the effect of gender on charging and plea-bargaining outcomes, but neither of them controlled for the presence of evidence of the suspect's guilt or the strength of evidence, when present. Thus, we still cannot be sure that the findings of gender effects are meaningful.

Later multivariate research that included measures of the presence and strength of evidence reported that gender does not exert a significant effect on the initial decision to charge a suspect with a felony. Specifically, M. A. Myers and Hagan (1979) found that evidence of guilt, the defendant's age, the race of the defendant and victim, having a record of prior charges, and the victim-defendant relationship influenced the initial decision to charge a felony. Albonetti (1987) found that evidence of guilt, the victim-suspect relationship, type of offense, record of prior convictions, and whether the victim was an individual or an organization influenced the initial decision to prosecute. Miethe's (1987) study, controlling for use of a weapon and prior offenses, found that males are more likely to be charged than females.

Only a few studies have examined prosecutorial discretion to discontinue prosecution. Spohn, Gruhl, and Welch (1987) and Albonetti (1986) found that among felony cases surviving the initial decision to prosecute, females were more likely to have charges dropped than males. Strength of evidence against the defendant, the victim-defendant relationship, whether the offense was somehow provoked by the victim, the defendant's race, and the type of felony offense all significantly affected the prosecutor's decision to discontinue prosecution. These studies point to the importance of including measures of evidence in an examination of charging decisions.

Most research on plea-bargaining has not examined the influence of a defendant's gender on whether the defendant pleads guilty or on the favorability of the bargains negoti-

ated. Instead, research has focused on whether the likelihood of a plea-bargain is affected by informal organizational controls, the defendant's prior convictions, the defendant's role in the alleged crime, and the strength of the evidence. A few exceptions are noteworthy. Bernstein et al. (1977) reported that females received less favorable bargains than males, and Figueira-McDonough's (1985) study suggested that women plea bargain less frequently than males due to the less serious nature of the crimes they are alleged to have committed. Albonetti (1998a) found that being female reduced the likelihood of pleading guilty among white-collar defendants. However, Daly (1994), Albonetti (1992), M. D. Holmes, Kaudistel, and Farrell (1987), and Bishop and Frazier (1984) found that a defendant's gender was irrelevant in the plea-bargaining process. Some theorists suggest that informal relationships among the prosecuting attorney, defense counsel, and judge may influence plea negotiations, while others believe that social constructions of the defendant as sinister may have this effect.

Taken together, studies of charging and plea-bargaining point to the need to investigate whether a defendant's gender is related to leniency of plea-bargains indirectly through crime seriousness, prior convictions, susceptibility to informal prosecutorial pressures, and the amount of leverage the defendant brings to the plea-negotiation process. Women who fit the "evil woman" stereotype may be disadvantaged in plea-bargaining and other court processes. *See also* CASE PROCESSING AND GENDER; CHIVALRY EXPLANATION OF COURT OUTCOMES; GENDER DISCRIMINATION AND SENTENCING.

Further Reading: Albonetti 1998a, "Direct and Indirect Effects"; Chesney-Lind 1977, "Judicial Paternalism"; Daly 1994, *Gender, Crime and Punishment.*

Celesta A. Albonetti

Child Abuse by Women

Although one of the primary social roles for women is that of mother, some women engage in child abuse, a category that includes neglect and physical and sexual maltreatment. According to the U.S. National Clearinghouse on Child Abuse and Neglect Information, in 1996, state child protective services agencies investigated more than two million allegations of child abuse involving more than three million children. These investigations resulted in the confirmation of approximately one million cases of abuse, about one thousand of which were fatalities. The perpetrators in 77 percent of cases were parents, and in another 11 percent of the cases, the perpetrators were other relatives; approximately two-thirds of the perpetrators were women. It is commonly believed that women who mistreat their children suffer from some type of serious mental illness, but that is true in only a small percentage of cases. Most often, some combination of psycho-social risk factors is present that places a given family in jeopardy. The larger the number and more severe the risk factors, the higher the risk for child maltreatment.

According to the National Clearinghouse on Child Abuse and Neglect Information, 24 percent of confirmed cases of child abuse involve physical maltreatment. Slightly over half of the perpetrators of physical child abuse are women, many of them teen mothers. They tend to suffer from low self-esteem, depression, anxiety, and low frustration tolerance. They also tend to have deficits in empathy and intellect, as well as difficulty controlling their anger. These mothers may have been victims of child abuse themselves and are likely to have problems with interpersonal relationships. They may be isolated, with little support from family and/or friends. They generally lack knowledge about child development, and thus they may have unrealistic expectations of their children and be insensitive to their children's needs and abilities. They also tend to have poor communication and problem-solving skills. These parents tend to view the parenting role as stressful and to hold negative perceptions of their children. Perpetrators may be substance abusers or have other health problems in addition to a high overall level of life stress.

Sexual abuse is the main problem in about 12 percent of confirmed cases of child abuse. Most studies report that 90 percent or more of perpetrators of child sexual abuse are males. The few women who do engage in sexual abuse of children tend to be accomplices to males, isolated single parents, adolescent female babysitters, or women who become romantically involved with adolescent males.

Neglect, the most common type of child abuse, accounts for 52 percent of confirmed cases. About 75 percent of neglect cases involve female perpetrators. Generally, neglect refers to a failure to meet a child's basic needs, physically, educationally, and/or emotionally. Poverty is a strong predictor of neglect, with over half of the cases involving single-female-headed households in which the mother is unemployed. There is little research in this area, and what has been done tends to focus more on situational factors than on the caregivers' characteristics.

Contrary to popular belief, women do not necessarily possess an innate ability to be good mothers. Parenting skills can be learned, however, and most mothers are capable students. The challenge is to intervene in high-risk situations before a child suffers irreparable harm. *See also* DOMESTIC VIOLENCE BY WOMEN; INCEST VICTIMS; POVERTY AND CRIME; SEXUAL ABUSE OF CHILDREN.

Further Reading: Barnett, Miller-Perrin, and Perrin 1997, *Family Violence;* Briere, Berliner, Bulkley, Jenny, and Reid 1996, *The APSAC Handbook on Child Maltreatment;* U. S. Department of Health and Human Services 1998, *Child Maltreatment 1996.*

Sandra S. Stone

Child Homicide. *See* CHILD ABUSE BY WOMEN; INFANTICIDE; VICTIMIZATION PATTERNS, CANADA.

Child Witnesses

Children may observe or experience crimes and need to provide reports to authorities, thereby becoming child witnesses. The crime of child sexual abuse, to which young girls are especially vulnerable, is particularly likely to bring children in contact with the court system. But for both girls and boys, the experience of being a child witness may leave social and emotional scars such as post–traumatic stress disorder. Child witnesses differ importantly from adult witnesses because of children's less developed socio-emotional, linguistic, and memory abilities. Asking children to report information to the police or to testify in court raises many questions about the accuracy of children's testimony, whether interviewers can create false memories in children, and how best to protect children from the stress of legal involvement.

Children have testified in legal proceedings throughout history. However, in recent years, there have been important changes in U.S. laws regarding children's competence to testify, the need for corroborating evidence, and the use of video technology. These changes apply equally to girls and boys. Additionally, "taint hearings" have been authorized in several states to explore whether a child's memory has been tainted by suggestive questioning (*State v. Michaels* 1994). Notwithstanding these legal changes, if a case goes to trial, children are often treated much like adults: required to face the defendant; subjected to cross-examination; and asked double-negative questions in "legalese."

When a crime is reported, children may be interviewed by police or social workers. Children vary in the completeness and accuracy of their reports, but the variations seem to depend more on age than gender. Young children do not provide as much information during a "free recall" interview as older children. However, if the interviewer poses more specific questions, the questions may be deemed leading or suggestive. This is especially true when children are subjected to multiple interviews.

Props or cues such as anatomically detailed dolls may be introduced during interviews. Research shows mixed results, the most common being that props facilitate the accuracy of children older than about 5 years, while they add error to the reports of younger children. Although there is currently no "gold standard" method of interviewing children, different combinations of free recall, specific questions, and prop-assisted questions are being studied to determine which facilitates the most accurate and complete reports from children.

Another important consideration is whether children are regarded as competent witnesses by jurors and legal professionals. In mock jury studies of sexual abuse cases, jurors tend to decide that young children would not themselves fabricate such allegations but could be coerced or manipulated into making false reports. Jurors are also more likely to believe child witnesses if corroborating evidence exists. When children are allowed to testify through closed-circuit television or out of sight of the defendant, rather than in open court, jurors find the testimony less credible. Overall, female jurors are more likely to believe child witnesses than are male jurors.

As a result of legal involvement, children may experience social and emotional distress brought on by such stressors as multiple forensic interviews, speaking about traumatic experiences, lack of parental support, harsh cross-examination, facing the defendant, and being disbelieved. While testifying is helpful for some children, it causes others to recover from the criminal and legal experience more slowly than their non-testifying counterparts. To remedy these negative consequences, innovative legal procedures, multidisciplinary interview centers, and child advocate programs are being developed and tested in the United States and abroad. *See also* SEXUAL ABUSE OF CHILDREN; VICTIMS IN COURT.

Further Reading: Goodman and Bottoms 1993, *Child Victims, Child Witnesses;* J. E. B. Myers 1998, *Legal Issues in Child Abuse and Neglect Practice.*

Kristen Weede Alexander and
Gail S. Goodman

Child-Savers Movement

The term "child-savers," popularized by Anthony Platt's (1969) book on the founding of the juvenile court, refers to a group of upper-middle- and middle-class U.S. women reformers and philanthropists in the Progressive Era (1880–1920) who campaigned for the recognition and control of youthful deviance. The child-savers and their social movement brought activities that had previously been ignored or dealt with informally—such as drinking, begging, frequenting dance halls, fighting, and flirting—under government control. Regarding themselves as moral custodians, the child-savers supported programs and institutions designed to eliminate immoral behaviors of youth. Their most significant and lasting legacy was the establishment of the first juvenile court in Chicago in 1899.

The roots of the child-savers movement can be found in early child protection work. The Society for the Prevention of Cruelty to Children, founded in New York in 1874, was the first group dedicated to championing the cause of child protection against cruelty. It formed to address the abuse and neglect of a young girl, Mary Ellen Wilson.

The core group of child-savers consisted of feminist reformers and women identified with the more conservative social purity movement who championed the prohibition of alcohol and worked against such "social evils" as prostitution and "white slavery." In an era during which women could enter the public sphere only by capitalizing on their motherly virtues, child-saving was reputable philanthropic work for women. Upper-middle- and middle-class women saw it as their moral responsibility to rescue wayward children of working-class and immigrant origins. Reformers associated with the Chicago settlement movement such as Jane Addams, Julia Lathrop, and Florence Kelly mobilized the Chicago Women's Club to use its extensive political contacts and economic resources on behalf of poor children. These women spoke out against brothels, alcohol, amusement parks, and juvenile crime. They organized immigrant mothers and offered them character training. By 1920, a powerful network of Mothers' Clubs existed in many states, working on behalf of juvenile justice reform.

The juvenile court movement, with its origins in Chicago in 1899, is generally regarded as the child-savers' most important contribution to criminal justice administration. The juvenile court movement was part of a more general movement to shield adolescents from the criminal law process and create special programs for delinquent, dependent, and neglected children. The juvenile court expanded the discretionary authority of judges and made inquiries into the character, habits, and genetic background of youths who seemed to be in danger of falling into vice. The child-savers also founded institutions specifically devoted to the reformation of girls, a group whose morality was of special concern to social reformers and juvenile court judges.

The juvenile court was designed not only to help wayward children but also to protect society from future criminals. Progressive reformers were interested in persuading immigrant and lower-class families to adopt middle-class American values. However, achievements fell short of the child-savers' compassionate goals. Neglected and merely boisterous children were often institutionalized. The child-savers' reforms resulted in greater state control over the lives of poor and immigrant children and over the sexual activities of girls. *See also* JUVENILE INSTITUTIONS, HISTORY OF.

Further Reading: Gordon 1988, *Heroes of Their Own Lives*; Kasinsky 1994, "Child Neglect and 'Unfit' Mothers"; Ryerson 1978, *The Best-Laid Plans*.

Renee Goldsmith Kasinsky

Chivalry Explanation of Court Outcomes

The "chivalry" explanation of court outcomes, a theory associated in particular with the criminologist Otto Pollak, holds that "misplaced gallantry interferes with convictions of women offenders" (Pollak 1961:4). In other words, according to this theory, criminal justice personnel treat women defendants more leniently than male defendants out of a desire to be helpful or "chivalrous" to the former, whom they mistakenly regard as helpless and errant rather than criminal. Chivalry might explain leniency toward women at any decision point in the prosecutorial process: charging, offering bail, negotiating guilty pleas, deciding guilt at trial, or sentencing. For instance, one study of female criminals in the courts of Victorian England found that women felons were usually regarded as "mad, not bad" and were shut away in mental institutions rather than charged in criminal court (Knelman 1997). Sociologists examining American court records from the 1960s and 1970s have used chivalry to explain the fact that women were released pending trial more often than men, a difference with powerful positive effects on subsequent court stages.

Sentencing is the court procedure that has been most thoroughly scrutinized for gender disparities. Most studies find that there are significant differences between sentences imposed on men and women. However, unlike Pollak and other earlier criminologists, contemporary researchers seldom attribute these differences to chivalry.

Contemporary observers argue that socioeconomic and other "structural" factors may explain variation in court outcomes better than gender alone does. They point out, for example, that judges may treat women more gently than men because women's crimes and criminal histories are less serious, not because of chivalry.

Examining pretrial release and the "in/out" sentencing decision (i.e., prison/probation) in felony cases against men and women from 1965 to 1980, Kruttschnitt and Green (1984) found that women were released on bail significantly more often than men. Furthermore, this outcome increased in later years, when, presumably, the women's movement and the increase in women justice officials, such as probation officers and judges, would cause chivalrous responses to diminish. Finding little evidence of sentencing leniency, these researchers determined that the reason for variation in punishment really lay with women's social status. Defendants who were not self-supporting were more likely to be released before trial, suggesting that the courts were reinforcing "at least one existing mechanism of informal social control—the sexually stratified system of economic dependency" (Kruttschnitt and Green 1984:542), but not that the courts were being chivalrous.

More recently, Daly (1994) found significant differences between men's and women's sentences but attributed them to judges' conclusions that women are less blameworthy. Many of the women had been victimized themselves, they had led conventional lives, and they often admitted their guilt openly. Daly, too, recommended that criminologists discard the chivalry explanation, and at the beginning of the twenty-first century, that explanation for court outcomes is no longer considered valid. *See also* CASE PROCESSING AND GENDER; CHARGING AND PLEA-BARGAINING; CHIVALRY EXPLANATION OF FEMALE CRIME RATES; DEATH PENALTY; GENDER DISCRIMINATION AND JUVENILE JUSTICE; GENDER DISCRIMINATION AND SENTENCING.

Further Reading: Daly 1994, *Gender, Crime, and Punishment*; Kruttschnitt and Green 1984, "The Sex-Sanctioning Issue."

Candace McCoy

Chivalry Explanation of Female Crime Rates

Although nearly all available data indicate that females are less criminal than males, the chivalry explanation of female crime rates suggests that these differences are not real but rather the result of male officials' efforts to protect women offenders from prosecution.

Compared with men, women constitute a smaller proportion of arrestees, defendants, probationers, prisoners, and parolees—primarily because women are less actively involved in crime and commit less serious offenses. These "legal" factors explain why women have lower crime rates and why they appear to be treated more leniently by the police, courts, and correctional systems. However, some theorists have argued that "extra-legal" reasons better account for women's lower crime rates and their apparently more lenient treatment. They have put forth the chivalry hypothesis to explain these phenomena.

W. I. Thomas (1907) first used the term *chivalry* to suggest that female offenders are advantaged over similarly situated males because male criminal justice decision-makers are unwilling to inflict harm on women, whom they see as essentially innocent and guiltless. According to Thomas, police officers, judges, and other criminal justice decision-makers feel compelled to protect women, and they simply cannot believe that women can possess criminal intent as fully as men. Otto Pollak (1961) also cites chivalry to account for women's low official crime rates, indeed arguing that women commit crime at the same rates as men, but that their crime is "hidden." According to Pollak, women's "natural" attributes of deceitfulness and slyness, and their domestic lifestyles out of the public eye, help conceal the crimes they commit. Moreover, because of men's generally protective attitude toward women, criminal justice authorities are reluctant to investigate and prosecute women.

Many criminologists link the concept of chivalry to an argument that the criminal justice system reacts paternalistically toward women. The paternalism hypothesis states that regardless of women's criminal intent, their weaker and more childlike nature demands that they be cared for rather than punished. While either chivalry or paternalism could lead to more lenient treatment for women, paternalism is arguably more insidious because it may ultimately result in harsher treatment for women than men (Moulds 1980).

Scholars cite the 1913 Muncy Act of Pennsylvania to illustrate paternalism. This act was passed because legislators thought that women, being weaker than men, would benefit more from the rehabilitative effects of prolonged confinement (Armstrong 1982). The Muncy Act removed the discretion of trial judges to impose a lower sentence than the maximum punishment provided by law or to set a minimum sentence that would afford parole eligibility to women convicted of crimes punishable by imprisonment for a year or more. The result was that, under the guise of protection, women offenders routinely served longer sentences than men for the same offenses.

Scholars have investigated the validity of the chivalry/paternalism hypothesis through empirical studies. Few studies applying appropriate statistical controls for offense seriousness and prior record demonstrate uniformly lenient treatment for women (Belknap 1996). Rather, research suggests that gender may advantage women offenders under certain circumstances while it may play no part or even disadvantage them in others.

Nagel and Hagan (1983) suggest that chivalry/paternalism may operate for a subcategory of women offenders whose criminal behavior is interpreted as an extension of female gender roles. Conversely, women who do not fit the feminine stereotype by virtue of their race, class, or offense may suffer even more harshly than men accused of similar offenses. Recent studies reveal that the most likely recipients of preferential treatment are white, middle- or upper-class women who commit offenses that fit with "proper" gender roles and show deference to officials, especially police officers (Belknap 1996). Conversely, women who are young, poor, hostile, and of a minority background, or who commit offenses associated with males, may face more punitive treatment.

While an offender's sex *per se* may not lead to more lenient treatment, attributes of defendants that are related to gender roles are taken into account by criminal justice decision-makers. Daly (1989b) and Crew (1991) report that decision-makers work to keep families intact; thus, persons responsible for dependent children, most of whom are women, may receive special consideration.

The debate about the impact of gender on official crime rates and criminal justice processing has become less critical in recent years as increasing numbers of jurisdictions have enacted laws to reduce discretion in criminal justice decision-making. With mandatory arrest and sentencing laws, extra-legal factors such as gender have less room to affect arrest figures and sentencing. *See also* CASE PROCESSING AND GENDER; CHARGING AND PLEA-BARGAINING; CHIVALRY EXPLANA-

TION OF COURT OUTCOMES; FEMALE CRIME, PATTERNS AND TRENDS IN, USA; GENDER DISCRIMINATION AND JUVENILE JUSTICE; GENDER DISCRIMINATION AND SENTENCING; LIBERATION EXPLANATION OF CRIME; JUVENILE DELINQUENCY, AUSTRALIA.

Further Reading: Crew 1991, "Sex Differences in Criminal Sentencing"; Nagel and Hagan 1983, "Gender and Crime"; Pollak 1961, *The Criminality of Women.*

Lynne I. Goodstein

Chronic Offenders

Chronic female offenders—meaning women who continue to break the law long after others have "matured out" of criminal behavior—have received little criminological attention. The term "chronic" was coined in 1972 by Wolfgang, Figlio, and Sellin to describe offenders with five or more arrests. In the 1972 study by Wolfgang and his colleagues, 20 percent of sampled male juveniles arrested between 1948 and 1958 fit the "chronic" definition, and they accounted for 56 percent of arrests during that period. Estimates of the proportion of female offenders who are "chronic" by the same definition range from 1 percent among juveniles to 33 percent among incarcerated adults.

Because the vast majority of chronic offenders are incarcerated, increases in female prison populations almost certainly indicate that female chronic offenders are increasing in number. While males continue to significantly outnumber females in U.S. arrest statistics, accounting for over 80 percent of those arrested, the annual rate of females incarcerated continues to increase at approximately three to four times that of males. Between 1988 and 1997, the incarcerated male population increased 11 percent while the incarcerated female population increased 40 percent (U.S. Department of Justice, Federal Bureau of Investigation 1996, 1997, 1998). Since 1990, the annual growth of the female inmate population has averaged about 9 percent while that of the male inmate population has averaged about 7 percent. By 30

June 1999, females constituted 7 percent of all inmates nationwide.

Female chronic offenders are similar to their male counterparts in terms of a number of characteristics: they are likely to be members of a minority group, unmarried, substance abusers, and involved in intimate abuse/domestic violence. Unlike males, however, female chronic offenders are more likely to be the victims of abuse and violence rather than the perpetrators. Female chronic offenders are, on average, better educated, more likely to come from broken homes, and more likely to have had members of their families involved in criminal activities than male chronic offenders.

When compared with nonchronic female offenders, chronic female offenders are more likely to have been victims of child abuse, incarcerated for relatively minor offenses, and involved with male codefendants. Most important in discriminating between the two female groups is the age at first arrest (chronics are, in general, four years younger at age of first arrest), a history of substance abuse, and the fact of having served time for less serious offenses.

The social forces that contribute to multiple offending by females (abuse as children, single-parent households, substance abuse) may well increase in the future, resulting in the chronic female offender becoming a more common phenomenon than at present. Additional research on chronic female offenders is necessary in order to expand our understanding of, and ability to work with, this troubled group of offenders. *See also* DESISTANCE FROM CRIME.

Further Reading: Blount, Kuhns, and Silverman 1993, "Intimate Abuse within an Incarcerated Female Population"; T. Danner, Blount, Silverman, and Vega 1995, "The Female Chronic Offender."

Ira J. Silverman and William R. Blount

Co-correctional Prisons

Between 1970 and 1990, several co-correctional or "coed" prisons, housing male and female inmates in a single penal institution and under the same administration, were opened in the federal and various state prison systems in the United States. Co-corrections served administrative needs for more adequate programming for female prisoners, and they provided one solution to lawsuits charging that women's prisons discriminated by offering fewer resources than men's prisons. Nearly all of them had a predominance of male or of female prisoners, even though experts felt that the ideal ratio was 50 percent men and 50 percent women.

Co-correctional prisons enjoyed some popularity in the early 1980s. A survey published by *Corrections Compendium* in 1986 identified 25 prison systems that housed men and women together in settings where they shared food, recreation, and job services. By 1999, there were no co-correctional facilities on record, although some may well have existed informally.

Co-correctional facilities were established to solve administrative, operational, or economic problems or to respond to pressure from lawsuits charging discrimination. When they were established as a temporary solution to an immediate problem, they were frequently abandoned before long and with little fanfare.

When co-correctional prisons were established for more systematic reasons, they were usually based on the penal philosophy of reintegration or encouraging prisoners to learn to live, after release, in harmony with the outside community. The expectation was that prisoners who maintained ordinary relations with people of the opposite sex during incarceration would be best equipped to return to productive community life. Additionally, there is evidence that co-correctional prisons are less violent than those that house men only. These coed facilities were also an economical way to provide women with programs to which they would not have had access in a separate women's prison, and they provided career opportunities for women administrators, who are sometimes denied promotion in all-male facilities.

The greatest weaknesses of co-correctional prisons have to do with politics and with their tendency to disadvantage women prisoners. Co-correctional prisons are difficult for politicians to support in the current "get tough" era. Another disadvantage is the need to control interactions between males and females while at the same time maximizing the use of the facilities by both. Efforts to control interaction can lead to increased levels of supervision, especially of the female prisoners.

Countless rules and policies develop to regulate contacts and counter the strong motivation on the part of male and female inmates to control interaction themselves. As in the outside world, the burden of preventing pregnancies and the transmission of sexual diseases tends to fall on the women. Moreover, co-correctional policies must address prisoner decisions to seek divorces from partners outside of the prison after becoming involved with individuals inside the facility.

To be useful, co-correctional prisons must be integrated into state or local correctional systems. They must involve equal proportions of both male and female inmates so that neither group feels isolated. They must also provide opportunities for healthy male-female relationships. Although co-correctional prisons can be very useful, they are unlikely to be used to full advantage until the public again supports prisoner rehabilitation. *See also* GENDER DISPARITIES IN PRISONS.

Further Reading: Mahan 1986, "Doing Time Together"; Schweber 1984, "Beauty Marks and Blemishes"; Smykla 1979, "Does Coed Prison Work?"

Sue G. Mahan

Coffin, Rhoda (1826–1909)

Rhoda Coffin, a prime example of the religiously motivated, middle-class feminists in the nineteenth-century prison reform movement, was instrumental in the development of the first separate women's reformatory in the United States. Born Rhoda Johnson in 1826, she married Charles Coffin, a devout Quaker banker, in 1847. Together they participated in the 1870 national prison congress, which endorsed a *Declaration of Principles* supporting separate prisons for women and the movement to build reformatory prisons for adults.

Sexual scandals at the Indiana Prison provided the political impetus in 1869 for the Coffins to persuade the legislature to build the Indiana Reformatory Prison for Women and Girls. It opened in Indianapolis in 1873 with separate sections for adult women and delinquent girls.

In 1875, Rhoda Coffin became the first woman to present a paper at a meeting of the group known today as the American Correctional Association. In it, she argued that women's prisons should be under the control of women. This goal was achieved in her own state in 1877, when women replaced men on the board of managers of the Indiana Reformatory Prison for Women and Girls and Rhoda Coffin became head of the board. *See also* AMERICAN CORRECTIONAL ASSOCIATION; PRISON REFORM, USA; REFORMATORY MOVEMENT; WOMEN'S PRISON ADMINISTRATION, HISTORICAL; WOMEN'S PRISONS, HISTORY OF.

Further Reading: Freedman 1981, *Their Sisters' Keepers;* Rafter 1990a, *Partial Justice.*

Esther Heffernan

Community Policing

In the United States, two of the most significant changes in policing since the 1970s have been a commitment to community policing, in which officers work closely and cooperatively with area residents, and a significant increase in the number of women (and men of color) hired as patrol officers. The commitment to community policing grew out of a realization that traditional motor patrol policing is largely ineffective in deterring crime; it was reinforced by an interest in reducing police-community tensions and by the nationally televised police brutality case perpetrated by the Los Angeles Police Department against Rodney King, in which no officers were convicted. The hiring of more women of all races/ethnicities and more men of color into the profession is credited almost entirely to the enactment of Title VII, a 1972 amendment to the 1964 Civil Rights Act. In part, this amendment established that, except in rare cases, hiring decisions cannot be based on an applicant's sex, race, religion, or country of origin.

Although there is no single program designated as "community policing," police departments across the United States (and in many other countries) are attempting to design programs that provide more frequent and more positive interactions between the police and the citizens they serve. The goal of community policing is that citizens will encounter police in situations outside of crime victimizations and offending. The hope is that if citizens see police playing basketball with neighborhood teenagers or greeting community residents by name, they will regard the police more positively and be more inclined to report victimizations and other community concerns.

The commitment to community policing and the increased hiring of women of all races (and men of color) are interrelated in meaningful and beneficial ways. Specifically, hiring more officers of color (male or female) may help mitigate the police-citizen racial tensions of many communities, given that the officers more accurately reflect the populations they serve. Regarding gender, a substantial amount of research indicates that gendered differences in policing styles, behaviors, and practices make women, as a rule, ideal candidates for community policing.

It is important to note that not all women officers behave the same, nor do all men: There are no *men's* or *women's* policing styles. Nonetheless, the following research findings on gender differences in policing strongly suggest that women, as a group, are better suited for the community-policing role:

- Women police officers have better relations with, and more support from, the citizenry than their male counterparts.
- Women tend to have a less aggressive policing style than men.
- Compared with their male co-workers, female police officers are more likely to have empathy for rape and battering victims.

- Women police officers are generally more creative in their handling of problematic citizen encounters.

At the same time that women's policing behaviors have been evaluated favorably by the citizenry, however, women officers have faced a significant amount of hostility from male co-workers, supervisors, and police administrators. Thus the benefits women officers bring to the community-policing ideal are threatened by the everyday sexism (and racism) many of them experience in their departments.

In conclusion, the two major policy changes in policing since the 1970s go hand-in-hand: hiring more women officers (and men of color) increases the likelihood that police-community relations will be improved. Women officers tend to be more invested than their male counterparts in civil and respectful interactions with the citizenry and are less likely to escalate potentially volatile citizen encounters. Unfortunately, they still face considerable resistance from old-fashioned police administrators and fellow officers. *See also* POLICE OFFICERS, WOMEN OF COLOR AS; POLICING, MODELS OF; WOMEN PROFESSIONALS IN THE JUSTICE WORKPLACE.

Further Reading: Dreifus 1982, "Why Two Women Cops Were Convicted of Cowardice"; Grennan 1987, "Findings on the Role of Officer Gender in Violent Encounters."

Joanne Belknap

Compassionate Release from Prison

Compassionate release, a procedure by which dying or physically incapacitated prisoners are given early release, may be granted more readily to female than male inmates. Today, as U.S. prisons strain to the bursting point, compassionate release from prison is gaining broad support. But although the public and prison officials may be more willing to consider compassionate release for women than male prisoners, even in women's cases there can be enormous resistance.

Prisoners and their families remain the strongest proponents of compassionate release, but prison officials and medical staff have also endorsed this procedure for dying inmates. In California, for instance, a 1997 compassionate release bill was signed into law with endorsements from prisoners' rights groups, medical associations, and the prison guard union. Some opposition comes from victims rights groups and politicians worried about appearing "soft" on crime. But as the prison population continues to swell at unprecedented rates, even conservative legislatures are studying proposals for compassionate release from prison for those suffering from terminal illnesses such as AIDS and cancer.

The release procedure generally requires a prison physician's statement that the inmate has less than six months to live and agreement by corrections directors, judges, and sometimes the parole board that the inmate is no longer a danger to society. Women prisoners, incarcerated increasingly for nonviolent crimes, are often perceived as better candidates for compassionate release than male inmates.

Although studies show that it costs far less to treat a paroled prisoner in the community than to cover custody and care inside prison, compassionate release remains out of reach for most dying or incapacitated prisoners due to hostility against criminals. Even when policies are in place and the dying prisoner is a nonviolent, first-time female offender, institutions can be reluctant to unlock the doors. *See also* HIV AND AIDS IN PRISON.

Further Reading: Greenspan 1994, "Struggle for Compassion"; M. P. Russell 1994, "Too Little, Too Late, Too Slow."

Judy Greenspan

Control Explanations of Crime

Control explanations of crime have been advanced since the mid-nineteenth century but truly swept the field of criminology with the publication of Travis Hirschi's *Causes of Delinquency* (1969). Control theory is concerned with explaining why most people abide by the law rather than why some people violate it. This theory contends that most individuals obey the law because they fear that their relationships with family, friends, and others will be damaged if they become involved in crime. At the heart of control theory lies the perception that crimes are least likely to be committed by individuals who are strongly bonded to those conventional groups and institutions (family, school, work, church, and so on) that help to reinforce society's prevailing norms and values.

Four elements have been used to gauge the strength of that social bond: attachment, commitment, involvement, and belief. Attachment refers to the quality of one's relationships with parents, friends, school, and work. Commitment relates to the amount of time one devotes to achieving success through legitimate means such as education, hard work, and saving for the future. Involvement pertains to the extent to which an individual participates in school, work, and conventional extracurricular activities such as sports and church events. Lastly, belief refers to the degree that an individual accepts and agrees with the moral values and rules of society (Hirschi 1969).

Hirschi tested his theory by administering a self-report survey to 4,000 male high school students. In general, he found support for control theory. Specifically, youths with weak parental ties were the least committed to conventional values and the most likely to be engaged in delinquent behavior.

Early criticisms of control theory centered on Hirschi's decision to drop females from his study due to their low rates of participation in criminal activity. Some scholars argue that control theory may be useful in explaining gender differences in crime rates.

A number of studies have applied control theory to both males and females. In general, the results have been mixed. Hindelang (1973) found that control theory was better at predicting male delinquency. Conversely, Krohn and Massey (1980) reported that control theory was better able to explain female delinquency. Similarly, J. Rosenbaum (1989) found that lower female crimes rates were the result of stronger conventional ties or bonds.

Power-control theory, a variant of control theory, specifically focuses on gender and family relations. Comparing the crime rates of females raised in patriarchal and egalitarian homes, Hagan (Hagan, Gillis, and Simpson 1987) argues that females from egalitarian homes where parents share equal status are more likely to be involved in delinquency than females from patriarchal homes. Hagan maintains that young women from patriarchal homes are more closely supervised and come under greater scrutiny than their counterparts from egalitarian homes.

In sum, although women exhibit stronger ties to conventional institutions and have lower crime rates than men, control theory does not appear to sufficiently explain gender differences in crime. *See also* FEMALE CRIME, EXPLANATIONS OF; POWER-CONTROL EXPLANATION OF CRIME; SOCIAL CONTROL OF WOMEN; SOCIAL PROCESS EXPLANATIONS OF DELINQUENCY.

Further Reading: Hirshi 1969, *Causes of Delinquency*; Rosenbaum 1989, "Family Dysfunction and Female Delinquency."

Anne Sullivan

Corrections Officers, Contemporary.

See CORRECTIONS OFFICERS, HISTORY OF; WOMEN CORRECTIONS OFFICERS IN MEN'S PRISONS; WOMEN PROFESSIONALS IN THE JUSTICE WORKPLACE.

Corrections Officers, History of

With rare exceptions, women did not work as corrections officers or supervisors in institutions for adult offenders before the nineteenth century. Women's entry into the field was precipitated by the establishment of separate departments for female offenders within men's prisons. Separate departments first began to appear in the United States and Europe in the early nineteenth century, before which offenders of both sexes were housed in the same facilities, with male administrators making only nominal attempts at separation. The result of lack of separation for incarcerated women was often sexual abuse and exploitation. Pregnancies among long-term inmates were not uncommon, and in some particularly egregious cases, women inmates were forcibly employed in prison brothels that serviced male administrators, officers, and inmates.

Reformers, primarily white, middle-class women motivated at least partly by their religious convictions, began advocacy for female inmates during the nineteenth century. It was largely their efforts that led to the creation of separate women's departments in prisons and ultimately to the establishment of institutions specifically for female offenders. In Europe, the most prominent of these early reformers was Elizabeth Fry (1780–1845), and in the United States, women including Clara Barton (1821–1912) and Dorothea Dix (1802–1887) took up the cause. Reformers believed that female offenders should be supervised exclusively by women because such an arrangement would minimize the potential for sexual exploitation. They also argued that female offenders, being less hardened and more amenable to reform than male offenders, would benefit from the maternal care that could be provided by pious women serving as role models of acceptable femininity and domesticity.

The first woman known to hold the position that we would today call "corrections officer" was Rachel Perijo, appointed to the post of "matron" in charge of female offenders at the Baltimore men's penitentiary in 1822. By 1845, many state legislatures, particularly in the eastern United States, had created similar positions, in which women were appointed to supervise female inmates held in separate quarters in men's prisons. Typically, a prison hired only one matron. She lived in the institution, often in the women's section itself, and was on duty 24 hours a day, 6.5 days per week. Little biographical information is available on these women, but they appear often to have been older, widowed, and forced by economic hardship into the work. In other instances, they were wardens' wives. These early matrons performed largely custodial functions, had little authority or autonomy, and were invariably supervised by male officials.

With the creation of separate institutions for women, most of them "reformatories" meant to house young misdemeanants, op-

portunities for women's employment expanded, and state legislatures and boards of corrections granted female administrators more autonomy. Many of those who headed the new institutions came from the same middle-class ranks as the reformers. Staff, however, were typically single, working-class women, often required to resign their posts if they married. Their primary assignment was the supervision of cottages that housed the majority of inmates in reformatories, and their title was gradually changed, in most states, to "cottage officer" or "cottage supervisor" by the early twentieth century.

These women worked 12-hour shifts and lived and ate in inmate cottages, in accordance with the family model espoused by prison reformers. Their work situations differed dramatically from those of male corrections officers in men's prisons, who typically lived off the prison grounds and, as late at the 1940s, were paid up to three times more for their shorter, 8-hour shifts. In all women's correctional facilities, white women held the majority of staff positions. When minority (primarily black) women were hired, they commonly supervised minority inmates, who were segregated from white inmates, and women's prisons, particularly in the southern United States, well into the twentieth century.

Women working in women's facilities began to fill posts designated as "corrections officers" on a more equal footing with their male counterparts in the 1970s. It was also during this period that women began to be employed in prisons for men. The 1972 amendments to Title VII of the 1964 Civil Rights Act extended protection against discrimination on the basis of sex to public-sector employees, paving the way for women to move into jobs in male facilities.

Because most states barred women from posts in male prisons, women began to challenge such policies, winning most early cases in state and district courts. However, in the first such case to reach the U.S. Supreme Court, *Dothard v. Rawlinson* (1977), the Court ruled that the state of Alabama could bar women from jobs in maximum security men's prisons, reasoning that they were uniquely vulnerable to sexual assault from "predatory male sex offenders." Ironically, however, subsequent courts interpreted the decision as applying only to the deplorable conditions then present in Alabama's maximum security prisons, and no other state correctional department was successful in relying on *Dothard v. Rawlinson* to deny jobs to women.

The second wave of legal challenges to women's employment in men's facilities was initiated by male inmates and focused on privacy issues. Rather than barring the employment of women in men's facilities, however, courts generally held that states must balance male inmates' limited rights to bodily privacy with women's rights to equality in employment. States have dealt with these challenges in a number of ways, from restricting the deployment of women to making design and structural changes in facilities to increase inmate privacy. Although some restrictions on the assignment of women officers remain (most commonly, they are barred from performing strip-searches of male inmates), all states and the Federal Bureau of Prisons now employ women as corrections officers at every security level in both men's and women's institutions. *See also* FRY, ELIZABETH; PRISON REFORM, USA; REFORMATORY MOVEMENT; WOMEN CORRECTIONS OFFICERS IN MEN'S PRISONS; WOMEN'S PRISON ADMINISTRATION, HISTORICAL.

Further Reading: Freedman 1981, *Their Sisters' Keepers;* Rafter 1990a, *Partial Justice;* Zimmer 1986, *Women Guarding Men.*

Dana M. Britton

Crime Fiction Writers

Women novelists have made significant contributions to the field of crime fiction since the 1800s, and over time, the number of female crime fiction writers has steadily increased. Women crime fiction writers tend to be equal-opportunity storytellers: their protagonists include both males and females, and these characters vary in occupation. Typically, the main characters are police inspectors, detectives, police chiefs, and private in-

vestigators, but another common protagonist is the amateur sleuth whose primary profession lies outside crime-solving, in the academic world or that of finance, museum administration, or real estate.

Several women novelists stand out in the evolution of the mystery novel. Anna Katherine Green (1846–1935) created Ebenezer Gayse, the first detective to appear in a series by an American author, male or female. The first novel in this series, *The Leavenworth Case* (1878), was published nine years before the first Sherlock Holmes mystery. Green, known as the "mother of the detective novel," excelled in depicting detection as a battle of wits. She eventually developed an innovative technique of gradually unveiling the plot, piece by piece.

Green's work inspired others. Agatha Christie (1890–1976), one of the world's most famous mystery writers, acknowledged her debt to Green in an autobiography. The master of the "cozy" mystery, Christie became one of the best-selling authors of all time as well as a top mystery playwright. She was named Grand Master by Mystery Writers of America in 1954, the first year such an award was given.

Mary Roberts Rinehart (1976–1958) was also influenced by Green, writing that Green inspired her first mysteries. During World War I, Rinehart covered criminal trials for magazines and began her mystery writing career with serials. She was one of the highest paid writers in America, and in 1909, she became the first mystery writer to have a novel on the best-seller list.

The "big three" female authors in contemporary crime fiction are Sue Grafton, Sara Paretsky, and Marcia Muller. Grafton, author of a series in which the title of each volume begins with a new letter of the alphabet, is an eight-time award winner for her books in this series. Marcia Muller was the first American author to write a detective series starring a woman private eye. And Sara Paretsky is one of the founding members of Sisters in Crime, a support organization for women mystery writers, serving as its first president in 1986. She is also one of the few

American women to win the British Crime Writers' Association Silver Dagger Award, which she received in 1988 for *Blood Shot*. *See also* FICTIONAL CRIME VICTIMS.

Further Reading: Heising 1996, *Detecting Women 2*; K. G. Klein 1995, *The Woman Detective*.

Kristen J. Kuehnle

Crime Victimization

Crime victimization occurs when a person experiences physical injury, death, mental anguish, or the loss or damage of property as a result of actual or attempted illegal activity by another person. In violent crime, consequences to the victim can be devastating, with the physical, psychological, and emotional trauma lasting for years.

Until the onset of the women's movement in the late 1960s, crime victims generally received little in the way of support or services. Additionally, from the first crime victimization research in the 1940s through the 1970s, scholars portrayed female victims as complicit in their own victimization experiences. More recently, however, victimization studies have begun to explore the plight of victims, victims' needs, and victims' experiences in the criminal justice system. At the same time, as the general public and criminal justice officials have begun addressing crime victims' needs, a variety of victim-based treatment and support services and victim compensation programs have emerged, some targeting the specific needs of female crime victims. The United States has changed from a society that ignored or blamed crime victims to one that uses a restorative approach, emphasizing victims' rights, victim restitution, victim services, victim involvement in the criminal justice process, and offender accountability.

Victimology

Victimology, or the study of crime victimization, took root in the 1940s and at first conceptualized victimization as a partnership between the victim and offender, with each playing an important role in the criminal incident. The early studies also examined victims' contributions to their own victimization, especially in cases involving female victims. What resulted eventually was the development of victim-precipitation theory and victim-facilitation theory, both suggesting that the victim shares responsibility with the perpetrator for the criminal incident.

With the women's movement in the 1960s educating the public about the plight of female crime victims, victimologists in the 1970s shifted their attention to the treatment of victims and the social effects of victimization. Today, the field of victimology examines the special needs of female crime victims, the restoration and treatment of crime victims in general, and responses to victims by the criminal justice system.

Our knowledge of the extent and seriousness of victimization depends on victims' willingness to report crimes against them. Historically, crimes associated with female victimization have been the least reported. Trauma and the stigma of the "victim" label have prevented some female crime victims from reporting. For others, reporting the crime and participating in the criminal justice process constitutes a secondary victimization. Thus, due to inconsistencies in victim reporting, the extent and frequency of female victimization can only be estimated. However, reliable data are necessary if we are to calculate the seriousness of the problem, assess women's risks of victimization, test theories, and gauge the effectiveness of prevention and restoration measures. In the United States, the two ongoing national data sources used to measure crime victimization are the Federal Bureau of Investigation's *Uniform Crime Reports* (*UCRs*) and the National Crime Victimization Survey (NCVS).

The *UCRs* provide little information on female-specific forms of victimization such as domestic violence and sexual assault. The *UCR* database, established in the 1930s, combines arrest data from police departments throughout the United States. These data provide estimates for the types of crimes committed and help establish offender characteristics and profiles. However, due to underreporting, the *UCR* data underestimate the extent of female victimization. Moreover, these data provide little information for developing profiles of crime victims. In 1989, a new reporting structure, the National Incident-Based Reporting System (NIBRS), expanded the original *UCR* database by providing more detailed information on crime victims. As the NIBRS database develops, it will be useful for studying female victimization, although local police departments have been slow to phase-in the NIBRS.

The National Crime Victimization Survey, introduced in 1965, provides detailed information on violent victimizations of women and reveals how these differ from victimizations of men. The NCVS data are derived from household surveys that collect information on victimization experiences from respondents 12 years old or older. NCVS data show that the nature of female victimization is different from that of males in that most violent female victimizations involve domestic violence or sexual assault. NCVS data also show that women are most at risk at home, more likely than men to be victimized by someone they know, and more likely to suffer injuries when victimized. However, the NCVS data suffer from reliability and validity problems insofar as respondents underreport victimization experiences and overemphasize minor incidents. Moreover, they give us no information on victims under age 12, which makes it difficult to estimate rates of incest and other forms of sexual abuse to which girls may be especially vulnerable. The 12-year-old threshold also makes it difficult to know how much children, in general, suffer from crime.

Victims' Rights and Services

Feminists and rape victims were the first to organize for victims' rights, staging rallies for the restoration and healing of female sexual assault victims. Annual "Take Back the Night" marches continue to be held around the nation to raise public consciousness about sexual assault and domestic violence. Some advocates for sexual assault victims eventually expanded their agenda to fight for rights and services for all victims; they were joined by survivors and victims' families, who united and established support groups such as Mothers against Drunk Driving (MADD) and Families of Murder Victims. Reformers drew attention to the problems of interpersonal and domestic violence, highlighting typical forms of female victimization.

As victims' issues became important at the national level, two federal responses followed: funding for the NCVS and the establishment, in 1968, of the Law Enforcement Assistance Administration (LEAA). LEAA poured millions of dollars into state victim and witness protection and assistance programs. In 1975, LEAA established the National Organization for Victim Assistance to train service providers and to act as a clearinghouse for information on crime victims and victim assistance programs. Also established in 1975 were the National Coalition against Domestic Violence and the National Coalition against Sexual Assault. In 1976, victim advocates established the National Center for the Prevention and Control of Rape. These publicly supported agencies brought tremendous attention to the victims' rights movement and highlighted the need for increased support of victims.

Since the creation of these public agencies, major legal reforms have focused on crime victims' rights, victim services, and victim protection. Members of national organizations, primarily victims and their advocates, lobbied for changes in the criminal justice response to crime victims at both the federal and state levels. The changes include protections for rape victims from use of information on their sexual histories in court proceedings, mandatory reporting of child abuse and neglect by professionals, and use of victim impact statements in the sentencing phase of the criminal justice process. Victims' rights laws have been enacted in every state and in the federal system (see chronology on page 261 showing key developments in the crime victims' movement).

The first rape crisis centers opened in 1972, one in Berkeley, California, the other in Washington, D.C. Today, there are rape crisis centers and domestic violence crisis intervention centers in every state, although critics charge that these resources are woefully underfunded. In 1973, the first shelter in the United States, Rainbow Retreat, opened in Phoenix, Arizona (D. Martin 1976); since its establishment, more than 1,300 shelters have opened across the United States. Other resources that today are available to at least some crime victims include victim compensation programs and provisions for offenders to make restitution to victims.

In 1982, Congress enacted the National Victim and Witness Protection Act, designed to protect victims and witnesses of federal crimes and to promote changes in the criminal justice response to victims. This act made provision for keeping victims informed of the progress of their cases, creating separate waiting areas for victims in courtrooms, preventing felons from profiting from their stories, allowing victim impact statements, and creating protections for witnesses and victims from intimidation by defendants. While such provisions were not female-specific, they did grow out of feminist work on behalf of crime victims, and they covered women as well as men.

In 1982, President Ronald Reagan established a Task Force on Victims of Crime, which made 68 recommendations, including abolition of the exclusionary rule, elimination of parole and early release credits for violent prisoners, and amendments to bail laws to increase confinement of dangerous offenders and levy penalties for failures to appear for trial. The task force also advocated an amendment to the U.S. Constitution that would create specific rights for crime victims. Although this amendment failed, state constitutions and various state and federal statutes today generally give victims the following rights:

- to be treated fairly and respectfully
- to be protected from the defendant
- to be notified of, and present at, court proceedings
- to submit testimony ("victim impact statements") about the offense, confer with the prosecution, and make a sentencing recommendation

- to be informed about the conviction, sentencing, and release of the offender

Subsequent to the 1982 Task Force on Victims of Crime, many further federal programs were established to assist crime victims, but these generally fed into a conservative crime-control agenda, and few focused specifically on the victimization of women. *See also* DOMESTIC VIOLENCE AGAINST WOMEN, EPIDEMIOLOGY OF; FEAR OF CRIME; HOMICIDE VICTIMS; MEDIATION PROGRAMS; MOTHERS AGAINST DRUNK DRIVING; RAPE RATES; RESTORATIVE JUSTICE; SHELTER MOVEMENT; VICTIM ADVOCACY; VICTIM COMPENSATION; VICTIM-FACILITATION THEORY; VICTIM IMPACT STATEMENTS; VICTIM NOTIFICATION; VICTIM-BLAMING AND VICTIM-PRECIPITATION, CONCEPT OF; VICTIM SERVICES; VICTIMIZATION, FEMINIST PERSPECTIVES ON; VICTIMIZATION, REPEAT.

Further Reading: Fattah 1991, *Understanding Criminal Victimization;* Karmen 1996, *Crime Victims;* D. P. Kelly and Erez 1997, "Victim Participation"; Office for Victims of Crime 1998, *New Directions from the Field.*

Debra L. Stanley

Crime Victims and Definitions of Justice

To understand the experiences of women crime victims in the criminal justice process, it is useful to distinguish between individual justice and social justice. Historically, in an attempt to achieve social justice, a crime model of *State v. Offender* has been used—a model in which society is defined as the ultimate crime victim. While this has taken the burden of justice-seeking off individual victims and acknowledges the cumulative social impact of crime, it has simultaneously severed links between the concept of justice and the identity of the individual victim. Defining victimization as a social rather than an individual experience largely ignores the particular victims of an offense—those who are harmed, experience loss, and require redress. The outcome has been a justice system that tends to treat victims as witnesses to their own victimization. This role serves the organizational needs of criminal justice personnel, whose job is to achieve social justice, much better than it serves the personal needs of individual victims, who primarily seek individual justice.

Traditionally, when women victims were brought into the male-dominated system of justice, their victimization was ignored, discounted, or appropriated for social and political reasons. Women who were victims of marital rape, for example, found their husbands exempted from prosecution. Female victims of domestic violence were informed that wife-beating is a "private matter," beyond the control of justice personnel. In rape trials, the victim's sexual history was used to explain the attack, and in cases of child sexual abuse, the victims—even those younger than age 10—were sexualized by attorneys who blamed female victims and exonerated male offenders. Efforts by female victims to express their suffering and claim "victim" status were largely unsuccessful.

A new phase of victim involvement in the criminal justice system began in the 1970s, primarily due to the efforts of victims and of their supporters, many of whom were activists in the women's movement. Since that time, the justice system has included victims in the search for justice in two ways: by encouraging victims to voice their pain and by adjusting the system to consider victims' best interests. In the former strategy, state and federal laws have encouraged victims' voices through victim impact statements submitted to decision-makers at key stages of criminal justice processing. Particularly in cases involving child victims, means have been sought to enable victims to testify in settings that feel safe and comfortable. In addition, rape shield laws have been enacted to ensure that judicial decision-makers can hear victims' testimonies without eliciting from the defense prejudicial information about victims' sexual histories. Legislation has also encouraged the development of victim-offender mediation programs, which give victims opportunities to express their feelings to their offenders. As a result of these strategies, victims often report greater satisfaction with the justice process.

The second strategy initiative since the 1970s—seeking to reshape the system to serve victims' interests—has required different measures. Protection order legislation and victim notification laws have been enacted to protect victims from future victimization, and victim compensation and restitution programs have been enacted to mitigate the financial impact of crime. The 1994 Violence against Women Act expanded funding and service provision to victims of a variety of offenses while at the same time mandating that rape victims receive information about sexually transmitted disease testing and that restitution be available for domestic violence and other crime victims. Yet victim services in general are subject to ongoing legislative and funding approval, forcing service providers to adjust what they provide and how they provide it according to funding streams and political exigencies. The result is a system of victim services that is strong on idealism but inconsistent in delivery.

Although there has been much overlap between the two types of victim initiatives—encouraging victims to express their pain and seeking their best interests—a disjunction is also evident. Where once the female victim's voice was considered unnecessary and unwelcome, it has now become imperative to the extent it facilitates the goal of social justice. Examples can be found in policies requiring police officers to arrest—and prosecutors to prosecute—offenders in domestic violence cases (called mandatory arrest and no-drop prosecution, respectively). Women victims may choose not to participate in the justice system for a variety of reasons, including concern that justice will not be served and a fear of retaliation. Nevertheless, both mandatory arrest and no-drop policies are widespread and are considered by system professionals to serve victims' best interests. Victim advocates, on the other hand, note that both policies disempower victims by limiting their choices and excluding the voices of victims who say no to the system.

For many victims, the failure of the criminal justice system to respond effectively to either their current victimization or their fear of future victimization means that alternative responses (such as refusing to testify or fleeing an abusive environment) are legitimate strategic choices and may actually provide greater relief. But because these strategies require support and services outside of the justice system, and sometimes in confrontation with it, the system refuses to respect them. In sum, the justice system is currently designed to facilitate victim involvement in the justice process only as long as that involvement also serves the system's best interests.

Since 1990, there has been renewed advocacy for making victims central to the criminal justice process, many efforts focusing on victims' rights. Victim testimony before Congress at the beginning of the 1990s indicated that victims still experience blame for their victimization and a general feeling of disempowerment. A Victims' Bill of Rights was passed by Congress in 1982, and the Crime Control Act of 1990 took a stronger stance by placing the burden of encouraging victim involvement on justice system personnel, rather than on the victims themselves.

From the perspective of victims and their advocates, victim involvement is a crucial component of the justice system. Yet some criminal justice decision-makers portray victims who want to participate in the process as merely out for personal revenge. System professionals have also expressed concern about the future of prosecutorial discretion and plea-bargaining if victims' interests are incorporated into the justice system. Finally, some legal scholars have argued that victims' rights to be involved in the justice process may violate basic rights of the accused, such as the right to a fair trial. Judges still have the power to exclude victims from the courtroom if they feel a victim's presence will prejudice the proceedings. In general, victim participation in the justice system has been most acceptable when it has been nonconfrontational, routinized, and mediated by trained advocates.

A final issue ignored in the debate over the second strategy of focusing on victims' best interests is whether the criminal justice system is the proper place for victims to receive justice. Many policies enacted on behalf of victims (such as mandatory arrest, protection orders, and no-drop policies) fail to provide adequate support or relief, while at the same time mandating victim involvement in the justice system. Moreover, a victim's voluntary or involuntary involvement in the system can leave her open to emotional or psychological victimization by criminal justice personnel—what some victims describe as a "second rape" or "secondary victimization."

As crime victims, women experience the struggle for justice on both individual and social levels. As individuals, they become victims, experiencing harm and the threat of harm. As self-advocates, they find ways to voice their concerns to system personnel (sometimes meeting the system's needs at the same time, sometimes confounding the process). In turn, criminal justice personnel use victims' narratives to create a form of social justice that fits within current crime control models. Throughout, women victims in their individual quests for justice are often subordinated to the system's attempts to achieve social justice. *See also* DOMESTIC VIOLENCE CASE PROCESSING; MEDIATION PROGRAMS; PROTECTION ORDERS; RAPE SHIELD LAWS, CANADA; RAPE SHIELD LAWS, USA; VICTIM-BLAMING AND VICTIM-PRECIPITATION, CONCEPT OF; VICTIM COMPENSATION; VICTIMS, HISTORICAL TREATMENT OF; VICTIMS IN COURT.

Further Reading: Elias 1993, *Victims Still;* Hoyle 1998, *Negotiating Domestic Violence;* Sebba 1996, *Third Parties.*

Michelle Hughes Miller

Criminalization of Pregnancy, Canada

Canadian legislators and courts have proceeded with caution in the face of pressure for criminalization of pregnant women whose behavior endangers their fetuses. The *Charter of Rights and Freedoms* has been interpreted to deny the existence of prenatal fetal rights. In *Morgentaler v. The Queen* (1988), the Supreme Court of Canada struck down the abortion section of the *Criminal Code*, and in *Borowski v. The Queen* (1989), the Court confirmed that a fetus is not a person in law. In 1989, the Law Reform Commission of Canada recommended criminalization of certain conduct of pregnant women; however, the government has not done so.

In the area of criminal sentencing, an Ontario case is unique and relevant: in November 1998, a pregnant woman with a history of drug convictions pleaded guilty to a drug-related offense. She avoided a lengthy prison sentence by agreeing to be remanded in custody pending the birth of her baby. The plea agreement reflected the prosecution's concern that a "crack baby" might be born if she remained on the street.

Canadian courts have been loathe to extend the definition of "child" to include a fetus without express legislation (*Re A.* 1990; *Re Baby R.* 1988). The right of child welfare authorities to take custody of a newborn due to the prenatal (mis)conduct of its mother has, however, been accepted by Canadian courts, although, for some, this is too late. In 1997, one agency in Manitoba turned to the common law of torts and the *parens patriae* jurisdiction of the superior court for an order authorizing the forcible detention of an addicted pregnant woman.

In *Winnipeg Child and Family Services (NorthWest Area) v. G. (D.F.)* (1997), the agency attempted to have a 22-year-old pregnant Aboriginal woman (facing no criminal charges) detained for treatment because of her abuse of solvents. Evidence was introduced showing that three children had been permanently taken from her (two had been born seriously handicapped) as a result of her addiction. A judge initially granted the order and authorized the agency director to direct a course of treatment for the duration of her pregnancy. This order was appealed and stayed two days later; however, Ms. G. voluntarily remained in a treatment program until she was discharged. By the time her case reached the Supreme Court of Canada, she had delivered a healthy baby and had not resumed sniffing solvents.

The Supreme Court was next asked to impose a legally enforceable civil duty of care upon a pregnant woman toward her fetus, a duty which could then support an order for her detention and treatment during pregnancy, and to extend its *parens patriae* jurisdiction to the fetus. A minority of the Supreme Court agreed, holding that a live birth requirement is anachronistic and that a pregnant woman whose conduct threatened the life and health of her fetus could be ordered to be detained. However, the majority reaffirmed that live birth is a necessary precondition for legal personhood, that the Court's *parens patriae* jurisdiction does not extend to the fetus, and that "the common law does not clothe the courts with the power to order the detention of a pregnant woman for the purpose of preventing harm to her unborn child" (*Winnipeg Child and Family Services (NorthWest Area) v. G. (D.F.)* [1997] 3 S.C.R. 925, per McLachlin J. at 960).

Despite many attempts, initiatives aimed at "criminalization" and other forms of regulation of pregnant women have experienced little legal success in Canada to date. *See also* CRIMINALIZATION OF PREGNANCY, USA.

Further Reading: Dawson 1998, "First Person Familiar"; Gavigan 1992, "*Morgentaler* and Beyond"; S. Rodgers 1986, "Fetal Rights and Maternal Rights."

Shelley A. M. Gavigan

Criminalization of Pregnancy, USA

Beginning in the 1980s, the criminalization of pregnancy in the United States emerged as a response to pregnant women's use of illegal drugs. Since the mid-1980s, several hundred women in nearly two-thirds of the states have been arrested and charged with criminal offenses including child abuse and neglect, delivering drugs to a minor, assault with a deadly weapon, homicide, and feticide. Although the initial prosecutions targeted women who were accused of using cocaine, women have also been prosecuted for using other illegal drugs, as well as for using alcohol.

Twelve states now require health-care officials to inform child protection authorities about a pregnant woman's drug use, and three states require newborns to be tested for exposure to illegal drugs. South Dakota recently became the first state to allow judges to commit a pregnant woman who abuses alcohol or drugs into a treatment program for the duration of her pregnancy. The state also passed a law that makes alcohol use while pregnant a form of child abuse. A similar law in Wisconsin permits the detention of pregnant women who abuse drugs or alcohol, and under Minnesota's civil commitment law, pregnant women who use illegal drugs can be committed involuntarily to a treatment facility for the duration of their pregnancy.

Although nearly every court that has reviewed a prosecution of prenatal drug use has either dismissed the charges or overturned a guilty verdict, a glaring exception is the South Carolina Supreme Court. In 1996, the court ruled in *Whitner v. South Carolina* that the state's child abuse and endangerment statute could be used to protect viable fetuses. This ruling allows South Carolina prosecutors to file child endangerment charges against women for actions that may harm a fetus. A year later, the prosecutor in Rock Hill, South Carolina, filed a charge of unlawful neglect against a woman whose stillborn baby tested positive for cocaine. The prosecutor's office notified two other women who used illegal drugs while pregnant that they would be arrested for harming their fetuses.

Even in states where the courts have overturned such prosecutions, law-enforcement officials continue to file criminal charges against women for their behavior during pregnancy. For example, the Georgia Court of Appeals ruled in 1992 that the word "person" in the state's criminal statutes does not include the fetus. Nonetheless, in October 1999, a grand jury indicted a woman for murdering one of her newborn twins who died shortly after birth. The murder indictment was based on toxicology tests that indicated the woman had used cocaine and methamphetamine during her pregnancy.

Every major medical group in the United States opposes the criminalization of pregnancy. Furthermore, there is no conclusive evidence that a woman's drug addiction will result in severe mental or physical damage to her newborn. Although alcohol is a known teratogen, moderate alcohol consumption during pregnancy has not been shown to cause birth defects. The medical community favors a treatment approach to prenatal drug and alcohol use, yet few states provide comprehensive drug and alcohol services to pregnant women.

Attempts to criminalize drug and alcohol use during pregnancy reveal the extent to which social control policies to protect the fetus are gaining credibility in some areas of the country. These policies are directly linked to the anti-abortion movement, which has launched a multipronged strategy in the legislative and judicial arenas to obtain legal recognition of "fetal personhood." The criminalization of prenatal drug and alcohol use is part of this anti-abortion, fetal protection movement. Although most of the women prosecuted for prenatal drug or alcohol use have been poor and African American, that trend may change if the movement to protect fetuses from the behavior of pregnant women gains wider acceptance. *See also* ABORTION; CRIMINALIZATION OF PREGNANCY, CANADA

Further Reading: Center for Reproductive Law and Policy 1996, "Punishing Women"; Kleinig 1990, "Criminal Liability for Fetal Endangerment"; Paltrow 1999, "Pregnant Drug Users"; D. Roberts 1997, "Representing Race."

Karen J. Maschke

Cultural Deviance Theories of Crime.
See SOCIAL STRUCTURAL EXPLANATIONS OF DELINQUENCY.

D

Date Rape

Date rape and acquaintance rape—sexual assaults involving individuals who know each other—have occurred for centuries. It was not until 1982, however, that the term "date rape" (or "acquaintance rape," depending on the circumstances) began to be used by *Ms.* magazine, bringing much-needed public attention to the issue. Since then, an explosion of research has heightened public awareness to such a level that the term "date rape" is now a familiar concept. Although slower, the legal system has also begun to demonstrate awareness of the issue.

Research findings indicate that date rape and acquaintance rape occur in epidemic proportions. Mary Koss and her colleagues laid the groundwork for contemporary understanding of date rape with a large-scale, scientifically sound survey conducted at higher education institutions across the United States (Koss, Gidycz, and Wisniewski 1987). Her findings revealed that 27.1 percent of the 3,187 female participants in the study were victims of either rape (15.3 percent) or attempted rape (11.8 percent). Of these, 84 percent knew their attacker.

Subsequent research confirmed Koss's findings. In 1992, *Rape in America: A Report to the Nation*, based on research conducted by the Crime Victims Research and Treatment Center, announced that 13 percent of women surveyed reported having been victims of at least one completed rape and that of these, 78 percent knew their attacker. In 1993, the National Opinion Research Center conducted a National Health and Social Life Survey, which found that 25 percent of women aged 18–24 had been forced against their will to engage in a sexual activity and that 77 percent of these women knew their attackers.

But while date rape and acquaintance rape occur more often than stranger rape, they are less likely than stranger rape to be defined as rape. Even victims may not characterize their experiences as rape. Koss found that of those women who reported experiences that met the legal definition of rape, only 27 percent defined their experience as rape (Koss, Gidycz, and Wisniewski 1987; see also Allison and Wrightsman 1993; Warshaw 1988).

The psychological costs of identifying oneself as a rape victim are high, but rape has psychological consequences for nearly all victims, whether or not the victim identifies the experience as rape (Koss 1988a). Women raped by dates or acquaintances report high levels of anger and depression, just as women raped by strangers do. Many victims meet the criteria for a psychological diagnosis of post–traumatic stress syndrome. Many victims also suffer physical consequences not directly related to the rape for years after the event (Koss 1988b).

Despite increased awareness of date and acquaintance rape and sobering statistics on their incidence, most perpetrators are not held legally accountable for their crimes. One reason for this is that most date rape victims never report the crime. For example, only 5 percent of the victims in Koss's study reported the crime to the police. Most date rape victims never tell anyone about their experience. Even when date rapes are reported, however, perhaps no more than 2–3 percent of the cases result in convictions (Bienen 1983). *See also* RAPE LAW REFORM; RAPE LAWS AND SPOUSAL EXEMPTIONS; RAPE RATES.

Further Reading: Allison and Wrightsman 1993, *Rape;* Koss, Gidycz, and Wisniewski 1987, "The Scope of Rape."

Julie A. Allison

Davis, Angela Y. (1944–)

To speak of Angela Davis—author, teacher, and radical political activist—is to speak of an individual committed to racial justice and a progressive society. Davis's high profile as a criminal defendant in the early 1970s and her activism on crime and justice issues have raised Americans' consciousness of racism and other political dimensions of criminal justice. Her fame as an activist arose from the convergence of a social movement for social justice and her willingness to stand for her beliefs despite great personal cost.

Angela Yvonne Davis was born in 1944 in Birmingham, Alabama, to two progressive school teachers. She grew up in a newly integrated neighborhood and witnessed Klan attacks on her neighbors. Her parents had a number of socialist friends, many of whom were forced underground during the McCarthy era. At the age of 15, Davis moved to New York where she attended a private school and, moved by the writings of Karl Marx, joined the Communist Party's youth organization.

While studying in Paris at the Sorbonne, Davis received news of the struggles for civil rights in the United States and of the murders of several childhood friends by white racists. She returned to the United States to

Angela Y. Davis, 1975. *Agence France Presse/Archive Photos.*

pursue a doctorate under radical scholar Herbert Marcuse at the University of California–San Diego. Davis began teaching philosophy at the University of California–Los Angeles, and became active in prisoners' rights issues. Her work on the Soledad Brothers Defense Committee led to her friendship with George Jackson, a leader in the radical prisoners' movement, and his younger brother, Johnathan.

On August 7, 1970, an outbreak of violence at the Marin County courthouse left Johnathan Jackson dead, along with two prison guards and a judge. Davis, accused of conspiring with the Jackson brothers, was placed on the FBI's most wanted list.

In October 1970, Angela Davis was imprisoned on charges of kidnapping and murder stemming from the Marin County courthouse shooting, an imprisonment that lasted 16 months. An international movement led by social activists Kendra and Franklin Alexander of Oakland, California, campaigned for her acquittal and for an end to the use of prisons for social and political repression. As a result of the charges Davis faced and the successful movement for her acquittal, she became a central icon of the resistance movement of the 1960s. An account of her trial, imprisonment, and acquittal appears in *Angela Davis: An Autobiography* (A. Y. Davis 1974).

In early 2000, Angela Davis continues to be active in struggles for racial justice, women's rights, and prison reform and to speak around the world on these issues while teaching at the University of California–Santa Cruz. Her numerous articles include reflections on prisons and resistance, Marxism, racism, and women's struggles. In addition to her autobiography, she has published four books: *If They Come in the Morning: Voices of Resistance* (1971); *Women, Race and Class* (1981); *Women, Culture and Politics* (1988); and *Blues Legacies and Black Feminism* (1998).

In 1969, California Governor Ronald Reagan had fired Davis from her University of California teaching position due to her social activism and her Communist Party membership. He vowed that Davis would never again teach in the state's university system. However, in 1995, Davis was honored with the most prestigious award bestowed by the University of California on a faculty member: the Presidential Chair. *See also* POLITICAL OFFENDERS.

Further Reading: A. Y. Davis 1974, *An Autobiography;* A. Y. Davis 1998, *The Angela Y. Davis Reader.*

Renee S. Levant

Death Penalty

Between 1977 and 2000 in the United States, approximately 500 convicted criminals, of whom only 3 were female, were executed following death sentences. Since Colonial times, 20,000 persons have been put to death in punishment for crimes, of whom fewer than 600 have been women or girls.

The death penalty is now imposed only for the most heinous murders, although at one time, it could be imposed for any felony, and until the last quarter of the twentieth century, it was imposed for grave nonfatal felonies such as rape and armed robbery. In 1999, 40 states and the federal government permit-ted capital punishment. A small number of states, chiefly southern, carry out the majority of executions.

The three women executed since the U.S. Supreme Court reinstated executions in 1976 after a four-year moratorium include two grandmothers who had poisoned multiple family members, Velma Barfield in North Carolina and Judias Buenoano in Florida. The death of Barfield, the first woman executed, brought to a close a period of intense speculation about whether a contemporary U.S. governor would permit the execution of a woman. The second woman, Karla Faye Tucker—pretty, articulate, and like Barfield, a convert to Christianity while in prison—became a media star in the months leading up to her execution. Tucker had hacked two people to death with a pickax. The third, Buenoano (dubbed "the Black Widow" by the press), died a few weeks after Tucker in relative obscurity.

Contemporary scholars have offered two explanations of the comparative rarity of the execution of women. The first is that chivalry protects women from the full measure of punishment that the law might exact. In this view, women are spared because they are thought to lack the degree of reason and self-control necessary for full accountability. Chivalry may also inhibit those in power from killing a member of the life-giving and nurturing sex.

A second explanation for the male-female gap in executions is that women rarely commit homicides that merit the death penalty. Although women commit 1 in every 8 homicides, they commit less than 1 in 20 of the types of homicides that are heinous enough in society's eyes to merit execution. The death penalty is used to punish predatory murders. Women who kill typically kill family members and lovers in anger, crimes that do not result in capital punishment for either sex. Women killers are also much less likely than men to face sentencing with prior records for violent felonies, backgrounds that increase the likelihood of a death sentence. *See also* CHIVALRY EXPLANATION OF COURT OUTCOMES; DEATH

ROW; GRAHAM, BARBARA; JURY SELECTION; PUNISHMENT, AUSTRALIA.

Further Reading: Rapaport 1991, "The Death Penalty and Gender Discrimination"; Streib 1990, "The Death Penalty for Female Offenders."

Elizabeth Rapaport

Death Row

At the close of 1999, 50 women were on death row in 17 state prisons and none were on death row in federal prisons. Their ages ranged from 23 to 70, and over half were white. They included housewives, prostitutes, a police officer, and a serial killer, and they had been on death row for periods of time ranging from a few months to over 17 years. All were convicted of murder, with the victims including their farmhands, husbands, grandchildren, and entire families. Figure 1 illustrates the increases over recent decades in the number of women on death row.

Women's death rows are located in isolated parts of women's prisons, often in a former isolation cell area. These areas are quite small in comparison with men's death rows, each housing no more than a few women. This results in very little contact between female death-row inmates and other prisoners, guards, or outsiders.

Although "awaiting execution," almost all will have their death sentences converted to life imprisonment through commutation or through legal procedings that vacate the sen-

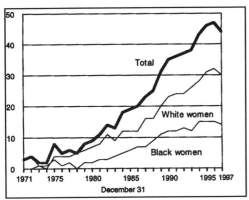

Figure 1. Number of Women under Sentence of Death [USA, 1971 to 1997]
Source: Bureau of Justice Statistics, U.S. Department of Justice 1999c, *Women Offenders*, page 11.

tence or conviction. In late 1999, only 0.5 percent of all executions since 1900 had been of women. *See also* DEATH PENALTY; GRAHAM, BARBARA; PREJEAN, SISTER HELEN; PUNISHING WOMEN OFFENDERS.

Further Reading: Rapaport 1991, "The Death Penalty and Gender Discrimination"; Schmall 1996, "Forgiving Guin Garcia"; Streib 1990, "The Death Penalty for Female Offenders."

Victor L. Streib

Desistance from Crime

The phenomenon of "maturing out" or "desistance from crime" refers to the fact that crime rates typically decline with age, with even chronic offenders committing fewer crimes as they mature into adulthood. Figure 2 illustrates this phenomenon. Although serious youthful offenders commit more crimes throughout their lives than individuals who did not get involved in crime during adolescence, researchers have documented considerable variability. For example, criminologists Sampson and Laub (1993) found that in follow-ups of adolescent males who had extensive involvement in delinquent behavior, those who had found stable employment and established good marriages were more likely than others to desist from criminal activity.

Until recently, research that focused on the long-term prospects of female juvenile delinquents did not exist. Thus, it was not clear whether the likelihood of desistance or the factors linked to desistance would be similar to those identified in studies focused exclusively on males. Some researchers have suggested that because offending by females is a relatively rare occurrence, it may involve a higher level of pathology on the part of the small number of young women who do engage in such behaviors. A somewhat contradictory viewpoint asserts that even when females engage in delinquency or criminal activity, their involvement is likely to be of a less serious nature than that of males. These contradictory images lead to different expectations about how gender might affect desistance processes.

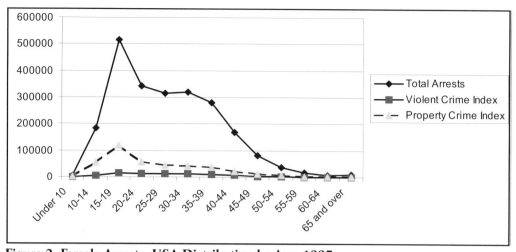

Figure 2. Female Arrests, USA Distribution by Age, 1997
Source: U.S. Department of Justice, Federal Bureau of Investigation 1998, *Crime in the United States 1997*, Table 40.

In the 1990s, the National Institute of Mental Health funded a longitudinal follow-up study of institutionalized female delinquents who were serious offenders during adolescence. This study, which also included a male comparison sample, revealed that a high percentage of females continued to have problems into adulthood. For example, at a 13-year follow-up, 72 percent of female delinquents had at least one arrest as an adult, and the mean number of arrests was 18, compared with the male rate of 87 percent and a mean of 12 arrests. In addition, the seriously delinquent women, when compared with a female control sample, experienced early and high fertility and were much more likely to have relinquished custody of one or more children (Giordano et al. 1997).

However, the study, like previous research on males, also documented considerable variability among female offenders. For example, by early adulthood, some women had completely desisted from any involvement in crime, violence, or drug use, and others decreased their levels of involvement. Analysis of factors linked to these declines suggests that stable employment was not a way out of crime for the majority of these women. The "good marriage effect" was observed for a subset of the sample but did not appear to be as critical to the desistance process, as has been shown in male-based studies. Some of the more successful women experienced radi-cal religious transformations, while others identified the birth or maturation of their children as a key factor in their movement out of deviant activities. Finally, for some women, additional time in prison or other rehabilitative settings became a catalyst for positive life changes (Giordano et al. 1997).
See also CHRONIC OFFENDERS; FEMALE CRIME, BRITAIN; JUVENILE DELINQUENCY AND AGE.

Further Reading: Sampson and Laub 1993, *Crime in the Making;* Uggen and Kruttschnitt 1998, "Crime in the Breaking."

Peggy C. Giordano

Deviance and Reform, Historical Overview of, Britain

The British criminal justice system for women has long been characterized by interchanges between "deviants," mainly lower-class women charged with crimes, and "reformers," mainly middle- and upper-middle-class women interested in improving the quality of justice for women and willing to go to jail for their beliefs. The reformers' work has often been directed toward revision or repeal of laws affecting women. Thus, the history of female crime and its control in Britain (England, Scotland, and Wales) has been one of shifting boundaries between "criminals" and those involved in order maintenance, with strong and infamous women on both sides of the line and movement back and forth across it.

As the first industrial society, Britain experienced a shift to early modernity which affected crime rates. In the eighteenth century, 45 percent of defendants at the Old Bailey (London's central criminal court) were women, but crime rates seem to have stabilized or even fallen in the nineteenth century, decreasing more for women than men (Zedner 1991). Experience in Scotland was somewhat different from England and Wales, with the large gap between male and female crime rates appearing later. Yet a general trend can be discerned in which industrialization, the development of welfare agencies, and reductions in harsh penalties for minor offenses such as drunkenness affected females more than males, greatly reducing women's rates of arrest.

Public concern about deviant women did not disappear, however, and nineteenth-century and early twentieth-century British criminal justice policies were characterized by strenuous attempts to control female behavior. The most notorious of these efforts were the Contagious Diseases Acts (of 1864, 1866, and 1868) which, together, required prostitutes living in garrison towns to submit to regular medical checks. If found to be infected with sexually transmitted diseases, these women were compulsorily treated in hospitals and morally reeducated. Although the Acts were intended to protect British soldiers and keep them fit for fighting, they engendered a fierce opposition campaign, led by moral reformer Josephine Butler, which succeeded in having them repealed in 1883.

The campaigns against the Acts were directed partly against the "double standard" of morality for men and women. As reformers pointed out, there was no enforced examination or treatment of the soldiers. The reformers' focus later widened to include campaigns against the regulation of prostitution in other European countries and sexual trafficking. Many prominent figures, including Florence Nightingale, supported the crusade against trafficking in women, as did most (though not all) of the first-wave feminists of the early twentieth century. This crusade was linked to many others that sought to rescue "fallen" women and protect girls and children from seduction and corruption. Women reformers played a major role in such campaigns.

Upper- and upper-middle-class women led many of the welfare developments in nineteenth-century Britain: provision of social housing (Octavia Hill, 1838–1912); broader access to nursing and public health (Florence Nightingale, 1820–1910); and reform of the poor law (Beatrice Webb, 1858–1943). These British reformers generally enjoyed greater freedom and scope in public life than activists in other European nations such as France and Germany and resembled American women in their status and achievements. Indeed, Jane Addams, the U.S. social reformer, took Toynbee Hall in London's East End as the prototype for Hull House, her famous neighborhood center in Chicago.

British female social reformers often held strong evangelical Christian beliefs. In the late nineteenth century, they became increasingly pragmatic about making alliances with government groups, working with and through the state. Unlike some American counterparts, they did not, on the whole, espouse radical ideas about marriage and the family.

Offending women—in addition to being targeted by the Contagious Diseases Acts and a generally more repressive regulation of prostitution—were the subjects of two short-lived penal experiments in the late nineteenth and early twentieth centuries. Reformatories were established for inebriate women and for women with low intelligence, designed both to reform females and to prevent them passing on antisocial behavior to their children. However, these projects were quickly recognized as failures (Zedner 1991).

For much of the twentieth century, women offenders were considered "too few to count" and were subject to penal policies designed for males. Penal practices based on women's needs were few in number and innovations were characterized, as in the story of the rebuilding of Holloway Prison, by much backsliding to male models.

Some early British feminists of the Victorian era continued their campaigns into the twentieth century, seeking both female suffrage (the vote for women) and a major role for women in social control and social welfare activities. The struggle to achieve votes for women in Britain was distinctive in its length, the strength of opposition to it, and the techniques of civil disobedience adopted by the suffragettes. Some campaigners fought for the vote on the grounds that it would bring female moral superiority into public life. A section of the policewomen's movement was founded by veterans of the suffrage struggle, with women who had themselves been arrested for throwing stones through the windows of the prime minister's residence seeking powers to arrest disorderly citizens a few years later (Lock 1979).

This phenomenon of "virtuous deviants"—of women prepared to challenge the law and even to be imprisoned for their beliefs—continued to reappear in Britain throughout the twentieth century. While most supporters of votes for women suspended their actions during World War I, some pursued the then-unpopular cause of peace, linking up with colleagues from other nations in the Women's International League for Peace and Freedom. Parallels to these protests occurred during the 1980s and 1990s with the Greenham Common protest against the siting of U.S. missile bases in Britain. Greenham Common protestors were regularly arrested, tried for various infringements, and fined or even imprisoned. The Greenham Common protesters attracted worldwide publicity and much vilification from sections of the press. After the Cold War ended, the missiles finally were removed.

Women willing to be cast as deviants for their beliefs also played prominent roles in other British peace campaigns, especially the Campaign for Nuclear Disarmament and the antinuclear Committee of 100 (which adopted a civil disobedience approach). While some, like the Greenham Common women, were from the working class, many shared with their early-twentieth-century counterparts relatively privileged backgrounds and education. Their accounts of trials, imprisonment, and punishments provided powerful critiques of the British criminal justice

system and its refusal to recognize gender differences. These critiques echoed the pleas made by the suffragette Emmeline Pankhurst on behalf of her fellow inmates in Holloway Prison.

Challenges to authority by women who themselves were close kin to elite figures reflect the slow pace of change in Britain. For example, it took 140 years to achieve the goals of Elizabeth Fry, who in the early nineteenth century campaigned on behalf of women prisoners for all-female prisons staffed by women, with regimes adapted to the needs of women prisoners. Imperialism, too, affected the development of criminal justice practices, especially in the colonies to which British practices were exported. Thus, Australia introduced female police at about the same time as Britain did, with India and South Africa eventually following suit.

Of greater long-term significance for Britain itself, however, has been the immigration of Commonwealth citizens from around the world to work and settle in the British Isles; in the late 1990s, 6 percent of the current population was born outside Britain. This immigration significantly affected Britain's criminal justice system in the late twentieth century, with a breakdown in trust between the police and some ethnic minority communities following scandals and miscarriages of justice. Women of color were the victims in several of these episodes.

Women's share of recorded crime in Britain is today low and relatively unremarkable. Nevertheless, due largely to the particular character of Britain's mass media, certain cases involving women perpetrators have received extraordinary and prolonged exposure. The British press is national, London-based, and competitive; much space, especially in the mass-market tabloid newspapers, is devoted to crime stories, and those featuring women (such as the notorious killer Myra Hindley) receive disproportionate coverage. Ruth Ellis, hanged in 1954, was the subject of two feature films and numerous books and articles. In the 1990s alone, worldwide coverage was given to the trial of Rosemary West for nine murders; to the history of nurse Beverly Allott, convicted of murdering children in her care; and to the case of Mary Bell, killer of two small boys in 1968, when she was only 11. Bell's life story was retold in a controversial book (Sereny 1998), and a furious debate ensued about the ethics of its revelations. Press coverage exaggerates the female contribution to serious violent crime, creating a disproportionately punitive public attitude toward some female offenders.

But the mass media has also been successfully exploited in Britain to aid certain causes for women, notably, campaigns against domestic abuse. Domestic violence was recognized as a social problem in the nineteenth century and was the subject of official inquiries at that time. However, it did not receive wide public attention until the launch of Chiswick Women's Aid in 1971 and the work of Erin Pizzey—and later of others in the refuge movement, an effort to provide shelters for women fleeing domestic violence. Pizzey (1973) proved adept at gaining media coverage of cases of battered women and at making the topic one of public and political concern. Her initiative was widely imitated elsewhere (in the United States, it contributed to the movement for shelters for battered women), and it achieved not only widespread recognition of the problem but also key policy changes. Pizzey later split from the main Women's Aid Federation, which continues to provide refuge to abused women.

Although Britain is a liberal democracy, some of its institutions have remained resistant to change. The criminal justice system has been notable in this respect; it has remained largely the preserve of men, with most senior judges and advocates drawn from a narrow group of white, middle- and upper-class males. England and Wales, the two countries for which employment statistics by gender are available, are ahead of France in terms of gender balance in criminal justice agencies but behind Canada and the United States.

At the beginning of the twenty-first century, there are some signs that the law and its enforcement agencies are recognizing that they need to represent the diversities of British society. This is due both to the crises in relations between the police and minority communities and the increase in the proportion of women (over 20 percent) elected to Parliament in 1997.

When feminist thinkers first addressed criminology in the late 1960s and 1970s, their work was a decidedly minor component of the overall criminological enterprise in Britain. As late as 1994, a handbook summarizing the state of criminology in Britain (R. Maguire, Morgan, and Reiner 1994) could omit feminist perspectives entirely. Yet, in a sign perhaps of feminist criminology's movement toward the mainstream, a second edition of this work (R. Maguire, Morgan, and Reiner 1997) included a chapter on feminist criminology. Gender issues still remain isolated as "women's" issues, but they are nonetheless becoming less marginalized. Criminology is a new area of the territory in which women reformers continue struggling to define the boundaries between deviance and normality. *See also* FEMALE CRIME, BRITAIN; FRY, ELIZABETH; GREENHAM COMMON WOMEN'S PEACE CAMP; HINDLEY, MYRA; HOLLOWAY PRISON; POLICE WORK, HISTORY OF WOMEN IN, BRITAIN; SOUTHALL BLACK SISTERS; SUFFRAGETTES; WOMEN IN PRISON, ENGLAND AND WALES.

Further Reading: Banks 1981, *Faces of Feminism*; Gelsthorpe 1997, "Feminism and Criminology"; Heidensohn 1997, "Gender and Crime"; Zedner 1991, *Women, Crime and Custody in Victorian England*.

Frances Heidensohn

Differential Association Theory of Crime.
See SOCIAL PROCESS EXPLANATIONS OF DELINQUENCY.

Domestic Violence against Women, Epidemiology of

Despite more than two decades of research, the epidemiology or extent of intimate- and family-perpetrated violence against women is frequently disputed. For many reasons, including the stigma historically attached to intimate-perpetrated violence, victims' fear of retaliation from their victimizers, and other safety concerns, estimating incidence rates of this violence has always been a difficult task. Not surprisingly, research employing diverse methodologies and definitions of these victimizations has yielded different estimates. This essay reviews the evidence on the epidemiology of family- and intimate-perpetrated violence against women in the United States and the methodological foundations on which these estimates are based. It focuses exclusively on acts of physical violence, meaning behaviors that threaten, attempt, or actually inflict physical harm, including rape. Violent behaviors by spouses, ex-spouses, boy/girlfriends, and former boy/girlfriends are referred to as "intimate partner violence." Violent incidents perpetrated by other family members such as parents, siblings, children, and grandparents are referred to as "other family violence."

Data on U.S. homicides that include characteristics of both the victim and offender are collected by the FBI for its Supplementary Homicide Report; they are part of the FBI's larger Uniform Crime Reporting (*UCR*) program. These homicide data indicate that a female homicide victim is more likely to have been killed by her husband, ex-husband, or boyfriend than a male victim is to have been killed by his wife, ex-wife, or girlfriend. For example, in 1992, approximately 28 percent of female victims of homicide (1,414 women) were known to have been killed by their husbands, ex-husbands, or boyfriends. In contrast, just over 3 percent of male homicide victims (637 men) were known to have been killed by their wives, ex-wives, or girlfriends. Female victims were also more likely to have been killed by other relatives (10 percent) compared to males (6 percent) (Bachman and Saltzman 1995).

The most enduring source of statistical information about nonfatal violent crime in the United States, the *UCRs* rely on incidents that are reported to the police. However, using police reports to estimate incidence rates of violence between intimates and family members is problematic, primarily because a large percentage of these crimes are never reported to police. Because of this and other weaknesses, random sample surveys of the population are the social science tool of choice for uncovering incidents of violence within families.

To date, three nationally representative surveys have provided magnitude estimates of violence against women by intimates and family members:

- The National Family Violence Survey (NFVS 1985)
- The National Crime Victimization Survey (NCVS, conducted annually)
- The National Violence against Women Survey (NVAWS 1995)

Each of these surveys has asked respondents about their victimization experiences somewhat differently, and consequently magnitude estimates vary considerably.

The 1985 NFVS was designed exclusively to measure violence within families and utilized a nationally representative sample of 6,002 married or cohabiting heterosexual persons age 18 and over. To obtain data on incidents of violence from respondents, the survey utilized what is known as the Conflict Tactics Scale (CTS) (Straus and Gelles 1990), which asks respondents to "think of situations in the past year when you had a disagreement or were angry with a specified family member" and to indicate how often they engaged in each of the acts included in the CTS. Physical violence by the CTS index is often subdivided into two categories:

- minor violence (including throwing an object; pushing, grabbing, or shoving; and slapping)
- severe violence (including kicking, biting, or hitting with a fist; hitting or trying to hit with an object; beating up; choking; threatening with a knife or gun; and using a knife or firing a gun)

Estimates from the 1985 NFVS indicate a violence rate of 116 per 1,000 couples; almost 1 out of 8 husbands carried out one or more violent acts during the year of this study, indicating that over 6 million women experienced at least one act of violence by their partners during the preceding 12 months. About 1.8 million of these women experienced severe violence. The NFVS also estimates, however, that rates of violence perpetrated by wives against husbands are very similar to rates of violence perpetrated by husbands against wives. Herein lies one of the most frequent criticisms of the CTS methodology—that it measures acts of violence in isolation from the circumstances under which the acts were committed. Critics point out that this symmetry in offending for males and females is obtained because the CTS ignores who initiates the violence, the relative size and strength of the persons involved, and the nature of the participants' relationship (R. P. Dobash et al. 1992).

The NCVS is an ongoing survey conducted by the Bureau of Justice Statistics and published since 1972 to monitor criminal victimizations experienced by U.S. citizens 12 years of age and older. Although the NCVS was redesigned starting in 1989 to provide more accurate estimates of violence occurring within families, in 2000, questions still do not ask specifically about incidents involving spouses and boy/girlfriends. In addition, questions soliciting information about rapes and sexual assaults are not as detailed as other contemporary surveys in the field, such as the NVAWS or the National Women's Study (National Victim Center 1992). For example, to uncover incidents of rape, the NCVS uses these words with respondents:

> Incidents involving forced or unwanted sexual acts are often difficult to talk about. Have you been forced or coerced to engage in unwanted sexual activity by — (a.) Someone you didn't know before — (b.) A casual acquaintance — (c.) Someone you know well?

If respondents reply affirmatively to one of these questions, interviewers next ask, "Do you mean forced or coerced sexual intercourse?" to determine whether the incident should be recorded as rape or as another type of sexual attack. However, the questions do not become more specific.

Estimates from the NCVS reveal that nearly 5 million violent victimizations are experienced by females over the age of 12 every year. Of those victimizations involving lone offenders, the NCVS estimates that 29 percent are perpetrated by intimates; 9 percent by other relatives such as siblings, parents, and children; 40 percent by other known offenders; and only 23 percent by strangers. Of these victimizations, over 500,000 are rapes or sexual assaults: 53 percent by friends and acquaintances, 26 percent by intimates, 3 percent by other family members, and 18 percent by strangers.

The NVAWS was conducted in 1995 by the Center for Policy Research (Tjaden and Thoennes 1998a) using a random sample of 8,000 women 18 years of age and older. The study was introduced as a survey on personal safety, and respondents were queried on a number of issues including violence they had experienced at any time in their lives at the hands of family members and other intimates.

Information on physical assaults was obtained by the NVAWS using a modified version of the Conflict Tactics Scale that controlled for assault context. Annual estimates of physical assaults from the NVAWS are higher compared to the NCVS results but are lower than results obtained from the NFVS. The NVAWS estimates that nearly 6 million

Table A. U.S. Persons Raped or Physically Assaulted by an Intimate Partner in Lifetime, by Sex of Victim

	Females		Males	
	Percent	Number	Percent	Number
Physical Assault	22.1	22,254,037	7.4	6,863,352
Rape	7.7	7,753,669	.03	278,244
Physical Assault and/or Rape	24.8	24,972,856	7.6	7,048,848

Source: Adapted from Tjaden and Thoennes 1998a, *Prevalence, Incidence, and Consequences of Violence*, page 7.

adult women experience a physical assault annually in the United States and that over two-thirds of these are perpetrated by intimates.

In contrast to the NCVS, the NVAWS obtained information on rape by using very specific questions, including the following:

> Has a man or boy ever made you have sex by using force or threatening to harm you or someone close to you? Just so there is no mistake, by sex we mean putting a penis in your vagina.

and

> Has anyone, male or female, ever made you have oral sex by using force or threat of force? Just so there is no mistake, by oral sex we mean that a man or boy put his penis in your mouth or someone, male or female, penetrated your vagina or anus with their mouth.

Because the NVAWS uses specific questions such as these, and because it asks a number of questions, it is not surprising that annual estimates of rape from the NVAWS are higher than those obtained from the NCVS. When making estimates comparable by restricting the sample to adult women (18 years of age and older) and using only completed and attempted cases of rape (not other sexual assaults), the NCVS methodology estimates that approximately 163,065 adult women are raped annually compared to 302,091 women estimated by the NVAWS (Bachman forthcoming). Table A compares male and female victimizations for physical assault and rape, as estimated from the NVAWS.

Regardless of absolute magnitude estimates across surveys, it is clear that both the NCVS and NVAWS contradict the stereotypical view that women are at greatest risk of violence from the stranger lurking in the bushes; both surveys reveal conclusively that women are most likely to be both raped and physically assaulted by people they know and often love. In addition, both surveys indicate that the same subgroups of the adult female population are particularly vulnerable to interpersonal violence: young women, eco- nomically deprived women, and women going through periods of separation from their partners. *See also* CRIME VICTIMIZATION; DOMESTIC VIOLENCE CASE PROCESSING; DOMESTIC VIOLENCE, POLICE RESPONSES TO; HOMICIDE, USA; RAPE RATES, USA; STALKING; VICTIMIZATION, FEMINIST PERSPECTIVES ON; VICTIMIZATION, REPEAT.

Further Reading: Bachman forthcoming, "Estimates of Violence against Women"; Tjaden and Thoennes 1998a, *Prevalence, Incidence, and Consequences of Violence.*

Ronet D. Bachman

Domestic Violence by Women

Considerable controversy surrounds the topic of domestic violence by women—violence that can be directed at husbands, unmarried partners, children, or elderly parents. Some scholars regard domestic violence by women (especially husband-battering) to be an important social problem while others consider it a much less significant problem than domestic violence against women.

A great deal of evidence indicates that the majority of incidents of partner- or spouse-battering are committed by men against women. Between 1992 and 1996, violence by a present or former spouse or intimate partner accounted for 21 percent of overall violence experienced by women; in contrast, only 2 percent of the overall violence experienced by men was committed by an intimate partner (Greenfeld et al. 1998). The National Violence against Women Survey (using 1995–96 data) found that 25 percent of women said they had been physically assaulted and/or raped by a current or former spouse, partner, or date in their lifetime. For comparison, this same study found that only 8 percent of men had been similarly victimized, as shown in Table A.

Research finds several important differences in male and female domestic violence killings. A female murder victim is far more likely than a male murder victim to have been killed by a partner or former partner. Overall, between 1976 and 1996, approximately two-thirds the victims in intimate-perpetrated murders were women (Greenfeld et al. 1998). As for wives killing husbands, there is evidence that a significant proportion of these killings occur in self-defense, which is rarely the case when men kill their wives (R. P. Dobash et al. 1992). In contrast to men, women kill after a long period of increasing physical abuse, when they perceive a lack of options, and when their own lives have been threatened.

Some research finds that women and men engage in equal amounts of violence in relationships. The National Family Violence Surveys of 1975 and 1985 found approximately equal rates of violence between husbands and wives (Straus 1977–78; Straus and Gelles 1986). The 1975 study found that women were more likely to "kick, bite, hit with a fist" and "hit or try to hit with something," while men engaged in more serious assaults. Straus (1997) states that violence by women against their partners should be seen as a major social problem, especially since even minor violence by women can increase the probability of severe reciprocal assault by men.

While the debate continues over the question of whether men or women are more violent in the home, we can draw several important conclusions. It is known that men tend to underreport their own violence (Edleson and Brygger 1986). Men have higher rates of inflicting injury upon their female partners, and they repeat violent acts more often. The greater physical strength of men makes it much more likely that women victims will be injured. Some violent acts by women occur in retaliation for abuse they have suffered, though the extent of this is unclear. Since women are more likely than men to be injured by partner violence, the priority must be treatment and prevention efforts aimed at women as victims.

To discuss women as perpetrators of child abuse is difficult because the very concept undermines images of women as mothers, nurturers, and caretakers. In addition, there are no clear, agreed-upon definitions of the forms the abuse can take; child abuse is variously defined to include physical abuse, emotional abuse, physical neglect, emotional neglect, and/or sexual abuse. Because women are the primary caretakers of children, children may be at higher risk of abuse from women. A number of family characteristics contribute to the risk of child abuse, including poverty, early and repeated pregnancy, inadequate education, insufficient knowledge of and experience with child rearing, single parenting, marital problems, and a history of victimization or the witnessing of family violence (Cappelleri, Eckenrode, and Powers 1993; Tolliver et al. 1998).

Child sexual abuse by women has been studied only since the late 1980s. While there are no definitive estimates of the prevalence of this type of offending, female sexual abuse of children may not be as rare as previously thought; it may account for 5 percent or more of child sexual abuse cases (Fromuth and Conn 1997; Jennings 1993). Finkelhor's (1984) review of the literature suggested that women are perpetrators in 5 percent of the cases of sexual abuse of girls and 20 percent of the cases of sexual abuse of boys. The extent of sexual activity between mothers and sons has not been sufficiently studied and therefore is unknown at this time.

Overall, in partner abuse situations, women are much more likely to be victims than perpetrators. In general, women seem to be more likely to commit child maltreatment than men, although men are responsible for the great majority of cases of child sexual abuse. *See also* Child Abuse by Women; Domestic Violence against Women, Epidemiology of; Homicide Victims; Homicide, USA; Incest Victims; Lesbian Partner Battering; Sexual Abuse of Children.

Further Reading: Cardarelli 1997, *Violence between Intimate Partners;* R. P. Dobash, Dobash, Wilson, and Daly 1992, "The Myth of Sexual Symmetry"; M. Elliott 1993, *Female Sexual Abuse of Children.*

Sylvia I. Mignon

Domestic Violence Case Processing

Since the mid-1980s, increasing attention has focused on domestic violence case processing. A case of domestic violence or battering enters the criminal justice system in three ways: arrest on the scene by responding police officers; arrest by warrant after a police-initiated investigation; or arrest by warrant on the basis of a victim complaint. Only a small fraction of battering incidents result in an arrest through any of these mechanisms, and at each subsequent step of the criminal justice process, cases are weeded out. The proportion of cases reaching the most serious level of response, a prison term, is minuscule in comparison to the approximately 1.8 million cases of battering that occur each year.

Three questions dominate current research and policy development in the area of domestic violence case processing.

- Are domestic violence cases processed differently than other forms of violent crime, and if so, in what ways?
- What is the evidence regarding the effects of various forms of prosecution in deterring future battering?
- What innovations in processing are most beneficial to women battered by their intimate partners?

A number of studies have found that domestic violence cases are treated less seriously than other violent crimes at every stage of criminal justice processing. Other research has found that leniency toward violent criminals generally is based on the shared class and race characteristics of the victim and the offender and on the existence of a prior relationship between them—circumstances that characterize domestic partnerships. Crimes that threaten public order are more likely to be prosecuted than those which occur in the private realm, particularly when offenders are of the same or lower social status than their victims. Interviews with prosecutors and examination of case files, moreover, indicate that victims of domestic violence are perceived as problematic.

Although victims of all types of crimes fail to follow through with prosecution, domestic violence victims are generally viewed as both less credible and less reliable than other victims.

The proportion of domestic violence victims who do not cooperate with prosecution varies widely among studies, ranging from 13 percent to 80 percent. Within any specific study, however, domestic violence victims are more likely than other victims to drop charges.

The reasons for lack of cooperation with prosecution reflect women's varied relationships with their abusers and with the criminal justice system. An abuser may threaten or cajole a woman into dropping charges; a woman may fear losing her partner's economic contributions; she may be threatened with criminal and civil actions such as deportation or loss of child custody; or she may believe that the threat of prosecution is a more powerful tool than actual prosecution for controlling her situation.

Many jurisdictions have adopted "no-drop" policies in an effort to make domestic violence prosecutions more successful. The Indianapolis Prosecution Experiment found, however, that the most important factor in deterring future violence is empowering victims to make their own choices about prosecution.

The Indianapolis Prosecution Experiment also compared three approaches to domestic violence case processing:

- pretrial diversion
- prosecution to conviction with the recommendation of counseling
- prosecution to conviction with presumptive sentencing

At a six-month follow-up, prosecution reduced men's repeated use of violence by 50 percent over the six months preceding arrest. However, there was no difference in effectiveness among the three prosecutorial outcomes. Counseling and other sentences are equally likely to deter offenders.

Recognizing the difficulties women face in prosecuting their abusers, many jurisdictions have adopted special domestic violence units and victim advocacy programs. Of 142 offices in large jurisdictions surveyed by the American Prosecutors Research Institute, half reported special domestic violence units and 71 percent had developed victim support programs. Specialized units allow prosecutors to develop greater knowledge of, and resources for, domestic violence cases. Victim advocacy programs provide referral to social services, information on civil remedies, court accompaniment, and court preparation. *See also* CRIME VICTIMS AND DEFINITIONS OF JUSTICE; DOMESTIC VIOLENCE AGAINST WOMEN, EPIDEMIOLOGY OF; DOMESTIC VIOLENCE, POLICE RESPONSES TO.

Further Reading: Buzawa and Buzawa 1996, *Domestic Violence;* Hilton 1993, *Legal Responses to Wife Assault;* U.S. Department of Justice 1998, *Legal Interventions in Family Violence.*

Kathleen J. Ferraro

Domestic Violence, Police Responses to

Because police are the first line of defense for victims of domestic violence, police response to domestic violence—whether dictated by law, department policy, or personal attitude—is an essential component in efforts to contain this type of crime.

The three predominant police responses to domestic violence are

- noninvolvement or "doing nothing"
- crisis intervention, which can include separation of the couple, mediation, and/or referrals to social service agencies
- arrest

For much of the twentieth century, "doing nothing" was the typical police response. Most police (and, indeed, most of the public) believed that domestic violence was a private matter, best handled within the home. In some jurisdictions, this practice continues.

The first change in the police response to domestic violence occurred in the 1960s and early 1970s. On the basis of information provided by social workers and psychologists, police officials decided that unless there was serious injury, officers should use mediation, reconciliation, or agency referrals as the preferred response. At the same time, a shift began to occur in the public's perception of domestic violence. As feminists raised awareness of the extent and severity of domestic violence, the public came to see it as a legitimate social concern.

In the 1980s, feminists' calls for change combined with conservatives' calls for solving social problems through law enforcement. The result was a demand for a more aggressive role for police officers in responding to domestic violence. This trend was reinforced by the 1984 Minneapolis Domestic Violence Experiment (L. W. Sherman and Berk 1984), the results of which suggested that arrest in domestic violence cases reduces the possibility of further violence. Shortly thereafter, the Minneapolis study was cited by the U.S. Attorney General's Task Force on Family Violence as sufficient evidence for adopting pro-arrest policies nationally.

Despite significant criticism of the Minneapolis study's methodology and interpretation of data (Binder and Meeker 1992), by 1990, 15 states had mandatory arrest laws for domestic violence, and all but a handful of states had amended their laws to allow for warrantless misdemeanor arrests in domestic violence cases.

The effectiveness of arrest as a strategy for policing domestic violence remains unclear. Some continue to advocate pro-arrest policies, arguing that only arrests of perpetrators will protect women and insure that the law is properly enforced. Others suggest that little is known about the possible negative impact of arrest, and that alternatives embodied in the crisis intervention approach provide viable options for domestic violence calls when no injury is involved.

Even when arrest is dictated by law or policy, the police have discretion in finding that a crime occurred. Ferraro (1989) found that at least four considerations affect a police officer's decision to arrest:

- legal factors, or what the officer understands the law to be
- ideological factors, or the beliefs the officer has about battered women
- practical considerations, or the amount of work involved processing an arrest versus the likelihood of a reprimand for failing to do so
- political issues, or the relationship between police department administrators and street officers

As a result, even when states enact mandatory or preferred arrest laws, the number of arrests may not increase significantly.

The future of police responses to domestic violence may be found in model programs that integrate the work of police, probation officers, and victim advocates. Such programs are already operating in Duluth (Minnesota), Denver (Colorado), and Quincy (Massachusetts). *See also* CRIME VICTIMS AND DEFINITIONS OF JUSTICE; DOMESTIC VIOLENCE CASE PROCESSING; VICTIMIZATION, FEMINIST PERSPECTIVES ON.

Further Reading: Buzawa and Buzawa 1996, *Domestic Violence;* Hofford and Harrell 1993, *Family Violence;* L. W. Sherman 1992, *Policing Domestic Violence.*

Susan T. Krumholz

Dothard v. Rawlinson. *See* CORRECTIONS OFFICERS, HISTORY OF; WOMEN CORRECTIONS OFFICERS IN MEN'S PRISONS.

Drug and Alcohol Treatment for Prisoners

A large proportion of inmates committed to U.S. correctional facilities were involved in drug or alcohol abuse at the time they committed their conviction offenses. Although there is some fluctuation in reported statistics, a safe estimate is that about 80 percent of women committed to state institutions and 60 percent of women committed to the Federal Bureau of Prisons have experienced problems with chemical dependency. Therefore, prison systems try to provide substance-abuse treatment to incarcerated offenders. Treatment can consist of Alcoholics Anonymous or Narcotics Anonymous meetings, substance-abuse education classes, group counseling, or participation in a therapeutic community within the prison walls.

Inmates who participate in therapeutic communities, or what are now commonly referred to as residential substance-abuse treatment (RSAT) programs, are generally segregated from the general prison population. The programs require 24-hour-a-day

participation and last from six months to one year. RSATs are probably the most effective form of treatment for offenders with histories of substance abuse.

Generally speaking, RSATs focus on the development of problem-solving skills and social skills such as stress and anger management. The treatment goals are to provide inmates with a foundation for recovery, relapse prevention, and pro-social behavior, including a crime-free lifestyle. Treatment can include cognitive restructuring, training in relapse prevention skills, and release preparation. Inmates learn concrete solutions to problems they may face upon release. Although much has changed since Synanon, the model therapeutic community of the 1960s, emphasis is still placed on achieving behavioral change through group pressure on program participants, mutual self-help, and the earning of privileges and rewards.

Female offenders have different treatment needs than male offenders. Thus, substance-abuse programs for women, in addition to dealing with issues of addiction, have also addressed incest and domestic violence, parenting and family issues, self-esteem, the development of positive interpersonal relationships, and educational and vocational training. Treatment providers are particularly aware of the relationship between early sexual abuse and subsequent chemical dependency among female substance abusers. A large percentage of women in the criminal justice system who seek treatment for substance abuse have been the victims of early childhood sexual abuse in the form of incest or sexual assault by a stranger. These women may have turned to drugs and/or alcohol as a way of coping with trauma. Some researchers have argued that unless treatment is given for these early childhood traumas, the women are more susceptible than men to relapse into drug or alcohol dependence, for the memories repressed by substance abuse become clear and painful when the women are sober.

Although substance-abuse treatment for women committed to prisons appears to reduce the rate of recommitment for women who successfully complete the programs, there are too few treatment slots to provide services for all the women identified as chemically dependent. Eighty percent of the women who need services either do not request treatment or are permanently wait-listed. (See Figure 11, page 204.) Thus, expanding substance-abuse treatment programs for female offenders will be a major challenge for correctional administrators of the twenty-first century. *See also* PRISONS, HEALTH CARE IN; PRISONS, TREATMENT PROGRAMS IN.

Further Reading: Center for Substance Abuse Treatment 1994, *Practical Approaches in the Treatment of Women who Abuse Alcohol and Other Drugs;* Early 1996, *Drug Treatment behind Bars.*

Susan E. Pease

Drug Dealers

Drug dealing has traditionally been a bastion of male privilege, a form of income generation that many believe requires people who are aggressive, ruthless, physically tough, and predisposed to violence. Studies conducted at all levels of distribution support the claim that women are underrepresented among drug dealers. Researchers have generally maintained that women form a small minority in distribution circles for several, often interlocking, reasons:

- a lack of the quintessential male characteristics that make for a successful drug dealer
- institutionalized sexism within illegal markets that prevents women from gaining a foothold in the business
- the easier availability of other employment opportunities (especially sex work)
- household and/or childcare responsibilities that preclude women's regular involvement

Women's participation in drug distribution has often been described as an outcome of their relationships with men. The few women who have enjoyed positions of power in drug distribution hierarchies have almost always been the wives (or former wives), girlfriends, or relatives of male drug dealers.

Women who enter the business from the bottom and attempt to work their way up without the assistance of, or connection to, a man in the business find few opportunities in retail and street-level drug markets, which tend to be highly stratified by gender and race/ethnicity.

During the U.S. crack cocaine epidemic of the 1980s and early 1990s, the relative number of female drug users clearly increased, and many researchers initially believed that women involved with crack, who were said to be as violent and crime-prone as men, would take advantage of new emancipatory opportunities to expand their share of roles in distribution circles. Subsequent research, however, found that while the number of females involved in distribution roles did indeed increase during the crack era, rather than providing new ways for women to escape their limited roles, statuses, and incomes, the crack economy further marginalized and impoverished those who participated in it. Far from gaining access to better and/or more income-generating opportunities, women found that participation in the drug economy was conditional and highly dependent on the availability of labor rather than an outcome of any reputed changes in their attitudes, skills, or availability.

Women's participation as drug distributors also varies considerably with the social organization of distribution within markets. For example, freelance crack markets offered opportunities for women, but the chaotic nature of such markets precluded women from advancing in any significant manner. In markets dominated by corporate-like organizations, women are generally consigned to the lowest-status jobs, performing such temporary or sporadic tasks as lookout, steerer, tout, stash-house sitter, or drug packager, and working during hours that are riskier and less financially rewarding than those offered to men. In short, the position of women within the illegal drug economy mirrors that within the legal sector.

By the late 1990s, crack markets had waned and street-level drug markets of all types had largely retired to indoor locales. As delivery services and other new styles of drug distribution began to appear, the increasingly gender-neutral market offered, in theory, new opportunities for newcomers, but there was little evidence that women's rate of participation actually increased. *See also* DRUG OFFENSES; SENTENCING, DRUG OFFENDERS.

Further Reading: Fagan 1994, "Women and Drugs Revisited"; Maher and Daly 1996, "Women in the Street-Level Drug Economy."

Richard Curtis

Drug Offenses

Of those arrested for drug abuse violations in the United States in 1997, 17.3 percent were women. The seriousness of the drug offense with which an individual is charged depends partly on whether the act falls into the category of "possession" or the more serious category of "trafficking" and partly on how the drug is classified by the federal Drug Enforcement Administration (DEA). Drugs are classified into five schedules, with Schedule I drugs the most serious in terms of legal consequences and Schedule V drugs the least serious. This classification scheme, a tool of law enforcement and the courts, is based on a legal—rather than scientific or pharmaceutical—assessment of drugs. For example, Schedule I and II drugs include heroin, marijuana, THC, LSD, and mescaline. These are drugs the DEA considers to have a high abuse potential, no medical value, and strong potential for leading to physical and/or psychological dependency. Schedule V drugs are defined in terms of a low abuse potential, accepted medical use, and low potential for creating physical and/or psychological dependency.

The number of Americans aged 12 or older who reported use of any illicit drug during the past year has decreased since 1985. Whereas 16.3 percent reported use in 1985, 11.2 percent reported such use in 1997. Whereas 9.7 percent reported use of an illicit drug other than marijuana in 1985, only 5.5 percent reported using any illicit drug other than marijuana in 1997. However, these declines are not reflected in the rate at which people are being imprisoned for drug use.

Women are significantly less likely than men to use any illicit drug. In 1997, 7.9 percent of women reported ever having used cocaine, compared with 13.2 percent of men; 23.3 percent reported ever having used marijuana as compared to 37.8 percent of men; and 0.6 percent reported ever having used heroin, compared to 1.3 percent of men (U.S. Department of Health and Human Services, Substance Abuse and Mental Health Services Administration 1999). Yet women's arrests and subsequent commitments to correctional institutions for drug offenses have increased dramatically since 1980.

The percentage of female state prisoners serving time for drug offenses has increased 300 percent since 1979. In 1997, 34.4 percent of female inmates were incarcerated for drug offenses, compared with 10.5 percent in 1979, 12 percent in 1986, and 32.8 percent in 1991 (U.S. General Accounting Office 1999). Moreover, drug offenses now account for the largest percentage of inmates committed to the Federal Bureau of Prisons (FBP).

Of all female prisoners committed to the FBP, 60.1 percent are committed for drug offenses. In 1998, 68 percent of white women, 70 percent of black women, and 44 percent of women classified as "other" who were incarcerated by the FBP were imprisoned for drug offenses (Bureau of Justice Statistics 1999b). Although black women are the least likely to self-report drug use, they are the most likely to be arrested and convicted of drug offenses.

Pregnant women are particularly susceptible to prosecution for drug offenses as they may seek medical treatment related to their pregnancy and then be prosecuted. In the name of protecting a fetus from the effects of illegal drugs, some states have enacted legislation designed to criminalize women who use illegal drugs while pregnant or to charge currently pregnant women with criminal offenses such as child abuse and neglect, contributing to the delinquency of a minor, assault with a deadly weapon, and causing the dependency of a minor. Even though drinking alcohol and smoking cigarettes probably cause more serious damage to the developing fetus, control of those substances has traditionally been left in the domain of public health, not moved into the jurisdiction of the criminal justice system. Unless policy changes occur that shift the problem of substance abuse to the realm of medicine and public health, it appears that the number of women arrested and incarcerated for drug offenses will continue to increase. *See also* CRIMINALIZATION OF PREGNANCY, USA; DRUG AND ALCOHOL TREATMENT FOR PRISONERS; PRISONER CHARACTERISTICS; SENTENCING, DRUG OFFENDERS.

Further Reading: Inciardi, Lockwood, and Pottieger 1993, *Women and Crack-Cocaine*.

Susan E. Pease

E

Elderly Victims

The category of elderly crime victims, which includes those age 65 years and older, comprises less than 2 percent of all victims of crime, yet the elderly are the age group most fearful of becoming crime victims. As shown in Table B, elderly women are less likely than elderly men to be victims of violent crime; this is particularly true of violent crimes involving strangers. On the other hand, elderly women are more likely to be victims of personal larceny in incidents such as purse snatchings. For both elderly men and women, household victimizations such as burglary, household larceny, and motor vehicle theft are the most frequent types of victimizations. Moreover, the elderly are relatively easy prey for crimes that have an economic motivation, such as fraud, theft of retirement checks from the mail, and home repair scams.

When the elderly become crime victims, the site of the incident is likely to be in or near the victim's home. The likelihood of crime victimization decreases with age, so that persons aged 65 and older are in the least victimized age category, and persons between 65 and 74 have a higher victimization rate than those who are 75 or older. Single elderly persons who live alone are the most vulnerable to victimization, while elderly members of racial minority groups are more often victimized (especially by personal crimes) than elderly whites.

Elder abuse and neglect, a problem not recognized until the 1970s, may affect one million victims each year. The deterioration of the body and mind that accompanies old age, such as vision and hearing impairment, physical injuries, and dementia, increases the possibility that an elderly person may be taken

Table B. Rate of U.S. Crime Victimizations per 1,000 Persons in Each Age Group, 1997

	Crimes of Violence*	Rape	Robbery	Aggravated Assault	Simple Assault	Purse-Snatching and Pick Pocketing
Female						
50–64 years	10.2	0.3	1.2	1.9	6.8	1.7
65 years and older	3.9	0.3	0.4	.5	2.6	1.5
Male						
50–64 years	19.3	.1	3.2	3.8	12.2	0.4
65 years and older	5.2	.0	1.4	0.8	3.0	0.9
* Rape, robbery, aggravated assault, and simple assault.						

Source: Excerpted from U.S. Department of Justice, Bureau of Justice Statistics 1998d: page 176.

advantage of by family members or other caregivers. Elder abuse includes abandonment and emotional, financial, physical, and sexual abuse. Congressional investigators estimate that only about 16 percent of abused elderly victims report their victimization experiences. With the elderly population growing, crimes against the elderly are expected to increase.

Most victims of elder abuse are women (68 percent); like their male counterparts, these women are most likely to suffer from neglect. Neglect is defined as the refusal or failure to provide reasonable care. The typical pattern is for the primary caregiver to perpetrate the abuse in the elderly person's home, refusing or failing to provide life necessities such as food, water, medication, shelter and clothing, help with personal hygiene and safety, and other essentials. Adult children are the most common abusers in cases of elder neglect, with other family members and spouses forming the second most common group of abusers. Abusers are equally distributed between males and females.

Elder abuse also occurs in extended care facilities such as nursing homes, where elders may be maltreated by those charged with providing care. While the states license these facilities, reported abuses in recent years have prompted many legislative bodies to enact specific laws prohibiting elder abuse. In addition, many states and local jurisdictions have created agencies to promulgate policies on standards of care in residential and daycare facilities for the elderly, to establish reporting requirements for law enforcement and protective service agencies, and to collect and disseminate data on elder demographics. Mandatory reporting laws, now enacted in all 50 states, require professionals to report any known incident of abuse or neglect. In addition, state and federal laws now define elderly abuse and neglect and provide resources for following up reports of abuse and resolving the problems. These measures reflect the current concern with elder abuse and, more generally, victimization of the elderly.

When the elderly become victims of violent crime, they are more likely than younger victims to suffer serious injury that requires medical attention. An important concern in addressing the problem of the victimization of the elderly is their physical vulnerability and sense of fear. Declining physical strength and increasing health problems reduce elderly people's ability to protect themselves during an attack and increase their level of injuries. In addition, social isolation and economic dependency can magnify the impact of elderly victimization, causing many elderly people to live in constant fear of crime. *See also* FEAR OF CRIME; VICTIMIZATION PATTERNS, CANADA; VICTIMIZATION PATTERNS, USA.

Further Reading: Bureau of Justice Statistics 1994b, *Elderly Crime Victims*; Bureau of Justice Statistics 1998b, *Criminal Victimization, 1997;* National Center on Elderly Abuse 1997, "The Basics"; Tatara and Blumerman 1996, *Summaries of the Statistical Data on Elder Abuse in Domestic Settings.*

Evelyn Gilbert

Employment Training in Prisons. *See* GENDER DISPARITIES IN PRISONS.

"Evil Woman" Thesis. *See* GENDER AND CRIME; GENDER DISCRIMINATION AND SENTENCING; HINDLEY, MYRA; MADONNA/WHORE DICHOTOMY.

F

Farnham, Eliza W. (1815–1864)

Abolitionist, author, criminologist, farmer, feminist, nurse, prison reformer, wife, and mother, Eliza W. Farnham was appointed matron of the female unit of Sing Sing Prison at Mt. Pleasant, New York, in 1844. As the first prison official in the United States to introduce methods for rehabilitating women prisoners, she charted new ground as a prison reformer and precipitated one of the first controversies about coddling criminals.

The prevailing attitude in the mid-nineteenth century was that offenders, particularly female offenders, were beyond redemption. Because they had betrayed their essential femininity by committing crimes, no punishment was too great for them; their lives in prison should be a living hell to deter them and others from committing crimes. Disagreeing strongly with this view, Farnham, who was not yet 30 years old at the time of her Sing Sing appointment, felt that crime was not a simple matter of free will but was caused by a variety of factors in peoples' lives including their education, intelligence, environment, and physical makeup. She based her beliefs on phrenology, the then-popular "science" according to which peoples' actions are attributable to over- or underdevelopment of certain areas or "faculties" of their brains. Problems such as crime, phrenologists taught, could be treated by stimulating the development of underdeveloped faculties and encouraging overdeveloped faculties to atrophy—

forms of treatment that involved retraining the individual offender.

Eliza Farnham believed that if offenders were treated brutally in prison, they would respond with further violence. If treated kindly, offenders would behave more positively. While she was a firm disciplinarian and even redesigned the facility's punishment cells, she believed that positive incentives should be used in place of coercive or corporal punishments. Farnham introduced education, had the walls whitewashed and added lamps with large reflectors to lighten the dark cells, arranged for inspirational speakers, had staff read to the women while they sewed uniforms for male prisoners, and added music and books to improve prisoners' mental faculties. Moreover, she refused to allow religious theology to be imposed on her charges by the Sing Sing chaplain, thus starting the first recorded battle between a woman prison administrator and a male supervisor who wanted to bring her under control.

Initially, Farnham received support for her theories both from the prison board of governors and influential members of the community. Soon, however, her views on religion and the biological roots of human behavior brought her in conflict with the prison chaplain and other conservatives. Her programs were attacked for being soft on inmates, and she was accused of corrupting her charges by introducing reading material other than the Bible. Although an investigation by the

New York Prison Association found no fault with Farnham's programs or her administration of the unit, she was forced to resign in 1848 when more conservative members were appointed to the prison's governing board.

Farnham's reforms came to an end with her departure from Sing Sing, and it would be another 20 years before progressive programming again became available to female inmates. Farnham continued her work in prison reform, abolition, and women's rights, dying in 1864 after contracting tuberculosis while nursing wounded soldiers at the battle of Gettysburg. *See also* PRISONS, TREATMENT PROGRAMS IN; WOMEN'S PRISON ADMINISTRATION, HISTORICAL; WOMEN'S PRISONS, HISTORY OF.

Further Reading: Hallwas 1988, Introduction to *Life in Prairie Land*; Kirby 1971, *Years of Experience;* Lewis 1965, *From Newgate to Dannemora.*

Joann B. Morton

Fear of Crime

Fear of crime has been a topic of major concern in modern criminology and victimology. Research findings, such as those displayed in Table C, consistently show that certain population groups, especially women and the elderly, are more afraid of becoming victims of crime than men and the young. Studies also show that women are more likely to alter their behavior because of the fear of victimization. These findings point to an apparent contradiction: although women and the elderly express more fear, they are actually less likely to be victims of crime. The contradiction between victimization rates and the levels of fear, one of the most perplexing issues in criminology, has come to be known as the "paradox" of fear (Warr 1984).

Different factors are used in attempts to explain the apparent contradiction between women's victimization rates and their fear of crime. According to some, gender differences in fear of crime reflect differences in physical vulnerability. Women feel physically more vulnerable than men because they tend to be smaller and therefore less able to defend themselves against physical aggression; thus, the fear of being a crime victim may emerge as a result of differences in strength and body size. Others argue that fear of crime among women may be related to the fear of rape, which some women consider the most terrifying type of criminal offense. In the United States, as well as in other cultures, warnings about sexual molestation are an important part of the socialization of girls. Women are taught to "sit like a lady," "keep your legs together," "keep your skirt down," and "avoid talking to strange men" because "something bad could happen to you."

Many studies of fear of crime fail to address the issue of domestic violence. Public policies, too, often ignore the relationship

Table C. Fear of Crime [USA, 1996]

Respondents' Fear of Walking Alone at Night in Own Neighborhood				
	Very Safe	Fairly Safe	Fairly Unsafe	Very Unsafe	Not Sure
Males	40%	41%	10%	8%	1%
Females	16%	39%	17%	23%	3%

Respondents' Feelings of Safety Alone at Night at Home			
	Very Safe	Somewhat Safe	Somewhat Unsafe	Very Unsafe
Males	56%	31%	9%	4%
Females	38%	40%	15%	7%

Source: Excerpted from Bureau of Justice Statistics 1997d, *Sourcebook of Criminal Justice Statistics*, pages 122, 123.

between women's fears and domestic violence. For example, policies aimed at reducing crime against women—such as safety tips given by police departments and security telephones in university campuses—address only the crime that occurs in public places. Underlying these efforts is an assumption that most crimes against women are committed by strangers in public spaces. However, recent data show that women are more likely to be victims of violence committed by someone they know.

An everyday reality for many women is life under a self-imposed curfew, based on a feeling that it is dangerous to freely walk city streets or to exercise the right to the use of public space. Indeed, fear of crime is a reality for most women. However, poor women lack some of the protection that most upper-class and upper-middle-class women have. For example, women of lower socioeconomic status use public transportation more often, and they may live in places where there is little or no security. Unlike many upper-class women, most poor women in cities do not have a security guard protecting the entrance of their buildings, and many have to enter their apartments by walking through dark, unprotected hallways. Often overlooked are class and racial differences that play a role in the fear of crime and its consequences on women's lives. Some Latina women's fear of crime, for example, is influenced by their "undocumented" status. If they are victims of crime, they cannot report the incident to the police because of the risk of being deported. Therefore, undocumented Latina women report higher levels of fear of crime than white women (Madriz 1997).

The possibilities of violence and the fear it produces are fundamental elements in the control of women's lives. Susan Brownmiller (1975:309) maintains that "even before we learn to read we have become indoctrinated into a victim mentality." Differences in the levels of fear of crime between men and women can be explained, at least in part, by dominant images that reflect structural gender divisions and that present women as comparatively vulnerable, weak, powerless, and passive and men as forceful, strong, powerful, and active.

The fear of crime, and specifically the fear of male violence, also feeds into the notion that women and men are not entitled to the same freedoms. There are places where women should not and cannot go, while men can; activities in which women cannot engage, while men can. Moreover, women should wear "proper" attire so they don't get molested by men. These attitudes reflect the idea that women must protect themselves from criminal victimization, so they had better stay home and be "good girls." These attitudes also reinforce the subordinate role of women: If a woman wants to be safe and protected, she had better be accompanied by a man.

In conclusion, fear of crime touches deep-seated beliefs and supports many assumptions about proper roles for men and women. Hence it contributes to the social control of women by limiting women's everyday activities. Fear of crime is an important element in the perpetuation of gender inequalities that maintain and reinforce patriarchal relations, undermining women's power, rights, and potential for achievement. *See also* DOMESTIC VIOLENCE AGAINST WOMEN, EPIDEMIOLOGY OF; VICTIMIZATION, FEMINIST PERSPECTIVES ON.

Further Reading: Madriz 1997, *Nothing Bad Happens to Good Girls;* Riger and Gordon 1991, "The Fear of Rape"; Stanko 1990, *Everyday Violence.*

Esther I. Madriz

Female Crime, Australia

There are no national statistics on female crime in Australia because the various states are responsible for the police and courts. The following data are drawn from the state with the largest population, New South Wales (NSW); however, the pattern of findings is similar in other states. Criminal matters are heard either in Local Court or Higher Court. In 1997, most (97 percent) of convictions occurred in the Local Court, which has jurisdiction over both state statutes and summary offense matters.

In 1997, women made up only a small proportion (16 percent) of all persons found guilty in Local Courts in NSW. As Table D indicates, the two offense categories for which women were most often convicted were theft (30 percent) and driving offenses (34 percent). A greater proportion of all female than all male convictions was for theft, but in raw numbers, male convictions far outnumbered those of females. Of women's theft convictions, 62 percent were for larceny, and 51 percent of their driving offenses related to alcohol consumption.

Women made up an even smaller proportion (8 percent) of convictions in the NSW Higher Criminal Courts, which have jurisdiction over indictable offenses. Again the most frequent offense category for women was theft (26 percent), followed in this case by drug offenses (23 percent). Two-thirds (68 percent) of women's theft convictions in the Higher Courts were for misappropriation. The most frequent offense category for men, on the other hand, was offenses against the person (32 percent).

In summary, women make up a small proportion of all offenders convicted in criminal courts. Their offending is most often trivial in comparison to patterns of male offending, consisting mainly of property or drug/alcohol-related offenses, and far less often involves violence.

Aboriginal Australians— men, women, juveniles, and adults—are arrested and detained at rates well above their proportion in the general population. Nearly half of the women arrested and held in custody nationally are Aboriginal Australians, even though they constitute less than 2 percent of the general population (Carrington 1998). In NSW, Aboriginal women make up 18.4 percent of women in full-time custody (Edwards 1995b). For Australia, 9 percent of Aboriginal women (and 32 percent of Aboriginal men) were arrested in 1994 (Mukherjee, Carcach, and McDonald 1998). Aboriginal women are mostly arrested and detained in relation to public-order offenses. In the state of Victoria, for example, Aboriginal women were arrested more often for "other summary offenses" (mostly offenses against "good order") than for any other offense category. They were nearly 10 times more likely to be arrested for this offense in Victoria than non-Aboriginal women (Mackay and Smallacombe 1996).

Table D. Convictions by Sex and Offense Type, 1997, New South Wales, Australia

Type of Principal Offense	Females	Males	Total
Local Court			
Against the Person	11% (n=1,678)	15% (n=11,234)	14% (n=12,912)
Theft	30% (n=4,401)	16% (n=12,474)	18% (n=16,875)
Property Damage	3% (n=419)	4% (n=3,181)	4% (n=3,600)
Environmental	0% (n=8)	0% (n=73)	0% (n=81)
Against Justice Procedures	7% (n=1,039)	8% (n=5,788)	7% (n=6,827)
Against Good Order	7% (n=1,051)	8% (n=6,516)	8% (n=7,567)
Drugs	8% (n=1,128)	8% (n=5,865)	8% (n=6,993)
Driving	34% (n=4,975)	42% (n=31,905)	40% (n=36,880)
Total*	100% (n=14,849)	101% (n=76,793)	99% (n=91,642)
Higher Court			
Against the Person	19% (n=36)	32% (n=745)	30% (n=781)
Robbery and Extortion	18% (n=37)	20% (n=482)	20% (n=519)
Theft	26% (n=55)	21% (n=492)	21% (n=547)
Drugs	23% (n=49)	17% (n=392)	17% (n=441)
Other	15% (n=32)	10% (n=247)	11% (n=276)
Total*	101% (n=209)	100% (n=2,358)	99% (n=2,567)

* Percentages may not total 100 due to rounding error.

Source: NSW Bureau of Crime Statistics and Research 1998, *New South Wales Criminal Courts Statistics 1997.*

In short, Australian women come to the notice of the criminal justice system far less often than men and for qualitatively different crimes. Female crime in Australia consists of minor nonviolent and often poverty-related offenses, for which Aboriginal Australians continue to be disproportionately arrested. *See also* ABORIGINAL WOMEN AND CRIME, AUSTRALIA; HOMICIDE VICTIMS AND OFFENDERS, AUSTRALIA; JUVENILE DELINQUENCY, AUSTRALIA.

Further Reading: National Corrective Services Statistics Unit 1998, *Prisoners in Australia, 1997.*

Sharon Pickering

Female Crime, Britain

Females in Britain generally commit far less crime than do males. Indeed, while criminal convictions are relatively common for males, they are still very unusual for females, as shown in Table E. In England and Wales, the general ratio of male to female offenders is currently 6:1 for indictable (that is, serious and largely imprisonable) offenses. Of those found guilty or cautioned (formally warned by the police) in 1997 in England and Wales, most offenders (about 82 percent) were male and just 17 percent female. While 34 percent of males born in 1953 have been convicted before the age of 40, only 8 percent of females fall into this category. The peak age of offending for females in 1997 was 18, up from 14 or 15 years since 1987. The peak age of offending for males in 1997 was 18 (the same since 1988). The change in the peak age of offending for females is attributable to a decline in the number of females cautioned aged 17 or under.

In Northern Ireland, the overall rate of conviction in 1997 was 219 per 10,000 of the population; this breaks down into 48 per 10,000 for females, in contrast to the much higher rate of 400 per 10,000 for males. In 1997, the rate of conviction was highest for females at 18 years, compared with 19 years for males.

In Scotland, too, women constitute a relatively small percentage of the criminal cases coming before the courts. Although 52 percent of the overall Scottish population is female, only 14 percent of those convicted in 1997 were women. It is estimated that 50 percent of men will be convicted of an offense at some time in their lives, in contrast to only 15 percent of women. The peak age of offending for females is 22 years of age, compared with 18 years of age for males.

There are some interesting historical fluctuations in the amount of crime committed by females in Britain. For instance, there was a surge in female prosecutions in the late seventeenth century and eighteenth century, resulting in a unique moment of female dominance among recorded offenders (Beattie 1995). More recently, a slight narrowing of the gap between males and females for overall convictions has been noted, changing from 7:1 during the 1950s and 1960s to around 5:1 at the beginning of the 1990s (Walklate 1995b); there have been claims that women's liberation has led to the narrowing of this gap, but such an argument is difficult to sustain (Box and Hale 1983).

One key question is whether females commit the same kinds of crimes as males. While such offenders as Myra Hindley have attracted enormous media and public attention because of the commission of sexual crimes and violent murders, and while females over 21 are found in all other offense groups (ranging from burglary, robbery, criminal damage, and drug offenses to motoring offenses, for instance), they form a numerical majority in only two: offenses relating to prostitution and failing to pay for a television license. When women are convicted, it is more likely to be for offenses involving theft and handling stolen goods, drug offenses, and fraud and forgery than anything else. Women seem to have much lower rates of involvement in murder, serious violence, and professional crime. In none of the categories does the female share reach even half the total.

The media have drawn attention to apparent increases in female violence in recent years (from 7 percent of indictable crimes in 1987 to 10 percent in 1997), though a closer look at the figures reveals that the biggest increase has been in the 14- to 18-year-old age group. Whether this change can be at-

Table E. Convictions by Sex and Offense Type, 1987–1997, England and Wales

Number of Offenders							(Thousands)				
	1987	1988	1989	1990	1991	1992	1993	1994	1995	1996	1997
Males—Indictable Offenses											
Violence against the Person	44.4	49.3	51.2	48.1	43.3	39.8	35.5	33.9	26.4	27.3	31.3
Sexual Offenses	6.2	7.1	7.2	6.5	5.5	4.9	4.3	4.4	4.6	4.4	4.5
Burglary	52.6	46.9	42.0	42.1	44.7	43.0	39.2	37.0	34.4	31.3	30.7
Robbery	4.2	4.1	4.4	4.6	4.5	4.8	4.8	4.5	4.8	5.5	5.1
Theft and Handling Stolen Goods	143.8	133.9	107.9	107.5	108.1	103.9	99.5	99.1	94.9	93.6	96.1
Fraud and Forgery	17.6	17.7	17.6	17.2	16.6	15.6	13.6	14.2	13.4	12.6	12.9
Criminal Damage	9.9	11.0	8.7	10.3	9.3	9.0	8.6	9.2	8.8	9.0	9.6
Drug Offenses	14.7	16.6	20.2	22.1	21.2	20.6	19.9	25.3	28.5	30.4	36.3
Other (Excluding Motoring Offenses)	17.4	23.2	26.4	29.7	31.6	33.1	34.2	35.5	38.2	39.2	42.4
Motoring offenses	28.1	30.4	10.8	10.6	10.8	10.3	10.3	11.4	10.7	9.4	8.9
Total Indictable Offenses	338.9	340.2	296.6	298.8	295.7	284.9	269.8	274.6	264.7	262.5	277.8
Females—Indictable Offenses											
Violence against the Person	3.4	4.1	4.4	4.4	3.9	3.8	3.4	3.7	2.8	2.8	3.3
Sexual Offenses	0.1	0.1	0.1	0.1	0.1	0.1	0.1	0.0	0.1	0.0	0.0
Burglary	1.6	1.5	1.3	1.4	1.4	1.2	1.0	1.0	1.0	0.9	1.0
Robbery	0.2	0.2	0.2	0.2	0.3	0.3	0.3	0.4	0.4	0.5	0.5
Theft and Handling Stolen Goods	32.1	29.6	26.6	26.8	25.5	24.0	22.1	22.5	21.2	20.9	22.3
Fraud and Forgery	4.9	5.0	4.7	4.6	4.5	4.4	3.9	4.2	3.8	3.7	4.1
Criminal Damage	0.7	0.8	0.7	0.9	0.9	0.8	0.8	0.8	0.8	0.9	0.9
Drug Offenses	2.2	2.2	2.4	2.4	2.2	2.1	2.0	2.5	3.1	3.7	4.4
Other (Excluding Motoring Offenses)	1.3	1.7	2.1	2.6	2.8	2.9	3.6	3.8	4.0	4.3	5.1
Motoring Offenses	0.9	1.0	0.4	0.4	0.5	0.4	0.5	0.6	0.5	0.5	0.5
Total Indictable Offenses	47.5	46.1	43.0	44.0	41.9	40.0	37.8	39.5	37.5	38.0	42.2

Source: Adapted from Home Office 1998a, *Criminal Statistics, England and Wales, 1997.*

tributed to actual crime rates or changing responses to crime, however, is difficult to discern.

Recent research does suggest that one idea about the relative absence of females from crime needs to be reassessed. Following an extensive self-report survey of over 2,500 young people, Graham and Bowling (1995) suggest that an increasing number of young women are lured by crime. Their findings indicate that teenage girls are just as likely as boys to become involved in crime (at around the age of 15), but while girls have generally grown out of it by their late teens, many young men are still involved as late as their middle twenties. One finding was that girls who disliked school or rated their performance below average were more likely to offend, but for boys, neither attitude nor performance were related to their starting to offend. The main factors in young women growing out of crime included leaving home, entering into a stable relationship with a member of the opposite sex, forming a new family, and eventually becoming economically independent.

Another key question is whether women commit crimes for the same reasons as men. The contributory factors in women's offending have received comparatively little research attention in Britain. Some women may be attracted by the excitement crime offers or may be drawn into crime by their associates or other factors in their lifestyle. Lack of money or a lack of opportunity to gain sufficient income through legitimate means is cited by many women offenders as a major explanation for having committed crimes. This would seem to be confirmed by the nature of women's offending—for example, theft and prostitution. The small number of women who commit violent crimes, particularly murder or culpable homicide, are more likely to do so following a history of being abused themselves. *See also* DESISTANCE FROM CRIME; DEVIANCE AND REFORM, HISTORICAL OVERVIEW OF, BRITAIN; HINDLEY, MYRA.

Further Reading: Heidensohn 1997, "Gender and Crime."

Loraine R. Gelsthorpe

Female Crime, Canada

Historically, Canadian legislators, policy-makers, academics, and the public have paid little heed to women and crime except in the rare, sensational cases involving serious violence. Grace Marks, a 16-year-old domestic servant who was convicted of killing her employer and his lover in 1843 and imprisoned for the next 30 years in Kingston Penitentiary, was the focus of much media, medical, and public attention at the time and, more recently, became the subject of Margaret Atwood's novel, *Alias Grace* (1996). Ann Hansen, a member of the Squamish Five who was sentenced to life imprisonment in 1986 for her part in politically motivated crimes (e.g., bombing a factory that produced parts for American weapons systems), likewise has received extensive coverage in both news and entertainment media. More typically, however, women are charged and convicted of much less serious offenses as shown in Table F. In 1997, minor assault, theft $5,000 or under, fraud, simple possession of illicit drugs, prostitution, and bail violations accounted for 69 percent of the 74,114 criminal charges laid against adult, Canadian women that year, whereas homicide and attempted murder charges comprised only .002 percent of the total.

Although systematic data are lacking, available research and statistics suggest that the "average" woman facing criminal charges in Canada is very similar to her counterpart in other Western countries. She is young (under 25), white, unmarried (although she may be a mother), and poor, with little formal education and few job skills. She has been charged with a nonviolent offense such as shoplifting and will receive a noncustodial sentence if convicted. "Averages" often conceal important differences, however, and a more comprehensive picture of Canadian women lawbreakers requires inter- and intra-gender comparisons.

For instance, official crime statistics reveal that men and women engage in more or less the same range of "street" crime but that they differ markedly with respect to the total number of charges laid each year. This gap

Table F. Police-Reported Incidents, by Most Serious Offense, Canada and the Provinces/Territories, 1997

Type of Offense	Women,[1] Percent of Total Charges[2]	Men,[1] Percent of Total Charges[3]
Criminal Code		
Theft	26	11.8
Fraud	10	4.3
Other Property	4.7	10.5
Violent Offenses	18.5	23.3
Impaired Driving	9.5	15.1
Other Criminal Code Violations	24.1	26.7
Other Federal Statutes[4]	7.3	8.3
Total	100.1[5]	100.0

Notes
[1] Charges against persons over the age of 18
[2] Total number of charges against women = 82,900
[3] Total number of charges against men = 426,600
[4] Includes drug-related offenses
[5] Does not equal 100 due to rounding error

Source: Adapted from Canadian Centre for Justice Statistics 1998, *Canadian Crime Statistics, 1997.*

has narrowed over time, yet in 1997, men still accounted for 84 percent of all criminal charges (excluding traffic offenses). The size of the gender gap also varies by type of offense. While the male-female charge ratio now is relatively low for prostitution and minor theft, men continue to be charged with the vast majority of traditional "male" offenses such as breaking-and-entering and motor vehicle theft. Women, however, are much more likely to be charged with welfare fraud under the so-called "spouse in the house" rule than are men. The assumption that if a woman lives with a man, he is supporting her and she is therefore ineligible for welfare, is not made about men who live with women and collect social assistance.

Despite predictions about the emergence of a "liberated, violent, female criminal" in Canada during the 1980s, women still are nowhere near equality with men with respect to crimes against the person. The drop in the male-female charge ratio for violent offenses, from 21:1 in 1968 to 6.5:1 in 1997, mainly

reflects an increase in the number of women charged with minor, nonsexual assault. Men retain their historical monopoly on serious crimes of violence: in 1997, they were charged with 98 percent of sexual assaults, 85 percent of homicides, and 90 percent of attempted murders.

Data on differences among criminally charged women reveal that age and marital status vary in relation to offense and type of sentence. However, the greatest divisions among accused women are related to race and ethnicity. Historically, women (and men) from the most marginalized racial and ethnic group(s) at a given time are overrepresented in official crime statistics. During the nineteenth century, it was Irish women immigrants to Canada who were statistically prominent. Today, although non-Aboriginal women comprise the majority of females accused of crimes, Aboriginal women (status and non-status Indians, Metis, and Inuit) are disproportionately present in criminal statistics relative to their numbers in the Canadian population. As well, Aboriginal women are more often convicted of violent crimes than are non-Aboriginal women who, in turn, are much more likely to be convicted and imprisoned for drug offenses.

However, research does not suggest that Aboriginal (or Irish) women are more innately criminal than are other criminally charged women and men. Rather, their overrepresentation in the criminal justice system and the types of offenses they commit are linked to their status as the most marginal people in Canada. Aboriginal women are more likely to be unmarried with dependants than are other criminally charged women, yet they also are the least educated and least self-supporting of all accused persons. While many criminally charged women (and men) are on the edges of conventional Canadian society, clearly some are closer to the boundaries than others. See also ABORIGINAL WOMEN AND CRIME, CANADA; BATTERED WOMEN AND SELF-DEFENSE, CANADA; CRIMINALIZATION OF PREGNANCY, CANADA.

Further Reading: Adelberg and Currie 1987, *Too Few to Count;* Adelberg and Currie 1993, *In*

Conflict with the Law; Backhouse 1991, *Petticoats and Prejudice;* Comack 1996, *Women in Trouble.*

Dorothy E. Chunn

Female Crime, Explanations of

In the last century and a half, criminologists have developed numerous theories to explain criminal behavior, but for the most part, they have ignored female criminality. The few criminologists who have studied female offenders have tended to describe these lawbreakers as immoral, corrupt, hysterical, manipulative, and devious.

The discipline of criminology emerged in the nineteenth century, when researchers began to apply scientific methods to the study of crime. The scientific or "positivist" approach emphasized the importance of objective empirical methods to collect data, develop theories, and verify hypotheses.

The earliest positivist theories attempted to explain crime in terms of criminals' biology. In the late 1800s, the Italian physician Cesare Lombroso, the most influential of the biological theorists, analyzed the physical characteristics of prisoners and concluded that male criminals are atavistic—throwbacks to a more primitive evolutionary stage of development. Lombroso portrayed the female offender as even more of a brute. With his son-in-law, William Ferrero, Lombroso asserted that women are less evolved than men and that female criminality results from women's biological inferiority. Lombroso and Ferrero (1895) concluded, somewhat illogically, that the female offender is masculine and biologically like a man.

Like Lombroso, Otto Pollak, author of *The Criminality of Women* (1950; reprinted 1961), attributed female crime primarily to deviant biology, but he also emphasized what he saw as the deceitful and manipulative nature of women. Pollak asserted that women conceal their criminal activity by using sex to manipulate men into committing crimes on their behalf. A more recent biological explanation proposes a link between the menstrual cycle and female crime, with Katharina Dalton (1961) claiming that a large percentage of female crimes are committed during the four days prior to menstruation.

Another branch of the positivist school focuses on the psychological causes of female crime. Like biological theories of female crime, psychological explanations characterize women as inferior to men. One of the more famous psychological explanations of female behavior is Sigmund Freud's theory of penis envy. Although Freud himself did not write about female crime, his ideas served as the basis for a Freudian perspective that views the female offender as a woman who wants to be a man. She resorts to crime as a way of rebelling against her gender role.

Both biological and psychological theories look at the individual offender to identify the cause of crime. In sharp contrast, sociologists locate the causes of crime in factors external to the offender. Like biological and psychological explanations, however, sociological theories often exclude women from analyses of criminal behavior. For example, Robert Merton (1949) hypothesized that crime results from the strain that men experience over being denied access to legitimate means (education and employment) of achieving universal goals (wealth, power, and status). Albert Cohen (1955) applied Merton's theory to juvenile delinquency, focusing mainly on boys but also stating that the only strain that females experience is the pressure to marry. As a result, Cohen argued, girls express their criminality through sexual promiscuity.

More recently, Travis Hirschi (1969) developed a control explanation of crime, according to which crime occurs when an individual's bonds to conventional institutions such as family, friends, and school are broken. Researchers have tested control theory extensively, in general finding that females exhibit stronger bonds to society than males but that these differences do not contribute to females' lower offending rates: However, Jill Rosenbaum (1989) did find that young girls with weak parental attachments are more likely to move from status offending to more serious crimes than young girls with strong familial ties.

Building on control theory, John Hagan (Hagan, Gillis, and Simpson 1987) developed power-control theory, which focuses on family structure and the relations between parents and their children. Hagan contends that in a patriarchal family where fathers typically have higher status than mothers, daughters are placed under stricter controls than sons, which may contribute to lower crime rates among girls. Conversely, in homes were parental power is shared, young girls are likely to be encouraged to engage in the same risk-taking behavior as their brothers, which may contribute to delinquency.

In the 1970s, labeling theory dominated the criminological literature, maintaining that when a person is negatively labeled, he or she will accept that label and act accordingly. In 1984, Edwin Schur examined the relevance of labeling theory to female crime. He concluded that females are more likely to be labeled mentally ill than criminal, mental illness being more in keeping with traditional gender roles for women than criminality.

In the 1970s, the groundwork for the feminist perspective was laid by two works, Freda Adler's *Sisters in Crime* (1975) and Rita James Simon's *Women and Crime* (1975), that advanced the liberation theory of female crime. According to this theory, women have lower crime rates than men because of their second-class economic and social status. Adler predicted that as women gain equal status with men, their crime rates will increase and become comparable to those of men.

Although most criminological theories were developed by men to explain the criminal behavior of men, women did contribute to the study of crime prior to the groundbreaking work of Adler and Simon. In the late 1800s, for example, Pauline Tarnowsky found that female murderers were biologically different from law-abiding women (Bowker 1978), a theory similar to Lombroso's, although Lombroso's work received more attention. Likewise, in the early 1900s, Jean Weidensall (1916) made an in-depth study of the relationship between low intelligence and crime in her comparative analysis of incarcerated and law-abiding women.

Criminology has been a male-dominated discipline. Not only have studies of criminal behavior ignored women, but the contributions of pioneering female researchers have been eclipsed by the work of their male contemporaries. More recently, considerable strides have been made in the study of women and crime. In particular, scholars have attempted to refute biological and psychological explanations of female crime, while at the same time focusing attention on its social, political, and economic causes. *See also* CONTROL EXPLANATIONS OF CRIME; GENDER AND CRIME; LIBERATION EXPLANATION OF CRIME; LOMBROSO, CESARE; MADONNA/WHORE DICHOTOMY; PREMENSTRUAL SYNDROME; POWER-CONTROL EXPLANATION OF CRIME; PSYCHOLOGICAL EXPLANATIONS OF DELINQUENCY.

Further Reading: Belknap 1996, *The Invisible Woman;* Datesman and Scarpitti 1980, *Women, Crime and the Criminal Justice System.*

Anne Sullivan

Female Crime, History of, Europe

Female crime of the past in Europe apparently bore many similarities to female crime patterns today in both Europe and the United States. In the seventeenth, eighteenth, and nineteenth centuries—as in the present—females tended to commit much less crime than males, especially less violent crime. Then, as now, females also committed fewer types of crime than males, engaging mainly in petty offenses and in those two female-specific constants through the centuries, prostitution and infanticide.

Research on the history of female crime is based primarily on two sources: contemporary journalistic accounts, which highlight sensational crimes, and official records, which provide general counts of women suspected of crime. Each source offers a partial, and sometimes misleading, portrait of female criminality. For example, the press in Victorian England and imperial Russia devoted extensive attention to women murderers, even though they were extremely rare (Frank 1996; Knelman 1997). The police arrested women on a selective basis. Just as selectively, courts prosecuted and convicted them. Knowledge about female crime is filtered, then, by agencies whose reaction was affected equally by female crime and by public anxieties about it. This filtering process ensures that the extent of female crime in the past can never be known with any certainty.

While imprecise, data from England (D. J. V. Jones 1992, 1996; Emsley 1996), Europe (B. F. Martin 1990; Shapiro 1996; Richter 1998), and Russia (Frank 1996) support four conclusions about female crime in Europe since the seventeenth century. First, female crime patterns generally paralleled those of today. Women constituted only a minority, usually less than 20 percent, of suspects who came to the attention of the police and the courts. They also committed a narrower range of offenses than men. Involvement in serious violence or major property crime was rare. Instead, most female suspects were accused of relatively minor offenses such as theft, vagrancy, disorderly conduct, and prostitution.

A second conclusion is that the rate at which women were suspected of crime fell dramatically in the seventeenth, eighteenth, and early nineteenth centuries (Boritch and Hagan 1990; Feeley and Little 1991), at least in England and perhaps in other countries as well. One reason for this decline was the development of capitalism, which initially restricted women to familial roles and imposed informal controls on their behavior. The third conclusion toward which the historical evidence points is that the women most likely to come to the attention of the authorities were single, young, working-class women who were immigrants or belonged to ethnic groups. (The same is true of men in these categories, who also attracted more attention from authorities than did their more advantaged counterparts.) Women living in urban areas were also more likely to be suspected of crime. While this difference could be due to greater criminality on the part of urban women, it could also reflect the tendency for rural areas to prefer informal rather than formal responses to crime.

Fourth and finally, the historical evidence indicates that the gender difference in minor property crimes and in assaults has narrowed

considerably since the late nineteenth century. This narrowing reflects, in part, women's recent participation in the labor force, which provides both motives and opportunities for criminality.

Prostitutes consistently constituted a significant component of the female criminal class, although they were often arrested for property and public-order offenses. Whether condoned as an inevitable evil, strictly regulated, or sharply attacked, prostitutes were an enduring feature of cities and small towns throughout Europe (A. R. Henderson 1997) and in England (Nash 1994). Many were single, young, propertyless women seeking to improve their precarious economic position. Their success depended on factors such as ethnicity and class background. Little is known of higher status prostitutes who worked in brothels or lived independently, since lower status prostitutes such as streetwalkers came to official attention more often. In addition to arrest and incarceration, low status prostitutes faced premature death through illness and substance abuse, and they were often exploited by their clients, pimps, and the police. Lower status prostitutes seldom achieved upward mobility within the profession or outward mobility through marriage.

Another (though much smaller) proportion of the female criminal class consisted of women accused of infanticide. Again, the true extent of infanticide will probably never be known because of underreporting and selective prosecution. In nineteenth-century Upper Bavaria, for example, whether a woman suspected of infanticide was actually prosecuted depended on her reputation as a reliable, honest worker and otherwise respectable woman (Schulte 1994). In places where punishment was harsh, juries were reluctant to convict, and women tended to be accused and convicted of the less serious offense of concealing a birth. Available records indicate, however, that like women accused of other forms of criminality, those suspected of infanticide were typically young, unmarried, and impoverished (Richter 1998).

Although the evidence is incomplete, available sources indicate that subjective factors such as reputation (which was closely associated with socioeconomic status) were as important as objective factors such as the nature of the offense committed in defining female crime in Europe between the seventeenth and nineteenth centuries. *See also* FEMALE CRIME, BRITAIN; FEMALE CRIME, HISTORY OF, USA; INFANTICIDE; PROSTITUTION; WITCHES.

Further Reading: Zedner 1991, *Women, Crime, and Custody in Victorian England.*

Martha A. Myers

Female Crime, History of, USA

The history of female crime in the United States, insofar as it can be reconstructed from court records, is one in which arrest patterns have remained largely the same from the Colonial period into the mid-twentieth century. Greatly outnumbered by males, females criminals were arrested mainly for minor property offenses, family violence, and sex or morals offenses. Consistently, women of color were arrested in numbers disproportionate to their share of the general population. Socioeconomic trends affected female crime patterns. And certain female criminals—witches in Colonial New England, shoplifters in nineteenth-century cities, and "gun molls" in the Great Depression—caught the public's attention, despite their relatively small numbers.

Some of the first colonists were female felons transported to the New World from England as a form of punishment. However, transportees made up only a small part of the female criminal populations of early Massachusetts (Hull 1987), New York (Greenberg 1974), Pennsylvania (Rowe 1985), and the Carolinas (Hindus 1980; Spindel 1989). As the influence of religion waned, so did prosecutions for fornication, viewed in the early Colonial period as a violation of God's rules. At the same time, prosecutions of illegitimate births, considered economic burdens on communities, increased. Sexual crimes (whatever their labels) and theft far outnumbered violent crimes. If women murdered, they killed those within their own households—children,

servants, and spouses—and in that order. Single women and African American and Native American females were overrepresented in arrest statistics. Overall in the Colonial period, female crime represented only about one-tenth of all recorded crime, with the lowest rates occurring in rural areas.

Arrests for prostitution grew in prominence—in both the public's eye and in recorded statistics—in the nineteenth and early twentieth centuries. Indeed, in nineteenth-century America, the prostitute became a symbol of the female criminal, who was conceptualized as a victim of, yet potent danger to, society. By the early nineteenth century, the public had begun viewing prostitutes as victims of male trickery and seduction (Hobson 1987). In truth, however, personal choice and economic realities such as low pay and few job opportunities outside the home were more influential in pushing women into prostitution.

Nineteenth-century prostitutes were almost uniformly young, poor, and single women, whether they lived in large, notorious vice districts such as San Francisco's Barbary Coast, in the smaller but persistent red-light districts of the Midwest or South, or in the transitory cattle and mining towns of the West. Violence, alcohol, disease, drugs, and suicide were constants. And few prostitutes ever moved beyond their original poverty. Those who plied their trade in the dance halls, "cribs," and "cat wagons" of the West may have led the harshest lives. Western prostitutes were fewer in number than Midwestern or Eastern urban prostitutes, but they also had fewer employment opportunities, less formal protection against violence, and greater economic burdens in an inflated economy (Butler 1985). In cities such as St. Louis and St. Paul, the same police who protected prostitutes from violent clients also closely regulated prostitution through sweeps of streetwalkers, informal licensing of brothels with periodic fines, and formal licensing after medical examinations (Best 1998). Early twentieth-century reformers used venereal disease and the moral depravity of prostitutes as justifications for their campaigns against vice districts, but ironically, their onslaughts scattered into the streets the same women they wanted to "save" and to isolate from upright citizens.

Although "white slavery" or prostitution captured the public's imagination in the early twentieth century, women were also committing other crimes in other contexts, including their own homes. Family violence by women attracted much less attention. It has been argued that if it were possible to discover how many of their own children women had actually killed, "the figures would perhaps reveal that women committed murder at a higher rate than any other identifiable subgroup in the population," at least in nineteenth-century Philadelphia (Lane 1979:100). Single women, whether divorced, widowed, or never married, were the most likely to kill, beat, and/or neglect their children. Economic pressures, personal isolation, a domestic service market that excluded dependents, and long hours in factory labor contributed to such abuse (Gordon 1988).

From the Civil War onward, black women figured disproportionately in arrests for both violent and property crimes. Systematic racism certainly shaped crime statistics, but so did other forces. A higher percentage of black than white women in Northern cities such as Philadelphia (Lane 1986) and the smaller, newer Columbus (Monkkonen 1975) were involved in domestic service, a type of work that offered opportunities for theft. In the South, delayed industrialization and urbanization after long reliance on labor-intensive field crops kept crime rates volatile until the first decades of the twentieth century (M. A. Myers 1995).

Although property and violent crime arrests have long been considered the best index of male criminal activity, public-order offenses have also played an important role, over time, in arrest and incarceration statistics for females. Disorderly conduct, public drunkenness, and out-of-wedlock sexual activity, when committed by women, were prosecuted from the nineteenth century into at least the Great Depression, if not the 1970s (Giordano, Kerbel, and Dudley 1981). Fe-

male public-order offenders dominated female jail populations (Crowley and Adrian 1992) and made up a half or more of the turn-of-the-century female reformatory populations (Rafter 1985b).

Over more than two centuries, then, female arrest statistics have formed consistent patterns. Women arrested for crimes were most likely to be public-order offenders or petty thieves and least likely to be violent offenders. Racism, beliefs about female sexuality, and lack of economic opportunities helped shape the profile of the criminal woman. That profile has always been lower—statistically, if not in terms of public notoriety—than that of males. *See also* BARKER, "MA"; BORDEN, LIZZIE; CALL GIRLS; FEMALE CRIME, HISTORY OF, EUROPE; INFANTICIDE; PARKER, BONNIE.

Further Reading: R. M. Alexander 1995, *The 'Girl Problem'*; Butler 1985, *Daughters of Joy, Sisters of Misery.*

Beverly A. Smith

Female Crime, Patterns and Trends in, USA

Scholars and others often overlook patterns and trends in female crime as they attempt to explain overall crime trends. When aggregate data (totals including both males and females) are used to describe or test propositions, differences in patterns of female criminality often go unnoticed due to females' relatively small contribution to the overall crime rate.

It has long been known that females account for far fewer arrests than males. This has provided the best evidence that women's participation in crime is much less common than men's participation. Females were arrested 2.3 million times in 1997 in the United States. This represents 22 percent of all arrests reported to the FBI that year, as shown in Table G. Just under 2 million people were arrested for FBI "index" crimes that year. (The index crimes, used to track the overall crime picture, include murder, rape, robbery, aggravated assault, burglary, larceny-theft, vehicle theft, and arson.) Of that number, 487,000 females were arrested, representing

26 percent of the total, again as shown in Table G.

When 1997 arrests for index crimes are examined by type, females were arrested 406,000 times for index property crimes (burglary, larceny-theft, motor vehicle theft, and arson) and 81,000 times for index violent crimes (murder, rape, robbery, and aggravated assault). Some crimes have higher percentages of female perpetrators than these numbers indicate. These tend to be economic crimes such as larceny-theft or forgery/counterfeiting. In 1997, females made up 34 percent and 39 percent of arrests for these two crimes, respectively. They accounted for 46 percent of fraud and embezzlement arrests combined.

The FBI's *Uniform Crime Reports* record only two categories of offenses with more females arrested than males: prostitution and runaways. Of 72,000 arrests for commercial sex activities in 1997, 60 percent were arrests of females. Females made up 58 percent of the juveniles taken into custody as runaways.

Although arrest data have consistently demonstrated that females are responsible for far fewer crimes than men, there is evidence that female crime and violence patterns are changing. Over the 10 years from 1988 through 1997, women consistently increased as a percentage of all arrestees (see Figure 3), indicating that they are committing more crimes relative to men. In one decade, women increased from 18 percent of arrests to nearly 22 percent. An even larger proportional increase was evident for violent crimes. Arrests of females rose from 11 percent to 16 percent of all arrests for violent index crimes. These changes in percentage of arrestees appear to reflect not just a change in police behaviors but an actual increase in female offending.

Published FBI data do not include enough information to make direct comparisons of female arrest rates across multiple years, due to changes in reporting agencies from year to year and a lack of population information by sex. However, reasonable estimates of trends can be determined by comparing the

Table G. Persons Arrested in the United States, 1997

Offense	Total	Men	Women	Percent Women
All Crime Categories	10,544,624	8,261,870	2,282,754	21.6
All Index Crimes*	1,910,953	1,423,611	487,342	25.5
Index Violent Crimes*	501,353	420,378	80,975	16.2
Index Property Crimes*	1,409,600	1,003,233	406,367	28.8
Murder and Non-negligent Manslaughter	12,764	11,447	1,317	10.3
Forcible Rape	22,133	21,855	278	1.3
Robbery	94,034	84,808	9,226	9.8
Aggravated Assault	372,422	302,268	70,154	18.8
Burglary	245,816	216,612	29,204	11.9
Larceny-Theft	1,033,901	676,219	357,682	34.6
Motor Vehicle Theft	116,052	98,651	17,401	15.0
Arson	13,831	11,751	2,080	15.0
Forgery and Counterfeiting	83,051	51,081	32,033	38.6
Fraud	274,950	148,271	126,679	46.1
Embezzlement	12,269	6,488	5,781	47.1
Prostitution and Commercialized Vice	72,385	28,785	43,600	60.2
Runaways	136,350	56,949	79,401	58.2

*Index violent crimes: Murder and non-negligent manslaughter, forcible rape, robbery, and aggravated assault. Index property crimes: Burglary, larceny-theft, motor vehicle theft, and arson.

Source: U.S. Department of Justice, Federal Bureau of Investigation 1998, *Crime in the United States 1997*, Table 42.

number of female arrests reported for each year per 100,000 total population of the covered jurisdictions.

Although men's arrest rates have generally leveled off and even decreased since 1992, arrest rates for women have increased noticeably. Although it is not known why, females do not seem to be sharing in the same kind of decrease in offending that the United States has seen in this decade among male offenders. Of particular interest is the increase in the arrest rate of women for violent index crimes. As reported crime declined during the 1990s, arrests per capita declined between 1990 and 1992 and then stabilized or continued downward. The same is not true of arrests for women, as Figure 4 demonstrates. At best, female arrest rates decreased from 1990 to 1992 and then stabilized. Female arrest rates for violent index crimes generally increased. This category saw nearly a 13 percent increase from 1990 to 1997, while male arrest rates for violent index crimes decreased by nearly 24 percent.

The troublesome task of explaining crime is aggravated by these divergent patterns of female and male crime rates. Criminologists, police administrators, and politicians are claiming to be able to explain the decline in serious crimes during the 1990s. However, they may be hard pressed to factor in the trends seen in female criminality at a time when those trends are becoming more noticeable. *See also* FEMALE CRIME, AUSTRALIA; FEMALE CRIME, BRITAIN; FEMALE CRIME, CANADA; FEMALE CRIME, HISTORY OF, USA; JUVENILE DELINQUENCY, USA.

Further Reading: Chesney-Lind 1997, *The Female Offender.*

W. T. Jordan and Jeffrie F. Jinian

Feminist Criminology, Australia

Feminist criminology was first published in Australia in the 1980s, somewhat later than in either England or the United States. A feature of Australian feminist criminology is its openness to feminist ideas from a variety of European and American sources. It is not uncommon for Australian feminist criminologists to have studied or conducted research in other countries.

Many Australian feminist criminologists have law degrees, and legal and criminal justice reform remains the subject of much of their work. Nevertheless, diverse subject matter, methodologies, epistemologies, and

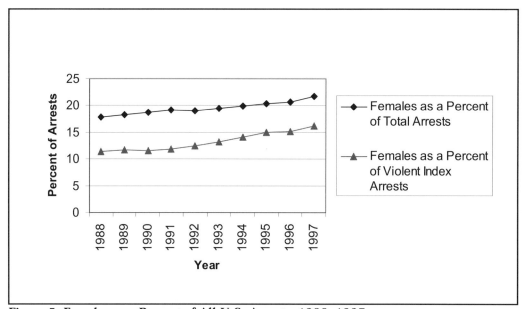

Figure 3. Females as a Percent of All U.S. Arrests, 1988–1997
Source: Derived from U.S. Department of Justice, Federal Bureau of Investigation 1989–1998 *Crime in the United States.*

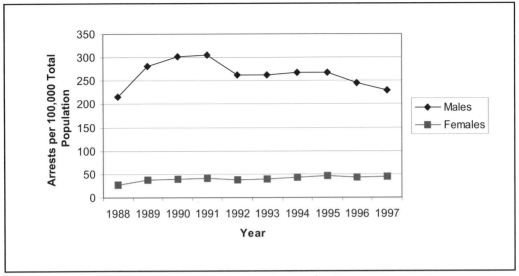

Figure 4. U.S. Arrest Rates for Violent Index Crimes, by Sex, 1988–1997
Source: Derived from U.S. Department of Justice, Federal Bureau of Investigation 1989–1998, *Crime in the United States.*

theories are represented in their work. Not necessarily bounded by traditiional under-standings of "crime," their concerns range across the breadth of women's lives and across institutions other than those of the legal and criminal justice systems. However, feminist criminologists have tended to neglect the study of Aboriginal women, even though these women are significantly overrepresented in criminal justice statistics.

Australian feminist criminologists frequently engage in both activism and academic work. They often work with government departments and community groups outside the universities. Up to the mid-1990s, such involvement was facilitated by the power of feminists ("femocrats") in government bureaucracies. The power of femocracy may be a distinctive feature of Australian feminism (McGregor and Hopkins 1991).

More recently, Australian feminist criminologists have started to question the pragmatism of their work and their law reform agenda. The working together of femocrats, activists outside the bureaucracies, and academics has not been without some tensions (Stubbs 1994:5). There are also concerns about unintended consequences of reforms, the co-option of reform agendas by conser-

vatives, and the subversion of apparent achievements. *See also* FEMINIST CRIMINOLOGY, BRITAIN; FEMINIST CRIMINOLOGY, ORIGINS OF, IN CANADA; FEMINIST CRIMINOLOGY, USA.

Further Reading: Alder 1995, "Feminist Criminology in Australia"; Grieve and Burns 1994, *Australian Women;* O'Malley and Carson 1989, "Contemporary Australian Criminology."

Christine M. Alder

Feminist Criminology, Britain

Feminist criminology in Britain shares a history and many characteristics with feminist criminology in the United States. Indeed, the two are often grouped together by foreign commentators. However, they also differ significantly in their concerns and impact, variations that reflect larger differences in the university systems of the two nations and their political organizations.

The history of feminist criminology in Britain can be divided into three stages. In the first stage, pioneers mapped out the major concerns of feminist criminology. The next stage was one of consolidation, with scholars producing both theoretical and empirical work. The most recent stage has been one of diversification of interests and diffusion of the work, with feminist criminology now having some influence (though not major impact) on mainstream criminology.

Feminist perspectives in criminology began to develop in Britain in the 1960s, a period of considerable intellectual ferment. To be sure, the major forum for discussing criminological matters in the 1960s and 1970s, the National Deviancy Conferences, paid little attention to female crime or women's experiences in the criminal justice system. Nonetheless, there was sufficient stimulus from new ideas in the field to inspire the first published article on the topic of women and crime (Heidensohn 1968), a work that raised some of the key questions that framed later debates. It pointed out that women have much lower recorded conviction rates than men and that there are very many fewer women in prison. (Indeed, female prisons were under-used at that time in Britain and for some years thereafter.) Although these patterns were widespread and stable over long periods, they had scarcely been noticed by mainstream criminologists—and when they were mentioned, they tended to be dismissed as irrelevant to the study of crime. In truth, however, studies that focused predominantly on male offending were distorted by their lack of attention to the impact of gender on rates of offending and incarceration.

The key text in the first stage of feminist criminology in Britain, one that had an international impact, was Carol Smart's *Women, Crime and Criminology* (1976). Smart devoted most of her book to a feminist critique of existing studies of female criminality, concluding with a tentative proposal for a feminist criminology. More recently, however, Smart has rejected the possibility of a feminist criminology, viewing the criminological enterprise as too deeply involved in repression for it to accommodate the feminist goal of freeing women from domination and male perspectives (Smart 1990).

Other feminist scholars in Britain have voiced variations on Smart's concern about an inherent tension between the goals of criminology on the one hand and feminism on the other. Such doubts are one of the distinguishing characteristics of feminist criminological work in Britain. Pat Carlen, another important theorist in this area, also rejects the label "feminist criminologist," but from a different point of view than Smart. Carlen (1992) advocates an alliance of feminism and "left realism," a left-liberal approach to criminological issues. While she has produced a series of influential studies of women in custody (1983), women offenders (1988), and alternatives to prison (1990), for Carlen, class may be a more important consideration than gender in research on power and punishment in this particular period of history.

Unlike Carlen, Maureen Cain, another leader in the area of feminism and criminology, argues that feminism can constitute a "transgressive criminology" (1990), challenging mainstream criminology and eventually replacing it. Although Cain shares Smart's skepticism about the possibility of renewing criminology, she advocates development of a "successor science" that can incorporate feminist perspectives. Another specialist, Loraine Gelsthorpe, at first doubted whether feminism ever had or could have any impact on mainstream criminology. In 1990, however, she and Allison Morris described feminism as a work-in-progress, with outcomes and boundaries as yet unknown; and more recently, Gelsthorpe spoke more hopefully of the possibility of "gender-aware criminologies" (1997:528). Nonetheless, the debate over the compatibility of feminism and criminology remains one of the distinctive features of British criminology.

Most characteristic of late-twentieth-century criminological work by British feminists is its concern with recording and analyzing women's encounters with the criminal justice system. Some researchers have asked whether the courts handle women in the same way as they do men, or more chivalrously (Eaton 1986; Allen 1987); others have examined the paternalism of discipline in women's prisons (Carlen 1983; R. P. Dobash, Dobash, and Gutteridge 1986). In a third approach, some scholars have studied the experiences of women who work in the criminal justice system. Sandra Jones pioneered this work with her book *Policewomen and Equality* (1986). Subsequently Heidensohn compared the professional experiences of female officers in Britain and United States (1992), and in the year 2000, she and Jennifer Brown published the results of a multinational study of women police officers.

Yet another aspect of feminist criminological work in Britain relates to the study and support of crime victims. The media began to rediscover domestic violence in the 1970s, when feminist activist Erin Pizzey led a group of women in setting up shelters for battered women in London. Pizzey's work and book (1973) almost immediately triggered the shelter movement in the United States. More research and theoretical work on the victimization of women followed (R. E. Dobash and Dobash 1992; Hanmer and Maynard 1987). Perhaps more so than in the United States, the study of victimization has retained an activist character, aimed at liberating women not only from violent relationships but also from the domination of patriarchal ideas and dependency on men (Lupton and Gillespie 1994).

Mainstream criminology in Britain was slow to take up the challenges posed by feminist thinking, but it is now acknowledging and including at least some of that work (Downes and Rock 1992). Feminist criminological ideas are widely recognized, if not always accepted or incorporated. Major texts and edited collections now include sections on women. More significantly, recognizing that the crucial factor in determining crime and incarceration rates is not sex but gender, criminologists are now focusing on masculinity as well as femininity as a criminological issue (Newburn and Stanko 1994; Jefferson and Carlen 1996; Davies 1998).

In Britain in the late twentieth century, feminist concerns also affected public policy, though not in a consistent or sustained manner. The government began to monitor the experiences of women in the criminal justice system, a sign that it accepted the feminist research finding that gender can have a significant impact on treatment. Apparently stung by feminist criticisms, the police have modified their methods of handling of victims of domestic violence and serious sexual crimes. However, in contrast to Canada and other nations, no country in Britain (England, Scotland, and Wales) undertook official research on women's experience of criminal justice, and the main public studies of flaws in Britain's beleaguered courts and prisons ignored women and women's issues (Heidensohn 1995).

A balanced assessment of the impact of feminist perspectives in Britain would probably conclude that they have influenced criminology and criminal justice but have not actually been incorporated in a way that would make their influence permanent. Engagement with the topics and debates raised by feminists became much more prevalent in the 1990s. For example, Zedner (1991) considered the history of the custodial treatment of women in the Victorian era, putting gender issues at the heart of her study. Rock (1996 and this volume) analyzed the rebuilding of the major prison for women in England, arguing that gender issues were contingent to the process but not central to it. Masters and Smith (1998) discussed integrating feminist principles of mercy and forgiveness into concepts of justice, and even official discourse occasionally, if obliquely, reflected feminist criticisms of judicial processes (Hedderman and Hough 1994).

Nevertheless, feminism has not become a permanent or even prominent feature of British criminology. As Rock reported (1994), only about 20 percent of British criminologists are women. Unlike the American Society of Criminology, the British Society of Criminology has no division on women and crime. And British feminists themselves remain divided over the wisdom of fully engaging with criminology. *See also* FEMINIST CRIMINOLOGY, AUSTRALIA; FEMINIST CRIMINOLOGY, ORIGINS OF, IN CANADA; FEMINIST CRIMINOLOGY, USA; HOLLOWAY PRISON.

Further Reading: Gelsthorpe and Morris 1988, "Feminism and Criminology in Britain"; Heidensohn 1996, *Women and Crime*; Heidensohn 1995, "Feminist Perspectives."

Frances Heidensohn

Feminist Criminology, Origins of, in Canada

One of the factors most responsible for the distinctive character of Canadian feminist criminology is its pioneer, Marie-Andrée Bertrand (1925–), a scholar from Canada's *société distincte*—Québec, also known as the French Province. After years of practicing social work with prostitutes and other women caught in the web of the criminal justice system, Bertrand decided to pursue an academic career to further her understanding of the relationship between women and crime. She received a Ph.D. from the School of Criminology at the University of California, Berkeley, in 1967 and subsequently took a teaching and research position at the Université de Montréal, an institution with which she remains affiliated.

In 1969, Bertrand published a groundbreaking article on the relationship between socially conservative ideas about femininity and women's low crime rate that challenged the claim that women's low rate of crime in comparison with men is due to inherent differences between the two sexes. After exposing criminology's biologism, Bertrand next attacked the then-dominant explanation for what was perceived as an increase in, and change in the nature of, crime by women. Whereas many criminologists blamed these apparent changes on the women's liberation movement, Bertrand argued that the idea that women were committing more crimes because they were becoming more "masculine" was simplistic. She also revealed problems with official crime statistics (Bertrand 1969).

Bertrand's own research (1992, 1994) explored the relationship between women's emancipation and crime, examining the specific effects that social, political, and economic changes have had on women's consciousness and behavior, as well as on the criminal justice system, in different historical epochs. Her findings reveal the inadequacy of isolating the women's liberation movement, or any other single variable, to explain women's criminality.

Bertrand's challenge to criminological assumptions about women's nature and the causes of their criminal behavior led to an epistemological project: to rethink the entire field of criminology by calling into question its gendered foundation. Drawing on contemporary social theory, Bertrand explored how feminist insights into gender, power, and knowledge could help criminology critically examine its taken-for-granted concepts such as criminality, victimization, and justice. Her critique of criminology, which culminated in her coorganizing with Kathleen Daly and Dorie Klein the first International Conference on Women, Law, and Social Control, in Québec in 1991, encouraged a whole new generation of feminist scholars to examine and challenge the deeply gendered nature of both criminology and law (Bertrand, Daly, and Klein 1992).

Bertrand's endeavor to radicalize criminology has not been limited to academic writings. Throughout her life, she has fought for social justice as an advocate for sex-trade workers, prisoners' rights, and the legalization of drugs. A highly committed pioneer, Marie-Andrée Bertrand has given Canadian feminist criminology part of its unique identity. *See also* FEMINIST CRIMINOLOGY, AUSTRALIA; FEMINIST CRIMINOLOGY, BRITAIN; FEMINIST CRIMINOLOGY, USA.

Further Reading: Bertrand 1979, *La Femme et le Crime;* Chunn and Menzies 1995, "Canadian Criminology and the Woman Question."

Dany Lacombe

Feminist Criminology, USA

Feminist criminology in the United States originated in the women's movement in the 1960s and has continued to this day. There are three defining features of this approach to the study of crime: first, interest in the well-being of female offenders, female crime victims, and females in the criminal justice system; second, a focus on gender in explaining individual and institutional behaviors related to crime and its control; and, third, a view of gender relations as socially constructed and asymmetrical, with females subordinate.

Topics of early interest in feminist criminology reflected both applied and theoretical concerns, including descriptive studies of criminal justice processing that suggested systemic gender bias, notably, the criminalization of female sexual activity. The handful of pre-feminist theories on women's offending, such as the biological theory of the early Italian criminologist Cesare Lombroso, were subjected to critiques which argued that mainstream criminologists had interpreted women's behaviors in gender-stereotyping ways.

Over the years, there have been conceptual and topical shifts within feminist criminology and between feminist and mainstream criminology. In the United States, theoretical debates over feminism have been mostly with mainstream criminologists, while internal controversies have tended to be empirical, e.g., over whether women's criminality has changed.

Of major importance to feminist criminology in the United States has been its links to advocacy. While there have been ties to movements for female prisoner rights, the strongest ties have been to organizations for female victims of male violence. It would be difficult to overestimate the impact on feminist criminology of the movements against violence against women, which arose in the 1970s and continue to this day. In the United States, attention first turned to reconceptualizing rape as an offense with its origins in sexism. Later, there was development of the newly visible crimes of wife-battering and sexual harassment.

In the 1980s, attention turned to detailed studies of the situation of females in the criminal justice system. By the end of the decade, there was a wealth of data on the circumstances of arrestees, defendants and inmates, and victims of crime, accompanied by policy recommendations.

In recent years, concern has focused on new aspects of women's criminal justice involvement, such as changing arrest policies toward male partner-abusers, rising women's imprisonment rates, concerns about whether female juvenile violence has increased, and enforcement policies targeting drug use by pregnant women or mothers of newborns.

At the theoretical level, there have been two noteworthy recent developments, both of which reflect feminist criminology's deepening connection to wider feminist scholarship in the United States. One is the effort to more fully acknowledge ethnicity and racism, leading some scholars to question the early feminist premise that female experiences cut across ethnic or class lines, divisions which, in the United States, are highly intercorrelated. The other is the reconceptualizing of male criminal behaviors and their control as reflective of male roles and gendered subcultures (the study of "masculinities" and crime). Other emerging trends include developing feminist methodologies within criminology and redefining criminal justice on the basis of feminist legal and philosophical concepts.

In conclusion, in considering feminism's impact on criminology, whether one concurs with those who argue that the academic mainstream is as yet largely unaffected or with those who cite the growing literature on feminist-related topics, one is observing a body of work still in progress. *See also* FEMINIST CRIMINOLOGY, AUSTRALIA; FEMINIST CRIMINOLOGY, BRITAIN; FEMINIST CRIMINOLOGY, ORIGINS OF, IN CANADA.

Further Reading: Daly and Chesney-Lind 1988, "Feminism and Criminology"; D. Klein 1995, "Crime through Gender's Prism."

Dorie Klein

Fictional Crime Victims

Literature that examines the female victim is as old as Aeschylus's *Oresteia* and as recent as the nightly television movie. In stories of female victimization, we discover how Western culture often suppresses women's quest for justice.

In Aeschylus's *Oresteia*, for example, King Agamemnon slaughters his innocent daughter. Bound like a lamb on the altar and gagged to silence her pleas, Iphigenia dies because her father/king recognizes only the legitimacy of his will. It therefore falls upon Iphigenia's mother, Clytaemestra, to avenge her daughter's death and challenge Agamemnon's belief system with one that honors the mother and the life of the child. The tragedy illuminates how gender affects victimization when the god Apollo denies Clytaemestra's rights as a parent, declaring that a woman is only a "vessel" for the male's "seed."

In many ways, the fictional women of twentieth-century literature, from Joseph Conrad's Winnie Verloc in *The Secret Agent* to Toni Morrison's angry and vengeful Sethe in *Beloved*, resemble Clytaemestra. Their desire to protect innocent children locks them into a similar pattern of violent conflict with patriarchal law that denies them rights as mothers.

Contemporary concerns about victims, as well as familiar patterns in the psychology of female victimization, can be found in dramas of the early modern period. Shakespeare's *Othello* depicts a victim of wife abuse and murder, blaming herself for her degradation. John Webster's *The Duchess of Malfi* shows male attempts to regulate and control female sexuality in the humiliating and ultimately deadly restrictions placed on a widow's freedoms. "She-tragedy," a popular genre on the English stage during the late seventeenth and early eighteenth centuries, recalls the punishments (forfeiture of land, public humiliation, and even death) meted out to wives guilty of adultery, most famously in Nicholas Rowe's *The Tragedy of Jane Shore*.

Female victims in the eighteenth-century novel, from Samuel Richardson's *Clarissa* to Matthew Lewis's gothic *The Monk*, illustrate predatory violence by men and the general absence of punishments against rape, particularly for aristocratic or wealthy perpetrators. Later novels underscore how female victims are especially vulnerable to established legal practices when the laws that should protect them only enforce their victimization. Richard Wright's Bessie in *Native Son* is a striking case in point. The murder of a poor, uneducated, and abused black woman is forgotten while the court and the media rush to convict Bigger of the murder of a wealthy white girl. Wright's story bears striking parallels to Fedor Doestoevsky's nineteenth-century novel *Crime and Punishment* and its account of the murder of a poor, simple, and abused woman named Lizaveta. This classic murder novel and psychological thriller traces male cruelties toward women as part of a socially constructed masculine identity evidenced in the quiet erasure of Lizavita's murder, open hostility toward prostitutes such as the self-effacing Sonia, and the predatory impulses of the serial killer who preys upon the weak and helpless women.

Influenced by film and television, twentieth-century novels that examine female victims often recognize the connections between masculine objectification and control of the female body and the voyeuristic impulse of film. Anthony Burgess's *A Clockwork Orange* is one example of fiction's interest in the impact of film on masculine behavior, and popular culture testifies to the range of forms film can assume—from relatively benign advertisements, to pornography on the Internet, to the murderous violence of a "snuff" film. In acknowledging the tenuous boundaries between fiction and real life, novels and films often ask whether representation in art is not just another kind of victimization of women. *See also* CRIME FICTION WRITERS.

Further Reading: Bronfen 1992, *Over Her Dead Body;* Tanner 1994, *Intimate Violence;* Tennenhouse 1989, "Violence Done to Women on the Renaissance Stage."

Kathy M. Howlett

Filicide. *See* INFANTICIDE.

Forensic Psychiatry and Gender, Canada

The discipline of forensic psychiatry is concerned with the medico-legal assessment and treatment of persons in conflict with the criminal law. Since the mid-nineteenth century, psychiatrists have become increasingly involved in the regulation of "insane" women. Asylums have operated to confine those who violate culturally accepted standards for feminine conduct. Women found "criminally insane" have included those who trespass against moral convention, exhibit "manlike" qualities, and allegedly fail as wives and mothers. Women patients have been more likely than men to experience such somatic interventions as sterilization, insulin coma, electroshock, lobotomy, and psychotropic drug treatment (Chunn and Menzies 1998).

The male-dominated psychiatric profession has encouraged medical interpretations of women's criminal behavior (Allen 1987; Ussher 1991). The Diagnostic and Statistical Manual of the American Psychiatric Association (DSMIV) lists an assortment of diagnostic classifications (e.g., borderline personality disorder and depression) that are predominantly applied to women. Infanticide provisions of the Canadian Criminal Code reflect medical theories about the biological determinants of women's irrationality (Grant, Chunn, and Boyle 1994). Experts have promoted legal defenses such as premenstrual syndrome, battered woman syndrome, and postpartum psychosis on the presumption that women who experience such conditions have diminished capacity to form criminal intent.

In Canada, judges can divert defendants suspected of psychiatric illness to forensic clinics. Most of the approximately 1,000 Canadian women remanded annually are found fit. However, between 15 and 20 percent of them are found unfit, and clinicians may address various other issues including treatability, criminal responsibility, and suitability for release. Patients found unfit or not criminally responsible on account of mental disorder are potentially subject to indeterminate hospitalization.

Researchers have documented the gendered impact of forensic psychiatry on the criminal trial process. One project was undertaken at the Metropolitan Toronto Forensic Service (METFORS), a pretrial forensic remand center that, since 1978, has conducted evaluations on defendants arriving from the city's courts. Studies demonstrate that women are disproportionately represented among METFORS patients; that women are more likely than men to have a history of psychiatric institutionalization; that forensic psychiatrists invoke a wide array of gender-specific medical and moral labels; that women are more apt to be characterized as "double deviants" (both "mad" and "bad");

that women are more frequently rerouted into general psychiatric or forensic hospital settings; and that, for many women, forensic assessments trigger a protracted series of encounters with psychiatric clinics, hospitals, jails, prisons, and community agencies (Chunn and Menzies 1990).

Over the past decade, dangerousness and risk to self and others have become key constructs in the forensic processing of women defendants. Canadian clinicians and researchers have been at the forefront of a rapidly proliferating technology of psychometric instruments including the PCLR (Psychopathy Checklist Revised), VRAG (Violence Risk Assessment Guide), and SARA (Spousal Assault Risk Assessment guide) that purportedly enable the accurate identification of risky people. However, many people argue that the "riskification" of criminal justice and mental health systems endangers the human rights of forensic subjects. While the gender dimensions of this trend have yet to be fully charted, the concept of risk will likely be the single greatest influence on the psychiatric processing of women defendants in the twenty-first century. *See also* BATTERED WOMEN AND SELF-DEFENSE, CANADA; MEDICAL EXPLANATIONS OF DELINQUENCY; PREMENSTRUAL SYNDROME; PSYCHOLOGICAL EXPLANATIONS OF DELINQUENCY.

Further Reading: Chunn and Menzies 1990, "Gender, Madness and Crime"; Menzies 1989, *Survival of the Sanest;* Ussher 1991, *Women's Madness.*

Robert Menzies

Framingham Eight

The Framingham Eight were a group of women incarcerated at the Massachusetts women's prison in Framingham who, while serving time for attacks they perpetrated on intimate partners, sought to be paroled or have their sentences commuted. Between 1986 and 1990, all eight were found guilty of manslaughter or second-degree murder. Their sentences to the Framingham prison ranged from a minimum of eight years to life. Due to *pro bono* legal assistance and a high-profile campaign on their behalf, between

1993 and 1994, seven of the eight women were paroled, had their sentences commuted, or had their sentences reduced to time served.

Legal arguments supporting their release were based on the grounds that these women were victims of battered woman syndrome, a condition that psychologists attribute to learned helplessness or post–traumatic stress syndrome. Because the Framingham Eight had killed their batterers, proponents of their release argued that they needed therapy, not punishment in prison.

National recognition of these women and the larger issue of domestic violence followed the release of the Academy Award–winning film, *Defending Our Lives,* featuring the story of the Framingham Eight and made with their help. Their legal predicament led to important changes in the handling of domestic violence. In 1993, Massachusetts enacted legislation permitting the introduction of evidence of abuse in criminal trials.

Many of the Framingham Eight have had difficulties since their release. While aware-ness of domestic violence issues has been greatly expanded, some argue that little has been done to ensure that the Framingham Eight were offered the necessary help to change their lives. By 1999, two of them were back in prison. *See also* HOMICIDE, USA; DOMESTIC VIOLENCE AGAINST WOMEN, EPIDEMIOLOGY OF; VICTIMIZATION PATTERNS, USA; VIOLENT CRIME.

Further Reading: Goldfarb 1996, "Describing without Circumscribing."

Maureen A. Norton-Hawk

Fry, Elizabeth (1780–1845)

Elizabeth Fry, an English Quaker, focused public attention on prison conditions for women. These efforts arose out of her religious convictions, and she put this work above the domestic claims of home and family.

In 1816, appalled at the squalor, degradation, and violence in London's Newgate Prison, Fry, with a group of other Quaker

Elizabeth Fry reading to prisoners at Newgate. *Courtesy of the Charles Roberts Autograph Letters Collection, Haverford College Library.*

women, determined to intervene in behalf of women prisoners. The authorities feared for the visitors' safety, but Fry addressed the women prisoners as fellow mothers and asked if they would work with her in helping their children. It is significant that in the early years of her work, Fry always involved prisoners in the plans for their improvement. A school was established for the Newgate prisoners' children, with a schoolmistress chosen from among the prisoners.

Fry and her companions formed the Association for the Improvement of the Females at Newgate. The association provided clothing and a regime of useful work through which the prisoners acquired skills and habits to fit them for a life beyond prison. A monitorial system operated whereby some prisoners oversaw the work of others. Cooperation and collaboration between the visitors and the prisoners was key to the entire enterprise. The transformation of the situation in the prison was dramatic and gave rise to attention from the press and the public.

In 1818, Fry set out with her brother, Joseph John Gurney, to tour the country and establish ladies' associations elsewhere. By 1827, she had published *Observations on the Visiting, Superintendence, and Government of Female Prisoners,* setting out her ideas. At this point in her work, she had begun to place less emphasis on the participation of prisoners in the creation of improved conditions, instead presenting routine and continuous surveillance as central to a reforming discipline. Religious instruction, basic literacy, and needlework remained important, but now as part of a system of classification whereby women made progress through stages according to their degrees of rehabilitation. Each stage was marked by a reward or a privilege, and prisoners were categorized by uniforms and badges. By 1827, Fry no longer recommended that prisoners hold positions of authority, but she did emphasize that at all times, women prisoners were to be segregated from men and supervised only by women.

Fry put women prisoners on the penal system's agenda. In arguing for a system geared to the needs of women, she raised an issue that still remains to be fully addressed. *See also* DEVIANCE AND REFORM, HISTORICAL OVERVIEW OF, BRITAIN.

Further Reading: R. P. Dobash, Dobash, and Gutteridge 1986, *The Imprisonment of Women;* E. Fry 1827, *Observations;* Rose 1980, *Elizabeth Fry.*

Mary Eaton

G

Gangs: Cabra Girls (Australia)

During the early 1990s, the Cabra Girls, a loose-knit group of young women, roamed the streets of Cabramatta, a small suburban enclave situated in Sydney's southwest. Affiliated with male gang members and involved in extortion and petty crime, they were simultaneously streetwise and vulnerable. Bound by economic desperation and gender roles, their stories are not unlike those of other marginalized women (Maher 1997). On the street, sexism is just another burden.

In North America, the legendary characteristics of urban gang subculture (territoriality, brotherhood, and do-or-die loyalty) have emerged out of a culture of boystudy: systematic documentation and empathetic accounts of gang life by successive generations of male researchers and journalists. By contrast, explorations of gang girls have, with notable exceptions (e.g., Campbell 1984; J. A. Miller 1996), been scattered and sensationalist. Accounts, such as those by journalist Gini Sikes (*8 Ball Chicks,* 1997) and sociologist Carl Taylor (*Girls, Gangs, Women and Drugs,* 1993), warn of a growing cadre of "gangsta bitches" more violent and more brutal than their male counterparts. In Australia, despite periodic waves of media interest, there have been few empirical studies and gang girls are notably absent from the literature.

Cabramatta, the primary field site for the research reported here, is the nucleus of the 200,000-strong Vietnamese community in Australia. The suburb also has the dubious distinction of being Australia's "heroin capital." In 1994, the local member of parliament was murdered outside his home, and the following year, a 20-year-old gang leader and one of his lieutenants were shot dead in their apartment. In 1997, 35 people died from heroin overdoses and 5,881 crimes were recorded in the area, the majority of them heroin related (Maher and Dixon 1999).

During the late 1980s, loosely structured youth gangs began to emerge in and around Cabramatta. Many first-wave gang members had spent their formative years in Vietnam, growing up amid the turmoil and hardship that followed the war. Some had already been exposed to street life as "children of the dust" (*bui doi*) and many had endured harrowing journeys to Australia. Upon resettlement, they confronted language and cultural barriers, as well as issues of loss, family separation, and economic marginality.

Displaced and alienated, some young people turned to the street, seeking friendship and support from similarly situated peers, and using the expression "coming out to play" (*ra choi*) to describe this process. These groups, or gangs, initially functioned as surrogate families whereby young people provided each other with familial resources— love, loyalty, respect, and physical protection.

As one of the young men who participated in the research said:

> Living this life, you stay in a group. The group is like your family. You look out for them and they look out for you. Like our group, we've been through a lot together. Like getting into fights, being on the run from police, getting locked up, mainly bad things. So we try and make a family, make something good for us. (Vu, 23-year-old Vietnamese Australian)

Predominantly Indo-Chinese in their membership, the gangs functioned much like traditional Southeast Asian families: private and patrilineal, with official membership restricted to males. Characterized by the pooling of resources, gang leaders often adopted parental roles, particularly when it came to economic functions. Perhaps the most notorious of these groups was the 5T, which took its name from the 5 T's tattooed on members' forearms. While observers have offered various interpretations, members insist that the T's stand for the Vietnamese words *tuoi, tre, thieu, tinh* and *thuong* which roughly translate as "young people who lack love and care."

While gang members initially relied on robberies, burglaries, and extortion in order to survive, by 1990, drug distribution was the favored source of income. Despite its increasing reliance on the heroin trade, strong normative codes within the gang prohibited heroin consumption. The structure and function of 5T as a cohesive social unit served to protect its members from becoming their own best customers for heroin.

During the early 1990s, reports began to emerge of a group of young Indo-Chinese women, known as the Cabra Girls, who were affiliated with the 5T. Some of these young women had become involved in street life through romantic liaisons with male gang members. Others, estranged from their families, solidified their relationship with the street through their identity as Cabra Girls.

Initially, the 5T re-created traditional Vietnamese gender roles. The men did the crime work and the women did the cooking, cleaning, and childcare. The Cabra Girls were not so much a gang as a group of young women engaged in domestic service provision to criminally involved young men. However, around 1992, some of these young women began to "chase the dragon" (smoke heroin). One of the young women recalled her initiation:

> First time with a friend. She asked me "Do you want to try white [heroin]?" I didn't know what white was at the beginning and she opened it up and she took the foil out and the straw and everything and that and then I just tried first puff and then vomit. That's how I started. (Linh, 15-year-old Vietnamese Australian)

With the lucrative wholesaler roles taken by the boys, young women were relegated to street-level dealing positions in order to support their heroin use. However, as they grew more dependent on the drug, smoking became a less efficient route of administration. In their work as street sellers, young women came into contact with injectors and most made the transition from smoking to intravenous use (Swift, Maher, and Sunjic 1999).

> Sometimes one of my customers would come with me when I go pick up. I'd smoke say three caps and they tell me, "What a waste." They'd tell me, "Half of that and you could be smashed off your face and you could be saving gear and making more profit, by shooting up." And then I tried it. (Lien, 17-year-old Vietnamese Australian)

In the absence of "true" gang membership, the Cabra Girls did not have the benefit of strong normative codes to regulate their conduct. While at first they tried to hide their use, reports began to filter back to the 5T. As one young woman recalled:

> It was shameful. They guys didn't accept it, especially Minh—he hated heroin.... No one knew before. We only used with best friends who used and if they told we could tell about them, so no one said anything. (Phuong, 19-year-old Vietnamese Australian)

Initially, male gang members reacted swiftly, using violence to punish the girls. Linh, a 15-year-old, recounted her experience:

I used to stay with my boyfriend, with the 5T. There was heaps of us living in one flat. But they don't use the white, just sell it…. When I started using the needle … my boyfriend bashed me. (Linh, 15-year-old Vietnamese Australian)

However, as their dependence on heroin increased and their use became more problematic, most of the Cabra Girls were ostracized by the 5T. As one young woman explained:

Sometimes they try to teach you a lesson. You know, how they're all brothers and just say one of the brothers' girlfriends is a junkie or whatever. Like they'd all know about it and it would be pretty embarrassing for the guy. All the brothers stick up for each other, listen to each other. Tell him "Oh you have to leave that girl." That's how it is. That's how much they stick together. (Trinh, 17-year-old Vietnamese Australian)

With their estrangement from the 5T, heroin use among the Cabra Girls intensified. Most continued to sell heroin as freelancers in order to support their habits. However, rather than solidifying their relationships, girls were forced into competition against each other. Longstanding friendships broke down, leaving them isolated and vulnerable. Over the next few years, most were imprisoned, some died, and a few left the area. Few of the original Cabra Girls remained on the street in 1999, and those who have remained are destitute, in poor health, and often homeless. They are looked down on by the community, offer little support to each other, and no longer associate with the 5T, who continue to remain active in heroin distribution in the area. *See also* DRUG DEALERS; DRUG OFFENSES; JUVENILE DELINQUENCY AND DRUG AND ALCOHOL ABUSE; JUVENILE DELINQUENCY AND GANGS, USA. JUVENILE DELINQUENCY, AUSTRALIA.

Further Reading: Maher 1997, *Sexed Work;* Maher and Dixon 1999, "Policing and Public Health"; J. A. Miller 1996, "Female Gang Involvement"; Swift, Maher, and Sunjic 1999, "Transitions between Routes of Heroin Administration."

Lisa Maher

Gender and Crime

Public perceptions of the extent and characteristics of female crime and criminals have changed dramatically during the twentieth century. The same is true of empirical evidence about the nature of female crime. These changes follow shifts in our perceptions of women's roles and abilities in general. Ideas about crime reflect ideas about human nature and gender roles. Moreover, this relationship tends to be reciprocal. Today, as a result of the women's movement, empirical research on women offenders and their offenses is flourishing and influencing public policy at every level, and in turn, it is feeding back into public beliefs about gender.

Beliefs about gender lie at the heart of conceptualizations of female crime. Deeply rooted in culture, preconceptions about the nature of men and women affect all aspects of understandings of female criminality. A society that does not believe that women are equal or even equivalent to men will not perceive women's criminal behavior as equal or equivalent to men's criminal behavior. Traditionally, criminologists and the general public have pictured female criminals not merely as bad people—equivalent to male criminals—but also as bad women, violators of gender-role prescriptions.

The Biblical story of the Fall of Man illustrates this tendency to blame female offenders for breaking not only the law but gender prescriptions as well. When Eve fails to resist Satan's temptation and eats the apple, Adam and Eve are expelled from the Garden of Eden, and all humans are condemned to lead painful lives. One common interpretation of this story holds that Eve lacked strong faith in God, a lack that made her susceptible to Satan's evil. Adam, more loyal to Eve than to God, ate the apple so that Eve would not die alone. Note that in this interpretation, Adam is strong, even though his loyalties are misplaced. Eve is simply weak, an interpretation strengthened by religious scholars who hold that Eve was in fact incapable of resisting temptation due to her inferior character.

While interpretations of the story of the Fall of Man vary, most of them reiterate tra-

Sin, by Flemish painter Hugo van der Goes, 1479. *Courtesy of the Kunsthistorisches Museum, Vienna.*

ditional ideas about why women who break the rules do so. The story depicts Eve as mentally weak and morally corrupt, much as nineteenth- and twentieth-century criminologists have argued that women in general tend to be mentally weak and gullible. In the traditional view, women are (or should be) nurturing, irrational, compliant, dependent, and incapable of strong critical thought. From that follows the traditional claim that women who commit crime are bad at being women. Lacking strength of character, they are easily tempted, and they are all too willing to corrupt male associates with their soft charms.

In contrast (the traditional view continues), men who commit crime are strong and aggressive, but in them, these fundamentally desirable male tendencies are exaggerated or unchecked. In traditional thinking, criminal women are no more likely to be strong or forceful than are non-criminal women. The types of crime women commit, largely sex and property crimes, reflect the sins of lust and greed. This traditional view was stron-

ger in the early and mid-twentieth century than today, but beliefs about male-female differences continue to color our thinking about female crime and criminality.

Historically, when women and girls were found guilty of crimes, gender roles affected them in two ways. Females found guilty of nonviolent offenses, especially sex offenses, were more likely to be punished (or "treated") than males who had behaved the same way. But at the same time, females found guilty of "masculine" offenses were likely to be punished more severely than males committing those offenses, since these "out of character" offenses were interpreted as danger signs. Both effects related directly to traditional perceptions of women and girls: Females were expected to need more supervision and guidance (thus the increased attention to their minor offenses, especially when sexuality was involved), and they were expected not to be aggressive or anti-social (thus the perception of betrayal when legal or moral codes were broken).

Early criminological theory reinforced these stereotypes of women and girls as simultaneously less serious and more dangerous offenders than men and boys. Early explanations of female criminality focused on biological defects. For instance, Lombroso's theory of the "born criminal" held that criminal women are biologically monstrous, more similar to men in their physical characteristics than to other women (Lombroso and Ferrero 1895). Similarly, defective delinquency theory held that "feebleminded" women of childbearing age should be institutionalized and thus prevented from producing criminal children (Rafter 1997). These women of supposedly low mental ability were considered promiscuous and a general detriment to society, no matter how minor their offenses. Later theorists identified traits (considered to be physiological) such as passivity, deceitfulness, and reproductive drive, common to all women, that predisposed females to specific types of criminal behavior. Both the biological and the psychological schools of thought viewed extramarital sexual behavior by women as evidence of criminality. However, they did not apply the same definition of criminality to men.

The historical impact of gender-role beliefs on the identification and reaction to female crime and criminals is well accepted; what is less clear is the effect of gender roles today. There has certainly been a significant change in our perception of the appropriate roles for women and girls (although we continue to have different expectations for men and boys). There have also been changes in our knowledge of the extent and characteristics of female crime and criminals.

Can some portion of the change in female criminality documented in the United States in the past 30 years be attributed to changes in ideas about gender? The answer is almost certainly yes. However, the magnitude of that effect is difficult to measure. One approach is to compare crime measurements by official agencies with measurements obtained from other sources.

The annual *Uniform Crime Reports* (*UCRs*), the most comprehensive source of arrest data in the United States, indicate that about one quarter of all juvenile arrests are of female offenders. While the majority of those arrests are for nonviolent offenses, the violent crime rate for female juveniles has increased recently. A special report on juvenile crime based on the 1997 *UCRs* (U.S. Department of Justice, Federal Bureau of Investigation 1998) highlights the increases in juvenile crime, especially the increase in the proportion of violent crimes committed by females. From 1988 to 1997, the number of male juvenile arrests increased by less than one-third, while the number of female juvenile arrests more than doubled. During this same period, male juvenile violent crime arrests increased 42.0 percent, while female juvenile violent crime arrests increased 100.7 percent.

Adult females also account for an increasing amount of officially recognized criminal activity. According to the *UCRs*, the majority of adult female arrests are for non-violent offenses, but the proportion of arrestees who are female has increased in recent years. From 1988 to 1997, the number of male arrests rose 10.3 percent, while female arrests rose

39.8 percent. It is clear that the criminal justice system has identified an increase in female crime.

Those skeptical of the influence of the criminal justice system on crime measurement might argue that the observed increase in official counts of female crime and criminals reflects nothing more than increased crime committed by women and girls. Victimization data contradict this claim, however. Although victimization data do measure an increase in female crime, the magnitude of this increase is less than that found in the *UCRs*. Data from the National Crime Victimization Survey indicate that from the mid-1970s to the early 1990s, female crime accounted for a small, stable proportion of all offenses. These data show that female offending has increased slightly since the early 1990s, but in much smaller proportion than the *UCRs* suggest.

Although neither the *UCRs* nor the National Crime Victimization Survey data can be considered accurate counts of the true amount of crime that is occurring, both have been shown to be consistent measures of the behaviors that they do capture. It is likely that the discrepancy between the increase in the official or *UCR* count of female crime and the victimization reports of female crime reflects a change in the system's ability to detect female crime. Other comparisons of official data with alternate crime measures provide further evidence that much of the change in official reports of crime and delinquency since the 1970s is an artifact of changes in public policy (Curran 1984). There is substantial evidence of the recent increase in the criminal justice system's ability to recognize female crime.

As perceptions of women have changed, so have perceptions of their behavior (both criminal and noncriminal). But even this direct effect of our culture on our knowledge of female crime and criminality, related to our identification and punishment of female offenders, may not be the strongest influence on our identification of female crime.

In the 1970s, with the advent of the women's liberation movement, criminologists began to focus on the ways changing gender roles might affect women's criminal behavior. However, this period failed to produce drastic changes in the level of female crime and criminals, leading to even closer scrutiny of the interaction between gender roles and criminal behavior. John Hagan's power-control theory (Hagan, Gillis, and Simpson 1985) focused on the interaction among gender roles and factors such as the power structure of a patriarchal capitalist society. Other theorists, such as Chesney-Lind (1989), emphasized the interaction between gender roles and judicial processing. In general, current theories explain female crime in the context of gender roles while working to specify the nature of that relationship.

Moreover, recent work on female crime addresses specific kinds of criminal behavior, examining the effect that gender roles have on the type of crime committed. It tries to integrate what is known about pressures such as poverty and extreme deprivation with understandings of the constraints placed on females by gender roles. For example, discussions of prostitution now emphasize an interaction between social forces (poverty, laws prohibiting prostitution) and gender roles (especially the expectation of chastity on the part of women and girls) that lead to the labeling of some women as criminal prostitutes. Current theoretical explanations of female crime and criminals far surpass the simplistic explanations offered just a few decades ago.

Despite this more enlightened approach to studying the causes of crime, gender roles probably continue to bias our understanding of female criminality. For example, the public's fear of juvenile crime is still essentially the fear of crime by boys. Although girls' rates of violent crime are indeed lower than boys' rates, the public apparently resists accepting girls as violent. It is difficult, if not impossible, to study that which we do not believe exists.

Much as gender roles affect understandings of crime, so too do they affect treatment options. For girls and women who come into contact with the criminal justice system, there are far fewer programs than those available for boys and men. Ironically, lack of treatment increases the probability that a young girl will slide further into the system and thus, as in the past, receive harsher treatment than a boy for a less serious initial offense. Thus, the cycle is self-feeding, with gender expectations affecting criminology and treatment options, and both criminology and treatment cycling back to reinforce gender expectations. *See also* FEMALE CRIME, EXPLANATIONS OF; FEMALE CRIME, PATTERNS AND TRENDS IN, USA; JUVENILE DELINQUENCY, USA; LOMBROSO, CESARE; MADONNA/WHORE DICHOTOMY; MASCULINITY EXPLANATION OF CRIME; OFFENDERS; PROSTITUTION; SEXISM AND RACISM IN CRIMINAL JUSTICE POLICY; SOCIAL CONTROL OF WOMEN; VIOLENT CRIME.

Further Reading: G. M. Anderson 1994, "Juvenile Justice and the Double Standard"; Chesney-Lind 1998, "Women in Prison"; Eisenstein 1979, *Capitalist Patriarchy and the Case for Socialist Feminism;* Rafter 1990b, "The Social Construction of Crime and Crime Control."

Mary Ann Zager

Gender and Judicial Decision-Making

Recent decades have seen considerable debate over the issue of whether a judge's gender affects the process of judicial decision-making and, if so, what this implies for judicial appointments. Some people maintain that there should be more women judges because women are entitled to their "fair share" of all governmental positions, including judgeships. Others believe that there should be more women judges so that women, as well as men, feel that courts represent them and make legitimate decisions. Still others argue that there should be more women judges not solely for symbolic reasons but for substantive reasons as well; they contend that women are likely to make different decisions than men.

Some feminist legal theorists claim that women on the bench would have a different perspective, just as women in general have a different perspective than men. Women put more emphasis on community than on individuality, and on relationships and responsibility than on rights and rules. As judges, they might favor experiential or anecdotal evidence over the more abstract empirical and statistical evidence.

Research on gender and judicial decision-making has been hampered by the relatively small number of women judges on any given court or in any given jurisdiction. On most courts and in many jurisdictions there are not enough women to make valid comparisons with men.

Surveys of the literature show that studies have generally found mixed results: The presence of women judges has made a difference in some ways but not in others. In a study of federal court of appeals judges, for instance, women appeared more liberal than men in cases involving employment discrimination and racial discrimination. But women did not decide differently than men in cases involving obscenity or search-and-seizure.

In studies of state trial court judges, women and men convicted defendants at similar rates but sentenced them slightly differently. In one city, women judges sentenced female defendants to prison more frequently than men did. In borderline cases, men treated female defendants more leniently, giving them probation and allowing them to avoid prison. In another city, women sentenced rapists to longer prison terms than men did.

One unique study that overcame the problem of the small number of women judges focused on one legal issue decided in one year (1988) by hundreds of federal district court judges—the constitutionality of federal sentencing guidelines. The study examined the decisions of 28 women judges and found that they ruled the same as the men judges.

More pronounced differences have appeared in areas most directly related to gender. Thus, U.S. Supreme Court Justice Sandra Day O'Connor, who generally votes as a judicial conservative, usually votes with the liberal bloc in sex discrimination cases. Moreover, her presence on the Court apparently has sensitized her male colleagues to gender issues. Most of them began to vote against sex discrimination more frequently after she joined the Court.

Women justices on state supreme courts exhibit similar patterns. They tend to support women's rights in cases ranging from sex discrimination to child support and property settlement. Even women justices from opposing political parties often agree on these issues.

In most areas, however, the research has not found differences, or at least no large differences, between men and women judges, despite the expectations of numerous theorists. Perhaps the socialization of women though law school and the legal profession influences them so they think more like men lawyers. Or perhaps only the women who think like men lawyers are appointed or elected to the bench. It also is possible that trial court judges experience the subtle pressure of the "court workgroups," the judges and attorneys who work together to process cases day after day, while appellate court judges experience the subtle pressure of their small group, both of which might diminish any differences between the genders.

Nevertheless, newspaper and magazine articles, as well as gender bias task force reports, have reported many instances in which the presence of women judges has a less direct effect. Sometimes men judges and lawyers in court refer to women lawyers and witnesses by their first name or by a term such as "honey," "sweetie," or "young lady." Or in the midst of the proceedings, men sometimes comment on a woman's clothing or appearance. Although these remarks may be innocent, they also may be sly ways to undermine the credibility of the woman, especially if the case is being tried before a jury. Women judges and lawyers do not make these comments, and they often warn men lawyers against making them. In this way, women judges protect the credibility of women lawyers and witnesses. *See also* Gender Bias Task Forces; Judges; Jury Selection; Lawyers and Gender Difference; Legal Profession, Women's Current Participation in; O'Connor, Sandra Day; Women Professionals in the Justice Workplace.

Further Reading: S. Davis, Haire, and Songer 1993, "Voting Behavior and Gender on the U.S. Courts of Appeals"; Eich 1986, "Gender Bias in the Courtroom"; Finley 1989, "Breaking Women's Silence in Law."

John R. Gruhl

Gender and Policing

The policing occupation has long been associated with images of masculinity, aggression, physicality, and crime-fighting. The paragon police officer was the physically large and intimidating man who could use his authority—and force, if needed—to enforce the law. Police officers and the public alike viewed women as unable to assertively handle the rough underworld or to command respect and obedience from offenders and the community.

In the nineteenth century, when full-time, salaried police positions were created, women performed limited roles as police matrons in jails. Women's supposedly nurturing nature was seen as appropriate to the tasks of searching female prisoners and dealing with female victims and girls who were in trouble. In this restricted capacity, police matrons merely extended women's traditional caretaker role into the municipal sphere, where they were called "municipal housekeepers" (Schulz 1995). Police matrons did not threaten the male stronghold of power since these women did not seek the same jobs or responsibilities as men had, nor did male police personnel desire to perform the police tasks associated with women and girls.

However, once women sought expanded police duties, such as armed patrol, men resisted their inclusion. In fact, it was not until 1972 that women were granted the legal right to function as patrol officers. That year, the passage of the Equal Opportunity Act extended the provisions of Title VII of the 1964 Civil Rights Act to state and local governments and prohibited discrimination based on sex.

Legislative and executive action, in conjunction with court orders, were needed to address discrimination in eligibility criteria, selection standards, and assignment and promotion practices in police departments. The overall climate following the urban riots of the 1960s and the burgeoning women's movement also helped open up traditionally male professions for women. The Kerner Commission report on civil unrest specifically advocated the increased hiring of women and non-white police officers to avoid the divisiveness and violence that was sweeping the nation.

Legal hurdles, however, were not the sole obstacle that women faced. Many male police officers resented women's presence in police departments, and many officers and members of the community believed that women were not capable of performing police work. In particular, men believed that women were weaker, both physically and emotionally, and thus incapable of handling the tasks associated with the job or exercising authority as police officers. Rigid gender roles and social expectations of men and women shaped the view that it was "unmanly" for men to rely on women. If women became police officers, it would be clear that policing was no longer a job that only men could do, a possibility that threatened the masculine image and subculture associated with policing (S. E. Martin and Jurik 1996).

Women's entrance into patrol functions in the early 1970s stimulated studies that evaluated policewomen's competence. These studies revealed that women were not only capable of performing patrol functions but that they also brought a different repertoire of skills to the job. Some research indicated that women even contributed to policing in unique ways due to more finely developed interpersonal communication skills that enabled them better to de-escalate conflicts.

Susan E. Martin studied female police officers in Washington, D.C., in the early 1970s to learn how these women adapted their behavior to fit into the male policing environment. Her groundbreaking work revealed two ways that women adapted to the police role. Some women accentuated their femininity in order to gain acceptance from the male police subculture. These policewomen were more passive, deferential, and flirtatious and less likely to threaten men's power. The alternative adaptation taken by policewomen emphasized skills and competence rather than traditional feminity. These policewomen identified with male officers, embraced masculine characteristics, and adopted tough, aggressive, street-oriented styles. Instead of gaining full acceptance by their male counterparts, however, they were chastised by both male officers and other policewomen by being labeled "bitches" or "dykes" (S. E. Martin 1980).

Other researchers have identified a third, more androgynous approach (Jurik 1988; Zimmer 1986; S. E. Martin 1994), in which female officers strive for an occupational style that balances their femininity with job success. Susan E. Martin (1994) contends that regardless of a policewoman's adaptive style, many male officers continue to trivialize women's participation and mistrust them or diminish them as sexual targets. She finds that racism further divides women, with black women receiving far less protection and experiencing more fear because of white hostility and intimidation. Men of color may assimilate more easily than women of color into policing because they possess masculine traits and do not threaten the police subculture in the same way that women do.

Despite these obstacles, women have been hired and promoted, with Bureau of Justice figures showing that, in 1997, women officers constituted 8.8 percent of sworn police officers in all sizes of departments, and 14.6 percent in departments serving populations of one million or more. However, women police officers remain concentrated at entry-level positions, and women and non-white officers still face an ambivalent welcome in many police departments.

Community policing, in which officers patrol a single neighborhood and get to know its residents, challenges the gender assumptions of traditional policing and its emphasis on aloof, detached, professional officers. Instead, community policing seeks officers with traits that, in the past, have been viewed as "feminine," and thus unwelcome, such as informality, a conciliatory approach, attachment to community residents, and involvement with their problems (S. L. Miller 1998a). As more and more police departments embrace community policing, it is likely that police officers, regardless of gender, will align themselves with the goals of community policing in order to stay professionally competitive.

The traditional police department is changing due to women's successes in gaining and articulating police jobs for themselves over the past century. As attitudes change and the police working environment becomes more hospitable to diversity, roles and responsibilities may become less tied to gender-based role expectations and more reflective of gender-neutral skills and competence levels. Communities are growing more supportive of police departments that foster a problem-solving style, as opposed to a strictly law-enforcement style. In addition, citizens are calling for police departments that are similar in racial, ethnic, and gender composition to the communities in which they serve. *See also* COMMUNITY POLICING; POLICE SUBCULTURE AND GENDER; POLICE WORK, HISTORY OF WOMEN IN, BRITAIN; POLICE WORK, HISTORY OF WOMEN IN, USA; POLICING, MODELS OF; WOMEN PROFESSIONALS IN THE JUSTICE WORKPLACE.

Further Reading: S. E. Martin 1980, *Breaking and Entering;* S. E. Martin and Jurik 1996, *Doing Justice, Doing Gender;* Schulz 1995, *From Social Worker to Crimefighter.*

Susan L. Miller

Gender Bias Task Forces

Gender bias task forces are high-level investigative bodies appointed in the United States by state supreme courts and federal circuit councils to discover the nature, extent, and consequences of gender bias in their own judicial systems and to recommend and implement reforms. These task forces emerged in response to the judicial education programs of the National Judicial Education Program to Promote Equality for Women and Men in the Courts, a project of the NOW Legal Defense and Education Fund, initiated in 1980 and co-sponsored by the National Association of Women Judges.

The first gender bias task force was established in 1982 in New Jersey. By 1998, the national gender bias task force movement had grown to include 40 states and 8 federal circuits. Although the severity of the problems documented varies from jurisdiction to jurisdiction, there is an overall uniformity. In the words of the New York Task Force on Women in the Courts (1986–87:17–18), "gender bias against women litigants, lawyers and court employees is a pervasive problem with grave consequences. Women are often denied equal justice, equal treatment and equal opportunity."

The gender bias task forces examined an array of issues pertaining to women as victims and perpetrators of crime and made findings in the following areas:

- **Rape.** The courts' handling of stranger rape cases has improved, but in non-stranger cases (the vast majority of rapes), it is still often the victim who is on trial. Her dress, demeanor, conduct, associations, and lifestyle—rather than his threats or use of force—become the focus. Judges and jurors want evidence of physical resistance and injury, even though most rapes involve neither. Women of color have even less credibility than white women, and if there is a conviction in their cases, the sentence may be lighter than for the rape of a white woman.
- **Domestic violence.** Despite many improvements in the protection of battered women and the punishment of their abusers, there are ongoing problems. Many judges and gatekeeper court personnel know nothing of the dynamics of domestic violence and thus ask why the victims provoke it or why the women do not just leave. Many perpetrators receive scant or no punishment. Mediation is used inappropriately. Violence against women of color is assumed to be normative in their communities and thus unworthy of court intervention.
- **Battered women who kill their abusers.** There is greater understanding of the

battered woman syndrome, but women who do not neatly fit that paradigm, especially women of color, are not benefited.
- **Prostitution.** Male customers are never jailed, and non-white prostitutes are jailed more often than white.
- **Women in prison.** Facilities are even worse for women than for men, with fewer opportunities for education and work release.
- **Juveniles.** Girls are placed in secure facilities for status offenses for which boys are not. There is little understanding of the extremely high rate of sexual abuse in these girls' lives that leads them to run away and to prostitute themselves.

The gender bias task forces made recommendations for judges, court administrators, judicial educators, judicial selection and disciplinary commissions, lawyers, bar associations, prosecutors, police, legislators, law professors, and others to ameliorate the problems documented. Implementation of these recommendations is proceeding at different rates in different jurisdictions. *See also* BATTERED WOMEN AND SELF-DEFENSE, USA; GENDER DISCRIMINATION AND JUVENILE JUSTICE; GENDER DISCRIMINATION AND SENTENCING; GENDER DISCRIMINATION AND STATUS OFFENSES; JUDGES; RAPE VICTIMS, DISCREDITING OF; WOMEN PROFESSIONALS IN THE JUSTICE WORKPLACE.

Further Reading: A list of the Gender Bias Task Force Reports and information on how to obtain them is available from the National Judicial Education Program, 395 Hudson Street, New York, NY 10014; 212-925-6635; fax 212-226-1066; e-mail njep@nowldef.org; actions taken to implement task force recommendations that can be replicated in any jurisdiction are catalogued in *Gender Fairness Strategies Project: Implementation Resource Directory,* available from the National Judicial Education Program; Schafran 1990, "Overwhelming Evidence."

Lynn Hecht Schafran

Gender Discrimination and Juvenile Justice

Three types of juveniles fall into the jurisdiction of the juvenile court:

- status offenders, or persons committing acts such as truancy that are illegal only for underage individuals
- delinquent offenders, or juveniles who have committed an act that would be considered a crime if committed by an adult
- young people who are dependent and neglected

Gender discrimination occurs when female offenders are treated more harshly than their male counterparts, or when male offenders are treated more harshly than their female counterparts, at any stage of the juvenile justice process, including referral (i.e., arrest), pre-detention, adjudication, and disposition.

Research exploring gender discrimination within the juvenile justice system has traditionally concentrated on the treatment of female and male status offenders, because in the first half of the twentieth century, there were obvious differences in the definition of, and responses to, girls and boys in this category. Historical accounts of juvenile justice processing indicate that police, as well as juvenile justice personnel, purposefully treated female status offenders more harshly than male status offenders primarily in order to prevent girls' sexual activity prior to marriage. Quantitative studies prior to the 1980s also provided strong evidence that female status offenders were treated more harshly than their male counterparts, but these studies rarely accounted for important factors such as prior offense history, age, and type of offense. When these factors were considered in later studies, evidence of gender discrimination became far more tenuous, leading researchers to question more closely whether the contemporary juvenile justice system reacts differently to male and female status offenders.

Harsher treatment of girls than boys appears less prevalent when delinquent behavior is considered. Although fewer researchers have explored the possibility of differential treatment of female and male delinquent offenders, findings indicate that female offenders are treated similarly or receive more lenient outcomes than their male counterparts. However, there are at least two exceptions to this pattern. First, research indicates that racial/ethnic minority female delinquents often receive harsher treatment than either white female or white male offenders. Secondly, female offenders who are charged with atypical offenses (e.g., assaults) or with moral offenses (e.g., prostitution) appear to receive harsher treatment than their male counterparts.

To date, little research has explored gender discrimination in the handling of dependent/neglect cases. It is important to note, though, that there is a substantial amount of overlap between dependent and neglected girls and female status offenders. In fact, historically, girls who were neglected or dependent on the state were often sent to the same institutions as female status offenders in order to provide for them, but also to indoctrinate them with proper moral standards of behavior.

Two theories, chivalry and paternalism, have been put forth to account for the differential treatment of male and female juvenile offenders. According to the chivalry explanation, the system attempts to protect female offenders from the harshness of the system by not arresting girls as readily as boys and by removing them from the system sooner than male offenders. Many have used chivalry theory to account for the low number of apprehensions of female offenders and their more lenient treatment throughout the juvenile justice process. Yet chivalry cannot explain the high rates of female status offenders compared with male status offenders and the harsher treatment that girls often receive for status offense charges. Consequently, paternalism has often been used to explain this pattern of findings. According to the paternalism explanation, female status offenders are treated more harshly than male counterparts because police officers and juvenile justice personnel intervene in an effort to "save the female offender from herself." This explanation implies a double standard of morality which holds female offenders more accountable for deviant behavior than their male counterparts.

Based on the mixed results found in this area of research, it seems reasonable to conclude that both chivalry and paternalism operate in the juvenile justice system, depending on the charge and the jurisdiction in question.

Many questions still need to be examined in this area of investigation. Further research is needed to understand how gender discrimination operates in the handling of delinquency and neglected/dependent cases. It is also necessary to explore how gender discrimination may operate through the race of the offender and to determine the impact of gender discrimination on the use of different types of social control (e.g., secure placements vs. mental health placements). Research findings on gender and racial discrimination in juvenile justice also must be interpreted within the context of system resources, cultures, and pressures. Such understanding will permit both theoretical and policy development to more adequately address gender discrimination within the juvenile justice system. *See also* CHILD-SAVERS MOVEMENT; CHIVALRY EXPLANATION OF COURT OUTCOMES; CHIVALRY EXPLANATION OF FEMALE CRIME RATES; GENDER DISCRIMINATION AND SENTENCING; GENDER DISCRIMINATION AND STATUS OFFENSES; JUVENILE INSTITUTIONS, HISTORY OF; STATUS OFFENSES.

Further Reading: Chesney-Lind and Shelden 1998, *Girls, Delinquency, and Juvenile Justice*; Smart and Smart 1978, *Women, Sexuality, and Social Control*.

Denise C. Herz

Gender Discrimination and Sentencing

Despite the assumption that "justice is blind" in determining the fate of defendants in U.S. criminal courts, researchers have found gender discrimination in sentencing. Unlike patterns of discrimination in the larger society,

where women are disadvantaged compared to men, for the most part women are treated more leniently than men when it comes to punishing criminal behavior. This finding has prompted scholars to come up with a variety of explanations for this difference in criminal sentencing and has raised the question of whether women's advantaged status is warranted.

Over the past three decades, a number of statistical studies have been conducted on criminal court sentencing. While the data used in these studies vary greatly in terms of quality, time period, type of court (felony versus misdemeanor), and region of country, in general, researchers have found "sex effects" favoring female defendants after controlling for important variables such as type of offense and prior record. Women are between 8 and 25 percent less likely to be incarcerated than men convicted of similar offenses and with similar prior records. Sex effects favoring women are more likely to be found in studies of felony offenses, courts in urban areas, and incarceration decisions. In addition, some scholars have found that the gender gap in criminal sentencing is greater for black defendants than for white defendants. An exception to this general tendency toward greater leniency for female defendants is found among juvenile girls sentenced for status offenses, such as truancy and running away from home. Studies show that girls are treated more harshly than boys by the juvenile justice system for status offenses.

Why do women, in general, receive more lenient sentences than men in criminal court? A number of explanations have been offered over time. Early attempts to explain the preferential treatment of women in the criminal justice system include the chivalry thesis, judicial paternalism, and the "evil woman" thesis. Chivalry is an informal code of manners that leads to a protective attitude of men toward women. According to the chivalry thesis, when male judges give women offenders lighter sentences compared to their male counterparts, they are simply reflecting this protective attitude. In contrast, paternalism implies an unequal power relationship. According to the paternalism thesis, when male judges sentence women more lightly than men, they do so because they are viewing women as childlike; incapable of making decisions on their own, women cannot be held responsible for their behavior. The "evil woman" thesis holds that women are treated less harshly than men if they commit crimes that conform to sex-stereotypic roles, but that they will be treated more harshly than men if their criminal behavior violates these conventional roles. Despite their plausibility, all three of these explanations lack empirical validation.

More recent explanations for the disparity in criminal court sentences between men and women have been supported empirically. In addition, unlike earlier explanations, they suggest that the differential treatment may, in fact, be well-founded. For example, some have shown that female offenders are subjected to less formal social control (criminal sentencing) because they already experience various types of informal social control in their daily lives (for example, dependency on the government for welfare support or on particular men). Others argue that the differential sanctioning of men and women is a function of differences in their familial caretaking responsibilities. Women are more often than men responsible for the daily care of family members. Thus, the cost of incarcerating women is viewed as much higher by sentencing judges. Last, differences in men's and women's sentences may reflect a belief among judges that women are less blameworthy and have a greater potential for reform compared to men. This belief is grounded in a qualitative understanding of the differential history and social organization of women's lawbreaking compared to men's. See also CHIVALRY EXPLANATION OF COURT OUTCOMES; GENDER DISCRIMINATION AND JUVENILE JUSTICE; GENDER DISCRIMINATION AND STATUS OFFENSES.

Further Reading: K. Daly and Tonry 1997, "Gender, Race, and Sentencing"; K. Daly and Bordt 1995, "Sex Effects and Sentencing."

Rebecca L. Bordt

Gender Discrimination and Status Offenses

In terms of processing youthful offenders, a key question concerns how status offenses—behaviors that are considered violations of the law only when youth, not adults, commit them—have worked over time to foster gender discrimination in the juvenile justice system. Status offenses include running away from home, truancy from school, promiscuity, and drinking alcohol. Although self-report data indicate few gender differences in the *occurrence* of status offenses, research on the *processing* of youth for status offenses routinely points to profound gender differences.

Historically and currently, a major component of the significant gender differences in the processing of status offenses has been the social and legal desire to control girls, particularly their sexual activities. A historical account of the efforts between 1885 and 1920 to raise the age of consent in U.S. statutory rape laws found a preoccupation with policing girls' consensual sexual experiences (Odem 1995). The reformers hoped to protect girls (particularly white girls) from devious men wanting to have sex with them. The end result, however, was the criminalizing of girls' consensual sexual activity, while the men usually went uncensored (unless they were African American, in which case they, too, were harshly sanctioned).

Ironically, efforts to control girls' consensual sexuality can lead to girls' sexual victimization. A study of court records in Memphis, Tennessee, between 1900 and 1917 (Shelden 1981) found that girls received harsh sanctions for any kind of sexual experiences, consensual or forced. Similarly, even recent studies of the juvenile justice system charge that the juvenile courts are sometimes unable to distinguish sexual abuse *victimization* from sexual *offenses*. That is, girls who have been sexually abused are sometimes processed similarly to girls charged with "promiscuity" (a word and charge never associated with males) and prostitution. A classic study analyzing juvenile court cases in Honolulu, Hawaii, between 1929 and 1964 reported that girls stopped for *any* charges, including nonsexual offenses such as larceny, were routinely subjected to gynecological exams to determine whether they had sexually transmitted diseases (STDs) and whether they were virgins (Chesney-Lind 1973; also see Federle and Chesney-Lind 1992). Any indication of sexual activity resulted in increased charges for the girls. There is no account of boys' subjugation to any processes to account for their sexual activities or STDs. Finally, more recent feminist research on girls' pathways to offending highlights how sexual abuse in the home is frequently related to girls' running away and (ab)using alcohol, increasing their risks of status offense charges.

Accounting for gender differences in the processing of status offenders requires examining the behavior of various authorities: parents, police, and the courts. Research has consistently shown that parents are more alarmed by their daughters' than their sons' status offenses and thus are more likely to report their daughters to the police or juvenile justice authorities. Research on gender differences in the processing of offenders reports that for both police and court decision-making, gender disparities are most pronounced (and disadvantageous to girls) when the female is a youth and the offense is a status offense.

The Juvenile Justice Delinquency Prevention Act of 1974 (JJDPA) was designed and implemented to divert status offenders from the juvenile justice system and keep them out of institutions. As hoped, the JJDPA initially resulted in a significant decrease in youth in institutions for delinquents. However, subsequent research indicates that the long-term effects of the JJDPA are more complicated, with white male youth being the major benefactors and girls being "trans-institutionalized" into other nondelinquent institutions (e.g., mental health facilities). Efforts in 1992 to address the sexism girls still face regarding status offenses also seem to have failed. Clearly, the problem of sexism in the processing of status offenses is far from resolved. *See also* CHILD-SAVERS MOVEMENT; GENDER

DISCRIMINATION AND JUVENILE JUSTICE; JUVENILE INSTITUTIONS, HISTORY OF; STATUS OFFENSES.

Further Reading: Belknap and Holsinger 1998, "An Overview of Delinquent Girls"; Chesney-Lind 1973, "Judicial Enforcement of the Female Sex Role"; Sarri 1983, "Gender Issues in Juvenile Justice."

Joanne Belknap and Kristi Holsinger

Gender Disparities in Prisons

Since the first women were incarcerated in early penitentiaries, their programs, supervision, work, types of quarters, and even punishments have differed from men's, revealing pervasive inequalities or gender disparities in prison.

While men held at New York's Auburn Penitentiary in the early nineteenth century were isolated at night in single cells and beaten if they violated the rule of silence, Auburn's women prisoners were housed in one large attic room above the kitchen. For their first seven years at Auburn, the women had no matron. Once a day, a steward delivered their food and removed waste (Rafter 1985b:6). Harriet Martineau, a middle-class visitor to Auburn, was shocked to see the instruments used for women's punishment: "[S]tocks of a terrible construction [and] a chair with a fastening for the head and for the limbs" (1838:202).

Early legislators and prison officials did little planning for women. Occasionally, women sentenced to penitentiaries were pardoned and sent home because of inadequate space. Sometimes they were placed in separate cells in male cellblocks. As exemplified by Auburn, women were also housed in makeshift quarters separate from the men or in a different building on the grounds of the men's facility, and often they were supervised only by male guards. Women did traditional women's tasks—washing, ironing, and sewing—while men did crafts or industrial labor, which contributed to the institutions' financial profits.

Although women prisoners lived in the same institutions with men, they were not treated equally. Rarely included in any penitentiary policy, criminal women were viewed as more depraved than criminal men. Believing they were irredeemable, prison officials did not attempt to transform women (as they did men) into productive citizens. Since the women did not receive any training for work, they left penitentiaries no better off than when they entered. Some women were even less fortunate: Due to lack of supervision, they may have been sexually attacked by male inmates or guards or forced into prostitution while in prison.

Appalled at the treatment of imprisoned women and believing that women were essentially different from men, nineteenth-century women reformers lobbied for separate prisons for women. To protect women from sexual attacks, the reformers argued that only women should be employed in the new reformatories.

Many of the women's reformatories opened in the late nineteenth and early twentieth centuries consisted of a series of cottages on grounds without any walls or fences. With the objective of sexual and vocational regulation of young working-class women,

programs were designed to teach female offenders the skills and behaviors necessary to become dutiful wives, mothers, and servants. Reformative efforts focused on training in homemaking and other domestic skills. However, the seemingly better housing and programs for women actually resulted in a new set of gender disparities. Reformatory programs based on female stereotypes tried to shape imprisoned women into narrow images of proper womanhood. Homemaking skills did not prepare poor women, needing work, for jobs with adequate pay. Finally, reformatory women had been convicted of crimes for which men were never prosecuted. The male reformatories housed young, first-time-offender felons. However, reformatory women had been convicted of public intoxication, waywardness, vagrancy, and prostitution, which are only misdemeanors. Thus, women served time in state prisons for behaviors that were ignored in men.

While reformatories spread throughout the country during the late nineteenth and early twentieth centuries, women's prison units of the custodial type continued to de-

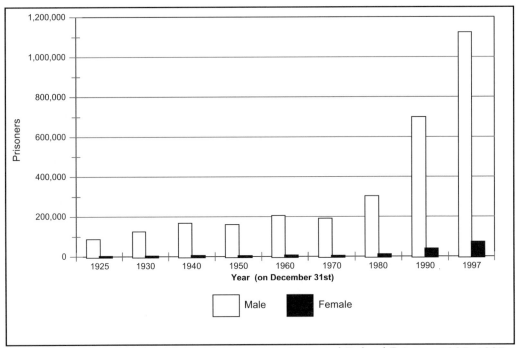

Figure 5. Number of Male and Female Inmates in State and Federal Prisons, 1925–1997
Source: Bureau of Justice Statistics, 1999b, pages 488–489 and *Bureau of Justice Statistics* 1999c, page 9.

velop. They included special departments in men's prisons, prison farm camps in the South, and institutions separate from men's prisons, without the reformatory architecture and philosophy.

The white working-class women sent to reformatories fit the popular view of women who could be "reformed" into ladies, but the reformatory system discriminated against African American women, who comprised the majority of the female felons in custodial facilities. Stereotypically portrayed as more masculine than white women, African American women offenders were presumably beyond redemption and, therefore, unsuitable for reformatory training.

Women's reformatories were phased out in the late 1930s; after the Depression, states could not afford to incarcerate misdemeanants. Only female felons were left in women's state prisons, although the cottages and traditional sex-role training remained. However, heightened attention to women's issues since the 1960s and an unprecedented women's imprisonment rate by the end of the 1990s resulted in a movement to achieve parity in the treatment of male and female prisoners. Advocates of parity urge that women prisoners be treated as well as male prisoners—though not identically—to allow for gender differences.

Women prisoners have used the courts to address sex discrimination, arguing that gender disparities in penal institutions violate the Equal Protection Clause of the Fourteenth Amendment. These suits have addressed inequalities in basic education, vocational training and work, medical care, and access to legal assistance. Whether due to these suits or other factors, there have been some changes in the number and quality of programs for women prisoners. Most women's prisons today provide basic education and vocational training, and some even include a few nontraditional programs such as auto repair, carpentry, and plumbing. Designed to address women's special needs, parenting classes and child visitation programs are offered by many women's prisons, although few

serve more than a small fraction of the inmate population.

Even with such improvements, however, 20 years after a decision favorable to women prisoners in *Glover v. Johnson* (1979), Michigan's sex discrimination suit, disparities are still being litigated. Claimants argue that Michigan has not provided programs for women equal to those for men. Women continue to be more controlled than men in prison. According to a Texas study, women are given more disciplinary reports for very minor infractions, and they are punished more harshly than men (McClellan 1994). Nationwide, imprisoned women still do not have services, educational programs, or facilities comparable to those of men.

Prison administrators argue that it is too expensive to provide the full range of programs available to men for a relatively small number of women (see Figure 5). Small numbers also result in there being only one institution for women in some states, making it more difficult for women than men to have access to their families and social services, and further reducing women's opportunity to participate in furloughs or community-based pre-release programs. Moreover, vocational education programs still emphasize stereotypical female occupations such as clerical work and cosmetology, neither of which is likely to lead to an adequate income for women and their dependent children (Morash, Haarr, and Rucker 1994).

In a political climate that emphasizes a "get tough" approach to crime, efforts to overcome gender discrimination have ironically led to the unanticipated consequence that Chesney-Lind calls "vengeful equity" (1998:68). Although women's prison programs still are inferior to those of men, women now have equal opportunity to be on chain gangs, go to boot camps, serve long mandatory sentences for drug offenses, and be executed at the same rate as men. While conditions are not as bad as they were for women in the first penitentiaries, critics of the equality/parity movement warn that pure equality is resulting in the "worst of both worlds" for imprisoned women. *See also* IN-CARCERATED MOTHERS; PRISON DISCIPLINE; PRISON TREATMENT PROGRAMS, LEGAL ISSUES IN; PRISONS, HEALTH CARE IN; PRISONS, TREAT-MENT PROGRAMS IN; SEXUAL ABUSE OF PRISON-ERS.

Further Reading: Butler 1997, *Gendered Justice in the American West;* "Female Offenders" 1998; Pollock-Byrne 1990, *Women, Prison, and Crime.*

Marianne Fisher-Giorlando

Glueck, Eleanor T. (1898–1972)

Born and raised in New York City, Eleanor Touroff Glueck was educated at Barnard College (A.B., 1920), the New York School of Social Work (diploma in community organization, 1921), and Harvard University (Ed.D., 1925). She married Sheldon Glueck (1896–1980) in 1922. In the late 1920s, the Gluecks began their life-long affiliation with Harvard Law School, where Eleanor was a researcher and Sheldon a professor. The Gluecks codirected large-scale research projects on the causes of delinquency, adult offending, and recidivism, and together published over 200 books, articles, and monographs. For their contributions to criminology, they received numerous awards and honors from universities and professional organizations in the United States and abroad.

The Gluecks' four major research projects involved over 3,000 human subjects and a then-novel research approach: longitudinal study of subjects using multiple sources, such as institutional records and interviews with a wide circle of informants and the subjects themselves. One of these projects, *Five Hundred Delinquent Women* (1934), was among the first to study recidivism among female offenders.

The findings from their best-known and most methodologically sophisticated project were published in *Unraveling Juvenile Delinquency (UJD)* (1950) and *Delinquents and Non-Delinquents in Perspective* (1968).

UJD involved the longitudinal study, from childhood to age 32, of 500 delinquent, low-income boys matched with 500 nondelinquent, low-income boys, on the basis of in-telligence, ethnicity/race, and area of residence. The Gluecks found that, even in poverty, children who enjoyed a stable and nurturing family life were much less prone to delinquency than those who did not. Another major finding of the *UJD* project involved the age-crime relationship: aging, with its attendant life changes, promoted desistance from offending, although the earlier the onset of delinquency, the longer offending persisted.

In the United States and abroad, the Gluecks' studies and publications (some of which were translated) were familiar to a diverse audience of academics, justice system officials, and the public. The Gluecks were always interested in practical applications of their research, creating prediction tables used by juvenile and criminal justice agencies to assess the likelihood of recidivism and propensity to delinquency. These tables were also published in mass media outlets, allowing parents to assess the risk of delinquency in their own children. In addition to the projects on which the Gluecks collaborated, which consumed most of her professional life, Eleanor Glueck individually researched and published on topics such as parenthood training, delinquency prediction, the role of schools in servicing and strengthening neighborhoods, and the benefits of females serving in police forces.

In attempting to explain what causes delinquency and offending, the Gluecks' research was informed by sociology, psychology, and biology. The Gluecks were critical of narrow theoretical approaches to the study of crime, while criminologists rooted in single theoretical perspectives criticized what they perceived as the Gluecks' atheoretical approach. In the 1960s and 1970s, sociological explanations of crime gained wide currency among criminologists, causing the Gluecks' multifactor, empirically driven approach to be discredited. In recent years, however, the multifactor approach—and in particular, study of family life factors—has regained legitimacy among criminologists, prompting the rediscovery of Eleanor and Sheldon Glueck's body of work. In addition, the archives of the Gluecks' rich data sets (particularly *UJD*) are being used by contemporary researchers to test a variety of new criminological, psychological, and sociological theories.

Further Reading: Laub and Smith 1995, "Eleanor Touroff Glueck"; Sampson and Laub 1993, *Crime in the Making.*

Jinney S. Smith

Graham, Barbara (1923–1955)

Barbara Graham was one of four women executed in California's gas chamber before the United States Supreme Court ruled the death penalty unconstitutional in 1972. She died at age 32, at 11:42 AM on June 3, 1955, after two stays of execution. After the second delay she reportedly cried out: "Why do they torture me? I was ready at 10 o'clock" (*Time*, 13 June 1955). Graham, who was condemned to die for her part in the pistol-whipping and strangulation of Mabel Monahan of Burbank, California, claimed she was framed for the "caper" and steadfastly maintained her innocence to the end.

In prison, Graham was known for her beauty, style, and sardonic wit, but she may best be remembered today for the Hollywood version of her life and death played by a tough-talking Susan Hayward in the 1958 blockbuster movie *I Want to Live!* Despite the brutality of the crime for which she was convicted, Graham won the respect, if not the hearts, of certain newspapers reporters and prison officials, including "death watch" officer Joseph Ferretti, who brought her slippers to wear the night before she died and served her a hot fudge sundae as a last requested meal. Ferretti told a newspaper reporter that after he strapped her into the gas chamber, patted her on the knee, and backed through the door, he went home and wept (*Marin Independent Journal*, 12 December 1984). Executing a woman then was as much a novelty as it is today, and Graham, during those months leading up to her death, became a local media celebrity with an extra edition of the *San Francisco Call-Bulletin* published the morning she died. It carried a picture of her, composed and looking straight ahead, as she was transported by car to the gas chamber.

Graham became a ward of the court in her early teenage years when she was committed to the Ventura School for Girls in Ventura, California, for being "wayward and unmanageable." She married several times and had three sons, including her youngest child, Tommy, who occasionally visited her in prison and is pictured with her in various newspaper accounts of the time. Initially sent to the state's women's prison in Corona, California, Graham was later moved north to the all-male San Quentin Prison near San Francisco, reportedly for security reasons based on reports that her life was in danger. There, in a specially prepared cell with a cordoned off "bedroom" and a sitting area, Graham chain-smoked, read poetry, and listened to classical music on a Victrola she was allowed to keep in her cell. Prison psychiatrists examined her frequently during those days leading up to her execution and found her to be, among other observations, "attractive," above average in intelligence with an IQ of 114, "well nourished," and free of mental illness. She always insisted that doctors "just put down housewife" as her occupation on medical forms. (Papers on Barbara Graham and her case are maintained in the Barbara Graham Archives, San Quentin Museum Association, San Quentin, California.)

In 1999, there were 8 women on California's death row, and 48 women nationally under sentence of death. No California woman had been executed since 1962, although the death penalty was reinstated in 1976. *See also* DEATH PENALTY; DEATH ROW.

Further Reading: Freeman-Davis 1961, *The Desperate and the Damned.*

Teresa Allen

Greenham Common Women's Peace Camp

The Greenham Common women's peace camp, the most visible and sustained example of British women's politics in the 1980s, mobilized thousands of women in protest against nuclear weapons, leading to mass

Protestors at the Greenham Common Women's Peace Camp, 1987. ©*Reuters/Corbis.*

arrests and heightened public awareness of the political dimensions of definitions of deviance and criminality. Media coverage tended to depict the women as sexually deviant (lesbians) and negligent mothers, while their actions were criminalized by the local authorities.

In August 1981, 36 women, 4 men, and 3 children marched 110 miles from Cardiff in Wales to the Royal Air Force base at Greenham Common in Berkshire to protest NATO's decision to site American Cruise missiles there. On arrival, they set up the peace camp outside the main gate. This became known as Yellow Gate as more protesters arrived and built camps at other entrances to the base, all named after the colors of the rainbow. The camps consisted mainly of "benders"—plastic sheets draped over branches, which were regularly bulldozed by the local council.

The camp was declared a women-only space in 1982, and feminist politics became more apparent, with no hierarchy in decision-making, little formal organization, and an emphasis on nonviolent protest. The next two years saw a sustained program of action with women regularly blockading the gates and breaking into the base. This led to arrests, and women were charged with offenses such as breach of the peace and criminal damage. Some of the women continued their protest in the local courts by refusing to take the oath or singing instead of answering questions. Magistrates imposed fines and prison sentences.

Greenham became a site of symbolic feminist protest. For example, 30,000 women linked hands around the nine-mile perimeter fence to "embrace the base." The barbed wire fence was also regularly "darned" with colored wool and decorated with flowers, photos, toys, and peace symbols.

In 1991, the last Cruise missiles left the base. By 1999, all of the Greenham Common women had left except for three who continued to campaign for a nuclear-free future. *See also* DEVIANCE AND REFORM, HISTORICAL OVERVIEW OF, BRITAIN.

Further Reading: Junor 1997, *Greenham Common Women's Peace Camp;* Roseneil 1995, *Disarming Patriarchy.*

Shirley Koster

H

Harris, Jean (1923–)

In 1981, Jean Harris was convicted of the shooting death of physician Herman Tarnower, author of the then-popular diet book, *The Complete Scarsdale Medical Diet*. She was sentenced to 15 years to life at the Bedford Hills Correctional Facility in Westchester, New York. The circumstances surrounding Harris's trial and subsequent incarceration are not typical of women in the criminal justice system, although—like many other women who kill—she is responsible for the death of an individual with whom she was intimately involved. But there the similarity ends. Harris came from a privileged background, had received an elite education at Smith College, and, at the time of Tarnower's death, was the headmistress of the exclusive Madeira School in Virginia.

Harris has maintained that the shooting death of Tarnower was accidental; she claimed at her trial that she had returned to the home of her former lover to say goodbye and then commit suicide. She was depressed and angry about his affair with a younger woman and was suffering from withdrawal from a strong amphetamine that Tarnower had prescribed. However, there was a physical struggle during the visit, her gun discharged, and Tarnower was killed.

Because of Tarnower's fame and Harris's background and position, the trial was a media event, widely covered in the United States and abroad. A movie entitled *The People vs.* *Jean Harris* was made in 1981 based on the trial testimony.

While incarcerated, Harris wrote three books about her trial and prison experiences: *Stranger in Two Worlds* (1986), *They Always Call Us Ladies* (1988), and *Marking Time: Letters from Jean Harris to Shana Alexander* (1991). These books provide insight into her life and the circumstances that led to the death of Tarnower. Her writing also provides an inside view of some of the major issues confronting female prisoners, such as health care, rehabilitation, inmate relationships with correctional personnel, and the welfare of dependent children. In prison, Harris established herself as an authority on the special problems faced by children of incarcerated women.

Aware that children of prisoners lack parental nurturing and often become offenders, Harris taught parenting and sex education classes to incarcerated mothers at Bedford Hills. She encouraged pregnant female inmates to participate in the facility's nursery program, which allowed them to keep their infants in the prison nursery. Harris established the Children's Center at Bedford Hills, a program designed to increase the amount of time that incarcerated mothers have with their children. Proceeds from Harris's first book go to The Children of Bedford Fund, a nonprofit foundation that pays for the education of children of inmates.

After serving 12 years of her sentence, Harris was granted clemency by the New York State Parole Board on December 29, 1992, and paroled in early 1993. Since her release from prison, she has continued to write, raise money, and lecture on behalf of inmates' children. *See also* BEDFORD HILLS REFORMATORY; INCARCERATED MOTHERS.

Further Reading: S. Alexander 1983, *Very Much a Lady*; Trilling 1981, *Mrs. Harris.*

Becky L. Tatum

Hindley, Myra (1942–)

Britain's longest-serving woman prisoner, Myra Hindley was sentenced to two life sentences in May 1966 for two counts of murder and for harboring her accomplice, Ian Brady, after a third killing. Subsequent confessions revealed that together they killed five young people between the ages of 10 and 17, burying them on Saddleworth Moor outside Manchester and earning the label of the "Moors Murderers." Influenced by Nazism, de Sade, and Dostoevsky, Hindley and Brady sexually tortured a 10-year-old girl; when audiovisual evidence of this torture was pre-

Myra Hindley, 1966. Hulton Getty/Archive Photos.

sented during their trial, Hindley became Britain's most notorious and reviled woman.

Offending public assumptions of women's maternal nature, Hindley's photograph on arrest (bleached blonde hair, scowling features, defiant stare), her sanity, and her lesbianism all compounded the image of a deviant woman as pure evil. Public antipathy has repeatedly obstructed Hindley's bids for parole, despite her fulfillment of normal requirements. Her case raises significant legal issues around the punishment of women who do not match the standard picture of femininity. *See also* DEVIANCE AND REFORM, HISTORICAL OVERVIEW OF, BRITAIN; MADONNA/WHORE DICHOTOMY.

Further Reading: Bradley 1995, "Myra Hindley"; Cameron and Frazer 1987, *The Lust to Kill.*

Oliver Charles Phillips

HIV and AIDS in Prison

Incarcerated women are more likely than incarcerated men to be infected with the human immunodeficiency virus (HIV), which causes acquired immunodeficiency syndrome (AIDS). According to the U.S. Bureau of Justice Statistics, in 1996, 3.5 percent of women incarcerated in state prisons were HIV-positive, compared with 2.3 percent of male state inmates (see Table H). If the number of women incarcerated continues to increase as dramatically as it has in the last 15 years, the incidence of HIV-infected female inmates will be much greater in the next 10 years.

The overrepresentation of women with AIDS is explained, in part, by intravenous drug use. Women drug users constitute a significant percentage of the female inmate population, and a large number of women are currently serving sentences for drug offenses. Conditions where drug users share needles without proper sterilization foster the transmission of the disease. Additionally, on the streets, many women who are illicit drug users engage in sex work in order to secure drugs or the money to buy drugs, or they may have heterosexual partners who are also intravenous drug users. The transmission of

Table H. U.S. Prisoners Known to Be HIV-Positive, by Sex and Region, 1996

Region	Male Prisoners		Female Prisoners	
	Number of HIV Cases	Percent of Total Custody Population	Number of HIV Cases	Percent of Total Custody Population
All Regions	21,799	2.3	2,135	3.5
Northeast	10,985	7.2	1,105	13.0
Midwest	1,741	1.0	633	1.3
South	7,375	1.8	787	3.0
West	1,698	0.8	110	0.7

Source: Adapted from Bureau of Justice Statistics 1999b, *Sourcebook of Criminal Justice Statistics, 1998,* page 524.

the virus from an infected partner can occur through unprotected sexual activity.

Sexual activity and drug use do not necessarily cease once women are incarcerated, and the risk of infection continues. In prison, there are also other risks associated with contracting HIV. For example, inmate tattooing frequently involves the use of unsterilized needles that can spread the virus.

Prison systems have implemented a number of policies concerned with inmates who are HIV-infected or have AIDS. Current procedures include testing inmates for the virus, deciding whether to segregate infected inmates or house them with the general inmate population, developing and providing AIDS education and prevention programs, supervising the treatment regimen for infected inmates, and establishing the process for compassionate release (also known as medical parole) for terminally ill AIDS victims. One difficulty associated with treating AIDS inmates in a prison setting has to do with the diverse medications that are required. Inmates often have to take 30 or more pills a day at specified time intervals. Such treatment protocols cannot always be strictly maintained in a prison setting. In addition, the cost of treating inmates who have been diagnosed with AIDS in a prison setting is exorbitant. As a strategy to prevent the spread of the disease, a small number of prisons now authorize the distribution of condoms to inmates and/or bleach to sterilize needles.

Because most inmates will be released to the community after completing their sentences, education and prevention programs appear to have the greatest likelihood of success against the HIV virus. Prisons continue to develop new education initiatives and to include both inmates and staff in the process. These programs provide information about the risk of infection and the kinds of treatment available. Institutional life also provides an opportunity to deliver sustained treatment to HIV-infected inmates. However, much depends on the availability of treatment and support services once the inmate is released into the community. Rather than exclusively relying on institutional programming, there are efforts to establish programs and services that involve a long-term collaborative community strategy that incorporates social support, education, drug treatment, and medical care while the women are in prison and after they return to the community.

In 1998, the United States Supreme Court decided two cases that may affect inmates with the HIV infection. In *Pennsylvania Department of Corrections v. Yeskey* (118 S. Ct. 1952), the Court determined that the Americans with Disabilities Act (ADA) of 1990 protects disabled inmates. In *Bragdon v. Abbott* (118 S. Ct. 2196), the justices established that individuals who are HIV-infected can be covered under the ADA. These rulings may bring considerable change to the treatment of prisoners with the HIV infections and AIDS in the years ahead. *See also* COMPASSIONATE RELEASE FROM PRISON; PRISONER CHARACTERISTICS; PRISONS, HEALTH CARE IN.

Further Reading: Kantor 1998, "The AIDS Knowledge Base"; MacDougall 1998, "HIV/AIDS behind Bars."

Alida V. Merlo

Holloway Prison

The New City Prison at Holloway in north London, founded in 1852 and constructed on the then-new radial principle, originally housed men, women, and children, but it became a prison for women only in 1903 and remains one today. Over the course of the twentieth century, it was a focal point for battles over the treatment of women prisoners. A secure prison, devised for the silent system, Holloway was regarded almost from the first as unsuitable for women, who were characteristically defined as unsophisticated, petty offenders, and particularly so during the rise of the new therapeutic ideology of the 1960s.

The physical structure of Holloway came to be dismissed as an anachronistic obstacle to an enlightened regime, and a case was made for its replacement by a more appropriate institution, a "secure hospital" that might eventually be ceded to the Health Service. The new Holloway, it was decided, would have to be built phase by phase as the old prison was razed. It would be an "anti-panopticon," with an open, green center rather than a central surveillance point, and it would be arrayed as a therapeutic continuum, consisting of a string of small, linked, flexible spaces that plotted a moral career for the inmate. Externally, the new institution was to be a prison that would not look like a prison, its boundaries with the outer world being designed to be as slight and reassuring as minimum security would allow.

By 1970, the old Holloway was undergoing simultaneous demolition and replacement on site. Such a difficult operation took time, and it was only in 1977 that the inmates were transferred and in 1985 that the new building was finished. By the 1980s, however, the original authors of the proposal had all moved on, ideologies had shifted, the initial planning assumptions had almost all been modified, the inmate population had grown in size and changed in composition, and an experimental building experienced as a mass of confrontational spaces, hazardous bends, and contested boundaries was put to use as a conventional prison. Management, officers, and inmates competed for control over territory inside a edifice that did not permit easy cohabitation. A spiral of conflict, spatial segregation, and repression ensued that fostered an image of the prison as brutal and its inmates as "disturbed," and Holloway become a scandalous icon of state oppression.

So crisis-laden did Holloway become that, by 1985, a charismatic male governor was appointed expressly to "open up" the prison. He placed men in key positions to undermine the cohesiveness of the women staff, and he reintroduced education and periods of free association. There was to be continuing strife about authority and control, and one outcome was the first full-blown prison officers' strike in England. The governor maintained the regime for six weeks in the summer of 1988 with only a skeletal staff, proving for a while, and amidst publicity, that women inmates could be "reasonable" and "co-operative" and that repression and spatial exclusion were not imperative. The prison officers returned, however, and the governor was transferred as a face-saving measure for the returning strikers. Since that time, the prison has tended to lurch between equilibrium and crisis under the gaze of observers who continue to see in it an important representation of the state's posture towards criminal women. *See also* FEMALE CRIME, BRITAIN; WOMEN IN PRISON, ENGLAND AND WALES.

Further Reading: Casale 1989, *Women Inside;* R. P. Dobash, Dobash, and Gutteridge 1986, *The Imprisonment of Women*; Rock 1996, *Reconstructing a Women's Prison.*

Paul Rock

Homicide, Filipino Women in Australia as Victims of

Filipino women residing in Australia are almost six times more likely than other Australian women to be victims of homicide. Homicides of Filipino women in Australia are distinctive. Offenders are typically men who are not Filipino; that is, unlike other homicides, these are not intra-cultural but inter-cultural. Generally, there is a large age difference between the partners, with the man consistently older. The man, unlike the woman, has frequently had prior marriages. Often the couple met in the Philippines.

As in the case of homicides of women generally, Filipino women are typically killed by a man with whom they have been in an intimate relationship. Often there has been a history of prior violence by the man against the woman, and separation and disputes about child custody may heighten the risk.

Within Australia, Filipino women face obstacles in dealing with domestic violence. They often have limited access to service provision and to information about legal rights and entitlements. They may also suffer the effects of racism, including disadvantages in the employment market.

The international context also contributes to their increased vulnerability to homicide. Large numbers of Filipino women immigrate to other parts of the world for work and marriage. Emigration is actively promoted by the Philippine government because of the poor conditions within that country and as a means of earning foreign exchange from Filipinos living abroad.

Due to Australian immigration policy, the majority of Filipino women enter Australia as sponsored partners of Australian resident men. Some men actively seek inter-cultural relationships. There are a number of commercial agencies and informal networks, including some on the Internet, that facilitate men's access to women from the Philippines and other countries. These operate internationally and are not confined to Australia. Some of these agencies also promote sex tourism.

Commonly, these services use racialized and sexualized imagery to promote inter-cultural relationships by representing Filipino (and other Asian) women as compliant, loyal, accommodating, and ultra-feminine. Such images, reinforced by other media, can function to justify men's domination of women by implying that it is "natural" for Filipino (or Asian) women to be submissive. Serious violence may arise in relationships where men seek to enforce their stereotyped image of Filipino femininity and the women resist.

It is likely that Filipino women also face an increased vulnerability to homicide in other countries where men engage in inter-cultural relationships based on myths about the submissive nature of Filipino women. In addition, such imagery may contribute to the abuse of Filipino women immigrant workers in numerous countries. Filipino organizations actively work to challenge such misrepresentations. *See also* HOMICIDE VICTIMS; HOMICIDE VICTIMS AND OFFENDERS, AUSTRALIA.

Further Reading: Cunneen and Stubbs 1997, *Gender, "Race" and International Relations;* A. Wallace 1986, *Homicide: The Social Reality.*

Julie Stubbs and Chris Cunneen

Homicide, USA

In any given year, only a small percentage of all people arrested for homicide in the United States are women. *Uniform Crime Report (UCR)* statistics show that in 1998, only 11.2 percent (1,385) of the people arrested for murder or willful killing were female. In contrast, 10,950 were male. Similarly, in any given year, only a very small number of all women living in the United States are arrested for homicide. From 1981 to 1997, for every 100,000 women, each year fewer than 3 were arrested for homicide, a rate reflected in Figure 6. In contrast, over the same period of time for every 100,000 U.S. men, each year between 14 and 21 were arrested for homicide.

Further, in any given year, homicide represents only a very small proportion of all the crimes for which women are arrested. In 1998, women were arrested for 2.2 million crimes, including 81,072 violent crimes, but less that 0.1 percent of the total arrests were for homicide. Notably, only a slightly higher proportion (0.1 percent) of all arrests of men that year were for homicide.

Women arrested in the United States for homicide are less likely than their male counterparts to have a record of prior criminal activity. In addition, they are more likely to have acted alone, to have killed someone with whom they shared an intimate relationship, and to have killed in a domestic situation.

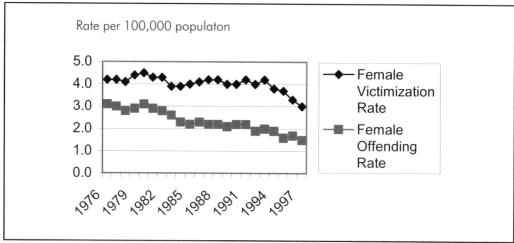

Rate per 100,000 populaton

Figure 6. Female Homicide, Offending and Victimization, USA, 1976–1997
Source: Derived from Fox and Zawitz 1998, "Homicide Trends."

Historically, studies of homicide by women have focused on women who kill in domestic settings, particularly on battered women who kill abusive partners. However, women also kill for a variety of other reasons. Some women kill their children, most often through abuse or neglect. Others kill in the furtherance of other crimes, most often offenses involving money or illicit drugs.

Criminologists have tried to understand why women have a lower homicide offending rate than that of men and why their patterns of killing are somewhat different. Some theorists argue that if women are liberated from their traditional roles, their rates and types of violence will more closely approximate men's as their social, economic, and cultural opportunities became more like those of men. Others argue that even if women are given the same opportunities as men, their behaviors will continue to differ because gendered traits are unchangeable. *See also* DOMESTIC VIOLENCE AGAINST WOMEN, EPIDEMIOLOGY OF; DOMESTIC VIOLENCE BY WOMEN.

Further Reading: Brownstein, Spunt, Crimmins, Goldstein, and Langley 1994, "Changing Patterns of Lethal Violence"; A. Jones 1996, *Women Who Kill*; Rasche 1990, "Early Models for Contemporary Thought on Domestic Violence."

Henry H. Brownstein

Homicide Victims

According to official U.S. statistics, in 1998, there were 14,088 homicide victims, 3,419 (24 percent) of whom were females. This figure represents a slight increase from previous years in the 1990s when females represented 23 percent of all homicide victims. The United States continues to have the highest overall criminal homicide rate of any industrialized country in the world. As Figure 6 indicates, the female victimization rate is higher than the female offending rate in homicides.

Popular stereotypes notwithstanding, the most frequent homicide victims are males, specifically young, non-white males who are killed by other young, non-white males. Males are also the most common killers of women; in 1998, 9 out of every 10 female victims were murdered by men. As in the male case, non-white females, especially African American women, are the most frequent female homicide victims. These victims, both male and female, are usually shot; firearms are the most commonly used weapon in American homicides.

Homicide victims typically know their assailant, but there are important gender differences in the nature of the relationship. For male murder victims, the perpetrator is most likely a friend or acquaintance. For female murder victims, the killer is often an intimate, such as a husband, former husband, or boy-friend. About one-third of female homicide victims are killed by intimate partners, often marking the lethal conclusion of a battering relationship. Although women do not kill very often, when they do, the victim is frequently a male intimate who is killed in response to a prior history of abuse. The context for female involvement in lethal violence, both as victims and perpetrators, is spousal violence.

The typical homicide develops somewhat spontaneously out of a fight, disagreement, or argument, which helps explain why most perpetrators are friends, acquaintances, and family members rather than strangers. Thus, criminal homicide is a process, not an event. A common homicide situation involves a weekend social gathering, where alcohol or other drugs are present, and two people who know each other get into a fight that escalates from words to violence; weapons appear, and one person ends up a homicide victim. For females, the most dangerous time is when they seek to end an abusive relationship by divorcing or leaving the abuser, which often precipitates a lethal response from the male. *See also* DOMESTIC VIOLENCE BY WOMEN; HOMICIDE, USA; HOMICIDE VICTIMS AND OFFENDERS, AUSTRALIA; SERIAL KILLERS; SERIAL KILLERS, VICTIMS OF; VICTIMIZATION PATTERNS, CANADA.

Further Reading: Harries 1997, *Serious Violence;* R. M. Holmes and Holmes 1994, *Murder in America;* Polk 1994, *When Men Kill;* M. D. Smith and Zahn 1999, *Homicide.*

Alexander Alvarez

Homicide Victims and Offenders, Australia

The rate of homicide in Australia in recent years has hovered around the level of 2.0 per 100,000 people in the general population. This rate is much lower than the rates observed in such high homicide countries as the United States and Mexico, but slightly higher than those of low homicide countries such as Norway and Japan.

In 1997, men were more likely than women to be homicide victims, with a rate of 2.2 victims per 100,000 males compared with 1.3 victims per 100,000 females. These levels have remained relatively constant over recent years (James and Carcach 1997).

Female murder victims tended to be younger than male victims. In 1997, the highest rate of victimization for females was in the group aged 15–19, while for males it was in the group aged 25–34. The offender was known to 64 percent of female victims, as compared with 49 percent of male victims. In other words, males are much more likely to be victimized by a stranger, a pattern seen in other countries as well.

Women make up a much smaller proportion of homicide offenders than they do homicide victims. Currently in Australia, women make up only 1 in 10 of homicide offenders (Mukherjee, Cook, and Leverett 1998). When women do kill, their victim is likely to be either their sexual partner or a natural child. In comparison, men's victims are likely to fall outside of the family network. When women kill their sexual partner, their violence is most often in reaction to precipitating violence by the male (Polk 1994).

Homicides involving child victims are unique because of the high proportion of women offenders. The proportion of women offenders involved varies with the age of the child victim. When a woman kills her child, the child is likely to be under the age of six. While women are approximately as likely as men to kill young children, after the age of 11 years, a child is unlikely to be killed by a woman. *See also* BATTERED WOMEN AND SELF-DEFENSE, AUSTRALIA; HOMICIDE, FILIPINO WOMEN IN AUSTRALIA AS VICTIMS OF; INFANTICIDE; VICTIMIZATION AND MANLY RITUALS, AUSTRALIA; VIOLENT CRIME VICTIMIZATIONS, AUSTRALIA.

Further Reading: Alder and Baker 1997, "Maternal Filicide"; Polk 1994, *When Men Kill;* Stubbs 1994, *Women, Male Violence and the Law*; A. Wallace 1986, *Homicide.*

Kenneth Polk

I

Imprisonment in the South, Pre–Civil War

Leading historians claim pre–Civil War imprisonment in the South was limited primarily to men. While it is true that few women could be found in pre–Civil War penitentiaries of Alabama, Georgia, Tennessee, and Virginia, Louisiana was an exception. Between 1835 and 1862, approximately 60 women were admitted to the Louisiana State Penitentiary at Baton Rouge. Women imprisoned in pre–Civil War Louisiana constituted an average of 5 percent of the total prison population during the 1850s, a percentage higher than most twentieth-century rates for women in Louisiana and elsewhere in the United States.

Although Maryland imprisoned slaves until 1818, Louisiana was the only Southern state to continue this practice. Consequently, in the 1850s, African American women always constituted at least 75 percent of the female offenders at the Baton Rouge penitentiary. Most imprisoned women were not from Louisiana. Only four of the slave prisoners had been born in Louisiana, and most of the white women were apparently immigrants from Ireland, Scotland, and Germany or migrants from northern states.

Sentencing patterns reveal an urban-rural dichotomy. Most slave women came from cotton and sugar plantations or smaller farms, while all the white women (except one from Baton Rouge) were sentenced in New Orleans.

The majority of slave women had been convicted of capital crimes—arson, poisoning, attempted poisoning, murder, and striking a white person. Substitution of life imprisonment for the death penalty (legislated in 1823) and commutation of death sentences saved some slave women from execution. In an offending pattern persistent into this century, most of the antebellum white women in Louisiana were convicted of property offenses—shoplifting, stealing clothing or cloth, receiving stolen goods, and counterfeiting. Their sentences ranged from six months to two years.

Seven white women had committed violent crimes; only three received a life sentence (two for homicide and one for arson). All three obtained early release; not one spent more than five years in the penitentiary. Of 13 slave women who received life sentences, only three were pardoned, one after three years. Free women of color served sentences more comparable to white women. Most sentences were from one to five years. The most common offense, being in the state illegally, was a result of their marginal status, for free women of color had to produce papers proving they were not slaves. Many incarcerated women were mothers. They left children behind or brought them to the penitentiary, and they conceived and bore children at the institution. Children born to slave women sentenced for life were auctioned at age 10 by the Baton Rouge sheriff. Profits were deposited in the free school fund.

Prisoners and their children, originally housed in two large rooms, were moved in 1857 into a new three-story facility with a wash-house and drying yard. Protecting these prisoners was not a priority. A fence was built around the facility to ensure the women did not distract men from their work. Although other southern states provided a matron, Louisiana's first matron of record in the penitentiary, Mrs. Elizabeth Edwards, was not hired until December 1860, 25 years after the first woman prisoner entered the institution. Technically sentenced to hard labor, the women did washing, ironing, and sewing, activities different from those of male prisoners, whose work contributed to the subsistence and profits of the institution.

Southern incarceration practices after the Civil War and into the present day reflect the early patterns. In 2000, the majority of Louisiana's imprisoned women are African Americans, just as before Emancipation. As in Louisiana's antebellum penitentiary, white women came and went; black women came to stay. *See also* SEXISM AND RACISM IN CRIMINAL JUSTICE POLICY; WOMEN'S PRISONS, HISTORY OF.

Further Reading: W. Crawford 1969, *Report on the Penitentiaries of the United States;* Fisher-Giorlando 1995, "Women in the Walls."

Marianne Fisher-Giorlando

Incarcerated Mothers

Of the women housed in jails and prisons, between 65 and 80 percent are mothers, the majority of them with children under the age of 18. As the population of women behind bars has increased, the number of children affected by the imprisonment of their mothers has also grown and in 1999 was estimated to be in excess of 100,000.

Due to the gendered nature of childcare, the imprisonment of a mother is usually much more disruptive to a child than the incarceration of a father. While 90 percent of the children of male inmates remain with their usual caretakers after their fathers' imprisonment,

the children of female inmates face disruption in where they live, where they attend school, and who their caretakers are. When their mothers go to prison, children usually end up residing with grandparents, fathers, or other relatives, or they come under state care in foster homes or group homes.

In addition to the penalties imposed by the criminal justice system on inmate mothers, incarceration may also bring the family to the attention of child welfare agencies. In some jurisdictions, a woman's sentencing to more than one year in prison is equivalent to an act of child abandonment (Genty 1995). This sets the legal system in motion to terminate legal custody. Termination of parental rights suggests that the parent is unfit to care for the child and frees the child for adoption.

Demonstrating fitness to care for children while incarcerated is a significant challenge for inmate mothers, especially for those with few community resources. Due to persistent drug use and the inability to reject criminal life styles, about one-third of inmate mothers lose custody of their children (M. Martin 1997).

Separation from children and the attendant concerns about their well-being are the major stresses of incarceration for women. In some cases, visiting with children to maintain the family bond is complicated by the long distances of women's correctional facilities from women's homes. Nurseries and visiting programs that include overnight stays for children are available in only a small number of prisons. These programs have beneficial effects not just for the maintenance of family bonds but also for demonstrating to child welfare and other agencies that the mother is working for family reunification (Boudouris 1996).

Maternal incarceration has both short-term and long-term destructive effects on children. These include psychological distress, traumatic stress reactions, delinquency, school problems, substance abuse, and early sexual behavior. To mitigate these problems, researchers, psychologists, and professional organizations recommend that community-based programs be provided for incarcerated mothers and their children in lieu of incarceration. Moreover, prison workers must recognize the special needs of inmate mothers and their children. *See also* HARRIS, JEAN.

Further Reading: Enos 1997, "Managing Motherhood in Prison"; Gabel and Johnston 1995, *Children of Incarcerated Parents;* Garcia Coll, Surrey, Buccio-Notaro, and Molla 1998, "Incarcerated Mothers: Crimes and Punishments."

Sandra L. Enos

Incest Victims

Incest is a form of child sexual abuse that occurs within the child's family. Among sexually abused girls, between 33 and 50 percent of perpetrators are family members, whereas 10 to 20 percent of sexually abused boys are assaulted by family members. The most common perpetrators of intra-familial abuse of girls are fathers, stepfathers, uncles or cousins, brothers, and grandfathers. The vast majority of incest perpetrators are male, but mothers and other female relatives also commit incest. Fathers' involvement in early caretaking may make them less likely to sexually abuse their daughters (Finkelhor 1994; Kendall-Tackett and Marshall 1998).

Unique legal issues occur when a child is sexually abused within the family. The non-abusing parent may have to choose between the child and the abuser. A separation or divorce may ensue. The highest-profile cases are those in which allegations of incest are made during a custody dispute. Despite the allegations of false charges in such cases, false allegations appear to be fairly rare. In one study of 9,000 divorces, only 2 percent (180 cases) involved allegations of incest, and of those 180 cases, only between 9 and 14 of them were determined to be false reports—less than 1 percent of the total number of divorces studied. Further, professionals who regularly evaluate children report that only a small percentage make false allegations of abuse, with the smallest percentage occurring among preschool age children.

Many factors contribute to the severity of the incest experience. Sexual abuse by a biological relative is not automatically more traumatic than abuse by a non-blood relative, especially if the victim is emotionally close to the perpetrator. For example, girls might be seriously affected by a stepfather's abuse even though he is not related to them by blood. Other factors that make the experience severe include sexual penetration (oral, vaginal, or anal), use of force, long duration and frequent contact, and lack of support from a non-abusive parent. Incest may start earlier than other forms of child sexual abuse, go on longer, and involve increasingly more serious sexual acts.

A range of symptoms appear among incest victims as children and adults. Severity of the experience is related to the severity of the symptoms. Symptoms among preschoolers include anxiety, nightmares, and inappropriate sexual behavior. Among school-age children, symptoms include fear, mental illness, aggression, nightmares, school problems, hyperactivity, and regression. For adolescents, symptoms include depression, withdrawal, suicidal or self-injurious behaviors, physical complaints, illegal acts, running away, and substance abuse.

Among adults, depression is the most commonly reported symptom. Relationship problems are also common, and they in turn can affect parent-child relations, relations with partners (including increased risk for revictimization), and availability of effective social support. Substance abuse, dissociative behaviors, and eating disorders also appear in the victims of incest. *See also* CHILD WITNESSES; SEXUAL ABUSE OF CHILDREN.

Further Reading: Herman 1994, *Trauma and Recovery*; D. E. H. Russell 1986, *The Secret Trauma.*

Kathleen A. Kendall-Tackett

Infanticide

Infanticide is one of the most common forms of homicide by women. The term "infanticide" is usually defined as the killing of a child less than one year of age by his/her mother, and that definition is adopted here. However, the term is also sometimes used to cover the killing of a child under one year of age by anyone, or the killing of a child of any age by anyone, or the killing of a disabled infant.

"Infanticide" is a specific form of "filicide," the killing of a child (of any age) by a parent or parent substitute. The discussion below focuses on filicide, with an emphasis on infanticide.

Studies reach different conclusions as to whether women or men constitute a greater proportion of filicide offenders. Some studies find a greater proportion of men, others a greater proportion of women, while some studies find similar proportions. It should be remembered, however, that women have much more time "at risk," since they are much more likely than men to be the sole or primary caregivers of children.

The research also indicates that the sex of the child does not have any significant impact on the risk of filicide in Western countries. However, in some non-Western countries such as India and China, girl children are reported to be at much higher risk of filicide than boy children, due to traditional social attitudes about girls' lesser worth.

The risk of filicide is generally highest for children under one year and declines steadily with age. Women are particularly likely to kill children aged under one year, with their filicide rate declining sharply thereafter. One of the most common forms of female filicide is neonaticide, the killing of a newborn child within 24 hours of birth. This typically involves a young single girl who becomes pregnant unintentionally, conceals and denies her pregnancy, and gives birth alone at home. The baby dies either from neglect or an act of violence shortly after the birth. In contrast to women, men are generally most likely to kill children slightly older than one year (1–4 years).

Some countries such as Canada, England, Wales, New Zealand, and certain Australian states have laws prohibiting infanticide as a special type of homicide, but no American states have laws of this type. Jurisdictions with infanticide legislation generally define the offense in terms of a woman killing a child of her own who is under age one when the balance of her mind is disturbed because of not having fully recovered from the effects of childbirth or lactation. Section 178 of the New Zealand *Crimes Act* 1961 has an interesting variation on this, in covering a child aged up to 10 years killed when the offender has not recovered from the effect of giving birth of that or *any other* child, or lactation, or any disorder *consequent* upon childbirth or lactation. A lower penalty applies if a woman is convicted of infanticide rather than murder.

In practice, women convicted of infanticide almost always receive a noncustodial and/or psychiatric sentence. In countries such as England, Wales, and Australia, this is also true of most women who kill older children, although they are at greater risk of a custodial term. American women who kill their children are more likely to be sentenced to prison (often for some time) than are women in other countries. Men who kill their children—in whatever jurisdiction—usually receive a prison sentence.

Feminist and other writers are sharply divided as to whether jurisdictions with infanticide laws should retain, amend, or abolish them. Another debate concerns the advisability of introducing such laws in the United States.

The medical basis for infanticide legislation—the notion that female infant killing is caused by a mental disorder due to disturbed hormones at childbirth—has been clearly discredited. It is now known that the causes are primarily social and psychological rather than hormonal. For example, the stresses of childcare, lack of social support, unrealistic expectations of parenthood, and personality problems can all lead to maternal infanticide. Fathers, too, kill very young children, often for similar reasons.

The basis for the infanticide provisions is unsatisfactory for two reasons. Firstly, not all women who kill their infants are mentally ill; in one English sample, for example, mental illness accounted for only half of the cases (Wilczynski 1997:157). Secondly, very few women suffer from the extreme hormonally based disorder "puerperal psychosis" after childbirth; new mothers are much more likely to suffer from "postnatal depression," a disorder whose causes are primarily psychosocial.

Since the legislation's medical basis is outdated, some writers argue that it serves no purpose. Some view infanticide laws as evidence of the legal system being inappropriately "chivalrous" to women by relying on outdated notions of women's frailty. Feminist scholars have argued that the legislation reinforces stereotypes of women (particularly violent women) as "mad," driven by their hormones, and not responsible for their behavior. Feminists also argue that such assumptions mask the social causes of child-killing, such as women's disproportionate childcare responsibilities. On the other hand, some have suggested that the leniency granted to women via infanticide is justifiable for pragmatic reasons because of their greater child-rearing role. Some favor amending the legislation to include "the circumstances *consequent* upon the birth" (in addition to the birth itself, as in New Zealand) and thus incorporating the social causes of child-killing and better reflecting court practice.

In sum, while patterns of infanticide are similar in the United States and other countries, legislation is not. Although infanticide legislation has been a topic of legal debate in the United States, there is no clear indication that it will be enacted and no sign of what form it would take. *See also* CHILD ABUSE BY WOMEN; FEMALE CRIME, HISTORY OF, EUROPE; FEMALE CRIME, HISTORY OF, USA; HOMICIDE, USA; HOMICIDE VICTIMS AND OFFENDERS, AUSTRALIA.

Further Reading: Maier-Katkin and Ogle 1993, "A Rationale for Infanticide Laws"; Reece 1991, "Mothers Who Kill"; Wilczynski 1997, *Child Homicide*.

Ania Wilczynski

International Association of Women Police

The International Association of Women Police (IAWP), originally called the International Association of Policewomen (IAP), was founded in 1915 by Alice Stebbins Wells. The first American woman to officially hold the rank of sworn police officer, Wells organized the association and served as its first president. In 1916, the organization developed and adopted a charter, and a decade later it was incorporated as the International Association of Policewomen. In 1932, the IAP dissolved due to the Depression and policewomen's lack of interest in maintaining a work identity separate from that of policemen.

At the Women Peace Officers of California meeting held in San Diego in 1956, Lois Lundell Higgins (a veteran Chicago policewoman) and others resurrected and reorganized the IAP as the International Association of Women Police. Higgins envisioned the IAWP as an information clearinghouse and a way to professionalize policing for women.

In 1915, the IAP had supported establishment of separate women's bureaus within police departments because they provided advancement opportunities in types of work associated with women—especially the provision of social services to other women and children. However, by 1956, when the IAWP was reorganized, a number of the members identified more with law enforcement than social service, a change that encouraged younger officers to seek equal access and opportunity in the 1970s. In 1972, the clause encouraging the establishment of women's bureaus was deleted from the IAWP's constitution. Recognizing that both male and female officers are necessary for effective operation of the criminal justice system, the IAWP admitted male police officers as members in 1976.

The IAWP sponsors annual training conferences where members exchange information and research findings through seminars, lectures, and workshops. The IAWP has established 14 regions (11 in the United States plus one each in England, Canada, and the West Indies). In 1996, the first IAWP-sponsored annual training conference outside of North America convened in Birmingham, England. *See also* POLICE WORK, HISTORY OF WOMEN IN, USA.

Further Reading: Appier 1998, *Policing Women;* International Association of Women Police <http://www.iawp.org/history.htm>; Schulz 1995, *From Social Worker to Crimefighter.*

Donna C. Hale

J

Jails, Issues for Women in

Women in jails—local institutions that hold pretrial detainees and sentenced misdemeanants—have concerns that reflect their criminal involvement, their status in our culture, and the ways in which the justice system operates. Whereas in 1978, women constituted approximately 6 percent of the total jail population, by 1997, they made up 11 percent of the total (see Table I), an increase caused mainly by drug-war initiatives. Notwithstanding this increase in female prisoners, jails continue to be designed and operated primarily for male inmates, and jail programs and policies reflect masculine needs and issues.

Jailed women tend to have an impoverished background, limited education, a poor employment record, history of substance abuse, and the experience of physical or sexual abuse as a child and/or adult. Yet jails, which are high-turnover institutions, seldom have programs that address these deficiencies and needs. The very few programs that jails do offer tend to be aimed primarily at male inmates, or for some other reason they are unlikely to assist women in addressing problems that contribute to criminality or a poor quality of life. To ensure that participants can complete programs while incarcerated, some programs accept only sentenced women, with the result that women who have not yet been tried or sentenced are excluded from the few programs that do exist. In addition, very few communities have programs that women can begin in jail and continue after release.

Jailed women are often unable to maintain connections with loved ones in the community. Restricted contact with the outside, particularly with their children, results in an acute pain of imprisonment for jailed women. Between 65 and 80 percent of incarcerated women have children under the age of 18 whom they nurtured and financially supported before arrest. Usually, jail rules prevent mothers from having contact visits with their children, and jail visitation hours are limited. Poverty, lack of transportation, and work or other obligations constrain children's caretakers from bringing them for a visit. Jailed women's limited resources can make it impossible for them to make phone calls, and illiteracy can make writing and reading letters impossible, thereby further isolating some women.

The jail setting itself presents problems for women offenders. Sexual abuse or harassment by staff or, in mixed-sex jails, by other inmates, has been reported. In an effort to prevent abuse, some jails have instituted special training programs for staff, and some have developed protective policies ruling, for example, that only female officers can perform pat-down and body-cavity searches.

Mental and physical health care for women in jails has typically been inadequate. While most medium and large jails have nursing and other medical personnel on staff, few small jails are so staffed. When medical problems arise, they are not always handled expeditiously. Moreover, since women are a minority in jail populations, the focus of medical programming is usually on male, rather than on female, needs.

Finally, women exiting a jail are faced with a plethora of problems associated with their need to simultaneously secure employment, housing, and childcare. Rarely are there transition services to assist with these needs. Thus, women depend heavily on family and friends to support their transition. Otherwise, they rely on overtaxed social services, and if these prove inadequate, some women are rendered homeless along with their children. *See also* GENDER DISPARITIES IN PRISONS; JAILS, WOMEN IN; PRISONS, HEALTH CARE IN; SEXUAL ABUSE OF PRISONERS.

Further Reading: Gilliard and Beck 1997, *Prison and Jail Inmates at Midyear, 1996*; Gray, Mays, and Stohr 1995, "Inmate Needs."

Mary K. Stohr

Jails, Women in

In Colonial-era jails in the United States, women were incarcerated together with men and children. By the mid-twentieth century, males and females, and adults and children, were for the most part separated in jails. Today, not only are jailed women physically separated from men, but they also differ considerably from men in their numbers, commitment offenses, and the conditions and nature of their confinement.

Before the latest version of the war on drugs was implemented in the 1980s, women typically accounted for only 6 percent of jail inmates. By the mid-1990s, as Table I shows, women jail inmates constituted over 10 percent of jail populations. Between the 1980s and 1990s, the general jail incarceration rate doubled, changing from 108 per 100,000 people in the general U.S. population in 1985 to 212 per 100,000 people by 1997.

The simultaneous increases in the general jail incarceration rate and the proportion of jailed people who are women has resulted in an unprecedented number of women in jails. Moreover, the growth in the jail incarceration rate is characterized by an increasingly disproportionate number of minority (African American and Hispanic) jail inmates. By 1997, African Americans were six times more likely than whites, two times more likely than Hispanics, and eight times more likely than people of other races or ethnicities to be incarcerated in U.S. jails.

The adult female jail population has grown 9.9 percent annually since 1985, whereas the adult male jail population has grown only 6.4 percent. However, even with a higher rate of growth than men, women still constitute a small fraction of people in jail, which makes it easy for jail administrators to overlook them and their distinctive needs.

Jails hold both unconvicted prisoners who are awaiting trial and people convicted of relatively minor crimes (misdemeanors) for which the sentence is one year or less in confinement. The commitment offenses of convicted women in jail are mainly for drug and stereotypically "female" property crimes such as fraud and theft. At midyear 1996, 28 percent of men in jail were there for a violent offense, as compared with 15 percent of the women. Twenty-seven percent of women inmates were held for a drug law violation, as

Table I. Local Jails, USA: Inmates by Sex, 1990–1998

	Percent of Jail Inmates								
	1990	1991	1992	1993	1994	1995	1996	1997	1998
Male	90.8%	90.7%	90.8%	90.4%	90.0%	89.8%	89.2%	89.4%	89.2%
Female	9.2%	9.3%	9.2%	9.6%	10.0%	10.2%	10.8%	10.6%	10.8%

Source: Adapted from Bureau of Justice Statistics, 1999, *Prison and Jail Inmates at Midyear 1998,* Table 7.

compared to 21 percent of the men. Women inmates were twice as likely as men to be held for fraud or theft (24 percent versus 11 percent). Female jail inmates were also more likely to be unconvicted or first-time offenders than male inmates. In short, women in the nation's jails are generally much less serious offenders than their male counterparts.

Most jails are not able to effectively classify women to living units, jobs, or programs. Instead, it is typical for one living unit to hold a mix of female first-time and repeat offenders, women who are not yet convicted and those who have been convicted or sentenced, women who are mentally disturbed and those who are unimpaired, offenders whose crimes are petty and those whose crimes are serious, and both female trustees (inmates appointed as workers) and inmates with disciplinary problems. Whereas male inmates are often separated based on these distinctions, jails rarely can or will separate the women. An important outcome of this mix is that programs and policies cannot be tailored to the characteristics and situations of jailed women. *See also* GENDER DISPARITIES IN PRISONS; JAILS, ISSUES FOR WOMEN IN.

Further Reading: Gilliard and Beck 1997, *Prison and Jail Inmates at Midyear, 1996;* Gray, Mays, and Stohr 1995, "Inmate Needs."

Mary K. Stohr

Judges

Women have served as judges in the United States for more than a century, but they still are greatly underrepresented on the bench. The first female judge in the United States, Esther Morris, was appointed justice of the peace in South Pass Mining Camp, Wyoming, in 1870. However, women like Morris were extremely rare before 1920 because women were not legally eligible to serve as judges in many jurisdictions until after passage of the Nineteenth Amendment.

Within weeks of women winning suffrage in 1920, Florence Ellinwood Allen became the first woman elected to serve on a court of general jurisdiction. Two years later, she became the first woman to serve on a state's highest court when she was elected to the Ohio Supreme Court. In 1934, she became the first woman to serve on an Article III court when she was appointed to the United States Court of Appeals for the Sixth Circuit by President Franklin Roosevelt. No other women joined her on the federal bench until President Harry Truman appointed Burnita Shelton Matthews to the U.S. District Court for the District of Columbia in 1949. In 1958, Judge Allen also became the first chief judge of a federal appellate court.

While a debt is clearly owed to these trailblazers, they were the exception, not the rule. No more than a token female presence was tolerated in the federal judiciary until President Jimmy Carter made a concerted effort to open the federal nominating process to women and minorities.

Carter appointed 40 women to federal judgeships and in so doing surpassed all prior administrations combined. Even so, female judges remain relatively uncommon. According to the Administrative Office of the U.S. Courts, as of September 30, 1999, only 332 of the 1,612 judges serving in the federal judiciary were women. Thus, males continue to dominate the federal judiciary by a ratio of almost four to one.

At present, two of the nine justices serving on the United States Supreme Court are female. Sandra Day O'Connor, the first woman to serve on the Court, was appointed by President Ronald Reagan and took the oath of office on September 25, 1981. O'Connor remained the only woman on the Supreme Court until President Bill Clinton nominated Ruth Bader Ginsburg in 1993.

The United States Court of Appeals is divided into 13 circuits. As of April of 2000, there were 240 judges, including both active and senior judges, serving on the Court of Appeals. All 13 circuits had at least one woman serving on the Court of Appeals. The First, Eighth, and Federal Circuits each had one female judge. The District of Columbia, Fourth, Fifth, and Seventh Circuits had two female judges apiece. The Second and Tenth Circuits had three female judges, while the Sixth and Eleventh Circuits had four female judges. The Third Circuit had five female judges and the Ninth Circuit had nine, the largest complement of female judges of any circuit. Two circuit courts were presided over by women: Stephanie K. Seymour is chief judge of the Tenth Circuit, and Carolyn D. King is chief judge of the Fifth Circuit.

In addition, each state has its own court system. As of 1980–81, there were only 10 women serving on state courts of last resort (normally designated the state supreme court). By the year 2000, there were female judges on the supreme courts of almost every state. New Hampshire and Wyoming, among the last of the states to appoint women to their supreme courts, finally did so in April of 2000. South Dakota, as of that date, stood alone as the only state that had yet to appoint a woman to its highest court. South Dakota also had no women on its intermediate appellate court as of April 2000. Although most states now have women serving on their supreme courts, female representation is often token in nature. According to the National Center for State Courts, as of April of 2000, 21 of the 49 states with women on their supreme courts had only one woman serving.

Despite obstacles, a few women in the state judiciaries have risen to supervisory positions within their courts. Judge Susie Marshal Sharp of North Carolina, for example, became the first woman to hold a state's highest judicial post when she was elected chief justice in 1974. Since then, a number of women have risen to the rank of chief justice, including Ellen Ash Peters of Connecticut, Rosemary Barkett of Florida, Rose Elizabeth Bird of California, and Ann Kettering Covington of Missouri. Judge Covington, during her tenure as Missouri's chief justice, was also the first woman to hold an executive office (second vice president) in the Conference of Chief Justices.

As sensitivity to the problem of sex discrimination in this country has grown, most of the states and a majority of the federal circuits have instituted task forces to study gender bias within their court systems. Most of these task forces have reported evidence of gender bias, which adversely affects female litigants, witnesses, attorneys, and even judges. Over a quarter of the female judges who responded to the survey administered by the Third Circuit Task Force on Equal Treatment in the Courts reported that they had been treated with less respect than their male colleagues.

One frequent suggestion for combating gender bias in the courts is to put more women on the bench with the expectation that if their numbers are sufficiently large, female judges will be able to ensure that women are treated with fairness and respect. While inclusion of more women within the judiciary certainly enhances the appearance of fairness, it does not necessarily guarantee increased substantive fairness because just as some men embrace feminism, some women embrace patriarchy. At this point, due to their small numbers and comparatively short tenure on the bench, it is difficult to evaluate the impact female jurists will ultimately have. *See also* GENDER AND JUDICIAL DECISION-MAKING; GENDER BIAS TASK FORCES; LAWYERS AND GENDER DIFFERENCE; LEGAL PROFESSION, HISTORY OF WOMEN IN; O'CONNOR, SANDRA DAY; WOMEN PROFESSIONALS IN THE JUSTICE WORKPLACE.

Further Reading: E. Martin 1990, "Men and Women on the Bench"; S. E. Martin and Jurik 1996, *Doing Justice, Doing Gender.*

M. Dyan McGuire

Jury Selection

Jury selection in the United States is a multistage process. It begins with a sample of citizens who each receive a questionnaire designed to assess their eligibility for jury service and culminates in a jury chosen to decide a particular case. The group of jury-eligible citizens that is brought to the courtroom (the venire) is whittled down to the trial jury in a question-and-answer session called voir dire. Potential jurors may be dismissed by the judge "for cause" if they indicate bias for or against one side or the other. An attorney can also exercise peremptory challenges to remove a limited number of potential jurors. Attorneys do not give reasons for their peremptory challenges, but they are prohibited from basing these challenges on the juror's race or gender.

Under English common law, women were excluded from jury service due to "the defect of the sex." Change was slow; it was not until 1957 that legislation was passed that guaranteed women the right to serve on federal juries, and some states excluded women from jury service as late as the 1960s. It was 1975 before the U.S. Supreme Court overturned state laws that limited jury service by women to those who volunteered *(Taylor v. Louisiana).*

In 1994, the U.S. Supreme Court held that using gender as the basis for a peremptory challenge is prohibited by the Equal Protection Clause of the Fourteenth Amendment because it violates a potential juror's right to nondiscriminatory jury selection procedures *(J.E.B. v. Alabama).* Although the Court in *J.E.B.* specified that gender may not be used as a proxy for bias when making a peremptory challenge, the Court explicitly noted that other characteristics can still be an acceptable basis for a challenge, even if one gender is disproportionately represented in the group of jurors who share that characteristic. For example, unemployed spouses could be challenged because of their lack of employment, even if women are more likely than men to be unemployed spouses.

Research has revealed few systematic differences between men and women in their verdict preferences in criminal cases. The few differences that have been detected have emerged in cases involving sexual assault, domestic abuse, physical and sexual abuse of children, and the death penalty. In the abuse and assault cases, women appear to be more willing to convict. It is unclear if this difference arises because women empathize more with the victims, because they identify less with the defendants, or because they find the victims' stories more plausible due to their own life experiences.

When gender and child abuse are not implicated in the alleged offense, the gender of the juror is generally not related to verdict preferences. The one exception arises in capital cases—litigation for which the death penalty can be the sentence. In capital cases, jurors are excused if they say they would be unable to follow the law in deciding on a verdict due to their views on the death penalty. Thus, because women are more likely than men to oppose the death penalty, they are less likely to be seated on a jury in a capital case.

Overall, gender tends to be a poor predictor of jury verdicts. Its impact is confined to particular types of cases. In addition, the rare studies of real cases (as opposed to simulations) have revealed few differences, and studies that include judicial instructions and deliberations appear to mute gender differences. *See also* GENDER AND JUDICIAL DECISION-MAKING.

Further Reading: Hastie, Penrod, and Pennington 1983, *Inside the Jury;* Krauss and Bonora 1995, *Jurywork: Systematic Techniques*; Van Dyke 1977, *Jury Selection Procedures.*

Shari S. Diamond and Leslie Ellis

Juvenile Delinquency and Age

Current research examining the relationship between age and delinquency reveals that age is related to specific types of delinquent behavior. For example, studies find that youths under the age of 15 are more likely to engage in crimes against persons or property than are youths aged 15 and older. By contrast, the studies also reveal that those aged 15 and older are more likely to engage in drug-related offenses than their younger counterparts. Overall, between 1986 and 1995, juvenile crime increased 57 percent for youths under age 15 and 39 percent for youth aged 15 and older. However, the violent crime rates have declined for both groups for the period 1994–96 (Puzzanchera 1998).

Little attention has been paid to the gendered nature of offending patterns among juveniles. Since 1987, juvenile arrest rates have increased for females at a faster rate than for males. In fact, arrest data indicate that an increasing proportion of the FBI's total index crime, as well as violent index crime, is accounted for by females. (The FBI's crime index includes the violent offenses of murder and nonnegligent manslaughter, forcible rape, robbery, and aggravated assault, as well as the property crimes of burglary, larceny-theft, motor vehicle theft, and arson.) Despite the fact that female participation in violent crime still falls far below that of males, percentage increases since the 1960s reveal increasing female representation. For example, violent crime arrest rates for 1967–96 increased 124 percent for male juveniles, whereas for female juveniles, the increase was approximately 345 percent (Bureau of Justice Statistics 1997b).

Although changes in juvenile offending patterns have been occurring since the 1960s, more noticeable changes have occurred since 1990. Female representation in total juvenile index crime arrests has increased from 13 percent to 25 percent, while male representation has decreased from 87 percent to 75 percent. At present, criminologists have failed to offer any compelling explanations to account for this rapid increase in offending behavior by young females. Figure 7 shows the age categories victimized by female and male juvenile delinquents.

A recent and important theory of offending behavior offered by psychologist Terrie Moffitt posits significant differences between delinquent girls and some delinquent boys in terms of the ages at which they begin offending and the seriousness and length of their criminal careers. Moffitt identifies two dif-

ferent types of offenders characterized by their ages at the onset of delinquency. Her theory holds that early participants in delinquency, or "life-course persistent offenders," exhibit neuropsychological deficits, antisocial behavior patterns as children, delinquent conduct before age 14, future risks for chronic offending, and persistence in crime as adults. Her second group of offenders, "adolescent-limited offenders," initiate delinquent behavior in mid-adolescence, by age 15 or after, largely due to the influence of their peer group. These late onset delinquents stop offending soon thereafter as they leave school and mature into adulthood (Moffitt 1993).

According to Moffitt's theory, female delinquency overwhelmingly falls in the adolescent-limited category. While Moffitt acknowledges that females can be found among life-course persisters, she asserts that the phenomenon is rare. In short, serious, early-initiating, persistent offending is largely a male phenomenon.

Recent evidence has been somewhat supportive of Moffitt's theory, but no studies have been undertaken that comprehensively examine gender differences in her two offender groups. Additionally, one of the main risk factors for serious female offending, sexual abuse, is missing from Moffitt's theory.

In sum, there are significant age-related differences in delinquency, although recent research indicates that these are less pronounced for females than for males. This re-

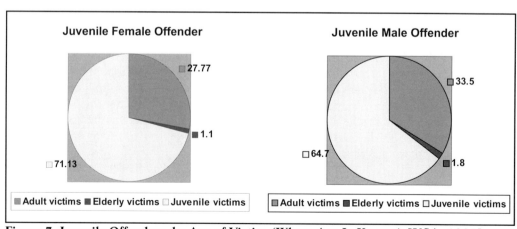

Figure 7. Juvenile Offenders, by Age of Victim (Where Age Is Known) [USA, 1997]
Source: U.S. Department of Justice, Federal Bureau of Investigation 1998, *Crime in the United States 1997*, Sec. V. Fig.5.6.

cent research is not definitive, however, since key factors in the age-delinquency relationship, such as sexual victimization, have not been examined. *See also* DESISTANCE FROM CRIME; FEMALE CRIME, PATTERNS AND TRENDS IN, USA; JUVENILE DELINQUENCY, USA.

Further Reading: Moffitt 1993, "Adolescence-Limited and Life-Course-Persistent Antisocial Behavior"; Uggen and Kruttschnitt 1998, "Crime in the Breaking."

Sharon Schnelle

Juvenile Delinquency and Drug and Alcohol Abuse

Juvenile delinquency and drug and alcohol use are strongly correlated for both females and males. Although there is a gap between male and female juveniles in terms of self-reported delinquency and arrests, as reflected in official police records, the gap is considerably smaller for drug and alcohol use. In other words, drug and alcohol use by males exceeds that of females, but the differences are smaller when compared with other crimes. While violent offenses are considered stereotypically masculine delinquent behavior, and while status offenses and certain kinds of property offenses such as shoplifting are considered stereotypically feminine delinquent behavior, drug and alcohol offenses are essentially gender-neutral, even though the circumstances surrounding the use of drugs and alcohol may differ for males and females.

According to police records, males are more likely to be arrested for drug or liquor violations than females, and this disparity is larger for drug-law violations, especially drug sales. By contrast, some self-report studies have revealed few significant gender differences in drug and alcohol use. In some surveys, females are about as likely to report using alcohol, marijuana, barbiturates, amphetamines, and cocaine as males, although males report slightly more selling of drugs and procurement of alcohol. In other surveys, such as the *Monitoring the Future Survey*, the prevalence of illicit drug use by males exceeds that of females (National Institute on Drug Abuse 1996).

The *Monitoring the Future Survey* is the largest study of self-reported drug and alcohol use among adolescents in America. On an annual basis, approximately 50,000 eighth-, tenth-, and twelfth-grade youth in 420 private and public schools are surveyed. Information from the survey reveals that for drugs such as cocaine and heroin, males report higher use than females, while for alcohol and stimulants, females report using as much or more than males. Marijuana appears to be the illicit drug of choice for both males and females, with 45 percent of male and 38 percent of female twelfth-graders reporting using marijuana at least once.

The gender disparity in drug and alcohol involvement might reflect differences in drug and alcohol use patterns. For example, females are more likely to use drugs or alcohol in private residences than in more visible locales, whereas males tend to expand their use to vehicles or public streets, locations that render them more vulnerable to an arrest. Moreover, surveys of college students have revealed that females are more likely to have been given their drugs, whereas males are more likely to have purchased them—in both cases, from male suppliers. This might be evidence for the claim made by many researchers that females tend to become involved in drug use initially through a relationship with a male.

Social concern over girls' drug and alcohol involvement relates to the belief that such activities might lead to more serious delinquent or criminal activity. Indeed, the precise nature of the connection between drug and alcohol use and other kinds of delinquent activity remains hotly debated. It has been established, however, that serious drug and alcohol use play a significant role in female criminal behavior, just as they do in male criminal behavior. Like males, once females are addicted to drugs or alcohol, they are likely to increase their delinquent behavior. *See also* ALCOHOL ABUSE AND ALCOHOLISM; DRUG OFFENSES; JUVENILE DELINQUENCY, USA.

123

Further Reading: Merlo and Pollock 1995, *Women, Law, and Social Control;* Tonry and Wilson 1990, *Drugs and Crime.*

Miriam D. Sealock

Juvenile Delinquency and Family Conflict

The relationship between juvenile delinquency and family conflict is complex, especially for girls. Events early in a child's life can have a profound impact on future behavior. Research has established that children who are rejected by parents, who grow up in homes with considerable conflict, or who are inadequately supervised are at an increased risk of becoming juvenile delinquents. Additionally, there is evidence that family conflict has more damaging effects on the adjustment of children than divorce. This stems from the fact that the family is the key socializing agent of children; it fosters the development of respect for institutions, responsibility, and prosocial values. In families plagued by conflict, key aspects of effective socialization are compromised. While the impact of family conflict on delinquency is well documented, the differential impact of family conflict on girls and boys is less clearly understood.

Early in the twentieth century, juvenile delinquency experts recognized the important role families play in shaping a child's behavior. It was observed that dysfunctional families often do great harm because they teach negative attitudes, values, and behaviors to their children. By contrast, supportive, affectionate, and nurturing families are critical for positive child development because they impart socially acceptable attitudes, responsibility, commitment, and behavior patterns.

Family conflict can lead to delinquency in a multitude of ways. For example, it can lead to difficulty in adaptation, communication, and establishing meaningful relationships early in life. The lack of these core socialization skills often results in feelings of emptiness, solitude, and frustration, feelings that present risks for aggressive and delinquent behavior. Family conflict can also facilitate a flight to delinquent peers as youth search for support and emotional connection from others.

Research suggests that experiencing family conflict may be especially damaging for girls (J. Rosenbaum 1989). Females have been found to value emotional relationships to a greater degree than males. Moreover, evidence suggests that females are likely to internalize stress, blame themselves for noxious situations that arise, and become depressed. Males, by contrast, are more likely to respond to stressful situations by getting angry and externalizing blame.

There is also evidence that the home lives of serious female delinquents are almost universally dysfunctional. Criminologists now think that a substantial amount of female delinquency may be related to sexual and physical abuse at home (Chesney-Lind and Shelden 1992). Family turmoil and conflict are consistently related to delinquency for females, and there are good reasons to expect that negative events in the family, including sexual victimization, have more serious consequences for females than for males.

As families are the most important socializing influence in the lives of children, perhaps more important for females than for males, programs that strengthen the family and reduce conflict should reduce the onset of delinquent behavior. Possible programs may include crisis intervention, family life education for youths and parents, family systems support groups, and behavioral contracts between youths and parents. The implementation and assessment of these programs is vital to the future of today's young girls. *See also* INCARCERATED MOTHERS; JUVENILE DELINQUENCY, USA.

Further Reading: Chesney-Lind and Shelden 1992, *Girls, Delinquency, and Juvenile Justice;* Laub and Sampson 1988, "Unraveling Families and Delinquency"; Nye 1958, *Family Relationships and Delinquent Behavior.*

Nanette Graham

Juvenile Delinquency and Gangs, USA

Young women's involvement in juvenile delinquency and gangs was largely ignored or stereotyped until fairly recently, perhaps due to the fact that female participation in delinquent activity has always been on a smaller scale than that of males. On the basis of male gang members' views of female gang members, rather than firsthand reports of young women actually involved in gangs, researchers traditionally characterized female gang members as "sex objects" or "tomboys." According to this research tradition, girl gang members served as girlfriends to male members, providing sexual services, carrying weapons and drugs for them, luring rival gang members to fighting locations, and spying on rival gangs.

Beginning in the mid-1970s, ethnographic research delved more deeply into the role of the gang for young females and revealed that females' gang activity was not wholly dependent upon gang males, although some degree of sexism and subordination could still be found within most gangs. Anne Campbell's (1991) study of female gang involvement, the most in-depth to date, focuses on three different New York City "girl gangs" that she studied in 1980. Campbell finds that young females seek asylum in a gang to escape the limitations of poverty and the difficulties they expected to face in the future. Other research on Mexican American gang members in Los Angeles barrios (Moore 1991) finds similar motivations and reveals that female gang members are more likely than male members to come from extremely troubled home environments—families with alcoholic, drug-addicted, and/or criminally involved siblings or parents.

Traditionally, gangs with female members have been classified into three general types: auxiliaries to male gangs, sub-units of coed or mixed-sex groups, and autonomous female gangs. Today, most female gangs are auxiliaries of male gangs, although some evidence supports the notion that independent female gangs became more common in the 1990s and played a more central role in drug dealing and violence. Other studies suggest that females' gang activity is not dramatically shifting but only seems to be because the media

and scholars report on it more than in the past.

The limited data available on female participation in gangs suggest that young women constitute no more than 10 percent of all gang members nationwide. However, recent longitudinal youth surveys in selected cities reveal a higher rate of female gang participation. In Rochester, New York, for example, the proportion of females admitting gang participation (22 percent) was even higher than that of males (18 percent) (Bjerregaard and Smith 1993). Several self-report surveys also indicate that gang-involved female youths exhibit significantly higher rates of delinquency and drug use than non-gang female peers and, in some cases, even non-gang males.

Overall, recent examinations of female gangs and their members reveal tremendous variation in the forms the groups take, their relationships with male gangs, and the activities gang members engage in. While some gangs are highly organized—with formal initiation rites and membership rules—and are involved in drug sales and other types of criminality, many others are loosely knit groups with minimal criminal involvement. Despite these variations, females' reasons for joining gangs are similar to males' and fairly consistent across cities and gangs: protection, the support and friendship of fellow gang members, opportunities to achieve status and boost self-esteem, and fun and excitement. In sum, although female gang participation is less common than that of males, understanding this behavior is vital to a clear understanding of female delinquency. *See also* GANGS: CABRA GIRLS (AUSTRALIA).

Further Reading: Bjerregaard and Smith 1993, "Gender Differences in Gang Participation"; Campbell 1991, *The Girls in the Gang*; Chesney-Lind and Hagedorn 1999, *Female Gangs in America*.

Dana M. Nurge

Juvenile Delinquency and Intelligence

The relationship between juvenile delinquency and intelligence has been an important issue since the late nineteenth century, although only during the early twentieth century did researchers find what they interpreted as significant gender differences in delinquents' intelligence and use these findings to recommend gender-specific treatment of delinquent girls.

Late-nineteenth-century researchers attempted to study the effects of intelligence on delinquency through, for example, craniometry or skull measurement, but the scientific measurement of intelligence remained an elusive goal until Alfred Binet developed a method of intelligence quotient (IQ) testing in France in the early 1900s. In contrast to later psychologists, Binet did not believe these tests should be used to label slower students as unteachable; in fact, Binet believed that IQ could be enhanced via training.

Psychologist Henry H. Goddard was the principle proponent and manipulator of Binet's ideas in America. In the early part of this century, Goddard used IQ tests to further the eugenics movement by administering these tests to immigrants, inmates, and other groups deemed socially undesirable, to justify the deportation of "morons," "idiots," and "imbeciles" whom authorities thought would corrupt future generations with their inferior genes. Goddard was also alarmed by the menace of native-born "feebleminded" women to the vitality of the nation's "stock." When he and other early intelligence testers measured the intelligence of institutionalized delinquent girls, they found that up to 90 percent of these girls were feebleminded and hence a reproductive threat.

Even though most early research that identified a link between IQ and delinquency found this relationship in males, females were more likely to be sterilized, an operation performed to prevent them from bearing delinquent children. Not until World War I did Goddard and his colleagues test a cross-section of Americans and, due to the very poor scores, conclude that something might be wrong with their intelligence testing techniques. By that time, however, the ball had been set in motion, and in 1927, in *Buck v. Bell, Superintendent,* the U.S. Supreme Court

ruled that IQ test scores could be used to identify "feebleminded" individuals (typically women) and to sterilize them in order to prevent crime in the next generation. Such sterilizations were legal until the 1970s.

Studies of intelligence and criminality decreased after the *Buck v. Bell* decision, only to increase again in the 1970s. Since then, studies have shown a small, persistent, significant association between low IQ and delinquency, even when the influences of social class and race are taken into account. In contrast to the early intelligence testers like Goddard, however, late-twentieth-century researchers have not found significant gender differences among delinquents. Most recent studies conclude that it is low verbal IQ (as opposed to quantitative, or spatial ability) that is responsible for most of the intellectual discrepancy between delinquents and nondelinquents. This finding is consistent with criminological strain theory, according to which delinquents are inhibited and frustrated by their inability to interact with others, to succeed in daily tasks, and to accomplish goals.

The question that remains unanswered is, "Does low intelligence cause delinquency?" Although some scholars have claimed that IQ tests are culturally biased, there is a consistent and significant correlation between low verbal IQ and criminality. However, many studies have shown that effects of intelligence on female and male delinquency are primarily indirect, operating through variables such as school performance or language achievement. Furthermore, the effects of IQ may be negligible due to other influences, such as birth delivery complications or sustaining an early head injury, which may cause both low intelligence and delinquency. Recent studies, such as Herrnstein and Murray's *The Bell Curve* (1994), have fueled the ongoing controversy over the effects of intelligence on life outcomes.

The best conclusion that can currently be drawn is that low verbal IQ has been established as a consistent predictor, but not necessarily a direct cause, of both female and

male delinquency. *See also* STRAIN EXPLANA-
TION OF CRIME.

Further Reading: Gould 1981, *The Mismeasure of
Man;* Rafter 1997, *Creating Born Criminals.*

Stephen G. Tibbetts

Juvenile Delinquency and Peer Influences

The relationship between juvenile delinquency and peer influences has been among
the most frequently studied areas in the field
of criminology. A substantial body of research
has, in fact, established that one of the more
effective predictors of a juvenile's level of
delinquency is the level of peers' criminal involvement, regardless of his or her sex. Although there has been difficulty in establishing
the exact nature of that relationship—specifically, whether delinquent youth flock to other
delinquents, or whether youth engage in delinquency only after becoming associated with
delinquent peers—it is clear that a youth's
peer associations are highly associated with
his or her delinquent activity.

These findings have been proffered as support for Edwin Sutherland and Donald
Cressey's differential association theory,
which postulates that delinquency develops
as a result of an individual being exposed to
an excess of definitions favorable to crime
through his or her associations with delinquent others. According to this theory, criminal behavior and the motives, attitudes, and
rationalizations fueling it, are learned within
the context of close friendships. These theorists did not elaborate upon the influence of
peers upon girls' delinquency as compared
with boys' delinquency, although such an
elaboration would be useful in better understanding why boys engage in more delinquent
activity than girls. To explore this issue, one
would have to examine whether girls have less
opportunity to form associations with delinquent peers and become exposed to definitions favorable to crime than boys, perhaps
because they are traditionally more restricted
in their activities.

From this perspective, recent increases in
certain types of crime among girls may be
related to increases in equivalent or similar
socialization experiences for boys and girls.
Many criminologists, however, disagree with
this premise, and it has not been established
that parental restrictions on girls' behaviors
and associations have become more lax in
recent years. In short, no evidence supports
the assertion that girls are any more likely
now to be associating with delinquent peers
than they have been in the past.

Criminologists have, however, attempted
to understand the influence of peers on female delinquency since the mid-twentieth
century. Sociologist Albert J. Reiss (1960)
claimed that sexual activity and promiscuity
may be a way in which girls gain and maintain status among their peers, as relationships
with boys are their primary source of status
and prestige. Complications resulting from
that activity, such as pregnancy or disease,
may rob the girl of that status and may pro-
pel her into more serious forms of delinquent
activity. (This rationale, as well as related
predictions that girls become delinquent because of sexual promiscuity or romantic relationships with delinquent boys, are considered outdated today.) Sociologist Anne
Campbell (1990) presents evidence that it is
not a girl's relationship with boys, but her
relationship with other girls, that produces
delinquent behavior.

The differential impact of peers upon male
and female delinquency remains an area of
particular interest. Researchers Rachelle Canter (1982) and Merry Morash (1983) have
argued that among females in particular, peer
influences may be more critical than familial
bonds in the development of delinquency.
Girls spend at least as much time, if not more,
interacting with peers than their male counterparts. Other studies have indicated that delinquent girls are not only influenced by their
peers, they are in fact more influenced by their
female than their male peers (Giordano
1978), with their likelihood of offending increasing as their female friends' approval of
criminal activity increases (Naffine 1987).
Additionally, it appears that female peer networks may involve fewer pressures to engage
in delinquency than male peer networks.

Criminal activity is less likely to be considered an appropriate or desirable behavior among female peer groups, and female peers are, on average, less likely than males to encourage members to engage in such behaviors.

In short, there appear to be somewhat different processes at work for males and females in the relationships between peers and delinquency. While there is evidence that delinquent girls can and do encourage their friends to become delinquent, there is also evidence that nondelinquent girls have a parallel positive effect on their peers. *See also* JUVENILE DELINQUENCY AND SCHOOL INFLUENCES; JUVENILE DELINQUENCY, USA.

Further Reading: Belknap 1996, *The Invisible Woman;* Carrington 1993, *Offending Girls.*

Miriam D. Sealock

Juvenile Delinquency and Race

Identifying juvenile delinquency patterns across race and gender is often problematic because official statistics are typically reported for gender and race separately. To further complicate this, many sources of official statistics classify race and ethnicity as separate variables, and most reports (particularly those published before the 1990s) lack any reference to Hispanic girls. More recent research includes the Hispanic/non-Hispanic breakdown of delinquency, but this analysis is separate from racial breakdowns. It is also difficult to find official statistics that refer to races other than white or black. While most government data include an "other race" category (which would include Asians and Native Americans), offense rates for these groups are low (especially among females). For example, juvenile court data from 1988–97 indicate that nationwide, delinquency cases involving girls were decreasingly white (ranging from a high of 70.4 percent in 1988 to 66.7 percent in 1997), and increasingly non-white. For this period, cases involving black girls accounted for an average of 29.1 percent of all cases disposed; the figure for girls of other races was 3.9 percent (Office of Juvenile Justice and Delinquency Prevention 1998).

As with most crime statistics, minority representation increases as we look deeper into the justice system. Bergsmann (1994) reports that 13 percent of females in secure detention are Hispanic and that nearly half of those girls are black. Self-report statistics, however, help overcome the mixing of ethnicity and race by measuring and reporting female juvenile delinquency rates across race. Based on these statistics, non-white females have higher rates of offending than white females, but an accurate measure of race differences depends on offense type. Whereas offending rates for burglaries and assaults tend to be similar for girls across race, rates vary when other offenses are considered. White females, for example, are more likely to rival or surpass non-white females for drug and alcohol offenses and status offenses, but non-white females are more likely than white females to commit personal crimes. Similarly, victimization also varies across white and non-white female juvenile offenders. Although female offenders are generally more likely than male offenders to be the victims of sexual and physical abuse, African American female offenders are more likely than their white counterparts to be victimized. Despite these apparent differences in female juveniles' offending and victimization, however, girls of color are often invisible in theoretical discussions of offending.

Researchers who attempt to address these differences contend that female experiences and responses to experiences are structured differently across race and class. Studies consistently provide evidence that many factors such as family, peers, school, and social structural variables, including economic status and urban residency, affect white and African American female behavior differently. More specifically, African American female juvenile delinquency appears to be affected by economic status and living in urban areas, whereas social-psychological factors such as self-esteem and peer relationships mediate the effect of such variables on white female delinquency.

The treatment of female offenders within the juvenile justice system also reinforces the need for more research on how gender, race, and class affect female experiences. Research on juvenile justice processing typically examines the impact of the offender's gender or race on outcomes while neglecting the interaction of gender and race. Findings from studies that have examined this interaction effect show that African American female offenders receive more punitive outcomes, while their white counterparts receive either less severe or more rehabilitative interventions from the court.

In sum, race differences in female offending have traditionally been ignored in both theoretical and empirical research, but the importance of these differences is crucial to understanding female delinquency and to developing appropriate interventions for preventing and reducing it. This neglect applies to all girls of color, including Latina girls, who are often excluded from consideration due to low numbers or to their classification as white offenders. Yet to gain a clearer understanding of female delinquency, studies must explore how the intersection of race, ethnicity, gender, and class creates different experiences and defines different responses across all female offenders. *See also* JUVENILE DELINQUENCY, USA; SEXISM AND RACISM IN CRIMINAL JUSTICE POLICY.

Further Reading: Chesney-Lind and Shelden 1998, *Girls, Delinquency, and Juvenile Justice;* D. Elliott 1994, "Serious Violent Offenders."

Denise C. Herz

Juvenile Delinquency and School Influences

Much has been written about the relationship between juvenile delinquency and school influences. School factors have consistently been shown to be associated with delinquent involvement and are prominently featured in several delinquency theories. While delinquency is related to school factors for both boys and girls, that association tends to be stronger for boys, but to have longer-lasting consequences for girls.

The critical school factors related to involvement in delinquency are low attachment to school, poor academic performance, and low commitment to educational success. Each of these factors has been shown to be associated with a higher likelihood for delinquent behavior, primarily by contributing to stronger ties with delinquent peers and by enhancing the likelihood of dropping out of school. The relationships described here are stronger for males than for females, but they are present for both groups.

Socialization plays a role in the development of commitment to educational success and attachment to school. Girls tend to be socialized to be concerned with their attractiveness to others (especially to boys), even at the cost of reducing their own ambitions. Thus, by the end of high school, girls have lower occupational aspirations and are more concerned with their popularity than are boys. This dynamic is particularly evident in the case of lower-income and minority girls. Popularity for these girls is often achieved through fighting, toughness, and using drugs, rather than through educational success.

Lower-income girls are more likely to focus on marriage as an outcome of high school. African American and Hispanic girls are particularly alienated from educational success. Some of them must learn to function and survive within the context of youth gangs and pervasive violence among their peers. These young women have a higher likelihood of dropping out of school and becoming pregnant as teenagers.

Dropping out of school because of pregnancy is related to a higher likelihood of involvement in violent crime for teenage girls. Forty-four percent of dropouts in the United States have indicated pregnancy or marriage as the primary reason for leaving school, and females are more likely than males to drop out for those reasons. Given that the value of a high school education is often lower for females, they are less likely to return to school in the future. In fact, 80 percent of teenage mothers do not finish high school. This has serious long-term consequences for these girls, who are less likely to achieve educational and occupational success. It also leads to negative long-term outcomes for their children, many of whom will grow up in poverty. Since the educational expectations of youths are influenced greatly by the educational attainment of their same-sex parents, the female children of these young women will have a higher likelihood of following a similar pattern.

On a more positive note, girls are just as receptive as boys to the preventive potential of preschool interventions. Preschool programs have been shown to have positive effects on the long-term educational success of the youths, and to reduce the likelihood of teenage pregnancy and delinquency. *See also* JUVENILE DELINQUENCY AND PEER INFLUENCES; JUVENILE DELINQUENCY AND SOCIAL CLASS; STRAIN EXPLANATION OF CRIME.

Further Reading: Chesney-Lind and Shelden 1998, *Girls, Delinquency, and Juvenile Justice*; Maguin and Loeber 1996, "Academic Performance and Delinquency."

G. Roger Jarjoura

Juvenile Delinquency and Social Class

Criminologists have long been interested in the relationship between juvenile delinquency and social class. Early theories that examined this relationship focused their attention on the delinquency of boys, in particular, lower-class boys. Girls were either ignored, or their delinquency was believed to be unrelated to social class. The majority of early research simply ignored females because these projects were largely unconcerned with the role of gender in delinquency causation. The studies that did examine this relationship, however, found the rate of delinquency for both males and females was highest among the lower class.

The rise of feminist criminology in recent years has increased the attention given to the relationship between social class, gender, and delinquency. Two theories in particular have been developed to explain this relationship: power-control theory by Hagan and his colleagues (1979, 1985, 1987, 1989) and masculinities and crime theory by Messerschmidt (1993a).

Central to Hagan's work is the argument that social class shapes the way gender relationships are reproduced in families and the way this ultimately affects the distribution of delinquency in society. He argues that America is basically a male-dominated, patriarchal society with traditional, male-dominated households. However, as women have moved into the workforce, alternative familial arrangements have arisen, including female-headed and egalitarian families. According to Hagan, in patriarchal families, where fathers have the power, daughters are more closely controlled than sons. In egalitarian families, where mothers have power as well as fathers, daughters are controlled to the same extent as sons. The greater control that daughters receive in patriarchal families leads to a lower preference for risk-taking and, thus, lower levels of delinquency for girls relative to boys. In egalitarian families, less control leads to a greater preference for risk-taking and thus more delinquency for daughters. From this, Hagan predicts that boys of all classes will be freer to be delinquent than girls, but that differences in offending by gender will be greatest in the lower classes, where patriarchal families are more prevalent.

Messerschmidt (1993a), while interested in how gender shapes delinquency across social class, pays little attention to females in his theory of masculinities and crime. He argues that crime for males is not simply an extension of the male role but is shaped by class position. According to this theory, crime is a way of "being" masculine for lower-class male youth, for whom other ways of doing so are unavailable. Though less concerned with the delinquency of girls, Messerschmidt does argue that their criminality, too, is an expression of their powerlessness and lack of resources.

Despite the development of these theories, relatively little research examines their key components. To date, there have been no direct tests of Messerschmidt's work, although Hagan's theory has received some support. For example, some research indicates that differences between males and females in rates of delinquency are less pronounced in upper-class, egalitarian households. On the other hand, contrasting research finds that differences by gender in delinquency are consistent across social classes.

In recent years, the work of theorists such as Hagan and Messerschmidt has advanced our knowledge about the way class and gender interact to shape delinquency. Most criminologists would agree, though, that there is still a great deal of work, both theoretical and empirical, to be done in this area. *See also* MASCULINITY EXPLANATION OF CRIME; POVERTY AND CRIME; POWER-CONTROL EXPLANATION OF CRIME.

Further Reading: Hagan 1989, *Structural Criminology*; Messerschmidt 1993a, *Masculinities and Crime*.

Ruth Ann Triplett

Juvenile Delinquency, Australia

The marked changes that most Australian juvenile justice systems have undergone in recent decades have significantly affected the position of female juvenile delinquents. Of particular importance has been the shift from a welfare to a justice model and the attendant elimination of status offenses, which in the past resulted in disproportionately high numbers of young women being dealt with in the Children's Court for such charges as "being uncontrollable" or "in moral danger."

Young women annually account for only a small proportion (generally less than 20 percent) of those dealt with by Australian juvenile justice systems. The recorded offending profile of these young women is fairly similar to that of young men. The less serious types of property offenses—notably "larceny" and "receiving"—account for a relatively high proportion of all juvenile female apprehensions, with offenses against "good order" and drug offenses also prominent.

These three offense groupings also dominate the offense profiles of young males. Nevertheless, there are some areas of difference between male and female juvenile delinquents. Young men, for example, are still more likely than young women to be charged with the more serious property crime of "break and enter," while recent figures indicate that a higher proportion of young women than young men are charged with offenses against the person (mainly "minor assault") and, although numbers are very low, with "robbery."

The other major change to Australian juvenile justice systems in recent years has been the introduction of a range of informal processing options designed to divert young people from prosecution in court. These alternatives, too, have significantly affected young women, with a high proportion in this group being diverted. In South Australia, for example, almost two-thirds of young women who annually come to police attention are dealt with by way of either an informal or a formal caution, while a further 10 percent are referred to a family conference. In contrast, males have a greater likelihood of being directed to court.

Apprehended young women are less likely than young men to receive the most serious options of those available at each key decision-making point in the system. Not only are they less likely to be referred to court than their male counterparts, they are also less likely to be arrested (as opposed to be issued with a summons or court attendance notice), and if brought before a court, they are less likely to be sentenced to detention in a youth training center.

Various reasons for these gender differences have been postulated. Some argue that young women actually commit fewer and less serious offenses than their male counterparts. Others, however, believe that young women are actually treated more leniently—with more chivalry and paternalism—by the predominantly male decision-makers in the system. Any explanation, however, is likely to be complex, particularly in view of the fact that young women's experiences with "the law" are not homogenous. Instead, the nature and extent of their involvement with the juvenile justice system varies according to race, ethnicity, and class.

To take race, for example, it is noteworthy that although young women as a whole are underrepresented in the system, indigenous or Aboriginal young women are substantially overrepresented. In South Australia, where indigenous young women accounted for only 2 percent of the state's female population in the 10–17 year age range in 1997, this group constituted 17 percent of all young women apprehended. On a per capita basis then, their level of representation was 7 times higher than expected. Moreover, their level of overrepresentation exceeded that of indigenous males, who in 1997 accounted for 13 percent of all young men apprehended.

The outcomes recorded for young indigenous women once in the system also differed from that of non-Aboriginal young women, and from nonindigenous males as well. Again using South Australia as an example, in 1997, almost half of all Aboriginal female apprehensions were arrest-based, compared with only 20 percent of the apprehensions of non-Aboriginal young women and 29 percent of non-Aboriginal boys. Sixty-one percent of arrested Aboriginal girls were referred to the Youth Court, compared with 33 percent of non-Aboriginal young women and 45 percent of non-Aboriginal males.

Other marginalized young women—such as those living on the streets, those who are long-term unemployed, and those from neighborhoods and family structures that the system tends to label "dysfunctional"—also receive harsher treatment. These differences highlight the dangers of generalizing about young women's juvenile justice experiences.

Many of the young women in the juvenile justice system are not only perpetrators of criminal behavior but also victims, particularly of sexual and physical abuse, and efforts by the juvenile justice system to respond appropriately to the offending behavior of young women must take into account this fact. *See also* ABORIGINAL WOMEN AND CRIME, AUSTRALIA; CHIVALRY EXPLANATION OF FEMALE CRIME RATES; FEMALE CRIME IN AUSTRALIA; JUVENILE DELINQUENCY, CANADA; JUVENILE DELINQUENCY, USA; STATUS OFFENSES.

Further Reading: Alder 1997, "Theories of Female Delinquency"; Alder and Baines 1996, *And When She Was Bad?;* Carrington 1993, *Offending Girls.*

Joy Wundersitz

Juvenile Delinquency, Canada

Laws concerning juvenile delinquency in Canada are the responsibility of the federal government. The federal government also partially funds youth custody facilities and specific youth programs. Provincial, territorial, and municipal governments are responsible for administrating and funding the police, courts, and correction services. Approximately 80 percent of the funds spent for the Canadian youth justice system goes to fund custody, leaving little for community-based programs. Few services are geared specifically to girls.

The Juvenile Delinquents Act (JDA) of 1908 was in force until 1984. Under it, girls 7 to 15 years of age in Canada's two territories and eight provinces, and up to 17 years in Quebec and Manitoba, could be cautioned by police or charged for breaking municipal, provincial, or federal criminal laws, or for the status offenses of immorality, truancy, and unmanageability. Any of these violations could result in a conviction of delinquency in a juvenile court closed to the public. A judge could suspend sentence, levy a fine, or for an indeterminate period, sentence a girl to probation, a social welfare agency, or a youth custody facility for rehabilitation or until she turned 21.

Before 1984, juvenile courts laid fewer than 10,000 charges annually against Canadian girls under federal criminal laws, as indicated by Table J. Far more girls than boys were charged with status offenses. More than 60 percent of the girls sentenced to custodial facilities had been convicted of minor offenses.

In 1984, the paternalistic, rehabilitative JDA was replaced by the Young Offenders Act (YOA). It aims to balance the protection of society, respect for legal rights, and recognition of specific needs of youth. Its mandatory provisions specify due-process proce-

Table J. Comparison of Charges against Girls in Canada's Youth Court for Criminal Code and Federal Statute Offenses in 1980 and 1995–1996

	Nature of Delinquency for Girls Aged 7–15 in 1980[1]		Cases by Principal Charge for Girls Aged 12–18 in 1995–96	
	N	Percent	N	Percent
Murder; Attempt	9	.11	6	.03
Robbery	89	1.12	369	1.69
Arson	42	.53	53	.24
Against Person[2]	710	8.97	4,434	20.25
Theft Over/Auto	504	6.36	525	2.40
Break & Enter	1,152	14.55	1,087	4.96
Fraud	457	5.84	559	2.55
Theft Under/Stolen Goods	3,411	43.01	6,820	31.15
Trafficking/Possession	265	3.35	573	2.62
Mischief	446	5.63	662	3.02
Nuisance/Disorderly	240	3.03	171	.78
Immorality/Vice/Soliciting	98	1.24	198	.90
Failure to Comply[3]	450	5.68	5,985	27.33
Other/Unknown	46	.58	456	2.08
Total	7,919	100.00	21,898	100.00

Notes
[1] 16- and 17-year-old girls included in statistics from Manitoba and P.Q.
[2] Includes major assaults, minor assaults, intent to use weapons, possession of weapon, kidnapping, and impaired driving. In 1980, there were fewer than 25 major assaults (.32% of total charges) while in 1995–96, 693 (or 3.16%) of the cases were charged with aggravated assault or assault with a weapon.
[3] Includes charges of escape custody, failure to comply with a disposition or to appear, and against the YOA.

Sources: Unpublished Table 12 "Nature of Delinquency by Sex and Age of the Accused" for 1980 provided by the Canadian Centre for Justice Statistics, *Youth Court Statistics*, 1995–96, Table 3.

dures and limits on the discretion of justice officials.

The YOA eliminated the offense of delinquency and informal judicial procedures. Status offenses were decriminalized. Violations against municipal and provincial laws were removed from federal law. In every part of Canada, girls 12 to 18 years could be charged only with federal criminal offenses. Girls younger than 12 were dealt with under child welfare laws. Alternative measures to the formal adversarial youth court procedures were encouraged but not mandated under the 1984 YOA or its amendments.

At every stage of criminal justice proceedings, a girl must be informed in a language she can understand of her right to a lawyer without delay (irrespective of her parents' ability to pay), and of her rights to bail and special hearings. Dispositions are made by a judge, usually after consideration of a pre-disposition report from a youth worker regarding a girl's circumstances and needs for guidance and assistance. Time-limited dispositions proportionate to the offense include absolute discharge, fine, restitution, community service, probation, and open or secure youth custody. Initially, the maximum sentence was 3 years for murder, amended to 5 and then to 10 years in 1995. If a girl 14 or older is charged with a serious offense, prosecutors can apply for an adult trial. With the 1995 amendments to the YOA, it is presumed that all 16- and 17-year-old youth should be dealt with in adult court for the most serious offenses.

Since 1984, the number of Canadian girls charged has increased, although the patterns vary by province and by race. Murder and murder attempts by girls remain at less than

15 cases annually (see Table J). The rates of serious violent and property offenses also have remained constant and low. Charges for minor property and assault offenses have increased. From 1986 to 1996, there was a 1,000 percent increase in administrative charges against girls such as failures to attend court and failure to comply with probation conditions and other court orders. In 1995–96, as Table J shows, 27.3 percent of charges against girls were for failures to comply with orders of the Youth Justice Administration; 19.7 percent was the comparable figure for boys.

Custody dispositions have increased in most provinces, despite the YOA's intent to promote alternatives to custody and the 1995 amendments requiring judges to impose custody only when all available and reasonable alternatives have been considered. A custody disposition was made for 23.4 percent of the principal charges against girls in 1995–96. More girls are in custody for noncompliance offenses than for assault. Most custody dispositions are for less than six months. There is no provision for parole or remission, but the youth courts must review (and can modify) custody sentences longer than one year.

The Canadian federal government is considering a new youth criminal justice statute for 2000 to include the provision that adult sentences must be presumed for serious violent offenses committed by youths 14 years and older. More prevention programs and community-based sentences will be encouraged by modest interim government grants. There are no mandatory provisions to reduce the gender, geographic, or racial variations in charging and sentencing practices. *See also* Juvenile Delinquency, Australia; Juvenile Delinquency, USA; Gender Discrimination and Juvenile Justice; Status Offenses.

Further Reading: Bala 1997, *Young Offenders Law;* Reitsma-Street 1991, "A Review of Female Delinquency"; Reitsma-Street 1998, "Still Girls Learn to Care."

Marge Reitsma-Street

Juvenile Delinquency, USA

Female juvenile delinquency in the United States has historically been underresearched, and consequently, it is a poorly understood area within the field of criminology. Two major reasons account for this. First, many researchers have been most interested in what they define as serious delinquent behavior, and therefore they have focused on male delinquency and ignored female delinquency. Second, many researchers believed there were few reasons to examine female delinquency because it was assumed that the processes generating delinquent behavior were largely the same for both sexes. Consequently, researchers and theorists alike ignored the female context and inferred that the major predictors of delinquent behavior applied to both male and female participation.

Two recent trends in criminology have revealed new information on female delinquency. First, researchers are increasingly examining the sex-specific influences on important predictors of delinquency. These approaches consider whether certain influences, such as intelligence, differ in their relationship to male and female delinquency. A better understanding of whether differences exist between males and females in predictors of delinquency is vitally important for developing effective prevention programs.

A second trend concerns exploring the nature of female delinquency on its own terms, independent of how it compares with male delinquency. The study of female delinquency is important regardless of whether it is similar to, or different from, male delinquency. Moreover, research in this area is examining the complex dimensions of female delinquency, with some researchers asking whether important differences exist among females in the characteristics associated with delinquency. Factors related to delinquent behavior are not necessarily the same for all females.

Estimates of delinquent behavior are drawn from three main sources: police arrest statistics, juvenile court records, and self-report surveys. These sources reveal some consistent themes and at the same time have

Table K. Police Arrest Statistics for Juvenile Delinquency, USA, 1998

Crime Type	Percent Male of Total Juvenile Arrests	Percent Female of Total Juvenile Arrests	Gender Ratio (M:F)
Total Crime	73	27	3:1
Index Crime	74	26	3:1
Violent Index Crime	83	17	5:1
Murder	92	8	12:1
Forcible Rape	98	2	49:1
Robbery	91	9	10:1
Aggravated Assault	78	22	4:1
Property Index Crime	72	28	3:1
Burglary	89	11	8:1
Larceny-Theft	65	35	2:1
Motor Vehicle Theft	83	17	5:1
Arson	89	11	8:1
Non-Index Crime	73	27	3:1
Other Assaults	69	31	2:1
Forgery/Counterfeit	64	36	2:1
Fraud	67	33	2:1
Stolen Property	87	13	7:1
Vandalism	88	12	7:1
Weapons	90	10	9:1
Prostitution	49	51	1:1
Sex Offenses	93	7	13:1
Drug Abuse	86	14	6:1
Gambling	97	3	32:1
Offenses against Family/Children	63	37	2:1
Liquor	70	30	2:1
Drunkenness	82	18	5:1
Disorderly Conduct	72	28	3:1
Vagrancy	84	16	5:1
Curfew	70	30	2:1
Runaways	42	58	1:1
DUI	83	17	5:1

Source: U.S. Department of Justice, Federal Bureau of Investigation 1999, *Crime in the United States, 1998.*

implications for how we currently understand female delinquency.

Information on the participation of males and females in various forms of delinquency, as measured by recent police arrest statistics, is reported in Table K.

Inspection of Table K leads to two general conclusions. First, males participate much more frequently than females in official juvenile delinquency (that is, delinquency that comes to the attention of the police). These differences are most pronounced for serious offenses, especially violent offenses.

Second, participation rates differ for most offenses, although female participation is more similar to males' for certain crimes such as theft, forgery, prostitution, and running away.

It is important to point out that arrests depend on the ability of the police to identify an offender and the decision to make an arrest. Persons suspected of delinquency are not always arrested (for various reasons), and decisions not to arrest take the seriousness of the behavior under consideration. Moreover, most delinquent behavior does not come to

Table L. Annual Self-Reported Delinquency, USA, 1997

	Percent of Juveniles Reporting Involvement	
	Females	Males
Argue/Fight with Parent	90	87
Hit Instructor	2	5
Serious Fight	13	22
Group Fight	16	27
Hurt Someone Badly	6	23
Armed Robbery	1	6
Theft under $50	27	42
Theft over $50	8	18
Stole from Store	30	38
Auto Theft	4	8
Stolen Car Parts	2	9
Break and Enter	19	31
Arson	1	5
Damage School Property	10	21
Damage Work Property	3	10
Been Arrested	4	14

Source: Johnson, Bachman, and O'Malley 1998, *National Survey Results.*

the attention of the police. In short, most juvenile delinquency is not officially recorded; researchers, therefore, need to examine self-reports of delinquent behavior directly from juveniles.

Self-reported information on delinquent behavior for males and females appears in Table L. It reveals that females' self-reported delinquency is lower than that of males, especially for violent behaviors. However, female delinquency is relatively high for certain acts. For example, approximately 30 percent of female adolescents report having stolen from a store and 19 percent report having committed a break-and-enter crime in the past year.

It is important to point out that self-report studies of delinquency rely on youths, primarily youths from high schools, to accurately report their deviant activities. Of course, some youths lie, and many of the most serious delinquents are not in school. However, overall, self-reports reveal consistent information about the delinquent activity found among most adolescents. In sum, while self-reports do not always capture information on the most serious juvenile offenders, they do reveal useful data for the majority of

youths who engage in offending behavior, most of which is trivial in nature.

Available evidence, then, suggests that females are less delinquent than males and that for certain behaviors, such as violence, the gap is especially large. At present, three explanations account for these differences. First, females, on average, score lower on many of the major risk factors for delinquent activity (impulsivity, school failure, etc.). Second, even when they have the same risks for delinquency, female adolescents are subjected to greater supervision and control than males. Third, females tend to cope somewhat differently than males with many of the conditions that foster delinquent behavior. In short, they embrace nondelinquent responses to a greater extent than males, even when faced with similar criminogenic conditions.

At present, there are two answers to the question, "What accounts for female delinquency?" First, the majority of females who become delinquent, especially in terms of the delinquent behaviors revealed by national self-report studies, do so for reasons very similar to males. Most delinquent conduct is trivial, and the reasons why females get involved in these activities are related to experiences in their families, schools, and peer groups, just as with male delinquents. Much evidence suggests, then, that the pathways leading to delinquency are very similar for females and males when relatively trivial forms of delinquent conduct are being considered.

A second body of information has emerged in research on serious female delinquency. Serious delinquent behavior is often characterized by an early onset age, as well as by high frequency and severity of activity. At present, we know very little about serious female delinquents. Recent evidence suggests, however, that these females have had especially traumatic experiences in their lives, including sexual victimization and additional dysfunctional experiences (e.g., parental alcohol and substance abuse, crime, or parental conflict) at home. These noxious experiences often lead to escapist behaviors such as drug abuse and running away, which place these youths at significant risk for more serious delinquency and crime in the future.

While information on the unique characteristics of female delinquency still falls far behind that of males, progress is being made. Research on female delinquency routinely appears in the top academic criminological journals. New theories of delinquency increasingly consider whether there are specific characteristics for females that need to be addressed.

Several areas need further development and exploration, however, if we are to increase knowledge of female delinquency. For example, researchers need to explore more fully the dimensions of female delinquent and criminal careers. Questions such as why females begin, persist, and ultimately cease offending have not been adequately addressed. Moreover, at present, the early childhood precursors of delinquency, as well as the long-term life outcomes of former delinquents, are not well understood for females. Finally, the unique role of sexual victimization in serious female delinquent behavior needs to be examined more comprehensively. Sexual victimization is a risk factor for participation in serious delinquent conduct for females. Clearly, however, not all females who experience sexual victimization become involved in delinquent behavior. Understanding the characteristics that lead to delinquency under these circumstances is crucial.

Females are no longer ignored in research and theories of delinquent behavior. Significant progress is occurring. However, there is an important need for future research that will unravel the complex nature of female delinquency. *See also* DESISTANCE FROM CRIME; JUVENILE DELINQUENCY AND FAMILY CONFLICT; JUVENILE DELINQUENCY, AUSTRALIA; JUVENILE DELINQUENCY, CANADA.

Further Reading: Broidy and Agnew 1997, "Gender and Crime"; Moffitt 1993, "Adolescence-Limited and Life-Course Persistent Antisocial Behavior."

Paul Mazerolle

Juvenile Institutions

Over the 1990s, juvenile institutions in the United States experienced growth in their number of female inmates. In the past, most female delinquents were status offenders, but today increasing numbers of female youths are convicted of violent crimes, leading to longer sentences and more secure lock-up facilities. Between 1981 and 1997, violent offending by girls increased by 89 percent, and property offending by 39 percent. Subsequent arrest figures suggest that the trend is continuing. The burgeoning number of more serious female offenders has added a tremendous strain to the juvenile justice system.

Juveniles accused of committing crimes or status offenses such as truancy or running away are usually referred to the juvenile justice system, which differs from the adult criminal justice system in its greater degree of record confidentiality, its limits on sentence lengths, and its primary goal of rehabilitation. In most states, when a juvenile of 15 years or older commits a serious offense, the case may be transferred to an adult court. When an adult sentence is imposed, juveniles are moved at some point into the adult prison system. However, the majority of cases are not transfer-eligible, and they remain in the juvenile system.

Although probation is the most common type of sentence for juvenile female offenders, rising numbers of girls are being incarcerated temporarily in detention centers or sentenced to secure juvenile correctional facilities. On an average day in 1997, nearly 106,000 juveniles were confined in detention or correctional facilities, 14 percent of them female. As to detention center custody, approximately 16 percent of delinquency cases involving females resulted in detention, compared with about 22 percent for male offenders. However, the rate of detention is increasing faster for girls than boys. Most detention center custody of females is for nonviolent offenses involving drugs, prostitution, and breaches of the peace.

Juvenile females are also less likely to be ordered to long-term correctional facility custody than juvenile males. Between 1989 and 1993, less than one quarter of female offenders were removed from the home, whereas 29 percent of male delinquent offenders were in long-term out-of-home placements (Poe-Yamagata and Butts 1996:10). The average length of stay for female youths in a secure correctional facility is approximately 201 days, compared with 250 days for male youths.

Of female youths confined in 1997, about 49 percent were Caucasian, more than one-third black, about 13 percent Hispanic, and another 5 percent Native American. Most were 15 to 16 years old, and almost 19 percent were parents. The majority of institutionalized female juveniles have a history of childhood abuse; over 60 percent were victims of physical abuse and 54 percent were victims of sexual abuse. More than one-half of them have attempted suicide. Incarcerated juvenile females also report high rates of drug use, including alcohol, marijuana, and cocaine. In 1992, Congress amended the Juvenile Justice and Delinquency Prevention Act (JJDP) to require states applying for federal grants to review their juvenile justice systems and analyze their gender-specific services for the prevention and treatment of juvenile delinquency. With this encouragement, some

states have begun to recognize the special needs of incarcerated juvenile females.

U.S. juvenile institutions for female offenders number in the thousands if one includes all the public and private facilities and institutions that range from the most secure facilities available to halfway houses. Recently, many state legislatures have passed laws providing alternatives to the traditional incarceration of juveniles. Legislatures are attempting to reduce the significant burden on state-owned and operated juvenile correctional facilities. Many states are using "blended sentencing" for juveniles, allowing judges to impose juvenile punishments, adult sanctions, or a combination of both. Programs for female juvenile offenders that use blended sentencing tend to focus on prevention, intervention, and provision of community-based services. *See also* FEMALE CRIME, PATTERNS AND TRENDS IN, USA; JUVENILE DELINQUENCY, USA; JUVENILE INSTITUTIONS, HISTORY OF; STATUS OFFENSES.

Further Reading: Budnick and Shields-Fletcher 1998, *What about Girls?;* Chesney-Lind and Shelden 1998, *Girls, Delinquency, and Juvenile Justice;* Snyder and Sickmund 1999, *Juvenile Offenders and Victims.*

Walter E. Lippincott

Juvenile Institutions, History of

Institutions for female juvenile delinquents in the United States did not appear until the early nineteenth century, and even then, they were slow in developing. The first institution for delinquent boys was the New York House of Refuge, opened in 1824. During the next 30 years, several other cities opened houses of refuge, many of which housed girls and boys in separate quarters. In fact, one of the most important court cases in the area of delinquency, that of *Ex Parte Crouse*, involved a girl of 16 who was committed, at the insistence of her mother, to the Philadelphia House of Refuge on a charge of being "incorrigible." This was the first case where the English doctrine of *parens patriae* was affirmed by a court. The Pennsylvania Supreme Court rhetorically inquired: "May not the natural parents, when unequal to the task of education, or unworthy of it, be superseded by the *parens patriae* or common guardian of the community?" This logic prevailed, even though one of Crouse's parents (her father) felt able to care for her. Many other parents committed their daughters and sons to institutions because they could not provide adequate care or found the children uncontrollable.

The first separate institution for girls was the State Industrial School for Girls in Lancaster, Massachusetts, established in 1856. As Barbara Brenzel notes, the Lancaster school was intended "to be a school for girls— for the gentler sex ... with all the details relating to employment, instruction, and amusement, and, indeed, to every branch of domestic economy" (Brenzel 1975:41). Institutions for girls, like those for boys, focused not on children who had committed crimes, but rather on youngsters who seemed likely to become criminals. Thus, it is not surprising to find that both in the houses of refuge and the Lancaster Industrial School, most of the inmates had not actually committed crimes. Most were brought into the system because of status offenses, behaviors that trigger state intervention only when committed by persons under a certain age (usually 18); these behaviors included running away and a catch-all known variously as "incorrigibility" or "immorality."

A look at the specific offenses of the earliest inmates of the Lancaster institution reveals that over two-thirds had been accused of moral rather than criminal offenses: vagrancy, beggary, stubbornness, deceitfulness, "idle and vicious behavior," "wanton and lewd conduct," and running away. Similarly, many girls in what was called the Home of the Good Shepherd, in Memphis, Tennessee, had been brought into the juvenile court because of running away, incorrigibility, or various charges labeled by the court as "immorality," including "sexual relations" that ranged from sexual intercourse to "kissing and holding hands in the park" (Shelden 1981). A study of juvenile court records in four cities around the turn of the century arrived at the same conclusion: "immorality"

seems to have been the most common charge against females. Included under the rubric were "coming home late at night," "masturbating," "using obscene language," "riding at night in automobiles without a chaperon," and "strutting about in a lascivious manner." As was also the case for institutionalized boys, many of these girls were the children of immigrants, most of whom were extremely poor (Schlossman and Wallach 1978; Schlossman 1977).

The building of institutions for girls continued well into the twentieth century. The titles of these institutions gradually changed, evolving from "industrial schools" to "reform schools" and then to "training schools." Meanwhile, the juvenile court was founded in 1899 in Chicago, and within 20 years, such courts could be found in almost every major city. The juvenile court continued the pattern of previous (mostly county) courts, focusing mostly on various status offenses, especially "morals" offenses in the case of girls, but ignoring almost identical behavior for boys. One study of several different courts found that in 1920, 93 percent of the girls accused of delinquency were charged with status offenses; of these, 65 percent were charged with immoral sexual activity. The researchers found that 51 percent of the referrals had come from the girls' parents, a situation they explained as working-class parents' fears about their daughters' exposure to the "omnipresent temptations to which working class daughters in particular were exposed to in the modern ecology of urban work and leisure" (Odem and Schlossman 1991:196; Odem 1995).

A study of the Los Angeles Juvenile Court found that in 1920, 77 percent of the girls were detained before their hearings, most commonly to look for the presence of venereal disease. (This was during a period when there was a widespread movement to ferret out venereal diseases, especially among the immigrant population.) Thirty-five percent of all delinquent girls and over half of those held for sex offenses had gonorrhea, syphilis, or other venereal infections. The researchers noted that the presence of venereal disease, and the desire to impose treatment (which in those times was lengthy and painful), accounted for the large numbers of girls in detention centers. Analysis of court actions revealed that although probation was the most common court response (61 percent were accorded probation), only 27 percent were released on probation immediately following the hearing. Many girls were held for weeks or months after initial hearings. Girls not given probation were often placed in private homes as domestics or placed in a wide range of private institutions, such as the Convent of the Good Shepherd or homes for unmarried mothers. Ultimately, about 33 percent of the "problem girls" during this period were sentenced to institutional confinement (Odem 1995; Odem and Schlossman 1991).

A follow-up to the 1950s of this same court found that 31 percent of the girls were charged with running away from home, truancy, curfew, or "general unruliness at home." Nearly half of the status offenders were charged with sexual misconduct, though "usually with a single partner; few had engaged in prostitution." The rate of venereal disease had plummeted; only 4.5 percent of all girls tested positive. Despite this, the concern for female sexual conduct "remained determinative in shaping social policy" in the 1950s, according to these researchers (Odem and Schlossman 1991).

Studies continue to note problems with the vagueness of contemporary status-offense categories, which are essentially "buffer charges" for suspected sexuality. As Chesney-Lind (1973) reported, many girls who came to the attention of the juvenile court were subjected to vaginal exams. Studies of institutionalized girls in the 1960s showed that although most were incarcerated for behaviors like running away from home and incorrigibility, the underlying offenses in many cases remained sexual misconduct (Vedder and Sommerville 1970).

As studies continued to demonstrate a "double standard," a widespread social movement to deinstitutionalize status offenders began in the 1970s, resulting in a significant decrease in the detention and institutionalization of such offenders. Despite this movement, we can still find girls much more likely to be detained and sent to institutions (and even placed in adult jails in some jurisdictions) on what researchers have called "bootstrapping": Girls originally charged with a status offense are subsequently rearrested for "probation violation" (technically a delinquent offense, which can result in detention and institutionalization) if they commit another status offense (Chesney-Lind and Shelden 1998). *See also* JUVENILE INSTITUTIONS; STATUS OFFENSES.

Further Reading: Brenzel 1983, *Daughters of the State*; Chesney-Lind 1973, "Judicial Enforcement of the Female Sex Role"; Chesney-Lind and Shelden 1998, *Girls, Delinquency and Juvenile Justice*; Pisciotta 1982, "Saving the Children."

Randall G. Shelden

K

Kellor, Frances A. (1873–1952)

Frances A. Kellor, one of the first female criminologists in the United States and certainly the first to have received formal training, was born in Columbus, Ohio, in 1873. She graduated from Cornell University Law School in 1897, at a time when most law schools refused to admit women, and enrolled one year later in the University of Chicago's graduate program in sociology. However, Kellor never completed the doctorate due to opportunities to pursue applied studies.

Kellor was the first American to empirically critique Cesare Lombroso's biological interpretation of female criminality. Her research led her to recommend an environmental analysis of crime. In 1901, she published *Experimental Sociology Descriptive and Analytical: Delinquents,* one of the earliest American books on criminology. This text included a critique of then-current criminological methods, empirical data on criminal behavior, and an analysis of race and crime based on her study of Southern prisons.

In 1902, Kellor accepted a fellowship at the New York Summer School of Philanthropy. During her first two decades in New York, she researched and published extensively on the plight of Southern black migrants and European immigrants. In 1904, Kellor organized and served as general director of the Inter-Municipal League on Household Research, an agency that advocated legal change to improve the conditions of child labor and tenement houses.

In 1906, the National League for the Protection of Colored Women was established in New York City with the help of Kellor, who sought to facilitate black women's relocation from the South. Kellor was appointed secretary of the New York State Immigration Commission (1908) to investigate immigrants' living and working conditions. From 1910 to 1913, she served as director and chief investigator of the Bureau of Industries and Immigration, established to protect the welfare of immigrants. From 1926 until her death in 1952, she was the vice-president and chief administrator of the American Arbitration Association.

Perhaps Frances Kellor is best remembered as one of the first empiricists in criminology and as a legal scholar and activist who helped transform the lives of many early-twentieth-century immigrants and Southern migrants from extreme marginality to stability. *See also* LEGAL PROFESSION, HISTORY OF WOMEN IN; LOMBROSO, CESARE.

Further Reading: A. Davis 1967, *Spearheads for Reform*; Fitzpatrick 1990, *Endless Crusade;* Freedman 1981, *Their Sisters' Keepers.*

Donna C. Hale

Kingston Penitentiary. *See* PRISON REFORM, CANADA; WOMEN IN PRISON, CANADA.

Kleptomania. *See* SHOPLIFTING AND KLEPTOMANIA.

L

Labeling Explanations of Female Crime

"Labeling" explanations of female crime hold that attempts to control crime can actually create more crime. Although labeling explanations of crime initially developed in the late 1930s, it was not until the late 1970s that these explanations were expanded explicitly to include females. Labeling theory is usually seen as beginning with the work of Frank Tannenbaum (1938), but it received the most attention in the 1960s and 1970s, drawing on the work of Edwin Lemert (1951) and Howard Becker (1963).

The central idea behind the work of early labeling theorists is that attempts to formally control crime actually generate crime. Lemert's (1951) discussion of the movement from primary to secondary deviance explains how this happens. According to Lemert, primary deviance is the set of initial deviant acts, behaviors in which almost everyone engages. Secondary deviance, however, is the deviance that results when one takes on a deviant role. Lemert believed that labeling an individual ("delinquent," "criminal," "weird," and so on) is critical in the move from primary to secondary deviance because the label leads others to exclude the labeled individual from conventional activities. This exclusion changes the self-image of the labeled person, and that change leads, in turn, to the acceptance of a deviant social role.

The first theorist to explicitly include females in labeling explanations of crime was Anthony Harris (1977). In the move to include females, Harris applied labeling theory to informal processes of social control. Harris argues that while males are more often the focus of formal control, females are more often dealt with informally. He discusses "type-scripts" that define role-appropriate conforming and deviant behavior for the various groups in society, including males and females. Harris then argues that females are less likely to commit crimes than males because crime is not role-appropriate for females either as conforming or as deviant behavior.

Edwin Schur (1984) built on Harris's work in *Labeling Women Deviant*. Schur argues that the deviance of women emerges, like that of men, through a process in which other people react to a behavior as if it is deviant. Females, however, have lower levels of offending than males because gender norms and role expectations shape the opportunities for involvement in crimes and define role-appropriate behavior for females. Schur maintains that females' high rates of mental illness and low rates of criminal behavior result from the fact that mental illness is a role-appropriate deviant behavior for females while crime is not.

Since Schur's work, attempts to include females in labeling explanations of crime have been of two types, both maintaining the earlier focus on the way gender norms shape informal social control. Among the first is work by Bartusch and Matsueda (1996), who argue that socialization processes make females more relationship-oriented than males. This difference in orientation makes females more susceptible to the reactions of others and, thus, more likely to be deterred by negative labels than males. Bartusch and Matsueda recognize that females are labeled more frequently for certain activities than males. Running away from home is a good example of a behavior that females are more likely to be arrested for than males.

The second explanation is John Braithwaite's (1989) theory of crime, shame, and reintegration. Integrating control, social learning, strain, and subcultural theories with the labeling perspective, Braithwaite develops his theory around the concept of shaming, which he defines as "all social processes of expressing disapproval which have the intention or effect of invoking remorse in the person being shamed" (1989:100).

Braithwaite argues that there are two types of shaming. The first, reintegrative shaming, is followed by efforts to reintegrate the offender back into the community. The second, stigmatization, actually leads to increases in crime because there is no effort to return the offender to the community. According to Braithwaite, reintegrative shaming is more likely to occur in communitarian societies that are characterized by a high degree of interdependency among the members.

In his explanation of crime by females, Braithwaite argues first that the same process explains both male and female offending. Like earlier theorists, Braithwaite then argues that gender-role socialization leads to greater interdependency for females, which increases the likelihood that they will be deterred from crime by social reactions. Braithwaite then goes a step further, arguing that females are also more likely than males to be deterred by social reactions because they are more likely to be reintegratively shamed, whereas males are more likely to be stigmatized.

While labeling theory ignored the crimes of females when it was first developed, as it stands today, it has the potential for adding to our understanding of female crime. The potential of labeling theory arises largely from its greater sensitivity to issues of informal social control and gender-role socialization than other criminological theories. *See also* SOCIAL CONTROL OF WOMEN; SOCIAL PROCESS EXPLANATIONS OF DELINQUENCY.

Further Reading: Becker 1963, *Outsiders*; A. Harris 1977, "Sex and Theories of Deviance"; Schur 1984, *Labeling Women Deviant*; Braithwaite 1989, *Crime, Shame and Reintegration*.

Ruth Ann Triplett

Lawyers and Gender Difference

The increasing number of women lawyers in the American legal profession has made it possible for professional women to explore the legal issues implicated in the scientific and theoretical controversies about the significance of gender difference.

While historically, women who entered the medical profession did so by claiming a difference from men in their ability to nurture and care for the sick, women who sought entrance to the legal profession argued that they were the same as men, intellectually and in their ability to perform in the courtroom or law office. Supreme Court Justice Ruth Bader Ginsburg, when she was a practicing lawyer, litigated for women's rights successfully in the Supreme Court by developing arguments based on the idea of equality.

In 1974, however, when the Supreme Court ruled that discrimination on the basis of pregnancy was not discrimination on the basis of sex *(Geduldig v. Aiello)*, some women lawyers who were seeking to establish women's reproductive rights began to argue that women's biological (and other) differences from men need to be acknowledged in the law. From that point on, women lawyers were actively engaged in theoretical debate and practical legal work that explored the "gender differences" debate. Are women different from men in ways that the law should acknowledge, in cases involving (for example) the "special needs" of pregnancy, the battered spouse defense of "learned helplessness," statutory rape, military and combat service, and single-sex schools? Or are men and women more alike than different for purposes of legal regulation and the avoidance of inappropriate stereotypes?

As women lawyers strategized about the appropriate legal treatment to be given gender categories, they also acknowledged possible differences in the way women lawyers practice their profession. After the publication of Carol Gilligan's *In a Different Voice: Psychological Theory and Women's Development* (1982), many women lawyers argued that they practiced law differently from some men. These differences included seeking solutions to problems, redefining legal categories (as Catharine MacKinnon did in her work on sexual harassment [1978] and pornography [Mackinnon and Dworkin 1997]), using more mediational and less aggressive and "macho" approaches to legal work, and employing more egalitarian and participatory approaches to the management of legal work.

As women lawyers and law teachers rediscovered Susan Glaspell's short story ("A Jury of Her Peers" 1917) and play (*Trifles* 1916) about the female reaction to a murder of an abusive husband, women argued that men and women reason differently in factfinding, conclusion development, and understanding of such legal concepts as justification and excuse.

Within the profession itself, which remains deeply stratified, women lawyers are still found disproportionately in public service work, as compared with private practice, and they are still less likely to be managing partners and to hold leadership positions. But as the gender hierarchy of the profession slowly changes—with, in 1999, two women lawyers on the Supreme Court, a woman lawyer as first lady, and another woman serving as the first female attorney general of the United States—women lawyers are in a better position to work on the issues of what impact gender differences should have on the law. *See also* BATTERED WOMEN AND SELF-DEFENSE, AUSTRALIA; BATTERED WOMEN AND SELF-DEFENSE, CANADA; BATTERED WOMEN AND SELF-DEFENSE, USA; GENDER AND JUDICIAL DECI-

SION-MAKING; GENDER BIAS TASK FORCES; LEGAL PROFESSION, HISTORY OF WOMEN IN; LEGAL PROFESSION, WOMEN'S CURRENT PARTICIPATION IN; O'CONNOR, SANDRA DAY; RENO, JANET; WOMEN PROFESSIONALS IN THE JUSTICE WORKPLACE.

Further Reading: Littleton 1987, "Reconstructing Sexual Equality"; MacKinnon 1987, *Feminism Unmodified*; Menkel-Meadow 1994, "Portia Redux"; Menkel-Meadow 1985, "Portia in a Different Voice."

Carrie J. Menkel-Meadow

Learned Helplessness. *See* BATTERED WOMEN AND SELF-DEFENSE, AUSTRALIA; BATTERED WOMEN AND SELF-DEFENSE, CANADA; BATTERED WOMEN AND SELF-DEFENSE, USA; VICTIMIZATION, FEMINIST PERSPECTIVES ON; FRAMINGHAM EIGHT; LAWYERS AND GENDER DIFFERENCE.

Legal Profession, History of Women in

The history of women in the U.S. legal profession is fairly short. An almost total exclusion of women continued well into the late 1800s. Only recently, as Table M shows, has a significant percentage of law school graduates been women, and women still tend to cluster in certain legal specialties (Table N).

Up until the 1900s, a degree from a law school was not a prerequisite to admission to the bar in most U.S. states. Rather, individuals could engage in apprenticeships or clerkships with practicing attorneys before applying for admission. The few women who engaged in such clerkships did so with husbands or fathers. One of the first women lawyers noted in history was Margaret Brent, who "read" under an attorney until she took the bar exam. In the 1600s, she executed land deals and litigated the estate of Maryland's governor. Very few women appeared to have practiced law in any way in the next century, although one noteworthy exception was Lucy Terry Prince, an African American woman who successfully defended a land claim in a case that went to the Supreme Court. In 1869, Arabella Babb Mansfield was admitted to the Iowa State Bar. During the same year, Myra Colby Bradwell passed the Illinois bar exam but was denied admission to the Illinois bar because she was a woman. Her case fighting this barrier led to a landmark decision regarding women's entry into the legal profession.

Table M. Number and Proportion of Female Lawyers in Selected Years, USA

Year	Percent Women	Number of Women Lawyers
1870*	0.01	
1880*	0.1	
1890*	0.2	
1900*	0.9	
1910	0.5	
1920	1.4	
1930	2.2	
1940	2.4	
1950	2.5	
1960	3	7,434
1971	3	9,947
1980	8	44,185
1985	13	85,542
1991	20	159,377
1995	23	207,738
2000 (projected)	27	269,068

* Includes semiprofessions.

Sources: Data for 1870–1940 from Halliday 1986, "Six Score Years and Ten"; Pear 1987, "Women Reduce Lag"; and Abel 1989, American Lawyers, page 264. Data for 1950 from Curran et al. 1986, Supplement. Data for 1960–2000 from American Bar Association, Commission on Women in the Profession 1995, Women in the Law.

In 1873 in *Bradwell v. Illinois*, the U.S. Supreme Court enunciated what has come to be known as its "mother of the species" argument. Basically, the Court held that women had a special role to fulfill, but it was as mothers, not lawyers. The Court also held that as a married woman, Bradwell would have been unable to enter into contracts and therefore was disabled as an attorney (married women at that time had no legal entity apart from their husbands and, thus, were unable to enter into contracts). The Court also held that the Illinois legislature, in creating the statute authorizing the Illinois state bar, never intended women as admittees; and, finally, in a portion of the opinion that had more far-reaching consequences for individual liberty rights, the Court held that the federal Constitution did not protect women (or evidently men) from being barred from any particular occupation or profession.

Despite the *Bradwell* case, other women continued to apply for admission to state bar associations, and some succeeded. Lavinia Goodnell was formally admitted to a local bar association in Wisconsin in 1875 but was denied admission to the state bar. She fought the decision and was successful in 1879 in her campaign to change the admissions statute that had excluded women. Interestingly, upon her death at the age of 41 from rheumatic fever, newspaper articles attributed her early demise to the fact that she practiced law.

Table N. U.S. Female Lawyers by Type of Practice, 1980 and 1991

	1980			1991	
Type of Practice	Number of Women	Percent	Type of Practice	Number of Women	Percent
Private Practice	24,592	6.6	Private Practice	110,961	19.0
Judiciary	1,653	8.6	Judiciary	4,006	18.6
Government	7,626	15.1	Government	18,802	28.4
Private Industry	4,937	8.4	Private Industry	15,078	19.6
Legal Aid/ Public Defender	2,141	26.0	Legal Aid/ Public Defender	3,342	37.9
Education	893	13.5	Education	2,127	26.0
Retired	2,343	8.2	Retired	5,062	13.7
Total	**44,185**	**8.1**	**Total**	**159,377**	**19.8**

Source: American Bar Association, Commission on Women in the Profession 1995, Women in the Law.

States slowly started to remove language from state bar admissions criteria that excluded women. By 1900, 34 states had admitted women to the practice of law, and by 1920, all states had removed language that barred women from admittance.

However, as state bars removed exclusionary language toward women, the prerequisite of a law school degree gained ascendancy. Thus, women had a new battle to fight, since many law schools denied admission to women. The first female graduate of a law school, Ada Kepley, graduated from the University of Chicago Law School in 1870 (although it took her another 11 years to gain admission to the Illinois bar). Most western and midwestern law schools opened their doors to women much earlier than eastern schools. In the northeast, the rejection of women led to alternative programs such as the Portia School of Law in Boston, founded in 1908, which eventually became the New England School of Law. Yale opened its doors to women in 1918 and Columbia in 1927, but Harvard Law School barred women until 1950.

In the early 1900s, women practicing law often did so in the newly emerging juvenile or family courts. This was a choice that raised less objection since it was seen as an extension of women's "natural" role with children. Even today, women tend to cluster in family law, public interest law, and other specialties such as appellate law rather than litigation. *See also* Judges; Lawyers and Gender Difference; Legal Profession, Women's Current Participation in; O'Connor, Sandra Day; Paralegals; Reno, Janet; Women Professionals in the Justice Workplace.

Further Reading: Bernat 1992, "Women in the Legal Profession"; Morello 1986, *The Invisible Bar.*

Joycelyn M. Pollock

Legal Profession, Women's Current Participation in

Although Arabella Babb Mansfield was admitted to the Iowa bar in 1869, the number of women in the U.S. legal profession remained extremely low (less than 3 percent) until the 1980s. During the 1980s, as Table M shows, gender differences in law school admittance subsided substantially. However, only 16 percent of legal practitioners were female at the time. Today, the percentage of lawyers who are female is continuing to increase, and a select few are obtaining employment and partnerships in the most prestigious sectors of law.

Given recent increases in the proportion of female law students, one might conclude that gender differences in this elite profession have all but disappeared. However, substantial gender differences remain in the prestige of law schools attended by men and women and the specialties and professional sectors in which they work. Moreover, even greater gender differences persist in salaries, rates of promotion to partner, proportion engaged in full-time work, and numbers leaving the profession.

When women first began entering law schools, they were seldom admitted to elite law schools but instead often attended local law schools or those specially designed for the training of women, such as the Portia School of Law in Boston. After Columbia Law School admitted its first woman student in 1920s, other elite schools began following suit, but women's admissions to law schools, especially elite law schools, remained relatively low until the 1980s. While women today have more than a token status in law schools, the continuing gap between men and women in law school entry cannot be explained by differential ability; female applicants have better undergraduate records and slightly better LSAT scores than men. These differences are particularly prominent at the elite law schools, attendance at which is associated with entry into the most prestigious jobs.

Women and men vary in the types of law they practice and the occupational settings where they work. Men are more likely to enter the more prestigious specialties such as securities and tax law, while women typically enter low-ranked specialties associated with traditionally female roles such as divorce, family, and poverty law. In addition, men are more likely to practice in lucrative private firms or the corporate sector, while women almost equal men in the lower-paying government sector. Table N shows the proportion of women lawyers in various types of practice in 1980 and 1991.

Even within these sectors, there are significant differences in the types of work performed by male and female lawyers. In the private-firm sector, male lawyers are most likely to practice in the core group of large prestigious law firms, while women often work for medium-to-small peripheral law firms. Moreover, the few women entering prestigious law firms seldom enter the Fortune 500 firms (i.e., firms whose clients are primarily Fortune 500 companies). Even within Fortune 500 law firms, women are seldom assigned to the high-profile Fortune 500 clients who pave the way to partnership. In the private corporate sector, the chief corporate councils are predominantly male, with the staff lawyers being both male and female. Although males also occupy most of the supervisory positions in the government sector, women are more equally represented there than in either private firms or the corporate sector.

The most egregious gender differences among lawyers involve remuneration and promotion. Although male and female lawyers begin with virtually equal salaries, within only a few years, men are earning considerably more than their female counterparts, especially in the private-firm sector. Moreover, the earnings gap between male and female lawyers is amplified as they ascend the mobility ladder. The pinnacle of success for lawyers in the private-firm sector is the ascent to partnership. Although women have constituted more than 20 percent of graduating law students over the past 20 years, they represent less than 10 percent of partners in major law firms. Thus, while women have begun to establish legal careers, their career patterns look very different from those of their male counterparts. Due mainly to gender differences in family responsibilities, female lawyers are more likely than males to practice part-time and/or to enter into "mommy-track" positions that limit career advancement.

Given the gender differences in remuneration and mobility following women's increased entry into the legal profession, it is not surprising to find that there are also gender differences in departures from law firms, with women exhibiting much higher attrition rates than their male counterparts. *See also* Lawyers and Gender Difference; Legal Profession, History of Women in; Legal Training; Women Professionals in the Justice Workplace.

Further Reading: Abel 1989, *American Lawyers*; Hagan and Kay 1995, *Gender in Practice*.

Jo Dixon

Legal Training

Until the twentieth century, men studied law by apprenticing themselves to practicing lawyers while women studied law with their fathers or husbands and encountered resistance when they attempted to practice. As professional law schools became the predominant sites of legal training in the United States, many barred women from attendance. At law schools in which women were permitted to enroll, their scarce numbers made them targets of distinctive treatment and even outright hostility. Some professors engaged in the practice of "ladies' day," in which they called exclusively on women in class; others questioned why women were taking "men's seats" in the law school classroom.

In 1967, women accounted for under 5 percent of law degrees, but today, close to 40 percent of those entering law school are women. White women account most for this striking shift; racial and ethnic minority women are still substantially underrepresented.

As women are entering law school classrooms in greater numbers, they have created some pressure on faculties to reexamine traditional methods of law teaching. Several studies have shown that women are less comfortable than men in law classes and do not perform as well as would be expected given their prior academic achievements. In a study of the experiences of students at the University of Pennsylvania Law School, researchers found that even though women and men entered with virtually identical credentials, women law students participated less in class discussions and did not graduate with comparable honors and awards. Many women said that they felt uncomfortable in the use of the Socratic method and in the competitive atmosphere of law school classes, preferring seminars and more cooperative learning settings.

An extensive study sponsored by the Law School Admission Council and based on some 28,000 students entering law schools in 1992 discovered small but statistically significant discrepancies in the grades earned by women and men in first-year courses. However, men and women reported similar satisfaction with their decisions to go to law school. An observational study of law school classrooms discovered that women's experiences were influenced by a number of contextual factors, including the teaching method, the gender of the teacher, and the elitism of the law school.

Some observers have urged that a diversity of teaching methods be adopted and tested to promote the learning of women and minority law students. Although there is resistance to changing the traditional method of law school teaching, the evidence that law school teaching may compromise the achievements of women and minority students is causing many law school professors to reevaluate the reliance on traditional methods of legal training. *See also* LAWYERS AND GENDER DIFFERENCE; LEGAL PROFESSION, HISTORY OF WOMEN IN.

Further Reading: Drachman 1998, *Sisters in Law;* Guinier, Fine, and Balin 1997, *Becoming Gentlemen.*

Valerie P. Hans and Frederika E. Schmitt

Lekkerkerker, Eugenia (1899–?)

In 1931, Eugenia Lekkerkerker, a Dutch woman, published *Reformatories for Women in the United States*, the first overview of reformatory prisons for women and a book that remains a valuable source for histories of women's prisons. Lekkerkerker came to the United States in the late 1920s to study women's reformatories for her Ph.D. dissertation. The group with which she traveled was interested in learning how best to institute women's reformatories in Holland, which at that time had no penal institutions of this type.

Lekkerkerker's book, published in Holland but written in English, provides an in-depth discussion of women's criminality and analyses of the history, goals, and distinctive methods at these all-female rehabilitative institutions. *See also* REFORMATORY MOVEMENT; WOMEN'S PRISONS, HISTORY OF.

Further Reading: Lekkerkerker 1931, *Reformatories for Women in the United States.*

Aviva M. Rich-Shea

Lesbian Partner Battering

Lesbian partner battering is a pattern of violent or coercive behaviors through which a lesbian tries to control the thoughts, emotions, and behavior of her partner or to punish the partner for some perceived transgression. Lesbian partner battering is similar in many ways to heterosexual partner battering, but there are also important differences.

Some of the forms of abuse most common in heterosexual battering relationships—e.g., pushing, shoving, being hit with open hands or fists, threats, being demeaned in front of others, disruption of sleeping and eating patterns—are also common in lesbian partner battering relationships. The motives for the abuse also appear to be similar: manipulation, control, coercion, and punishment. However, one important difference between lesbian and heterosexual partner battering is that the former is affected by widespread homophobia. Unique to abusive homosexual relationships is the threat (or act) of "outing," whereby the abuser threatens to reveal (or does reveal) to others, such as employers, relatives, and landlords, that her partner is a lesbian, when the partner wishes to conceal her sexual orientation. Outing can produce various discriminatory outcomes such as shunning, job loss, and even violence, with little or no legal recourse for the victim.

The prevalence of lesbian partner battering is not known, since large, random samples of the lesbian population are needed to measure prevalence. All studies of lesbian partner battering to date have used small, self-selected samples because random sampling is not possible with a largely hidden population. Studies of lesbian partner battering have found, however, that the abuse often grows more frequent and more serious over time. If abuse occurs, it is likely to recur.

Several factors have been identified as possible contributors to lesbian partner battering. Some researchers have found that lesbians who witnessed and/or experienced abuse in their families of origin are more likely than those who grew up in nonabusive families to be victimized as adults, to abuse their own partners, or both (Lie et al. 1991). This finding, however, does not receive consistent empirical support (see V. E. Coleman 1990; E. E. Kelly and Warshafsky 1987; Renzetti 1992). Similarly, some researchers have found a strong relationship between substance abuse and lesbian partner battering (V. E. Coleman 1990; E. E. Kelly and Warshafsky 1987; Schilit, Lie, and Montagne 1990), while others have not (Renzetti 1992). Other studies report that lesbian batterers seen in clinical practices often exhibit personality disorders, especially the borderline and narcissistic disorders (V. E. Coleman 1994). Lesbian batterers may also have poor self-concepts and high dependency needs (Renzetti 1992).

Unfortunately, very little research has been undertaken on either the victims or perpetrators of lesbian partner battering, so many questions about the problem remain unanswered. Future research should explore further the various contributing factors identified here as well as others, such as institutionalized homophobia and internalized homophobia (acceptance by homosexuals of society's negative evaluations of them and the incorporation of these evaluations into their self-concepts). *See also* DOMESTIC VIOLENCE AGAINST WOMEN, EPIDEMIOLOGY OF; DOMESTIC VIOLENCE BY WOMEN.

Further Reading: Leventhal and Lundy 1999, *Same-Sex Domestic Violence*; Lobel 1986, *Naming the Violence*; Renzetti 1992, *Violent Betrayal*.

Claire M. Renzetti

Liberation Explanation of Crime

The "liberation" explanation of female crime, according to which women's emancipation from traditional gender roles will lead not only to new freedoms but also to higher crime rates, was developed about 1975. Before 1975, the low incidence of female crime was attributed to various psychological and physiological differences between men and women; to the limited role that women as homemakers, child-rearers, and shoppers play in public life; and to the reluctance of the police to arrest females (the so-called chivalry factor). By the mid-1970s, the role of women in the United States had undergone a marked change. Women were entering the labor force en masse, even at the professional level, and in the political world as well.

Working independently, Freda Adler (1975) and Rita James Simon (1975) conducted statistical analyses of female crime rates and found that these rates were increasing far faster than male crime rates, especially with regard to property offenses (Simon), but also with respect to other forms of criminality, even drug offenses and terrorism (Adler). In *Sisters in Crime*, Adler posited that as the social and economic roles of women change in the legitimate world, women's participation in crime changes accordingly. She argued that the temptations, challenges, stresses, and strains to which women were increasingly subjected caused them to act or react in the same manner in which men have consistently reacted to the same stimuli. In other words, equalization of social and economic roles leads to similar behavior patterns, both legal and illegal, on the part of both men and women. To embezzle, one needs to be in a position of trust and in control of funds. To get into a bar fight, one needs to be in a bar. Previously, women had seldom been either in positions of economic trust or in bars. Now these opportunities existed.

Adler further suggested that the new opportunities, positive and negative, that women began to experience in the 1970s were the result of the changing social roles that the women's liberation movement helped to bring about. Hence, some scholars have named Adler's explanation the "liberation theory (or explanation) of female crime," with the implication of antifeminism. This is both an oversimplification and a logical fallacy (specifically, the fallacy of the undistributed middle). Consider that the suffragette movement of the early twentieth century created the opportunity for women to swim at public beaches. In consequence, the drowning rate of women increased—yet nobody contends that the suffragettes promoted the drowning of women. In the same way, the women's liberation movement vastly changed the social, political, and economic opportunities for women. If, in consequence thereof, female crime rates increased for women who experienced increased illegitimate opportunities, women's liberation bears no blame. The liberation explanation of female crime is best conceptualized in terms of the "opportunity" theory of crime, according to which people who cannot meet their goals through legitimate means will do so through illegitimate means, if they have them.

The theories of Adler and Simon were initially subjected to considerable criticism on both statistical and ideological grounds. Hundreds of articles and dissertations have been devoted to the subject. More important, as a result of the work of Adler and Simon, the issue of gender and crime has become a recognized area of concern in the continually growing body of research dealing with contemporary criminological issues. While scholars may still disagree on the extent and form of contemporary female crime, they generally agree that the crimes women commit are closely associated with their socioeconomic position in society. *See also* CHIVALRY EXPLANATION OF FEMALE CRIME RATES; FEMALE CRIME, EXPLANATIONS OF; MASCULINITY EXPLANATION OF CRIME; STRAIN EXPLANATION OF CRIME.

Further Reading: Adler 1975, *Sisters in Crime*; B. R. Price and Sokoloff 1995, *The Criminal Justice System and Women*; Simon 1975, *Women and Crime*.

Freda Adler

Lifestyle and Victimization

Lifestyle theories of crime victimization, which focus on the characteristics and activities of individuals that contribute to their victimization, begin with the premise that some situations are more favorable to crime than others. However, lifestyle theories and their close relative, the routine activities theory, are contradicted by data on female victimizations. Moreover, to the extent that they seem to blame victims, these theories are incompatible with feminist perspectives on victimization.

Lifestyle theories direct attention to lifestyle factors that may lead to victimization, such as how much time victims spend outside the home, their typical activities, and their overall patterns of movement. Routine activities theory moves beyond a focus on the lifestyle characteristics of the victim to state that crime is likely to occur when at least three elements or risk factors converge in space (Birkbeck and LaFree 1993; Felson 1996):

- a likely offender
- a suitable target of crime
- absence of a capable guardian

Routine activities theory implies that the victimization of women will likely increase as a result of women's increasing employment in the paid labor market and other important social trends such as increases in divorce rates and in the number of single-parent households. It also implies that women's paid employment and changes in the family structure indirectly contribute to increasing crime because they result in less supervision of children, especially of delinquency-prone teenagers. Finally, routine activities theory implies that women's employment outside the home directly increases women's chances of being victimized.

These implications of routine activities theory and, more generally, of the lifestyle explanation of victimization, are contradicted by data in a study of femicides (homicides with female victims). Despite lifestyle changes, women are still more likely to be killed at home, by someone they are involved with in an intimate relationship. This reality has led to the conclusion that women's homicide victimization, because of its intimate nature, is distinct from lethal violence against men (Gartner forthcoming). Research in Canada supports the contention that femicide is most likely committed at home by an intimate partner (M. Crawford and Gartner 1992), and this pattern is even more pronounced in the United States, where the rate of homicide within families is higher than in most Western nations (Browne and Williams 1993).

The research on women's risk from homicide, then, shows that the lifestyle and routine activities theories fail to address the larger sociocultural context, including gender relations, that contributes to changes in lifestyles and trends in crime and victimization. Moreover, routine activities theory does not help us understand why femicide continues to occur mainly in the home despite women's recent lifestyle changes. In addition, the theory's prediction that women's employment outside the home will increase their chances of victimization does not hold across all societies.

Likewise, lifestyle theories in general do not shed light on why overall homicide rates are much higher in the United States than in other North American and European countries. Nor do they help to explain why men are more likely to be killed by strangers, while women remain more likely to be killed by someone they are close to. One of the strongest criticisms of lifestyle theories from a feminist perspective is that they fail to account for situations, such as intimate homicide, that are a product of unequal power relationships between men and women. In short, these theories presume "an equality between participants where none may exist" (Walklate 1995a:31).

Lifestyle and routine activities predictions may be useful for explaining only certain types of crimes, particularly those that occur outside the home and among strangers. These theories have proven useful in directing our attention to the situational aspects of crime, and they have led to the designing of crime-reduction strategies. However, these theories appear to be based on the assumption that crime and victimization are phenomena that occur only in public spaces. And these theories, despite their increasing influence, have been criticized for promoting the idea that individuals contribute to their own victimization. A singular focus on how people's lifestyles increase their risk of being victimized can easily be interpreted as blaming the victim for the occurrence of crime. *See also* DOMESTIC VIOLENCE AGAINST WOMEN, EPIDEMIOLOGY OF; HOMICIDE, USA; HOMICIDE VICTIMS; VICTIM-BLAMING AND VICTIM-PRECIPITATION, CONCEPT OF; VICTIMIZATION, FEMINIST PERSPECTIVES ON.

Further Reading: Birkbeck and LaFree 1993, "The Situational Analysis of Crime and Deviance"; L. E. Cohen and Felson 1979, "Social Change and Crime Rate Trends"; Craven 1997, *Sex Differences in Violent Victimization, 1994*; Walklate 1995a, "Criminology, Victimology and Feminism."

Deborah Marie Plechne
and Robert Nash Parker

Lombroso, Cesare (1835–1909)

A pioneer in criminology, Cesare Lombroso established the influential theory that women's biology, particularly their sexuality, determines female patterns of crime. Born into a Jewish family of Verona in 1835, Lombroso studied medicine and psychiatry in Italy and Austria. As a professor at the University of Turin, he founded the discipline of criminal anthropology, or the study of the physical and psychological features of the criminal. Although borrowing from earlier theories like phrenology, Lombroso claimed to have revolutionized research on the etiology of crime by introducing a scientific, or "positivist," approach. To gain empirical data about criminals, Lombroso put them through a battery of tests including physical measurement and psychological interviews.

Lombroso is best known for his concept of the "born criminal," who represented a throwback on the evolutionary scale and could be identified by physical and psychological "atavisms," or anomalies. After applying this theory first to male deviancy in 1876 in his famous book *Criminal Man* (Lombroso-Ferrero 1911, 1972), Lombroso then incorporated it into one of the earliest criminological treatises on women. Entitled *La Donna Delinquente* (1893), co-authored with his son-in law, and soon published in English as *The Female Offender* (1895), this book argues that female "born criminals" exhibit numerous physical and psychological anomalies including small cranial size, an impaired sense of touch, muscular strength, cruelty, vanity, and dishonesty. Such a portrait provided supposedly scientific underpinnings for the traditional stereotype of the fe-

PHYSIOGNOMY OF RUSSIAN FEMALE OFFENDERS.

PLATE I.

Illustration from *The Female Offender* (1895), accompanying a discussion of "facial and cephalic anomalies of female criminals."

male criminal as more monstrous and deceitful than her male counterpart.

Lombroso also shaped future conceptions of female deviancy by equating prostitution with crime. Claiming that the dominant characteristic of "primitive" women is sexual license, he labeled any woman who violated nineteenth-century bourgeois sexual norms as atavistic and possibly a "born prostitute." Female crimes that were not obviously sexual, like theft and murder, were also frequently attributed by Lombroso to the deterministic grip of women's unalterable sexuality. According to Lombroso, women are impressionable by nature and easily susceptible to states of hysteria and moral insanity during which they may commit a range of crimes. The sexual causes of psychological imbalance, according to Lombroso, include clitoral insensitivity, the early onset of puberty, menstruation, or the instinctual willingness of

women to assist their male sexual partners in criminal activity.

During the 1880s and the 1890s, Lombroso's theory of the "born criminal" became the center of debate at the international Congresses of Criminal Anthropology (Rome, 1885; Paris, 1889; Brussels, 1892; Geneva, 1896). His international reputation was confirmed by the rapid translation of *The Female Offender* into German in 1894, English in 1895 (with editions issued in both London and New York), French in 1896, and Russian in 1897. Controversy over his theory of biological determinism was not confined to scientific circles but entered the general debate about women's equality at the turn of the century.

In a setback for the first wave of feminism, Lombroso argued that biological inferiority prevented "normal" women from reaching the higher stages of psychological and mental evolution typical of white men. Women's ambitions should be restricted to motherhood, the "natural" female role in the struggle for existence.

While many criminologists in both Europe and the United States quickly contested Lombroso's theory of biological determinism as the explanation of male crime, they were generally uncritical of its application to women. Until the 1970s, studies of female crime were rare and continued to echo Lombroso (W. I. Thomas 1923; Glueck and Glueck 1934; Pollak 1961). Beginning with the work of Dorie Klein (1973) and Carol Smart (1976), feminist criminologists have severely critiqued the Lombrosian dogma that the etiology of female crime can be traced to women's sexuality, arguing instead for the importance of sociological, economic, and cultural factors. *See also* FEMALE CRIME, EXPLANATIONS OF; MASCULINITY EXPLANATION OF CRIME; MEDICAL EXPLANATIONS OF DELINQUENCY.

Further Reading: Gibson 1990, "On the Insensitivity of Women"; D. Klein 1973, "The Etiology of Female Crime"; Smart 1976, "Women, Crime, and Criminology."

Mary S. Gibson

M

Madonna/Whore Dichotomy

The madonna/whore dichotomy, which underlies many theories of female crime and victimization, assigns all women to one of two categories: *madonna* ("good girl" or virgin) or *whore* ("bad girl" or slut). The opposing images of this duality are among the most powerful stereotypes and myths of western thought.

As analyzed by Clarice Feinman (1980), the dichotomy characterizes madonnas as "ladylike" in every respect: proper, pure, perfect, and passive. Madonnas assume their natural roles by becoming virtuous wives and mothers. These women are not only the bearers of children but also the keepers of social values and public morality. Beyond reproach, madonna-like women are sweet, unsullied, obedient, and submissive to male authority.

The other side of the opposition, the "whore" or evil woman, is a deviant rule-breaker and role-breaker. As nonconformists, "whores" are those women who refuse to abide by society's rules and break from their socially prescribed feminine roles. They challenge traditional beliefs, attitudes, and practices. Unscrupulous, seductive, rebellious, manipulative, and deceitful, whorish women defy the authority structure, thereby damaging themselves and society. They are threats to social order and stability.

Clearly, the dichotomous classification of women as either madonnas or whores does not accurately depict the complexity or diversity among women. The nature and reality of females is not this simple, yet these dual images of madonna/whore, virgin/slut, good girl/bad girl persist. Historically, they have strongly informed discussions of female offenders and victims.

Underlying earlier theories of female criminality was the assumption that women are inferior to men, passive and dependent creatures. It followed that women who deviate from this "feminine" nature are abnormal and masculine. Females with criminal inclinations were defined not only as criminal but also as evil. They violated not only the law but also deeply ingrained beliefs about gender.

The madonna/whore dichotomy has played an active part in maintaining men's power and control over women. Either as protectors of madonnas or punishers of whores, men took it upon themselves to restrict women's freedom. "Madonnas" were expected to defer to their defenders and serve them. Men also set themselves up as punishers of deviant women, retaliating against "whores" for not only what they had done but also for who they were.

The madonna/whore dichotomy undergirds discussions of female victimization as well. "Madonnas," paragons of virtue, can legitimately complain about victimizations. "Whores," epitomes of evil, are blamed for precipitating or contributing to crimes against themselves. They get what they deserve. The application of this dichotomy to victimization prediction implies that being a "good woman" and behaving properly prevents victimization, especially from crimes of a sexual nature. Madonnas thus must not engage in unseemly behavior, travel alone, socialize in public establishments without a companion, drink alcohol with men, wear provocative clothing, and go to secluded or private places with new acquaintances. By being "good girls," they prevent physical or sexual assault. If some random act of violence is committed against them, it will be by a stranger and through no fault of their own. Only "bad girls" engage in provocative behaviors, thereby "inviting" sexual or physical confrontation. They are to blame for such victimizations.

The madonna/whore dichotomy reinforces stereotypical images of women with its simplistic, two-type classification. It also has a racist dimension, since it has been applied mainly to white women and not to women of color. For any typology to have valid application, it must consider the complexity and diversity of women and include such major factors as race, class, and age. *See also* GENDER AND CRIME; OFFENDERS; VICTIM-BLAMING AND VICTIM-PRECIPITATION, CONCEPT OF.

Further Reading: Belknap 1996, *The Invisible Woman;* Benedict 1992, *Virgin or Vamp;* Feinman 1980, *Women in the Criminal Justice System;* Merlo and Pollack 1995, *Women, Law, and Social Control.*

Carol A. Facella

Mahan, Edna (1920–1968)

In 1928, toward the end of the women's reformatory movement, Edna Mahan was appointed superintendent of the New Jersey Reformatory for Women, where she remained until her death in 1968. In her 40-year tenure at Clinton Farms, as the reformatory was informally known, Mahan made significant contributions in implementing the ideals of the women's reformatory movement, reweaving them into a progressive, rehabilitative program. Equally important were her efforts on behalf of women who worked in corrections, whose status Mahan promoted through

Edna Mahan. *Courtesy of Mary Q. Hawkes.*

the American Correctional Association, where she served on the board of directors and the executive committee.

Mahan's philosophy for working with female offenders was based on her belief in human dignity, trustworthiness, and the value of all individuals, and on her conviction that behavioral change could most easily be effected in an open atmosphere. Soon after she arrived at Clinton Farms, she had bars removed from all cottage windows and abolished degrading punishments. Student government, as Clinton Farms' system of inmate self-regulation was called, formed the core of the reformatory's program. Mahan carried it further than any other administrator of an adult penal institution.

Mahan's efforts on behalf of female staff aimed at raising their salaries and working conditions to be comparable to those of staff at men's institutions. To professionalize the role of cottage officers, she offered in-house training, support for education, and funds for attending professional meetings.

Mahan kept the rehabilitative spirit of the reformatory movement alive long after it had died in nearly every other women's institution. At the time of her death, she was one of the best connected and most respected prison administrators of either sex in the United States. *See also* Reformatory Movement; Women's Prison Administration, Historical; Women's Prisons, History of.

Further Reading: Freedman 1981, *Their Sisters' Keepers*; Hawkes 1998, "Edna Mahan"; Rafter 1990a, *Partial Justice*.

Mary Q. Hawkes

Masculinity Explanation of Crime

The masculinity explanation of crime, according to which female criminals are more masculine than other women and male criminals are more masculine than other men, has been used for over 100 years to explain sex differences in rates and types of offending. One of the first to formulate this theory was the Italian criminologist Cesare Lombroso, who argued (Lombroso and Ferrero 1895) that females who are "born" or biological criminals resemble men more than law-abiding women. Another version of the hypothesis argues that men and boys who are high-rate offenders are motivated to commit crime by a need to "prove" their masculinity.

In the mid-twentieth century, several criminologists advanced a more general masculinity hypothesis that applies to the offending patterns of both men and women. This revised version of the masculinity hypothesis has been expressed in two basic forms. The first is based on the idea of gender-specific roles and is rooted in the work of Talcott Parsons, one of the first to theorize a link between masculinity and offending. This theory focuses on gender roles as they are expressed in personality traits or personal characteristics. It argues that the more masculine a female (or male) is (i.e., the more masculine traits she or he possesses), the more likely she or he is to become delinquent or criminal.

The second branch of the general masculinity hypothesis, formulated and popularized in the 1970s by Rita Simon and Freda Adler, has alternatively been referred to as the "liberation hypothesis" or the "gender equality hypothesis." While the gender-role masculinity hypothesis focuses on gender-based socialization, this second version focuses on the structural location or opportunities of the genders. In its simplest form, the "liberation masculinity hypothesis" states that as women's structural positions (i.e., labor force participation, economic power, and so on) more closely approximate men's, so too will their participation in crime and delinquency.

In the 1990s, James W. Messerschmidt (1993a) brought together the ideas of class relations, gender relations, and race relations to explain crime as structured action in a conflict framework. He maintains that crime is not an expression of masculinity, as the gender-role or the liberation versions of the masculinity hypothesis propose. Rather, crime is a way for men to construct gender when conventional methods for establishing masculinity have been obstructed. Masculinity is not, according to this conceptualization, a characteristic one possesses but something that one creates and must continually reinforce.

As its many different formulations attest, the masculinity explanation of crime is one of the most fertile and flexible general theories in the field of criminology. *See also* Liberation Explanation of Crime.

Further Reading: Adler 1975, *Sisters in Crime*; Messerschmidt 1993a, *Masculinities and Crime*; Simon 1975, *Women and Crime*.

Carolyn Uihlein Nilles

Mediation Programs

Victim-offender mediation (VOM) programs bring offenders face-to-face with the victims of their crimes in a meeting facilitated by a trained mediator. VOM usually proves successful for both victims and offenders, although it may not be a suitable approach for female victims of domestic abuse or rape. Most women victims of domestic violence are already at a disadvantage in terms of physical and emotional power—bringing them face-to-face with their victimizers may merely replicate the underlying problems. For many rape victims, a confrontation with the offender could be traumatic and re-victimizing. On the other hand, in VOM programs, women victims—who often feel ignored by the traditional criminal justice system—have an opportunity to express their feelings and ask questions of the offender, a process that may contribute to healing. VOM is always voluntary for victims, and in most cases it is voluntary for offenders as well.

VOM may be useful at any stage of the criminal justice process. Its goals are dialogue, understanding, empathy, healing, closure, and making amends. Mediators first meet separately with the victim and offender to screen cases and prepare the participants for mediation. Offenders become accountable through restitution agreements, either monetary or symbolic, which may include work for the victim or community service. Voluntary agreements reflect justice that is meaningful to the victim and offender, rather than narrowly prescribed by law. In severely violent crimes, victim-offender mediation is always an adjunct to criminal prosecution.

In appropriately screened cases, some VOM programs have found that mediation can be helpful for rape victims and rehabilitative for their offenders. In a Canadian study of mediation in cases of severe violence (46 percent of them sexual assaults), all of the victims and offenders expressed satisfaction with the process and outcomes (T. Roberts 1995). Moreover, in national and international studies, the overwhelming majority of victims and offenders who participated in VOM programs reported a just and satisfying result. Victims typically report resolution of fears of re-victimization, a particularly critical issue for women. *See also* CRIME VICTIMIZATION; RESTORATIVE JUSTICE.

Further Reading: M. Price 1997, "Can Mediation Produce Justice?"; T. Roberts 1995, *Evaluation of the Victim-Offender Mediation;* Umbreit 1994, *Victim Meets Offender;* Zehr 1990, *Changing Lenses.*

Martin E. Price

Medical Explanations of Delinquency

Medical explanations of delinquency, which view criminality as a disease that affects both society and individual offenders, profoundly influenced the treatment of criminal behav-

ior in the late nineteenth and early twentieth centuries.

In the late nineteenth century, Cesare Lombroso and other criminal anthropologists identified a group of "born criminals," moral and biological throwbacks to an earlier evolutionary period. According to Lombroso, born criminals can be identified by physical characteristics indicative of lower levels of evolution. Among born female criminals, these physical characteristics include a sloping forehead, moles, large jaw and skull, small cranial capacity, and a masculine appearance.

In the early twentieth century, proponents of the then-popular theory of defective delinquency—according to which criminals tend to be mentally retarded and persons with mental retardation tend to be criminalistic— argued that intellectual capacity is a heritable trait and equivalent to moral capacity. Defective delinquents, in this view, are people deficient both intellectually and morally. Female defective delinquents pose an especially severe threat to society because their low mental and moral capacities lead to promiscuity and criminality; moreover, they inevitably give birth to morally and intellectually deficient children, thus passing the problems on to the next generation. These beliefs were reinforced by the fact that large proportions of incarcerated men and women scored poorly on early intelligence tests. Treatment strategies for female defective delinquents aimed at preventing their reproduction through lengthy incarceration or use of voluntary or forced sterilization.

Although medical models of delinquency had a great impact in the early twentieth century, their influence was on the wane by the 1950s. Yet explanations of female criminality, and to a lesser extent male criminality, still retained a focus on the potential relationship between biology and crime. For instance, Gisela Konopka (1966) argued that girls' sexual misbehavior stems from hostility and low self-esteem brought about by inadequate parental support during their physical maturation. Similarly, Ellis and Austin (1971) argued that the aggression levels of incarcerated women are correlated with hormonal changes associated with women's menstrual cycles. Specifically, they argued that hormonal changes influence a woman's emotional stability, which then influences aggression levels.

More recently, several explanations of criminality have reformulated a relationship between biology and crime. For instance, James Q. Wilson and Richard Herrnstein (1985) argued that criminal involvement is an outcome of biologically based constitutional differences that influence an individual's calculations of the costs and benefits of crime. Constitutional deficits that are present at or soon after birth may be caused by drug and alcohol use during pregnancy or by poor prenatal and infant nutrition. The authors also argue, however, that constitutional differences may in part be genetic; specifically, they contend that intelligence levels are genetically based. Wilson and Herrnstein's theory, like earlier explanations, implies that reductions in criminality can be achieved by decreasing the likelihood of biologically based deficits. *See also* FEMALE CRIME, EXPLANATIONS OF; FORENSIC PSYCHIATRY AND GENDER, CANADA; JUVENILE DELINQUENCY AND INTELLIGENCE; LOMBROSO, CESARE; PREMENSTRUAL SYNDROME; PSYCHOLOGICAL EXPLANATIONS OF DELINQUENCY; SHOPLIFTING AND KLEPTOMANIA.

Further Reading: Rafter 1997, *Creating Born Criminals.*

Lori A. Elis

Mothers against Drunk Driving

Mothers against Drunk Driving (MADD) is a national organization whose mission is to stop drunk driving and to support the victims of this crime. MADD's advocacy work has been welcomed by a broad spectrum of highway safety experts, governmental officials, media representatives, and members of the public. As a result of MADD's work, drunk driving is no longer shrugged off as the inevitable cost of modern life. Rather, most Americans now view it as a serious public danger, a violent crime that results from a person's decision to drive while impaired. This change in public attitudes, which has led to the passage of numerous tougher anti–drunk driving laws, has produced a drop in alcohol-related traffic fatalities from 25,165 in 1982 to 17,126 in 1996.

MADD was founded in 1980 by an angry mother, Candy Lightner, who lost her 13-year-old daughter to a repeat drunk driver and who saw a lenient criminal justice system as the cause of the problem. Through her efforts, MADD led the way in reforming that system through enactment of tough laws that impose firm and consistent punishments on convicted drunk drivers.

MADD has grown to include more than 400 local chapters in the United States, their work coordinated through a system of state, regional, and national offices. With nearly three million members and supporters, MADD is the largest victim-advocate and anti–drunk driving organization in the world.

MADD has taken the lead in pushing for a number of prevention-oriented policies, including increases in the national minimum drinking age to 21, administrative license revocation, sobriety checkpoint roadblocks, and stricter definitions of alcohol-impaired driving. In addition, chapter-based advocates help victims cope with the emotional trauma of a drunk driving crash, contend with the vagaries of the justice system during the criminal investigation and trial, identify other community resources, and achieve emotional recovery. In another key activity, MADD has also taken the lead in promoting a Constitutional amendment to protect the rights of victims in criminal justice proceedings. *See also* CRIME VICTIMIZATION.

Further Reading: DeJong and Hingson 1998, *Strategies to Reduce Driving under the Influence;* Ross 1992, *Confronting Drunk Driving.*

William DeJong

Muncy Act. *See* CHIVALRY EXPLANATION OF FEMALE CRIME RATES.

O

O'Connor, Sandra Day (1930–)

Sandra Day O'Connor, born on March 26, 1930, is the first woman justice of the United States Supreme Court, the nation's final court of appeals for criminal matters. She was appointed in 1981 by President Ronald Reagan. Despite initial indications that she would vote with the politically conservative faction of the Court, O'Connor has emerged as a centrist whose opinions often define new directions in the law. Her pragmatic decisions generally are case-specific rather than ideologically based. She advocates a limited role for the federal government. Her opinions in affirmative action, sex discrimination, and sexual harassment cases have been pivotal in moving the Court toward a more expansive view of equal protection.

O'Connor grew up on a remote Arizona ranch and attended an El Paso, Texas, boarding school until graduation at age 16. She earned her law degree in 1952 from Stanford University and married John Jay O'Connor III the same year. O'Connor's legal career has included experience as a civilian attorney for the Army, her own private practice (which she established when law firms would not hire her), volunteer activities while raising three children, and public service as an assistant attorney general and elected state senator. She served on the Arizona Court of Appeals before joining the United States Supreme Court. *See also* GENDER AND JUDICIAL DECISION-MAKING; JUDGES; LAWYERS AND GENDER DIFFERENCE.

Further Reading: Maveety 1996, *Justice Sandra Day O'Connor;* Van Sickel 1998, *Not a Particularly Different Voice.*

Roxann Ryan

Offenders

Over time, it has been very difficult to form an accurate view of female offenders due to the preconceptions and prejudices that have riddled criminological works on the subject. The first large-scale study of women offenders was Cesare Lombroso's *The Female Offender* (Lombroso and Ferrero 1895), which argued that women are criminals as a result of biological factors—survival of primitive traits. Other early criminologists were also unanimous in the view that individual flaws—biological, psychological, or both—are the cause of women's criminal behavior. These criminologists tended to view women as either good or bad, overlaying their writings with a moral righteousness.

W. I. Thomas's *The Unadjusted Girl* (1923) explained that girls who are adjusted do not commit crimes. As late as the 1930s, Eleanor and Sheldon Glueck, working at Harvard University, spent years attempting to classify types of delinquent women and girls by physiological and psychological abnormalities, an investigation they reported in *Five Hundred Delinquent Women* (1934). It was not until the 1970s, as criminology matured as a social science, that scholars began to develop a more accurate picture of female offenders and why they commit crime by looking at societal factors in their explanations.

Women offenders have far less power in the criminal world than men and thus engage in different criminal activities than their male counterparts. Moreover, women are far less likely than men to participate in criminal activity and even less likely to engage in violent behavior. In 1996, men constituted over 75 percent of all people arrested for major or "index" crimes (as defined by the Federal Bureau of Investigation, these include murder and non-negligent manslaughter, forcible rape, robbery, aggravated assault, burglary, larceny-theft, motor vehicle theft, and arson). As Figure 8 shows, of all females arrested in 1997, more than three-quarters were arrested for non-index crimes, and violent crimes constituted a very small proportion of the index crime arrests. For as long as crime statistics have been collected in the United States, women have constituted only a small percentage of the offender population.

Women offenders are generally ignored by the correctional system. Jails and prisons have failed to expand their rehabilitative,

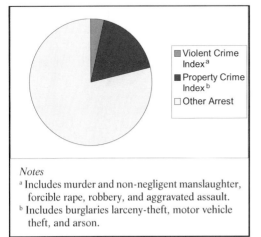

Notes
[a] Includes murder and non-negligent manslaughter, forcible rape, robbery, and aggravated assault.
[b] Includes burglaries larceny-theft, motor vehicle theft, and arson.

Figure 8. Female Arrests by Offense Type, United States, 1997
Source: U.S. Department of Justice, Federal Bureau of Investigation 1998, *Crime in the United States, 1997.*

medical, and childcare services to meet the needs of women inmates. Until the 1980s, corrections officials justified the lack of services for women on the grounds that there were insufficient numbers of these inmates to justify using already scarce budgetary resources. In recent years, as women's presence in jails and prisons has grown, the justification for few programs is that the public does not want the criminal justice system to coddle inmates; thus, services to men have been reduced, and no new programs have been initiated for women. Only prison construction has been responsive to the escalating population, with women's prisons being built at a faster rate than ever before in U.S. history. But little money is allocated for shelters for battered women, domestic violence programs, or drug treatment.

Crime holds a powerful fascination for the public, which on the one hand fears offenders as a threat to their safety and on the other hand is fascinated by criminal behavior. Historically, criminal women have captured the attention of the public and the press when their acts have violated traditional views of women as soft and nurturing. Traditionally, women have been expected to serve as the transmitters of patriarchal culture. In their role as mothers, women are considered pure and entitled to chivalrous treatment by men. But this protection and respect has come at a high price. Women who defy society's standards do not receive chivalrous treatment; indeed, in the cultural phenomenon often referred to as the "madonna/whore dichotomy," they are viewed as evil. Moreover, traditionally only middle-class white women enjoyed the benefits of chivalry; poor women and women of color did not have a place on male-created pedestals, and little was expected of them except hard physical labor.

The typical woman offender does not much resemble the few women who have achieved notoriety as a result of their crimes. Instead, the profile of most women offenders closely parallels the profile of those for whom the American dream of the good life is out of reach. The typical female prisoner is, on the average, about 30 years of age and a single parent with several children. She is likely to have been the victim of sexual abuse as a young girl and to have begun abusing drugs or alcohol by the age of 14 years. She was arrested several times by the age of 19, typically for property crime. She is also likely to be a high school dropout who has worked in sales, services, or clerical work at low wages.

In crime, gender clearly does matter. Women today are still not equals with men in the criminal world, just as they are not equals in the noncriminal world. For the most part, as women venture into the criminal world, they choose practical strategies and forms of behavior that take into account their lesser physical strength as compared with men and their lesser ability to intimidate and gain advantage by force. They serve as lures or decoys for the male robber, or they engage in prostitution and then steal from sleeping customers, or they engage in nonphysical crimes such as shoplifting and credit card fraud. When they use violence—killing their children or their partners in self-defense—they become notorious, fulfilling society's worst expectations about the dark side of women. And for most women who violate gender norms, severe punishment is assured. *See also* FEMALE CRIME, HISTORY OF, USA; FEMALE CRIME, PATTERNS AND TRENDS IN, USA; FEMINIST CRIMINOLOGY, USA; GENDER AND CRIME; GLUECK, ELEANOR; MADONNA/WHORE DICHOTOMY; PRISONER CHARACTERISTICS.

Further Reading: Daly and Chesney-Lind 1988, "Feminism and Criminology"; Leonard 1995, "Theoretical Criminology and Gender."

Barbara Raffel Price

Organized Crime (The Mafia)

Little is known about the involvement of women in the ongoing criminal enterprises collectively called "organized crime" or "the mafia." It is difficult to obtain reliable information on organized criminal enterprises in general because one of the strongest principles of many organized criminal enterprises is the importance of secrecy. Even less is known about women in organized crime because investigators have long believed that women were unlikely to participate in such enterprises. Men who run criminal organizations may be reluctant to acknowledge women's role out of fear of diminishing their image as heads of the business. Moreover, women are sometimes used to hide valuable information or undertake risky activities precisely because they are less likely to come under suspicion, and members of organized criminal enterprises do not want this situation to change.

There are a number of myths about the role of women in organized crime. The most prevalent is that women are unaware of the organized-crime activities of their husbands and other family members, and that they do not participate. Recent information from informants in Italy and the United States indicates that this is not the case. When the husband is killed or incarcerated, the wife will sometimes take over the business to survive financially. The increased freedom of women has led to increased participation in organized crime activities. While some organized crime groups (like La Cosa Nostra) go to considerable length to exclude women, especially from the higher levels of the organization, others (such as the Camorra and some U.S. mafia groups) are characterized by more flexibility. Women are likely to participate in nonviolent activities like drug trafficking and loan sharking, although the powerful image of the widow can be used by a woman to encourage male members of the family to engage in a violent vendetta on her behalf.

Mafia culture does not closely resemble that portrayed by the U.S. movie industry. Law enforcement officials note that members of the Italian mafia are avid fans of movies like *The Godfather* and *Goodfellas* and take on the rituals and characteristics of actors in the movies. But the public culture of the mafia and the private roles that women play in actual organized crime enterprises differ greatly. While women are not the primary players in organized crime, they sometimes step in to help or take over a certain aspect of the business if necessary. *See also* PROPERTY CRIME.

Further Reading: Calder 1995, "Mafia Women in Non-Fiction"; Longrigg 1999, *Mafia Women.*

Taj C. Carson

P

Paralegals

In the late 1960s, the increasingly competitive market for legal services created a niche for a new job category: paralegals or legal assistants. Typically college-educated women, paralegals perform many of the same tasks that lawyers do, such as researching legal issues, summarizing court transcripts and depositions, reviewing and analyzing documents, and interviewing clients and witnesses. But they do this work at a fraction of the cost in annual salary to law firms. Studies have found that paralegals are also expected to perform emotional tasks such as nurturing the lawyers for whom they work. In sum, paralegals play an important, though nearly invisible, role in the processing of criminal and civil cases.

Although paralegals do work similar to that of attorneys, as members of a "satellite occupation" (Johnstone and Wenglinsky 1985), they must work under the supervision of lawyers. Consequently, they lack exclusive control and autonomy over their work. Like many other semi-professions, the occupation is female dominated: More than 85 percent of paralegals are women. Like many other feminized occupations, the job itself is low in status, poorly paid, and offers no possibilities for upward mobility in law firms. *See also* LEGAL PROFESSION, HISTORY OF WOMEN IN; WOMEN PROFESSIONALS IN THE JUSTICE WORKPLACE.

Further Reading: Johnstone and Wenglinsky 1985, *Paralegals*; Pierce 1995, *Gender Trials*.

Jennifer L. Pierce

Parker, Bonnie (1911–1934)

Bonnie Parker is among the most notorious and romantic of America's outlaw women. She has been described as both beautiful and

Bonie Parker, 1933. *Courtesy of the UT Institute of Texan Cultures at San Antonio.*

homely; as a Robin Hood and selfishly greedy; as diabolical and simpleminded; and as in love with both Clyde Barrow and infamy. Few other criminal women have inspired such public fascination.

Bonnie's flair for the dramatic helped inspire her involvement in the criminal exploits of her lover, Clyde Barrow. However, Bonnie's early life hardly seemed to be leading her toward the excitement and lure of stardom. She was married to Roy Thornton at age 16, only to be left behind when Roy was periodically sent to prison. When Bonnie met Clyde Barrow in 1929, she had just lost her café job and was living with and assisting a friend who had broken her arm—hardly the stuff of legends.

However, within a few months of meeting Clyde, Bonnie was a well-known criminal. She first gained notoriety in 1932 when she slipped a gun to Clyde so that he could escape from his jail cell. In the two years that they crisscrossed the South and Midwest, Bonnie and Clyde continued to shape their romantic image by their deeds and by sending striking photographs to the newspapers. Bonnie enhanced her own visibility by writing poems idealizing their exploits.

Between 1932 and 1934, Bonnie accompanied Clyde in numerous robberies of stores and banks as well as in 12 murders, including the killing of 9 law enforcement officers. Had she restricted her crimes to bank robberies, she might have retained her romantic, folk-heroine status as a "gun-slinging moll," because hers was an era of gangsters and of popular support for those who victimized the wealthy and powerful. However, Bonnie and Clyde's role in the deaths of law enforcement agents aroused public ire.

In spite of her diminutive stature—less than five feet tall, and under 100 pounds— Bonnie was one of the nation's most wanted fugitives by 1934. Lee Simmons, Texas state prison director, finally called on former Texas Ranger Frank Hamer to hunt down Bonnie and Clyde. Three months later, Hamer led an ambush that trapped Bonnie and her lover on a deserted road in Louisiana. It was a fitting close to the life they had led: Bonnie died under a barrage of gunfire, in Clyde's arms, in a car they had stolen.

While Bonnie was unwilling to give up the daring life she was living, she was not unaware of its likely outcome. Her poems published in newspapers of the day both mocked the efforts of law enforcement and recognized that they would nonetheless succeed in their efforts to end her outlaw career. *The Story of Bonnie and Clyde,* written by Bonnie in 1933, concluded with a chilling prediction:

> They know that the law always wins;
> They've been shot at before,
> But they do not ignore
> That death is the wages of sin.
> Some day they'll go down together;
> And they'll bury them side by side;
> To few it'll be grief—
> To the law a relief—
> But it's death for Bonnie and Clyde.

See also OFFENDERS.

Further Reading: Milner 1996, *The Lives and Times of Bonnie and Clyde;* Phillips and Gorzell n.d., *Legendary Ladies of Texas—Bonnie Parker;* Treherne 1984, *The Strange History of Bonnie and Clyde.*

Barbara Perry

Paternalism. *See* CASE PROCESSING AND GENDER; CHARGING AND PLEA-BARGAINING; CHIVALRY EXPLANATION OF FEMALE CRIME RATES; CHIVALRY EXPLANATION OF COURT OUTCOMES.

Pizzey, Erin. *See* DEVIANCE AND REFORM, HISTORICAL OVERVIEW OF, BRITAIN; SHELTER MOVEMENT.

Police Academy Training

The training and socialization of U.S. police officers, of whom 10.5 percent were female in 1996, remains primarily the responsibility of municipal police departments and state agencies charged with preparing new recruits at police academies. Larger departments are more likely than smaller departments to actively recruit women. The length, type, and curricula of police academy programs vary dramatically. Nationally, programs range in length from weeks to months, in substance from basic traffic procedures to sophisticated multicultural training, and in entrance requirements from high school equivalency to two or more years of college. The issues for women in police training extend from understanding the masculine work culture to issues of acceptance once they hit the street. As both the communities served by the police and the police force itself become more complex, so too do the challenges of training.

Anchored in a traditionally military model of policing, police academy culture is characterized by an emphasis on developing an occupational role model of the strong, cynical, and typically masculine, street-wise police officer. Thus, much of academy training—for both male and female recruits—contrasts with society's dominant gender characterization of women. At the same time, recruits are socialized to take on an organizational role. Female recruits often find that their gender is viewed as both an asset—strengths in communication and in dealing with women and children—and as a liability—lingering concerns by colleagues about women's physical strength and suitability for the work. Thus, as women begin to learn the details of their department's operation and the skills necessary to succeed on the job, they face the additional challenge of adapting to a masculine occupational and organizational culture.

Female recruits experience differential treatment during training. Pike's research (1992) on police academy behavior revealed that academy personnel characterize women in three ways: as wives and sex objects, as victims and suspects, and as police officers. For example, "wife jokes" are a standard part of humor in academy teaching, despite the concomitant acknowledgment that wives are taken seriously as supporters of their officer-husbands. The portrayal of women as sex objects is commonly a source of entertainment in and out of the academy classroom, and concerns about female officers having to "hustle more than men" to do the job are widespread.

Recent expansion in police departments has posed the challenge of rapidly increasing the number of officers while maintaining entrance requirements and training integrity. One key issue is the balance between what can be taught in the classroom and what must be learned through experience on the street. Furthermore, departments must adjust to changes mandated by the recruitment of more minorities and women. These changes require continued attention to improving the effectiveness of police academy training. Academy instructors and male recruits need to deal respectfully with their female counterparts. Training programs must establish physical fitness standards that adequately prepare officers for street patrol while allowing for the biological differences between men and women. And finally, to enhance the retention, promotion, and success of female officers, departments must combat sexual harassment and continue to improve gender integration. *See also* GENDER AND POLICING; POLICE SUBCULTURE AND GENDER; POLICE WORK AND STRESS; POLICING, MODELS OF; WOMEN PROFESSIONALS IN THE JUSTICE WORKPLACE.

Further Reading: Pike 1992, *Women in Police Academy Training;* Van Maanen 1973, "Observations on the Making of Policemen."

Diane L. Pike

Police Administrators and Supervisors

The underrepresentation of women in the higher ranks in police departments—as police administrators and supervisors—demonstrates that vast gender disparities still exist in municipal and state police departments. Overall, the representation of women in police departments across the country has increased steadily since the 1972 Equal Employment Opportunity Act and subsequent legal challenges to ensure equal employment and promotion opportunities for women. Between the late 1970s and early 1990s, the proportion of women in municipal police agencies more than doubled. However, by 1997, women held only 6.5 percent of top-command law enforcement positions and 9.2 percent of supervisory positions. More than 20 percent of the 100 largest law enforcement agencies reported no women in top-command positions, and nearly 80 percent of these agencies had no women of color in the higher ranks (National Center for Women and Policing 1998).

While part of this underrepresentation can be attributed to women's lack of seniority (women have not been on the force as long as men), underrepresentation probably also reflects gender bias in selection and promotion practices. Police departments are paramilitary organizations with a steep organizational hierarchy; all supervisors are selected from a pool of officers within the department and rise through the ranks on the basis of standardized written and oral examinations plus other promotion criteria. The influence of prior experience, supervisors' recommendations, and informal political influence varies among departments but generally has declined in the past 25 years with the impact of affirmative action. This has opened more opportunities for women and ethnic minorities. However, beyond a certain rank (usually sergeant or lieutenant), the selection process becomes more political; top-command staff members are chosen by the chief with approval of the mayor and/or city managers. As the figures suggest, the higher the rank, the smaller the proportion of women. Nevertheless, in seven law enforcement agencies, women held at least 20 percent of the top-command positions in the late 1990s: the police departments of Pittsburgh, Atlanta, San Diego, Dallas, Birmingham, and Seattle, and the Jacksonville, Florida, sheriff's department. Moreover, women have headed or currently head large departments as in the case of Houston, Austin, and Atlanta.

Promotion procedures for first-level managers vary, but in the great majority of departments they begin with a written exam. Other elements considered in promotion include an oral interview, assessment center exercises, performance evaluation, seniority, and military service. The assessment center exercises simulate the tasks the candidate will face as a supervisor, such as dealing with typical papers in the in-basket. Assessors may be outside examiners or selected from within the department.

Historically, men have been reluctant to put women in police department positions in which they exercise authority over men. The presence of women threatens group solidarity and men's identity, problems that are exacerbated once women attain advanced positions of authority. Male subordinates sometimes refuse to acknowledge a female supervisor's rank, and structural barriers within departments such as inadequate family leave policies, tolerance of sexual harassment, and sex stereotyping in assignments further reduce female officers' potential to advance within their department.

Promotion boards are typically dominated by male administrators, which may advantage male candidates. Men who study together for promotional examinations may exclude outsiders such as women from these informal work groups. In many departments, an oral interview is a component of the promotion process, and this component, in which men are the likely examiners, can inject bias and subjectivity into the evaluation process, to the disadvantage of women.

As women officers move beyond token numbers and achieve a critical mass, more women will advance into middle management and command positions. That there remains a dearth of female supervisors and administrators even now, after women have been active patrol officers for almost 30 years, indicates that discrimination continues to play a role in promotion decisions. See also GENDER AND POLICING; POLICE ASSIGNMENTS AND SPECIALIZATIONS; POLICE WORK, HISTORY OF WOMEN IN, USA: POLICING, MODELS OF; WOMEN PROFESSIONALS IN THE JUSTICE WORKPLACE.

Further Reading: S. E. Martin 1989, *Women on the Move?*; S. E. Martin and Jurik 1996, *Doing Justice, Doing Gender.*

Amy S. Farrell

Police Assignments and Specializations

Women have been integrated into every level of law enforcement but still suffer from negative attitudes, stereotypes, and gender discrimination. This has resulted in the overrepresentation of women in certain assignments and underrepresentation in others. Nonetheless, despite barriers to equal opportunities, observers of the police recognize that women are effective street officers and managers.

Police agencies offer their officers a variety of career opportunities. Officers may work as administrators, community service officers, evidence technicians, investigators, jail guards, patrol generalists, and so on. Historically, women were excluded from patrol; they worked in a limited number of specialized assignments (i.e., juvenile services) and administrative areas of policing. In the larger departments, women were assigned to women's bureaus but had limited promotion opportunities. Despite changes since the early 1970s, women's gains have been difficult and slow.

Today, both male and female police begin their careers as patrol officers and then move into specialized areas as they gain experience and the positions become available. The move from the general duty of patrol to a specialized assignment is formally based on officer interest, training, and performance evaluations. Informally, however, decisions often are made on the buddy system, perceptions of supervisor, and "whom you know." This contributes to the disproportionately small number of women who are in the highest-status assignments including detective/investigators and Special Weapons and Tactics (SWAT) team members and to their assignment to stereotypic "women's jobs" including community service and administrative units.

Female officers are victims of the false stereotype that they are not physically or emotionally able to perform police work. Contrary this negative image, experience and research have demonstrated that female officers are as effective, and in some cases more

effective, than men. Studies have reported that policewomen can often de-escalate potentially violent encounters better than male officers because they are less aggressive (Belknap and Shelley 1992; Brecci 1997). However, many male officers still prefer making arrests to cooling-out situations, and most departments reward officers for arrests and not for the more difficult decisions and actions required to defuse a potentially violent situation. A positive stereotype of women police is that they are more compassionate and effective in responding to situations in which communication skills are seen as more important than physical ones (Belknap and Shelley 1992; Brecci 1997).

Women police excel in many other areas of policing when given the proper opportunity. For example, as undercover officers, many women can handle extreme pressure without raising suspicions that they are officers. As training academy instructors, they can provide recruits a different perspective on policing. In most cases, the problems of women police are not due to a lack of knowledge or talent, but to the double standards and stereotypes that they must face (Herrington 1997).

The next critical step is for women to be provided a fair opportunity to perform well in all areas of law enforcement, particularly those specialties that open doors to promotions to middle management ranks and thus for entry into command staff positions that historically have been male oriented and continue to be reserved for men. *See also* GENDER AND POLICING; POLICE ADMINISTRATORS AND SUPERVISORS; POLICE SUBCULTURE AND GENDER.

Further Reading: S. E. Martin 1997, "Women Officers on the Move."

Geoffrey P. Alpert and Kimberly Coxe

Police Attitudes toward Police Work

Early studies of police attitudes toward police work failed to acknowledge the influence of attitudes toward gender and race on boundary maintenance within the police organization, especially in terms of hiring practices that excluded women and non-whites.

Although most of this early research was carried out in all-male work environments, scholars ignored or downplayed the extent to which police work served as a critical resource for reinforcing ideas about masculinity among predominantly white, working-class men. Instead, social scientists developed several typologies designed to explicate the complex relationship between officer attitudes about the role of police in society and styles of policing. Muir's (1977) typology, for example, demonstrated that differing conceptions of the police role (law enforcement, public service, order maintenance) and contrasting moral beliefs about the use of force influence the manner in which officers do their jobs.

Today it has become clear that police organizations maintain a set of tightly held beliefs about masculinity and the personal qualities necessary to perform adequately on the job. Indeed, the centrality of gender for how police conceptualize their jobs and identities became increasingly obvious as greater numbers of women began to serve in patrol capacities following the Equal Opportunity Act of 1972. Although research studies have consistently demonstrated that women are as capable as men in performing police work, women's emergence as patrol officers generated tremendous hostility among male colleagues who felt that policing (particularly the crime-fighting component of the job) was "men's work." Policewomen have had difficulty being accepted by male officers and supervisors—as both women and as police officers. Studies of police organizations from the early 1970s report that sexist stereotypes and erroneous beliefs about women's limited physical strength and "passive" nature continue to be used to justify major and minor forms of harassment, as well as discriminatory hiring, promotion, and assignment policies.

Despite the fact that exclusionary practices and harassment place additional demands on policewomen, research suggests that there are few performance and attitudinal differences between men and women officers. For example, studies find that men and women choose policing as a career for similar reasons, such as a desire to help others, attractive salaries, and job stability. Further, policewomen and policemen have comparable philosophies regarding the role of law enforcement in society, and they share similar perceptions of the public, their co-workers, and the police department. Attitudinal similarities are attributable largely to occupational socialization and the police subculture. Indeed, the militaristic style of organization and persistent pressure to meet public demands, combined with two critical elements of the police role, danger and authority, generate a distinct world view and "working personality" shared among all police officers (Skolnick 1966).

Nonetheless, the experience of tokenism and harassment in the workplace does generate additional sources of stress and concerns about the workplace environment among policewomen. Studies have found that policewomen experience "invisibility" on the job and that the majority feel pressured into downplaying their professionalism in favor of serving in the role of sex object, mother, or sister to gain the acceptance of male colleagues. Additionally, the overwhelming majority of women officers express concern over a perceived lack of support from male colleagues and, beyond this, report at least one incident involving race and/or gender discrimination (S. E. Martin 1995; Morash and Haar 1995; Jacobs 1987). These negative experiences contribute to lower self-confidence in regard to on-the-job performance and a lower set of expectations for promotion among policewomen. These concerns are particularly acute among African American policewomen, who report even fewer positive experiences with their colleagues than white policewomen (A. P. Worden 1993).

In response to the obstacles they face, policewomen bring an enhanced style of professionalism to policing. One study reported that over 80 percent of policewomen rejected the belief that there is "one style" of policing. Instead, respondents maintained that women often do engage in a different style of policing than men (Belknap and Shelley 1992).

This style merges elements of the traditional, masculinist crime-fighting model with a greater respect for citizens, a stronger emphasis on communication, and a reduced reliance on the use of force. *See also* GENDER AND POLICING; POLICE ADMINISTRATORS AND SUPERVISORS; POLICE ASSIGNMENTS AND SPECIALIZATIONS; POLICE SUBCULTURE AND GENDER; POLICE WORK AND STRESS; POLICING, MODELS OF.

Further Reading: Belknap and Shelley 1992, "The New Lone Ranger"; A. P. Worden 1993, "The Attitudes of Women and Men in Policing."

Jill A. McCorkel

Police Foundation, The

The Police Foundation (PF) is a private, nonprofit organization established by the Ford Foundation in 1970 to improve American policing, which was under pressure to reform procedures, end police misconduct, and reduce rising crime rates. Accompanying and complementing the federal effort to reform policing, the PF sought to change policing through experimentation and research challenging traditional police practices and by testing innovations related to personnel policies, organizational practices, and the policing environment.

Efforts to change organizational practices included experiments in preventive patrol (Kelling et al. 1974), community-oriented policing (Pate et al. 1986), the handling of spouse abusers, and use of women officers on patrol. The Minnesota Spouse Abuse experiment concluded that arrest is more effective than mediation in reducing subsequent spousal violence (L. W. Sherman and Berk 1984). Studies related to women's opportunities in policing documented gender-related barriers to equal employment opportunities (Milton 1972); evaluated the first group of women on patrol, concluding women can police as effectively as men (Bloch and Anderson 1974); and assessed the progress of women officers (Sulton and Townsey 1981; S. E. Martin 1990). *See also* COMMUNITY POLICING; DOMESTIC VIOLENCE, POLICE RE-SPONSES TO; GENDER AND POLICING; POLICE WORK, HISTORY OF WOMEN IN, USA.

Further Reading: Uchida 1997, "The Development of American Policing"; S. Walker 1977, *A Critical History of Police Reform.*

Susan E. Martin

Police Officers, Lesbian

Lesbians have become one of the most recent "outsider" groups to explicitly seek positions as police officers, thereby challenging the traditionally male and masculine profession of policing. Historically, police departments overtly resisted employment of officers who did not fit into the dominant group of white, masculine, heterosexual men. Outsiders were excluded through recruitment and selection practices, including physical competency tests (to exclude women), written tests or educational requirements (to exclude blacks and other racial minorities), and background investigations and personal interviews (to exclude anyone who did not express the "correct" attitudes about masculinity, such as homosexuals). Court orders and the enforcement of equal employment opportunity laws facilitated the integration of women and/ or people of color into the traditional police force, but nontraditional officers still face obstacles of exclusion, harassment, and limited advancement. Reform efforts to professionalize the police have increased the number of educated, middle-class officers, which has helped to challenge entrenched racist, sexist, and homophobic attitudes.

Gay men and lesbians have sought access to the policing occupation and, once hired, have demanded workplaces free of harassment. Lesbian police officers face both structural and subcultural barriers within policing. While many issues for lesbian officers are similar to those experienced by gay men, lesbians often occupy a unique position: they are assumed to be masculine and thus more competent than heterosexual female officers to handle the job, yet they still are harassed because of their gender and also because of the curiosity and hostility of heterosexual male officers. Another issue raised by homosexual officers on the force concerns the fact that police officers are charged with a legal duty and responsibility to protect citizens from constitutional and civil rights violations. Yet lesbian officers routinely face discrimination within police department, which leads to officers' hiding their sexual orientation or resigning from the force. In addition, some states still have sodomy laws, which can be used to create a legal barrier to disqualify homosexual applicants despite the fact that many heterosexuals also violate these statutes. Opponents of gay and lesbian officers claim that heterosexual officers might not provide adequate backup for homosexual officers in danger, and that gay officers might force unwanted sexual attention on heterosexual officers. Lesbian officers must deal with internal harassment from homophobic officers, as well as antagonism from members of the gay and lesbian community who have experienced decades of violence and repression by police and thus view lesbian police officers as disloyal (Buhrke 1996).

On the other hand, many people believe that job performance and competence are unrelated to sexual orientation. Citizens now generally accept the premise that a police force must be diversified so as to accurately reflect the community which it serves. Another argument in favor of hiring lesbian officers is that police officers who are from an oppressed group themselves may have greater cultural sensitivity in dealing with citizens from other oppressed groups.

Several cities have formed organizations for lesbian and gay officers that offer occupational support and provide educational resources, particularly in larger cities. As of 1992, at least 11 departments explicitly recruited gay and lesbian officers: Atlanta, Boston, Chicago, Los Angeles, Madison, Minneapolis, New York City, Philadelphia, Portland, San Francisco, and Seattle. The New York City Police Department, with its 26,000 members, for instance, has created a Gay Officers Action League, estimating in 1990 that at least 10 percent of the department was gay or lesbian (Leinen 1993).

Social change, court mandates, and other legal and social pressures are coalescing to challenge and change existing discriminatory practices so that all qualified applicants, regardless of sexual orientation, can serve as police officers. *See also* GENDER AND POLICING; POLICE ATTITUDES TOWARD POLICE WORK; POLICE SUBCULTURE AND GENDER; POLICE WORK AND CIVIL RIGHTS LAWS; POLICING, MODELS OF.

Further Reading: Buhrke 1996, *A Matter of Justice;* Burke 1993, *Coming Out of the Blue;* Leinen 1993, *Gay Cops.*

Susan L. Miller

Police Officers, Women of Color as

Although women of color have been sworn law enforcement officers in the United States since 1916, at the beginning of the twenty-first century, they still are underrepresented in many of the nation's police agencies, particularly in supervisory positions. The majority of women of color in sworn law enforcement positions work in municipal agencies and sheriffs' departments. They are most underrepresented among state level law enforcement agencies. Most of the women officers of color are African American.

A 1997 survey of the 125 largest law enforcement agencies in the United States (including the 26 state, 17 county, and 57 municipal police agencies that provided responses), found that women constitute 12 percent of sworn law enforcement officers, including 14 percent in municipal, 13 percent in sheriffs' and county departments, but only 5 percent of officers in state law enforcement agencies. Women of color (the study did not distinguish among racial/ethnic groups) hold 4.5 percent of these sworn law enforcement positions. At the supervisory level in these same large agencies, women hold 9 percent of all positions above entry rank, and 7 percent of the top-command positions. The proportions of supervisory and top-command positions held by women of color are, respectively, 3.1 percent and 2.4 percent. In addition, more than 20 percent of agencies report no women in top-command positions, and nearly 80 percent have no women of color in the highest ranks. Nevertheless, African American women have become chief of police in Atlanta, Georgia, and in Tuskegee, Alabama; and sheriff in Dekalb County, Georgia. They also have risen to the positions of deputy commissioner and commander in law enforcement agencies in Pittsburgh, the District of Columbia, New York City, Philadelphia, Miami-Dade, and Detroit.

The agencies with the highest percentage of women of color in their sworn ranks, not surprisingly, tend to be those that have large proportions of women and that are in cities with high minority populations. For example, in the Metropolitan Police Department of Washington, D.C., a city with a black majority population, 23 percent of all officers are women and 22 percent of sworn police personnel are women of color. Similarly, in the Miami Police Department, 21 percent of all officers are women and 14 percent are women of color (all figures from the National Center for Women and Policing 1998).

Women's increased representation in law enforcement is attributable to affirmative action policies that were put in place in the early 1970s. Affirmative action policies may be court-ordered or voluntary efforts to address racial discrimination; many also include plans to address sex discrimination. It is notable that 8 of the 10 large departments with the highest proportion of women officers are (or have been) under consent decrees resulting from lawsuits in which departments agreed to increase hiring and promotion of persons of color and women. Other agencies seeking to avoid similar litigation and to maintain control of their personnel policies adopted voluntary affirmative action plans.

Women of color have been largely invisible in the policing literature. The few examinations of race/ethnicity focus principally on black women and have generalized about their experiences related to race on the basis of black men's experiences, and about their gender perspectives on the basis of data on white women. One of the few studies focused on black women officers' experiences found that they encounter "a double whammy" of discrimination based on both gender and race that results in their being isolated from (1) black male police because of sexism, and (2) other women police because of racism (S. E. Martin 1995). In addition, they are the biggest losers with the demise of affirmative action. Another report (Haarr 1997) found that black women have little on-the-job interaction with whites, do not socialize much with the other officers off duty, receive more disciplinary penalties for off-duty activity, and are less likely than white women to be accorded "chivalrous" treatment by male officers. Whether these findings generalize to Hispanic, Asian American, and Native American women officers is unclear.

To address their isolation within police agencies, minority women officers have established the National Organization of Black Women in Law Enforcement or NOBWLE (pronounced *noble-ee*). This agency gives them a focal point through which they network, mentor women officers, and address issues unique to women of color. *See also* INTERNATIONAL ASSOCIATION OF WOMEN POLICE; POLICE WORK, HISTORY OF WOMEN IN, USA; WOMEN PROFESSIONALS IN THE JUSTICE WORKPLACE.

Further Reading: Dulaney 1996, *Black Police in America;* Fletcher 1995, *Breaking and Entering;* Haarr 1997, "Patterns of Interaction in a Police Patrol Bureau"; S. E. Martin 1995, "The Interactive Effects of Race and Sex on Women Police Officers"; National Center for Women and Policing 1998, *Equality Denied.*

Evelyn Gilbert

Police Organizations, Federal, Statistics on

As of 1998, U.S. federal police organizations and other federal agencies with law enforcement authority employed about 83,000 full-time personnel with the authority to make arrests and carry firearms. About 12,000, or 14 percent, of these federal officers were women. Figure 9 shows the proportion of female officers in various federal law enforcement agencies.

The largest federal law enforcement agency, the Immigration and Naturalization

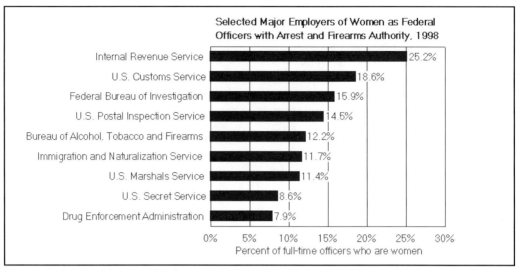

Figure 9. Selected Major Employers of Women as Federal Officers with Arrest and Firearms Authority, 1998

Service (INS), was established within the Department of Justice in 1891. Nearly half of the 16,552 officers employed by the INS in 1998 were border patrol agents, with most of the remainder serving as immigration inspectors, criminal investigators, and detention officers. About 1,900 of these officers were women.

The Justice Department is also home to the oldest federal law enforcement agency, the U.S. Marshals Service, established by Congress in 1789. The Marshals Service, which accounts for a majority of the arrests of federal fugitives, employed about 2,700 full-time officers in the U.S. in 1998. This total included about 300 women. U.S. marshals and their deputies also protect the federal judiciary, transport federal prisoners, and manage the federal witness protection and asset forfeiture programs. Other Justice Department agencies include the Federal Bureau of Investigation (FBI) and the Drug Enforcement Administration (DEA). The FBI, which began as a small unnamed force of special agents appointed by the attorney general in 1908 to conduct investigations, employed more than 11,000 agents in 1998. FBI agents have broad investigative responsibilities covering more than 250 federal crimes. About 1,800 women served as FBI agents in 1998.

The DEA was created in 1973 when all federal antidrug forces were unified under a single command. In 1998, more than 3,300 DEA agents were employed nationwide to investigate major narcotics violators and enforce narcotics regulations. There were more than 250 female DEA agents in 1998.

After the Justice Department, agencies within the Treasury Department are the largest employer of federal officers. The largest, the U.S. Customs Service, employed more than 10,000 officers in 1996. About 2,000 of these officers were women. About two-thirds of customs officers work as inspectors, while the remainder are criminal investigators. The next largest employer in 1998 was the Internal Revenue Service with about 3,400 officers, including about 900 women. Nearly all were agents assigned to investigate tax fraud.

Also within the Treasury Department is the U.S. Secret Service, which was created in 1865 to deal with counterfeiting. After the assassination of President William McKinley in 1901, it was authorized to protect the president and the president's family. In 1998, the Secret Service employed about 2,200 agents with criminal investigation and enforcement responsibilities mostly related to financial and computer crimes. Another 1,400 Secret Service officers were employed within the Uniformed Division to provide various protection services. There were about 300 women serving as Secret Service agents or officers in 1998.

The Treasury Department's Bureau of Alcohol, Tobacco and Firearms (ATF) employed about 1,700 agents in 1998, including more than 200 women. The ATF has enforcement and investigation responsibilities related to federal laws covering alcohol, tobacco, firearms, explosives, and arson.

Outside of the Justice and Treasury departments, the largest employer of federal law enforcement officers in 1998 was the U.S. Postal Inspection Service with 3,490 officers, including about 500 women.

Federal law enforcement employment grew about 11 percent from 1996 to 1998. This growth is expected to continue as a result of Congressional authorization for the hiring of 1,000 additional border patrol agents per year through 2000. Additional immigration inspectors were also authorized. *See also* POLICE ORGANIZATIONS, MUNICIPAL AND STATE.

Further Reading: Reaves 2000, *Federal Law Enforcement Officers, 1998.*

Brian A. Reaves

Police Organizations, Municipal and State

Municipal and state police organizations in the United States first opened up to women in 1910, when Los Angeles hired Alice Stebbins Wells, the first female sworn police officer. The entry of women into what has traditionally been a hyper-masculine profession occurred during a period—the early decades of the twentieth century—when crime prevention and citizen protection became a legitimate police concern. Thus, room was opened up for functions other than patrol—preventative and protective work that seemed suitable for women. Pioneer policewomen served as social workers, working with female victims and offenders and with children, rather than as conventional armed crime-fighters. But in spite of their limited roles, female officers enjoyed only marginal

support. Policewomen remained at the periphery of police departments, sequestered in separate women's bureaus, until the 1960s, when they began to seek a role equal to that of male police officers.

Starting in the 1960s, pivotal legal and legislative reforms transformed the practice of employment discrimination on the basis of sex and race, practices that had subjected women and minorities to separate selection criteria and job function restrictions. Job discrimination suits, the enactment of the Civil Rights Act in 1964 and the Equal Employment Opportunity Act in 1972, and modifications in hiring practices and requirements paved the way for women and minorities to demand an increased presence and greater scope of duties in policing.

Nonetheless, breaking into this gender-stratified occupation as fully vested, uniformed police officers did not come easy for women. Nearly all U.S. police agencies follow a paramilitary model that dictates the chain of command and spells out the responsibilities of officers at each level. In addition, police departments are rigid bureaucracies where officers are expected to perform specific functions and follow the rules and regulations of their superiors while routinely making independent and discretionary decisions in the line of duty. Male police officers feared that women were too emotional and passive to fit into the military structure. They also worried about women's ability to provide adequate backup help to male colleagues in times of danger.

Although opportunities for female police officers have expanded, women remain underrepresented in policing. There are roughly 18,000 police agencies in the United States at the municipal, state, and federal levels. Nearly 17,000 of these are city police departments, county sheriffs' departments, and special police agencies such as park, airport, transit, and campus police (Reaves 1996). According to data collected by the Federal Bureau of Investigation (U.S. Department of Justice, Federal Bureau of Investigation 1998), women account for 10.2 percent of municipal law enforcement personnel.

Table O. Percentage of Women Employed as Sworn Officers, USA, in Selected Years

	Year			
	1980	1985	1990	1997
Total Cities	3.8	6.2	8.3	10.3
Cities with pop. >250,000	4.6	8.6	12.6	15.4
Cities with pop. 100,000–249,999	4.2	6.6	8.2	9.7
Cities with pop. 50,000–99,999	3.1	4.5	6.2	7.7
Cities with pop. 25,000–49,999	3.0	4.0	5.1	6.7
Cities with pop. 10,000–24,999	2.9	3.8	4.3	5.8
Cities with pop. <10,000	3.2	4.7	5.5	6.9
Suburban Counties	8.1	9.7	11.3	12.4
Rural Counties	9.9	5.7	6.3	7.3

[1]*Source:* Derived from U.S. Department of Justice, Federal Bureau of Investigation 1981, 1986, 1991, 1999 *Crime in the United States.*

Table O shows the proportion of women employed as sworn officers in cities of various sizes.

While most police work at the local and state level is field or patrol work, larger departments conduct a variety of other tasks. For instance, about 90 percent of state and large municipal agencies operate SWAT teams, and most have drug enforcement units. In addition, over half of the sheriffs' departments with 100 or more officers provide services in search and rescue, underwater recovery, and bomb removal. Despite the tendency of these organizations to offer the types of specialized services that have historically been considered "men's work," it is within these police agencies that females have made the greatest inroads in terms of representation. Currently, 15 percent of all sworn officers in large municipal and sheriffs' departments are women. However, even when women are successful at entering the profession, their upward mobility within law enforcement is likely to be curtailed. For example, less than 4 percent of supervisory positions within police organizations of all sizes are held by female officers, although these percentages are higher in larger departments.

With the exception of Hawaii, every state has a state-level police agency, yet only 5.2 percent of state troopers are women. State police departments were originally formed to address rising crime rates in nonurban jurisdictions, increases that resulted from population growth, demographic shifts, the popularity of the automobile, and the expansion of national highways. Municipal departments simply could not handle mobile, multi-jurisdictional criminals. In many states, the general police powers of municipal and state agencies are similar, although state police provide law enforcement services for the entire state. Yet the primary role of the state police remains that of patrolling highways and major thoroughfares. The large territories governed by state police increase the likelihood of job transfers from one region of the state to another. Women, particularly those with families, may be hesitant to enter an organization in which they may be transferred far from home. Women may also be more reluctant to seek positions in rural areas where back-up assistance is slower to materialize.

The entry requirements of state police departments and the likelihood of relocation may help explain the exceptionally low presence of female officers in state police organizations. The overall token status of policewomen subjects them to gender stereotyping, increased job performance pressure, and isolation from male officers. However, in state police organizations and small, rural departments (where the representation of female officers is generally lowest), the effects of tokenism are likely to be the most severe. *See also* GENDER AND POLICING; POLICE ASSIGNMENTS AND SPECIALIZATIONS; POLICE ATTITUDES TOWARD POLICE WORK; POLICE ORGANIZATIONS, FEDERAL, STATISTICS ON; POLICE RECRUITMENT

AND SELECTION; POLICE SUBCULTURE AND GEN-
DER; POLICE WORK, HISTORY OF WOMEN IN,
BRITAIN; POLICE WORK, HISTORY OF WOMEN IN,
USA.

Further Reading: Fletcher 1995, *Breaking and
Entering;* S. E. Martin 1980, *Breaking and
Entering;* Schulz 1995, *From Social Worker to
Crimefighter.*

Michelle L. Meloy

Police Recruitment and Selection

One issue confronting police departments
today is the recruitment and selection of
women. Many people believe that a diverse
police organization is more effective than an
agency that is homogeneous. It is also believed that police departments should resemble the communities they police. Recruiting females and other minorities might not
only improve the relationship that police
agencies have with their communities, it
might also improve the quality of police services. Female police officers may bring with
them skills and styles of policing that would
benefit both police departments and citizens.
Therefore, strong recruiting efforts based on
eliminating sexism and sex-role stereotyping
can professionalize departments, modernize
them, and improve their flexibility in the provision of services.

In 1972, Congress amended Title VII of
the 1964 Civil Rights Act, extending the principle of equal opportunity to women in law
enforcement. While police departments have
made some gains in recruiting females over
the years, women still constitute but a small
percentage of sworn police officers (Martin
1997).

Legal changes over the past 35 years have
helped increase the representation of females
in police departments. Typically, the selection process includes a written exam, a physical agility test, an interview, a medical exam
including drug screening, a background investigation, and a polygraph. Historically,
women were eliminated from consideration
by physical agility and/or height requirements. However, in 1971, the U.S. Supreme
Court ruled in *Griggs v. Duke Power Co.* that

an agency could not discriminate against
women, due to Title VII. Moreover, in
Dothard v. Rawlinson (1977), the U.S. Supreme Court made it a requirement for police agencies to demonstrate that selection
criteria such as height and weight requirements are job-relevant and valid. Today, most
departments have eliminated their height and
weight criteria to comply with the law, thus
enabling more women to meet the eligibility
criteria.

Some argue that more subjective aspects
of the selection process, such as the interview or even the background investigation,
can perpetuate gender discrimination. Yet
many police departments have now taken
steps to recruit women and other groups like
minorities and college-educated persons by
offering special pre-entry training and other
inducements to attract them to their agencies. *See also* GENDER AND POLICING; POLICE
ACADEMY TRAINING; POLICE ATTITUDES TOWARD
POLICE WORK; POLICE ORGANIZATIONS, FED-
ERAL, STATISTICS ON; POLICE ORGANIZATIONS,
MUNICIPAL AND STATE; POLICE WORK, HISTORY
OF WOMEN IN, USA.

Further Reading: Belknap and Shelley 1992, "The
New Lone Ranger"; S. E. Martin 1990, *On the
Move.*

*Laure Weber Brooks and
Jeremy Raymond Krum*

Police Subculture and Gender

The police subculture, an informal system of
shared norms, beliefs, and behaviors by which
police distinguish themselves from outsiders,
has traditionally constituted a barrier to
women's entry and survival in policing.

Three key assumptions characterize the
traditional police subculture. First, officers
assume that a contradictory relationship exists between the formal world of the academy and the informal world of the street. The
academy instructs rookies in the formal rules
of law and in department rules restricting the
use of force, participation in corruption, and
other immoral conduct. On the street, however, rookies learn to tolerate the routine use
of extralegal force as "normal," to accept gra-

tuities and certain kinds of bribes (i.e., "clean" money), and to participate in conduct that contradicts the department's moral code (i.e., "acceptable" lying). Second, rookies learn that seasoned officers assume they will obey a subcultural code of silence that forbids discussing legal violations in officer conduct with outsiders. Third, rookies absorb the subcultural assumption that "real police work" involves attributes, values, and behaviors such as arresting criminals that are considered masculine. All three of these assumptions have worked to exclude women from policing.

Two processes facilitate rookies' learning of subcultural norms and perpetuate the exclusion from policing of outsiders such as women. Rookies are exposed to a system of reward and punishment which helps them distinguish and adopt new categories of "normal force," "clean money," and "acceptable" lying. Simultaneously, they learn culturally shared ways of explaining their behavior that help neutralize guilt and keep their moral identity intact. Rookies who demonstrate a proper understanding of informal norms are rewarded by veteran officers who take them under their wing, show them the ropes, protect them in the event of trouble, and begin to include them in the inner circle of "real police." Officers who do not understand or who violate informal rules are punished by gossip, negative labeling, isolation, discrimination, limited job mobility, and on occasion, physical injury.

Police distinguish their world according to a gendered system in which activities associated with femininity are viewed as lower in status and further away from real police work than those linked to masculinity (Martin 1980). Thus, the informal world of the street, clean money, normal violence, and routine lying are linked to masculinity and the police occupation. The academy and assorted "inside" jobs involving secretarial and administrative tasks are perceived as feminine. Women police are, therefore, viewed as threats who might expose the informal dimensions of police work and undermine masculine identity by bringing feminine at-

tributes and values to the street. Resistance to women through harassment and stereotyping helps to reduce men's fears of exposure and maintain the status quo.

Police officers and departments differ in the degree to which they adopt subcultural values and evince hostility to women officers. The acceptance of subcultural norms varies depending on individuals' vulnerability to informal socialization, capacity to neutralize moral tensions, and where they decide to stop on the spectrum of illegal force, corruption, and lying. Norms also vary among police units and departments, according to their political and social organization and whether or not high-level city and police officials informally collude with the views of rank-and-file officers.

Increasing numbers of women, gay men, and racial and ethnic minority officers have entered police work since the 1970s. Most police departments also have reorganized to embrace styles of policing that emphasize some combination of professionalism, order maintenance, and community relations. However, because studies of police in the 1980s and 1990s have largely relied on survey research rather than intensive fieldwork and unstructured interviews, researchers have focused on surface norms and behaviors. They have failed to probe possible changes in the police subculture's hidden understandings, latent values, and behaviors through which police define their occupation and distinguish themselves from outsiders. Whether the presence of increasing numbers of women officers has changed the informal policing subculture thus remains a largely unexamined issue for future research. *See also* GENDER AND POLICING; POLICE ACADEMY TRAINING; POLICE ATTITUDES TOWARD POLICE WORK; POLICE WORK AND STRESS; POLICING, MODELS OF.

Further Reading: Hunt and Manning 1991, "The Social Context of Police Lying"; Kappeler, Sluder, and Alpert 1994, *Forces of Deviance.*

Jennifer C. Hunt

Police Work and Civil Rights Laws

Women's participation in police work in the United States was profoundly changed during the 1960s and 1970s as a result of civil rights legislation and several significant court cases. The civil rights movement, the women's movement, and the due-process revolution gave women and people of color assistance they had not previously had in addressing the discriminatory employment practices that had long plagued police organizations.

Although women have worked in policing as sworn officers since 1910, their early participation was limited and confined to what were considered gender-appropriate tasks. Policing has been characterized as requiring physical strength and the ability to control potentially violent situations, which are deemed inherently masculine characteristics. Since women were perceived as lacking these characteristics, they were viewed as unable to perform police work competently. Because of the characterization of the job as appropriate for men only and inconsistent with appropriate female activities, women have experienced discrimination in various forms throughout the history of policing.

It was not until the passage of Title VII of the Civil Rights Act of 1964 that women began to see some relief from these discriminatory practices. Title VII made it unlawful for private employers with 25 or more employees to discriminate in recruitment, hiring, working conditions, promotion, or other employment practices based on race, color, religion, sex, or national origin. The Equal Employment Opportunity Act of 1972 extended the application of Title VII to state and local governments, which included police departments. This act also created the Equal Employment Opportunities Commission (EEOC) to oversee its enforcement.

Women were allowed into uniformed patrol in the late 1960s and early 1970s, on the heels of antidiscrimination laws. Shortly after women's entrance into uniformed patrol, an abundance of evaluative studies measuring women's competence as patrol officers were undertaken. Without question, research indicated that women performed in policing as ably as their male counterparts, and in some cases, better than their male counterparts (Grennan 1987).

Significant court cases, including *Griggs v. Duke Power Co.* (1971), *Meritor Savings Bank FSB v. Vinson* (1986), and *Harris v. Forklift Systems, Inc.* (1993), helped to clarify civil rights legislation and have also increased women's participation in policing.

In *Griggs v. Duke Power Co.*, the Court held that a plaintiff does not have to prove intentional discrimination on the part of an employer. Once a plantiff proves that job qualifications exclude a certain group or class more than another, the burden of proof falls on the employer to prove that the job requirements are bona fide occupational qualifications (BFOQ) and that no other means of selection could be used. The *Griggs* standard was used to evaluate height and weight requirements that had previously excluded women from employment in policing.

Meritor Savings Bank FSB v. Vinson clarified issues relating to sexual harassment, which has been identified as problematic for women in policing (Gomez-Preston and Trescott 1995; Hale and Menniti 1993; S. E. Martin 1980) and is also a form of sex discrimination prohibited under Title VII. In *Meritor*, the Court held that both quid pro quo harassment and hostile work environments are prohibited by Title VII. The Court held that for harassment to be a cause of action in a hostile work environment, the plaintiff must suffer severe or pervasive treatment that affects the conditions of the plaintiff's employment. However, in *Harris v. Forklift Systems, Inc.*, the Court ruled that a hostile work environment does not have to seriously affect a plaintiff's psychological well-being or cause injury. Instead, the Court articulated a midpoint between what is merely offensive behavior and what is psychologically detrimental to the plaintiff.

These court cases, along with legislation, provided for the development of affirmative action programs, which in some cases required quotas and timetables for hiring women. Affirmative action programs were intended to address the results of past discrimination.

Although women represented only 2.2 percent of sworn personnel in municipal police organizations in 1975, representation had increased to 9 percent by 1993, a gain of nearly 7 percent that more than tripled the number of women officers. Had it not been for civil rights legislation and other legal mandates, these increases might have never occurred. However, while these increases are noteworthy, the significance of issues such as the sexual harassment of women in policing as a potential barrier to women's employment and retention should be at the forefront of organizational concerns in police departments. *See also* POLICE ATTITUDES TOWARD POLICE WORK; POLICE OFFICERS, LESBIAN; POLICE SUBCULTURE AND GENDER; POLICE WORK, HISTORY OF WOMEN IN, BRITAIN; POLICE WORK, HISTORY OF WOMEN IN, USA; WOMEN PROFESSIONALS IN THE JUSTICE WORKPLACE.

Further Reading: S. E. Martin and Jurik 1996, *Doing Justice, Doing Gender;* S. E. Martin 1990, *On the Move;* S. E. Martin 1980, *Breaking and Entering.*

Kathryn E. Scarborough

Police Work and Stress

Work-related stress is an important issue for police officers, particularly for women, who frequently face distinctive workplace problems and pressures due to their subgroup status. Work-related stress is an important issue because of the physical, emotional, and job performance consequences it has for a police officer. Specifically, high stress has been linked to job dissatisfaction, absenteeism, "burnout," work performance problems, and physical illness.

The literature on police work and stress uses various definitions and conceptualizations of stress. Sometimes "stress" refers to the sources, or stressors; more often "stress" is conceived as an inner state reflected in anxiety or frustration, or as a response characterized by behaviors such as yelling, by adrenaline flow, and/or by a sense of physical and emotional discomfort.

Most of the cited studies on police work and stress do not distinguish between types of stress or stressors experienced by men and women officers. When women have been included in a sample, it has usually been assumed that they experience the same stressors as men; therefore, the measurement of women police officers' stress has been carried out using variables that predict male police officers' stress. A comprehensive list of stressors that have been identified by researchers, most of them studying white male officers, includes:

- relationships within the police organization, such as relations with supervisors and co-workers
- the organizational structure and climate, including lack of managerial support, office politics, and frustrating organizational policies
- circumstances intrinsic to the job, such as shift work, facing situations that may call for use of deadly force, and the possibility of being injured in the line of duty
- the officer's role in the organization, including role conflict or ambiguity and degree of participation in decisions
- factors related to career development, including job security and promotions
- individual employee characteristics, including age, gender, race, rank, and years of service

In the 1980s, several studies (Ellison and Genz 1983; Goolkasian, Geddes, and DeJong 1985; Wexler and Logan 1983) finally concluded that structural features of the police work organization and cultural features governing male-female interactions in the occupation contribute to unique female-related stressors, including lack of acceptance by the male police subculture; an atmosphere of disrespect, bias, and prejudice against women; and the denial of needed information, alliances, protection, and sponsorship by supervisors and colleagues. In a pivotal study, Morash and Haarr (1995) concluded that while women police officers do not appear to experience more stress than men, they experience it under somewhat different circumstances. In particular, women's stress stemmed from their subgroup status in the workplace, notably bias and language harassment through profanity and sex jokes.

Most police research has focused on one dimension of the stress process, the stressors. However, how a police officer copes with stress and stressors is also of central concern, because coping strategies can either moderate stress or become stressors in and of themselves. Police officers report using a wide array of coping strategies in dealing with occupational stress, and to a large extent male and female police officers report using similar methods of coping. Haarr and Morash (1999) did find, however, that women police officers reported using escape mechanisms (ignoring the situation, suffering in silence, avoiding colleagues) at a significantly higher level than men. Among the few studies that have been conducted on police officers and stress coping mechanisms, most find that police tend to utilize maladaptive strategies (e.g., resorting to use of alcohol and drugs, or escape/avoidance) that may provide immediate relief but easily degenerate into self-defeating strategies that create even more stress over time. *See also* GENDER AND POLICING; POLICE ACADEMY TRAINING; POLICE ATTITUDES TOWARD POLICE WORK; POLICE SUBCULTURE AND GENDER; WOMEN PROFESSIONALS IN THE JUSTICE WORKPLACE.

Further Reading: Ellison and Genz 1983, *Stress and the Police Officer;* Goolkasian, Geddes, and DeJong 1985, *Coping with Police Stress;* Hurrell 1995, "Police Work, Occupational Stress, and Individual Coping"; White and Marino 1983, "Job Attitudes and Police Stress."

Robin N. Haarr

Police Work, History of Women in, Britain

The history of women in police work in Britain is distinctive in several ways, while still having parallels with that of the United States and other nations. In Britain, the story is marked by the length and vigor of the campaign to gain entry for women into policing,

by the more radical vision for females in law enforcement held by some of the pioneer policewomen and their supporters, and by the "colonial" impact of the British model in several other countries. In later periods, although developments in Britain converged with those in the United States, certain distinctive characteristics remained.

Britain is widely regarded as having introduced the first modern police force with the setting up of the new Metropolitan Police of London in 1829. During the nineteenth century, this body and the other forces set up throughout the country recruited only men. When female suspects were searched, policemen's wives were often employed. Among the campaigns mounted during the second half of the Victorian era by first-wave feminists were several focused on moral reform, especially the protection of women and young people from "vice." At the beginning of the twentieth century, members of these reform groups joined forces to promote the entry of women into policing. Also involved in this movement were suffragettes, who had campaigned for votes for women using direct action, as a result of which many had themselves been arrested and imprisoned.

The outbreak of the First World War gave them their chance. Having lobbied earlier for the appointment of women constables "with powers equal to men," Margaret Damer Dawson and Nina Boyle recruited members to the Women Police Volunteers. The volunteers were allowed to patrol the streets of London to offer protection to girls and women at risk and to those soldiers thought to be in moral danger. The volunteers wore uniforms and undertook training in police work. Later, other volunteer groups were formed, although all were disbanded at the end of the war.

Peacetime patrols were set up again in London in 1919, and vigorous lobbying continued until 1931 when at last women achieved the status of attested police officers. The campaign had involved petitions to the home secretary; parliamentary debates; a major enquiry into the handling of a young woman alleged to have behaved indecently;

the support of Nancy Astor, the first woman member of Parliament actually to take her seat; as well as the publication of a journal, *The Policewoman's Review*, which promoted the cause.

The pioneer policewomen in Britain had a somewhat different concept of their role than their U.S. counterparts. They did not ally themselves with social workers but instead sought to emulate professional police officers. They wore distinctive uniforms and developed training that followed conventional policing paths. In the early days, there were real conflicts among the first volunteers over the enforcement of wartime curfews imposed on women in garrison towns (Radford 1989). A few feminists were outraged, but the majority split away and reformed as the Women Police Service, determined to police as they were instructed. When they were accorded sworn officer status, they wore uniforms, and they had their own command structures, within which they could be promoted. They did not, however, perform the full range of tasks undertaken by male officers.

The British model was exported to some of Britain's colonies, including some Australian states and nations in the Caribbean. However, Britain's African and Asian colonies followed a more military pattern of policing based on the Royal Irish Constabulary (later to form the basis of the Royal Ulster Constabulary). However, it was in Europe and specifically in Germany where, after each of the two world wars, British policewomen brought in to deal with vice and juveniles strongly influenced later developments by providing a model.

After a long latent period, women's role in law enforcement developed quickly in the 1970s. The 1975 Sex Discrimination Act required the integration of police forces, and this was achieved rapidly and abruptly. Numbers of female recruits expanded, reaching up to a quarter of the total, although at the end of the twentieth century, women still constituted only about 16 percent of all officers. While as yet underrepresented at senior levels, two female chief constables were appointed in the mid-1990s, and women took on every policing task.

All forces are required to have Equal Opportunities Codes, and Britain is a major supporter of the European Network of Policewomen, a nongovernmental organization geared to the promotion of the role of female officers. In the late twentieth century, the main problems faced by British policewomen were found *within* police organizations, where harassment and discrimination, supported by a resistant police culture, persisted (Halford 1993).

While police in Britain face many twenty-first century challenges, issues of equality in gender and ethnic issues remain among the most significant. *See also* POLICE WORK, HISTORY OF WOMEN IN, USA; SUFFRAGETTES; WOMEN PROFESSIONALS IN THE JUSTICE WORKPLACE.

Further Reading: J. M. Brown and Heidensohn 2000, *Gender and Policing;* Carrier 1988, *The Campaign for the Employment of Women as Police Officers;* Heidensohn 1992, *Women in Control?*

Frances Heidensohn

Police Work, History of Women in, USA

The appointment of Alice Stebbins Wells to the newly created rank of "policewoman" by the Los Angeles Police Department in 1910 is usually cited as the start of women's history in police work in the United States, but women had served as matrons in prisons, jails, and in some police stations since the late 1800s. The idea that women could serve as police was part of a municipal reform agenda in the late nineteenth and early twentieth centuries by educated, native-born American men and women who sought a role for women in public life, particularly in areas concerning morality and temperance, children's issues, and the care of less fortunate women.

The first policewomen were primarily upper-middle-class women, many educated as social workers, who were supported by groups such as the Women's Christian Temperance Union and the General Federation of Women's Clubs, feminists, Progressives, and juvenile court advocates and other "child-savers"—but rarely by male police chiefs. In 1915, Wells and a few others, representing policewomen in 28 U.S. and 4 Canadian cities, attended the National Conference of Charities and Corrections (later the National Conference of Social Workers) annual conference and formed the International Association of Policewomen (IAP). These women did not see their roles as similar to policemen; quite the contrary, they used the IAP to publicize their views that policewomen should be well educated, should work in plainclothes, should refrain from competing with men by avoiding general patrol work, and should be segregated in a women's bureau supervised by a woman officer. While policewomen were rarely able to achieve all of these goals, they were successful in Washington, D.C., New York City, Detroit, Indianapolis, and few smaller cities.

By 1917, 30 U.S. cities employed policewomen. With few exceptions, they enforced laws concerning dance halls, movie theaters, and other places of recreation where women and children might mingle with adult males. They searched for missing persons, patrolled train stations for runaways, and provided social service information to women. Because they were concerned with the activities of young women, whom they viewed as easily lured into amoral conduct and prostitution, they exercised governmental authority in assuring that women—usually poor or immigrant women—raised their daughters appropriately. Unknown to them, they set the pattern for policewomen's duties for more than 50 years, until well into the 1970s and even the 1980s.

During World War I, concerns with women's morality and keeping soldiers free from venereal disease led to increases in the number of policewomen. By the end of the war, there were approximately 300 policewomen, including a small number of African Americans, employed in more than 220 cities. Their ranks remained stable until the 1930s, when the Great Depression and the development of the crime-fighter ideology combined to diminish their numbers.

Policewomen reemerged during World War II, again to police morality. After the war, policewomen were assigned to undercover and decoy work, primarily because policemen accompanied by women were less conspicuous. Although this work moved women into a more direct crime-fighting role, their selection was still based on sex. Some women, particularly military veterans, chafed at their limited roles, but it would be another two decades before real change came.

Despite a few lawsuits in the 1950s by individual women seeking to expand opportunities in some police departments, and the re-creation of the IAP by Chicago policewoman Lois Lundell Higgins as the International Association of Women Police, little changed until September 1968. It was then that Indianapolis policewomen Betty Blankenship and Elizabeth Coffal reminded their chief, Winston Churchill, that as a sergeant he had said he would permit women to do patrol work if he ever became chief. With one day's preparation, the women put on uniforms and gun belts and climbed into Car 47, setting in motion the patrol era for policewomen.

Media attention to Car 47 notwithstanding, real change did not come until passage in 1972 of Title VII of the 1964 Civil Rights Act, which, among other things, extended to police agencies prohibitions against discrimination on the basis of sex in such employment areas as recruitment, hiring, working conditions, promotions, and benefits. Additionally, in 1973 the Crime Control Act, responsible for dispensing federal funds to local agencies, specified that grantees were prohibited from discriminating in employment practices. These laws, as well as a number of court rulings, convinced police departments that women would have to be hired and assigned on the same basis as men, not only in municipal police departments but also in county, state, and federal agencies.

Legal equality has been achieved, but whether actual equality exists is open to question. Although women are hired by most agencies in percentages equal to their applications, and women pass through academy training in percentages equal to their acceptance into training, the percentages of women in policing remain small. At the end of the 1990s, women constituted 13.3 percent of all police officers, ranging from over 25 percent in a few urban departments to 0 percent in some small departments and about a dozen state police agencies. Women make up 9.2 percent of first-line supervisors and 6.5 percent of command positions below chief. About 16 percent of FBI agents are women.

Women chiefs are a rarity. Penny E. Harrington, a 20-year veteran of the Portland, Oregon, Police Department served as chief from January 1984 to June 1986. By 1999, only two women had reached the top of large departments: Elizabeth Watson in Houston, who served from 1990 to 1992, and Beverly Harvard, appointed in Atlanta in 1994 and still serving in 2000. Harvard, the first female African American chief of a major department, is one of about 125 female chiefs, the vast majority of them in small agencies of under 100 officers. *See also* GENDER AND POLICING; INTERNATIONAL ASSOCIATION OF WOMEN POLICE; POLICE ADMINISTRATORS AND SUPERVISORS; POLICE OFFICERS, LESBIAN; POLICE WORK AND CIVIL RIGHTS LAWS; POLICE WORK, HISTORY OF WOMEN IN, BRITAIN.

Further Reading: S. E. Martin 1990, *On the Move;* S. E. Martin and Jurik 1996, *Doing Justice, Doing Gender;* Milton 1972, *Women in Policing;* Schulz 1995, *From Social Worker to Crimefighter.*

Dorothy Moses Schulz

Policewomen on Television

A television viewer who pushes the remote-control power button today might well encounter a police drama starring women. This was not always the case.

In early television, detectives and other police officers were men. Women appeared as femme fatales or damsels in distress. Later, television and advertising executives targeted a women's audience. This targeting became more pronounced in the 1970s as more women entered the labor force, including criminal justice occupations.

Tyne Daly as Detective Mary Beth Lacey and Sharon Gless as Detective Christine Cagney in *Cagney and Lacey. American Stock/Achive Photos.*

Two 1970s programs featured women detectives. *Police Woman* starred Angie Dickinson as Sgt. Pepper Anderson. She frequently went undercover and had to be saved by her male partner. *Charlie's Angels* featured glamorous ex-cops who fought crime under the direction of their male superior. Women enjoyed starring roles, but the programs were sexually exploitative.

Cagney and Lacey was a watershed for women. The series, which ran from 1982 to 1988, depicted two women friends working in a nontraditional occupation—policing. They solved crimes, often with little help from male colleagues, and negotiated sexism and other issues facing real women. Yet, there was a constant tension between television's penchant for glamorous, subordinated women and attempts to develop a woman-centered narrative (D'Acci 1994).

The most significant woman-centered police program today is *Prime Suspect,* a series of British made-for-TV movies aired on PBS. Helen Mirren stars as Detective Chief Inspector Jane Tennison. The first movie involved Tennison's efforts to head a largely male criminal investigation unit as it solved a series of brutal murders of women.

Prime Suspect features a strong woman who is trying to succeed in a formerly all-male world. Like Cagney and Lacey, Tennison is subjected to sexist insults and discrimination. However, Tennison is the detective in charge. She pays a high personal price, however: she is typically alone at movie's end.

In sum, as women entered occupations like policing, television followed suit with police dramas starring women. Despite some advances in depictions of policewomen, notions of stereotypic beauty and dependence on men are ever-looming. *See also* FICTIONAL CRIME VICTIMS.

Further Reading: Benedict 1992, *Virgin or Vamp;* Cavender and Jurik 1998, "Jane Tennison and the Feminist Police Procedural"; D'Acci 1994, *Defining Women: Television and the Case of Cagney and Lacey.*

Gray Cavender and Nancy C. Jurik

Policing, Models of

Models of policing are concepts used to explain the operating styles of police organizations, including their responses to female victims and female police officers. Models of policing emerged in the 1960s when James Q. Wilson (1968) developed three models to understand police work: the watchman, legalistic, and service styles. Wilson's models were based on observations of virtually all-male police departments that emphasized the typically masculine work culture, stressing obedience under a paramilitary command structure and assuming police officers are "rational men." Although these models provided a foundation for understanding police behavior, they made invisible the gendered nature of policing. Gender is a characteristic that permeates all aspects of society. Models that do not address gender can only be considered partial explanations of policing.

In the last 25 years, the proportion of female police officers has grown from less than 2 percent to more than 10 percent, and women have moved from being confined to specialized units into all ranks and units.

Comprehensive models of policing should reflect the status of women in police departments and society's views of gender roles. Moving in this direction, the democratic model (Angell 1971) encourages the empowerment of *all* officers through education, training, professionalism, and opportunity.

Community policing, a philosophy of police work that emerged in the 1980s, expands upon the ideas originally formulated in the democratic model to include a partnership-style relationship with the community. This concept of policing also reveals how the gendered nature of police organizations has changed. Whereas previous models emphasized the stereotypically masculine traits of suspicion, cynicism, and aggression, the community policing model also recognizes interpersonal skills and intelligence as valued police characteristics.

Despite these improvements to models of policing, female officers have yet to be completely accepted into the masculine profession of policing. The association between the traditional gender roles that continue to dominate policing and the negative experiences of female officers has been well established, including women's experiences of sexual harassment (J. M. Brown 1998), restriction of promotion opportunities (Holdaway and Parker 1998), and unique workplace stressors (Morash and Haarr 1995). However, research has also suggested that an officer's police identity may be more important than her or his gender identity in shaping work related attitudes (A. P. Worden 1993). The role of women in society also continues to change.

Accordingly, a future model of policing may emerge that is gendered in ways equally accommodative of the skills and resources of male *and* female officers. This egalitarian model of policing could be advanced if police departments were to

- afford greater support services to officers, including recourse from discrimination and harassment
- revise promotion procedures to measure performance using nonsexist and

nonracist criteria and promote better accountability

- encourage disciplinary procedures that place heavier emphasis on formal, rather than informal, control of police behavior

See also COMMUNITY POLICING; POLICE ATTITUDES TOWARD POLICE WORK; POLICE SUBCULTURE AND GENDER; POLICE WORK, HISTORY OF WOMEN IN, USA; WOMEN PROFESSIONALS IN THE JUSTICE WORKPLACE.

Further Reading: S. E. Martin and Jurik 1996, *Doing Justice, Doing Gender;* A. P. Worden 1993, "The Attitudes of Women and Men in Policing."

Peter K. Manning and Amanda L. Robinson

Political Offenders

There are many instances in which women have acted or been treated as political offenders, but very few studies have been conducted to determine the extent and nature of their involvement in oppositional politics. If political crime is defined as actions in defiance of societal authority, women have rarely initiated or led such challenges. In most times and places, the traditional subordination of women has been reflected in their typically supportive rather than active roles in antiauthority operations, especially when violence is intended or anticipated (Vetter and Perlstein 1991). However, there have been notable exceptions, and women since the nineteenth century have been increasingly active in both nonviolent and violent radical political movements.

Even where freedom of belief and expression come to be enshrined in law, as in the American Constitution, the dissident and disobedient are always suspect in the eyes of authorities, who tend to dislike and distrust those who challenge the correctness of their actions or their claims to higher status or superior wisdom. American history provides many examples.

The most notable female dissident in early Colonial times was Anne Hutchinson of the Massachusetts Bay Colony, whose spirited criticisms of the (male) Puritan clergy led to her banishment in 1638 for persisting in unwomanly activities. Two centuries later, the women's suffrage movement—led by such redoubtable activists as Susan B. Anthony—protested, despite insults and physical assaults, against the legal subordination of women practiced by excluding them from the electoral process. For voting in the 1872 presidential election, Anthony was convicted without being allowed to speak (women's testimony being inadmissible) and fined $100, which she refused to pay.

Despite relative inactivity in larger political spheres, women have been notably active in antiwar movements. One of the mightiest voices against American involvement in the First World War was that of anarchist Emma ("Red Emma") Goldman, who fought for women's rights, sexual emancipation, educational reforms, and free speech. She was convicted of conspiracy to violate a federal law—i.e., opposing military conscription (which in itself was not an offense at the time of her arrest), imprisoned, and then deported to Russia.

It is not always clear when the line between nonviolent and violent politics, or between ordinary criminal and extraordinary political violence, has been crossed. A sensational instance of debatable ambiguity is the transformation of "brainwashed" Patty Hearst from kidnapped heiress in 1974 to armed bank robber and self-described "urban guerrilla" of the Symbionese Liberation Army, to prison inmate (released after two years by President Jimmy Carter's commutation order), to suburban housewife. An equally controversial case is that of the militant black Marxist Angela Y. Davis, who was arrested on a fugitive warrant for murder, kidnapping, and conspiracy in the 1970 attempt to free the revolutionary George Jackson, imprisoned for 18 months, then acquitted in 1972 after a highly publicized and politicized trial.

Beyond such debatable cases, there are numerous examples of women who have not only participated but also led in efforts to achieve political objectives through violence. One of the most notorious was Ulrike Meinhof ("the brains of the Baader-Meinhof Gang"), a prominent left-wing German journalist whose violent exploits in the late 1960s and early 1970s included organizing a raid to free the terrorist Andreas Baader and culminated in her imprisonment and apparent suicide in 1976.

While women clearly may challenge authority, the available evidence suggests that the likelihood of their doing so depends on the resources made available or denied by the cultural contexts and class structures in which political struggles occur. Least likely to be involved are rural, poor, and uneducated women in traditionally male-dominated societies, presumably because it is difficult for most women under these conditions to envision, much less engage in, outspoken dissent, civil disobedience, and political violence. Limited support for this hypothesis is provided by Brent Smith's (1994) finding that in the United States, women adherents of contemporary right-wing terrorist groups are far less involved in decisions and operations than were their left-wing counterparts of a generation ago. But given that they are typically as extremist as the men in their views, often knowledgeable about firearms, and not necessarily subjugated, why right-wing women have been less violent is a question still to be answered. Clearly, what is known about the political criminality culminates in a research agenda rather than an established body of knowledge. *See also* Davis, Angela Y.; Rosenberg, Ethel; Suffragettes; Terrorism.

Further Reading: Lessing 1985, *The Good Terrorist;* Turk 1982, *Political Criminality.*

Austin T. Turk

Pollak, Otto. *See* Chivalry Explanation of Court Outcomes; Female Crime, Explanations of.

Pornography

Until the 1970s, debates over pornography or sexually explicit materials typically were a struggle between liberal advocates of sexual freedom and conservative proponents of traditional morality. That changed with a radical feminist critique of pornography, which emerged out of the larger struggle against sexual violence during the second wave of the women's movement in the 1960s. Radical feminists argued that discussions of pornography should focus not on questions of sexual mores, but on its harm to women, both those used in making pornography and those who suffer violence at the hands of men incited by pornography.

Many debates about pornography center on the question of effects. Does pornography, particularly material that explicitly eroticizes sexual violence, result in sexual violence against women, children, and other vulnerable people? Pornography's supporters, including many self-identified feminists, argue that there is no conclusive evidence for such a claim. Many social scientists say the studies so far do not produce a clear answer. Radical feminist critics of pornography, on the other hand, have argued that the evidence clearly suggests a connection and that, even without definitive scientific proof, women's accounts of their experiences with the making and use of pornography demonstrate that pornography causes harm.

Many of those experiences have been publicized during attempts in the United States to pass legislation that would allow people hurt by pornography to bring civil actions against pornography makers and users. The first of those efforts, sponsored by radical feminist law professor Catharine MacKinnon and feminist writer Andrea Dworkin, came before the Minneapolis, Minnesota, City Council in 1983. That ordinance defined pornography as the graphic sexually explicit subordination of women and a systematic practice of exploitation and subordination based on sex. So far, those legislative efforts have either failed to be passed or have been struck down by the courts on First Amendment grounds after enactment. Opposition to such legislation has come from not only pornographers but also from the wider publishing industry and feminists who believe that restrictions on sexual material do not serve women's interests.

Whatever the future of legal strategies, the radical feminist critique of pornography has changed the nature of the debate. The issues now include not only constitutional and moral questions, but questions about the ways in which women may be

- coerced into pornography
- forced to view pornography
- victimized by assaults linked to pornography
- defamed through unauthorized use of their images in pornography
- subordinated through the trafficking of women in pornography

The radical feminist critique of pornography is part of a wider movement to address the harms to women in prostitution, other parts of the commercial sex industry, and the international trafficking in women. *See also* VICTIMIZATION, FEMINIST PERSPECTIVES ON.

Further Reading: Burstyn 1985, *Women against Censorship;* Dines, Jensen, and Russo 1998, *Pornography;* MacKinnon and Dworkin 1997, *In Harm's Way.*

Robert W. Jensen

Portia School of Law. *See* LEGAL PROFESSION, HISTORY OF WOMEN IN; LEGAL PROFESSION, WOMEN'S CURRENT PARTICIPATION IN.

Poverty and Crime

Links between poverty and crime have been demonstrated by criminological research, although that research has largely been based on samples of men. Recent analyses of the relationship between women's economic status and their criminal behavior indicate that, although women's opportunities for economic crimes remain limited, there has been an increase in female petty property crime such as shoplifting, passing bad checks, and credit card fraud. These rising rates of petty property crimes may reflect a struggle for economic survival. Darrell Steffensmeier (1993) suggests that increased economic adversity for females and increased opportunity for theft and fraud related to the growth of electronic banking services are two primary factors shaping female crime trends. In essence, poor women who are unemployed or underemployed may turn to property crime as the most easily available solution to the problem of supporting their children.

Recent census trends demonstrate a potentially worsening economic situation for women, as shown in Figure 10. Those hardest hit are young, single, minority women. Criminal activity may serve as a way to supplement a legitimate but meager income

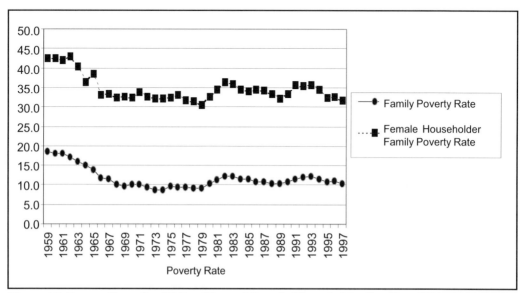

Figure 10. Poverty Rates for All Families and Female Householder Families, USA, 1959–1997

Source: U.S. Census Bureau 1999, "Historical Poverty Tables—Families," Table 13.

or to provide a primary source of income. Economically marginalized communities often cannot provide sources of employment. Many women work in entry-level positions or in temporary, federally funded training programs, neither of which provide benefits. Female offenders convicted of embezzlement, forgery, and fraud have indicated that while the monetary gains were, in actuality, very small, the criminal activity supplemented their legitimate incomes. The motive was to meet family financial needs.

Education is also related to poverty and crime, particularly for women. High school dropout rates are high in poor communities. Young females who have dropped out often report that they want legitimate work, but their choices are limited to temporary, entry-level positions. Access beyond the entry level is denied to these women; job stability with advancement is not present. Yet like other Americans, such women value material goods, which may be accessible only through an illegitimate source of income.

Although the research on female drug users is limited, there is evidence that poverty feeds into this problem, also (Mann 1984). For example, during the 1980s, some impoverished women chose to run drug franchises that provided far more income than menial jobs. Through the income from drug dealing, they received instant rewards. Unfortunately for these same women, drug use often became a part of the drug dealing, and prostitution sometimes became a way to get extra income to support the drug addiction. This downward spiral from drug dealing to prostitution may lead to violent victimization as well as participation in violent criminal activities. Community context—the environment of a distressed neighborhood—can also reinforce criminal behavior.

Most women in impoverished communities do not resort to criminal activities for an income. But the stigma attached to poor communities is difficult to alter. Federal programs, with the current get-tough approach, offer training programs as incentives to leave welfare. Unfortunately, training without continued job security and benefits does not necessarily address the multiple problems related to an impoverished woman's status.

Further Reading: Alder 1986, "Unemployed Women Have Got It Heaps Worse"; Carlen 1988, *Women, Crime and Poverty;* Chesney-Lind 1986, "Women and Crime."

Kristen J. Kuehnle

Power-Control Explanation of Crime

Power-control theory, in its most generic form, argues that authority relations involved in work outside the home influence mothers' and fathers' relational power within the family (Hagan, Gillis, and Simpson 1985, 1987; Hagan 1989). In turn, mother-father relational power within the family affects the social control of sons and daughters, having implications for gender differences in risk preferences and resulting risk-taking behaviors, including common forms of delinquent behavior. In more patriarchal families, daughters are objects of more intense control than sons, and sons are generally more strongly encouraged to take risks. Consequently, patriarchal parental relations produce daughters who have lower risk preferences than sons, and thus, daughters from such families engage in less risk-taking behavior than sons. In contrast, less patriarchal parental relations reduce gender differences in the control experiences of daughters and sons, and daughters come to resemble sons in risk preferences and in risk-related behaviors (Grasmick, Blackwell, and Bursik 1993).

LaMar Empey and Mark Stafford (1991:432–43) suggest that the theory's distinct contribution is its emphasis on the role of power in conceptualizing the influence of control in the causation of common delinquency (see also Simpson 1989; R. O'Brien 1991). John Braithwaite (1989:93) acknowledges core ideas of power control by noting that

> in elaborating the seminal work of Hagan, Gillis, and Simpson (1979), we predict that females will more often be the objects and the instruments of reintegrative shaming, while males will more often be the objects and instruments of stigmatization.

Concepts from power-control theory have been used to explain gender-linked aspects of computer crime (Hollinger and Lanza-Kaduce 1988), minority delinquency (Heimer 1995), violence (Simpson 1991), rape (R. O'Brien 1991), and fear of crime (Sacco 1990).

Recently, McCarthy et al. (1999) have drawn on Sewell's rethinking of structural theory to offer an elaborated power-control theory of gender and delinquency that is sensitive to gender differences across families in the roles of resources and schemas, and especially to assertions and reassertions of agency. Power-control theory proposes that transformations in women's workforce experiences, the resulting increase in their control of work and home-based resources, and their enhanced opportunities to exercise agency in family relations, represent important changes in family life. These changes are accentuated by comparisons between more- and less-patriarchal households and may include alterations in familial control practices and reduced support for traditional, patriarchal schemas.

Changes in familial control undoubtedly influence both sons and daughters, in the latter case possibly lessening the proportionately greater controls to which mothers traditionally expose their daughters, and thereby allowing increases in daughters' preferences for risk and involvement in delinquency. *See also* CONTROL EXPLANATIONS OF CRIME; FEMALE CRIME, EXPLANATIONS OF; JUVENILE DELINQUENCY AND SOCIAL CLASS.

Further Reading: Grasmick, Blackwell, and Bursik 1993, "Changes in the Sex Patterning of Perceived Threats of Sanctions"; Hagan and Kay 1990, "Gender and Delinquency in White-Collar Families"; Hagan, Gillis, and Simpson 1987, "Class in the Household."

John Hagan

Prejean, Sister Helen (1939–)

Helen Prejean, spiritual advisor to death row inmates and author of the best-seller *Dead Man Walking*, was born in Baton Rouge, Louisiana, on April 21, 1939. She became a member of the Sisters of St. Joseph of Medaille of Louisiana in 1957. Prejean earned a B.A. in English from St. Mary's Dominican College in New Orleans and an M.A. in Religious Education from St. Paul's University in Ottawa, Canada. In her work with the Roman Catholic Church, Prejean assisted inner city residents of the St. Thomas Housing Development in New Orleans and taught local high school students as part of Project Hope.

In 1982, Prejean began working with death row inmates at the Louisiana State Penitentiary at Angola, first as a pen pal to condemned inmates and later as their spiritual advisor. Drawing on her experiences at Angola, Prejean wrote her 1993 book, *Dead Man Walking*. The book was made into a movie that was released in 1995. Both the book and the movie provide thought-provoking accounts of the people involved in executions, including the condemned person, the executioner, and victims' family members. Popular successes, the book and movie stimulated public debate about the death penalty.

Further Reading: Prejean 1993, *Dead Man Walking*.

Barbara A. Koons

Premenstrual Syndrome

A link between premenstrual conditions and crime, suggested by a number of empirical studies, has led some scholars to propose that the insanity defense be expanded to recognize the impact of premenstrual syndrome. Reviews of the literature indicate, however, that the association has not been firmly established and that alternative interpretations of the data are possible.

Although several reports of a link between menstruation and crime appeared in the early criminological literature (e.g., Lombroso and Ferrero 1894), the first scientific studies on this topic appeared in the 1960s. Dalton (1961) interviewed incarcerated women, obtaining information about their menstrual cycles. From their self-reports, Dalton calculated the women's cycle phases at the times their crimes were committed. If crimes were randomly distributed across a 28-day cycle, approximately 29 percent of crimes would be expected to occur in any eight-day period. According to Dalton's calculations, however, 49 percent of all the crimes were committed during the four days preceding menstruation and the first four days of menstruation. She speculates that symptoms of premenstrual tension, such as irritability, lethargy, and water retention could be causally related to certain crimes.

A number of other studies followed, with sometimes contradictory results. Epps (1962) used a similar methodology with shoplifters in an English prison and concludes that their crimes were not influenced by menstrual cycles. D'Orban and Dalton (1980) studied 50 women imprisoned for violence against persons or property and did find a relationship between cycle phase and commission of the crime, but they found that the significant increase was during the menstrual phase and not the premenstrual phase. Other research has considered the relationship between menstruation and behavior such as schoolgirls' unpunctuality, forgetfulness, avoiding games, and talking (Dalton 1960b); prison inmates' verbal attacks and physical attacks (Ellis and Austin 1971); and acting out by patients in a security hospital (Hands, Herbert, and Tennant 1974). Most have found some evidence of a relationship between these behaviors and phase of the menstrual cycle, although findings are inconsistent with regard to the particular phase of the cycle that influences behavior.

Methodological problems have led other researchers to question the results of these studies. Reliance on self-reports of menstrual cycles may produce biased results because many women do not accurately report the date of their last menstruation or the length of their cycle. Research has shown that most women report average cycles of 28 days, although very few women actually have 28-day cycles. The considerable variability in cycle length that exists across women is problematic for calculating phases of the cycle and for determining the phase associated with a particular behavioral incident. Because of these issues, some have questioned whether a link between menstrual cycle and crime actually exists.

If the statistical association is accepted as valid, there remains an important question of causal interpretation. Most of the researchers in this area have assumed that the association between criminal behavior and menstrual cycle reflects the impact of premenstrual tension on a woman's behavior. A plausible alternative hypothesis, however, is that psychosocial factors associated with the behavior and its consequences affect the menstrual cycle. Such effects on hormonal processes have been frequently noted in the medical literature and cannot be ruled out by any of the designs used to research the connection between menstrual cycles and crime. We are left with a number of intriguing studies which cannot at this time definitively establish whether or how menstrual cycles and crime are related. *See also* FEMALE CRIME, EXPLANATIONS OF; LOMBROSO, CESARE; MEDICAL EXPLANATIONS OF DELINQUENCY.

Further Reading: Harry and Balcer 1987, "Menstruation and Crime"; Horney 1978, "Menstrual Cycles and Criminal Responsibility"; Wallach and Rubin 1971, "The Premenstrual Syndrome and Criminal Responsibility."

Julie Horney

Prison Accreditation

Prison accreditation is a means for certifying that correctional facilities and services meet minimum professional performance standards. Neither of the two major prison accrediting organizations in the United States, the American Correctional Association (ACA) and the National Commission on Correctional Health Care (NCCHC), has developed separate standards for the accreditation of women's facilities and services. Instead, both groups include some standards specific to women's needs, such as screening for pregnancy, housing separate from male prisoners, and equal access to programs and services, in their general sets of standards for prisons and jails.

Until about 1980, the ACA did not include criteria specific to women's needs in its accreditation standards, under the assumption that all standards applied equally to all offenders. However, the standards evolved in practice as ACA members began to recognize important differences between male and female prisoners in terms of health needs. In one sign of that growing awareness, in 1975 the health-care concerns of incarcerated women were addressed in a U.S. Department of Justice publication designed specifically for them (Brecher and Della Penna 1975); it covered pap smears, information on sexually transmitted diseases, contraception, pregnancy tests, abortion advice, childbirth and infant care information, and information about feminine hygiene. NCCHC included a standard on pregnant women in its 1981 jail standards (American Medical Association 1981), and women's needs in prisons and jails have been covered by recent ACA standards calling for pregnancy screening, separate housing, and program equality.

By 1996, 30 women's facilities had achieved accreditation in 26 states, representing 8.2 percent of all such facilities and holding about one-third of the adult female incarcerated population. Twelve adult community correctional facilities had also been accredited, or 5.6 percent of all 214 such facilities, as had 5 institutions and 4 community programs for juvenile females (4.1 percent of 98). Standards mandate that accreditation audit teams give comparable attention to women's facilities and services during the accreditation process.

The decision to seek accreditation by an administrator of a correctional agency is voluntary. A small number of the standards in each of the ACA's 19 manuals are mandatory and must be met for accreditation; 90 percent of the remaining nonmandatory standards must be met. There are no government requirements for accreditation, although certain standards may be mandated as part of a court order.

As the standards are revised, issues specific to women are likely to continue being addressed. Women administrators have participated in this process from the beginning, and their continuing involvement is essen-

tial. *See also* GENDER DISPARITIES IN PRISONS; JAILS, ISSUES FOR WOMEN IN; PRISON TREATMENT PROGRAMS, RATIONALES FOR AND PROBLEMS WITH; PRISONS, HEALTH CARE IN; WOMEN'S PRISONS, HISTORY OF.

Further Reading: American Correctional Association 1990b, *Standards for Adult Correctional Facilities;* American Medical Association 1981, *Standards for Health Services in Jails;* Branham 1998a, "An Inside Look at Accreditation"; National Commission on Correctional Health Care 1995, *Standards for Health Services in Correctional Facilities.*

Dale K. Sechrest

Prison Discipline

Women experience prison discipline as an elaborate system of rules, policies, and procedures designed to order and control their behavior. Scholars in growing numbers and of increasing sophistication have turned their attention to the distinctive features of women's prison regimes and the mechanisms used by prison authorities to impose order on prisoners who fail to conform.

Recent studies of discipline in women's prisons (Dobash, Dobash, and Gutteridge 1986; McClellan 1994; Pollock 1986; Zedner 1991) have examined three interrelated questions: Do disciplinary rules and practices in women's prisons differ from those in men's prisons? Are there significant differences between men and women in the nature and extent of citations for prison rule violation? What is the relationship between prevailing notions of female propriety and the disciplinary regimes in women's prisons?

Studies that examine the distinctive problems of discipline and control of women prisoners point to the following conclusions: Compared with men's prisons, rules and regulations in women's prisons are greater in number and pettier in nature. Even when rules are the same, women are more strictly supervised than men. For instance, women are cited for behavior that would not be considered worthy of action in male facilities, such as cursing, failing to eat all the food on one's plate, sharing shampoo in the shower, and lighting another prisoner's cigarette.

Thus, women receive a greater number of disciplinary citations than men. The offenses for which women are cited are less serious than men's, yet, overall, women prisoners are punished more often and more severely (McClellan 1994).

Women prisoners have, historically, been characterized by their keepers as emotional, temperamental, excitable, and difficult to manage. However, as early as 1864, Mary Carpenter, in her classic work, *Our Convicts*, concluded that women prisoners were *not* more poorly behaved than men. Instead, Carpenter noted, they were subjected to far more intense surveillance, resulting in their higher rate of punishment. Carpenter decried the "remarkable disparity in the punishments inflicted on the two sexes" (1864:222).

Recent studies of British and U.S. women's prisons continue to find keener surveillance of female inmates, with the inevitable consequence that women are reported and punished for behaviors tolerated in men's prisons. The conscious policy of bringing the full weight of institutional authority to bear on every infraction of rules generates prisoner resentment and resistance. As night follows day, omnipresent surveillance elicits the behavior it is installed to control.

Feminist scholars argue that gender-based assumptions lie at the heart of distinctive prison regimes for women. Intensive surveillance of women prisoners is a historical vestige in the field of corrections; it reflects the broader societal belief that women should conform to gender-based stereotypes stressing obedience, dependence, and deference. The successful adjustment of women prisoners is measured by their conformity to the cultural stereotype of the "good woman"— compliant, submissive, and passive. The women's prison disciplinary regime seeks to bring the behavior of women in line with this ideal by punishing nonconformity through reprimand, loss of privilege, solitary confinement, loss of good-conduct time, and reduction in time-earning status. *See also* GENDER DISPARITIES IN PRISONS; PUNISHING WOMEN OFFENDERS; WOMEN'S PRISONS, HISTORY OF.

Further Reading: R. P. Dobash, Dobash, and Gutteridge 1986, *The Imprisonment of Women;* Freedman 1981, *Their Sisters' Keepers;* McClellan 1994, "Disparity in the Discipline of Male and Female Inmates."

Dorothy S. McClellan

Prison Reform, Australia. *See* PUNISHMENT, AUSTRALIA.

Prison Reform, Britain. *See* FRY, ELIZABETH; HOLLOWAY PRISON.

Prison Reform, Canada

The history of women's prison reform in Canada predates confederation (1867), with the opening of the country's first penitentiary in Portsmouth in 1835. The Kingston Penitentiary (KP) was built to house men sentenced to confinement (then a new alternative criminal penalty to corporal or capital punishment), but it was soon compelled to accommodate women as well. The first women prisoners in KP were confined in temporary locations, such as the prison's hospital and a small area above the mess hall of the male convicts. This situation was noted in 1836 by the president of the Penitentiary Board of Inspectors to have caused "some inconvenience" to the "peculiar discipline of the prison."

The first reform in the imprisonment of women came in 1839, when a part of KP's north wing was opened as a prison for women. As the population of women in the prison grew, they were moved to different temporary locations within KP. The lack of a permanent facility for women was pinpointed again as an impediment to penitentiary discipline, prompting the Brown Commission (1848) to recommend the establishment of a separate facility for women. This recommendation was to be repeated several times by the prison's warden and in various Inspectors' Reports between 1867 and 1909. In 1913, a separate prison for women was finally constructed within the walls of KP.

Concerns were soon raised about the conditions of confinement in the new women's prison. In 1921, the *Report on the State and Management of the Female Prison* (Nickle Report) outlined several reforms to ameliorate the working and living conditions of prisoners. To facilitate these reforms, the report recommended the construction of a new facility outside the walls of KP. The new Prison for Women, often referred to simply as P4W, was built across the street from KP and received its first prisoners in 1934. However, the reforms suggested by the Nickle Report were not realized in the new P4W, prompting the 1938 Royal Commission to Investigate the Penal System of Canada (Archambault Report) to recommend the closure of the prison. This recommendation appeared repeatedly in the many government inquiries into federal prisons that followed.

A common criticism of the conditions of women's imprisonment in government reports and critical analyses has been the lack of meaningful programs, a situation rationalized by the relatively small numbers of women prisoners and the economy of scale. In 1980, the relative absence of programs for incarcerated women in comparison to incarcer-

ated men was the basis of an equality challenge before the Canadian Human Rights Commission on behalf of women prisoners. Another attempt at program reform was the development of a specialized psychiatric facility for women prisoners in the 1980s. This unit was established in the Regional Health Centre in the men's Kingston Penitentiary, a location that has sparked criticism from prisoner advocates.

The treatment of women prisoners was later the focus of a Commission of Inquiry (1995–96), headed by Louise Arbour, which investigated and made recommendations regarding an incident in 1994 involving the strip-searching of women in a segregation unit of the P4W. However, the impetus for the most significant reforms in Canada was *Creating Choices* (Canada, Ministry of the Solicitor General 1990), the report of the Task Force on Federally Sentenced Women. The task force recommended the closure of the P4W and the creation of regional facilities in which women could serve their sentences closer to their home communities. The latter recommendation, first suggested in the

The Okimaw Ohci Healing Lodge. *Courtesy of the Correctional Service of Canada.*

1914 Royal Commission on Penitentiaries and repeated in numerous other government reports, was finally implemented as a result of the task force's report. Federally sentenced women in Canada currently serve their sentences with provincially sentenced women in regional institutions located in British Columbia, Alberta, Saskatchewan, Ontario, Quebec, and Nova Scotia. The P4W remained open, however, until 8 May 2000.

Another of the task force's recommendations was to create an institution modeled on the concept of a spiritual healing lodge for aboriginal women. The Okimaw Ohci (Thunder Hills) Healing Lodge was built using a circular eagle design and opened in 1995 in Maple Creek, Saskatchewan. Aboriginal teachings form the basis of the healing lodge's programs, which are designed and implemented by First Nations elders. Today, the challenge confronting this unique reform rests on the issue of how to employ aboriginal healing strategies in a penal environment. *See also* GENDER DISPARITIES IN PRISONS; HOLLOWAY PRISON; PRISON REFORM, USA; WOMEN IN PRISON, CANADA.

Further Reading: Canada, Ministry of the Solicitor General 1990, *Creating Choices;* Cooper 1993, "The Evolution of the Federal Women's Prison"; Faith 1995, "Aboriginal Women's Healing Lodge."

Liz M. Elliott

Prison Reform, USA

U.S. prison reform has long involved the struggle to improve the conditions of women's imprisonment, although that struggle has waxed and waned in intensity. Since the first U.S. prisons were founded soon after the Revolutionary War, the small number of female prisoners and lower status of women in American society have worked together to create conditions for women prisoners that are inferior to those of their male counterparts. Because the number of women sentenced to prison was low, until the late nineteenth century women were housed in the same institutions as male prisoners and were controlled through segregation and isolation. This treatment resulted in gross limitations on the number and variety of activities available to women. As the numbers of women prisoners increased, so did the need for larger, separate facilities to house them.

The modern American reform movement for women in prison began in the 1870s as an offshoot of the wider women's movement of the time. Middle-class reformers started looking at women's issues such as young women's moral improprieties and the lack of a right to vote. From their perspective, female criminals were deviant not only in a criminal sense but also in a gendered sense: women who betrayed the essentially moral nature of their sex. Many reformers saw an opportunity to stave off further immorality by rehabilitating women in prison. They attempted to shift imprisonment from a punishment model to rehabilitative model. Their intent was to resocialize female prisoners to adopt the dominant domestic roles of the period. The reform movement in the 1870s also aimed at establishing separate women's facilities, run by women, in order to prevent abuse of women prisoners by male staff. With female staff, these separate institutions would be able to focus on rehabilitation.

For the next century, women's prisons reaffirmed this mission of policing gender-role conformity despite changes in prison staff and the prisoners themselves. Even though more women were hired to staff the new separate facilities, they remained beholden to male authority. By the early 1900s, the top women administrators were well educated and invested in the scientific model of classification popular at the time. This professional stance further reinforced the class differences between staff and inmates and tended to reaffirm earlier models of discipline in men's prisons, which emphasized control and retribution.

During the Great Depression, prison reform ceased and even regressed due to the lack of funds. After World War II, prison reform recommenced by echoing the larger society's effort to return women to domestic roles. The 1950s corrections movement was similar to early reform efforts in that it, too, focused on teaching female inmates to behave in socially acceptable ways (Faith 1993). Since that time, little has been done in the way of prison reform, and there has been little overall change despite the rise of the feminist movement in the 1960s and 1970s.

While some women's institutions have broadened their range of programming, female offenders still receive lower quality housing and less programming than male offenders. With the recent increases in the number of female inmates, the building of newer facilities could have been an opportunity to make significant changes in the way women are imprisoned. Yet women's prisons are still modeled after male prisons. While there continues to be discussion over whether women have different physical and psychological needs, little has been done to acknowledge those needs and see that they are met within the prison system. *See also* FRY, ELIZABETH; GENDER DISPARITIES IN PRISONS; PRISON REFORM, CANADA; REFORMATORY MOVEMENT.

Further Reading: Belknap 1996, *The Invisible Woman;* R. P. Dobash, Dobash, and Gutteridge 1986, *The Imprisonment of Women;* Faith 1993, *Unruly Women.*

Amy C. Miller

Prison Security

Prison security for women encompasses the prison's physical setting, the degree to which prisoners' behavior is monitored and controlled within the prison, and prisoners' personal safety while incarcerated. These factors shape daily life and the experience of imprisoned women.

To understand security in women's prisons requires consideration of the inmates' criminal histories, the institution's approach to rule enforcement, prison architecture and classification, and opportunities for sexual abuse of prisoners by staff.

Women are typically incarcerated for nonviolent crimes. The estimated proportion of female offenders who have been convicted for drug or property crimes ranges from 60 to 70 percent. In contrast to male prison populations, with almost 50 percent of their inmates convicted of violent crimes, less than one-third of female inmates are violent offenders (Bureau of Justice Statistics 1998c). Compared with men, women in prison also commit fewer violent offenses while incarcerated. Thus, prisons for women require much less restrictive physical security than prisons for men.

Despite less violent behavior prior to and during incarceration, women receive disciplinary infractions at a high rate. Because correctional institutions attempt to exert more stringent social control over women's everyday lives than is characteristic of institutions for men, infractions committed by the women are usually petty behaviors (McClellan 1994). Just as women's behavior outside of prison is more closely monitored than that of men, so too are incarcerated women subjected to stricter rule enforcement patterns than incarcerated men.

Prison architecture is an additional influence on prison security for women. Prior to the late 1800s, women were often held in penitentiaries along with male prisoners. Women confined in these prisons were vulnerable to brutalization and sexual attack by other prisoners and by guards. Beginning around 1870, the reformatory movement led to the development of separate women's prisons, typically unwalled reformatories built on large parcels of land, usually in rural areas, with small cottages instead of a cell-block structure. Alderson Prison in West Virginia and the California Institute for Women in Frontera followed this model, which enabled women to move freely through the institution. However, after the 1930s, the architecture of prison facilities for women returned to the custodial model, and the facilities became more similar to prisons for men, with their severe restrictions on inmate movements (Rafter 1990a).

In the 1980s and 1990s, as female prison populations exploded due to punitive sanctions against drug offenders, women's prisons became increasingly crowded. Some states began to build new facilities for women, again using designs modeled after men's prisons. These "new generation" prisons typically have two types of housing: special units intended to hold women who pose disciplinary problems, and either dormitories or rooms holding six to eight women for the majority of inmates. While contemporary prisons, particularly those based on the design of men's prisons, control physical movement to a great degree, they differ from men's prisons insofar as they tend not to classify prisoners by security level.

Most states have just one or a relatively small number of prisons for women and thus house women prisoners at one or two geographically isolated locations. Women are often housed far from home, friends, and family, and distant from services available in urban communities. Unlike male prisoners, the majority of incarcerated women are confined in prisons that encompass all classification and security levels in one facility. These facilities, often rated as "administrative security level" institutions, either commingle women of all security levels or attempt some internal housing categories.

With the exception of newly arrived prisoners and the minority held in the more restrictive special housing units (such as administrative segregation or security housing units), most women remain in what is referred to as the general population. Regardless of security level classification, women prisoners work, attend school, and participate in other programs in close contact with all other inmates, whose classification may range from minimum to maximum security.

The disproportionate sanctioning through disciplinary procedures and the commingling of women of all custody levels within few "general purpose" facilities often results in the "over-classification" of women prisoners. Few prison systems in the United States have developed classification instruments that adequately assess the custody and security needs of women. Women often receive classification scores much higher than their degree of risk due to disciplinary infractions rather than the actual degree of threat posed by these infractions. Moreover, the majority are subjected to the more severe custody conditions required for the smaller number classified as

high risk. Additionally, women who represent a minimal risk to the community are often "over-confined" due to the lack of community corrections and "camp" facilities for women.

The few women confined to administrative segregation units are either detained while under investigation or held for brief periods of time ranging from a few days to one month. Administrative segregation functions much like a jail in the free community. Women housed in security housing units are usually confined to their cells for six months or more and experience the most restrictive custody. In their cells for an average of 23 hours a day, they eat their meals there and are allowed minimal recreation and visiting privileges (Owen 1998). Only a small percentage the total female prison population is held in security housing units, but the conditions for these women are often severe.

Security procedures often interfere with privacy and personal integrity in women's prisons. While privacy is eroded by crowded conditions, shared housing units, and the need for surveillance, the presence of male staff undermines inmates' ability to attend privately to personal hygiene and grooming. Male staff, who make up between 50 and 80 percent of the custody staff in women's prisons, supervise housing units, observing showers, toilets, and rooms or cells where women dress. Personal integrity is also compromised by search procedures. While most prisons prohibit strip-searches and body-cavity searches by male staff, Human Rights Watch has found that males sometimes observe these procedures when conducted by female staff.

While women in prison are not particularly dangerous to one another and to staff, they are often at risk of sexual abuse by prison staff. Human Rights Watch investigators, in a careful review of sexual abuse in selected U.S. prisons, identified four specific concerns related to sexual abuse of women prisoners:

- their inability to escape the abuser
- ineffectual or nonexistent investigative and grievance procedures
- lack of employee accountability (either criminally or administratively)

• the absence of public concern

The investigators bluntly concluded: "Our findings indicate that being a woman in U.S. state prisons can be a terrifying experience" (Human Rights Watch 1996:1).

The physical setting, the nature of organizational and individual behavior, and the degree to which women are safe from abuse by prison staff and other prisoners all contribute to the general issue of prison security for women. These architectural, procedural, and social factors shape the daily life of women prisoners and structure their reactions to the experience of imprisonment. *See also* GENDER DISPARITIES IN PRISONS; PRISON DISCIPLINE; PRISON VIOLENCE; PRISONER CLASSIFICATION; SEXUAL ABUSE OF PRISONERS.

Further Reading: Human Rights Watch 1996, *All Too Familiar;* McClellan 1994, "Disparity in the Discipline of Male and Female Inmates"; Rafter 1990a, *Partial Justice;* Watterson 1995, *Women in Prison.*

Barbara Owen

Prison Treatment Programs, Legal Issues in

Women often lack access to the prison treatment programs available to male inmates, including vocational, educational, and employment programs. This lack of access is part of a historical pattern of differential treatment of women prisoners in the U.S. criminal justice system (Rafter 1990a). Women's prison administrators have traditionally offered such training programs as cosmetology, food preparation, and sewing, and new programs such as boot camps have not always been made available to women (*West v. Virginia Department of Corrections* 1994).

Incarcerated women have challenged these inequities on the grounds that they violate the Fourteenth Amendment's guarantee of equal protection, but the suits, filed in several federal district courts, have met with varying degrees of success. In *Glover v. Johnson* (1979), the court found that women are entitled to facilities "substantially equivalent" to those provided to men. In *Mitchell v. Untreiner* (1976), the court ordered remedies for disparities in educational opportunities between an all-male and a coed jail. By contrast, in *Pargo v. Elliott* (1995) and *Klinger v. Department of Corrections* (1994), the courts found that the conditions of incarceration for men and women were so different that an equal protection analysis was not appropriate.

Female prisoners have also challenged inferior training programs under Title IX of the Education Amendments of 1972. In *Jeldness v. Pearce* (1994), the Ninth Circuit found that Title IX requires equality, not parity, of programs (D. G. O'Brien 1996). In an earlier case, *Canterino v. Wilson* (1982), the court found that Title IX required the state to "offer equivalent programs" to females. However, in contrast, the District of Columbia Circuit Court of Appeals found that neither Title IX nor equal protection principles were applicable because the situations of the male and female prisoners were not sufficiently similar (*Women Prisoners of the District of Columbia Dept. of Corrections v. District of Columbia* 1996).

Thus, with the circuit courts of appeal in disagreement, the stage is set for an appeal to the U.S. Supreme Court to settle the following issues: Under what circumstances are female and male prisoners similarly situated so as to require an equal protection analysis? What standard of review does Title IX require; or, in other words, how compelling a reason does the government have to offer in order to justify differential treatment on the basis of sex?

Rosemary Kennedy (1997) argues that a move toward the new "heightened scrutiny" standard of review may be strengthened by the Supreme Court's decision in the Virginia Military Institute (VMI) case (*United States v. Virginia* 1996). In that case, the Court rejected Virginia's plan to create a separate military college for women so as to avoid integrating all-male VMI. However, Kennedy (1997) also notes that the Supreme Court in 1995 established a new "hands-off" approach to prison regulation and expressed a preference for deferring to the states and to prison officials in managing prisons (*Sandin v.*

Conner 1994). The Prison Litigation Reform Act of 1995 attempts to limit the power of a federal or state court to go beyond finding that a violation of a federal law has taken place in a prison setting. Under this law, a court might be prohibited from ordering prison authorities to take specific steps to remedy the situation.

In response to these concerns, Marya P. McDonald (1997) recommends that courts utilize the principles of administrative law to refocus the constitutional review of inmate challenges concerning prison programming in order to limit agency discretion and protect the rights of inmates. Under an administrative procedures act, a court could examine both what training programs are offered and how that decision was made. If this type of recourse proves fruitful, in the twenty-first century, prisons may begin to offer the same or at least equivalent treatment programs to incarcerated women and men. *See also* GENDER DISPARITIES IN PRISONS; PRISON DISCIPLINE; PRISON SECURITY; PRISONER LITIGATION; PRISONS, TREATMENT PROGRAMS IN; WOMEN'S PRISONS, HISTORY OF.

Further Reading: R. M. Kennedy 1997, "The Treatment of Women Prisoners after the VMI Decision"; M. P. McDonald 1997, "A Multidimensional Look at the Gender Crisis in the Correctional System"; D. G. O'Brien 1996, "*Jeldness v. Pearce*"; Rafter 1990a, *Partial Justice*.

Randall P. Grometstein

Prison Treatment Programs, Rationales for and Problems with

Rationales for providing treatment to incarcerated women can be found in the history of the American prison system, in the needs of the typical female offender, and in the many problems found in women's prison programs over time. Although the first U.S. prisons aimed at "reformation" (later termed "rehabilitation" and more recently "treatment"), this goal does not fuel the development and implementation of services in contemporary practice.

About 1820, prison reformers developed plans for "penitentiaries," institutions based on principles of penitence, redemption, and reform that applied to both women and men. Between the 1870s and 1920s, the reformatory movement attempted to address the specific needs of women offenders, albeit within a framework that now seems sexist and elitist (Rafter 1985b). The early-twentieth-century progressive movement also supported efforts in inmate rehabilitation.

After the 1920s, the emphasis on rehabilitation gradually diminished as the U.S. prison system moved toward a more punitive, custodial orientation in both women's and men's facilities. Despite a resurgence of the rehabilitative ideal during the 1950s and 1960s, today's criminal justice system places a low priority on the treatment needs of female offenders.

Women manifest treatment needs that are generally unmet within the sanction-based juvenile justice and criminal justice systems. Girls and women in the juvenile and criminal justice systems have often experienced victimization, unstable family lives, school and work failure, and mental health and substance abuse problems. Social factors that marginalize their participation in mainstream society include poverty, minority group membership, single motherhood, and homelessness. They are also likely to have committed nonviolent offenses, such as property or drug-related crimes.

The criminal justice system lacks the capacity to simultaneously offer women offenders prevention, intervention, punishment, and treatment. Probation and parole are contexts in which these women's needs might be addressed, but the system often fails to provide a continuum of care, consistent supervision, and coordination of community resources. Jails and prisons are also uneven in the provision of treatment to female offenders. Moreover, the juvenile and criminal justice systems often miss opportunities to provide aftercare and follow-up community services when an offender is released. The availability of treatment within the criminal justice system seldom matches the needs of women under its jurisdiction.

The most pressing treatment needs of incarcerated women occur in the following interrelated areas:

- **Health care.** The physical needs of women offenders are often neglected, if not ignored. In addition to basic health care, women offenders often have specific health needs related to risky sexual and drug-using behaviors prior to arrest. Pregnancy and reproductive health needs are also neglected.
- **Mental health services.** While estimates vary, it may be that over 60 percent of the female prison population requires mental health services. Many inmates experience problems with both substance abuse and mental health. It is common for women offenders to have experience with both the criminal justice and mental health systems. Few criminal justice systems provide adequate mental health services. Closely related to mental health problems is the need to recognize the impact of the physical, sexual, and emotional abuse experienced by women offenders. Many female prisoners have experienced violent victimization, both as children and adults. This abuse has implications for their emotional and physical well-being and may be tied to drug-abusing and offending behaviors.
- **Substance abuse treatment.** The vast majority of women offenders have a need for substance abuse services. Although women offenders are quite likely to have an extensive history of drug and alcohol use, a relatively small percentage of women receive any treatment for these problems within the justice system. Programs are often hampered by insufficient individual assessment; limited treatment for pregnant, mentally ill, and violent women offenders; and lack of appropriate treatment and vocational training.
- **Gender-specific counseling.** The criminal justice system often fails to develop a diversity of options for dealing with the gender- and culturally spe-

cific problems of female offenders. Gender-specific services should address women's physical, psychological, emotional, spiritual, and sociopolitical issues.

The criminal justice system lacks any comprehensive approach to meeting the needs of female offenders, particularly in terms of prevention and intervention. With institutionalization often the only system option, there are few programs that adequately address women's rehabilitative needs and seek to modify self-destructive behaviors and reduce recidivism. *See also* DRUG AND ALCOHOL TREATMENT FOR PRISONERS; GENDER DISPARITIES IN PRISONS; INCEST VICTIMS; MAHAN, EDNA; PRISON TREATMENT PROGRAMS, LEGAL ISSUES IN; PRISONER CHARACTERISTICS; PRISONS, TREATMENT PROGRAMS IN; REFORMATORY MOVEMENT; WOMEN'S PRISONS, HISTORY OF.

Further Reading: Singer, Bussey, Song, and Lunghofer 1995, "The Psychosocial Issues of Women Serving Time"; Wellisch, Anglin, and Prendergast 1994, "Treatment Strategies for Drug-Abusing Women Offenders"; Zaplin 1998, *Female Offenders.*

Barbara Owen

Prison Violence

Prison violence includes inmate assaults on other inmates or staff, as well as larger group disturbances such as prisonwide riots. Historically, explanations of prison violence have focused primarily on institutions for men and on whether inmate violence is behavior imported from the street (importation model) or is a response to the deprivations experienced by inmates while incarcerated (prisonization model). Factors that can encourage prison violence include the mishandling of gangs, problems introduced by staff turnover, prison overcrowding, and failures in inmate classification.

Although there is little research on violence in women's prisons, the evidence available indicates that female inmates are less likely than male inmates to engage in violent acts, and that when women do behave violently, their actions result in less serious injury. Riots occur infrequently in women's prisons, where violence grows out of daily interactions among those who live and work in the institution.

The differences in violence in men's and women's prisons are shaped by the composition of inmate populations and gender differences in the way inmates adapt to the prison environment. Gangs and the racial violence associated with them are uncommon in women's prisons. Instead, the social networks of women's prisons are organized around friendships, homosexual liaisons, and "pseudo-families" or make-believe family units (Stojkovic and Lovell 1997). Leadership roles within women's prisons often are assumed by inmates who take on the traditional male role in a prison "family" setting. Like male inmates, female prisoners appear to support a code of behavior that prohibits "ratting" and promotes inmate solidarity. However, their adherence to this code and the use of violence to enforce it are weaker than among male prisoners. Violence in women's prisons tends to be more personal, much of it stemming from problematic friendships or intimate relationships. *See also* PRISON DISCIPLINE; PRISON SECURITY; PRISONER SUBCULTURES.

Further Reading: Belknap 1996, *The Invisible Woman;* Pollock-Byrne 1990, *Women, Prison and Crime.*

Marie L. Griffin

Prisoner Characteristics

The characteristics of prisoners—their socioeconomic class, gender, race, and offense histories—determine (or should determine) the development of correctional policies and interventions to meet their specific needs. Women prisoners have different personal histories and pathways to crime than their male counterparts. They have, more often than not, experienced physical and/or sexual victimization as children and adults; they may have lengthy substance abuse histories; their offenses tend to be less serious than those of male offenders; and they are often the primary caretakers of their children prior to entering prison.

Table P. Characteristics of U.S. Female State Prison Inmates, 1991

Characteristics	Percentage or Median
Race/Origin	
White Non-Hispanic	36.2%
Black Non-Hispanic	46.0%
Hispanic	14.2%
Other	3.6%
Age	
<18	.1%
18–24	16.3%
25–34	50.4%
35–44	25.5%
45–54	6.1%
>54	1.7%
Median Age	31
Marital Status	
Married	17.3%
Widowed	5.9%
Divorced	19.1%
Separated	12.5%
Never Married	45.1%
Education	
8th Grade or Less	16.0%
Some High School	45.8%
High School Graduate	22.7%
Some College or More	15.5%
Pre-Arrest Employment	
Employed	46.7%
Full-Time	35.7%
Part-Time	11.0%
Unemployed	53.3%

Source: Snell and Morton 1994, *Women in Prison.*

According to the Bureau of Justice Statistics (1994c), over half of the women in U.S. prisons are African American (46 percent) or Hispanic (14.2 percent). In 1996, African American women were more than twice as likely as Hispanic women, and eight times more likely than white women, to be in prison (Bureau of Justice Statistics 1998c). Table P gives information on race/ethnicity and other characteristics of incarcerated women.

The average woman in prison is 31 years old, undereducated (only 22.7 percent have completed high school), and was unemployed at the time of arrest (53.3 percent). Most incarcerated women are unmarried (45 percent have never been married), and more than three-quarters have children, two-thirds of whom are under age 18. The majority of imprisoned women's children live with maternal grandmothers or other relatives. Approximately 10 percent of women prisoners' children are in foster care, a group home, or another agency. Most incarcerated mothers do not see their children regularly, and they have significantly fewer visits from their children than do men in prison. Bloom and Steinhart (1993), found that over half (54 percent) of the children of incarcerated mothers never visited their mothers during the term of incarceration, in part because women's prisons are usually located in rural areas far from urban centers and are inaccessible by public transportation.

According to the Bureau of Justice Statistics (1994c), compared with men, women prisoners are at least three times more likely to have been physically abused and at least six times more likely to have been sexually abused since age 18. An estimated 40 to 80 percent of imprisoned women have been physically or sexually abused at some time before incarceration (Bureau of Justice Statistics 1994c; Owen and Bloom 1995). For many incarcerated women, their problems began as girls. According to the American Correctional Association (1990a), nearly half (46.7 percent) of the women in U.S. prisons and jails had run away from home as girls, and two-thirds of these women ran away more than once.

Incarcerated women are less likely than incarcerated men to be serving sentences for violent crimes. In 1996, approximately two-thirds of women in U.S. prisons were serving sentences for either drug or property offenses. In a study of California female inmates, 71.9 percent of women had been convicted of a drug or property offense, versus 49.7 percent of men (Owen and Bloom 1995). Of the women incarcerated for violent offenses, many committed their crimes against a spouse or partner who had physically and/or sexually abused them.

Substance abuse plays a critical role in women's imprisonment. According to the Center for Substance Abuse Treatment (1997), up to 80 percent of women in state prisons have severe, longstanding substance abuse problems. Drug law violators make up more than a third (37.4 percent) of the female state prison population (Bureau of Justice Statistics 1998c). Nearly 84 percent of the growth in the female federal prison population between 1990 and 1996 was a result of convictions for drug offenses. Women of color have been disproportionately incarcerated for drug offenses: between 1986 and 1991, the number of women in state prisons for drug offenses increased by 828 percent for African Americans, by 328 percent for Hispanics, and by 241 percent for white offenders.

The rate of HIV infection is higher for women than men prisoners. At the end of 1995, 4.0 percent of female state prisoners were infected with HIV, compared with 2.3 percent of male prisoners. From 1991 to 1995, the number of male prisoners infected with HIV increased 28 percent, while the number of female prisoners infected with HIV increased at a much faster rate of 88 percent (Bureau of Justice Statistics 1997a).

The characteristics of women prisoners reflect a population that is triply marginalized by race, class, and gender. They are primarily poor, women of color, and single mothers who are serving prison sentences for nonviolent drug and property offenses (Bloom 1996). These characteristics suggest a need for gender-sensitive correctional policies and programs that specifically target female offenders. *See also* Drug Offenses; HIV and AIDS in Prison; Incarcerated Mothers; Offenders; Prisons, Treatment Programs in; Women in Prison, USA.

Further Reading: Bloom and Steinhart 1993, *Why Punish the Children?;* Owen 1998, *In the Mix.*

Barbara E. Bloom

Prisoner Classification

Prisoner classification, a basic technique that agencies use to manage the diversity among prisoners, is crucial to the operation of criminal justice institutions. The major goal of classification is to bring order, discipline, fairness, and rationality to decisions affecting vastly different kinds of prisoners. Classification is essentially a decision-making and gate-keeping procedure that channels prisoners into various security levels, programs, services, and treatment options. All institutional processing decisions depend on a preliminary act of classification.

In criminal justice, classification functions in a manner analogous to diagnostic processes in hospitals: new prisoners (or patients) cannot be effectively processed, housed, or treated until a classification (or diagnosis) is established.

Currently, classifications are designed around two broad principles. First, prisoners can be classified according to risk prediction (e.g., risk of violence, suicide, escape, etc.). Such classifications typically govern the prisoner's security and supervision arrangements. Second, prisoner classification can focus on treatment and rehabilitation. This aspect of classification assesses various social, psychological, medical, and rehabilitative needs (drug problems, abuse trauma, employment history, educational problems, financial problems, family history, etc.). The goal of such classification is to provide guidance in treating the prisoner while incarcerated, designing rehabilitation programs, and identifying special needs that must be addressed during incarceration. Classifications typically govern the prisoner's security and supervision arrangements.

From the prisoner's viewpoint, classification has enormous implications for her life while incarcerated. For example, it governs the security level to which she is assigned (maximum, medium, or minimum security), and this, in turn, determines the kinds of people she is housed with (murderers, drug offenders, drunk drivers, lifers, first-time offenders, and so on). Classification also affects many other aspects of prison life: eligibility for work assignments, access to programs, eligibility for early release, access to community placements, visitation arrangements, and so on. Moreover, classification labels appear to profoundly influence how a prisoner is perceived by both staff and other prisoners.

Classification methods, until about the mid-1970s, were based on the subjective judgment of correctional staff. Such procedures were challenged by prisoner litigation as inconsistent, lacking in validity, open to bias and prejudice, and unfair. Consequently, during the 1980s, more objective, numerically based classification methods were widely introduced.

These statistically based classification procedures were offered as "gender-neutral" and objective, with seemingly equal applicability to male and female prisoners. Unfortunately, these procedures were developed and designed predominantly using male samples, and they were tightly aligned with the risk and needs factors of male prisoners. It has become obvious that these procedures have limited validity or relevance for women prisoners and that their use with women may produce disparate and unfair treatment. For example, rates of violence among women prisoners are far lower than among males. A well-documented statistical consequence of using risk-based methods to predict very infrequent events is that they unavoidably make a large percentage of "over-classification" errors (i.e., falsely classifying women prisoners into the high-risk category). Thus, since high-risk and dangerous violence among women prisoners is far rarer than among male prisoners, relatively more women than men will be erroneously assigned to the high-risk categories. More generally, it has also been discovered that risk-based classifications have very poor predictive accuracy for women prisoners. Yet, most agencies continue to use these "gender-neutral" risk-based classification techniques.

Increasing demands are now being made for classification procedures specifically designed for women prisoners, to assess their specific needs and provide more valid classifications for both risk and rehabilitation. An urgent need exists for an expanded research effort to develop classification methods for women prisoners. Yet research into classification for women prisoners remains poorly supported, and little progress has been made in this area of correctional practice. *See also* GENDER DISPARITIES IN PRISONS; PRISON DISCIPLINE; PRISON SECURITY; PRISON VIOLENCE; PRISONER CHARACTERISTICS; PRISONS, TREATMENT PROGRAMS IN.

Further Reading: Bershad 1985, "Discriminatory Treatment of the Female Offender"; Brennan 1998, "Institutional Classification of Females"; Widom 1978, "An Empirical Classification of Female Offenders."

Tim Brennan

Prisoner Litigation

Most prisoner litigation consists of lawsuits concerning prison issues that are filed by prisoners without assistance from an attorney, although inmates are sometimes assisted by "jailhouse lawyers," other prisoners self-taught in the law. Because over 90 percent of the prison population is male, most lawsuits are filed by male prisoners. However, female prisoners also file lawsuits and, based on statistics available from the Michigan Department of Corrections, the percentage of lawsuits filed by women prisoners is roughly commensurate with their numbers. In 1996, female prisoners were responsible for 5.3 percent of the prisoner lawsuits served on the department, and in 1997 they were responsible for 4.6 percent of the new lawsuits, an increase from earlier years. The recent increase may be due to the cumulative effects of changes brought about by the 1981 federal court order discussed below, although it also could be due to other factors, including the changing role of women in society or greater availability of legal materials and assistance in filing lawsuits.

A court order that had considerable impact on women offenders resulted from the case *Glover v. Johnson*, decided in 1979 with a final order in 1981. This was one of the first federal court decisions that addressed the types of programming provided to female prisoners as compared with that provided to male prisoners. The judge ruled that equal protection rights required "parity of treatment" for female prisoners and ordered a variety of educational and vocational opportunities, as well as increased assistance in obtaining access to the courts. The decision was not appealed.

More recent appellate court decisions regarding equality of treatment for female prisoners have been far less favorable to inmates. For example, in a 1996 decision, the District of Columbia Court of Appeals said that before comparing what is offered to female prisoners versus what is offered to males, courts must determine if the groups being compared are similar with regard to several factors, including size and security level of the facilities, the length of sentences being served, and other relevant factors. The U.S. Supreme Court has not decided a case that addresses the issue of parity, meaning comparable—though not identical—treatment.

One area of litigation that is more prevalent in women's than men's prisons is sexual harassment and abuse claims. Although the U.S. Department of Justice has filed lawsuits against at least two departments of corrections under the Civil Rights of Institutionalized Persons Act, alleging systemic sexual abuse and invasion of privacy in women's prisons, most such claims are filed by individual women prisoners. Such cases have resulted in several damage awards of thousands of dollars and are a matter of concern to prison administrators as well as to women prisoners and their supporters. Adequate supervision and training of staff, as well as prompt and thorough investigations of claims of abuse, are crucial to defending against, and preventing, litigation in this area.

Both male and female prisoners have filed lawsuits alleging invasion of privacy due to searches and visual surveillance by opposite-sex officers. Although search and surveillance procedures may involve touching sexual areas and observing prisoners' unclothed bodies, courts generally have rejected such claims as long as reasonable accommodations are made to ensure as much privacy as possible without compromising prison security. The U.S. Supreme Court has not decided a case directly on this issue.

The Prison Litigation Reform Act enacted by Congress in 1996 and several recent U.S. Supreme Court decisions have resulted in some decline in prisoner litigation. Yet an overall and dramatic increase in prisoner litigation remains a major twentieth-century development in the field of corrections and continues to be a major factor in prison administration. *See also* GENDER DISPARITIES IN PRISONS; PRISON TREATMENT PROGRAMS, LEGAL ISSUES IN; PRISONER RIGHTS; SEXUAL ABUSE OF PRISONERS.

Further Reading: Branham 1998b, *The Law of Sentencing, Corrections, and Prisoners' Rights;* Jackson 1998, "The Legitimacy of Cross-Gender Searches and Surveillance in Prisons"; Scalia 1997, *Prisoner Petitions in the Federal Courts, 1980–96.*

Marjorie M. Van Ochten

Prisoner Rights

Women inmates have made, and in some cases have won, substantial legal claims in the area of prisoner rights. Legal issues of equal protection, cruel and unusual punishment, and privacy rights have been the most prominent claims made by female inmates, and the unique conditions of women's imprisonment have presented the court system with complex challenges to commonly held doctrine.

The majority of legal challenges from female inmates have focused on sex discrimination and their right to equal protection of the law, as guaranteed by the Fifth and Fourteenth Amendments. In most states, the small number of women's prisons limits access to health-care programs, rehabilitative work programs, legal resources, and community corrections programs that are alternatives to incarceration. Additionally, many states have just one correctional facility for women, forcing female inmates to reside at considerable distance from families and virtually eliminating the possibility of inmate classification.

A series of federal court cases have established that prisons are required to offer only "parity of services" between male and female prisoners (*Glover v. Johnson* 1979). Furthermore, many courts have been reluctant to grant women's claims of unequal treatment because female inmates are not "similarly situated" or comparable to their male counterparts (*Klinger v. Department of Corrections* 1994). Following the standard of "intermediate scrutiny" (*Craig v. Boren* 1976), the federal courts have often concluded that any differences between services at male and female prisons are rationally related to legitimate penological interests, such as security and rehabilitation, and that the women therefore have no case. In short, many courts have refused to scrutinize differences in programming or services between male and female inmates.

As an alternative to claiming equal protection rights, women inmates can challenge unequal educational and vocational programs under Title IX of the Educational Amendments of 1972. In *Jeldness v. Pearce* (1994), the court held that state prisons receiving federal funds are required to make "reasonable efforts" to offer the same educational opportunities to women as those offered to men.

Pregnancy and abortion in prison present unique questions about the Eighth Amendment guarantee against cruel and unusual punishment. National statistics indicate that 6 percent of female offenders are pregnant at the time of intake. In order for a prisoner to substantiate a claim of cruel and unusual punishment, she must allege acts or omissions sufficiently harmful to prove a deliberate indifference to serious medical needs (*Estelle v. Gamble* 1976). *Estelle* requires more culpability on the part of prison officials than malpractice, but the harm need not be truly intentional. Thus, a series of negligent acts or omissions, proved to be outside the reasonable expectations of punishment, may cumulatively become a constitutional violation.

In federal cases such as *Niantic West v. Manson* (1983), prisons have been found to be in violation of pregnant inmates' Eighth

Amendment rights for gross violations such as shackling pregnant women in leg irons, denying them access to showers, and failing to provide adequate nutrition. However, since *Estelle*, the courts have not explicitly stated that pregnancy, by definition, is a serious medical need. Though many states have adopted broad prenatal care and programming for pregnant inmates, the courts have been reluctant to mandate that prisons and jails provide services beyond basic lifesaving measures to pregnant mothers and their newborns.

In a limited number of federal decisions (e.g., *Monmouth County Correctional Institution Inmates v. Lanzaro* 1987), the courts have explicitly indicated that policies requiring a court-ordered release to obtain an abortion are unconstitutional. Female inmates have successfully claimed that a prison's refusal to provide inmates with all medical care related to pregnancy, including abortion, constitutes "deliberate indifference" to their medical needs in violation of the Eighth Amendment, since childbirth in prison is not a routine part of punishment. Federal regulations give inmates the responsibility to choose to have an abortion or bear the child (28 C.F.R. section 551.23(a) 1992). Currently, the federal government pays for abortions only when the life of the mother is endangered or the pregnancy resulted from rape.

The courts have recognized very limited privacy rights for prisoners in relation to searches of their private body parts, particularly by guards of the opposite sex, or to having their naked bodies exposed unnecessarily to guards of the opposite sex. In *Gunther v. Iowa State Men's Reformatory* (1980), the Circuit Court held that a prison must rearrange guard duties for a woman guard in a male prison to limit invasions of the inmates' privacy. However, in *Forts v. Ward* (1980), the court held that privacy rights of women inmates do not extend to protection against being viewed by male guards while sleeping, so long as suitable sleepwear is provided and they are permitted to cover their cell windows while changing clothes. According to the Supreme Court, the line between acceptable punishment and cruel and unusual punishment is crossed when the prison conditions of confinement are "objectively" cruel and when the prison officials inflict pain in a "subjectively" cruel state of mind. In *Jordan v. Gardner* (1993), the Circuit Court found that the psychological impact of clothed body searches by male prison guards of women inmates with a history of sexual abuse amounted to an unconstitutional "infliction of pain."

While civil suits against individual guards for sexually abusing female inmates have occasionally prevailed (*Carrigan v. Delaware* 1997; *Fisher v. Goord* 1997), class action suits under the Eighth Amendment have emerged as the best option for women prisoners wishing to obtain relief from custodial abuse in American prisons. Following the highly publicized case of *Women Prisoners of the District of Columbia Dept. of Corrections v. District of Columbia* (1996), the City Council for the District modified its sexual assault legislation to make any type of sexual intercourse or sexual contact involving an incarcerated individual a felony. However, the courts have been slow to recognize the uniquely vulnerable position of women prisoners and the great power disparity between inmate and guard that increase the risk of custodial sexual abuse in prison.

State and federal jurisdictions have established conflicting standards and interpretations of issues associated with discrimination, rape, pregnancy, and body searches by guards of the opposite sex. Until these legal issues are resolved by the Supreme Court, women prisoners' rights will remain in flux. *See also* GENDER DISPARITIES IN PRISONS; PRISON TREATMENT PROGRAMS, LEGAL ISSUES IN; PRISONER LITIGATION; SEXUAL ABUSE OF PRISONERS.

Further Reading: Dale 1990, "The Female Inmate"; Herbert 1985, "Women's Prisons"; R. M. Kennedy 1997, "The Treatment of Women Prisoners after the VMI Decision."

Amy S. Farrell

Prisoner Subcultures

Some women adapt to imprisonment by becoming involved in a prison subculture, an informal social organization that is at least partly concealed from prison officials and exists within, but is distinct from, the formal culture of prison and society. An inmate's role within a prisoner subculture is shaped by many factors, including her personal characteristics, the policies of the prison administration, the prison's size, and gender norms of the broader society. Other inmates remain aloof from inmate subcultures and their roles.

According to many penologists, an inmate code, establishing the rules of prison life, is a crucial feature of inmate subcultures. The inmate code was originally described in the 1940s and 1950s and was assumed to be the same for both male and female inmates. As described by penologists, the code included such precepts as "Don't interfere with inmate interests," "Never squeal," and "Do your own time." Today, penologists recognize that women differ from men in their adherence to the inmate code. For example, women usually do not subscribe to the rule, "Do your own time." Nor do they have proscriptions regarding interactions with correctional officers. Compared with male prisoners, women prisoners also show a greater propensity for informing on other inmates and gossiping.

According to the classic literature on women's prison subcultures, inmates assume social roles characterized by specific behavior patterns. Common roles include the "square" (an inmate who holds middle-class values) and the "real woman" who, like the "real man," is responsible, loyal, and willing to stand up for what she thinks. In fact, many of the social roles of female prisoners are similar to those of male prisoners.

Again according to the classic literature on women's prisons, the subcultures revolve around pseudo-families, friendships, and homosexual liaisons. Although research has reported that a large proportion of women in prison engage in homosexual relationships, only a small portion of these women are committed to a homosexual orientation as a lifestyle. In addition, although the women re-ceive affection and attention from their partners, homosexuality in women's prisons does not always include sexual relationships. While most homosexuality in men's prisons is an expression of domination, consensual homosexual relationships are typical in women's prisons, and rape of women by other prisoners is almost unheard of.

Pseudo-family relationships among female prisoners are modeled after parent-child, sibling-sibling, and even extended family relationships (grandparents, aunts, and uncles). The mother-daughter relationship is the most common. Prison staff often legitimate the presence of pseudo-family systems by rewarding leaders for controlling their inmate family members. According to recent research, inmates' participation in pseudo-families has become less common since the mid-1970s, when visiting policies and programs were liberalized. Whereas racial gangs are common in male prisons, racial problems do not usually exist in prisons for women; instead, racial integration is the norm.

Other subcultural aspects of women's prison life include drugs and fights. However, drugs and violence are much less common in women's prisons than in prisons for men, and when violence does occur, it rarely involves weapons. Apparently, a major function of women's prison subcultures is to provide emotional support and distraction from the boredom and indignities of incarceration. *See also* RACE RELATIONS IN PRISON.

Further Reading: Fox 1990, "Women in Prison"; Giallombardo 1966, *Society of Women;* Heffernan 1972, *Making It in Prison.*

Hoan N. Bui

Prisons, Health Care in

Maintaining a good health-care program is difficult even in the best correctional institutions. Punishing systems and healing systems are not easy partners. Incarceration and the associated lifestyles are often pernicious to physical and mental health. The environment is highly stressful and counter-therapeutic.

Women's health issues fare particularly poorly in correctional settings. Because of

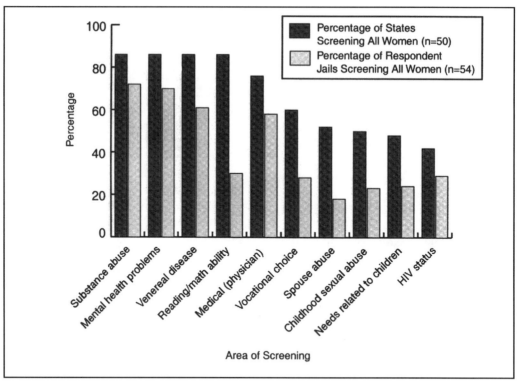

Figure 11. Proportion of U.S. State Correctional Department and Jail Administrators Reporting All Women Inmates Screened for Problems

Source: Morash, Bynum, and Koons 1998, *Women Offenders,* page 4.

their small numbers, women are typically housed in facilities designed for men, and their lives are governed by rules designed for men. They are afforded little privacy, and their physical, biological, psychological, emotional, and maternal health needs are inadequately met.

Additional problems arise for women housed in primarily male facilities, such as small and medium-sized jails. These women are restricted to their section of the building and require an escort to seek medical or mental health care. Consequently, care and attention may be delayed by hours or days, in contrast to the more immediate attention given to male prisoners.

Good health care for incarcerated women includes prompt arrival screenings and intake health evaluations that are gender-specific and address issues of possible pregnancy; obstetric and gynecological history; substance use and withdrawal; recent physical, sexual, or emotional trauma; sexually transmitted

diseases; mental illness, including depression; and verification of adequate care and protection for dependent children. Yet as figure 11 shows, U.S. jails and prisons often fail to screen women inmates adequately. Good health care for imprisoned women further includes a timely follow-up by qualified health professionals for each condition identified during arrival screening and intake evaluation, including a comprehensive individualized treatment plan and regular follow-up for ongoing or chronic conditions.

The majority of incarcerated women come from abusive backgrounds. Many experience mental disorders as a result of severe head trauma from beatings or abuse. Most have a history of chronic addiction and are at high risk for HIV infection. Serious medical and dental problems are common. All of this is compounded during incarceration by increased exposure to infectious disease, poor diet, crowded living conditions, violence, and traumatic stress associated with prison life.

The high incidence of pregnancy among women admitted to jails and prisons is of considerable concern. Prompt medical evaluation and care are essential. Drug and alcohol withdrawal can harm a fetus as well as a mother. Early detection and treatment of venereal disease can prevent long-term consequences. High-risk pregnancies, typical among expectant inmates, require perinatal care from qualified professionals, either in the community or at the prison itself. Delivery, however, should always be planned and accomplished in an appropriate community obstetric setting.

Adequate space and time must be set aside for prenatal and parenting classes. Pregnant women should never be locked in a cell without a toilet, should be offered lower bunks, and should be allowed opportunity for frequent movement and moderate exercise to avoid discomfort and serious complications. Pregnant women should never be shackled for prolonged periods, or at all during labor. Because an incarcerated mother's separation her newborn infant usually is accompanied by significant emotional pain and depression, great sensitivity is required on the part of health-care and correctional staff.

In most other respects, a good correctional health-care program for women is similar to that required for men. Emphasis on unimpeded access, regular follow-up, good documentation, suicide prevention, and continuing quality improvement are all important. *See also* DRUG AND ALCOHOL TREATMENT FOR PRISONERS; GENDER DISPARITIES IN PRISONS; HIV AND AIDS IN PRISON; PRISON ACCREDITATION; PRISONER RIGHTS.

Further Reading: Faiver 1997, *Health Care Management Issues in Corrections;* Keamy 1998, "Women's Health Care in the Incarcerated Setting"; Richardson 1998, "Preferred Care of the Pregnant Inmate."

Kenneth L. Faiver

Prisons, Treatment Programs in

Treatment programs in women's prisons are generally inadequate: few in number, poor in quality, based on gender stereotypes, yet insensitive to gender-specific needs. Even at the beginning of the twenty-first century, prisons still reflect the old-fashioned idea that the best roles for women are as mothers and wives. Despite this view, however, women's prisons only recently began instituting programs to promote contacts between incarcerated mothers and their children.

Historically, prisons have provided fewer and less varied programs for women than for men. One reason is that women have always formed a minority of those confined in prisons. Another lies with the fact that funding for beds, programs, and services for women prisoners has not been a priority for policymakers, possibly because incarcerated women do not evoke the same level of public fear as male prisoners. Furthermore, programs in women's prisons continue to be shaped by stereotypical notions about the nature of women, offering training in occupations such as cosmetology, sewing, and food preparation.

Even though many women prisoners have substance abuse problems, drug and alcohol treatment programs are available to only a fraction of those who need them. Mental health, educational, and vocational programs, when they are offered at all, are often minimally implemented. Moreover, the programs and services that can be found in women's prisons are often based on models of male development. Female inmates have different needs, and both crime and incarceration affect them differently than male inmates.

Programs for women in prison can take the form of education, vocational training, recreation, health care, personal and family counseling, and substance abuse treatment. Normally "treatment" refers to some type of service or program that helps the woman to achieve a better self-image, whether this happens through counseling or therapy. The fact is that many incarcerated women have been subjected to sexual crimes as children, adults, or both. Furthermore, many have children for whom they are the primary caregivers. And finally, these women have often been through relationships in which physical, mental, or emotional abuse was not uncommon. They bring their histories, problems, and needs into the institutions with them. Without adequate treatment programs, these women will return to society older but still without job skills, education, or counseling.

A recent trend in women's programming calls for a more complete approach to treatment in which programs are designed to treat a host of related issues simultaneously, rather than one at a time. This would be ideal, but the fact remains that few incarcerated women receive any treatment whatsoever. *See also* DRUG AND ALCOHOL TREATMENT FOR PRISONERS; GENDER DISPARITIES IN PRISONS; PRISON TREATMENT PROGRAMS, LEGAL ISSUES IN; PRISON TREATMENT PROGRAMS, RATIONALES FOR AND PROBLEMS WITH; PRISONER CHARACTERISTICS; PRISONS, HEALTH CARE IN.

Further Reading: Albrecht 1996, "Gender-Specific Programming in Juvenile Detention and Corrections"; Morash, Haarr, and Rucker, 1994. "A Comparison of Programming for Women and Men in U.S. Prisons"; Morash, Bynum, and Koons 1998, *Women Offenders.*

Rebecca D. Petersen

Privacy of Records in Sexual Assault Trials, Canada

In Canada, as elsewhere, the privacy of complainants' personal records in sexual assault (formerly rape and indecent assault) trials has become a contentious issue. How can the rights of complainants be protected while, at the same time, ensuring fair trials for accused persons? Perhaps in response to limitations on the use of evidence about the sexual history of complainants in such cases, defense lawyers increasingly have sought pretrial access to the confidential, private records of accusers, including information from therapists, rape crisis centers, schools, child protection agencies, and health-care providers. This development has probably also been encouraged by a strengthening of defense rights of access to the prosecution's case.

One view is that the disclosure of private records in sexual assault cases infringes on the equality, privacy, and security rights of complainants, and that accused persons can have a fair trial without such access by defense counsel, just as they do in trials for other crimes. There also is a concern that forced

access to records creates grave difficulties with respect to trust and recordkeeping for people offering therapeutic assistance to victims, such as psychologists, and people offering support and solidarity, such as workers in rape crisis centers.

The other view is that the only way in which an accused person can prepare a defense is to examine complainants' private records with the hope of finding inconsistent statements, a motive for lying, and/or material supporting the theory that therapists might have encouraged false memories of sexual abuse in their clients.

The leading Canadian case on the question of record disclosure is *R. v. O'Connor* (1995), which is part of a larger movement to hold people in positions of power, such as doctors, priests, and employees in residential schools for Aboriginal children, accountable for sexual assault. Bishop O'Connor, the director of St. Joseph's Mission School in British Columbia, was prosecuted on a number of charges of rape and indecent assault, the complainants being four Aboriginal women who were former students or employees of this residential school. Prior to O'Connor's trial, his lawyer obtained a court order that directed the four complainants to authorize disclosure to O'Connor's lawyer of all their records currently in the hands of third parties such as therapists, counselors, psychologists, psychiatrists, and school officials. The issue of whether such an order was proper generated a great deal of public debate and eventually made its way to the Supreme Court of Canada.

That Court, for the first time, recognized a defense right of access to "likely relevant" records in the hands of third parties, but it split on the process required to protect both complainants and fair trials. It did not address the argument raised by intervenors, including the Women's Legal Education and Action Fund (LEAF), that a justice system committed to equality would not have allowed records generated in residential schools that were committed to the eradication of Aboriginal culture to be searched for material to discredit survivors of such schools. O'Connor himself ultimately was acquitted on most charges. The prosecution did not proceed to a new trial on the final charge after O'Connor agreed to participate in an Aboriginal healing ceremony with the women who had come forward to testify that he had assaulted them.

Following the Supreme Court of Canada decision, "O'Connor" applications became commonplace, so that people who are deciding whether they are prepared to testify that they were sexually assaulted have to face the possibility that their records will be handed over to the defense. Because of public concern on this issue, the Parliament of Canada introduced in 1997 *An Act to Amend the Criminal Code (Production of Records in Sexual Offence Proceedings)* to limit, though not totally prohibit, defense access to complainants' private records. This legislation has since been upheld as constitutional by the Supreme Court of Canada.

The continuing debate about how to accommodate the rights of both complainants and defendants in sexual assault trials has given rise to a broader phenomenon. Case law, including *O'Connor*, has developed new rules about notice to third parties in a criminal trial such as complainants and record holders, their right to make arguments, and their rights of appeal. These rules mean that third parties, as well as the prosecution and the defense, can now present arguments about their interests. Thus the criminal trial process has been enriched by recognition that complainants and witnesses are a part of that process and entitled to be heard. *See also* RAPE LAW REFORM; RAPE SHIELD LAWS, USA; RAPE VICTIMS, DISCREDITING OF.

Further Reading: Bennett 1996, "Disclosure of Complainants' Medical and Therapeutic Records"; Factum of the Intervenors et al. 1996, *Equality and the Charter;* H. J. Holmes 1977, "An Analysis of Bill C-46"; MacCrimmon 1996, "Trial by Ordeal."

Christine Boyle

Private Prisons, Australia

The first private prison for women outside the United States opened in Australia in 1996. The Metropolitan Women's Correctional Centre (MWCC) is owned and managed by the Australian arm of the world's largest private prison corporation, Corrections Corporation of America.

The MWCC is located 16 miles from Melbourne, Australia, on a former defense industry rocket fuel and ammunitions testing site. The prison can accommodate 150 women and a handful of children who can live there until school age.

The MWCC holds 80 percent of women prisoners in the state of Victoria, the highest proportion of female or male prisoners in private prisons in any state in the world. Anticipation of this high proportion was, in itself, a cause of opposition to the prison's opening.

Privatization of prisons was part of a conservative government agenda that privatized services and assets that were formerly government owned or run. The government argued that privatization would improve services to women prisoners by establishing performance standards in the contracts for the prisons, with financial penalties for noncompliance. These standards created a contract monitor who would report annually to Parliament, providing greater accountability than previously. The government also claimed that a private prison would be cheaper and better in terms of facilities, and that under privatization, reform-resistant unions would lose their power, enabling corporations to change the entrenched prison officer culture.

Opponents of privatization argued that the profit priority of corporations could clash with the social objectives of imprisonment, that privatization would entrench prison as the primary response to crime, and that corporations would rely whenever possible on cheap technology rather than human beings. Opponents further maintained that freedom-of-information requests would be shunted aside by the corporations with arguments of commercial confidentiality, that privatization would increase prisons' tendency to secrecy, and that public debate would be compromised by the corporations' use of defamation threats.

The MWCC does have better facilities than the prison it replaced. There are fewer full-body strip-searches, many women spend longer times out of cells, and a women's committee of prisoners has been established as a forum to discuss issues of concern with representatives from the administration.

On the other hand, in the first two years after the prison opened, there was one hanging suicide. (There had been only one suicide in the previous 40 years of the prison that MWCC replaced.) Moreover, women prisoners have been tear-gassed for the first time ever, visits from children have been restricted, there is no public transport to the prison, staff numbers are low and turnover is high, the corporation relies on cameras for surveillance, and it has issued two defamation threats against critics.

The company has been fined for inadequate staff training and for drugs within the prison. The government has had to subsidize the prison for suicide prevention training and drug education. In freedom-of-information court challenges by community legal centers, the courts have found that the corporation's performance standards, contracts, and contract monitors' reports are "commercially confidential" and should not be released. In the prison's first two years of operation, there were no financial or contract monitors' reports to Parliament. *See also* PRIVATE PRISONS, USA; WOMEN IN PRISON, AUSTRALIA.

Further Reading: George and Lazarus 1995, "Private Prisons"; Harding 1997, *Private Prisons and Public Accountability*; S. Russell 1997, "Private Prisons for Private Profit."

Amanda George

Private Prisons, USA

The term "private prisons" generally refers to private-sector involvement in the operation of jail and prison facilities, although it is the construction, financing, or management of entire correctional institutions that is usually the center of concern in discussions of private prisons.

Most private jails and prisons are facilities for men, but private jails and prisons for women do exist. Unfortunately, reliable data on the exact number of such facilities for women are difficult to locate. The National Council on Crime and Delinquency reports at least three such facilities (Gadsden Correctional Facility in Quincy, Florida; New Mexico Correctional Facility in Grants, New Mexico; and South Nevada Correctional Facility in North Las Vegas, Nevada). Other sources note at least two other private prisons for women, the McPherson Unit in Newport, Arkansas, and the Central Oklahoma Correctional Facility in McLoud. The design capacity of these five facilities is approximately 2,050 women. Issues raised by these facilities, as by public jails and prisons, include the extent and quality of programming, sexual harassment by correctional staff, operational costs, and management and staffing concerns.

It is not clear why so few "private" prisons for women exist, particularly in a period of rapid expansion of women's prison populations. Profitability is no doubt a primary consideration—the much larger, and potentially more profitable, male inmate population has driven the market for private prisons. Additionally, public-sector prisons for women are experimenting with new forms of incarceration, such as gender-specific treatment, whereas private-sector involvement in prison construction, financing, and operations has not generally shown a flair for innovation. Thus, private sector companies may be focusing their attention on male facilities, which take a traditional security- and control-oriented approach. *See also* PRIVATE PRISONS, AUSTRALIA; WOMEN IN PRISON, USA.

Further Reading: Logan 1990, *Private Prisons: Cons and Pros;* D. C. McDonald 1990, *Private Prisons and the Public Interest;* Shichor 1995, *Punishment for Profit;* U.S. General Accounting Office 1996, *Private and Public Prisons.*

Russ Immarigeon

Probation and Parole

Neither probation (an alternative to prison in which the offender serves time in the community) nor parole (early release from prison, after which the offender serves the remainder of her or his sentence in the community) is administered in ways that systematically take into account the offender's gender.

Nonetheless, research indicates that the experience of probation and parole can be quite different for women and men. Figure 12, on page 215, shows the proportion of women on probation and parole relative to the proportion in prison for the United States in 1996.

First, the problems that affect female offenders under community supervision are substantively different from those of male offenders and may lead more often to probation or parole revocation. Some studies indicate that female offenders more often report family problems, such as difficulties with spouses or partners, children, and childcare (Norland and Mann 1984; Stanley 1976). Probation and parole officers are sometimes overwhelmed by the complexities of these problems, dismissing them as beyond the scope of their own expertise. When agents feel unable to solve problems effectively, their relationship with their client is jeopardized.

Second, female offenders may present more, and more complex, medical problems to their parole officers than male offenders, again complicating the relationship of officer to client. Incarcerated women have disproportionately high rates of HIV infection, gynecological problems, and other medical problems. Because women's prisons often do not have the medical technology needed to provide adequate medical care, health issues are carried over into the community during parole and beyond.

Third, female parolees frequently experience child custody loss. Although male offenders may experience this as well, considerably more female offenders have custody of their children just prior to incarceration than male offenders. The forced separation between female offenders and their children creates particular stress, and after release to the community, female parolees may encounter unique difficulties in reacquiring their children, reestablishing family ties, and managing a household.

Fourth, female parolees are less likely than male parolees to be sufficiently prepared for release. There are fewer female than male inmates, and women's prisons are not budget priorities. As a result, departments of correction allocate insufficient resources to meet the needs of the female population, including pre-release preparation. This puts female parolees at a distinct disadvantage.

Fifth and finally, studies indicate that female parolees have more severe drug problems than their male counterparts (MacKenzie, Robinson, and Campbell 1995; Bureau of Justice Statistics 1994c). Yet there are not enough community-based substance abuse treatment programs to meet present demand. Again, circumstances conspire to disadvantage female parolees relative to their male counterparts.

One major concern for the future of female offenders on probation and parole relates to the lack of adequate resources, a problem that will worsen as the "war on drugs" incarcerates ever more women. A second major concern also relates to the increasing incarceration rates of female drug offenders: an ever greater number of children in destabilized home environments, which creates a cycle of hardship for female offenders and further endangers their ability to succeed under community supervision. *See also* DRUG AND ALCOHOL TREATMENT FOR PRISONERS; DRUG OFFENSES; INCARCERATED MOTHERS; SEXISM AND RACISM IN CRIMINAL JUSTICE POLICY.

Further Reading: Bershad 1985, "Discriminatory Treatment of the Female Offender"; Neto and Bainer 1983, "Mother and Wife Locked Up."

Carolyn Petrosino

Property Crime

Historically, property crime has been the most frequent type of offense committed by females. Women tend to specialize in larceny and fraud—specifically, the offenses of shoplifting, bad-check writing, and embezzlement—while they tend to avoid such property offenses as arson, burglary, car theft, and vandalism.

Although the overall incidence of property crime has dramatically decreased since the 1970s, the number of females arrested for property offenses has increased. For 1996, the FBI reported 420,417 female arrests for "index" property crime (a category in which the FBI includes burglary, larceny-theft, motor vehicle theft, and arson), a 23.6 percent increase over the previous 10 years. Males continue to dominate in arrests for index property crimes, yet the female proportion increased from 24 percent in 1986 to 28 percent in 1996. Tougher responses to even petty criminal acts may help explain this increase in female arrests for property (and other types of) crime.

Much of the literature on women and property crime has focused on shoplifting. This focus reflects not only the actual involvement of women in property crime but also the way that criminologists and journalists have constructed it. Female crime has traditionally been described as less serious than male crime, much as women have been taken less seriously than men in criminal justice processing and in society in general. According to many commentators, women avoid "masculine" forms of offending, such as robbery and assault, in which offenders directly confront their victims. Instead, women engage in more minor forms of property crime such as shoplifting.

A study of women in prison (Bureau of Justice Statistics 1994c) reported that, historically, women most often served time for property crimes, larceny-theft and fraud being the most common. Specifically, 41 percent of imprisoned women in 1986 were convicted of property crimes. Today, however, female arrests for drug sales and possession outpace those for property crimes. By the 1990s, the majority of female prisoners were serving time for drug offenses, while the proportion of female prisoners incarcerated for property crimes dropped to 29 percent in 1991 (Bureau of Justice Statistics 1994c).

There is, in fact, a close relationship between drug and property offending for females: a significant portion of arrestees held for property crimes test positive for drugs (National Institute of Justice 1998). About 60 percent of women arrested for property offenses in 1997 tested positive for at least one illicit drug. "Boosting" or shoplifting is one of the most common ways that female

drug abusers support their habits; another is prostitution. Careers in shoplifting often begin in early adulthood, around the time drug abuse sets in, and continue throughout the drug career. Items stolen include everything from clothes and shoes to VCRs.

Drug abusers describe the gendered nature of "boosting": Women typically report stealing more "feminine" goods, such as clothing and incidentals, while men more often report stealing more "masculine" items, such as electronics equipment. Goods stolen are sold in the underground economy for a fraction of their retail value, and monies obtained are typically spent on drugs such as heroin and crack cocaine. *See also* DRUG OFFENSES; FEMALE CRIME, HISTORY OF, USA; GENDER AND CRIME; SHOPLIFTING AND KLEPTOMANIA.

Further Reading: Chesney-Lind 1997, *The Female Offender;* R. E. Dobash and Dobash 1995, *Gender and Crime;* Simon 1975, *Women and Crime.*

Tammy L. Anderson

Prostitution

Often referred to as the world's oldest profession for women, prostitution is sex for sale. Most statutes against prostitution specify that money is exchanged for sexual activity, but some laws include a more general reference to anything of value as potential payment. Both males and females engage in prostitution; however, female arrests for this offense outnumber arrests of males. Of the more than 72,000 arrests in 1997 for prostitution and commercialized vice in the United States, females accounted for approximately 60 percent (U.S. Department of Justice, Federal Bureau of Investigation 1998).

Males play two roles in female prostitution. They are usually the customers ("johns") and they are usually the financial managers ("pimps"). Law enforcement policy throughout the United States appears to favor arresting those who are on the supply side of prostitute activity, although periodic crackdowns on the demand side result in arrests of "johns" for soliciting prostitutes. Pimps can serve any of several roles, including recruiters and trainers of prostitutes, protectors, panderers, business managers, employment agents, legal liaisons, coaches, and companions. In houses of prostitution, however, many of the functions of a pimp are assumed by a madam—a female employer.

Prostitutes differ with regard to income, working conditions, and occupational hazards. The "call girl" is considered to be at the top of the status hierarchy of prostitution, able to be the most selective of customers and to command the highest fees. Generally, the streetwalker is perceived to be at the bottom of the hierarchy, although the "lot lizard"—a newly documented type of prostitute who works truck stops and the rest areas along interstate highways—appears to have slightly lower status.

The conditions in American society that give rise to prostitution and encourage its continued existence are probably best understood by looking at the demand side of this economic activity and the social context of women's sexual place in a patriarchal society. The male double standard for sexuality in such a culture dictates that men can be sexually promiscuous, but women must be chaste. Prostitution arises as a solution to this dilemma. It provides for a relatively small number of women to be reserved for meeting the sexual needs of many men without diminishing significantly the pool of women available for marriage (Jolin 1994).

Factors predisposing women to gravitate to this line of work are varied. An in-depth study by Silbert and Pines (1982) of 200 female juvenile and adult current and former street prostitutes found that, rather than experiencing an attraction to the life of a prostitute, subjects were propelled into it by negative circumstances and precipitating events.

Prostitutes' rights groups have debated the issue of whether prostitution is a profession voluntarily chosen by women. COYOTE (Call Off Your Old Tired Ethics), founded by ex-prostitute Margo St. James in 1973 in the San Francisco Bay Area, views prostitution as a freely chosen line of work. COYOTE directs its efforts at decriminalization, as does the Atlanta-based group HIRE (Hooking Is

Real Employment) founded by Dolores French. Others, such as the New York City–based group WHISPER (Women Hurt in Systems of Prostitution Engaged in Revolt), reject the notion that prostitution is a profession and dismiss the idea that women freely choose to enter prostitution. WHISPER supports decriminalization only as an initial step toward its goal of the abolition of prostitution.

Prostitution is considered a "victimless crime" because it involves consenting parties engaging in a mutual exchange which, though in demand, is publicly prohibited. Although some other countries have legalized prostitution, the predominant policy in the United States has been to criminalize it. In Nevada, however, the majority of counties have legalized houses of prostitution. To work legally, a prostitute must be hired by a licensed brothel. Proponents of legalized prostitution point to Nevada's system as an example of the benefits of such a public policy. The screening of applicants (and routine testing of those hired) for intravenous drug use, sexually transmitted infections, and the human immunodeficiency virus (HIV) are all seen as advantages of this system of regulating prostitution. Those favoring legalization also point to the revenue collected through the taxes paid by these legitimate businesses. Another argument for legalization is the money saved by cities, which would otherwise be spent on arrest, prosecution, the provision of public defenders, court administration, and incarceration.

Since public policy toward prostitution in the United States rests heavily on the belief that sex for hire is morally wrong, it is unlikely that this victimless crime will undergo any significant change in the direction of decriminalization (the removal of criminal penalties) or legalization (gaining lawful status). To the contrary, in the wake of the acquired immunodeficiency syndrome (AIDS) epidemic, there has been an increase in laws regarding prostitution. Many states are passing laws targeting prostitutes that enhance penalties for a subsequent conviction for prostitutes who become aware that they are

HIV-positive. These laws have been enacted, despite the lack of scientific evidence suggesting that female prostitutes in the United States are vectors of transmission of HIV through sexual activities (Luxenburg and Guild 1993). *See also* CALL GIRLS; FEMALE CRIME, HISTORY OF, EUROPE; FEMALE CRIME, HISTORY OF, USA; PROSTITUTION, FORCED.

Further Reading: Jenness 1993, *Making It Work;* Winick and Kinsie 1971, *The Lively Commerce.*

Joan Luxenburg

Prostitution, Forced

The distinction between voluntary and forced prostitution has become extremely contentious. Some commentators argue that all prostitution is forced—a violation of women's human rights and a form of inhumane and degrading treatment. Others contend that women have the right to individual self-determination and therefore should have the choice to work as prostitutes. Despite disagreement over what constitutes coercion, there is fundamental agreement that the most obviously coercive aspects of the prostitution trade—for example, the kidnapping and selling of women—are intolerable breaches of women's basic human rights. It is these practices, therefore, that are most often used to define forced prostitution.

Despite international and national sanctions, forced prostitution has become an enormous global enterprise and a serious worldwide problem. Prostitution is extremely profitable, which motivates individuals, organized crime networks, and sometimes even governments to engage in the trade. Every year, increasing numbers of women are enticed, coerced, or trapped into prostitution and forced to work in brothels against their will. While any woman, regardless of age, race, or economic class, can be forced into prostitution, poor women from developing countries are the predominant victims.

Women are procured for prostitution by kidnapping, purchase, or fraudulent promises of jobs and a better life. Kidnapping has become increasingly violent, involving drugging, rape, or gang rape before sale; beating; selling the person more than once; and im-

prisonment for an extended time before sale. Parents may sell a daughter into prostitution to escape the payment of an expensive dowry, or they may believe the sale of their girl child is recompense for the expense of raising a daughter. For others, the issue is more basic: prostitution is better than starvation. Women are also often forced into prostitution after "friends" lure them away from their homes with the promise of legitimate work or an introduction to a prospective partner.

Women who are forced into prostitution are often forcibly trafficked between brothels, cities, and countries in what has become the modern slave trade. They experience rape, sexual assault and harassment, physical injury, drug addiction, depression, chronic pain, and serious health problems, including constant exposure to AIDS. Brothel living conditions are usually appalling: women are often underfed, denied medical treatment, and exposed to ongoing psychological trauma and physical violence. Reports of prostitutes who become sick being killed by brothel owners are not uncommon.

Forced prostitution is maintained through overt force, subtle coercion, and physical and emotional abuse. Once in the brothel, it is extremely difficult to escape. Debt bondage is widely used to control women and prevent their escape. They are often given drugs to force their addiction and increase their dependence, and in some cases, they are chained to their beds. For many women who do consider escaping, there is the fear of being stigmatized and rejected by the community. Women forced into prostitution may endure slavery until they die.

A range of explanations for the rise in forced prostitution have been suggested. The primary factor in developing countries is poverty, while in the West it is the rampant development of capitalism. Other explanations include broader social and economic factors such as women's subordinate position in society and the moral depravity of those who buy and sell women. *See also* HOMICIDE, FILIPINO WOMEN IN AUSTRALIA AS VICTIMS OF; PROSTITUTION.

Further Reading: Altink 1995, *Stolen Lives;* Brock and Thistlewaite 1996, *Casting Stones;* Human

Rights in China 1996, "Caught between Tradition and the State"; Jeffreys 1997, *The Idea of Prostitution*.

Sandy E. Cook

Protection Orders

Legal and court responses to domestic violence in all U.S. states now include victim protection orders. This is one of the important changes to arise from the *Final Report* of the United States Attorney General's Task Force against Domestic Violence (1984), which recommended a more active criminal justice system response to domestic violence. Victim protection orders are known by different names in various states, including temporary restraining orders, injunctions against harassment, orders of protection, and civil orders of protection.

State laws also vary by the forms of relief provided by the court, the methods by which orders are obtained, the distribution of the costs involved, and ways in which the orders are served and enforced. Typical victim protection orders prohibit further abuse, set limitations on the nature of the contact between victims and offenders, designate temporary child custody, set up supervised visitation, and order support or compensation and possibly the offender's eviction. Most states allow civil protection orders to be obtained with or without collateral criminal prosecution of the offender. Unlike the earlier temporary restraining orders, which often required victims to retain an attorney, the new civil protection orders may be obtained on an *ex parte* or emergency basis.

Research on the effectiveness of civil protection orders is complicated, and, to date, it reports mixed results. A study by Molly Chaudhuri and Kathleen Daly (1992) found that about two-thirds of the men complied with the court order during the first two months of its issuance, that police were more responsive to the subsequent calls from women who had obtained a court order, and that women's experiences with the legal process were generally favorable. Another set of researchers (Horton, Simonidis, and Simonidis 1987) reported that fewer than 50 percent of the women who had obtained court orders later called in the police, and another research team (Grau, Fagan, and Wexler 1985) concluded that orders were generally not effective in reducing the rate of abuse. The latter group also found that victim protection orders tended to be more effective in cases where the domestic violence was not severe.

An Arizona study (Adhikari, Reinhard, and Johnson 1993) found violations in over half of the victim protection orders, with subsequent violent acts in 65 percent of these. In 45 percent of those cases, the women victims surmised that obtaining a court order was an important factor in precipitating the repeat violence. These researchers argued that protection orders protected only in cases where offenders had little knowledge or experience with the criminal justice system.

Police enforcement of victim protection orders is what seems to vary the most from one community to the next, making research results uncertain. Court orders are also more effective in those communities where the criminal justice system directs victims to receive other services such as advocacy, welfare benefits, employment services, and personal and legal counseling. *See also* CRIME VICTIMIZATION; DOMESTIC VIOLENCE AGAINST WOMEN, EPIDEMIOLOGY OF; HOMICIDE VICTIMS; LESBIAN PARTNER BATTERING; STALKING; VICTIMS IN COURT.

Further Reading: Adhikari, Reinhard, and Johnson 1993, "The Myth of Protection Orders"; Buzawa and Buzawa 1996, *Domestic Violence;* U.S. Attorney General's Task Force against Domestic Violence 1984, *Final Report*.

John M. Johnson

Psychological Explanations of Delinquency

Psychological explanations of delinquency arose in the latter half of the nineteenth century in conjunction with the development of medical models of deviance. Proponents of early psychological theories attributed criminality to a mental disease or defect that could be treated and potentially cured through the help of psychologists and/or psychiatrists.

Additionally, psychological dysfunction, particularly among women, was often thought to have a biological basis. For instance, nineteenth-century explanations for kleptomania attributed women's shoplifting to a mental disease associated with reproductive functions.

It was not until the early part of the twentieth century, however, that psychiatrists and psychologists gained a prominent role in the treatment of offenders. At that time, the behavioral problems exhibited by some accused and convicted offenders, including delinquent girls, were attributed to psychopathy, a mental disorder considered less severe than insanity yet serious enough to produce negative behavior.

Psychological factors have been emphasized most often in explanations of girls' rather than boys' delinquency, and theorists often allege that the prevalence and severity of psychological problems is higher among institutionalized girls than boys. One of the earliest studies of delinquent girls, W. I. Thomas's *The Unadjusted Girl* (1923), examined the factors that led to delinquency among a group of girls in Chicago. Thomas noted, as did other researchers, that girls were institutionalized predominately for sexual offenses. Sexual delinquency, according to Thomas, occurs when lower-class girls use their bodies as sexual capital to achieve material needs as well as to satisfy an emotional need for fun and excitement.

Sigmund Freud (1933) attributed women's deviance to their inability to psychologically adjust to their biological inferiority to men. Freud argued that most girls, after realizing they are biologically inferior to boys, develop normally and exhibit normal feminine characteristics, including a tendency toward narcissism and masochism. But some girls, in Freud's view, cannot accept their biological inferiority and thus develop a masculinity complex, exhibiting exaggerated masculine characteristics and engaging in masculine behaviors, including crime.

Several studies of institutionalized girls in the 1960s and 1970s also addressed the perceived relationship between psychology and delinquency. For instance, Gisela Konopka

(1966), after examining a sample of institutionalized girls in the United States, classified them as lonely, hostile, and suffering from low self-esteem. The emotional problems that characterized these girls, according to Konopka, were a response to factors including a lack of parental support during puberty, changes in the cultural position of women across time, and conflicts between mothers and their daughters. Konopka also argued that female delinquents are more apt than male delinquents to exhibit emotional problems, specifically low self-esteem. Konopka, like earlier theorists, implied that curing girls' delinquency requires individual treatment and adjustment.

Characteristics identified by these early psychological theorists, especially low self-esteem and depression, remain important correlates of female delinquency in studies today. *See also* FEMALE CRIME, EXPLANATIONS OF; JUVENILE DELINQUENCY AND FAMILY CONFLICT; JUVENILE DELINQUENCY AND INTELLIGENCE; MEDICAL EXPLANATIONS OF DELINQUENCY; PREMENSTRUAL SYNDROME; SHOPLIFTING AND KLEPTOMANIA.

Further Reading: Cowie, Cowie, and Slater 1968, *Delinquency in Girls;* Glueck and Glueck 1934, *Five Hundred Delinquent Women.*

Lori A. Elis

Punishing Women Offenders

In the United States, punishments for female and male offenders are the same in type and range, but they can have very different consequences. Research is beginning to document gender differences in the effects of punishment, and some judges, drawing on their own experience or research findings, consider differential effects in making sentencing decisions.

Various means are used to punish women offenders. Most severe, of course, is the death penalty. Women also are punished with jail and prison terms, probation or parole supervision in the community, and various types of alternative sanctions. The proportion of women sentenced in 1996 to probation, parole, prison, and jail is shown in Figure 12. In many cases, a particular response to crimi-

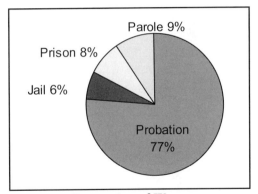

Figure 12. Proportion of Women on Probation, in Jail or Prison, or on Parole in 1996 [USA]
Source: U.S. Department of Justice 1997, *Correctional Populations in the United States, 1996.*

nal behavior (for example, confinement in a boot camp or probation supervision) includes both punishment and treatment, and there is variation in whether the response is intended and/or experienced as punishment, treatment, or both. Some experts argue that a simultaneous use of appropriate treatment and punishment options characterizes highly effective programming.

The severity of punishments used for women has varied over time depending on their status and related attitudes toward women. In the American Colonial period, women were, to some extent, considered equal agricultural partners with men. In some cases, they were similarly treated by the courts, though both courts and church punished women more severely than men for adultery (Feinman 1984). In the nineteenth century, there was a tendency to idealize at least some women as purer than men, and thus when white women broke the law, they were viewed as more depraved than men and deserving of harsher punishment.

Motherhood status and courts' perceptions of a defendant's adequacy as a mother can also affect punishment. In today's courts, some women are treated especially harshly because they are viewed as failures in providing motherly care for their children, but others are treated leniently so that they can continue nurturing their children.

As in the past, the severity of punishment continues to be affected by the race and

ethnicity of women offenders. There is evidence that prosecutors are more likely to dismiss cases against white women than those against African American and Hispanic women, though for each of these groups, women are treated more leniently than their male counterparts (Spohn, Gruhl, and Welch 1987). Not only are minority women more often prosecuted, but after conviction, they are sentenced to prison more often than are whites (Mann 1995). Compared with men, few women are on death row or have been executed, but like African American men, African American women are disproportionately represented in comparison to their numbers in the general population.

Conditions of confinement affect the severity of punishment resulting from incarceration. When prisons and jails were first established, women and men were housed together, and often women were subjected to physical and sexual abuse by male inmates and staff. In the nineteenth century, reformers, including Dorothea Dix, Mary Wister, and Abigail Hopper Gibbons, fought to establish separate facilities for women prisoners, administered and staffed by women. The reformatories that were established housed a small proportion of all women prisoners, typically young, white prostitutes or other moral offenders. A higher proportion of African American women remained in harsh penitentiaries, work camps, and agricultural prisons than in the more home-like reformatories. Also, even reformatories used "dungeons" for inmates considered to pose a threat, and some were marked by overcrowded conditions and scandals precipitated, for example, by physically abusive punishments by staff. Overcrowding also provided a breeding ground for illness and limited the ability of programs to achieve reform. When overcrowding was coupled with physical abuse, conditions deteriorated far below the ideal envisioned by reformers.

In many contemporary prisons and jails, staff attempt to control women's behavior and communications to a much greater extent than occurs in men's facilities, with the result that women are subjected to higher levels of supervision and serious and frequent

Punishing Women Offenders

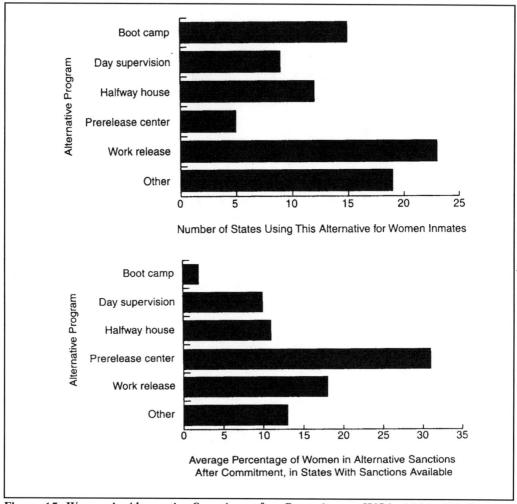

Figure 13. Women in Alternative Sanctions after Commitment [USA, 1993–1994]

Source: Morash, Bynum, and Koons 1998, *Women Offenders,* page 5.

sanctions for relatively minor infractions of rules. Also, because most states lack women's facilities with minimum levels of supervision and many use classification tools developed for men, many women are misclassified, overclassified, and housed in more restrictive environments than is necessary to ensure safety.

Although some facilities for women do have positive environments, such as rooms or living areas that would be described as "homey," many are characterized by stark institutional designs, gun towers, and high barbed-wire fences. The pain associated with incarceration is increased for women by the separation from family and friends that often

occurs when they are housed far from home due to the limited number of facilities for women. African American and Hispanic women, particularly those from urban areas, can feel especially isolated, for prisons often are located in rural areas due to political pressures to locate facilities to create employment or obtain inexpensive land. Prison staff typically are rural, white, and not bilingual.

Beginning in the 1960s, there was considerable emphasis on diversion from jails or prisons and the use of alternative sanctions. A recent national study estimated that in 1995, in states where the sanctions were available, the average proportion of female state prisoners involved in various alternative sanc-

216

tions was 31 percent for pre-release centers, 18 percent for work-release programs, 10 percent for halfway houses, 10 percent for day supervision programs, and 2 percent for boot camp programs (Morash, Bynum and Koons 1995) (see Figure13). The same study revealed that female jail inmates have even less access to alternatives to incarceration. Moreover, fewer than 20 percent of jails offer women drug abuse programs, electronic monitoring, or job training.

Many women are punished through restrictions imposed as a part of probation or parole. These restrictions can include requirements to stay in a particular geographic area, submit to urine testing for substance abuse, report to a probation or parole officer, and participate in work, educational, or other programming. Even though some offenders and many correctional staff view such requirements as rehabilitative, others consider them punitive.

In the United States, for both women and men, the most commonly used form of punishment is probation, and many people serve a period of time on parole as a condition for early release from prison. The result is that there are many more women on probation or parole than in prison or jail.

Given the large numbers of offenders on probation and parole, it is important to note that the rate of increase for women on probation and parole is higher than for men. In 1996, 515,600 women on probation made up 21 percent of the total probation population, up from 18 percent in 1990. A total of 79,300 women made up 11 percent of the parole population, up from 8 percent in 1990. There is no definitive explanation for the increases, but it is likely that intensification of efforts to curb and to punish drug-related violations of the law are contributing factors. Despite the widespread use of probation, little is known about the ways in which women's experiences with this form of punishment may be different from those of men.

Counteracting the push to use alternative sanctions, in the 1980s, "get tough on crime" and "war on drugs" policies resulted in increased use of jail and prison terms. The increase has disproportionately affected women, whose rate of incarceration has grown more quickly than has men's. Starting in 1980, a large number of prisons were built for women, and instead of planning for alternatives to incarceration, temporary facilities, such as converted juvenile facilities, were used to house the influx of women. By midyear 1997, the female prisoner population had grown to 78,067. Similarly, the female jail population rate was increasing faster (an average of 9.9 percent per year) than the rate for males (6.4 percent per year), and by midyear 1997, there were 24,700 convicted women and 34,600 unconvicted women in jails. The higher growth rates for women are due to laws restricting judicial discretion in drug-related cases; these laws have had a greater impact on women than men because women who would have previously been sentenced to community programs are now sentenced to prison or jail terms.

The media have drawn attention to the influx of women into prison and concentrated on a small number of unusually violent women offenders; additionally, many reporters have assumed in their coverage that because more women are in prison, their crimes are becoming more like the crimes of men. However, careful study reveals that the vast majority of women in prison continue to be incarcerated for nonviolent crimes, and that the media have often been misleading, particularly in their coverage of minority racial and ethnic groups. In their efforts to generate interesting stories, journalists tend to neglect changes in the law, social conditions that negatively impact women (especially minority women), and the reality that the majority of incarcerated women were sentenced for drug or property crimes.

Punishment of battered women who kill their abusers is controversial, with some people claiming such women should not be punished at all because they acted in self-defense. Even more complex is the issue of how the criminal justice system should react to female offenders whose pathway to criminal behavior began with childhood sexual abuse and other forms of victimization. Childhood experiences of abuse frequently lead to running away from home and from there to teenage drug abuse and prostitution. Adult women involved with abusive men may be forced to sell or carry drugs. As a result of laws that require judges to impose severe sentences for all kinds of drug activities, such women can end up serving extremely long prison terms for minor accomplice behaviors. When such women are punished, are they in fact being revictimized?

Another controversial issue regarding the use of incarceration to punish women is its secondary effects on children. Children of incarcerated mothers frequently suffer considerable trauma due to the separation. Despite some mothers' efforts to arrange for positive living situations and to help with school and other activities, the children need extra support services (Bloom and Steinhart 1933; Gabel and Johnston 1995). Advocates for the use of alternative sanctions argue that many women offenders who are not a threat to the community should not be incarcerated but should be allowed to remain in the community with their children. To alleviate separation trauma, a number of prisons have developed programs that facilitate mother-child visits, including overnight stays and daily visits for a week during the summer.

Since the Colonial period, women's status has had important effects on how women are punished and on the experience of punishment. Women often have been ignored, or their circumstances and needs have been ignored, because they were but a small proportion of all offenders or were considered less important than men. In recent times, by reinforcing stereotypes about women of color and focusing on a small number of unusually violent female offenders, the media have further clouded understanding of the lives and circumstances of the majority of women offenders. A result is that women are caught in a "get tough" emphasis on severe punishment. Attention is diverted from the utility of punishment in bringing about reform, and away from the injustices that result when women's criminality stems from their prior victimization. Similarly, attention is diverted from the degree to which mothers' incarceration traumatizes their children. *See also*

DEATH ROW; FRAMINGHAM EIGHT; INCARCERATED MOTHERS; JAILS, ISSUES FOR WOMEN IN; PRISON DISCIPLINE; PRISONER CLASSIFICATION; PROBATION AND PAROLE; PUNISHMENT, AUSTRALIA; SEXISM AND RACISM IN CRIMINAL JUSTICE POLICY; SEXUAL ABUSE OF PRISONERS; WOMEN'S PRISON ADMINISTRATION, HISTORICAL; WOMEN'S PRISONS, HISTORY OF.

Further Reading: Belknap 1996, *The Invisible Woman;* Daly 1994, *Gender, Crime and Punishment;* Feinman 1994, *Women in the Criminal Justice System.*

Merry Morash

Punishment, Australia

White settlement of Australia in 1788 as a British penal colony made the country a laboratory for experiments in punishment. Until the mid-1800s, transportation to the Australian Colonies was a major alternative to the death penalty in British courts and one of the most common sentences imposed by them. Twenty-five thousand of the 160,000 convicts who arrived in Australia were women, their numbers probably reflecting Britain's desire to populate the Colonies as much to punish these women for crimes. While at the time, women convicts were perceived as far more morally degenerate and troublesome than their male counterparts, recent research suggests that they were able workers who made an active and positive contribution to the founding of a new society.

From the 1840s, the reluctance of the Colonies to accept further convicts made the penitentiary the preferred punishment for criminals, both overseas and in Australia. Women defendants were more likely than men to be sentenced to imprisonment. Their crimes, however, were less serious than men's, largely relating to prostitution, vagrancy, and larceny, and women generally served much shorter prison terms, rarely exceeding two years. While Australian women prisoners were subject to the same punishments as men, bans on the flogging of women exposed them much earlier to harsh alternative disciplinary regimes such as solitary confinement.

Historically, offenses by Australian women involved reproductive offenses such as abortion, concealment of birth, and child murder. These crimes could have earned very harsh sentences, including the death penalty. The harsh punishments, however, were inconsistently and arbitrarily applied. Juries often refused to convict young servant girls for reproductive offenses, and courts preferred to impose medical treatment and other forms of social control. Until well into the twentieth century, the release of women from custody was sometimes contingent on their marrying within a given period.

The falling birth rate and women's growing emancipation in the late nineteenth century resulted in severe punishments for the few women convicted of child neglect and murder as well as for "murdering adulteresses." Of the five women executed in the state of Victoria over the 150 years leading up to the last hanging (of a man) in 1967, three took place in the two-year period 1894–1895. One of these women had murdered children left in her care, the second was a prostitute who killed her own child, and the third was a mentally unstable serial poisoner. The remaining two women put to death in this 150-year period were Elizabeth Scott, executed in 1863 for the murder of her husband, and Jean Lee, a prostitute hanged in 1958 for the killing of an elderly client. Both these executions involved triple hangings, with the women coming to grief for murders that were evidently carried out by their male accomplices. Since Jean Lee's death, no women have been executed in Australia.

The imprisonment of much smaller numbers of women than men creates its own problems. While there has always been—in principle—acceptance of the need for segregation of male and female prisoners, resources for the building of separate facilities were slow in coming. In Victoria in the nineteenth century, women prisoners were incarcerated for 11 years in hulks (unseaworthy docked ships) long after these vessels had been declared unfit for (male) prisoners. There was little incentive to provide the kinds of work and rehabilitation opportunities afforded to the more numerous male prisoners with their longer sentences.

Early feminists in nineteenth-century Australia, such as Catherine Spence and Rose Scott, were active in raising public consciousness about the need for reform of the criminal justice system and improvements in the lot of women prisoners. Nevertheless, many of the same issues remain relevant in the present day. Although one-half of women prisoners are held in minimum security prisons, there are ongoing concerns about the needs of women prisoners with children, Aboriginal women prisoners, and women prisoners with medical and substance abuse problems, particularly in Australia's less populous states. *See also* ABORIGINAL WOMEN AND CRIME, AUSTRALIA; FEMALE CRIME, AUSTRALIA; GENDER DISPARITIES IN PRISONS; WOMEN IN PRISON, AUSTRALIA.

Further Reading: Finnane 1997, *Punishment in Australian Society;* Oxley 1996, *Convict Maids;* Summers 1975, *Damned Whores and God's Police.*

Kathy Laster

R

Race Relations in Prisons

There are two particular dimensions to race relations in women's prisons: relationships among the women prisoners and those between prisoners and staff. Race is an increasingly important fact of contemporary prison life. Minority women are disproportionately represented in the U.S. prison population, and their percentage of the total women's population is increasing. In 1991, African American women made up approximately 40 percent of the female prison population; by 1995, this proportion had grown to 48 percent. The percentage of Hispanic and Latina women also is growing, though at a somewhat slower rate. The disparate increases are one result of the "war on drugs" in the United States, which has had its most pronounced effects on minorities.

Despite the diverse racial and ethnic composition of the female prison population, race relations and conflict have not been primary features of the social order in women's prisons. Women in prison typically live and work in integrated housing units and work settings, and they form personal relationships that often cross racial lines. Race and ethnicity play some role in the development of prison identities and prison culture among the women, but they do not usually result in racial conflict and antagonism.

Both historically and currently, scholars have found that pseudo-families and other supportive intimate relationships are the foundation of prison culture among women. Racial issues are likely to be a secondary or tertiary contributor to associations within this world. Thus, racial conflict is much more likely to be personal rather than grounded in the subcultural norms of the women's prison. Racial and ethnic conflict is brought to the foreground in situations involving crowded living or programming conditions, competition for scarce resources, or cultural expressions such as music or slang.

Racial and ethnic gangs of the sort found in men's prisons have not appeared in women's prisons. While a small number of women may enter the prison with some street gang or clique affiliation, the subculture of the women's prison is a more powerful force in shaping their prison identities. Women seeking the personal and community ties found in street gangs are likely to find substitutes within the prison pseudo-families or other personal relationships. There is very limited violence among women inmates, and racially motivated violence is rare.

Housing assignments in women's prisons, in contrast to those of some male prisons, are not routinely segregated according to demographic or gang affiliations. Women also do not informally segregate themselves according to the patterns of "ordered segmentation" and avoidance as do men in prison (Carroll 1988). Most recreational and social activities are integrated, as are some pseudo-families and other personal relations.

Race relations with staff, however, are potentially more antagonistic. The majority of correctional staff is both white and male in most U.S. prisons for women. Minority women prisoners have reported race-based instances of name-calling, job and program discrimination, and unfair disciplinary practices. Some studies have found that African American prisoners are more likely than other women to be cited for disciplinary infractions (Bloom 1996; Faily and Roundtree 1979).

Sharon McQuiade and John Ehrenreich (1988) assert that we know virtually nothing about the characteristics of women prisoners across the racial and ethnic groupings. This is evident in the lack of knowledge about race relations among women prisoners and with prison staff. Further research on the dynamics of race and ethnicity is necessary to articulate these relationships and their impact on the prison experience of women. *See also* PRISONER SUBCULTURES.

Further Reading: Kruttschnitt 1983, "Race Relations and the Female Inmate"; Mann 1995, "Women of Color in the Criminal Justice System"; Owen 1998, *In the Mix*.

Barbara Owen

Racism in Rape Case Outcomes

Racism in the processing of rape cases has been a concern of criminologists second only to racism in death penalty cases. Rape is an explosive topic, especially when combined with race. A whole mythology has been built around allegations about the sexuality of blacks, especially around the alleged desire of black males to rape white women. "No single event," writes Brownmiller (1975:230), "ticks off America's schizophrenia with greater certainty than the case of a black man accused of raping a white women." In the past, even the suspicion of such a rape led to lynching. Some researchers suggest that the frequency with which blacks select white victims (about 55 percent of the time) may add to white America's paranoia and fuel its racism (R. O'Brien 1987).

According to the so-called sexual stratification hypothesis, the rape of a white woman by a black male violates not only the victim but also a powerful racial taboo. American culture considers women to be the "property" of men of their own race, and it attaches more value to women who "belong" to men of the dominant (white) race than to women of other races. Any sexual assault of a white woman by a black man threatens both the white man's "property rights" and his claim to racial dominance. Because whites hold most positions of power in the criminal justice system, they have the opportunity to protect their race's dominant position by punishing the rape of white women by black men more severely than they punish any other assailant/victim racial dyad. According to the sexual stratification hypothesis, the next most severely punished dyad should be white/white, followed by white/black, and finally black/black.

The few empirical tests of the sexual stratification hypothesis are supportive. One study found that the rape of black, Hispanic, and white women results in an average of 2, 5, and 10 years imprisonment, respectively (R. Kennedy 1997). Another found that blacks who sexually assaulted whites were four times more likely to be imprisoned than blacks who sexually assaulted blacks, and 2.2 times more likely to be imprisoned than whites who sexually assaulted whites (Walsh 1987). These findings seem to provide strong evidence of racism. The more lenient treatment of assailants of black women indicates that black women are less valued than white women. Additionally, the harsher penalties for black men who violate white women than for white men who violate white women indicate the power of white males to react strongly to threats posed by non-white males to the sexual status quo.

Critics of a racial interpretation of these data point out that black-on-white sexual assault tends to take place in the context of another crime such as robbery (South and Felson 1990) and to be committed by strangers (R. Kennedy 1997), both factors that lead to harsher punishment, irrespective of race.

But when these and many other relevant factors were held constant in the Walsh (1987) study, blacks who assaulted whites were still punished more severely than whites who assaulted whites and blacks who assaulted blacks.

Contemporary data, then, tend to show that racism in the processing of rape cases persists mainly in disregard for minority victims of crime. Black defendants in sexual assault cases receive both the most lenient and the most severe sentences, depending on the race of their victims. These different sentences send the message that black women are less valued than white women, and that therefore the penalty for violating a black woman can be expected to be lenient.

To be completely consistent with the sexual stratification hypothesis, the sentences received by whites who sexually assault blacks should be considered. The hypothesis would predict that whites who raped blacks would, like their black counterparts, receive less severe sentences than whites who raped whites. However, reported rapes of blacks by whites are too rare for any meaningful comparisons. One study found only two such cases at the sentencing stage (LaFree 1980), another only four cases (M. A. Myers 1979), and yet another only nine cases (Walsh 1987).

Despite this lack of comparative data, the evidence that we do have indicates that racism is still a factor in the processing of rape cases. The evidence shows up in the devaluation of black female victims by treating their assailants more leniently than would have been the case if the victims were white. It does not show up (as many expected it to) in the more severe sentencing of black than white defendants in all sexual assault cases. *See also* RAPE VICTIMS, DISCREDITING OF.

Further Reading: R. Kennedy 1997, *Race, Crime, and the Law;* Mann and Zatz 1998, *Images of Color, Images of Crime;* South and Felson 1990, "The Racial Patterning of Rape."

Anthony Walsh

Rape Law Reform

The history of rape has been one of the persecution of victims rather than the prosecution of crimes. The rape law reform movement, an offshoot of the "women's liberation" movement, attempted to reverse this history, primarily through legal change. Every jurisdiction in the United States and many throughout Canada, England, and Australia, implemented rape law reform during the 1970s and 1980s. Michigan led the way with the earliest and most extensive revisions in 1974.

Many jurisdictions eliminated the crime of "rape" per se, replacing it with a series of gender-neutral offenses graded according to degree of seriousness and defined by the presence or absence of specified aggravating circumstances. The model Michigan Code, for example, replaced traditional statutes defining rape in terms of "carnal knowledge" with statutes distinguishing four degrees of "criminal sexual conduct." The new statutes defined the degree of severity in terms of objective crime circumstances such as the presence of a weapon or of aiders and abettors, the age and incapacitation of the victim, and the victim's degree of injury. Roughly half of the U.S. states adopted terms akin to "criminal sexual conduct," replacing the term rape with phrases such as "deviate sexual conduct," "sexual assault," and "sexual battery." They also broadened the definition of the crime to include male victims, assaults with objects, and oral and anal penetration.

In an attempt to focus on the offender and crime rather than on the victim, rape law reforms also got rid of the traditional requirement, unique to rape cases, that victims prove they had resisted and not consented. With the same objective, rape law reforms enacted in Michigan and numerous other jurisdictions eliminated corroboration requirements that forced victims to provide evidence (evidence that typically is unavailable) to substantiate rape charges. Reforms also did away with unique cautionary instructions advising jurors that "rape is a crime hard to defend against," advice that encouraged jurors to think of the defendants as victims. Another important reform was the enactment of "shield" provisions prohibiting defense attorneys from interrogating victims about irrelevant past sexual activities and relationships.

Reformers anticipated that the rape law reforms would lead to an increase in the number of reports of rape; they also predicted that the reforms would make arrest, prosecution, and conviction for rape more likely. The limited research on whether or not the law reforms have achieved such goals reports mixed results. On the one hand, success in realizing objectives has been noted in terms of more rape reports, prosecutions, and convictions in some jurisdictions. Relatedly, sexual assault cases have been found to be processed in a manner more comparable to other crimes than they were in the past. Furthermore, victims are less likely to be "doubly victimized" or revictimized by accusatory or leering criminal justice personnel, thanks to the improved attitudes toward rape victims that reforms fostered.

On the other hand, the weight of the evidence indicates that rape law reforms have failed to achieve their goals. The research has been unable to document improvements in areas relating to arrest, charging, and conviction in many research jurisdictions. Moreover, there is evidence that victims continue to be asked to provide corroboration of the charge and to prove their own resistance to their assailants. (Victims of other violent crimes are not forced to prove that they are not lying.) Critics also claim that victims are discredited by "back door tactics" used by defense attorneys to raise questions about their "promiscuity" and to create doubts in the minds of judges and jurors. These factors are particularly salient in cases where the parties are known to one another (i.e., date, acquaintance, and marital rape). Thus, it may still be true that only the stereotypical—but atypical—stranger-out-of-the-bushes rape is defined as "real rape" (Estrich 1987) and punished accordingly.

Some scholars suggest that the primary reason the reforms have fallen short of their goals is that criminal justice officials and the public continue to believe in rape myths, such

as "She asked for it," "She deserved it," "She could have resisted it," and "She falsely cried rape." These misogynous beliefs not only revictimize rape victims, they also encourage rape by providing a set of justifications for men to rape (Scully 1990). These harmful attitudes prejudicially affect the way in which laws are implemented by police, prosecutors, defense attorneys, judges, and jurors. This is why the law on the books so often differs from the law in action.

The erroneous and dangerous beliefs that underlie the historic mishandling of the crime of rape and its victims need to be seriously targeted if rape law reforms are to make headway. This needs to become a national priority if further gains for women's equality are to be realized in the realm of rape victimization and prosecution. *See also* RAPE LAWS AND SPOUSAL EXEMPTIONS; RAPE RATES, USA; RAPE SHIELD LAWS, CANADA; RAPE SHIELD LAWS, USA; RAPE VICTIMS, DISCREDITING OF; SEXUAL ASSAULT CASE PROCESSING.

Further Reading: Z. Alder 1987, *Rape on Trial;* Caringella-MacDonald 1996, "Rape"; Feild and Bienen 1980, *Jurors and Rape.*

Susan Caringella-MacDonald

Rape Laws and Spousal Exemptions

Until recently in the United States, a husband could legally force his wife to have sexual relations because spousal exemptions in state laws defined rape as sexual intercourse by a male with a female "not his wife," by force and against her will. The origin of the spousal exemption is generally credited to Sir Matthew Hale, a chief justice in seventeenth-century England who observed that "the husband cannot be guilty of a rape committed by himself upon his lawful wife, for by their mutual matrimonial consent and contract, the wife hath given up herself in this kind unto the husband which she cannot retract" (as quoted in Drucker 1979:181). In this view, marriage provides a husband with an irrevocable right to have sex with his wife, over whom he gains complete control through the act of marriage.

During the past two decades, there have been many changes to rape laws in the United

State Marital Rape Laws

Alabama	Nebraska*
Alaska	Nevada
Arizona	New Hampshire
Arkansas	New Jersey*
California	New Mexico*
Colorado*	New York*
Connecticut	North Carolina*
Delaware*	North Dakota*
Florida*	Ohio
Georgia*	Oklahoma
Hawaii	Oregon*
Idaho	Pennsylvania
Illinois	Rhode Island
Indiana*	South Carolina
Iowa	South Dakota
Kansas	Tennessee
Kentucky	Texas*
Louisiana	Utah*
Maine	Vermont*
Maryland	Virginia
Massachusetts*	Washington
Michigan	West Virginia
Minnesota	Wisconsin*
Mississippi	Wyoming
Missouri	District of Columbia*
Montana*	

Notes

Adapted from a chart prepared by the National Clearinghouse on Marital and Date Rape, Berkeley, CA, July 1995.

On July 5, 1993, marital rape became a crime in all 50 states under at least one section of the sexual offense codes. In 18 states (marked with asterisks), there are no exemptions from rape prosecution granted to husbands under the law. However, 33 states still have some exemptions from prosecuting husbands for rape, usually with regard to the use of force. In four states, Connecticut, Iowa, Minnesota, and West Virginia, these exemptions are also extended to cohabitors.

States, particularly with regard to spousal exemptions. In the 1970s, many involved in the women's movement began the fight to criminalize rape in marriage, campaigning to eliminate any exemptions from prosecution. In 1978, John Rideout of Oregon became the first man in the United States to be prosecuted for raping his wife while they were living together. In 1984, the New York Court of Appeals struck down husbands' exemption from rape prosecution on the grounds that it denied equal protection, bodily pro-

tection, and privacy for married women (*People v. Liberta* 1984). As of July 5, 1993, marital rape became a crime in all 50 states—under some circumstances.

Variations among the states' marital rape laws are shown in the list preceding. In 18 states and the District of Columbia, and on federal lands, the law grants husbands no exemptions whatsoever from rape prosecution. These states include Colorado, Delaware, Florida, Georgia, Indiana, Massachusetts, Montana, Nebraska, New Jersey, New Mexico, New York, North Carolina, North Dakota, Oregon, Texas, Utah, Vermont, and Wisconsin. However, in 32 states, there are still some exemptions from prosecuting husbands for rape. In the majority of these states, husbands cannot be prosecuted for raping their wives when their wives are most vulnerable and legally unable to consent—for example, when they are incapacitated from drugs or alcohol, mentally or physically impaired, or unconscious (Bergen 1996; National Clearinghouse on Marital and Date Rape 1998; Lehrman 1996). Wives in these conditions are not protected because their consent is presumed.

In 1995, at the United Nations Women's Conference in Beijing, China, delegates unanimously passed a resolution stating that a wife has a right to refuse sexual demands by her husband. But in 1997, the Mexican Supreme Court legalized rape in marriage in that country by ruling that forcing a spouse to have sexual intercourse is not rape, but the undue exercise of a right (Molina 1997). Mexican women's groups, supported by the international women's movement with a campaign coordinated by the National Clearinghouse on Marital and Date Rape, successfully pressured the Mexican Congress into overturning this decision.

Legislative efforts continue within the United States and around the world to totally eliminate spousal exemptions from rape. *See also* RAPE LAW REFORM; RAPE RATES, USA; SEXUAL ASSAULT CASE PROCESSING.

Further Reading: Bergen 1996, *Wife Rape;* Finkelhor and Yllo 1985, *License to Rape;* National Clearinghouse on Marital and Date Rape (Web

site), http://members.aol.com/ncmdr/index.html;
D. E. H. Russell 1990, *Rape in Marriage*.

Raquel Kennedy Bergen

Rape Rates, USA

Rape rates are notoriously difficult to measure. The quality and quantity of information obtained by a survey reflects the substance of the questions and the manner in which they are asked. Victimization surveys have the potential for being the most accurate source of data on the incidence of sexual assault. They attempt to bypass the underreporting of rape to police by contacting a sample of the population directly. Surveys also collect data about the circumstances of the assault more systematically than other methods of sexual assault data collection.

The only longitudinal (ongoing) national survey of United States residents is the National Crime Victimization Survey (NCVS), conducted by the U.S. Bureau of the Census in cooperation with the U.S. Department of Justice, Bureau of Justice Statistics. The NCVS polls over 45,000 households, totaling over 90,000 individuals, in the United States annually, using a multistage sample of housing units. Other national survey efforts include the 1992 National Women's Study conducted by the National Victim Center and the Crime Victim Research and Treatment Center, and the National Violence Against Women Survey conducted by the Center for Policy Research.

In 1994, the NCVS estimated that 433,000 rapes were committed in the United States. Approximately 32 percent were reported to a law enforcement agency. The rape rates were 1 rape for every 270 females and 1 rape for every 5,000 male residents 12 years or older. Rape rates were highest among those 16 to 19 years of age, low-income residents, and urban residents. Rape rates did not differ significantly among racial groups. Ninety-one percent of rape victims were female. Ninety-nine percent of single-victim incidents involved male perpetrators. Almost 60 percent of the incidents took place in the home of the victim or the home of a friend, relative, or neighbor. Ninety-one percent of rapes involved single offenders. Only 24 percent of incidents involved strangers. Victims reported that approximately 25 percent of perpetrators were under 21 years of age; 40 percent were 30 years of age or older.

The NCVS rape measurement has been criticized for several reasons. One criticism is that the definition of rape used by the NCVS is vague and not in line with state or federal rape statutes. Second, the question format requires respondents to personally define rape and choose to apply that label to their unwanted sexual experiences. If respondents specifically request a definition, they are told rape is "coerced sexual intercourse." However, because many people interpret intercourse as involving the penis and vagina, they may decide not to report other experiences that fall within the legal definition of rape but outside the NCVS definition. Third, the NCVS uses a short bounding period, 6 months, to ensure that the dates of crimes are accurately reported. For many crimes, this is helpful. However, the high salience and the low annual incidence of sexual assault should allow for a longer recall period. In addition, such a short period does not capture the health and mental health effects of sexual assault, which may take longer to unfold and may last for extended periods, even permanently.

The National Women's Study (NWS), a longitudinal survey of a national probability sample of 4,008 American women, uses clearer questions that do not leave the definition of sexual assault to the respondents. The NWS questions are removed from a heavy crime context, and additional questions ask about oral and anal sex and penetration with objects. The NWS found in 1992 that 13 percent of women surveyed had been victims of at least one completed rape their lifetime. Extrapolating from the United States Census, the authors estimated that approximately 12.1 million American women have been forcibly raped in their lifetimes, or 683,000 forcible rapes per year. The NWS estimate is approximately 1.5 times larger than the NCVS estimate.

The National Violence against Women Survey (NVAWS), designed by the Center for Policy Research and conducted between November 1995 and May 1996, used nearly the same questions and found nearly the same results as the NWS. Some of its findings are shown in Table A on page 51. Although questions from both limited the sex of the perpetrator to male, they improve on the NCVS questions by defining the acts that are under consideration and not limiting the timeframe of when the acts may have occurred.

A major disadvantage of victimization surveys is that they are extremely expensive. In addition, the small number of rapes within various racial/ethnic and socioeconomic groups surveyed means that the estimated rape rates have low reliability, especially within specific geographic areas or subgroups of the population. These limitations reduce the usefulness of crime victimization data for local service planning or development of prevention interventions.

The measurement of rape involves many decisions that are driven by the values of those doing the measurement. There will never be one number that definitively answers the question of how much rape there is. Nonetheless, social scientists and rape advocates must continue to monitor the resources devoted to national data collection and insist on continued improvement in the implementation of future data collection systems. *See also* DATE RAPE; DOMESTIC VIOLENCE AGAINST WOMEN, EPIDEMIOLOGY OF; RAPE VICTIMS, DISCREDITING OF.

Further Reading: Koss 1992a, "The Measurement of Rape Victimization in Crime Surveys"; Koss 1992b, "The Underdetection of Rape."

Janine I. White and Mary P. Koss

Rape Shield Laws, Canada

Canada's Rape Shield Law, which seeks to place limits on an accused man's use of a woman's prior sexual experience to defend himself in a rape prosecution, has been the site of feminist struggle over both form and content since the mid-1970s. Prior to 1976, the use of women's sexual history in sexual

assault prosecutions was governed by the common law, which permitted the defense to undermine credibility by asking the victim/witness about her sexual experience and to contradict her answers, although it did not force her to testify in response.

Three versions of the Rape Shield Law have been implemented in the intervening years. The first version was passed in 1976 when section 142 was added to the *Criminal Code*. It required the defense to give particulars and notice of intention to use evidence of sexual history at an *in camera* (nonpublic) hearing, after which a judge would determine whether excluding the evidence would preclude "just determination" of factual issues, including credibility. In *R. v. Forsythe* (1980), the Supreme Court of Canada interpreted this enactment to have expanded the common law such that the victim/witness could now be compelled to respond to questions regarding her past sexual history—thus worsening, not improving, her position.

In 1983, Parliament enacted the second Rape Shield Law as part of a wholesale revision of Canadian sexual assault legislation. Section 276 prohibited adduction of sexual history evidence with someone other than the accused unless it fell within one of three exceptions: rebutting prosecutorial evidence, establishing identity, or supporting a defense of mistaken belief in consent. But the Supreme Court, in *R. v. Seaboyer; R. v. Gayme* (1991), declared section 276 inoperative because it conflicted with the accused's rights to a fair trial and a presumption of innocence, and because hypothetically relevant and probative evidence could be excluded without any opportunity for judicial determination. *Seaboyer* dictated a return to the common law position that recognized judicial discretion to determine "relevance" and "admissibility," subject to new "guidelines," and to the principle that the "twin myths" that women who are sexually active are more likely to consent or to lie must not be the basis for relevancy determinations.

The negative reaction of the Canadian public and the women's movement prompted the federal government to pass a third Rape

Shield Law, Bill C-49, in 1992. The new section 276 governs the admissibility of evidence of all sexual activity, including that between the victim/witness and accused; admissibility is determined at an *in camera* hearing in which the victim/witness is not a compellable witness. The law prohibits reliance upon the "twin myths" to determine relevance; the onus is on the defense to demonstrate that the proposed evidence pertains to "specific instances" of the victim/witness's sexual activity; and the judge must determine whether the evidence has significant probative value not outweighed by its prejudicial effects, taking into account the need to remove discriminatory biases from the trial process and the need to protect the victim/witness's dignity and privacy, among other factors.

This third Rape Shield Law has had checkered success in terms of protecting victims/witnesses from discriminatory admissibility decisions. Its impact has also been blunted by defense efforts to obtain women's personal records to achieve discreditation and intimidation. Finally, although section 276 has been unsuccessfully challenged in the lower courts in *R. v. Darrach*, its constitutional validity remains to be determined in the Supreme Court's response to an appeal argued in February 2000. *See also* Privacy of Records in Sexual Assault Trials, Canada; Rape Shield Laws, USA; Victimization Patterns, Canada.

Further Reading: Boyle and MacCrimmon 1998/99, "The Constitutionality of Bill C-49"; Chapman 1999, "Section 276"; Sheehy 1991, "Feminist Argumentation before the Supreme Court of Canada"; Sheehy 1996, "Legalizing Justice."

Elizabeth A. Sheehy

Rape Shield Laws, USA

Rape shield laws are designed to restrict at trial what has traditionally been an unlimited inquiry into a woman's sexual history in order to negate her claim of nonconsensual sex. Under common law, evidence of previous sexual conduct outside of marriage was used to assess whether a woman had a "character for unchastity," i.e., a propensity to engage

in consensual nonmarital sexual relations, which was considered relevant for determining if the woman had consented to sex on the occasion in dispute. Evidence of unchastity was sometimes also used to impeach a complainant's credibility, for it was believed that promiscuity impaired a woman's moral sense, rendering her prone to lie.

In response to pressure from feminists, legal scholars, and social scientists, rape shield laws were passed at both federal and state levels

- to protect the privacy of those victimized by rape
- to eliminate the harassment and humiliation that deter the reporting and prosecution of rape
- to resolve cases on more rational grounds by excluding irrelevant or prejudicial evidence
- to deter would-be rapists by conveying the message that rape will be punished even if the victim was sexually experienced

Less restrictive shield laws allow admission of evidence of the complainant's prior sexual conduct after determination of its relevance. More restrictive laws create a general prohibition of sexual history evidence but designate specific allowable exceptions, e.g., evidence of previous sexual contact between the complainant and defendant. The more restrictive statutes have been criticized for not sufficiently accommodating the accused's right to present relevant defense evidence, the less restrictive for providing inadequate protection of the complainant's right to privacy.

Research suggests that when a courtroom work group's goal of processing cases efficiently or its norms concerning the relevance of sexual history evidence conflict with shield law, the law is frequently circumvented. *In camera* (closed) hearings required before evidence is admitted are often not held. Even when they are, the law's intent can be undermined, for it is "a human mind, subject to prejudice" (Althouse 1992:761) that applies the law, determining how "probative" or "prejudicial" the evidence is. *See also* Pri-

VACY OF RECORDS IN SEXUAL ASSAULT TRIALS, CANADA; RAPE LAW REFORM; RAPE SHIELD LAWS, CANADA; RAPE VICTIMS, DISCREDITING OF; SEXUAL ASSAULT CASE PROCESSING.

Further Reading: Galvin 1986, "Shielding Rape Victims"; Spohn and Horney 1992, *Rape Law Reform*.

Patricia Searles

Rape Victims, Discrediting of

Discrediting of rape victims occurs when people justify their disbelief of a rape allegation on the basis of the victim's character, behavior, or some other aspect of her account. Despite legal changes and education about sexual assault, discrediting of rape victims continues to be an obstacle to the successful prosecution of rape cases.

Women who report being raped have commonly been treated with skepticism or disbelief by legal agents. The attitudes of legal agents, however, reflect those of society at large.

Rape victims' accusations may be discredited because their behavior, relationship with the perpetrator, or the location of the incident stand in contrast to socially defined rules for appropriate women's behavior. Thus, a victim's allegation might be discredited because she was drunk, because the perpetrator was an acquaintance, or because the incident occurred in the victim's home or in a neighborhood associated with prostitution activity. A victim's account might also be discredited if it does not match the image of a "typical" (and therefore believable) rape. For example, it might be discredited if the victim does not immediately report the incident, or if the incident did not follow the typical sequence of events, or if there are inconsistencies in the accounts she tells to different law enforcement officials, or if she maintains a relationship with the perpetrator.

The implications of discrediting rape victims are numerous. Victim credibility is important in police decisions to investigate and make arrests in sexual assault cases; it also influences prosecutors' decisions about whether to pursue cases. Prosecutors often do not file rape cases because they anticipate that jurors will discredit victims' accounts, leading to acquittals. Women may not file rape allegations because they fear not being believed. A broader social consequence is that traditional beliefs about gender relations and sexuality are reinforced. These beliefs have been shown to promote violence against women. *See also* MADONNA/WHORE DICHOTOMY; RAPE LAWS AND SPOUSAL EXEMPTIONS; RAPE LAW REFORM; RAPE RATES, USA; RAPE SHIELD LAWS, CANADA; RAPE SHIELD LAWS, USA; SEXUAL ASSAULT CASE PROCESSING; VICTIM-BLAMING AND VICTIM-PRECIPITATION, CONCEPT OF; VICTIMS IN COURT.

Further Reading: Matoesian 1993, *Reproducing Rape;* Searles and Berger 1995, *Rape and Society*.

Lisa Frohmann

Reformatory Movement

The women's reformatory movement in the United States emerged shortly after the Civil War. During the nineteenth century, nearly all states housed female convicts within male penitentiaries. Due to wretched conditions and scandals involving sexual abuse, female reformers began to campaign for entirely separate women's prisons. These reformers believed that "fallen women" could be reformed under the guidance of proper, middle-class, female role models. In 1873, Quaker reformers in Indiana succeeded in establishing the nation's first independent women's prison, followed by Massachusetts in 1877, yet both institutions were modeled on a traditional cell-block design. At the end of the century, New York emerged at the forefront, establishing three reformatories (the Western House of Refuge at Albion, the State Reformatory at Bedford, and the House of Refuge for females aged 12 to 21 at Hudson) built on a radically new cottage architectural style, which became the hallmark of the women's reformatories. These cottages were to be run as idealized homes and were intended to promote the idea of family life. Female inmates were trained in sewing, cooking, serving, and other domestic arts.

Women's reformatories also broke radically with traditional male prisons in their commitment policies. Women could be sentenced for such "crimes" as adultery, disorderly conduct, fornication, "lewd and lascivious behavior," public drunkenness, "willful stubbornness," vagrancy, and other minor offenses. Previously such misdemeanors had been punishable by, at most, short stays in local jails. Thus, the women's reformatories significantly expanded the power of the state to police and penalize female behavior. In contrast, men's reformatories received only young men who had committed felonies.

By 1900, the ideal of a distinctive women's reformatory prison was fully formed, yet in all, only 17 states would establish women's reformatories. Most of these were in the northeast or midwest, and the great majority were a product of the World War I era. In most states, women continued to be sentenced to traditional "custodial" prisons attached to men's penitentiaries. Race was often the defining determinant. According to the 1923 prison census, 65 percent of women in the nation's state prisons were African American, as opposed to only 12 percent of women in reformatory prisons. Thus, women's prisons were "bifurcated" into two distinct branches: "one custodial and black, the other reformatory and white" (Rafter 1985b:240).

By the mid-1920s, the reformatory movement was in decline. Many administrators, reformers, and criminologists judged these institutions to be failures. Women prisoners evidenced active resistance and high recidivism rates. By the 1930s, the reformatory movement had passed in all but a few states such as New Jersey, where it lived under the leadership of Edna Mahan. States were no longer interested in incarcerating women for minor misdemeanors, nor could they afford the cost of maintaining two separate prisons for women. During the Depression, several states closed their custodial women's penal unit and transferred the prisoners to the former reformatory institutions, thereby undermining the distinctive character of the latter. Thus these institutions remained in op-

eration, housing a mixture of female felons and misdemeanants who continued to be subjected to highly unequal and gender-biased treatment, disciplined according to outmoded standards of "proper" feminine behavior, and offered limited educational and vocational programs. *See also* ALDERSON PRISON; BEDFORD HILLS REFORMATORY; COFFIN, RHODA; LEKKERKERKER, EUGENIA; MAHAN, EDNA; PRISON REFORM, USA; WOMEN'S PRISONS, HISTORY OF.

Further Reading: R. M. Alexander 1995, *The "Girl Problem"*; Freedman 1981, *Their Sisters' Keepers*; Rafter 1985a, "Gender, Prisons, and Prison History"; Rafter 1990a, *Partial Justice*.

L. Mara Dodge

Reno, Janet (1938–)

In 1993, Janet Reno became the first woman to be appointed United States attorney general. As the chief law enforcement officer in the federal government, the attorney general has ultimate responsibility for all criminal prosecutions in federal courts. In that posi-

Janet Reno. *Courtesy of the U.S. Department of Justice.*

tion, Reno created a Violence against Women Office to implement federal legislation targeting domestic violence and sexual assault crimes. Her tenure also was marked by controversies involving an attack by federal police agencies on an extremist group in Waco, Texas, as well as numerous requests to appoint independent counsel to investigate allegations of wrongdoing by President Bill Clinton and Vice President Al Gore.

Before her appointment, Reno worked in the Florida legislature and the Dade County state's attorney's office in Miami, Florida, where she developed a juvenile division, a career criminal unit, child support recovery programs, prevention programs targeted at young children, and the Miami Drug Court. She also practiced law in several private law firms. *See also* LEGAL PROFESSION, HISTORY OF WOMEN IN.

Further Reading: P. Anderson 1994, *Janet Reno*.

Roxann Ryan

Restorative Justice

The modern idea of restorative justice, which beginning in the mid-1970s emerged around the world with various names (including community justice, reparative justice, and transformative justice) and practices, has not been greeted enthusiastically by all feminists because to some it appears to be merely a form of mediation that will not serve women's interests as victims of crime (for debate, see Braithwaite and Daly 1994; Stubbs 1995). However, some appraisals, especially those from the perspective of Australian indigenous women, are more positive (Coker 1999).

Restorative justice emphasizes the repair of harms and of ruptured social bonds resulting from crime; it focuses on the relationships among crime victims, offenders, and society; and it assumes that those who are directly affected by crime should have a key role in deciding how to respond to it. A typical practice is for a crime victim to meet with an admitted offender to discuss the consequences of a crime and agree on a sanction that reflects the harm done to the individual and the broader community. The process is used not only in juvenile and adult criminal matters but also in child protection and family welfare cases.

Practices vary: victim-offender *mediation* typically includes only the victim and the offender, along with a mediator, whereas *conferencing* includes a larger group of people, typically the offender's and the victim's supporters, along with a police officer and a conference facilitator. To date, restorative justice practices in criminal cases are used only when an offender has admitted to an offense; thus the process occurs not in the fact-finding but in the sanctioning phase of the criminal justice process.

Because there are diverse meanings, practices, and sites where restorative justice is used, and because women and girls participate in these meetings as victims, offenders, supporters of victims or offenders, and professionals (e.g., mediators, police officers, and social workers), there is no simple way to characterize the merits of restorative justice practices "for women." Almost all commentary to date has focused solely on one group of women and girls in the restorative justice process, that is, female crime victims, and on only one set of harms, that is, sexual and family violence. In these contexts, a major concern is that gender power relations in the wider society will be reproduced, not checked in an informal process. Female crime victims may be revictimized by male offenders who deny the harm they have caused, are not remorseful, or offer insincere apologies. While this group of victims and offenses is important to study, a broader view is needed: Female victims of other offenses may be revictimized just as easily, and little is known about how the restorative process may work differently for men and women (or boys and girls) as offenders, supporters, and professionals.

While gender power imbalances may affect decision-making processes in restorative justice practice, with adverse effects for women, Daly's (2000) preliminary research on conferencing in Australia finds that men did not dominate discussions or have more sway in decision-making. However, Daly did find that conferences are gendered events. Although few offenders in her study were female (15 percent), women were 52 percent of the offenders' supporters. Results were mixed for whether women were expected to do more unpaid work for the community by participating in conferences: More mothers than fathers of offenders were present at conferences, but there were no gender differences in those nominated to supervise offenders' agreements.

The strength of restorative justice lies in the potential for frank and open discussion among offenders, victims, and their supporters on the consequences of crime and how these should be addressed. Because the process is typically used to divert youthful offenders from court, an added benefit is that a case can be satisfactorily resolved without the offender receiving a criminal record. From the viewpoint of females as offenders and as supporters of offenders, this would be a plus. Some have wondered whether Braithwaite's (1989) concept of "reintegrative shaming" has a different meaning and impact for female offenders, but evidence is lacking on this question.

The recognized world leaders in restorative justice are New Zealand and Australia. Major research projects have been conducted or are underway in New Zealand (Maxwell and Morris 1993) and Australia (Daly et al. 1998; L. W. Sherman et al. 1998) to determine how this new justice idea works in practice and to address arguments raised by feminists, critical race theorists, and youth advocates (Bargen 1996, 2000; Blagg 1997; B. Hudson 1998). *See also* Crime Victimization; Mediation Programs.

Further Reading: Braithwaite 1999, "Restorative Justice"; J. Hudson, Morris, Maxwell, and Galaway 1996, *Family Group Conferences;* Van Ness and Strong 1997, *Restoring Justice.*

Kathleen Daly

Restraining Orders. *See* Protection Orders.

Rosenberg, Ethel (1915–1953)

Ethel Rosenberg was the first woman in the United States to be executed for treason. She and her husband, Julius Rosenberg, were convicted of spying for the Union of Soviet Socialist Republics (USSR) and executed at Sing Sing prison within minutes of each other on June 19, 1953. The political context within which they were charged, convicted, and sentenced was that of the Cold War between the USSR and the United States and the rabid anticommunism associated with Senator Joseph McCarthy.

Ethel Rosenberg was born Esther Ethel Greenglass on September 28, 1915, in Manhattan's Lower East Side. She joined the Young Communist Party and on June 18, 1939, married Julius Rosenberg. Their first son, Michael Allen, was born in 1943, and a second son, Robert Harry, was born four years later.

During the development of the atomic bomb during World War II, the U.S. intelligence community decided that this technology must not fall into the hands of foreign governments, particularly those not allied with the United States. Some key scientists in the development of the atomic bomb believed that it was only a matter of time before the USSR developed its own nuclear capabilities, but the U.S. government was convinced that communist spies were attempting to garner this information and destroy the American way of life.

In fact, spies were attempting to steal U.S. military secrets, but whether Ethel and Julius Rosenberg were guilty of such treasonous activity is less clear. They maintained their innocence of all charges and went to their deaths proclaiming they were the victims of a massive miscarriage of justice and political fanaticism. The only evidence produced against the Rosenbergs came from Ethel's brother, David Greenglass (who confessed to transmitting a handmade sketch of the atom bomb to the USSR at the behest of Julius) and David's wife, Ruth. These witnesses may have been coerced into their testimony.

Although the guilt of Ethel and Julius Rosenberg continues to be debated, the evidence suggests that at least one of them may have been involved in spying for the USSR. However, some people continue to claim that both were political martyrs, victims of a national hysteria against communism complemented by anti-Semitism. *See also* POLITICAL OFFENDERS.

Further Reading: Philipson 1993, *Ethel Rosenberg;* Neville 1995, *The Press, the Rosenbergs, and the Cold War;* Radosh and Milton 1997, *The Rosenberg File.*

Aviva M. Rich-Shea

Routine Activity Theory of Victimization. *See* LIFESTYLE AND VICTIMIZATION

S

Secondary Victimization. *See* Crime Victimization; Crime Victims and Definitions of Justice; Rape Law Reform; Victim Impact Statements; Victimization, Feminist Perspectives on; Victims in Court.

Sentencing, Drug Offenders

The number of women imprisoned for drug offenses increased dramatically during the 1990s, leading some researchers to conclude that the "war on drugs" had become a war on women and to suggest that contemporary judges do not take gender into account in sentencing drug offenders. Other scholars question these assertions, noting that there is a substantial body of research demonstrating that female offenders are sentenced more leniently than male offenders. Although the findings of these studies have not gone unchallenged, the weight of the evidence would lead one to expect preferential treatment of female drug offenders. This expectation is called into question, however, by assertions that the moral panic surrounding drug use has prompted criminal justice officials to regard drug offenses as serious crimes that generally deserve harsh punishment.

Studies comparing the sentences imposed on female and male drug offenders typically find that female offenders are sentenced more leniently than male offenders. This is true of studies conducted both prior to and during the war on drugs that began in the mid-1980s. A study of drug offenders sentenced in the Southern Federal District of New York during the 1960s and 1970s, for example, revealed that male drug offenders faced higher odds of incarceration and received longer sentences than female drug offenders. A study of sentences imposed under the Pennsylvania sentencing guidelines found that female drug offenders were less likely than male drug offenders to be incarcerated; among those who were incarcerated, on the other hand, females received slightly longer sentences than males.

A study comparing the sentences imposed on males and females convicted of drug offenses in Chicago during 1993 revealed that females were substantially less likely than males to be sentenced to prison (Spohn 1999). Further analysis revealed that preferential treatment of females was confined to certain categories of offenders. Most important, gender did not affect the likelihood of incarceration among offenders who had dependent children, but female drug offenders without dependent children faced significantly lower odds of incarceration than male drug offenders without dependent children. The author of this study concluded that these results were consistent with previous research demonstrating that preferential treatment was reserved for female offenders who were viewed as "good mothers," and that women who committed certain types of crimes were seen as "bad mothers" who did not necessarily deserve special consideration from the court.

Collectively, the results of these studies suggest that judges do take gender into account in deciding whether or not to sentence drug offenders to prison. Female drug offenders, and particularly female drug offenders without childcare responsibilities, are sentenced more leniently than male drug offenders. *See also* CHIVALRY EXPLANATION OF COURT OUTCOMES; DRUG OFFENSES; GENDER DISCRIMINATION AND SENTENCING; PRISONER CHARACTERISTICS; SENTENCING GUIDELINES.

Further Reading: Daly and Bordt 1995, "Sex Effects and Sentencing"; Daly and Tonry 1997, "Gender, Race, and Sentencing."

Cassia C. Spohn

Sentencing Guidelines

Since the 1970s, sentencing guidelines have been created by many states and the federal government to reduce disparity in sentencing by limiting the discretion of judges. Guidelines are developed by legislatures or sentencing commissions, groups of experts responsible for recommending sentences for particular offenses. Guidelines are designed to restrict sentencing decisions by requiring that judges sentence offenders within a relatively narrow sentencing range. The goal is to treat like offenses alike. Judges wishing to depart from the specified sentencing guideline range must provide a written explanation for their departure. Only a few justifications for departures are permitted, such as the nature of the offense, prior record, and certain offense characteristics, such as victim injury. In general, federal sentencing guidelines are more restrictive than state guidelines.

Guidelines were originally intended to reduce sentencing inequality by limiting the ability of judges to consider individual characteristics such as gender or race. Although research on the impact of guidelines is limited, there is evidence that they have been effective in reducing sentencing disparity in some jurisdictions, though it has not disappeared. Less understood is the specific impact of sentencing guidelines on women. While some research has found that most women are treated more leniently than men under sentencing guidelines, there is also evidence that women sentenced under the guidelines receive harsher sentences than those sentenced in the pre-guideline era. This is particularly true for drug offenders, women of color, and women who commit offenses inconsistent with gender stereotypes.

Although men far outnumber women in virtually every offense category, including drug offenses, women are far more likely than men to be serving a prison sentence for a drug offense. Similarly, people of color are more likely to be arrested and sentenced to prison for drug offenses than are whites, despite similar patterns of drug use. Thus, lengthened sentences for drug offenses have had the unintended consequence of increasing incarceration rates for women, particularly women of color.

Some scholars argue that sentencing guidelines have taken too much discretion away from judges, while giving more discretionary power to prosecutors and elected officials. Under guidelines, sentences are heavily determined by the nature of the offense the prosecutor charges. Thus, plea agreements have become a way for sentences to be manipulated by prosecutors. The power of elected officials is similarly increased, since they have the ability to write sentencing preferences into law.

Scholars have argued that shifting discretionary decision-making away from judges is most likely to harm those who are already socially disadvantaged, including women. Because some research has shown that judges tend to be more lenient to offenders with dependent children, it is not clear that women are better off under restrictive sentencing guidelines since parental responsibilities cannot be considered by judges, nor can pregnancy. This disproportionately affects women since they are far more likely to have dependents, and, of course, only women can become pregnant.

Sentencing guidelines were developed with the admirable goal of reducing disparity in sentencing; thus, guidelines are likely to continue to play an important role in criminal justice policy in the future. However, it is critical that continued research focus on the unintended consequences of sentencing guidelines to be sure that guidelines do not create new inequalities while reducing old ones. *See also* CHARGING AND PLEA-BARGAINING; GENDER AND JUDICIAL DECISION-MAKING; GENDER DISCRIMINATION AND SENTENCING; SENTENCING, DRUG OFFENDERS.

Further Reading: Albonetti 1998b, "The Role of Gender and Departures in the Sentencing of Defendants"; Raeder 1993, "Gender and Sentencing"; Tonry 1996, *Sentencing Matters.*

Nancy A. Wonders

Serial Killers

Serial killers are individuals, or groups of individuals acting in concert, who have murdered three or more people in separate crime incidents over a period of time. As the subject of both media coverage and academic literature, women tend to be linked to serial killing as victims but rarely as perpetrators. The public resists recognizing that women, too, commit serial murder.

The female serial killer is not a late entry into the annals of crime, however. Indeed, she is found among the earliest documented cases of what is now designated serial murder. Well known to historians of crime is the French nobleman Gilles de Rais who, in the early 1400s, killed scores of children while sexually assaulting them. Little known, however, is Hungarian Countess Elisabeth Bathory who sexually assaulted and murdered hundreds of girls and young women in the early 1600s. In 1992, Jeffrey Dahmer was tried for the murders of 15 young men in Wisconsin. The gavel-to-gavel live-television coverage of his trial eclipsed live broadcasting of the overlapping Florida trial of Aileen Wuornos for the first of her seven alleged murders. A recurring observation in this field is the apparent resistance of society to the image of women as predatory criminals in general, and certainly to according women the "status" of serial killers.

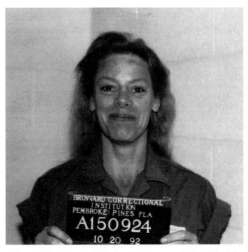

Aileen Wuornos, 1992. *Courtesy of the Florida Department of Corrections.*

Most known cases of female serial murderers are of women who kill a succession of husbands or lovers ("black widows") or family members. Others ("angels of death") use their custodial positions over children, the infirm, and the elderly to target vulnerable victims. Less frequent are cases of women who join with others to commit a series of murders. Methods of killing most often involve poisoning (especially arsenic) or suffocating, but women have also used more aggressive means including strangling, shooting, and drowning their victims. A recent examination of female serial killers relative to their male counterparts reveals that, just as other forms of crime change over time, the modus operandi of these women is evolving to incorporate more overt, traditionally "male" forms of violence (Skrapec 1993). In part because of her more subtle methods of killing and in part because we resist the image of woman as murderer, the female serial killer is often more successful at evading detection than the male serial killer.

Research on the prevalence of female serial murderers suggests they constitute approximately 10 to 15 percent of all serial murderers and are as prolific in terms of numbers of victims as their male counterparts. In nineteenth-century England, murder cases with the highest body counts involved female offenders. Nonetheless, serial killing by women constitutes an exceedingly rare homicide event, given the fact that, overall, less than 2 percent of all murder victims are killed by either male or female multiple murderers of any kind (i.e., including mass, spree, and serial murders).

Understanding the motivations of women who kill repeatedly over time demands an interdisciplinary approach that studies the psychological makeup of these women and the social forces that shape them as individuals. Without doubt, some murders go unsolved because of society's resistance to the very idea that a woman would willfully commit a series of murders. *See also* HOMICIDE, USA; INFANTICIDE; SERIAL KILLERS, VICTIMS OF.

Further Reading: Kelleher and Kelleher 1998, *Murder Most Rare;* P. Pearson 1997, *When She Was Bad;* Skrapec 1993, "Female Serial Murder"; Segrave 1992, *Women Serial and Mass Murderers.*

Candice A. Skrapec

Serial Killers, Victims of

Serial killers typically kill a number of people, usually strangers, in distinctive episodes often separated by long periods of time. Thus serial killers are distinguishable from mass killers who kill numerous people in one incident, and from spree killers who kill a number of people over a short period of time such as a weekend. Less often, serial killers victimize acquaintances or family members.

Women are disproportionately victimized by serial killers. Research shows that roughly four-fifths of serial killers kill at least one female victim. When acquaintances or family members are murdered by serial killers, young women and wives, respectively, are the most common victims.

Given that about 90 percent of serial killers are men, it is not surprising that it is mostly male serial killers who murder women. While the number of female victims of serial killers per year in the United States is not known, it is clear that women are much more likely to be murdered by an intimate or ex-intimate partner than by a serial killer.

Young women appear to be at greatest risk of being victimized by serial killers. Among these young women, prostitutes are the most commonly victimized, followed by other women engaged in activities that bring them into close contact with men not known to them. Thus, we find serial killers likely to kill female hitchhikers, young girls who are homeless and perhaps living on the streets, or, more often, women working as nurses, models, and waitresses. For example, the Green River Killer is thought to have killed at least 49 women in Washington and Oregon, many of whom were prostitutes or young "streetwise" girls. Many serial killings involve sex offenses, including sexual sadism.

The serial killing of women, like rape, is essentially a crime of domination and power. In this sense, serial killers resemble perpetrators of domestic homicides who kill the intimate female partners they have typically dominated, controlled, and battered, often for long periods of time. *See also* DOMESTIC VIOLENCE AGAINST WOMEN, EPIDEMIOLOGY OF; HOMICIDE VICTIMS; SERIAL KILLERS.

Further Reading: Egger 1998, *The Killers among Us;* Hickey 1997, *Serial Murderers and Their Victims.*

Neil Websdale

Sexism and Racism in Criminal Justice Policy

Sexism and racism in criminal justice policy refer to governmental activities related to crime control that have negative effects on a group defined by its members' sex and/or race. Sexist policies generally maintain men's domination and women's subordination. Racist policies generally maintain the domination of the majority racial group and the subordination of minority groups. Sexism and/or racism in criminal justice policy can be found in every arena of the criminal justice system (legislatures, policing, courts, and corrections). All actor groups (offenders, victims, agents, and family and community bystanders) may engage in, or be harmed by, sexist and racist policies.

Uncovering sexism/racism in criminal justice policy requires attention to the visible and hidden consequences of policies, wariness toward policies presumed to be gender- and/or race-neutral, evaluation of policy implementation, and clarity about feminist and antiracist goals (Renzetti 1998). At each stage, the essential question is: Who benefits and who suffers from this policy?

In some cases, as in laws concerning rape and domestic violence, the legal definition and/or the system processes are clearly sexist and/or racist. Historically, rape was viewed as the taking of a (white) woman who was another man's property, and wife-battering was not considered criminal. Prior to the Civil Rights movement and the second-wave women's movement, most state laws and justice officials did not recognize rape by white men against black women; sexual violence was an important weapon in the arsenal of white supremacy. Rape in marriage was ignored because husbands were assumed to have the right of sexual access to their wives. In addition, laws did not allow for the possibility that men might be victims of sexual assault, and neither police nor courts believed that prostitutes could be raped. With respect to domestic violence, because men were assumed to be the rightful authority of the household, they were allowed to "discipline" wives; thus, wife-battering was rarely treated by the police and courts as criminal assault.

In most cases, however, sexism and racism in criminal justice policy remain obscured by policies touted as gender-/race-blind or gender-/race-neutral, and only careful evaluation of the policies' implementation and consequences reveals sexism and/or racism. Examples of the hidden consequences to women of crime policies can be found in the modern "get tough on crime" movement incorporated in the 1968, 1984, and 1994 federal crime bills and their corresponding state laws. Despite the fact that the violent crime rate remained relatively stable for 20 years, political rhetoric at these points identified crime and drugs as serious and growing problems requiring punitive solutions. Politicians enacted mandatory sentence minimums and increased prison sentence lengths, with "three strikes and you're out" laws mandating life sentences upon the third felony conviction;

they also provided funds for more police and corrections officers. In most respects, such provisions in the federal and state crime bills appear gender- and race-neutral, but their effects have serious hidden consequences for women, especially minority women.

In 1997, these policies resulted in an institutional and community correctional population of over 5.7 million adults, 1.7 million of whom were incarcerated in federal and state prisons and local jails, a more than fourfold increase in just 20 years. Over 133,000 of those imprisoned were women. In the 1980s, women's imprisonment increased at a rate nearly twice that of men, and 34 new women's prison units were opened. African American men and women are 7 times more likely to be imprisoned than are white men and women. The numbers of black women imprisoned for drugs increased more than three times those of white women (Bush-Baskette 1998). Thus, the "war on drugs" initiated with the crime bills has been called a war on women, especially on black women.

Paying for more prisons to house the huge increases in offenders prompted by punitive policies requires cutting other governmental expenditures, thereby affecting community bystanders to crime. Social services, with their disproportionately poor, minority, and female clientele, and their largely female workforce, have been particularly targeted, as welfare reform demonstrates. In addition, hiring more police and corrections personnel disproportionately benefits men, who are more likely than women to fill jobs as agents of the criminal justice system due to institutional sexism and individuals' biases against women. Finally, most imprisoned men and women are also parents with young children and so must leave their children in the care of family members, most frequently women. The psychological and financial stress experienced by family bystanders to crime means that children and their caretakers also pay some of the hidden costs of increased incarceration. Since criminal justice policies result in unreasonably high imprisonment rates of minority people, minority communities suffer disproportionately. As these examples demonstrate, within the contemporary United States, criminal justice policies remain sexist, racist, and classist. *See also* Aboriginal Women and Crime, Australia; Domestic Violence Case Processing; Domestic Violence, Police Responses to; Gender and Policing; Imprisonment in the South, Pre–Civil War; Rape Laws and Spousal Exemptions; Rape Law Reform; Sentencing Guidelines; Women Professionals in the Justice Workplace.

Further Reading: S. L. Miller 1998a, *Crime Control and Women*.

Mona J. E. Danner

Sexual Abuse of Children

Sexual abuse of children, which includes any actual or attempted sexual exploitation of children by an adult or someone are significantly older, primarily affects girls and often leads to victims' later involvement in the criminal justice system as offenders. The offense includes exposing a child to pornographic materials and forcing a child to engage in pornography, sexual relations, or prostitution. Sexual abuse of children received little attention before the late twentieth century. In the 1970s, for example, some researchers still believed that incest, a common form of child sexual abuse, was a relatively rare event, occurring in perhaps one in a million families.

More recent research indicates that both girls and boys are sexually abused at alarming rates. In 1988, the National Center on Child Abuse and Neglect found that approximately two children per thousand were victims of sexual abuse, an estimate that would mean that there are currently 50–80 million Americans who were sexually abused as children. Moreover, recent research indicates that girls are three times more likely to be sexually abused than boys; that 75–90 percent of those who sexually abuse girls are males; and that 50 percent of the offenders violating girls are family members. At least one-third of all female victims are less than 11 years old when they are sexually abused. The crime thus often involves not only sexuality but also betrayal of trust by an adult on whom the child depends and exploitation of power differences in gender as well as age.

Most sexual abuse of children never comes to the attention of authorities. Often there are no apparent physical injuries; thus the abuse may continue unnoticed. Intense feelings of shame and secrecy are common responses to sexual abuse on the part of both the victims and the adults who know about it.

Child sexual abuse appears to have lifelong negative effects. Sexually abused children may exhibit physical, behavioral, and emotional symptoms well into adulthood. When compared to nonabused persons, those with a history of childhood sexual abuse show significantly higher levels of depression, anxiety, and suicidal impulses, together with lower self-esteem. A fifth of all victims develop serious long-term psychological problems and signs of post–traumatic stress syndrome. They also show higher levels of social aggression, and/or social withdrawal, antisocial behavior, sexual provocativeness, and alcohol or other drug abuse problems. In addition, victims of child sexual abuse are far more likely than nonvictims to be arrested for prostitution as adults (Widom 1995). Indeed, although the processes are not yet well understood, childhood sexual abuse seems to be a major factor in later female offending. One-third or more of the inmates of women's prisons report childhood sexual abuse.

The cultural taboo against the open discussion of child sexual abuse began to decrease as a result of the 1970s feminist movement and the establishment of rape crisis services. As women began to disclose adult sexual assault experiences, many also reported they had been sexually abused as children. Newspapers, magazines, radio, and television programs called attention to the incidence of sexual abuse and its serious consequences in Western societies, reducing the stigma associated with this type of victimization. People who had been sexually abused as children began to bring criminal and civil actions against those they considered responsible. Eventually, millions of dollars were awarded in high profile cases involving parents, teachers, clergy, and others in positions of authority.

In the 1980s, perhaps in reaction to the increasing influence of those reporting histories of childhood sexual abuse, some people began to doubt that sexual abuse was as common as researchers were stating. The media then began to print and broadcast stories on "false memory syndrome," which was alleged to be caused by unethical psychotherapists purposely or inadvertently implanting inaccurate memories of childhood abuse in patients. At first the court system became the primary arena in which the debate on memory raged, with those claiming to have been falsely accused of perpetrating abuse bringing lawsuits against psychotherapists. These actions then spurred an increase in the scientific study of human memory.

With the increase in attention to the victims of sexual abuse came an increase in information about the perpetrators. While the majority of perpetrators seem to be adult men who abuse girls, new research shows that women, too, sexually abuse children. New data further indicate that juveniles make up more than one-third of the sexual abusers of children (Finkelhor 1994).

Because sexual abuse of children is so prevalent in American society and seems to be intimately related to later criminal behavior on the part of victims, it will continue to be the focus of attention by the popular media, courts, and mental health system. *See also* Child Abuse by Women; Child Witnesses; Domestic Violence by Women; Incest Victims; Rape Rates, USA ; Victimization, Repeat.

Further Reading: Greenfeld 1996, *Child Victimizers;* Prentky, Knight, and Lee 1997, *Child Sexual Molestation;* U.S. Department of Health and Human Services 1999, *Child Maltreatment 1997.*

Mic Hunter

Sexual Abuse of Prisoners

Before 1873, when Indiana established the first separate women's prison, women in the United States were incarcerated with men,

either communally or in separate wings of the same prison, and they were supervised by male staff. Female inmates were vulnerable to abuse by their male keepers; some were sexually assaulted or forced into prostitution. One goal of the reformers who advocated separate institutions for women was to prevent the sexual abuse and exploitation of female prisoners.

In contemporary prisons and jails, sexual abuse is pervasive and extremely damaging in its outcomes. Over one-third of female prisoners report being sexually abused prior to incarceration. Such a history of abuse compounds the effects of sexual abuse in prison. Moreover, although there have been cases of female staff sexually abusing female prisoners, in most cases the abuse is perpetrated by male personnel (Human Rights Watch 1996). This is especially problematic because the ratio of male correctional officers to female correctional officers can be as high as two to one. Additionally, inadequacies within correctional systems make it difficult to address the sexual abuse of female inmates. For instance, few prison workers have been trained to prevent sexual abuse; many prisons lack policies and grievance procedures for female inmates to report violations; and female inmates need to be educated about sexual abuse as well as departmental and criminal law sanctions.

Human Rights Watch (1996), an international organization that conducts regular, systematic investigations of human rights abuses throughout the world, has identified various types of abuse that occur in prisons, including rape, sexual assault and abuse, and criminal sexual contact. Another form of abuse includes offensive and degrading language that refers to a prisoner's sexuality or body parts. There have been reports of administrators, clergy, correctional officers, medical doctors, psychologists, and teachers impregnating incarcerated women. Even in situations when sexual relations do not include the overt use or threat of force, the prisoner does not have an equal status in the relationship. This is especially evident when a prisoner attempts to free herself from the relationship.

In addition to their offender status, most women in prison are marginalized in other aspects: over 60 percent have less than a high school diploma; over 50 percent were unemployed prior to incarceration; and almost two-thirds are women of color. These factors increase women's vulnerability to men in powerful positions. To understand the sexual abuse of female prisoners, one needs to understand the abuse of power. *See also* COF-FIN, RHODA; PRISONER LITIGATION; PRISONER RIGHTS.

Further Reading: Human Rights Watch 1996, *All Too Familiar;* Zupan 1992, "Men Guarding Women."

Pamela J. Schram

Sexual Assault Case Processing

Are sexual assault cases processed in ways that deny justice to some victims of this type of crime? The empirical research on sexual assault case processing that began in the 1970s focused on this question. Gender bias in case processing was conceptualized in two ways. Using the notion of sexual property, some researchers hypothesized that a woman who was not attached to a man, either as an unemancipated daughter or as a wife, would not be protected as vigorously by the criminal justice system as a woman who was. The empirical research has produced only limited support for this hypothesis.

The second conceptualization of possible gender bias in sexual assault case processing drew on the idea of gender-role norms; it has had much greater impact, both theoretically and empirically. It states that if a woman fails to conform to standards of conduct deemed by society to be appropriate, and is then victimized by a sexual assault, the criminal justice system will ignore the incident or treat it less seriously than other sexual assaults. According to this perspective, women who are sexually "promiscuous" or who engaged in "risky" behaviors such as hitchhiking or using drugs at the time of the assault are less

likely to be seen as genuine victims who deserve protection under the law.

Empirical studies of sexual assault case processing have found evidence that gender-role norms do affect case outcomes. A study conducted in Indianapolis during the early 1970s, for example, disclosed that gender-role norms were significant in three of the six decisions examined: arrest, convictions by plea, and convictions as the result of trial (LaFree 1979, 1981, 1989; LaFree, Reskin, and Visher 1985). A study of case processing decisions in Chicago, distinguishing cases involving acquaintances from those involving strangers, found evidence of gender bias in 4 of the 18 decisions examined (Kerstetter 1990a, 1990b; Kerstetter and Van Winkle 1990). In cases involving acquaintances, whether the woman was a man's "sexual property" was significant in the arrest decision, while gender-role norms affected the decision to file a felony charge, to convict, and to incarcerate. In cases involving strangers, gender-role norms influenced the willingness of complainants to prosecute. In addition, the complainant's use of alcohol or drugs at the time of the incident—a factor which may reflect concerns about the credibility of the complainant as a witness—had a negative effect on the prosecutor's decision to file felony charges.

Research conducted in Detroit provides the strongest evidence that gender-role norms affect sexual assault case processing decisions (Horney and Spohn 1996; Spears and Spohn 1997). That research found that victim characteristics—in particular, the age of the victim and evidence of risk-taking behavior by the victim at the time of the assault—were more powerful than either case seriousness or evidentiary strength in explaining prosecutors' decisions to file charges or not.

There are both similarities and differences in the patterns of gender bias disclosed by these studies. The studies suggest that the police officer's decision to arrest, the prosecutor's decision to file charges, and the adjudication decision are the three decisions most likely to be affected by legally irrelevant victim characteristics. The Indianapolis and

Chicago studies see gender bias as influential but conclude that its influence is constrained by incident seriousness and by considerations connected with evidence, circumstances (e.g., is the suspect in custody?), and strategy. The Detroit study portrays gender-role norms as a starker, more dominating influence. The explanation for these differences may lie in the fact that the three studies were conducted in three quite different jurisdictions and at different times. *See also* DATE RAPE; RACISM IN RAPE CASE OUTCOMES; RAPE LAW REFORM; RAPE VICTIMS, DISCREDITING OF.

Further Reading: Kerstetter 1990a, "Gateway to Justice"; LaFree 1989, *Rape and Criminal Justice;* Spears and Spohn 1997, "The Effect of Evidence Factors and Victim Characteristics."

Wayne A. Kerstetter

Sexual Harassment

In 1992, Anita Hill declared the sexual harassment of women to be one of the nation's best known "dirty little secrets." One year earlier, her testimony to the all-male U.S. Congressional Judiciary Committee inspired women of many backgrounds to break their silence, organize, and act to stop this social problem. Women's organizations formed task forces and established legal action funds, and as a result, the number of sexual harassment complaints to government agencies more than doubled.

It was in 1975 that college students first coined the term "sexual harassment" to describe their experiences of having lost jobs as a result of refusing to respond to male co-workers' sexual attentions. In 1978, legal scholar Catharine MacKinnon published a treatise conceptualizing sexual harassment as more than inappropriate behavior by a few inconsiderate men. Instead, MacKinnon identified sexual harassment as an institutionalized practice that undermines the social and economic status of all working women.

The Equal Employment Opportunity Commission and the Office of Civil Rights put MacKinnon's conceptualization into practice by adding unwanted sexual attention to their list of potentially actionable forms of discrimination. They defined sexual harassment as unwanted sexual attention that becomes a condition of work. Responsibility for preventing sexual harassment rests with employers and educational institutions. As a result, most employers and schools have established special procedures for the processing of sexual harassment complaints.

Over the past 20 years, thousands of women and a few men have tested the legal limits of MacKinnon's theory and governmental guidelines through litigation. The Supreme Court has heard six sexual harassment cases and has consistently ruled in favor of the victims. Their opinions, along with those of many appellate judges, now form an impressive body of case law that prohibits sexual harassment, defines it as a civil rights violation, and holds employers and schools liable for such behavior.

Nevertheless, sexual harassment remains a fact of life for many women. Conservative estimates show that from 33 to 42 percent of U.S. women have experienced a legally actionable form of sexual harassment. Survey findings over time have failed to show decreases in prevalence rates.

While many women have experienced sexual harassment, they may find it troubling for different reasons. Lesbians, for example, often find the sexual attentions of heterosexual men more offensive than their heterosexual counterparts do and perceive such behavior as attacks on their sexual orientation rather than on their gender. For women of color, racism can intersect with sexism in ways that produce a form of harassment different from that experienced by white women or men of color and, therefore, not as easily remedied by law.

Although complaint mechanisms are available, only about 12 percent of sexually harassed women actually use them. Fear of retaliation and stigmatization, the effects of gender socialization, and a lack of adequate resources all conspire to make the act of reporting a stressful or impractical option. As a result, most women continue to solve their sexual harassment problems by quitting their jobs or by trying to ignore or avoid the harasser.

The risk of sexual harassment is highest among women working and learning in male-dominated settings. The prevalence of sexual harassment among women in the military, coal mining, construction work, and the criminal justice system is estimated to be 20–40 percent higher than in the general population. Some believe the problem will dissipate once a critical mass of women is employed in these areas. Others argue that the practice will continue as long as men are able to maintain control over economic resources.

As social, economic, and technological conditions shift, sexual harassment practices change, as do ways in which women protest and resist sexual harassment. For example, increased access to the Internet and the development of the World Wide Web have been accompanied by increases of sexual harassment in chat rooms, on electronic mail discussion lists, and at various Web sites. At the same time, women around the world are mobilizing their online resources to share their experiences and resources and to publicly protest electronic sexual harassment. *See also* POLICE WORK AND CIVIL RIGHTS LAWS; POLICE WORK, HISTORY OF WOMEN IN, USA; VICTIMIZATION, FEMINIST PERSPECTIVES ON; WOMEN CORRECTIONS OFFICERS IN MEN'S PRISONS; WOMEN PROFESSIONALS IN THE JUSTICE WORKPLACE.

Further Reading: Holcombe and Holcombe 1992, *The Search for Justice;* International Coalition against Sexual Harassment Web site, http://jan.ucc.nau.edu/~pms/sash.html; MacKinnon 1979, *The Sexual Harassment of Working Women;* U.S. Office of the Inspector General 1995, *The Tailhook Report.*

Phoebe A. Morgan

Shelter Movement

The shelter movement began in the early 1970s as a grassroots effort to help battered women by providing safe places to which they could flee with their children. The movement grew out of the anti-rape movement and other feminist efforts to address violence against women.

Volunteers with little financial backing ran the earliest shelters, which were located in rented buildings or activists' homes. Shelters were run informally, based on a feminist model of empowerment and egalitarianism that was an extension of the feminist belief that violence against women is rooted in patriarchy. Shelters provided safe spaces where battered women could talk with one another and find solutions through consciousness-raising. To raise public awareness and empower battered women, feminists held "speak-outs" where women publicly discussed their experiences of being abused. They documented the extent of woman abuse, pressured law enforcement for changes in policies and practices, and campaigned for tougher laws to protect victims and punish abusers. Before the shelter movement, there were no services specifically for battered women. Indeed, most people assumed that woman abuse was victim-precipitated.

The shelter movement began in 1971 in Chiswick, England, with the establishment of the first shelter in the world, Chiswick Women's Aid, under the leadership of Erin Pizzey. The same year, Women's Advocates of St. Paul, Minnesota, formed a consciousness-raising group in which the issue emerged. In 1972, Women's Advocates established a hotline to provide crisis counseling. The idea spread, and in 1973, Rainbow Retreat, the first U.S. battered women's shelter, opened in Phoenix, Arizona, soon followed by many others. In 1976, the National Organization for Women formed a task force on woman abuse. In 1978, the U.S. Commission on Civil Rights held a national "Consultation on Battered Women," a meeting involving hundreds of activists from throughout the nation. As a result, feminists formed the National Coalition against Domestic Violence to loosely coordinate the shelter movement.

As the public recognized woman abuse, nonfeminists got involved, sidestepping the issues of power and patriarchy. They assumed that domestic violence was part of a "family system" in need of treatment and in which women could be just as violent as men. Social service providers organized shelters bureaucratically and employed licensed professionals, providing established treatment plans and setting strict rules. Funders preferred the accountability of this mental health model, and by the 1980s, fewer than half of all U.S. shelters were affiliated with feminists. Although some activists and scholars argued that the movement had been co-opted, many feminists remained active on behalf of battered women, working to change public policy and defend women who had killed their abusers.

Today there are over 1,200 battered women's shelters in the United States, with many more crisis centers for abused women. Programs are based on a variety of models, but feminist goals of empowerment and social change are evident, particularly where feminist networks are strongest.

The shelter movement succeeded in criminalizing spouse abuse, institutionalizing safe space, and raising public awareness. But violence against women has not diminished despite three decades of activism. Moreover, in the late 1990s, funding for shelters was threatened by the turn toward social and political conservatism. *See also* DEVIANCE AND REFORM, HISTORICAL OVERVIEW OF, BRITAIN; FEMINIST CRIMINOLOGY, BRITAIN; STALKING; VICTIM-BLAMING AND VICTIM-PRECIPITATION, CONCEPT OF; VICTIMIZATION, FEMINIST PERSPECTIVES ON.

Further Reading: Gagné 1998, *Battered Women's Justice;* Schechter 1982, *Women and Male Violence;* Tierney 1982, "The Battered Women Movement."

Patricia Gagné

Shoplifting and Kleptomania

Shoplifting (theft from stores) and kleptomania (obsessive and senseless theft) have long been associated with women. Shoplifting is an ancient practice. Reports of criminal theft from shops and stalls appeared in sixteenth-century England, and shoplifters became key figures in American vaudeville

acts, plays, and even popular songs in the late nineteenth and early twentieth centuries. *The Kleptomaniac,* a silent film made in 1905, was one of the many movie depictions of what had by then become a ubiquitous social phenomenon.

Shoplifting in its modern form is tied inextricably to the urban department store and to gender, for with the emergence of large retail institutions in cities across the United States in the late nineteenth century, shopping became recognized as a female activity, a major domestic occupation linked to what were considered the innate and natural characteristics of women. "Next to mental improvement, shopping is now the business of life," *Woman's Journal* proclaimed in 1873 (26 April 1873:135). With a profusion of consumer goods, an unprecedented luxury of decor, and a multitude of customer services, department stores dramatically changed the very experience of shopping. Integrating the dual roles of work and leisure into new patterns of behavior, women shopped and shoplifted.

Nonviolent and impersonal, shoplifting was understood to be a particularly female form of crime. Whether motivated by opportunity, need, the very spectacle and diverse stimuli of the stores themselves, the crowds of other shoppers, or simple greed, women in untold numbers took large quantities of merchandise from the stores without the formality of payment. Shoplifting was, however, inseparable from other forms of department store life and shopping activity, for many shoplifters had legitimate purchases in their possession at the time of their apprehension.

As a defense against "the growing evil" and significant dollar losses, department stores became security-conscious in the 1880s, and a whole new industry emerged that was centered on protection, particularly on the attractive display of merchandise "without risk from the nimble fingers of the shoplifters" (*Dry Goods Economist,* 4 June 1892:13). Private detectives and in-house police became a permanent part of the store labor force; quiet surveillance became common. But not all women caught shoplifting were detained. Most cases were handled informally, for the new breed of shoplifter was indistinguishable from other shoppers, and merchants were reluctant to press charges against the very backbone of their clientele.

Many women, particularly if they were deemed "respectable"—white and middle- or upper-class—were let go with a warning; others were arrested and had to go through the disgrace of a court appearance and newspaper publicity. Judges released the majority of these first-time shoplifters, however, often viewing their actions not as real crime but simply as impulsive yielding to temptation—something women were expected to do. A few repeat offenders or professionals who had plagued merchants in the past and whose faces and methods of operation were known spent time in jail.

Explanations for the dramatic increase in shoplifting in the nineteenth century centered on both the special store atmosphere which reportedly "took hold of all the senses" and on the women themselves. Key elements of the nineteenth-century definition of "female" were worked into an image of gender weakness that made sense of the shoplifting phenomenon. Observers of these women, seeking a way to understand the paradox of theft that was costly to the department stores yet not taken very seriously and rarely punished, often called them "kleptomaniacs."

Physicians, store managers, detectives, newspaper reporters, and judges all worked within a framework that cast kleptomania as both a specific female disease and as a type of "unfortunate" antisocial behavior by women of a certain class. Gender, class, and scientific authority were at issue as the new breed of shoplifter seemed to fly in the face of all previously understood notions of crime. Men who lifted merchandise from department stores were rarely called kleptomaniacs, but many women shoplifters, betrayed by their social position and their own biology, were routinely seen as sick and labeled kleptomaniacs. The medicalization of kleptomania in the late nineteenth century depended upon an understanding of gender that, in turn, depended upon sexual polarity. Women and men were viewed as fundamentally different,

and only women were said to exhibit a type of "moral insanity" associated with their reproductive system.

The public discussion, not unlike the scientific, was an extended commentary on gender, class, role definition, and questions of sickness and health. Popular wisdom embraced a view of these women acting the way they did simply because they were women, shopping as they were supposed to do, behaving in appropriate fashion most of the time, but occasionally succumbing to a temporary aberration. Thus, kleptomania became a sickness of women not really in possession of themselves; such absurd behavior could be explained only by pathological motives.

Female shoplifting did not decrease over the course of the twentieth century, but long after the earlier, pre-Freudian understanding of kleptomania lost credibility, shoplifting was still understood to be a female crime. Even though men, as well as women, adolescents, and even the elderly make up the army of casual shoplifters today, the singular association of women with shoplifting has only recently begun to weaken. Although a shoplifter is more likely to be female, no longer is every woman shopper seen as a potential thief simply because she is female. The difference seems slight but is, in fact, significant.

Shoplifting has changed the way America shops. At the end of the twentieth century, the prevention of shoplifting has emerged as a major industry. Stores now make deterrence obvious. Tagged merchandise, electronic gates, and guards at the door reinforce the message that it is not acceptable to shoplift; gender and class no longer provide protection. Everyone is suspect. *See also* MEDICAL EXPLANATIONS OF DELINQUENCY; PROPERTY CRIME; PSYCHOLOGICAL EXPLANATIONS OF DELINQUENCY.

Further Reading: Abelson 1990, *When Ladies Go A-Thieving;* Abelson 1989, "The Invention of Kleptomania"; P. O'Brien 1983, "The Kleptomania Diagnosis."

Elaine S. Abelson

Social Control Explanations of Crime.
See CONTROL EXPLANATIONS OF CRIME.

Social Control of Women

Mechanisms of Social Control

Social control in criminology refers to the rules and standards imposed by society for regulating human behavior. It is both a concept and a social process. Broadly defined, the *concept* of social control refers to a set of belief systems that guide people's actions and behavior. As such, social control defines what is appropriate or inappropriate behavior, legal or illegal conduct, and morally acceptable or unacceptable action. Social control as a *process* refers to all constraints, strategies, and techniques aimed at circumscribing individual behavior, either through the inculcation of generally accepted norms or through the imposition of more formalized mechanisms, such as coercion and punishment.

Given the multiplicity of mechanisms and techniques utilized to achieve effective social control, it is helpful to differentiate between two major forms of social control: formal and informal. Informal social control refers to the socializing influences exerted by family, friends, school, peers, religion, workplace, and the community at large. The individual and combined efforts of these social institutions are instrumental in bringing about conformity and obedience to society's rules. A growing body of research confirms the effectiveness of informal social control, pointing to the significant and influential roles played by social institutions in generating conformity.

Formal social control refers to law and the criminal justice system. Law consists of officially promulgated rules and is enforced by legally authorized agents of the criminal justice system, representing the government. It differs from other forms of social control in that it relies primarily on the use of formal negative sanctions to punish those who violate it.

Examining the origin of criminal law as an agency of social control and the promulgation of specific criminal laws, scholars differentiate between two major perspectives. The first views society as a relatively stable entity and assumes a widespread normative consensus among its members. This *consensus model* sees law as the crystallization of the "will of the people" and a reflection of the common interests of society as a whole. The second perspective views society as a collection of different and competing interest groups. From this perspective, law originates in the inherent conflict between groups and in the prevailing inconsistencies of social norms. This *conflict model* views the law and the criminal justice system not as servants of the collective good but as protectors of the interests of the politically powerful. It follows that the law and the criminal justice apparatus protect the interests of dominant groups as they exert their substantial social, political, and economic power, often to the disadvantage of the less powerful.

In spite of the differences in these perspectives, both models agree that the law and its agents of social control are shaped by a society's political, economic, and social institutions. Empirical research on the making and implementation of laws, coupled with analyses of the well-known racial and gender disparities in the nation's arrest, adjudication, conviction, and sentencing statistics, clearly favor the conflict model. U.S. society is highly heterogeneous. Its diverse ethnic, racial, religious, and other social groupings gravitate toward maintaining the autonomy of their own individual cultures and enhancing their own special interests. Law on the books and the law in action fit into a pluralistic conflict model. This means that while there is some agreement on the more basic legal norms, there is much conflict among the multitude of competing interest groups in how laws are written and applied.

American criminal law is commonly defined as a body of specific rules regarding human behavior. It is promulgated by the legislative branches of the federal and state governments, applied uniformly to all persons to whom the rules pertain, and enforced by punishment meted out and controlled by the state. These characterizations describe an ideal. In reality, criminal law in action is neither impartial, nor is it always equitably enforced.

Even a cursory examination of arrest data reveals consistent age, racial, and gender patterns in the national crime rate. For example, young persons between the ages of 15 and 25 account for almost half of the nation's arrests for violent crimes and for well over half of property crime arrests. By contrast, persons aged 45 and over account for less than 8 percent of all arrests. The racial differences in arrest rates are equally pronounced. Minorities, especially African Americans, account for one-third of all arrests nationally, even though they consititute only 12.7 percent of the population. Arrest rates by gender reflect similar differences.

The explanation of sex differences in rates of crime and imprisonment is one of the main tasks for criminologists and theorists of social control, the formal and informal rules by which society regulates human behavior. About 80 percent of all persons arrested are male. Analysis of offender populations also points to pronounced differences in male and female crime patterns, with the latter clustering around larceny-theft, prostitution, shoplifting, and welfare fraud. Males, by contrast, commit significantly more crimes, especially personal crimes of violence. Further, delinquent boys commit significantly more property offenses and violence in the company of peers, while delinquent girls are overrepresented in cases of sexual offenses, truancy, and incorrigibility, with most of the latter violations being committed alone. Looking at conviction and incarceration rates, the number of women under the jurisdiction of state and federal prison authorities is growing more rapidly than that of men, raising important questions on whether the extent of female criminality is changing or whether criminal law is simply being more stringently applied to this offender population. That is, are we looking at changes in the power of social control to maintain obedience and conformity, or are we instead seeing an intensification of formal social control of women?

Social Control and Gender

Turning to gender as an important form of social control, the focus shifts to analyzing how gender functions to produce differences in crime patterns. As is the case with social control generally, gender is both a social structure and a social process. The social structure of gender refers to the gendered configurations of social life that characterize any contemporary or historical society or culture. It includes the imposition of differential cultural restrictions and proscriptions, as well as the extension of differential opportunities and freedoms to individuals based on their gender. Gender as a social process refers to the activities and practices through which females and males absorb and enact their roles as "women" and "men."

Gender is not destiny, but it plays a critical role in almost every facet of daily life. Gender affects peer relationships, the extent of parental control, risk-taking, sexual activities, and an individual's pursuit of power. Gender also defines the range of available opportunities. It plays a critical role in formulating definitions of "self" and clearly influences how society defines the individual.

Although the empirical evidence with regard to the cultural determinants of crime remains scant, gender differences in criminal behavior may at least in part be understood by drawing on a key concept of social control: differential cultural ascription of roles to males and females. In other words, analysis must focus on the concept of gender itself as a major form of social control.

Before discussing how gender roles affect criminal behavior, it is important to recall that, in the United States, the promulgation of laws and the development of normative systems that regulate human conduct and define social relationships are by and large dominated by males. Males are brought up to develop qualities deemed necessary for assuming their customarily dominant economic, political, social, and sexual roles. Women, by contrast, have traditionally been consigned to the roles of wife, mother, homemaker, and sexual object. These culturally and biologically conditioned roles form the foundation for the presumption of male dominance in most social spheres and human interactions. It is interesting to note the tenacious endurance of these cultural attitudes, even in the face of rapid and enormous social and economic change. Clearly, modern times have liberated women from the control of their fathers and husbands. Under the cover of law, women are now free to pursue their educational, employment, and social goals, along with men. Nonetheless, winds of social change bypass many women, while cultural determinants work to keep them tethered to their historical and traditional roles. The resulting dependency of the female on the male for support and subsistence, a vulnerability that rises with the number of children and with a woman's degree of reliance on the male for her very identity, go a considerable distance toward explaining existing gender differences in arrest rates and crime patterns.

Gender Differences in Crime

Explanations of these differences must begin with the recognition that gender exerts a powerful effect on the probability of engaging in delinquency and crime. Official crime statistics and self-report studies invariably show that females, as a group, commit fewer crimes and delinquencies. Society's gendered patterns of social life are forever created and transmitted through the processes of gender-role socialization. Together, they function to inhibit female delinquency and crime while increasing the likelihood of male offending.

Recent research illuminates some of the reasons for the observed gender differences in crime. For example, Bottcher (1995), examining the daily lives of young, urban males and females, notes significant differences in gender-related activity patterns and self-definitions. Specifically, she shows that males, compared with females, live under fewer social constraints. They experience comparatively limited informal social control for most of their lives. In general, male lifestyles are characterized by freedom, mobility, lack of accountability, and life in the "fast lane." Each of these factors has a potential for enhancing or encouraging the probability that males will engage in delinquency and crime.

Gender definitions, in turn, also function to enhance or inhibit criminal behavior. For example, male self-definitions consistently associate such notions as action, adventure, excitement, opposition to authority and rules, and delinquency itself with concepts of maleness. In a similar vein, peer pressure puts high values on toughness, agressiveness, combativeness, endurance, and strength in males. At the same time, it discourages such traits in females. Then there are parental gender definitions and those of related social institutions, which lead to closer supervision and more restrictions placed on females compared with males. One key reason for the greater control of females is the desire of parents and society to prevent unmarried females from getting pregnant. Even the physical differences between males and females carry important social connotations and gendered definitions; they translate into a greater acceptance of male exposure to physical risks and into pressure on females to devote themselves to domesticity, family care, and procreation. Finally, the social definitions of crime itself present criminal behaviors as quintessential expressions of maleness and as unacceptable for females. To the degree that the gendered role definitions and self-conceptions discussed here remain an integral part of the social structure and social process, they will continue to contribute to the gendered differences reflected in crime statistics.

Gender and Difference

As important as the assessment of the effects of gender is for explaining the differential crime rates, the approach presents only part of the picture. To complete the equation, a second consideration must be added to the discussion. It consists of the fact that the category "women" is anything but monolithic. Important distinctions exist between women in terms of class, race, ethnicity, and sexual orientation, along with other critical variables such as age and health. The intersections of gender with these characteristics creates significant differences among women in terms of status, resources, power, and opportunities. In addition, linkages among these variables help explain some of the differences noted in the types and degrees of criminality, the likelihood of victimization, and the opportunities women have for engaging in criminal activities or desisting from them.

For example, in the United States, the social milieu of many African American women and other minority females is frequently characterized by severe deprivation and powerlessness. It may include living in crime-ridden neighborhoods, experiencing abject poverty, and being a product of a single-parent home. It may also entail serious physical, sexual, and psychological abuse across the life cycle. Many such women may live in abusive relationships. Unable to leave their abusers for fear of deadly violence and/or the loss of what little support they may receive from them, such women and their children endure unending maltreatment and grief. Histories of drug and or alcohol abuse, coupled with limited education and work experiences, keep those affected tethered to a life of poverty. It should not be surprising that the combined effect of such social forces drives some of these women to engage in criminal activities such as drug offenses, prostitution, property crimes, and violence.

Contrasting with the experiences of so many women of color in our society are the lives of a majority of white, middle-class, and upper-class women, many of whom are able to enjoy the fruits of the capitalistic society. This entails, for the most part, a high material standard of living, considerable control over many aspects of their lives, access to education and health care, life in relatively safe neighborhoods, and varying degrees of personal success. The latter may be attained through family affiliation and marriage, or earned through educational and professional achievements. The combined effects of social class, personal control, high levels of socialization, and the absence of basic needs or criminogenic environments bring forth conformity and, for the most part, law-abiding behavior. By the same token, increases in opportunities to engage in white-collar crime lead some such women to commit such offenses.

In sum, the combined effects of gender as a critical form of social control and the differential impact exerted by social class, ethnicity, and race on the lives of women, help explain existing gender differences in the nation's arrest rates and crime patterns. However, while there is a good body of research on the effects of class and race on crime, research on gender and crime is still in its very early stages; much challenging research remains to be done in this important area.

Recent Increases in the Social Control of Women

As previously noted, analysis of differential crime patterns shows that crime, especially violent crime, remains predominantly a male problem. In addition, national crime statistics clearly reflect that crime has decreased significantly in recent years. Therefore, the critical question that needs to be asked is: Why are ever-increasing numbers of women coming under the formal social controls of the nation's criminal justice system at this particular point in time? Even though women account for only 6.4 percent of all state and federal prisoners nationwide, their number has risen more rapidly than that of males in recent years (Bureau of Justice Statistics 1999). Statistics also show that increasing numbers of women are coming under the control of probation, parole, and related community corrections authorities.

The explanation of the paradox of rising female correctional populations in the face of declining crime rates is complex. The single most important reason lies in the nation's current drug control policies. Over one-third of all state and federal female inmates are incarcerated explicitly for drug offenses. However, this statistic vastly understates the impact of drug laws on women, as recent prison statistics for the federal system indicate. In 1997, drug offenses constituted the single largest category of commitment offenses of women to federal prisons: 73.2 percent of African American women and 68.1 percent of white women had been sentenced to a federal prison explicitly for drug offenses (K. Maguire and Pastore 1998).

A second reason for the increase of women in prisons may be a decline in the "chivalry factor," which in the past may have led judges to sentence women more lightly than men. Today, the chivalry factor appears to be extinct.

Third, at least some of the growth of the female prison population must be attributed to an actual increase in violent crimes. In 1995, women's share of arrests for violent crimes, including murder, forcible rape, robbery, and aggravated assault, amounted to 17 percent of all arrests. This represents an increase of 6.1 percent for the previous decade (1985–1995)—hardly a serious female crime wave, but sufficient to account for some of the increase in women in prison.

Finally, the 1990s witnessed unprecedented changes in the nation's sentencing systems, shifts that led to a remarkable expansion of prison and jail populations. Mandatory sentencing legislation, such as "three strikes" legislation, "truth in sentencing" provisions, and "split sentences," under which an offender must serve at least part of her sentence in prison or jail, have all had a serious impact on women. It is also clear that particular groups of women have borne a greater part of the burden of these changes. Statistics reflect significant racial and ethnic disparities: African American women are twice as likely as Hispanic women and eight times as likely as white women to be sentenced to prison. Mandatory sentences, in particular, bring many more women into the prison system, thereby imposing serious hardship on their children as well as on their communities. Most important, criminal justice policies have failed to anticipate unintended social consequences of new sentencing policies, many of which are borne by the female offender.

Clearly, gender is a crucial aspect of social control, just as social control gives rise to gendered behaviors and gender differences. Crime statistics of all types bear the imprint of gender. Recent increases in incarceration rates for women reflect more general intensification of formal social control measures, especially in the realm of sentencing. They probably also reflect increases in the immiseration of women at the bottom of the social and economic ladders. To some small degree, they may further reflect changes in gender roles as women enter formerly all-male spheres. However, there is no evidence that women are becoming less vulnerable to either formal or informal social controls. See also CHIVALRY EXPLANATION OF FEMALE CRIME RATES; FEAR OF CRIME; GENDER AND CRIME; POVERTY AND CRIME; POWER-CONTROL EXPLANATION OF CRIME; PUNISHING WOMEN OFFENDERS; PUNISHMENT, AUSTRALIA; SENTENCING, DRUG OFFENDERS.

Further Reading: Chesney-Lind 1997, *The Female Offender;* Daly 1994, *Gender, Crime and Punishment;* S. L. Miller 1998a, *Crime Control and Women;* Tong 1984, *Women, Sex, and the Law.*

Edith E. Flynn

Social Disorganization Theory of Crime. *See* SOCIAL STRUCTURAL EXPLANATIONS OF DELINQUENCY.

Social Process Explanations of Delinquency

Social process explanations of delinquency focus on how the process of socialization affects delinquent behavior. Control theory, differential association theory, and labeling theory are all social process explanations of delinquency. While a quick glance at these theories reveals little commonality, they share an emphasis on social interaction. All begin with the idea that socialization is best understood through the process of social interaction.

Control theories—rather than trying to explain why some individuals break the law—seek to explain why people conform to the law. While many versions of control theory exist, all tend to be based on the assumption that humans are naturally motivated toward deviance. The most influential control theory was developed by sociologist Travis Hirschi in 1969. In his book *Causes of Delinquency*, Hirschi observes that the development of a social bond (consisting of attachments to conforming persons, commitment to conventional behavior, involvement in conventional activities, and belief in the moral validity of the law) is the process that insulates persons from delinquency. His theory asserts that the weaker the social bond, the greater the likelihood of delinquency.

Differential association theory, developed by sociologist Edwin Sutherland, explains delinquent behavior in much the same way that it explains nondelinquent behavior: individuals learn behavior within intimate personal groups. The key to becoming delinquent, however, involves more than just merely associating with delinquents. According to Sutherland, in order for delinquency to result, an individual must internalize norms and values supportive of delinquency and must have an excess of definitions favorable to law violations over definitions unfavorable to law violations.

Labeling theory, unlike most other criminological theories, has little interest in explaining the initiation of delinquency and is more concerned with accounting for why offending persists or increases over time. Labeling theorists believe that deviant behavior develops through a continuous process of action and reaction. The major emphasis of labeling theory is on "secondary deviance" or the "deviance amplification" hypothesis. This hypothesis identifies the damaging impact that formal criminal justice system reactions such as an arrest can have on the future likelihood of crime. According to labeling theory, an arrest sets in motion events that can lead to more crime in the future. Persons arrested are often marginalized from conventional groups and activities, which leaves them susceptible to deviant peer group influences. Additionally, persons labeled as deviant or delinquent often come to accept their label. In sum, labeling theory gives primary importance to the reaction of the criminal justice system to initial acts of deviance and the effects of those reactions on the future likelihood of serious forms of delinquency.

While social process theories of delinquency were not specifically developed with gender differences in mind, in recent years, these theories have been applied to the female context. The majority of studies that have applied social process theories to both sexes reveal that the theories work equally well in predicting male and female delinquency. Although there is some evidence that the effects of delinquent peer exposure are stronger for males, delinquent peers are still an important predictor of delinquency for females. Most of the studies that have tested social process explanations of male and female delinquency have focused on common forms of delinquency. Differences between males and female delinquents in the causes of serious forms of offending behavior have yet to be comprehensively investigated. *See also* CONTROL EXPLANATIONS OF CRIME; LABELING EXPLANATIONS OF FEMALE CRIME.

Further Reading: Akers 1998, *Social Learning and Social Structure;* Gottfredson and Hirschi 1990, *A General Theory of Crime;* Schur 1971, *Labeling Deviant Behavior.*

Nicole Leeper Piquero

Social Structural Explanations of Delinquency

Social structural explanations of delinquency identify the major structural dimensions of society that shape delinquent behavior. Factors such as social class, culture, and neighborhood social organization are examined to assess how these influences shape delinquent behavior. Structural explanations recognize that an individual's position in the class and cultural systems can affect delinquent behavior. Such explanations as social disorganization theory, cultural deviance theory, and strain theory exemplify social structural explanations of delinquency.

Social disorganization theory examines the impact of neighborhood characteristics on delinquent behavior. The theory developed out of research in Chicago that identified certain patterns of crime and delinquency throughout the city. Researchers observed that crime remained highest in areas near the center of the city where the industrial core was located. In adjacent areas, or transition zones, neighborhoods experienced rapid immigration, population heterogeneity and turnover, high rates of crime, and other forms of social breakdown. In such neighborhoods, crime and delinquency persisted even as the composition of the neighborhoods changed over generations. These neighborhoods were defined as socially disorganized because their ability to regulate or control behavior had been compromised. Absent neighborhood cohesion and shared values in socially disorganized neighborhoods, criminal values and traditions emerge (Bursik 1988).

Cultural deviance theories attribute delinquency to the socialization of some individuals to cultural values that approve of crime and deviance. According to these theories, some individuals are socialized into norms that are defined as deviant by traditional middle-class standards. By conforming to the standards of their cultural group, certain individuals may violate legal standards that reflect the dominant cultural group, the middle class.

Although various versions of strain theory exist, their main assertion is that crime and delinquency result when individuals are unable to achieve success goals through legitimate channels. Strain theorists contend that opportunities are blocked for some individuals by the structural constraints of society. For example, while most Americans are socialized to pursue material success, some are blocked from realizing this goal and turn toward crime and delinquency to achieve their goals illegitimately. A recent strain theory developed by sociologist Robert Agnew (1992) contends that individuals turn toward delinquency when their conventional goals are blocked, when they are exposed to aversive events and conditions, or when presented with noxious or negative stimuli. Such experience often generates anger, and delinquency becomes one possible solution for relieving anger and other negative conditions (Agnew 1992).

Social structural theories of delinquency conceive of deviance and delinquency as phenomena that arise from social conditions, not from individual characteristics. As a result, these theories tend not explore whether gender differences or gender-specific influences are associated with delinquency. In fact, early studies testing these theories simply focused on delinquency or crime without regard to gender. Overall, however, most research on structural theories has focused on male delinquency. In short, females have been largely overlooked in structural theories of delinquency.

Despite the fact that social structural theories have been largely applied to males, some scholars contend that these theories can also account for female delinquency. To do so, structural theories need to be refined to identify the specific conditions related to male and female delinquency. While research on social disorganization theory has largely overlooked gender, in recent years, studies have demonstrated that strain and cultural deviance theories can explain female delinquency. *See also* STRAIN EXPLANATION OF CRIME.

Further Reading: Agnew 1995, "The Contribution of Social-Psychological Strain Theory"; Bursik 1988, "Social Disorganization and Theories of Crime and Delinquency"; Wolfgang and Ferracuti 1967, *The Subculture of Violence.*

Nicole Leeper Piquero

Southall Black Sisters

Southall Black Sisters (SBS), a feminist organization founded in 1979 and based in West London, provides legal assistance to South Asian and African Caribbean women on issues of sexual and domestic violence. The project also advises on other areas of the law such as immigration and housing when they interface with a client's experience of sexual or domestic violence. SBS maintains a high profile through initiating and supporting campaigns to change discriminatory legislation and policies at both the regional and national levels in England. It has become a vehicle for raising public awareness of the argument that, to achieve true justice, courts and other criminal justice agencies must take a defendant's gender and cultural background into account.

One of SBS's best known campaigns concerned the case of Kiranjit Ahluwalia, a South Asian woman who had been physically and emotionally abused by her husband for many years and was convicted of his murder in December 1989. Although the case involved victim provocation, Kiranjit Ahluwalia was unable to defend herself using this fact or the traditional argument of self-defense due to restrictive interpretations of, and gender bias in, the law.

SBS claimed that the court had not fully understood the cultural context of Kiranjit Ahluwalia's married life, which included having come from a traditional Sikh family and having had an arranged marriage. SBS explained the concept of *izzat* (family honor) to the court, showing that izzat had bound Kiranjit to her husband during the long years of humiliating violence. Kiranjit Ahluwalia was released on appeal in 1992 on the grounds of diminished responsibility.

A more recent SBS campaign concerns Zoora Shah, a divorced Muslim woman from Pakistan serving a life sentence for the murder of a man who sexually and economically exploited her over a period of 12 years. In a moment of desperation, Zoora Shah poisoned him by lacing his food with arsenic. The case went to the Court of Appeal in April 1998 with important new evidence including her entire medical history and previously unheard testimony. However, the Court of Appeal upheld her conviction and sentence.

SBS maintains that the judicial reasoning of the Court of Appeal was riddled with prejudicial misconceptions based on cultural stereotypes. Here, the fact that Zoora Shah was divorced and forced to be a sex worker by the man she ended up killing worked against her. The court decided that she had no izzat, "no honour left to salvage," because she had been involved in sexual relationships. It overlooked the fact that her status as a divorced, isolated, and poverty-stricken Asian woman made her vulnerable to sexual and financial exploitation by a number of predatory men. In 1999, SBS made a submission to the Home Office appealing against Zoora's tariff of life imprisonment on the grounds that it was far too draconian. They argued that Zoora had, to date, served eight years and was not a danger to the public. In April 2000, the Home Office reduced Zoora Shah's tariff for imprisonment from 12 to 20 years (with four remaining to serve). SBC continues to campaign for her release.

SBS maintains that while courts must be fully informed and culturally aware of the ethnic background of defendants, they must also take care to avoid negative stereotypes. Both of these cases highlight the need for the criminal justice system to address the complex issues of both gender and cultural ethnicity if it is to apply the law fairly. Just as women's experiences differ, so do their cultural contexts differ depending on their class, religion, and marital and economic status. Until courts recognize this, SBS predicts, women will be punished twice, first by their abusers and later by the criminal justice system. *See also* CASE PROCESSING AND GENDER; DOMESTIC VIOLENCE CASE PROCESSING; SEXISM AND RACISM IN CRIMINAL JUSTICE POLICY.

Rita Rupal

Stalking

The criminal act of stalking involves the pursuit or harassment of a victim, not actual physical harm. "Stalking" originally referred to the hunting and tracking of an animal for the purpose of killing it; when the term is applied to humans, it implies similar conduct and motive. The criminalization of stalking is relatively new, but it has resulted in antistalking laws in all states, in the District of Columbia, and at the federal level. In addition, research is being conducted on types of stalkers, stalkers' effects on victims, and links between stalking and domestic violence. The issue was brought to national attention with the 1989 murder of an actor, Rebecca Schaeffer, apparently by a stalker. This murder occurred in California, which in 1990 became the first state to enact antistalking legislation.

State and federal statutes vary somewhat in their definitions of stalking, but in general, stalking involves repeated harassment that would cause a reasonable person to fear for her or his safety or for the safety of a family member. As with most criminal acts, intent is required, and some state statutes also require that the threat be "credible." Data from the National Violence against Women Survey (a telephone survey of a nationally repre-

Table Q. Persons Stalked in Lifetime and in Previous 12 Months, by Sex of Victim [USA]

	Percentage		Number[a]	
	Women (n=8,000)	Men (n=8,000)	Women (100,697,000)	Men (92,748,000)
Stalked in lifetime[b]	8.1	2.2	8,156,460	2,040,460
Stalked in previous 12 months[b]	1.0	0.4	1,006,970	370,990

[a] Based on estimates of men and women in the United States aged 18 years and older, U.S. Bureau of the Census, Current Population Survey, 1995.
[b] Survey conducted November 1995 to May 1996. Differences between women and men are statistically significant: p-value ≤ .001.

Source: Adapted from Tjaden and Thoennes 1998, *Prevalence, Incidence, and Consequences,* page 11.

sentative sample of 8,000 women and 8,000 men conducted from 1995 to 1996) indicate that 8 percent of women and 2 percent of men in the United States have been stalked at some time in their lives, meaning that an estimated 8 million women and 2 million men have been stalking victims (Tjaden and Thoennes 1998b). Findings from the survey are displayed in Table Q. Most stalking victims are women (78 percent) and most stalkers are men (87 percent). Victims are likely to be stalked by people they know; 77 percent of female victims and 64 percent of male victims knew their stalkers.

There is a strong link between domestic violence and stalking. The National Violence against Women Survey found that women are significantly more likely than men (59 percent and 30 percent, respectively) to be stalked by intimate partners, and that 81 percent of women who were stalked by a current or former husband or cohabiting partner were also physically assaulted by that partner (Tjaden and Thoennes 1998b:2). Only about half of stalking victims report their victimizations to the police, and only a small proportion (12 percent) of these cases are prosecuted. Most stalking victims do not obtain restraining orders or orders of protection, but of those who do, the majority report that their stalkers violated the order (Tjaden and Thoennes 1998b).

Typologies of stalkers classify offenders on the basis of personality traits, mental condition, victim characteristics, and the stalker-victim relationship. Stalker typologies that focus on mental condition distinguish the psychopathic-personality stalker whose stalking often ends in violence, from the psychotic-personality stalker whose target is unknown and unobtainable (Geberth 1992). Wright et al. (1996) divide stalkers into two groups, nondomestic and domestic, further subdividing the category of nondomestic stalkers into organized stalkers, who use anonymous communications to harass their targets, and delusional stalkers, whose harassment is based on romantic fantasies.

Although stalkers vary in their motives, types of victim, mental stability, and potential for violence, stalking is generally related to control and power over the person stalked. Whether the stalker is attempting to begin a relationship; to continue a real or fantasy relationship; or to harass, frighten, or physically harm the victim, the stalking behavior indicates a desire to control another person's life.

In many instances, stalking progresses in stages, becoming more serious in the degree to which it invades the victim's life and the likelihood of physical harm to or even death of the victim. Stalkers and victims have very different views of the situation. Whereas the stalker envisions a joining or rejoining of two lovers, the victim perceives a frightening intrusion into her or his life and wants the stalker to disappear. While the stalker perceives his or her attention, presence, and gifts as signs of romance and affection, the victim views such behavior as sinister (Emerson, Ferris, and Gardner 1998). Danger can increase significantly when the stalker realizes the victim is not interested in any type of relationship, a realization that sometimes comes only after repeated rejection.

The low prosecution rate in stalking cases indicates that the criminal justice system is not responding to victims in a comprehensive and coordinated manner. Criminal justice professionals must be trained to understand the dynamics of stalking, to treat these cases as crimes, and to recognize that the perpetrators are not pathetic Romeos but criminal offenders. *See also* CRIME VICTIMIZATION; DOMESTIC VIOLENCE AGAINST WOMEN, EPIDEMIOLOGY OF; DOMESTIC VIOLENCE CASE PROCESSING; PROTECTION ORDERS; VICTIMIZATION PATTERNS, CANADA.

Further Reading: R. M. Holmes 1998, *Stalking in America;* Meloy 1998, *The Psychology of Stalking.*

Gail Flint

Status Offenses

Status offenses, behaviors considered criminal only when committed by individuals under the legal age of maturity, were used in the United States in the nineteenth century and much of the twentieth century to regulate the morality and behavior of children and prevent troublesome behavior from escalating into delinquency. Status offenses originally included a wide range of behaviors, such as associating with criminal or immoral persons; breaking curfew; being habitually disobedient; endangering the welfare, morals, and/or health of self or others; engaging in dissolute or immoral life or conduct; loitering; flirting with sailors; and engaging in premarital sex. In addition to minors, sometimes young adult women were also punished for status offenses and sent to state prisons for correction (Rafter 1990a).

Historically, status offense laws were applied differently to male and female youth, resulting in substantial gender discrimination in the handling and institutionalization of status offenders. Far more female offenders than male offenders were charged with and institutionalized for status offenses; in particular, many girls (but few boys) were adjudi-

cated for sexual behaviors. Institutionalization, in turn, was used to teach female status offenders how to act properly and how to prepare to be good wives according to middle-class standards.

Official statistics continue to show that females are more likely than males to be arrested and institutionalized for status offenses, especially running away, but this disparity is much smaller than in the early 1900s. This reduction in the difference between male and female status offending can be attributed to at least two policy developments. First, due to the ambiguous nature and capricious enforcement of status offense statutes, states clarified the laws in the 1960s and 1970s by defining status offenses in terms of distinct categories of behavior, which currently include running away, incorrigibility, truancy, liquor law violations, and curfew violations. Second, Congress passed the Juvenile Justice Delinquency Prevention Act (JJDPA) in 1974, drastically changing the way in which status offenders are handled by the juvenile justice system. Specifically, the JJDPA required all states receiving federal funds to deinstitutionalize status offenders from secure confinement. As a result of this act, the number of status offenders held in secure facilities was reduced nationwide, and many juvenile courts either shared their jurisdiction over status offenders with social service agencies or transferred jurisdiction to them entirely.

Although the JJDPA drastically affected the handling of status offenders, it did not eliminate out-of-home placement entirely because the requirements of the act could be circumvented in several ways. For example, status offenders could be placed in nonsecure and/or mental health facilities without violating the act. Offenders could also be "bootstrapped," or charged with minor delinquency for status-offense behavior, in order to avoid placement constraints. In 1980, Congress further broadened JJDPA exceptions by passing an amendment allowing judges to place a status offender in secure confinement if the youth returned to court on a contempt charge.

Despite ways to circumvent the JJDPA, the act has been effective in reducing the overall number of status offenders held in secure confinement. The reduction in confinement rates for female status offenders, in particular, has been substantial. However, this change should be viewed with some skepticism since preliminary research indicates that status offenders, particularly female status offenders, may be displaced from secure facilities to residential treatment and mental health facilities. (Such a displacement has been termed "trans-institutionalization" or the "medicalization of deviance.") Consequently, many reformers and researchers advocate abolishing status offenses entirely or redefining them as a social services concern. Opponents to these positions argue that status offense behavior must be recognized and responded to immediately in order to provide the services that status offenders and their families need and also to prevent status offense behavior from escalating into delinquent offending.

Overall, status offenders, particularly female status offenders, present a dilemma to the juvenile justice system. Female status offenders are frequently the victims of physical and/or sexual abuse at home, and a return to their family may worsen the situation. Yet the juvenile justice system is mandated to treat status offenders in the community. Although juvenile courts are allowed to place female status offenders in residential treatment centers or mental health facilities, such placements may not be appropriate. Thus, while the current processing and dispositions of status offenders may be necessary, options for adequately handling these youths often do not completely address the underlying causes for their behavior. Despite the positive aspects of the JJDPA, juvenile justice and social service agencies continue to search for more equitable and effective ways to deal with status offenders. *See also* CHILD-SAVERS MOVEMENT; GENDER DISCRIMINATION AND JUVENILE JUSTICE; GENDER DISCRIMINATION AND STATUS OFFENSES; JUVENILE DELINQUENCY, CANADA; JUVENILE INSTITUTIONS, HISTORY OF.

Further Reading: Odem and Schlossman 1991, "Guardians of Virtue"; Maxson and Klein 1997, *Responding to Troubled Youth;* Weithorn 1988, "Mental Hospitalization of Troublesome Youth."

Denise C. Herz

Strain Explanation of Crime

The classic statements of the strain explanation of crime hold that strain or frustration results when individuals experience structural blockages to culturally prescribed goals, and that when individuals face such goal blockages, they may develop nonconformist or criminal responses as a way to compensate for the inability to reach their goals by conventional methods. Most strain theories point to blocked occupational or economic goals as the primary source of strain and a major cause of crime (Merton 1938; Cloward and Ohlin 1960). Because traditional gender roles dictate that personal economic success is of little importance to women, the classic statements of strain theory paid little attention to female crime—a glaring omission, given that women have historically made up a significant proportion of the poor.

In the past, career goals were not culturally emphasized as much for females as for males. But more recently, women have come to hold higher educational and career goals, and women increasingly occupy "breadwinner" roles due to changing trends in marriage and family arrangements. Thus, the potential for women to experience economically based strain should be increasing. This is especially true given the fact that women are often employed in "pink-collar" or traditional female jobs that do not pay as well as traditional male jobs. In addition, many women who aspire to high-paid positions have found their access to them blocked by the "glass ceiling."

Despite changing roles and economic situations for women, there has been surprisingly little empirical research examining female crime from the classical strain perspective. However, one line of research provides a partial test of strain theory by examining the differences between women who hold egalitarian gender-role attitudes versus those who hold more traditional gender-role attitudes. Women with liberal or egalitarian gender-role attitudes tend to have higher career goals, and thus have a greater potential to experience strain, in comparison with more traditionally minded women. In turn, liberal women should have higher crime rates, and their crime rates should be similar to those of males. However, several studies of this issue have failed to support this argument, finding instead that nontraditional females are no more likely to experience strain than traditional females (Lieber et al. 1994). It should also be noted that the empirical literature supporting classical strain theory in general has been limited at best (Burton and Cullen 1992).

Robert Agnew recently proposed a significant revision to classical strain theory. This "general strain theory" is broader in scope than traditional strain theories, holding that forces other than blocked economic goals can cause strain and crime (Agnew 1992). Broidy and Agnew (1997) have recently argued that general strain theory can be useful in explaining female crime, given that strain may result when an individual is presented with negative or noxious stimuli but lacks the resources to remove them. Thus, unhappy relationships, physical abuse, unfulfilling jobs, and responsibility for housework and childcare may lead to strain and crime among women. Future research on strain theory and female crime will likely build upon the idea that characteristics of the female gender role may contribute to strain and crime among women. *See also* GENDER AND CRIME; POVERTY AND CRIME; SOCIAL STRUCTURAL EXPLANATIONS OF DELINQUENCY.

Further Reading: Berger 1989, "Female Delinquency in the Emancipation Era"; Broidy and Agnew 1997, Gender and Crime"; Merton 1938, "Social Structure and Anomie."

Barbara J. Costello
and R. Gregory Dunaway

Suffragettes

Suffragettes—members of the movement to extend voting rights to women—became an important political force in Britain in the early twentieth century. Disillusioned and frustrated by the lack of success of existing women's political organizations, a new suffrage society was formed in 1903 by Emmeline Pankhurst, the Women's Social and Political Union (WSPU). It was the militant activity employed by the WSPU that brought the organization into prominence, and in 1906, its members were nicknamed the "suffragettes" by the Daily Mail newspaper to distinguish them from less militant groups agitating for broader voting rights.

The suffragettes raised the issue of votes for women whenever Liberal politicians spoke, and they participated in local and national suffrage demonstrations. By 1905, it became apparent that argument, persuasion, and peaceful demonstration were not enough to obtain the vote. The suffragettes then took "Deeds Not Words" as their motto and set about using more militant measures. They stormed the House of Commons, disrupted meetings, heckled cabinet ministers, and increased attacks against public and private property through window-smashing and arson.

By 1913, over 1,000 suffragettes had gone to prison for their beliefs, many repeatedly. In prison, many WSPU members went on hunger and thirst strikes. Faced with these tactics, the government responded with force-feeding and by passing the so-called Cat and Mouse Act, which allowed prisoners to be temporarily released to recover their health and then to be readmitted to prison. These militant suffragettes came to be classified as criminal rather than political prisoners.

Suffragette militancy peaked in 1913, notably with the death of Emily Wilding Davison, a WSPU militant who deliberately threw herself in front of the king's horse at the popular Derby Day race, shouting "votes for women" and carrying a WSPU banner under her coat. She had been to prison eight times, on hunger strikes seven times, and forcibly fed 49 times. Her funeral occasioned another large suffrage demonstration.

Great Britain's entry into World War I in 1914 abruptly ended the women's suffrage struggle. Alliances in the suffrage movement were overturned, and the nation's key political issue became the response to the war.

The Representation of the People Act in 1918 granted the vote to women over the age of 30 with property. In 1919, the WSPU disbanded, and thereafter the National Union of Societies for Equal Citizenship worked to finish the job of obtaining equal political and legal rights for women. In 1928, the Equal Franchise Act lowered the voting age to 21 and abolished the property qualification. *See also* DEVIANCE AND REFORM, HISTORICAL OVERVIEW OF, BRITAIN; POLITICAL OFFENDERS.

Further Reading: Atkinson 1988, *Suffragettes;* Liddington and Norris 1985, *One Hand Tied Behind Us.*

Marisa Silvestri

T

Terrorism

Terrorism is the calculated use of violent criminal action to achieve political goals through instilling fear in others with opposing ideologies. In 1980, the U.S. Central Intelligence Agency identified more than 370 terrorist groups operating in 63 countries, although they may not all be active today. Women have participated at every level in ter-

Patty Hearst. *Imapress/Archive Photos.*

rorist organizations. However, in the past, right-wing groups such as the Aryan Nation and the Ku Klux Klan seem to have had less allure for women than left-wing terrorist organizations such as the Symbionese Liberation Army and the Weather Underground (Weinberg and Eubank 1987).

Right-wing terrorist groups tend to idealize the past. Racism, sexism, and homophobia are often the foundation for their political ideologies. They take exception to policies—such as gender equality—that they believe threaten the traditional American way of life. Therefore, women have played a limited role and have been viewed as attachments to their male counterparts or as support for the men. Women who carry out attacks or who serve as leaders are exceedingly rare in right-wing terrorist groups.

On the opposite end of the political spectrum are left-wing terrorist groups whose goals are to bring about radical change and break with the past. They tend to argue that there are fundamental problems in the political and social institutions of society, problems such as patriarchy and racism. Leftist ideologies tend to support the feminist cause; thus women have played more extensive roles in leftist terrorist groups (Handler 1990). One study found that the women in these groups were well educated, middle or upper class, and in their mid-thirties (Benson, Evans, and Simon 1982). Whatever the profile of the leftist female terrorist, her goal is to generate momentum for her political cause through violent criminal activity.

Women participated in terrorist activities as far back as the 1780 revolutionary movement in Latin America and the Russian revolution of 1870. Several decades ago, women were also active as both leaders and members of such terrorist organizations as the Symbionese Liberation Army (SLA) and the Weather Underground. For example, newspaper heiress Patty Hearst joined the SLA after being kidnapped by it in 1974 and held for ransom; her participation in an SLA bank robbery led to two years in prison. Other late-

twentieth-century terrorist organizations with a strong female presence include the German Red Army Faction, the Japanese Red Army, the Italian Red Brigades, and the Popular Front for the Liberation of Palestine (Weinberg and Eubank 1987). With the current rise in fundamentalist terrorist groups, however, women's presence is diminishing. *See also* POLITICAL OFFENDERS.

Further Reading: Benson, Evans, and Simon. 1982, "Women as Political Terrorists"; Handler 1990, "Socioeconomic Profile of an American Terrorist"; MacDonald 1991, *Shoot the Women First.*

Joanne Ardovini-Brooker

V

Victim Advocacy

Over the past quarter century, victim advocacy has evolved to protect the dignity of women victimized by crime and other traumatic experiences, promote compassionate responses to their needs, and attain legitimization of the fact that many offenders target women because of their gender. The movement seeks to stop the secondary abuse frequently suffered by survivors, in male-dominated systems such as criminal justice, during the aftermath of victimization. Led by advocates from domestic violence and sexual assault programs at the local, national, and international levels, a large network of governmental, private, and volunteer victim services has emerged. Agencies now provide specialized interventions such as programs for girls through child victim assistance, for older women through elder abuse programs, for lesbians through hate crime action, and for other special populations through culturally appropriate measures. A chronology of the movement appears on page 261.

Essential themes in victim advocacy are recognition of the unique worth and experience of each individual and the pursuit of justice. As summarized by the United Nations Declaration of Basic Principles of Justice for Victims of Crime, the themes include respectful, fair, and dignified treatment; provision of judicial and administrative mechanisms for prompt redress of harm with minimal inconvenience; the right to be informed and heard; protection of privacy and security; restitution and compensation; skilled assistance; and remedies for abuses of victim rights. Women's advocates have insisted that healing is a critical component as well.

The methods of victim advocacy include personal and collective action. At the personal level, victims, moving forward as survivors, act as their own advocates while relying on trained supporters for information, problem solving, intercession with bureaucrats and employers, and assistance with transportation, paperwork, finances, and childcare. Collectively, victims and their advocates have promoted extensive legal reforms (most notably, passage of constitutional victim rights' amendments in most states), development of funds and resources, coordination of the complex services network, training for skilled services, and accountability of those responsible for assuring victim rights and services.

Each state has organizations that coordinate victim advocacy. U.S. national organizations particularly useful to female victims include:

National Coalition Against Sexual Assault
(717) 901-6757

Mothers against Drunk Driving (MADD)
(800) 438-6233

National Center on Elder Abuse
(202) 898-2586

Chronology of the Crime Victims' Movement

1965   First Victims' Compensation Program founded
        First national victims' survey compiled
1969   First Task Force on Child Abuse and Neglect (New York City) formed
1972   First victim assistance programs (St. Louis; San Francisco; Washington, D.C.) started
1973   First Victim Impact Statement (Fresno County, California) released
1974   First law enforcement victim assistance programs (Ft. Lauderdale and Indianapolis) founded
        National Center on Child Abuse and Neglect founded
1975   National Organization for Victim Assistance established
        First Victim Rights Week (Philadelphia) established
1977   Domestic violence arrests mandated in Oregon
1978   National Coalitions Against Sexual Assault and Domestic Violence formed
1980   First Bill of Rights for crime victims (Wisconsin) passed
        First Mothers against Drunk Driving chapters formed
1982   Victim and Witness Protection Act passed
1984   Victims of Crime Act (VOCA) passed
        National Center for Missing and Exploited Children founded
1985   National Victim Center (NVC) founded
1987   Victims' Constitutional Amendment Network established
1990   Victims' Rights and Restitution Act, Hate Crimes Statistics Act, and Campus Security
        Act passed by Congress
1991   First International Conference on Campus Rape (Florida) held
1994   Violence against Women Act passed
        First Victims' Bill of Rights constitutional amendment introduced into Congress
1995   National Victim Assistance Academy founded
1996   Sex Offender Notification Act and Interstate Stalking Acts passed
1997   Victim Rights Clarification Act passed

National Clearinghouse on Child Abuse
and Neglect
(800) 394-3366

National Domestic Violence Hotline
(800) 799-7233

National Organization for Victim Assistance
(800) 879-6682

National Center for Victims of Crime
(800) 394-2255

Office of Victims of Crime Resource Center
(800) 627-6872

Rape, Abuse and Incest National Network
(800) 656-4673

Working together, victim advocates focus on changing the environments in which victims recover. In supportive family and community contexts, victims should receive prompt, dignified, and fair treatment as they seek justice and healing. *See also* CRIME VICTIMIZATION; CRIME VICTIMS AND DEFINITIONS OF JUSTICE; SHELTER MOVEMENT; VICTIM COMPENSATION; VICTIM SERVICES; VICTIMS, HISTORICAL TREATMENT OF.

Further Reading: Burnley, Edmunds, Gaboury, and Seymour 1997, *National Victim Assistance Academy;* National Center for Victims of Crime, http://www.nvc.org/; Office for Victims of Crime, http://www.ojp.usdoj.gov/ovc/.

Arlene Bowers Andrews

Victim Compensation

Although women are not victimized by crime as often as men, they are more likely to benefit from compensation programs that provide services and financial reimbursement to crime victims. Prior to the development of victim compensation systems in the United States, some victim costs were met through Medicare, Medicaid, Workers' Compensation, mandatory automobile insurance, and other public and private means. In the early 1960s, however, the inability of these systems to meet the needs of many uninsured victims compelled states to experiment with victim-specific reimbursement, providing compensation for medical, mental health, and funeral costs that would otherwise have gone unpaid. Some programs also cover lost wages, rehabilitation, lost property, and attorney fees, and two cover pain and suffering.

Initially, it appeared that most victim compensation recipients were men. This may not have been so, because early programs primarily compensated homicides, which disproportionately occur to men, but on whose behalf widows and orphans receive benefits. But early programs also limited benefits to "worthy" victims, and they were reluctant to help victims who knew their assailants, as is more common with women victims. In 1984, the federal Victims of Crime Act (VOCA) began to offer matching funds to state programs that met minimal federal guidelines. These guidelines included a 30 percent minimum set-aside for "priority" victims (of sexual and domestic violence and child abuse) and a mandate to inform victims about support services available to them. As a result of the increased funding, each state now administers a program, and nearly all of them comply with federal guidelines. As the majority of funds go to priority victims, women now receive compensation greater than their proportion of victimizations. Eligibility for victim compensation has also been expanded, especially to victims of child sexual abuse, drunk driving, and family violence. Victims who do not report to the police can be referred to compensation programs by therapists and other service providers.

In the late 1990s, as crime rates fell but federal fines (from a few high-profile crimes) increased, victim compensation increasingly funded victim service programs and covered counseling for ever-expanding groups of victims, including witnesses; secondary victims; and victims of stalking, threats, and verbal or emotional violence—the crimes most often experienced by women. Policymakers observe that compensation still inadequately meets property losses and that service providers have benefited more from funding enhancements than have victims. In fact, while original allocations earmarked 70 percent of funds for victims and 30 percent for service providers, the 1999 allocation was 20 percent for victims and 80 percent for service providers. *See also* CRIME VICTIMIZATION; VICTIM ADVOCACY; VICTIMS, HISTORICAL TREATMENT OF; VICTIMS IN COURT.

Further Reading: T. Miller, Cohen, and Wiersema 1996, *Victim Costs and Consequences;* Parent, Auerbach, and Carlson 1992, *Compensating Crime Victims;* Sarnoff 1994, *A National Survey of State Crime Victim Compensation Programs;* Sarnoff 1996, *Paying for Crime.*

Susan Kiss Sarnoff

Victim Impact Statements

A victim impact statement is an oral or written statement tendered by a victim (or a family member, if the victim is deceased) that explains the emotional and financial impact of the crime. In response to women's groups' criticisms that the U.S. criminal justice system neglected crime victims, states began in the 1980s to pass victims' rights laws. Among these were laws calling for victim impact statements at critical points in the criminal justice process. These laws enable victims to have a "voice" in criminal justice processes and to share attention with offenders. Twenty-one states have championed victims' rights further by amending their state constitutions so as to provide for victims' bills of rights; 19 of these amendments provide for a victim's right to be heard.

Since 1995, every state provides for some type of victim impact statement at sentencing. Many states allow victims to provide the court with information about themselves, the victimization's effects, and their opinion about the appropriate sentence for the offender. Some states also call for an impact statement during a pre-sentence investigation (44 states), before a parole or furlough release decision (45 states), and/or before acceptance of a plea negotiation (21 states). Victim impact statements are most often allowed when the victim incurred personal harm from a violent crime.

Groups such as MADD (Mothers against Drunk Driving), Children of Murdered Parents, and the National Organization of Parents of Murdered Children provide victims with assistance in understanding their specific rights. Women who are victims of domestic violence and rape are provided assistance by victim advocates located within prosecutor offices or police departments. Victims, particularly rape and domestic violence victims, need to be informed about the extent to which their statements are confidential. In some states, a victim is required to have her statements subject to review by the offender or tendered in a room with the offender nearby. Rape victims and other victims of violent crime may be deterred from providing a victim impact statement if they have to physically face the offender. To address the needs of victims of violent crime and ensure that their rights to be heard, some states allow victims to submit video testimony or provide impact statements without the offender being present. Some states attempt to lessen the traumatic impact that giving an impact statement might have on a victim by accommodating the particular needs of the victim. While a number of states require that victim impact statements at the parole stage be given at the penal institution where the offender is housed, some states allow parole impact statements to be made at a location more comfortable to the victim, such as a parole board office or other convenient location. Thirty-seven states provide for separate and secure waiting areas for victims and their families to minimize contact with the offender.

Proponents of victim impact statements argue that criminal justice decision-makers must have victim input before rendering a decision. They argue that criminal records alone will not adequately reflect the extent of the harm done to the victims. Female victims of violent crime, in particular, have often found the criminal justice system hostile. Rape victims, for example, may experience "secondary" victimization by a legal system that focuses on offenders' due-process rights while ignoring victims' input. Many victims indicate that an opportunity to be active participants at critical points in the criminal justice process helps them deal with the impact

that the original victimization had on their lives.

Opponents of victim impact statements argue that victim input may make it more difficult for criminal justice decision-makers to be objective. In their view, adverse public reaction to an offender or emotional sensitivity to victims may result in unfair criminal justice outcomes. *See also* CRIME VICTIMIZATION; CRIME VICTIMS AND DEFINITIONS OF JUSTICE; VICTIM ADVOCACY; VICTIMIZATION, FEMINIST PERSPECTIVES ON; VICTIMS IN COURT.

Further Reading: Erez 1990, "Victim Participation in Sentencing"; Sarat 1997, "Vengeance, Victims and the Identities of Law"; Victims' Rights Sourcebook, http://www.ncvc.org/law/SBOOK/.

Frances P. Bernat

Victim Notification

Victim notification is a policy wherein criminal justice authorities contact victims, victims' families, or entire communities when offenders complete their prison sentences or relocate. Notification particularly affects female victims of sexual or physical abuse following the release from prison of abusive husbands, ex-husbands, or boyfriends. These offenders are sometimes fixated on retaliation against the women who helped prosecute them, putting those women at high risk for revictimization, including homicide.

While victim notification normally occurs shortly before an assailant's prison release, it may also occur prior to a parole hearing. At parole hearings, victims are sometimes allowed to offer victim impact statements justifying the denial of release privileges. Additionally, girlfriends, wives, and other individuals notified about impending felon releases can pursue safety options or contemplate relocation. Women victimized by domestic partners may be afforded an order of protection if there is a strong possibility of harm from the released offender. However, orders of protection generally fall short of providing security because they are difficult to enforce.

Notification to communities usually occurs when there is concern about child molestation (often involving female victims such as Megan Kanka) perpetrated by sex offenders. Legal stipulations under federal and state statutes involving habitual offenders (so-called "Megan's Laws") are a case in point. Released felons are supposed to register with local authorities. Offender classification systems sometimes stipulate that local officials must notify the community about the felon's presence. However, many felons circumvent the system by either avoiding registration or providing false addresses. Thus, the intended effect of community notification is undercut. *See also* PROTECTION ORDERS; VICTIM ADVOCACY; VICTIM IMPACT STATEMENTS.

Further Reading: Doerner and Lab 1995, *Victimology;* Karmen 1996, *Crime Victims.*

Lloyd Klein

Victim Rights Legislation. *See* CRIME VICTIMIZATION; VICTIM IMPACT STATEMENTS; VICTIMS, HISTORICAL TREATMENT OF.

Victim Services

Victim services in the United States grew from two sources, both related to the issue of female crime victims. One was the realization that many victims, and female victims in particular, fail to report crimes to the police. The other was the work of feminist grassroots activists on behalf of victims of battering and rape. Viewing sexual assault and domestic violence as important symbols of the subordination of women, feminist activists and victims founded rape crisis centers and shelters for battered women, at the same time vastly increasing public awareness of the extent and effects of these crimes.

The two separate streams from which victim services arose were philosophically quite distinct. Programs created by justice professionals were principally concerned with increasing victims' willingness to cooperate with justice authorities. The early programs they founded were well funded, served a wide spectrum of crime victims, and provided an array of services. In contrast, grassroots programs were poorly funded, typically served individuals victimized by specific crimes, and

---

Types of Victim Services
Crisis counseling
Follow-up contact
Shelter/safe house
In-person information and referral
Telephone information and referral
Emergency financial assistance
Criminal justice support advocacy
Emergency legal assistance
Personal advocacy

provided limited services. In many cases, the providers and recipients of such services distrusted the justice system and maintained their separateness from it.

A spirited debate still rages within the service community about how closely service providers ought to be aligned with the justice system. Advocates of grassroots programs maintain that caseworkers cannot truly serve the interests of victims if they are based inside the criminal justice system because caseworkers will inevitably side with justice officials when their interests and the interests of victims diverge. Victim advocates located within police or court agencies counter that they have far better working relations with police officers and prosecutors than grassroots service providers have. As a result, justice officials are more willing to refer victims to the service providers and are willing to listen to their advice about how to deal with difficult individual situations.

This divide between perspectives in narrowing. Over the past quarter century, victim programs have grown dramatically. Although many of these programs remain grassroots in orientation, federal dollars now form an essential pillar of support for most service programs. Funds for victim services provided by the 1984 Victims of Crime Act topped $363 million in 1998. With the passage of the Violence against Women Act in 1994 came dollars earmarked for female victims. In 1998, this act provided $172 million for victims of stalking, domestic violence, and sexual assault. Collaboration has become the buzzword, as some federal funding for domestic violence programming is contingent on the collaboration between criminal justice and social service agencies.

Crisis intervention is the foundation of services for victims. It begins with assisting victims in meeting their most immediate needs. Ensuring safety among abused women or responding to physical injury typifies this first phase of crisis intervention. The next phase usually focuses on emotional support or counseling. When an arrest is made, case-workers aid victims in negotiating the court system and assist them in preparing victim impact statements. Crisis intervention also extends to preventing future vulnerability. Data suggest that persons victimized once are at increased risk of future victimizations as well. Domestic violence against women, for instance, is seldom a singular episode.

Recently, service providers have begun to recognize that the victimization experience is conditioned by situational factors (e.g., the type of crime) and victim-related factors (e.g., the age of the victim). In response, services are increasingly offering specialized assistance aimed at, for instance, victims of stalking, immigrant victims of domestic violence, and elder-abuse victims.

In spite of the proliferation and specialization of victim services, many questions remain unanswered. Experience has shown that only a small percentage of victims receive aid from victim service programs. What explains the fact that many crime victims never connect with services? Federally funded research is underway to investigate the needs of victims and the reasons why they do or do not receive assistance. Questions of effectiveness present an additional challenge to the field. Researchers need to find answers to these questions to help service providers better confront issues of accessibility, delivery, and effectiveness. *See also* CRIME VICTIMIZATION; CRIME VICTIMS AND DEFINITIONS OF JUSTICE; SHELTER MOVEMENT; VICTIM COMPENSATION; VICTIM IMPACT STATEMENTS.

Further Reading: R. C. Davis and Henley 1990, "Victim Service Programs"; M. A. Young 1997, "Victim Rights and Victim Services."

Robert C. Davis and Catherine Stayton

Victim-Blaming and Victim-Precipitation, Concept of

Violent crimes against women and girls have often been explained by blaming the victim or at least accusing her of precipitating the violence. Violent crimes against men and boys have rarely been explained in this way; rather, in male cases, criminal justice officials have begun with the assumption that no one wants to be the victim of violent crime and that victims are unlikely to provoke assaults.

Stereotypical perceptions and cultural values related to gender roles play an important role in victim-blaming. When women victims violate gender stereotypes of "good" women by behaving "provocatively" or "promiscuously," or are excluded from that classification because they belong to minority racial or ethnic groups, they may be viewed as bearing responsibility for their own fate. Intoxication, assertiveness, and dressing in revealing clothing, for example, are violations of the "good" woman stereotype that may influence how victims are viewed by society and treated by the criminal justice system. In addition, the victim's relationship to her attacker may influence blame. Homicide, partner-battering, and rape are the crimes for which women victims have been most likely to be blamed.

While women victims have been held responsible for centuries, the concept of victim-precipitation was not formally integrated into criminology until 1958, when Marvin Wolfgang published his classic study of homicide, *Patterns in Criminal Homicide*. Wolfgang defined victim-precipitated homicides as killings in which the victim was the first to use physical force or display a weapon. Wolfgang found that alcohol was present in almost two-thirds of the cases of victim-precipitated homicides in his sample, and that in 44 percent of those cases, both victim and offender were drinking. In every case in which a victim-precipitated homicide occurred within a family, the victim was male, a batterer killed by his beaten wife.

More recent research, too, shows that homicide victims were often drinking before they were killed and that in domestic homicides, when women kill a partner, they do so after suffering repeated violent attacks. In short, domestic homicide research has long indicated that when women kill, the victim may indeed have done something to trigger or facilitate the event. Women victims of domestic homicide have long been blamed for precipitating the lethal event, at least by public opinion. Research indicates, to the contrary, that wife or partner-killing is more likely to be the culminating event in a history of abuse.

Victim-blaming is also common in partner abuse crimes that do not culminate in homicide. Because many people find it hard to understand why women stay in abusive relationships, stereotypes persist that wife abuse occurs because some women like to suffer or because these abused women do things to provoke assaults. The question commonly asked by the general public, "Why do they stay?" implies that the victimization occurs because something is wrong with the battered women. In the past, female victims of rape and battery were often treated as though they were the deviants, a reflection of society's overall devaluation of women. In fact, blaming the victim of wife-beating may serve as a justification for the batterer's violence. When women "nag," try to have an equal say in family decisions, go against their partner's wishes, or push or hit first, men may feel they are justified in using force. While women may be equally likely to use some form of physical aggression in partner assault situations, they are several times more likely to be injured than a man.

Victim-blaming may also occur through a mechanism called "intoxicated-victim effects." This perspective is based on the idea that women under the influence of alcohol and other drugs may be seen as "fair game" for male aggression. Many assume that intoxicated women, by violating norms for appropriate female behavior, lose the protection of traditional gender-role norms such as "never hit a women." Loss of this protection can then justify a physically violent response. Similarly, women under the influence of drugs or alcohol may be viewed as sexually

available, and indeed they are more likely to be victims of sexual aggression. However, studies suggesting that males increase their aggression towards women who violate gender-role expectations may not provide a complete explanation of why intoxicated women are at risk for victimization. Kaufman Kantor and Asidgian's (1996) research concludes that alcohol-linked victimizations have more to do with the male partner's drinking and violent inclinations.

Rape is another offense that has been excused by blaming the victim. Research shows that a rape charge tends to be doubted if the victim is lower class, has a reputation for promiscuity, or has a history of drinking, drug use, or psychiatric hospitalization. When women with such characteristics allege rape, their accusations have traditionally been discounted by the criminal justice system. Early studies concluded that the character of the rape victim determines whether or not a reported offense will be prosecuted. More recent reviews of research on victim-blaming and rape support early studies by finding that rape victims who dress in revealing clothing, are regarded as being of questionable character, or are acquainted with their attacker are held more responsible than rape victims who are perceived as more proper and/or who are attacked by a stranger.

Do victims ever share in the responsibility for the harms they experience? A review of homicide literature shows some support for victim-precipitation theory. This is evident in the finding that men killed by partners often have a long history of being the attacker. Research on wife-abuse and rape show that stereotypes can play a significant role in how the crimes are interpreted, but there is little recent research on whether the characteristics of victims might contribute to their victimization. Women growing up in violent families may be more likely to be victimized as adults because they have low self-esteem and have learned that assaults from a loved one are part of intimate relationships. They may also be more likely to engage in mutual assaults with their spouses. Moreover, poor self-esteem and depression may be intensified by denigration and physical abuse by the partner. In such cases, one might want to say that victim characteristics contributed to the probability of victimization while refraining from holding the victim responsible.

Awareness of victim-blaming phenomena is crucial to an understanding of ways in which social values and perception affect interpretations of crime. Innocent victims continue to be blamed for the behavior of their attacker or for contributing to their own violent victimization. *See also* CASE PROCESSING AND GENDER; CRIME VICTIMIZATION; MADONNA/ WHORE DICHOTOMY; VICTIM-FACILITATION THEORY; VICTIMIZATION, FEMINIST PERSPECTIVES ON.

Further Reading: Ryan 1971, *Blaming the Victim;* Whatley 1996, "Victim Characteristics Influencing Attributions of Responsibility to Rape Victims."

Glenda Kaufman Kantor

Victim-Facilitation Theory

Victim-facilitation, or the idea that victims sometimes contribute to their own victimization, has been a controversial concept, especially when applied to crimes such as rape and domestic violence in which women are likely to be the victims. The concept of victim-precipitation was developed as part of a larger effort, started in the 1950s and culminated in the 1970s, to articulate theories that might explain how the characteristics and behaviors of individuals can increase their likelihood of becoming a victim of a crime. Specifically, victim-facilitation refers to "acts of negligence, carelessness, recklessness, and imprudence, which create a temptation or an opportunity situation or make it easier for the potential offender to commit a certain crime" (Fattah: 1991: 297). In a similar vein, Sparks (1981) defines victim-facilitation as deliberate, reckless, or negligent behavior that involves the creation of special risks.

Victim-facilitation is often distinguished from more active behaviors such as victim-precipitation or provocation in which there is direct, face-to-face interaction between the offender and the victim, and the nature of that interaction creates the motive for the crime, as when an insult leads to an assault. Victim-facilitation, in contrast, can occur without face-to-face interactions and does not create the motive for the crime but makes the enactment of the crime easier. Victim-facilitation is also often distinguished from constructs that focus on perceptions of the victim, such as a sense of vulnerability (e.g., on the part of the elderly) or of attractiveness (e.g., on the part of the wealthy) which involve victim characteristics that increase their sense of likelihood of becoming victims. Sparks differentiates vulnerability from facilitation in that "vulnerability does not involve any deviation from standards of due care" (1981:48).

Victim-facilitation theory has not been equally applied to all types of criminal offenses. It has most commonly been applied to property crimes such as auto theft, burglary, and fraud. Failing to lock an automobile and remove the keys is a common example of facilitating behavior. Leaving a house unsecured is also viewed as facilitation. The concept of victim-facilitation has also been applied to violent crimes such as assault, sexual assault, and rape. For example, Fattah (1991) discusses sexual assaults of hitchhikers as involving victim-facilitation through the very act of hitchhiking. Often, the view that a certain type of crime may be facilitated by the victims' behavior is not suggested explicitly but rather implied in the focus on how the victims' behavior differed from that of nonvictims. Thus, while contemporary discussions and studies of sexual assault and rape do not always explicitly suggest victim-facilitation, some nevertheless focus on the behavior of the victim with the implicit assumption that, had the victim behaved differently in the situation, the crime might not have occurred.

While the construct of victim-facilitation is useful in certain crimes, it is also controversial. Because it implies some degree of responsibility for the criminal act, it has been described as victim-blaming. As a result, some argue that it places too much responsibility for crime prevention on the potential victim. Sparks (1981) notes that facilitation is context dependent: behaviors (e.g., failing to lock a car) may be facilitative in certain contexts (e.g., on the street in a large city) but not in others (e.g., on the street in a small town). In addition, behaviors considered facilitative have a probabilistic element to them. That is, victim-facilitation theory does not claim that the behaviors always result in the criminal act; rather, it holds that certain behaviors increase the probability of the criminal act, depending upon other aspects of the context (e.g., the presence of someone motivated to perform the act).

Certain behaviors may increase the probability of victimization so much as to clearly warrant the label facilitative. However, there are other behaviors that increase the probability of certain forms of crime to some degree. In practice, delineating facilitative from nonfacilitative behaviors is very difficult, in part because of the variability and vagueness of standards of due care. Moreover, there is a *post hoc* element to judgments about facilitative behaviors. That is, retrospectively, a behavior may seem facilitative because the evaluator knows that it led to a crime, but the same behavior might not seem facilitative if the crime had not occurred.

In summary, victim-facilitation is a useful construct that calls attention to victim behavior that may make the commission of a crime easier. In contrast to victim-precipitation theory, it does not make the victim responsible for the crime. However, the application of this construct to specific crimes has been marked by conceptual and pragmatic problems. As a result, with a few exceptions, it is difficult to determine the extent to which victim-facilitation is an important element of victimization. *See also* VICTIM-BLAMING AND VICTIM-PRECIPITATION, CONCEPT OF.

Further Reading: Karmen 1984, *Crime Victims;* Schafer 1977, *Victimology.*

Kenneth E. Leonard

Victimization and Manly Rituals, Australia

That men commit most known violence explains the criminological interest in a possible connection between manly rituals and patterns of criminal victimization. Ritual, as an anthropological concept, refers to the cultural production or affirmation of meaning systems that occurs at events or moments imbued with collective symbolism or significance. "Manly rituals" refers specifically to those regularized moments of cultural exchange between groups of men where shared assumptions and values are either reaffirmed or renegotiated. The mundane sites where manly rituals are performed on a daily basis include the pub, the workplace, the football match, and the street corner.

In Australia, over 80 percent of all homicide offenders, and well in excess of 90 percent of those charged with serious assault, robbery, and sexual assault, are men. Violent offenders tend to be young, male, single, and from blue-collar backgrounds.

The most comprehensive study of sexual violence in Australia found that almost 98 percent of known offenders were males, nearly half of whom were aged 18 to 25 and unemployed (Bonney 1985). Young men were more prone to attack in groups than alone, suggesting the importance of peer group rituals in the unleashing of violent inclinations. Most of the victims of sexual violence are young women. Young women aged 16 to 20 are three times more likely to be raped than any other age group of women in the population (Salmelainen and Coumarelos 1993).

While women are the most frequent victims of sexual and domestic violence, overall more men than women are the victims of violence committed by Australian men. Men account for 80 percent of all hospital presentations for intentional injuries (National Committee on Violence 1990:11). Where these injuries occurred reveals much about patterns of victimization and associated manly rituals. Whereas most female victims sustained their injuries in the home, making them primarily the invisible victims of domestic violence, men were more likely to be the victims of intra-male violence that occurs in public places. Sixty percent of the injuries that took place in public occurred at a leisure venue— on the street, at the sports field, at a pub, or at an entertainment outlet. These are places where men feel especially pressured to compete, to rival, and to demonstrate their masculine credentials through their participation in manly rituals such as fighting, brawling, and other risk-taking behavior leading to injury or violence.

The rape and murder of 14-year-old Leigh Leigh at a beach party on the east coast of Australia in November 1989 provides a detailed case study of the relationship between male violence and the rituals commonly associated with the passage from boyhood to manhood in Australian society (Carrington 1998). Leigh Leigh was subject to a series of callous assaults, insults, and sexual assaults, increasing in intensity and committed by a group of boys participating in a ritual to mark the coming-of-age of two local lads. Her attackers were playing out their place in a gender order where the recourse to sexual intimidation and the use of force were considered relatively normal.

Just what makes the passage from boyhood to manhood so dangerous is the subject of considerable controversy. Representatives of the men's movement argue that too few rituals celebrate a young man's entrance into puberty and transition from boyhood to manhood (Biddulph 1997). Frustration, combined with rising levels of the male hormone testosterone, is thought to lead to outbursts of uncontrolled male aggression.

Others argue that there are already too many sites (such as pubs and leisure venues) and rituals (such as football and other contact sports) that celebrate the display of maschismo and brute strength. Young men are pressured into participating in manly rituals that foster either their own victimization (as in intra-male violence) or the victimization of women (as in sexual or domestic violence).

Feminist scholars reject the notion that male violence has its roots in levels of testosterone. Biological accounts of aggression, they argue, provide a basis for understandings of male violence as inevitable. These accounts discourage prevention efforts and encourage tolerance of victimization.

While young men are undoubtedly responsible for the majority of violent crime in society today, this does not mean all young men are violence-prone. The fact that so many young men mature into responsible adults who eschew violence in their interpersonal interactions suggests that the rituals of aggression to which some are drawn in their youth is largely the product of their social environment. Most research also suggests that the perpetrators of violence are concentrated largely (though not entirely) within marginalized populations of the community (National Committee on Violence 1990:35; Deverey 1991). The weight of international research suggests that the prevalence of violent behavior among these cohorts of young men is at least partly due to the instability of masculine ideals being experienced in communities where social and economic change have disrupted established patterns of life (Segal 1990; Connell 1995). *See also* HOMICIDE VICTIMS AND OFFENDERS, AUSTRALIA; VICTIMIZATION, FEMINIST PERSPECTIVES ON; VIOLENT CRIME VICTIMIZATIONS, AUSTRALIA.

Further Reading: Carrington 1998, *Who Killed Leigh Leigh?;* Holland, Ramazanoglu, and Sharpe 1993, *Wimp or Gladiator;* Lees 1997, *Ruling Passions;* National Committee on Violence 1990, *Violence: Directions for Australia.*

Kerry Lynn Carrington

Victimization, Feminist Perspectives on

Theoretical conceptions of the victimization of women and girls have undergone a remarkable transformation since the 1970s. The prefeminist ideas that prevailed from the 1930s through the 1960s constituted an amalgamation of prejudices and unsubstantiated assertions masquerading as scientific truths. These accounts generally emphasized the supposedly unique biological and psychological characteristics of women, such as emotionality, impetuousness, and deceitfulness. Many of these notions explicitly or implicitly reflected Freudian, and more generally psychoanalytic, conceptions of women and girls. Women who were beaten by their husbands were described as unconsciously demanding violence, and girls who reported sexual abuse by their fathers were deemed irrational and prone to illusions, fabrications, and exaggeration. Masochism was enshrined as a feature of normal female sexuality, and as late as the 1970s, some commentators were arguing that girls subjected to sexual abuse and women experiencing violence from their intimate partners were responsible for their own victimization. These notions reinforced the historical legacy of neglect and impunity that characterized criminal justice responses to violence against women and girls.

With the rise of the new discipline of victimology in the 1970s, these ideas were extended to include the immediate circumstances surrounding crime and violence. Victim-precipitation theory, in particular, argued that women provoke rape and physical violence through their provocative verbal ("nagging") and sexual behaviors. According to victim-precipitation theory, women who are raped or sexually assaulted are culpable because they willfully put themselves in vulnerable situations and then did not resist strongly enough. In such accounts, male conceptions of women and girls are dominant. The supposed actions of the female victim are the focus of attention, not the motives, intentions, and actions of male offenders. Denial of women's autonomy and self-determination are integral to these conventional victimological approaches.

An important feature of conventional victimology and criminology has been surveys that attempt to directly assess victims' experiences of victimization, as well as to address a host of other issues, particularly fear of crime and attitudes toward the police. One persistent finding of these investigations is that women, particularly elderly women, are much more likely than men to express fear of crime, although their rates of crime victimization are much lower than those of men. On the basis of such findings, criminologists once again defined women's fears as irrational. More contextually specific and sophisticated forms of research have revealed that women's apprehensions and fears are indeed real and emerge not merely from their public experiences of crime but from a range of untoward, and often damaging, sexual and physical experiences that occur within public and private contexts.

Beginning in the 1970s, feminist analysis and evidence, coupled with community action through the rape crisis center and battered woman movements, challenged the prevailing ideas of culpable victims and "irrational fears." Feminist perspectives emphasized the social, familial, and cultural circumstances that made women susceptible to the predatory abuse and violence of men. Feminists identified male domination, control, and sense of entitlement as central components of the physical and sexual abuse of women. They characterized women subjected to violence as coerced and victimized within the context of male domination, and they argued that when these experiences occur over extended periods of time within intimate relationships, their effects are compounded. This is particularly so, feminists argue, when communities and institutions of the state are unwilling or unable to provide support and protection. Significantly, beginning in the 1970s, feminist scholarship and community work exposed the failure of state institutions to aid female victims and revealed that women and children often experience secondary victimization within the context of criminal justice responses to rape, battering, and child sexual abuse.

While recent analyses of the victimization of women and girls stress the importance of social, institutional, and cultural forces, a few researchers continue to emphasize the contribution of women's supposedly unique psychological traits. According to some commentators, women who are unable to leave violent relationships suffer from "learned helplessness" and a "battered woman syndrome." These ideas, in turn, have been challenged by research revealing that women who suffer from male violence in the home are controlled and restricted not merely by their partners, but also by cultural ideals that hold women responsible for dealing with male violence and by economic forces that make it difficult for them to leave and establish independent lives. Additionally, current criminological perspectives that emphasize routine activities and freely chosen lifestyles risk blaming victims. These approaches appear to suggest that all women need do is change their lifestyles, thus reducing their risks, and they will no longer be subjected to victimization. Again, the focus is on the victim and her attributes rather than on the offender and his motives or the circumstances of women's lives that require them to live and work in situations fraught with the risk of victimization from men. *See also* BATTERED WOMEN AND SELF-DEFENSE, AUSTRALIA; BATTERED WOMEN AND SELF-DEFENSE, CANADA; BATTERED WOMEN AND SELF-DEFENSE, USA; CRIME VICTIMIZATION; DOMESTIC VIOLENCE AGAINST WOMEN, EPIDEMIOLOGY OF; FEAR OF CRIME; LIFESTYLE AND VICTIMIZATION; VICTIM-BLAMING AND VICTIM-PRECIPITATION, CONCEPT OF; VICTIMIZATION AND MANLY RITUALS, AUSTRALIA.

Further Reading: R. E. Dobash and Dobash 1992, *Women, Violence and Social Change;* Stanko 1990, *Everyday Violence;* Walklate 1995b, *Gender and Crime.*

Russell P. Dobash and R. Emerson Dobash

Victimization Patterns, Britain

The available information about the victimization of women in Britain is dominated by information on violence against women. Yet violence is only one form of crime women worry about. According to the 1998 British Crime Survey (BCS), women express higher levels of concern about becoming victims of crime than do men. Furthermore, one of five women reports fear of the theft of her car and of encountering violence. Nearly one in five young women reported feeling in danger of attack from a stranger in the past 12 months (Mirrlees-Black and Allen 1998). Women are more likely than men to say they feel at risk and more likely to curtail their activities to avoid crime. Women are also victims of burglary, purse snatching, and motor vehicle theft. Households at greatest risk in Britain are single-parent households, and these in turn are largely female-headed households.

The emphasis on women's risk of violence at the hands of men has generated a variety of data about victimization; some appear in Figure 14. By far, women are most at risk to violence in Britain from men known to them. For example, official police reports show that women who report rape are likely to know their attacker. One in seven wives reported being raped by their husbands (Painter and Farrington 1998). A 1997 survey in Edinburgh, Scotland, found that nearly 3 of 10 women were made to take part in unwanted sexual activity (A. R. Henderson 1997). In England and Wales, a

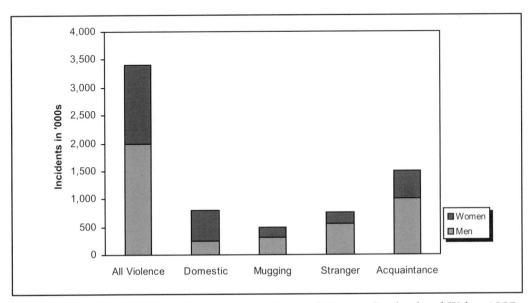

Figure 14. Number of Violent Crimes against Men and Women, England and Wales, 1997
Source: Mirrlees-Black, Budd, Partridge, and Mayhew 1998, "The 1998 British Crime Survey," Fig. 2.5.

recent study showed that 7 out of 8 rape cases involved assailants who were known to the women (Harris and Grace 1999).

Data about domestic violence come from a variety of sources. The 1998 BCS found that domestic violence is the most common form of physical assault against women. Over one-third of the victims of domestic incidents receive medical assistance. The 1996 estimated prevalence of domestic violence for the adult female population in England and Wales was 1 in 9 (Mirrlees-Black 1995), with divorced and separated women most at risk. Police data show that women are also attacked after they leave violent partners.

Prevalence of domestic violence has also been measured by feminist surveys conducted in small local areas. In the most recent study, Stanko and her colleagues (1998) found a prevalence rate for adult women in the London Borough of Hackney to be 1 in 9. In Mooney's (1994) crime survey in the London Borough of Islington, 1 in 8 women reported they had experienced domestic violence in the past year, and 1 in 4 women reported some form of domestic violence over their lifetimes. This finding corresponds to the results of the BCS, which found that among 16- to 59-year-old women, 23 percent said they had experienced an assault from a current or former partner at some time in their lives (Mirrlees-Black 1999). A study of the London Borough of Hammersmith and Fulham (McGibbon, Cooper, and Kelly 1989) found that nearly 40 percent of the respondents had experienced verbal or physical threats from a male partner. Nearly 1 in 5 had been beaten by their partners. Moreover, when women are killed in Britain, they are most likely to be killed by partners or ex-partners.

In general, research suggests that sexual and physical violence is common in the lives of many women in Britain. *See also* DOMESTIC VIOLENCE AGAINST WOMEN, EPIDEMIOLOGY OF; VICTIMIZATION PATTERNS, CANADA; VICTIMIZATION PATTERNS, USA; VICTIMIZATION, REPEAT.

Further Reading: Stanko 1985, *Intimate Intrusions.*

Elizabeth A. Stanko

Victimization Patterns, Canada

National victimization surveys of Canadians, including the first Violence against Women Survey in 1993, are primarily a development of the 1980s. As in other countries, the survey results are mirrored in police-recorded crime statistics and the victimization patterns that emerge from those statistics. Generally, the Canadian victimization surveys indicate that the country's victimization rates are low and stable. The International Crime Victimization Survey, conducted in 1989, 1992, and 1996, when a random sample of persons over 16 years of age in 34 countries were asked about their experience of selected violent and property-related offenses, also revealed relatively low and stable victimization rates in Canada. The 1996 Canadian rate—25 percent of the survey population reported being victimized in the previous year—was close to the average of 24 percent among 11 western, industrialized countries, including the United States (24 percent), and in the lower third of all participating countries. Data on violence against women appear in Figure 15.

Victimization rates in Canada are highly gendered. This gender patterning is most evident in relation to violent crimes over time. The vast majority of people accused of violent crimes are men (nearly 9 in 10 in 1996). Data from nonrandom samples of police agencies in 1996 and 1997 suggest that men are as likely to be victims of violence as are women, but for different offenses. Overall, men are more often the victims of homicide, attempted murder, nonsexual assault, and robbery, whereas women are disproportionately the victims of sex offenses and criminal harassment (i.e., stalking), an offense that was enacted in 1993. For instance, men constituted 88 percent of persons charged with criminal harassment in 1996 and women 80 percent of the victims.

Women and men tend to be victimized by different types of people. Historically in Canada, spouses or other intimates commit most violence against adult women, and acquaintances or strangers commit most violence against adult men. Between 1977 and 1996, for example, 1,525 wives (75 percent

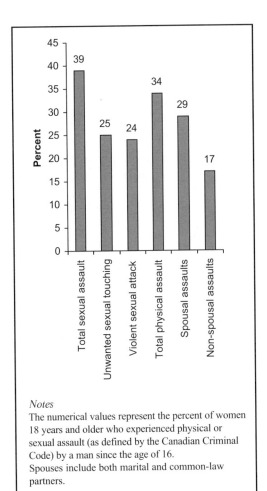

Notes
The numerical values represent the percent of women
18 years and older who experienced physical or
sexual assault (as defined by the Canadian Criminal
Code) by a man since the age of 16.
Spouses include both marital and common-law
partners.

**Figure 15. Violence against Women by
Type of Attack, Canada, 1993**

Source: Statistics Canada, Canadian Centre for Justice
Statistics 1993, *A Graphical Overview.*

and 1996, children under 18 years of age represented 13 percent of all homicide victims in Canada, and 58 percent of child homicides were committed by family members. In 1996, fathers were almost three times more likely than were mothers to kill children, most under the age of 12. From 1991 to 1997, however, women charged with the sex-specific crime of infanticide accounted for approximately 16 percent of homicide victims under the age of one. As well, girls under 18 more frequently are victims of intra-familial assaults than are boys. In 1996, girls constituted 79 percent of sexual and 56 percent of physical assault victims, with male family members accounting for 98 percent of the former crimes and 75 percent of the latter. The number of reported girl victims of intra-familial sexual assault was highest between the ages of 12 and 15; in contrast, most sexual abuse of boys occurred between the ages of 4 and 8. While physical assault increased with age for all children, boys under 13 more often experienced physical assault than did girls of the same age.

Police data indicate that older adults were victims in 2 percent of all violent crimes in 1996. From 1993 to 1996, family members committed about 20 percent of violent crimes against persons 65 years of age or over each year, most commonly physical assaults, which constituted 74 percent of police-recorded crimes against older adults in 1996. Like the patterns for children, trends from 1993 to 1996 show that older women are more likely to be abused by a family member than are older men; more than one in four older female victims were assaulted by a family member, compared with one in seven older males. Older women also are more often abused or killed by a spouse, and older men more often abused or killed by an adult male child.

Overall, victimization patterns for violent crimes in Canada contradict the widespread belief, particularly among women, that people are most at risk of being victimized on the street or in their own homes by strangers. *See also* BATTERED WOMEN AND SELF-DEFENSE, CANADA; VICTIMIZATION, REPEAT.

Further Reading: Gartner and Doob 1994, "Trends in Criminal Victimization"; H. Johnson 1996,

of the total killed spouses) compared with 513 husbands (25 percent) were killed by their partners. Likewise, women represented 89 percent of spousal assault victims in police-recorded crime for 1996. Moreover, women who are separated or are in common-law relationships are much more likely to be assaulted or killed by a spouse than are their male counterparts. In 1996, most criminally harassed women were stalked by ex-husbands, acquaintances, or ex-boyfriends, while the majority of men victims were stalked by acquaintances and relatively few by ex-wives or ex-girlfriends.

Patterns of violence against children and older adults also are gendered. Between 1974

Dangerous Domains; Sacco and Johnson 1990,
Patterns of Criminal Victimization in Canada.

Dorothy E. Chunn

Victimization Patterns, USA

Victimization patterns in the United States differ strongly by sex, as well as by age and race/ethnicity. Thus, although the majority of Americans fear becoming the victim of a crime (according to public opinion polls), there are actually marked differences in people's likelihood of victimization.

Females are less likely than males to become crime victims. For violent crimes, the male victimization rate is 49.9 per 1,000 males in the population, while the female rate is 34.6 per 1,000 females (Bureau of Justice Statistics 1998d).

With regard to age, those with the highest victimization rates are young, between the ages of 12 and 24, a pattern that holds for both violent crimes and property crimes. More specifically, individuals aged 65 and older have a violent crime victimization rate of just 4.9 (per 1,000 people in this age group). As Table R shows, violent crime victimization rates climb steadily for youths. The rate starts at 95.0 for those aged 12–15; it peaks at 102.7 for those in the 16–19 age bracket; it tapers off to 74.3 for those aged 20–24; and thereafter it drops steadily. For property crimes, the victimization rates are highest for those aged 12–19 (711.1), dropping to 380.6 for those aged 20–34, 388.9 for ages 35–49, 252.1 for ages 50–64, and 124.9 for those 65 and older.

Race and ethnicity also affect a person's chances of becoming a crime victim. For violent crimes, the rate of victimization for whites is 40.9, whereas the rates for African Americans and Hispanic Americans are 52.3 and 44.0, respectively. For property crimes, the victimization rate of whites is 272.9, while the rate for African Americans is 322.3, and for Hispanic Americans, 364.1 (Bureau of Justice Statistics 1998d).

In sum, if we look at the intersection of all three variables—sex, age, and race/ethnicity—we find that those most likely to be the victims of a crime are young, non-white

males (see Table R). However, this pattern masks some other important differences in patterns of criminal victimization, especially those between men and women.

Although women have lower rates of violent victimization, they are more likely than men to be the victims of particular types of violent crimes. For example, more than 98 percent of rape victims are females aged 12 and older. More than 81 percent of victims of attempted rape are females aged 12 and older, and females 12 and older make up 88 percent of victims of other types of sexual assault (Bureau of Justice Statistics 1998d). Similarly, women are nearly three times more likely than men to report having been physically abused by their spouse or companion, and almost four times more likely to report having been stalked (Bureau of Justice Statistics 1998d).

Both women and men are most likely to be victimized by a male rather than a female perpetrator. For example, 82.7 percent of victims of violent crimes involving a single perpetrator report that the perpetrator was male. Among victims of violent crimes with multiple perpetrators, 75.5 percent report that all the perpetrators were male, while only 12.9 percent report at least one female perpetrator and just 9.6 percent report being victimized by all female perpetrators (Bureau of Justice Statistics 1997c).

A second important difference in men's and women's criminal victimization patterns is the relationship between the perpetrator and the victim. Women are significantly more likely than men to be victimized by someone with whom they have an intimate relationship. Strangers account for nearly two-thirds of all violent crimes against male victims, whereas strangers account for only about one-third of all violent crimes against female victims. Women are almost three times more likely than men to be violently victimized by a relative (Craven 1996; Bureau of Justice Statistics 1997c). Most women are victimized not on the street, but in their homes or the homes of friends, relatives, and neighbors. Thus, the traditional advice to women who fear victimization—stay at home and keep your doors and windows locked—may do little to protect them.

In examining patterns of criminal victimization, we must also keep in mind that much of what we know comes from government statistics, which at best represent conservative estimates of actual rates of victimization, especially for those crimes of which women are the most common victims. For instance, research indicates women are somewhat more willing to report victimization experiences to survey interviewers than to the police. Nevertheless, many women have difficulty reporting being victims of certain crimes—e.g., sexual assault and domestic violence—to anyone, because they are embarrassed, ashamed, or fear reprisals from perpetrators. Consequently, it is estimated that, in a given year, the actual number of sexual assault, may be over five times higher than the number reported to interviewers for the National Crime Victimization Survey (D. Johnston 1992).

Researchers have found that women's criminal victimization is hidden in other ways as well. For example, criminologists who study corporate offending have not incorporated gender into their analyses. Yet women are frequently victimized by corporate crime and in some cases, such as the faulty Dalkon Shield contraceptive device and silicone breast implants, women are the only victims (Gerber and Weeks 1992; Rynbrandt and Kramer 1995). Similarly, in studies of homicide, differences in victimization by sex are usually included only in discussions of crimes of passion, but various data sources point to other important gender differences in homicide rates. For instance, while women account for only 8 percent of on-the-job deaths, one-third of women who die at work are murder victims compared with less than 15 percent of men who die at work. In fact, homicide is the most frequent cause of on-the-job death for women (U.S. Department of Labor 1997).

Thus, future analyses of victimization patterns should make gender a central independent variable. In addition, researchers need to examine more carefully how gender intersects with other factors, including race/

Table R. Violent Victimization Rates, USA, for Persons Age 12 and Older, by Race and Sex, 1994

Sex, Race, and Age of Victim	Rate of Violent Victimization (per 1,000 persons)
White Males	
12–15 years	135.6
16–19 years	146.0
20–24 years	123.3
25–34 years	65.0
35–49 years	44.5
50–64 years	15.2
65 years and over	5.7
White Females	
12–15 years	88.2
16–19 years	102.4
20–24 years	78.1
25–34 years	57.9
35–49 years	33.6
50–64 years	14.3
65 years and over	2.8
Black Males	
12–15 years	141.6
16–19 years	124.8
20–24 years	71.1
25–34 years	66.9
35–49 years	49.9
50–64 years	28.5
65 years and over	33.7
Black Females	
12–15 years	129.8
16–19 years	109.3
20–24 years	97.5
25–34 years	59.0
35–49 years	40.5
50–64 years	13.5
65 years and over	6.7

Source: Excerpted from Bureau of Justice Statistics 1997b, *Criminal Victimization in the United States, 1994*, page 15.

ethnicity, age, social class, and sexual orientation, if they are to detect variation in patterns of criminal victimization. *See also* DATE RAPE; DOMESTIC VIOLENCE AGAINST WOMEN, EPIDEMIOLOGY OF; ELDERLY VICTIMS; HOMICIDE VICTIMS; INCEST VICTIMS; INFANTICIDE; RAPE RATES; SERIAL KILLERS, VICTIMS OF; SEXUAL

ABUSE OF CHILDREN; STALKING; VICTIMIZATION, REPEAT; VIOLENT CRIME.

Further Reading: Chesney-Lind 1997, *The Female Offender;* Madriz 1997, *Nothing Bad Happens to Good Girls;* S. L. Miller 1998a, *Crime Control and Women.*

Claire M. Renzetti

Victimization, Repeat

Repeat victimization refers to a variety of situations in which an individual is repeatedly victimized by crime. Repeat victimization occurs frequently in the context of domestic violence, but it also has been reported to occur in individuals victimized in childhood by physical or sexual abuse or neglect.

In one study of victimization in the United Kingdom, half of those who were victimized were repeat victims, and they suffered 81 percent of all reported crimes (Walklate 1997). Using findings from the 1996 British Crime Survey of 16- to 59-year-olds (Mirrlees-Black and Byron 1999), this study classified 8.7 percent as chronic victims (three or more assaults during their lifetime) and 10 percent as intermittent victims. Women were more likely to be chronic victims than men, with 12 percent of the women, compared with 5 percent of the men, characterized by chronic victimization.

Another form of repeat victimization, particularly associated with the experiences of women in the context of domestic violence, refers to what have been called *series crime incidents*. A series crime incident is a crime in which a person experiences a number of similar victimization incidents during a given time period but cannot recall the date and details of each incident clearly enough to report it separately. Because spousal abuse sometimes represents a continual state of victimization, domestic assaults fall disproportionately into this type of victimization. In one study, about 20 percent of women victimized by their spouse or ex-spouse reported that they had been the victim of a series of three or more assaults in the last six months (Bachman and Taylor 1994). Repeat victimization of the sort characterized by these series incidents suggests an abusive relationship in which violence is likely to recur and is particularly problematic for women.

Revictimization refers to the phenomenon whereby a person victimized as a child or during adolescence is again victimized at a later point in time. A number of studies have found higher rates of sexual assault in community and college student samples among women who were victims of childhood sexual abuse or incest. Other studies have reported high rates of revictimization in adulthood in psychiatric patients. Someone physically or sexually abused as a child may be at high risk for some form of revictimization or repeat victimization.

Researchers have drawn conclusions about the characteristics of repeat victimizations based primarily on findings from British crime victimization surveys. These conclusions include the following (Farrell 1995; Polvi et al. 1990; Pease and Laycock 1996):

- An individual's past criminal victimization is a good predictor of his or her subsequent victimization, often by the same offender.
- The greater the number of prior victimizations, the higher the likelihood that the victim will experience future crime victimizations.
- Repeat victimization is highest in areas with the highest crime rates.
- If victimization recurs, it tends to do so soon after the prior experience.
- The same perpetrators seem to be responsible for the bulk of repeated offenses against a victim.
- Many factors contribute to an underestimate of the role of repeat victimizations in the general crime problem.

What are some possible explanations for repeat victimization? One theory postulates that offenders assess how easy or difficult it is to victimize an individual and then act on their risk assessment. Applied to the repeat victimization of women, this type of explanation would suggest that offenders perceive women as vulnerable, weak, and easy targets for crime.

A second possible explanation is that the victimization experience itself makes a repeat victimization more likely, especially if the offender has gotten away with the crime the first time. In the case of domestic violence, the perpetrator might perceive that since he was not caught or punished the first time, he can get away with it again. Furthermore, the perpetrator knows his way in and out of the home of the person he has previously victimized, which facilitates the repeat victimization. A third possibility is that in the case of domestic violence, the criminal victimization may reflect a pattern of behavior on the part of the batterer.

Some criminologists have also focused on *lifestyle and routine activity* theories to account for who becomes victimized, and these theories are relevant to repeat victimization as well. The routine activities approach (L. E. Cohen and Felson 1979) postulates that victimization experiences are associated with risk exposure, which is a function of particular lifestyles. There is some evidence that those who frequently go out at night for entertainment are more likely to be victims of violent crimes. One author (Wooley 1993) suggests that situational factors may influence revictimization rates through membership in a family characterized by high rates of violence (physical and sexual assault) or residence in an impoverished or dangerous neighborhood. Findings from the victimization surveys show a general pattern of high risk of crime victimization for groups that live in criminogenic environments and who engage in more risky behaviors on a daily basis.

Alcohol consumption may mediate the association between lifestyle and revictimization experiences. That is, people often drink or do drugs when they go out at night or for recreation, and it may be that substance use, not the risky behaviors, is associated with increased risk for revictimization. Substance abuse may contribute to disinhibited behaviors or impaired judgments that in turn expose one to more potentially risky situations. People who are intoxicated or under the influence of drugs may take fewer precautions to avoid victimization.

Until recently, little was known about repeat victimization, in part because traditional victimization surveys do not adequately count repeats. The effectiveness of prevention, intervention, and support can be improved by identifying the circumstances in which repeat victimization is most likely to occur. For women victims, understanding the principles underlying repeat victimization has led to more focused crime prevention efforts. Future work will tell us more about criminal victimization, the motivation of offenders, and consequences for victims. *See also* DOMESTIC VIOLENCE AGAINST WOMEN, EPIDEMIOLOGY OF; FEAR OF CRIME; LIFESTYLE AND VICTIMIZATION.

Further Reading: Farrell 1995, "Preventing Repeat Victimization"; L. W. Kennedy and Sacco 1998, *Crime Victims in Context.*

Cathy Spatz Widom

Victims, Historical Treatment of

Very little research has been done on the historical treatment of female crime victims. However, the limited existing research suggests that over time and on many continents, female victims have been treated quite differently, socially and legally, from male victims. For instance, in Western countries and at least some Asian nations, when females were victimized, the harm was often devalued by the victims themselves, members of their immediate families, and tribal or state authorities. When a female victim reported a crime, she was frequently disregarded and not taken seriously. A woman's complaint about victimization became an example of the powerless complaining about the powerful. Moreover, it was often assumed that she had played a role in her own victimization; thus the event was viewed as less socially threatening to the community than a male victimization, and sometimes the victim was even punished for allowing herself to be violated.

Examining the historical treatment of victims—and again, only some of the information deals specifically with women—reveals the ebb and flow of victim involvement in the criminal process. Recent trends toward greater victim participation are neither unique nor self-evidently beneficial.

In the West, northern Africa, the Mediterranean, and parts of the Middle East, before rudimentary government structures emerged, individual victims used revenge and retaliation to respond to harms, although this was probably less true for female than male victims. As organized institutions began to emerge in clans and tribes, the responses became more collective, even though (at least in male cases) the victim remained centrally involved. Individual victimization led to blood feuds, vendettas, and genocide. Besides retaliatory (and sometimes preemptive) violence, other responses included spells, exchanges, victim surrogates, and ritual suicides.

As societies developed, reparation began competing with retribution as a response to victimization, at least for crimes against men. In the 1750 BC Code of Hammurabi, reparation made by the offender to the victim was to be mediated by a third party. Restitution was used to settle disputes among the Greeks, the early Hebrews, the Hindus, and the Turks. It was part of the 450 BC Roman Law of the Twelve Tables and the Law of Moses. Reparations initially came in the form of property but evolved into money payments and finally into monetary fines for all offenses—most or all of which would go to victims. Disputes—even violent ones—were treated as torts or civil wrongs, rather than crimes. During the Middle Ages, this evolved into a "composition procedure" where third-party mediators would impose both punishment and compensation. Coupled with the emerging state and church, "crime" (or "sin") became viewed as an attack on society rather than on separate victims, and offenders became individually accountable for their actions.

In many of these early civilizations, females were considered the property of either their fathers or husbands. Consequently, when women were victimized, the damage was viewed as a victimization of the entire family, not so much of the woman herself. For example, the rape of a married woman was considered a disgrace to her father and infringement on the property rights of her spouse. A husband was exempt from prosecution for marital rape because he was considered entitled to sexual relations with his wife. Rape of an unmarried woman destroyed her value as a bride and sexual partner, and as a result, she might be sent away to fend for herself. In some cases, rape victims were expected to commit suicide, since their value to men had been ruined.

Medieval revenge was increasingly coopted by state power to promote dominant social and economic interests. Upper classes used the law to control the lower classes, who were increasingly limited in their recourse for crimes. Women's victimization was treated even more lightly: obvious harms against them were often not even defined as criminal.

The rise of monarchs further bolstered the state's role in criminal justice. In Europe, kings began taking part or all of victims' compensations as fines. (Whether this was the same for male and female victims, we do not know.) Fines gained increasing importance and eventually replaced restitution altogether. The combined civil/criminal process split into two parts, allowing most victims to bring actions against their offenders only in civil proceedings. By the end of the Middle Ages, the victim's role in the criminal process had substantially declined.

In less developed societies, the victim role survived somewhat longer. In the American Colonial period, for example, victims sometimes acted as police or prosecutors themselves or paid others to do so. Colonial law allowed victims—at least male victims—to collect damages from offenders, and wealthier victims could bind offenders into servitude. Yet soon community control proved inadequate and new laws and a greater state role emerged. Although laws created rewards for finding and convicting offenders, crime became a government activity and restitution was abandoned by the early 1800s. Criminal justice had become a means to promote social order, and punishment was calculated by the harm done to society, not to the victim.

In early U.S. history, criminal law was often used to protect propertied interests and to maintain order against organized opposition. Victims participated much less because the system no longer served them. Public police and prosecutors replaced private ones as the state's interest in punishments and fines increased. Thus, public officers rather than victims decided whom to arrest and prosecute, and reparations could be sought only in expensive civil suits against imprisoned and impoverished offenders.

In 1957, the English social reformer, Margery Fry, campaigned for state victim compensation, with the first such program established in 1963 in New Zealand, followed by England and California in 1964. In the U.S., growing support for victims coincided with the conservative backlash against U.S. Supreme Court criminal justice decisions that opponents believed "handcuffed the police." In response, law-and-order campaigns—beginning with President Richard Nixon's administration in the late 1960s—began strengthening law enforcement and state control, if not necessarily benefiting victims. Growing agitation by feminists increased the attention paid to victims. In 1972, Minnesota created the first modern restitution program, encouraging offenders to empathize with and repay victims. But this progress was short-lived. By 1975, with the formation of the National Organization for Victim Assistance (which would become the U.S.'s leading victim advocacy organization), the victim movement had been substantially seduced by America's increasingly conservative politics and by a perspective that equated progress for victims with restrictions on rights for the accused.

Two movements struggled against this trend in the 1970s. While the "official" victim movement was generating mostly symbolic victim policies, the women's movement was providing the most successful victim programs by challenging rather than collaborating with conventional criminal justice. The women's movement significantly improved the credibility of reports of female victimization and the status of female victims, especially victims of rape and domestic violence. And in the late 1970s, a human rights movement emerged that began again to broaden concepts of victimization beyond individual crimes—often indicting the very states upon which victims were increasingly relying for assistance.

The impact of these movements was undermined, however, when a new offensive for victims began in 1982 as a result of President Ronald Reagan's Task Force on the Victims of Crime. It triggered a proliferation of state and national victim legislation. In 1984, Congress provided subsidies for victim compensation and assistance through the Victims of Crime Act and in 1987 the National Victims Resource Center was opened. New programs promoted victim services, victim bills of rights, and increased victim involvement in the criminal justice process.

Yet this apparent new era of victim concern and involvement may have been more symbolic than tangible for most victims. Programs have received far less funding and delivered far fewer services to victims than many had hoped. Victim participation has not increased, partly because any greater involvement conflicts with criminal justice objectives. Indeed, new victim policies may have done more to enhance state power than to serve victim needs. Offender rights have declined, and punishments have dramatically increased.

To achieve any substantial decline in victimization or increase in victim involvement, the victim movement may need to abandon law-and-order strategies and constricted definitions of victimization. Reminiscent of earlier approaches, the victim movement might be more successful challenging rather than collaborating with state officials. For example, in 1985, the United Nations adopted a declaration that linked the victims of crime to the victims of state abuses of power. The implications would be profound if crime victims began viewing governments not as the cure for victimization but rather the cause. This would shift the victim movement's focus from offenders to political and economic institutions that might be responsible for generating crime and victimization in the first place. *See also* CRIME VICTIMS AND DEFINITIONS OF JUSTICE; MEDIATION PROGRAMS; SHELTER MOVEMENT; VICTIM COMPENSATION; VICTIM SERVICES.

Further Reading: Elias 1993, *Victims Still;* Karmen 1996, *Crime Victims;* H. Wallace 1998, *Victimology.*

Robert Elias

Victims in Court

In court, women crime victims have traditionally been treated in a manner that some have labeled "secondary victimization." The conception of crime underlying the U.S. criminal justice system is that crime is an offense against society. Crime victims most often serve as complainants who initiate proceedings against a perpetrator in the state's name. In court, victims are represented by a prosecutor, and their role is usually limited to being merely a witness. Victims have neither voice in the trial of their offender nor control over the process. For both women and men, the result has been victim frustration with—and alienation from—the system.

Women reach court most commonly as victims of violence, particularly sexual assaults and woman-battering or domestic violence. In addition to the hardships experienced by all crime victims in court, women suffer additional gender-related disadvantages. Tendencies of court officials (judges, prosecutors, and defense attorneys) to minimize the harm or the danger to victims of violence against women, to apply gender-role stereotypes to the dynamics that resulted in violence, to dismiss the violence as a private matter rather than a public concern, and to blame women for their victimization have been common experiences of women in court. Proceedings historically depersonalized and devalued women victims, and court officials discredited women's credibility as witnesses, transforming the trial of the defendant into an examination of the morality and character of the victim.

Recent efforts by victims and feminist activists to remedy secondary victimization by the courts have led to improved procedures and services to meet victims' financial, psychological, legal, and social needs. They include notification about proceedings, counseling, input rights at sentencing in the form of victim impact statements, restitution from the offender, and compensation from the state.

Over the last two decades, laws regarding the processing of violence against women in the courts have undergone radical reforms. Legislative efforts aimed at reducing gender bias in court and sensitizing the criminal justice system to the unequal treatment accorded female victims has included changes in substantive law and procedure. Definitions of rape have been expanded to include a variety of sexual acts hinging on the consent of the victim. Rape-shield laws were enacted to prevent attacks on the character of victims and witnesses' characters, and inappropriate questioning of victims about their past sexual behaviors. Spousal exemption laws, which excluded husbands from the definition of rape, have been eliminated, and marriage is no longer a legal license to rape. Special domestic violence laws provide women with protection orders, and no-drop policies allow prosecutors to proceed with a case without the cooperation of the victim. Courts now allow some women who kill partners to raise, in self-defense, a history of having been battered.

Yet women victims still experience unequal and denigratory treatment in courts. The conviction rate in rape cases has remained relatively low, and consent is interpreted in a way that leaves many unwilling victims outside the definition of rape. Charges of rape against husbands are still met with distrust by prosecutors and juries, and unless the assault has been accompanied by serious injury in these cases, the woman complainant is not likely to be recognized as a victim of rape.

Although significant changes have been legislated in the area of domestic violence, implementation has not been sensitive to the plight of battered women. Court officials still exhibit a lack of understanding of the reasons women may be unable to extricate themselves from abusive relationships: women's economic and emotional dependence on their batterer, lack of community and familial support for victims, and fear of future violence from the batterers. Reforms intended to benefit victims of domestic violence, such as no-drop prosecution policies, may actually disempower women, making them feel a further lack of control over their own lives.

Ultimately, proposed and enacted changes in the courts regarding female victims have not shifted the focus to punishing offenders but have remained firmly entrenched in stereotypes and assumptions that blame women for their victimizations. *See also* BATTERED WOMEN AND SELF-DEFENSE, USA; CRIME VICTIMS AND DEFINITIONS OF JUSTICE; DOMESTIC VIOLENCE CASE PROCESSING; PROTECTION ORDERS; RAPE LAWS AND SPOUSAL EXEMPTIONS; RAPE SHIELD LAWS, USA; VICTIM-BLAMING AND VICTIM-PRECIPITATION, CONCEPT OF; VICTIM COMPENSATION; VICTIM IMPACT STATEMENTS; VICTIMS, HISTORICAL TREATMENT OF.

Further Reading: Buzawa and Buzawa 1996, *Domestic Violence;* Erez 1994, "Victim Participation in Sentencing"; LaFree 1989, *Rape and Criminal Justice.*

Edna Erez and Carol Gregory

Violent Crime

Females have committed violent crime throughout the ages, although perspectives explaining their participation have varied greatly. Violent crime consists predominantly of homicide, assault, and robbery. Female-perpetrated homicide is the most documented of women's violent crimes. Other violent crimes such as kidnapping, terrorism, rape, and other forms of sexual assault are much less prevalent among women. While female-perpetrated violent crime represents but a small percentage of all violent crime, the very notion that females would engage in such acts has been counterintuitive to society's perception of women as nurturers and caretakers. As a result, when females do commit violent crime, their personalities are often subjected to minute scrutiny.

Typically, violent crime is characterized as either domestic or extra-familial in nature. But when this classification is imposed on our understanding of violence by women, it creates an artificial dichotomy. The earliest attempts at understanding why such acts occur classified violent women as either crazy or criminal—"mad" or "bad." More recently, another categorical layer has been introduced with the distinction between instrumental (means-to-an-end) and expressive (heat-of-passion) violent crimes. Most females are portrayed as committing expressive crimes, an explanatory perspective rooted in stereotypes about biology ("her hormones made her do it") and gender roles ("pent-up aggression led her to commit violence").

Unless serious injury occurs, intra-familial violent acts by women often are taken as signs of mental health problems. Thus, the female is "mad." Violent acts committed against family members have been considered either expressive (anger toward intimates and children) or, when they are responses to battering, as retaliatory or self-defensive. When women kill or physically assault infants and children, their behavior is usually interpreted as a sign of severe mental illness or of carrying discipline too far.

In the last few decades, the perception of the "bad" female has evolved to explain extra-familial participation in violent street crimes. These are usually robberies, simple or aggravated assaults, and (less frequently) homicides, crimes in which black females are markedly overrepresented. Some criminologists explain female participation in violent street crime involving friends, acquaintances, and strangers by arguing that women are becoming more like men in their aggressive interactions and economic endeavors. Others have suggested female participation as part of a lifestyle that includes involvement in drug markets and drug addiciton. They view these crimes as instrumental in nature.

Recent research indicates that the majority of female violent crime offenders may have histories of physical and/or sexual victimization. Current research is investigating linkages between psychologically traumatic victimization, substance abuse, and participation in violent crime by females. It suggests that any dichotomization of violent crime by females obscures the complexity of their violent acts. *See also* DOMESTIC VIOLENCE BY WOMEN; GENDER AND CRIME; INFANTICIDE;

LESBIAN PARTNER BATTERING; LIFESTYLE AND VICTIMIZATION.

Further Reading: Baskin and Sommers 1993, "Females' Initiation into Violent Street Crime"; Brownstein, Spunt, Crimmins, and Langley 1994, "Changing Patterns of Lethal Violence by Women."

Susan Crimmins

Violent Crime Victimizations, Australia

Violent crime victimizations in Australia resemble those of other countries in terms of specific crime types but form distinctive patterns when taken as a whole. While there are always difficulties in making definitive comparisons among countries on the basis of official statistics, Australia seems to fall in the middle-to-low range when it comes to homicide levels, its rate being considerably lower than that of the high-homicide-rate countries such as Mexico and the United States, but slightly higher than that of the low-homicide countries such as England and Japan (James and Carcach 1997). On the other hand, the picture with respect to assault and sexual assault is rather different, with the levels of these forms of violence being as high as those found in the United States, and roughly on par with the recent increases that have raised the level of these forms of violence in England and Wales (Mukherjee, Cook, and Leverett 1998, compared with Langan and Farrington 1998).

Statistics based on crimes reported to police by victims across Australia indicate that for women and men, the highest rate of victimization involves assaults (see Table S). The highest assault rates in 1997 for both men and women were experienced by those aged 20–24 years. Females were more likely than males to have been assaulted by someone known to them.

Police records of victims' reported crime indicate that men's victimization rates are higher than women's for all offenses except sexual assault (see Table S). In 1997, females represented 79 percent of sexual assault victims, and almost half of the victims were females aged under 20 years. Male children

Table S. Rate (per 100,000 Population) of Victimization in Australia: Crimes Recorded by Police, 1997

Offense Category	Males	Females	Total
Murder	2.21	1.26	1.74
Attempted Murder	2.50	0.91	1.72
Manslaughter	0.30	0.11	0.21
Assault	771.12	522.73	688.78
Sexual Assault	28.13	119.78	76.29
Kidnapping/ Abduction	2.05	3.74	3.01
Armed Robbery	35.59	16.83	27.34
Unarmed Robbery	69.82	46.68	59.77
Blackmail/ Extortion	2.04	0.84	1.47

Source: Australian Bureau of Statistics 1998b, *Recorded Crime, Australia, 1997.*

aged 0–9 represented the highest proportion of male sexual assault victims, accounting for about 6 percent of the total victims. The offender in both male and female cases was most commonly a non–family member known to the victim.

Problems with using police statistics as a measure of women's victimization have been well documented. Thus it is useful to turn to an Australian Bureau of Statistics survey of Australian women conducted in 1996 for additional information (McLennan 1996). In the previous 12 months, 7.1 percent of Australian women had experienced some form of violence. Most of that violence was committed by a male perpetrator. More specifically, 4.9 percent of women had experienced a form of physical violence, and 1.9 percent had experienced sexual violence at the hands of a male perpetrator. Almost half of the women who had been physically assaulted by a man sustained physical injuries in the last incident, with the most common injuries being bruises, cuts, and scratches.

The survey also asked victims about violence in their lifetime. Since the age of 15, over one-third (38 percent) of the women had experienced one or more incidents of violence, with 33 percent experiencing physical violence and 18 percent experiencing sexual violence (McLennan 1996:12–13).

What these patterns suggest, overall, is that while lethal violence in Australia has been relatively low, possibly due to rigorous forms of gun control, other types of violence are high enough to be of concern to policymakers. Although the patterns of victimization vary across the age span and by gender, there tend to be persistently high levels of offending on the part of males. In Australia, as in countries such as the United States and England, much more work is needed to uncover the factors that produce this distinctively masculine violence, and to describe in more detail the forms that it takes. *See also* HOMICIDE VICTIMS AND OFFENDERS, AUSTRALIA; HOMICIDE, FILIPINO WOMEN IN AUSTRALIA AS VICTIMS OF; VICTIMIZATION AND MANLY RITUALS, AUSTRALIA.

Further Reading: McLennan 1996, *Women's Safety in Australia;* Mukherjee, Cook, and Leverett 1998, *Australian Crime: Facts and Figures 1998.*

Kenneth Polk

W

White-Collar Crime

The term "white-collar crime" was coined by sociologist Edwin H. Sutherland (1940) to refer to violations of the law committed by persons in the course of high-status occupations. It now encompasses a wide variety of offenses, not all of them committed by people holding high positions. White-collar crimes are typically economic in nature and include such offenses as embezzlement, bank and insurance fraud, crimes against the environment, antitrust and securities violations, bribe-giving, and tax evasion.

Women traditionally have had very little involvement in white-collar crime. According to some criminologists, this has been due to women's place in the employment world. With women's increasing career opportunities, some predicted, gender differences in white-collar offending would become much smaller.

Currently available data suggest that women are, indeed, being arrested more for what are presumed to be white-collar offenses, particularly embezzlement and fraud. However, studies also indicate that women's crimes of this type are less serious than those of men, involving less harm and providing smaller gain. Furthermore, with a few well-publicized exceptions, women who commit white-collar offenses rarely are at the top of a corporate hierarchy. Women convicted of bank fraud, for example, tend to be tellers or clerks rather than bank managers or officers.

Criminologists also have found interesting differences in the motives of women and men convicted of white-collar offenses. Although women and men do share motives, women are more likely than men to commit their crimes to improve their family's economic status, fulfill a care-taking role, or maintain a love relationship. They are less likely than men to commit their crimes to advance their career or to obtain some long-desired status symbol (Daly 1989c; Zietz 1981).

Some research has suggested that women are less likely than men to be sentenced to prison for the same white-collar offenses (e.g., Weisburd et al. 1991). When lighter sentences do occur, they may be due to the small profit associated with women's crimes, shortages in prison space for women, and/or their responsibility for dependent children.

Any conclusions about women and white-collar crime must be tempered by the fact that statistics, particularly official statistics, can be misleading. Many white-collar crimes, if detected, are never reported to official agencies. When statistics are available, they often do not provide valid information on white-collar crime. Fraud and embezzlement, for example, are not necessarily committed by persons of high occupational status. Forgery may or may not be classified as a white-collar crime.

Studies that try to disentangle the types of offenses, the extent of harm, and the motives and characteristics of offenders are particularly helpful. Thus far, these studies indicate that white-collar offenses committed by women are fewer and bring less financial gain than those committed by men. Women also are more likely to commit their crimes alone and to be motivated by family-related financial needs rather than personal needs. Finally, there is little indication that increased opportunities for women in the corporate world have been accompanied by comparable increases in their white-collar offending. *See also* FEMALE CRIME, PATTERNS AND TRENDS IN, USA; GENDER AND CRIME; PROPERTY CRIME.

Further Reading: Albanese 1995, *White Collar Crime in America;* J. W. Coleman 1998, *The Criminal Elite;* Daly 1989c, "Gender and Varieties of White Collar Crime."

Anne M. Bartol

Witches

Witches are said to use the supernatural for the purpose of controlling aspects of the natural world. Because modern criminologists and historians do not believe witchcraft is possible, they study the beliefs of witches, beliefs about witches, and the judicial persecution of alleged witches, most of whom were women.

The belief that humans can manipulate supernatural forces can be found in many cultures. However, the image of the witch as exclusively evil and almost always female arises mainly in the Christian West. In Europe, millions of people were accused of witchcraft over the course of several centuries; 80 percent of them, or more, were women. Joan of Arc, burned at the stake in 1431, is the best-known victim of the European witchcraft persecutions. Though witch hunts occurred sporadically in earlier centuries, they intensified in Europe at the end of the fifteenth century. The major European witch-hunting craze lasted from 1560 to 1660, waning as demonology was replaced by more rationalistic explanations of evil.

In the American colonies, witch hunts lasted from the mid-seventeenth to the early eighteenth century, during which time several hundred people were accused of practicing witchcraft and at least 36 were executed. Of the accused, 80–95 percent were

Witchcraft investigation at Salem, Massachusetts. Courtesy of the Library of Congress, LC-USZ62-24187.

women. Most of these women were middle-aged and unmarried; many were midwives.

The largest and best-known Colonial witchcraft persecutions, in Salem, Massachusetts, in 1692, also signaled the demise of traditional beliefs about witchcraft in New England. By the time the last Colonial witch was accused (Connecticut, 1724), courts had come to believe that the accusers were mentally ill.

Beliefs about witchcraft took slightly different forms in Europe and America. In Europe, the Catholic Church defined witchcraft to include such practices as "keeping the devil's sabbath" and sexual relations with the devil. Women in Europe "confessed" to such offenses under torture. In Colonial America, on the other hand, prosecutors tended to believe that witches practiced maleficium (causing harm to people, animals, and other objects) and that they could perform such feats as raising storms at sea, making animals go wild, and walking in the rain without getting wet. Furthermore, New World witches were thought to have made a pact with the devil, thus becoming both heretics and traitors.

Explanations of beliefs about witchcraft and the attendant persecutions vary, although all must take into account the heavily female composition of the accused. Some scholars believe that a fear of female sexuality was the basis for witchcraft persecutions, especially in Europe, where ideas about witches were constructed by a celibate male clergy and included sadomasochistic erotic fantasies. Another explanation of European witchcraft suggests that the persecutions were an attempt by the Catholic Church to eradicate a rival, goddess-centered religion. Because many of the accused, in both Europe and America, were midwives and folk healers, some attribute the persecutions to an attempt to ensure male control of medicine, especially gynecology. Finally, because witch hunts typically occured during times of change in social structure, some scholars suggest that they served to reaffirm male dominance in fluid or new situations.

During the Renaissance, as feudalism was replaced by mercantile capitalism, the accompanying rise of individualism might have given new power to women. Instead, due to the witch hunts, women lost some of the power they had during the Medieval period. In Colonial America, where Puritans believed that individuals could directly communicate with God, the absence of a male intermediary priest might have empowered women. Indeed, Anne Hutchinson, a religious woman banished from the Massachusetts Bay Colony for heresy, felt so empowered and consequently threatened male rule. Witch hunts may have served to counter this sort of threat.

In both Europe and America, witch persecutions met threats to patriarchal control by the reaffirmation of a male god, a male priesthood, and male control of the natural world. See also GENDER AND CRIME.

Further Reading: M. Daly 1978, Gyn/Ecology; Karlsen 1987, The Devil in the Shape of a Woman; N. K. Wilson 1999, "Taming Women and Nature."

Nanci Koser Wilson

Women Corrections Officers in Men's Prisons

Women have been employed as administrators and matrons in penal institutions since the early nineteenth century, but it was not until the 1970s that they were permitted to work as corrections officers in men's prisons. A number of factors contributed to this change. One was the demand by women for increased job and promotional opportunities in corrections, and for better pay and higher job status. Another was the passage in 1972 of amendments to the 1964 Civil Rights Act that prohibited state, county, and local governments from employment discrimination based on gender.

During the mid-1970s, women used the act and its amendments to force administrators in men's prisons to hire them. Administrators who refused could be sued in court for gender discrimination. Considerable progress was made as courts nationwide generally supported the employment rights of women over the various objections of corrections officials. Even the U.S. Supreme Court's decision in *Dothard v. Rawlinson* (1977) could not halt the momentum. In this case, the Court upheld Alabama's policy of gender discrimination based on the belief that the presence of women corrections officers in a maximum-security men's prison threatened their own and the institution's security. The significance of the *Dothard* decision is not in its impact on the lower courts—which all but ignored the ruling and continued to support the employment rights of women—but in the outdated attitudes toward women expressed by the Supreme Court justices.

Other legal challenges over the last two decades focused on the deployment of women officers in men's prisons. Various states' corrections departments, as well as male inmates, charged that the assignment of women officers to strip-search or pat-search inmates, and to supervise inmates in shower, toilet, or dressing areas, violated inmate privacy rights. These cases were often resolved by the courts ordering prison officials to make changes in institutional policies or physical structures (i.e., to install translucent shower curtains) to accommodate the presence of women and balance their employment rights with inmate privacy needs.

Today, more than 80 percent of the women corrections officers currently employed in U.S. adult correctional institutions work in men's prisons. However, women still represent only a small proportion of the nation's total corrections officers force. As of January 1, 1997, only 20.6 percent of the 206,377 corrections officers working in U.S. adult (male and female) correctional institutions were female.

Some observers suggest that the reason that so few women are employed as corrections officers is that they are simply not attracted to the job because of the nature of the work, the clientele, and the physical work environment. Others believe that gender discrimination still exists in corrections systems' hiring and employment practices. Still others postulate that the inhospitable work environment that greets women in men's pris-

ons deters many from applying or drives them from the job.

The job performed by corrections officers is a difficult one, regardless of gender. But for women, the difficulties are compounded by the fact that they are working in a nontraditional occupation where they are in the minority and where male co-workers, supervisors, and administrators may resent their presence. Women corrections officers are highly visible within the prison. Their every action is closely watched, discussed, and critiqued. Their mistakes are taken as evidence of their individual inability, as well as of all women's inability, to perform the job. Those who perform effectively are viewed as an exception rather than the rule.

Male co-workers who believe women lack the physical and psychological strength to perform the job, and who may unconsciously fear that the presence of women reduces the masculine image of the job, subject them to all forms of sexual harassment. Women officers are often the victims of rumors and innuendoes, name-calling, joking, and teasing. Because they are viewed as outsiders by their male co-workers, they are also not allowed into the informal corrections officer clique or subculture. This subculture is vital in helping officers adapt to and survive the hardships of the prison work environment.

Paternalistic supervisors who feel the need to protect the women assign them to positions where they have limited contact with inmates. These assignments deprive women of opportunities to learn all aspects of the job, to gain confidence in their abilities to work with inmates, and to attain the experience necessary for promotion. Such assignments also increase the hostility of male co-workers, who may conclude that the women are getting the more comfortable and less-demanding jobs.

Male inmates are less hostile to, and more accepting of, women corrections officers than are the women's male co-workers and supervisors. At best, male inmates perceive the women as "softening" the harshness of the men's prison and making it a more livable and normal environment. At worst, women officers are viewed as no different from male "screws." Like male officers, women officers are subjected to an initial hazing process by inmates, one that in the women's case includes flirting, sexual propositions, whistling, and so forth. Once a woman proves her ability to perform the job, these types of behaviors taper off.

Despite the unique challenges faced by women corrections officers in men's prisons, research suggests that they do not greatly differ from male co-workers in terms of their evaluations of work conditions, their adjustment to the work, their levels of job satisfaction, their attitudes toward inmates, and their work styles. Also, no substantial differences have been found between female and male officers in evaluations of their performance, numbers of accommodations or reprimands, and amount of sick leave used. However, differences have been detected in work-related stress levels, assault rates, and attrition rates. Women corrections officers are more likely to suffer from higher levels of work-related stress, less likely to be assaulted by inmates, and more likely to resign. It should be noted, however, that the number of comparative studies on women and male corrections officers in men's prisons is limited and that these findings are based on studies of relatively small groups of officers. *See also* CORRECTIONS OFFICERS, HISTORY OF; WOMEN PROFESSIONALS IN THE JUSTICE WORKPLACE.

Further Reading: S. E. Martin and Jurik 1996, *Doing Justice, Doing Gender;* Morton 1991, *Change, Challenge and Choices;* Zimmer 1986, *Women Guarding Men.*

Linda L. Zupan

Women in Prison, Australia

As the indigenous or Aboriginal peoples of Australia had no prisons prior to European invasion in 1788, the first women prisoners in Australia were convict women transported from Britain to serve their sentences in the colony at Sydney Cove. From the earliest days, women prisoners were viewed with particular distaste and were considered more fallen and polluted than their male counterparts, an attitude that has persisted into the present.

Contemporary issues of concern in relation to women in prison in Australia include the large overrepresentation of Indigenous women in prison; the increases in numbers, rates, and proportions of women in prison since the early 1980s; discrepancies in rates of women in prison among various state/territory jurisdictions; the number of women in prison with a drug addiction; and the lack of services for women upon release.

In 1998 there were 1,100 sentenced women in Australian prisons and 180 unsentenced women in prisons awaiting a court hearing, sentencing, or deportation. The overall rate of women's imprisonment was 15.3 per 100,000 of the adult population. The rate for indigenous women was significantly higher at 200 per 100,000 of the adult indigenous population. The number of women as a proportion of the total prison population rose from 2.6 percent in 1977 to 5.7 percent in 1997. Sixty percent of women are serving sentences of under one year. Various forms of theft, robbery, and drug offenses account for more than half of the offense types for which women have been convicted.

It is estimated that over 80 percent of women in prison in Australia are addicted to alcohol, a prescription drug, and/or an illegal drug. Women prisoners are drawn overwhelmingly from the most disadvantaged groups and communities. The majority have not finished high school and were unemployed at the time of arrest.

There is ongoing debate regarding the harmfulness of putting women who have a drug addiction and/or who pose no threat to the community in prison rather than assigning them to nonprison options. A parliamentary team, the New South Wales Government Legislative Council Standing Committee on Social Issues, reported in 1997 that only a fraction of the women in New South Wales prisons needed to be there for society's safety.

In 1998, there were 230 indigenous Australian women in prison, an increase of 100 in just five years. Indigenous women in prison are younger than other women prisoners and are more likely to have served a previous prison sentence. The much higher rate of imprisonment of indigenous women has been attributed to a number of factors including the massive social and economic disadvantage they have experienced since 1788, indigenous peoples' separation from their land, and systematic colonial attempts to destroy their communities and cultures. It is estimated that more than half of the indigenous women in prison are part of "the stolen generations" (indigenous children removed from their families because they were indigenous) or children of the stolen generations.

Australian prisons are operated at the state/territory level, and thus there are eight different prison departments. There are also nine different criminal codes, one for each state and territory and one federal. Consequently, a woman may be convicted and sentenced to prison for an act deemed an imprisonable offense in one state but not another. In the Northern Territory, mandatory sentencing laws result in women being imprisoned for a first stealing offense, no matter how minor, whereas in most other states this would not carry a prison sentence.

States and territories vary significantly in their rates of female imprisonment. Victoria has a rate of 8.4 per 100,000 while New South Wales, very similar demographically, has a rate of 19.7. Rates for other jurisdictions range from 33.8 for the Northern Territory to 2.8 for Tasmania. While differences in criminal codes account for a fair proportion of these discrepancies, the use of nonprison sentences and the granting of more bail applications in jurisdictions like Victoria add to lower rates. The imprisonment rate of indigenous women is consistently high across the states, but there is also significant state/territory variation. For example, South Australia has an imprisonment rate of 401 per 100,000 adult indigenous people, whereas the Northern Territory (with a very high indigenous population) has a rate of 75.

Most jurisdictions have mothers-and-babies policies whereby infants of imprisoned mothers can live with their mothers during their first few years if the woman has a low security classification. All jurisdictions have work and training programs, but as most women are in prison on short sentences, these programs are of little help for the majority.

Women have different needs and post-release problems than males. However, the relatively small number of incarcerated women is used to argue that it is economically inefficient to provide services specifically for women. Despite a low security classification, insufficient resources mean women are sometimes held in higher security units than necessary. Post-release services specifically for women are scarce. Although there are small, poorly funded nongovernment post-release organizations in most states, very few of them have specialist services for women. Counseling, accommodation, and drug rehabilitation programs for women are also scarce. *See also* ABORIGINAL WOMEN AND CRIME, AUSTRALIA; FEMALE CRIME IN AUSTRALIA; PRIVATE PRISONS, AUSTRALIA; PUNISHMENT, AUSTRALIA.

Further Reading: Easteal 1992, *The Forgotten Few;* Hampton 1993, *Prisons and Women.*

Eileen Baldry

Women in Prison, Canada

Women sentenced to prison in Canada enter a two-tiered correctional system in which persons serving terms of two years or more fall under the federal Corrections and Conditional Release Act (CCRA), while those sentenced to less than two years are under the jurisdiction of provincial or territorial correctional authorities. In 1997–98, women constituted 5 percent of the 4,412 admissions to federal custody in Canada and 9 percent of the 98,646 admissions to provincial or territorial custody, proportions that have remained stable through the 1990s. Aboriginal and other visible minority women are overrepresented in prison; for example, 22 percent of the approximately 360 federally sentenced women in 1997–98 were Aboriginal, although Aboriginal women make up only 2 percent of the Canadian population.

A "one-day snapshot" of incarcerated adults in 1996 revealed that women prisoners also are disproportionately young; more than 40 percent were 25 to 34 years of age, though this group constitutes only 21 percent of the adult female population in Canada. On snapshot day, 64 percent of women in federal facilities and 28 percent of those in provincial/territorial institutions had been convicted of crimes against the person, as shown in Table T. The largest proportion of federally sentenced women (37 percent) were imprisoned for homicide or attempted murder and the second largest (27 percent) for drug offenses. In provincial/territorial institutions, the largest percentages of women had been convicted of theft and "other," nonviolent offenses respectively (13 percent each).

Historically, women in prison have been disadvantaged relative to men. They have been subjected to more intrusive forms of psycho-medical intervention and have been given fewer programs and other resources on the grounds that they are "too few to count." Reformers have worked hard to improve conditions for women prisoners in Canada, however, and during the 1990s, two issues generated considerable political activity by the Canadian Association of Elizabeth Fry Societies (CAEFS) and other groups.

The first of these issues grew out of a highly publicized assault in 1994 by the Institutional Emergency Response Team from Kingston Penitentiary against protesting prisoners at the Kingston Prison for Women (P4W), where about half of the more than 300 federally sentenced women were then interned. Madam Justice Louise Arbour subsequently headed a Commission of Inquiry that reviewed the policies of the Correctional Service of Canada (CSC) vis-à-vis federally sentenced women, as well as the specific events surrounding the stripping and shackling of women prisoners by male guards, the involuntary and illegal transfer of most of the women protestors to Kingston Penitentiary (a men's prison), and the subsequent illegal segregation of those women for approximately nine months at the P4W.

The *Arbour Report* (Canada, Commission on Inquiry into Certain Events 1996) provided a scathing indictment of both the CSC and Canada's historical treatment of women prisoners, which it described as involving a combination of stereotypical views of women, neglect, "outright barbarism," and "well-meaning paternalism" (1996:239). It chronicled

Table T. Women and Men in Prison, Canada, by Offense Type, 1996

Correctional Authority[1]	Number of Prisoners[2]	Crimes against the Person (percent of total)	Property Crimes (percent of total)	Other Criminal Code/Federal Offenses[3] (percent of total)
Provincial/Territorial.				
Female	1,453	28	37	34
Male	20,043	34	37	30
Federal (CSC)				
Female	210	64	7	29
Male	13,619	74	15	11
Total				
Female	1,663	33	34	34
Male	33,662	50	28	22

Notes
[1] Prisoners serve sentences of under 2 years under provincial/territorial authority and sentences of 2 years or more under federal (Correctional Services of Canada or CSC) jurisdiction.
[2] Based on a one-day snapshot of prisoners in adult correctional facilities, 5 October 1996. Missing data for 2,183 provincial/territorial inmates (9%) and 33 CSC inmates (under 1%).
[3] Includes drug offenses.

Source: Robinson et al. 1998, "A One-Day Snapshot," Table 6.

CSC's significant transgressions of the law and its own policies and professed practices, concluding that CSC had "a disturbing lack of commitment to the ideals of justice" 1996:198). The *Report* asserted that the rule of law applies in prisons and recommended the complete overhaul of policies and practices regarding women prisoners. At the time of the report, women serving sentences of two years or more were imprisoned in 11 locations across Canada, including new regional prisons and segregated maximum security units in men's prisons. However, despite the inquiry, the illegalities chronicled in the *Arbour Report*, with the exception of strip-searches by men, continued to occur.

A second issue in recent Canadian women's prison history involves women convicted of killing abusive male partners. The Supreme Court of Canada validated the need to consider women's own experiences of violence when they used lethal force to defend themselves from attacks by abusive male partners (see *R. v. Lavallee* 1990). Thereafter, women's groups campaigned strongly for a review of pre-*Lavallee* cases in which women had not been able to use evidence of past male violence to argue self-defense. In 1995, the minister of justice and solicitor general appointed Judge Lynn Ratushny to review 98 cases of women who had been jailed for striking back while defending themselves and/or their children.

Following extensive consultations and a stringent legal review of the cases, Judge Ratushny recommended that 7 of 98 applicants be granted relief and that longer-term law reform initiatives be undertaken, including the abolition of the mandatory minimum sentence for murder and the adoption of new guidelines for police and prosecutors who charge battered women with offenses of violence. The minister of justice and the solicitor general provided relief for five women; for example, two who had already finished their sentences were granted conditional pardons. However, no women were released from prison as a result of the *Self-Defence Review* (Ratushny 1997), and two of the

seven women for whom Judge Ratushny recommended relief were granted nothing.

Despite small numbers and the traditional "too few to count" attitude, Canada's women prisoners attract considerable attention from reformers. Although the long-term impact of the Arbour and Ratushny inquiries is uncertain, CAEFS and other national women's organizations continue to struggle for the rights of Canadian women prisoners, in coalition with academics, lawyers, and activists across the country. *See also* ABORIGINAL WOMEN AND CRIME, CANADA; BATTERED WOMEN AND SELF-DEFENSE, CANADA; FEMALE CRIME, CANADA; PRISON REFORM, CANADA.

Further Reading: Comack 1996, *Women in Trouble;* Sheehy forthcoming, "Review of the *Self-Defence Review*"; Canada, Task Force on Federally Sentenced Women 1990, *Creating Choices.*

Kim Pate

Women in Prison, England and Wales

Since 1992, the number of women in prison in England and Wales, which come under a single jurisdiction, has doubled to over 3,000. Academic observers and government inspectors alike state that most of the women pose no threat to the public. Of those held on remand prior to sentencing, three-quarters do not receive a custodial sentence. Of those receiving a custodial sentence, three-quarters are convicted of nonviolent offenses.

Most women prisoners share one or more of the following characteristics: a history of institutional care, poverty, abuse, unemployment, and responsibility for dependent children. Nearly one quarter of women prisoners come from non-white ethnic minority groups; many are foreign nationals sentenced as drug couriers. (For the latter, problems of poverty and childcare are compounded by distance.) The cost of imprisoning so many women is high: for each woman, an average of £512 ($837) a week or £26,624 ($43,504) a year. Community-based alternatives are cheaper and arguably more effective; for example, a drug rehabilitation program combined with a probation order costs £3,000 ($4,902) a year (Devlin 1998). Of course,

Table U. Prisoners, England and Wales, on 29 February 2000, by Type of Prisoner and Sex

Type of Prisoner	Male	Female	Total
Total	61,736	3,353	65,089
Young prisoners[1]	10,671	501	11,172
Aged 15–17	2,220	93	2,313
Remand	576	15	591
Sentenced	1,644	78	1,722
Non-criminal	0	0	0
Aged 18–20	8,451	408	8,859
Remand	2,096	129	2,225
Sentenced	6,346	276	6,622
Non-criminal	9	3	12
Adults	51,065	2,852	53,917
Remand	8,364	596	8,960
Sentenced	42,186	2,236	44,422
Non-criminal	515	20	535
All Remand	11,036	740	11,776
All Sentenced	50,176	2,590	52,766
All Non-criminal	524	23	547

[1] Young prisoners include all those aged 15–20 plus some 21-year-olds who were aged up to 20 on conviction and have not been reclassified as adult prisoners.

Source: White, Cullen, and Minchin 2000, "Prison Population Brief," Table B.

the financial price of imprisonment does not include its social costs to the women and their families.

Women form a small proportion (5 percent) of the total prison population, as indicated in Table U. There are 17 women's prisons for England and Wales, of which five are part of, or adjacent to, men's prisons. There are three open prisons for women. Four prisons have mother-and-baby units; in one of these, babies may stay until they are 9 months old, while in the others, they may remain until they are 18 months old. However, the number of places in these units is limited. Male prison officers work within all women's prisons. The presence of male guards with access to women's cells at any time can be particularly oppressive for women who have suffered sexual abuse (approximately one-third of all women prisoners).

There are fewer prisons for women than men because far fewer women go to prison. Due to the smaller number of women's prisons, women are more likely to be incarcerated a long way from their homes and families, making visits difficult. Since female prisoners are more likely than male prisoners to have responsibility for children, this separation is particularly painful for the women. Recent measures introduced in the interests of security following high-profile escapes from men's prisons are inappropriately applied to women. Women do not pose the same risk of escape, yet they, too, may be chained to an officer when outside prison attending a funeral or making a hospital visit. There is little recognition of the different criminal and social profiles of women prisoners or of the ways in which penal regimes are gender-differentiated in their impact on prisoners. *See also* FEMALE CRIME, BRITAIN; HOLLOWAY PRISON.

Further Reading: Carlen 1998, *Sledgehammer;* Devlin 1998, *Invisible Women;* Eaton 1993, *Women after Prison.*

Mary Eaton

Women in Prison, USA

The number of women in prison in the United States has jumped dramatically in recent years (see Figure 16 on page 294). In 1980, U.S. state and federal prisons held just over 12,000 women. By 1997, there were 79,624 incarcerated women, and by 1998, that number had increased by 6.5 percent to 84,427. In less than two decades, the number of women being held in the nation's prisons increased sevenfold.

The influx of women into prisons is a relatively new phenomenon. Throughout most of U.S. history, due to their small numbers, incarcerated women were correctional afterthoughts. As a result, the United States never developed a correctional system for women to replace the reformatory system that fell into disuse shortly before World War II. In fact, by the mid-1970s, only about half the states and territories had separate prisons for women, and many jurisdictions housed women inmates in male facilities or in women's facilities in other states.

Confronted with soaring rates of women's incarceration, states have been building new women's prisons at a rapid pace. Between 1930 and 1950, the U.S. opened only two or three facilities for women each decade, but over 34 were opened in the 1980s. By 1990, the nation had 71 female-only facilities; and just five years later, in 1995, the number of female facilities had jumped to 104—an increase of 46.5 percent in half a decade.

The dramatic increase in women's imprisonment is not a result of a need to incarcerate growing numbers of serious female offenders. The total number of arrests of adult women (one measure of women's criminal activity) increased by only 31.4 percent between 1987 and 1996, while the number of women in prison increased by 159 percent. Despite media images of hyperviolent women offenders, the proportion of women doing time in state prisons for violent offenses has been declining steadily from about half (48.9 percent) in 1979 to just over a quarter (27.6 percent) in 1997. In states like California, which runs the two largest women's prisons in the nation, the decline is even sharper. In 1992, only 16 percent of the women admitted to the California prison system were incarcerated for violent crimes, compared with

37.2 percent in 1982. Figure 17 on page 295 shows the most serious offenses of women committed to state prisons in 1996.

An increasing proportion of women in prison are drug offenders. (In contrast, an increasing number of men in prison have been convicted of violent offenses.) In 1979, 1 in 10 women in U.S. prisons was doing time for drugs. In 1997, the figure was more than 1 in 3 (37.4 percent). Although the policies that led to increased incarceration of women were intended to rid society of drug dealers and so-called kingpins, over one-third (35.9 percent) of the women serving time for drug offenses in the state prisons are serving time solely for possession. In 1979, in contrast, 26 percent of women doing time in state prisons for drug offenses were incarcerated solely for possession.

Nearly half of all women in prison are currently serving a sentence for a nonviolent offense and have been convicted in the past of only nonviolent offenses. By 1996, about two-thirds of women in the nation's prisons were serving time either for drug offenses or property offenses. Based on the nonviolent nature of women's offenses, it is clear that few pose much risk to public safety.

The characteristics of women in prison for violent offenses differ from the characteristics of men with violent offense histories. Many women convicted of murder or manslaughter killed husbands or boyfriends who repeatedly and violently abused them. In New York, for example, of the women committed to the state's prisons for homicide in 1986, 49 percent had been the victims of abuse at some point in their lives and 59 percent of the women who killed someone close to them were being abused at the time of the offense. For half of the women committed for homicide, it was their first and only offense.

Two-thirds of the women in prison have at least one child under 18, and most were responsible for providing for that child before imprisonment. Many women lose contact with their children during their imprisonment or have difficulty regaining custody after release.

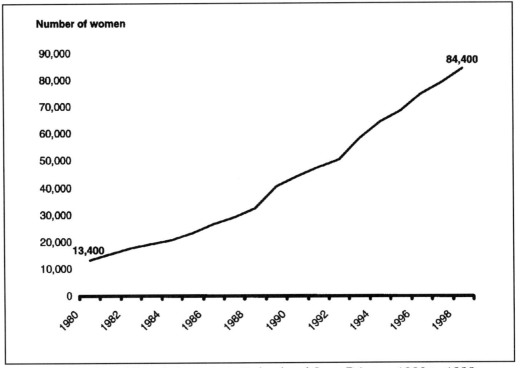

Figure 16. Number of Female Inmates in Federal and State Prisons, 1980 to 1998
Source: U.S. General Accounting Office 1999, *Women in Prison*, page 3.

The Bureau of Justice Statistics recently conducted a national survey of imprisoned women in the U.S. and found that in their personal histories, women in prisons have far higher rates of physical and sexual abuse than their male counterparts. Forty-three percent of the women surveyed reported they had been abused at least once before their current admission to prison; the comparable figure for men was 12.2 percent.

Changes in the characteristics of imprisoned women and increases in their number signal a major and dramatic change in the way the country is responding to women's offending, most of which is nonviolent. Without much fanfare—and certainly with little public discussion or debate—incarceration is being increasingly used as a response to women's crime, particularly women's drug problems. The policy shift has disproportionately affected women of color. More than half the women in the nation's prisons are African American (46 percent) or Hispanic (14.2 percent). Specifically, while the number of women in state prisons for drug sales in-

creased by 433 percent between 1986 and 1991, this increase is far steeper for Hispanic women (328 percent) and especially for African American women (828 percent), compared with the 241 percent increase in the incarceration of white women.

Inattention to gender difference by the correctional establishment (long focused on incarcerating men) means that many modern women's prisons encounter serious difficulties and unanticipated problems. Prisons are generally unprepared for the large number of women in their custody who are pregnant (some estimates put this at 1 in 10). The sexual harassment and sexual abuse of women inmates in U.S. prisons is an increasingly well-documented problem that is receiving both national and international attention. Finally, procedures such as strip-searches, which have been routine in corrections facilities for decades, are now being understood as problematic in women's prisons, particularly when dealing with victims of past sexual trauma. Gender matters a great deal in corrections, and a woman in prison is not, and

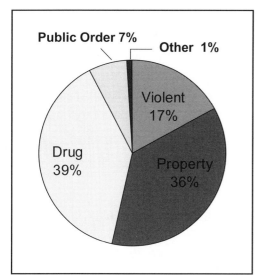

Figure 17. Most Serious Offense for New Commitments to [U.S.] State Prisons, Women Committed in 1996
Source: <http://www.ojp.usdoj.gov/bjs/dtdata.htm# most>, Bureau of Justice Statistics Web Site, July 1999

never will be, identical to her male counterpart. *See also* DEATH ROW; FRAMINGHAM EIGHT; GENDER DISPARITIES IN PRISONS; HIV AND AIDS IN PRISON; INCARCERATED MOTHERS; SEXUAL ABUSE OF PRISONERS.

Further Reading: Chesney-Lind 1997, *The Female Offender;* Rafter 1990a, *Partial Justice.*

Meda Chesney-Lind

Women Professionals in the Justice Workplace

Until the 1970s, criminal justice (CJ) occupations were gender-segregated, and women's participation was restricted to administrative support and social-service work dealing with women and children. Since then, broad social, economic, and legal changes and changes in the work and organization of CJ occupations have opened policing, law, and correctional work to women. Nevertheless, structural, cultural, and interactional barriers to equality in CJ work remain, disadvantage women, and force them to devise coping strategies.

Structural, Cultural, and Interactional Barriers in CJ Occupations

Gender pervades all aspects of life in social organizations. This includes divisions of labor and power, images of work tasks and of the workers appropriate to fill them, and the mechanisms and organizational policies that structure interactions in ways that foster cultural stereotypes and divisions based on workers' gender, race, and class. Because men control powerful positions in organizations, they are able to create rules and regulations (e.g., performance evaluations) based on their experience and behavior and to dominate jobs that offer more pay, social status, and power.

Within work organizations, workers develop informal occupational and organizational cultures that provide shared meanings and influence workers' activities, opportunities, and identities. In occupations where most workers are men, dominant work-culture images tend to associate effective job performance with prevailing ideals of masculinity. For middle-class men, including lawyers, this means suppressing emotions, displaying rationality, and dominating adversaries and clients through manipulating ideas. For working-class men, including police and corrections officers, this means displaying physical strength, courage, and aggressiveness. The job thus becomes a resource for constructing masculinity, and it enables men to magnify gender differences through social interactions in the workplace.

When women enter formerly all-male workplaces, they encounter these cultural and structural barriers, including the effects of their presence in only token numbers. As highly visible tokens, they face performance pressures, heightened in-group physical and social boundaries, and pressures to conform to stereotyped roles (Kanter 1977).

Women tokens also face overt hostility and more subtle discriminatory techniques that men use to undermine them. Exclusionary practices deprive them of learning opportunities and prestigious assignments. Verbal and nonverbal cues, such as comments on their appearance and "playful" touching, also serve as boundaries by sexualizing the workplace and highlighting gender differences.

Other interactional devices men use for constructing dominance and controlling women include undermining women by denying them information, preventing women's acquisition of on-the-job skills, sabotaging their work, excluding them from career-enhancing social organizations (e.g., social clubs or sports leagues), refusing to accept their authority, denigrating their work products, magnifying their failures, and attributing their successes to sexual favors or "reverse discrimination" (Cockburn 1991).

In the sexualized workplace, women must cope with sexual harassment including overtly sexual talk, unwanted contact, and physical advances that create a hostile work environment. Sexual double standards result in negative labels for women who return men's sexual humor or flirt; they also are blamed for "sexuality problems" arising at work. Women who ignore or reject men's advances are labeled prudes or lesbians.

Paternalism, or the practice of excusing or protecting women from difficult tasks in exchange for women's submission, also limits women. Because men's protection appears to be helpful, women may accept relief from hard assignments. But in doing so, they lose the chance to demonstrate their abilities, and they create resentment among other workers by violating the general sense of fairness.

Organizational policies, rules, and practices often operate to women's disadvantage. Work characteristically performed by women is devalued through formal organizational procedures like performance evaluations. These rely on ostensibly objective procedures but really are social constructions of male competence.

Women entering CJ occupations encounter dilemmas that are not encountered by men. The norms of "appropriate" or professional behavior for workers in CJ occupations are associated with enacting "masculine" behavior and interacting with fellow workers as peers and equals. But women workers are pressured by male co-workers to display "feminine" behavior, including deference to

men, which is deemed inappropriate for a CJ professional. In sum, women in CJ occupations must cope with discriminatory policies and practices, paternalism, men's hostility, a sexualized work environment, performance pressures, and organizational rules and expectations that disadvantage them. Nevertheless, these barriers affect women police and corrections officers differently from women lawyers and contribute to both differences and similarities in women's coping strategies in these two fields.

Barriers to Women in Police and Correctional Work

Policing and corrections work are stereotyped "men's jobs" because of certain characteristics of the work they entail. Policing involves diverse crime fighting, order maintenance, and service tasks. Across these activities, there remains the potential for unanticipated violence and the authority to use physical coercion on behalf of the state. These have resulted in an occupational culture characterized by officer suspiciousness, isolation from the community, and a cohesive, informal occupational group that resists integrating persons perceived as untrustworthy "outsiders." Similarly, corrections officers (COs) in men's prisons must control a hostile and dangerous population that far outnumbers them. To maintain order and discipline, COs enforce a myriad of rules but must rely on inmate cooperation through tacit agreements regarding which rules will be strictly enforced. Much corrections work is repetitious and uneventful, involving increased documentation of formerly routine decisions. However, danger makes COs dependent on each other for backup, while the unusual hours and isolated locations of prisons lead to formation of a cohesive work culture.

The most vocal objections of men correctional and police officers to women officers focus on their physical differences from men and are stated in terms of concern for physical safety and women's alleged inability to deal with violence. Additional concerns underlying their opposition to women include threats to the division of labor, work norms, work group solidarity, occupational status and public image, and sexist ideology that undergirds the men's definition of their work identity as masculine men. Women's presence on street patrol or in the prison cell block implies either that men's physical superiority is irrelevant (as it usually is) or that the man working with a woman officer will be at a disadvantage in a physical confrontation. For a man to be defended by, or dependent on, a woman officer may be regarded as an affront to his manhood. Men's opposition to women in policing also reflects the struggle over ownership of social control that Heidensohn (1992) characterizes as the real but unstated issue underlying men's assertions that women are unsuitable officers.

Organizational rules, policies, and practices put women at a disadvantage throughout their careers. Women entering policing or corrections work are less likely than men to have such "preparatory" experiences as military service, firearms training, or participation in team sports. The police training academy fosters inequality by emphasizing meeting physical fitness standards not proven to be job relevant, while permitting some physical education instructors to coddle women who seek exemptions. This has the negative consequence of allowing some women to enter patrol not fully prepared and undermines men's confidence in women officers in general. Police training also underemphasizes development of interpersonal skills, an area where women are likely to excel.

In field training, newcomers learn the tricks of the trade and develop the reputations that follow them through their careers. A police officer who does not have, or does not take, opportunities to develop street patrol skills because of limited assignments, under-instruction, or overprotection is likely to act hesitantly, be viewed as a threat to others' safety, and be deprived of subsequent opportunities to handle situations. New corrections officers receive little formal training, so new female COs' informal instruction is even more crucial to occupational survival. New women in both policing and corrections must overcome openly hostile and/or overprotective attitudes of some of their trainers, supervisors, and co-workers; a dual standard of evaluation; and pressures to prove their competence. In addition, men sometimes try to frighten women by "setting them up" or not providing backup in potentially dangerous situations. New women COs encounter hazing not only from male COs but men inmates, who haze all new COs but in gendered ways.

Other organizational barriers include restrictions on work assignments, inadequate women's toilet facilities, subjective performance standards based on masculine qualities that may be irrelevant to the job, the lack of adequate maternity leave and sexual harassment policies, retaliation and ostracism when complaints are filed protesting such harassment, and inadequate organizational commitment and resources to implement antidiscrimination policies. Although men's hostility appears to have subsided and overt barriers to promotion—including veterans preferences, seniority, and the need to have a sponsor—have diminished in their impact, women remain grossly underrepresented in the supervisory and administrative ranks of policing and corrections (S. E. Martin 1990; Morton 1991).

Women police and correctional officers also face interactional dilemmas. As officers, they are expected to interact with other officers according to occupational norms governing relations among equals; as women, they are expected to adhere to gender norms that maintain that women are subordinates of men. To keep women "in their place," men use physical and verbal harassment including excessive cursing, sexual jokes, gossip about or sexualized encounters with women, and leaving pornographic materials visible. Men cast women into gender stereotyped roles including incompetent "little sisters," "seductresses," manlike "iron maidens," or "mothers" in whom they confide. Those who fail to conform to acceptable gender stereotypes are labeled "lesbians" or "whores," implying a challenge to their sexual identity.

Race and ethnicity also differentiate the hostilities that women experience. Women of color often experience both racial and sexual harassment. Gender stereotypes of black women combine sexist and racist stereotypes that include the sexually promiscuous "Jezebel," "mules" who do the dirty work that white women will not do, or "uppity black women" who do not know their place (P. H. Collins 1991). Black women are rarely offered protection by white male colleagues, while protection and support from black male officers is inconsistent. Sometimes there is racial solidarity across gender lines; at other times, black men show resentment of women's encroachment on their space, or anger at women's rejection of their sexual advances (S. E. Martin 1995; Maghan and McLeish-Blackwell 1991).

To forestall even the appearance of impropriety, many women avoid interactions that might be viewed as having a sexual connotation. They maintain their moral reputation but lose the opportunity to build the close interpersonal relationships necessary for gaining sponsors or mentors. Social exclusion, sexual harassment, and performance pressures create a unique group of work-related stresses for women police and higher levels of work-related stress for women COs than for their male counterparts.

Barriers to Women in Law

Although women now constitute a quarter of the legal profession and about one-half of law students in the United States, their numerical gains have not led to equivalent increases in power or opportunities due to both overt and subtle barriers to full integration and equal participation in the legal profession. The phenomenal growth in the number of lawyers since the 1960s has contributed to new opportunities for women in law. At the same time, the shift from solo practice to large law firms with many salaried lawyers disadvantages women since a smaller proportion of lawyers today than in the past make the rank of partner. This, in turn, prevents them from moving up the rungs to the top of the legal career ladder (e.g., obtaining judgeships).

Women's lawsuits have ended the openly discriminatory policies that prevailed in law school admissions and job placement practices, law firms' recruiting and hiring practices, and partnership decision-making. In the past decade, gender bias task forces created by the bench and bar in many states and the American Bar Association's Commission on Women in the Profession have exposed patterns of discriminatory behavior in the courthouse. Nevertheless, the legal culture remains a quintessentially man's world, one in which women are disadvantaged.

Professional opportunities are defined by informal social networks, private clubs, and bar associations that order status and power. Each serves as a barrier reinforcing the other. The image of the law as masculine strengthens men's resistance to including women in informal socializing; women's absence from informal networks and professional activities then supports the view that women do not fit in. Professionalism means total commitment to a workaholic schedule of long days followed by informal socializing that assumes that there is a wife taking care of the home and family. Women lawyers who are married still have primary responsibilities for their families, and those who take parental leaves are less likely to be made partners, whereas men who have children are more likely to achieve partnerships (Hagan and Kay 1995).

Women attorneys face double binds that men do not. Success in law (particularly for litigators) rests on dominant behavior. A judge and other lawyers may defer to an aggressive man, while penalizing the same behavior in a woman as "shrill." Thus a woman lawyer who assumes a professional (i.e., tough, masculine) image is criticized for being difficult or unladylike, while one who "acts like a woman" by displaying characteristics incongruent with the professional stereotype is regarded as not tough enough.

In circular fashion, women lawyers are pressed into legal specialties (e.g., domestic relations) that yield low prestige and financial rewards. They lack mentors, are invisible in informal legal social circles, and are rarely given leadership roles in bar association activities that would advance their career by providing contacts with potential clients. Bringing such clients into a firm is a prerequisite for partnership. Thus both the structure of legal practice and the informal culture of the occupation interact and reproduce gender relations that affirm men's dominance and women's subordination.

The differential treatment of women lawyers has been termed gender bias and pervades the organizational logic, legal culture, work-related interactions, and professional identities of lawyers. Women lawyers encounter sexual harassment and are treated as sexual objects. They are questioned about their spouse's occupation and plans for pregnancy in recruiting interviews although such questions are illegal and are not asked of men. Gender bias in several types of settings affects women's assigned activities and rewards, contributing to negative views of their work environment (Rosenberg, Perstadt, and Phillips 1993) and more frequent moves out of law (Hagan and Kay 1995).

When gender-biased treatment occurs in a courtroom, it undercuts the woman lawyer's credibility and professionalism, creates double standards of performance, alters case outcomes, and affects interactional processes through which dominance and submission are displayed. Credibility is crucial for an attorney, particularly in the courtroom. Condescending treatment and displays of disrespect from judges and other attorneys undermine a client's confidence and diminish the lawyer's credibility in the eyes of jurors. For lawyers who need a winning track record to attract clients, disrespectful behavior may have devastating effects. Thus, displaying femininity and succeeding at trial work are often in conflict.

Sexual overtures and innuendoes, teasing, and exclusionary practices are systematic and patterned forms of harassment that create a working environment hostile to women lawyers. Frequent reiteration of gender differences through these practices maintains and reproduces the gendered structural features of the legal workplace where advancement decisions continue to rest on the masculine professional model in which work comes first, work-related social activities are essential in cultivating clients, family responsibilities are limited, and women who do not play by these professional rules tend to be disadvantaged.

Addressing Barriers: Individual and Collective Coping Strategies

Responses to gender-related problems and stresses vary among individuals and occupations; moreover, most women do not consistently adhere to a single coping strategy. One way that women minimize gender differences is by sharing the men's perspective on their work. Women police and corrections officers' attitudes toward work-related conditions and toward their clients (the public and prisoners) are similar to those of their male counterparts. Two other coping strategies are changing assignments or jobs and leaving the occupation. Women police and corrections officers are found disproportionately in administrative positions, and a higher proportion of women than men lawyers leave private practice for government or corporate legal work. The rates at which women are leaving all three occupations also are higher than those of men.

Researchers have described three individual-level styles of coping by women in CJ occupations. Some women adapt to the standards of the gendered organization and competently do the job by "doing" masculinity and emulating men's styles of reasoning, speech, and demeanor in work interactions. Others adopt constructions of femininity that accept inequality and men's protection; they gain personal acceptance but avoid competing with men either by taking less prestigious "women's jobs" or performing in stereotypically feminine ways. A third strategy is to construct a new femininity that also is compatible with images of competent job performance by striking a balance between these equally opposite but negative stereotypes. These women present themselves as "professionals," develop unique skills, and use humor to develop camaraderie and thwart unwelcome advances (Hunt 1984; Jurik 1988). Similarly, some women litigators embrace the adversarial (male) model, minimizing their feminine self; others reject it, embracing instead a caring role; a third group "split the role" by adopting a combative courtroom style but rejecting that style in relating to others in the firm (Pierce 1995).

Women in CJ occupations also have organized for change. They have brought lawsuits challenging discriminatory organizational policies related to entrance requirements, promotion practices, training opportunities, sexual harassment, and the lack of pregnancy and maternity leave. Professional associations for women in policing and corrections, while providing support for individuals, have floundered in many departments and national organizations have had limited impact. Women's bar associations have been more effective in providing women lawyers support and contacts at the local level and gradually have opened positions of responsibility to women in state bar associations and the American Bar Association. Women lawyers also have used their professional skills to bring antidiscrimination lawsuits on behalf of women in a range of CJ and other occupations, and they have pressured law firms to adopt more flexible career paths that permit childbearing and child rearing. Nevertheless, for women in these CJ occupations, there are tensions between work and family responsibilities. These arise from rigid work schedules and unexpected overtime and the need for noncontact assignments during pregnancy for police and COs, the open-ended demands of work for lawyers, and the absence or inadequacy of maternity leave policies in all three occupations.

In conclusion, legal challenges and women's accomplishments have weakened the barriers to equality in CJ occupations, particularly those barriers arising from openly discriminatory practices. However, altering gender-based occupational cultures that are hostile to women and organizational policies and practices that disadvantage women will require transformation of work organizations, gender relations, and the larger political-economic systems in which they are embedded. *See also* GENDER AND POLICING; GENDER BIAS TASK FORCES; LAWYERS AND GENDER DIFFER-

ENCE; LEGAL PROFESSION, HISTORY OF WOMEN IN; LEGAL TRAINING; O'CONNOR, SANDRA DAY; POLICE OFFICERS, WOMEN OF COLOR AS; POLICE WORK AND STRESS; POLICE WORK, HISTORY OF WOMEN IN, USA; RENO, JANET; WOMEN'S PRISON ADMINISTRATION, CONTEMPORARY.

Further Reading: Acker 1990, "Hierarchies, Jobs and Bodies"; Messerschmidt 1993b, "The State and Gender Politics"; Kanter 1977, *Men and Women of the Corporation;* S. E. Martin and Jurik 1996, *Doing Justice, Doing Gender.*

Susan E. Martin

Women's Prison Administration, Contemporary

A national survey of the head administrators of women's correctional facilities (Morash, Bynum, and Koons 1995) revealed that three-quarters of women's prison administrators are women. Half have held their positions for less than five years. Nearly all of the administrators had advanced to the position of prison administrator through a career in corrections, and most had worked in a women's correctional facility for at least 5 years, with many having worked in a women's correctional facility for 10 or more years. Half of the people who are wardens in women's prisons hold a master's degree, and nearly all of the rest have a bachelor's degree.

At levels of women's prison administration below the warden or correctional executive, other administrators handle oversight of various functions. These functions include security, food services, facility maintenance, and various types of programming, including educational, mental health, and drug rehabilitation programs.

Contemporary women's prison administrators handle a very wide variety of responsibilities. The head administrator, with support of other staff, typically spends a considerable amount of time communicating the needs of imprisoned women to the state department of corrections and advocating for resources and policies that will be responsive to both inmates and employees in women's facilities. High-level administrators also are responsible for maintaining a safe environment for inmates and employees, selecting and training employees, maintaining a system of employee supervision, keeping the physical plant in good shape, allocating funds according to the institution's budget, making budget requests, and ensuring adequate housing and food for inmates. Women's prison administrators are responsible for making sure that there is an effective procedure for handling inmate and employee grievances. They are on the front line in eliminating situations and circumstances that could result in legal action by either staff or inmates and in implementing changes ordered by the courts when there is a finding against the state correctional department. Finally, women's prison administrators also play a key role in insuring that the unique needs and characteristics of women are considered in the way that the inmate population is managed, in the training of employees and volunteers, and in the development of programs available to women within the institution.

An increase in the population of elderly offenders, and in the number of women inmates with AIDS or who are HIV-positive, in addition to inmates who have other medical problems, are pregnant, and have mental health problems, presents a tremendous challenge to the women's prison administrator. The administrators often must coordinate with state agencies and private contractors to ensure that specialized services are available to inmates, and they must monitor agreements and contracts to ensure the quality of these services.

According to women's prison administrators, the most common cause of management problems in processing women is overcrowding. Crowding leads to many difficulties in meeting the health needs of pregnant and older inmates, providing adequate mental health care, and separating prisoners by security level. It also results in disruptions when women must be moved between facilities due to space needs—and in a shift in institutional climate toward an impersonal atmosphere that contributes to inmate behavior problems. Other challenges facing many women's prison administrators are lack of appropriate programs, difficulties with an intake and classification system that was developed for men, and lack of resources.

Another major challenge that women's prison administrators face in operating an institution is with staff quality and turnover. Administrators must continuously arrange for the training and monitoring of employees in order to ensure that appropriate procedures are followed for searches, and to prevent overfamiliarity, harassment, and sexual assault. They must be aware of the unique communication styles and needs of women offenders. Unlike men in prison, women do not assume that there is a conflict between them and staff, and they typically move toward developing relationships with staff. Staff must be trained to respond to the wide variety of emotions that women exhibit during conversations, to set boundaries in order to maintain a professional relationship, and to make referrals to other sources of help.

The administrator of a woman's prison has a great deal of influence on how much contact inmates have with their children, other relatives, and community members. By allocating space and time for mother-child visits and providing appropriate furnishings and play equipment, the administrator can encourage interaction of mothers with their children. Institutions differ greatly in the degree of community involvement that is allowed inside the institution. Elaine Lord, warden at Bedford Hills Prison in New York, made possible the development of an AIDS education program, operated through a partnership between an inmate and a community volunteer who does work "on the outside" that the offender could not do, and who meets regularly to coordinate with the offender. Other wardens have spearheaded the development of programs that allow weekend visits of children and that train inmates for work in traditionally male occupations that provide good pay and benefits.

The majority of innovative programs for prisoners are designed and initiated by administrators and program staff within the institution. Thus, in addition to handling a myriad of responsibilities, women's prison administrators frequently take on a leadership role in advocating for women in prison and in promoting the development of programs to meet their needs. *See also* HIV AND AIDS IN PRISON; INCARCERATED MOTHERS; PRISON TREATMENT PROGRAMS, LEGAL ISSUES IN; PRISONER CLASSIFICATION; PRISONER LITIGATION; PRISONS, HEALTH CARE IN; PRISONS, TREATMENT PROGRAMS IN; SEXUAL ABUSE OF PRISONERS; WOMEN PROFESSIONALS IN THE JUSTICE WORKPLACE.

Further Reading: Cranford and Williams 1998, "Critical Issues in Managing Female Offenders"; Morash, Bynum, and Koons 1995, *Findings from the National Study of Innovative and Promising Programs for Women Offenders.*

Merry Morash

Women's Prison Administration, Historical

The creation of separate prisons for women in the late-nineteenth and early-twentieth centuries generated a need for specialized women's prisons administration. From the inception of the use of prisons as punishment in the United States, small numbers of women were incarcerated within men's institutions. Because this arrangement put women convicts at the mercy of male guards and encouraged sexual abuse, reformers advocated the segregation of women convicts into separate facilities run entirely by female staff. This meant that the prison superintendents and all other officers had to be women, a novel idea in the mid-nineteenth century. As it transpired, however, many early women's prison administrators were among the most highly qualified and enlightened correctional leaders of the period.

There were a few female administrators even in the late-eighteenth and very early nineteenth centuries when the first U.S. prisons were built. Philadelphia's Walnut Street Jail was run from 1793 to 1796 by Quaker Mary Weed, whose reformative ideas helped shape the early movement to punish offenders with imprisonment. Similarly, in 1822, Rachel Perijo was appointed matron at the Baltimore penitentiary, where she looked af-

ter women prisoners and offered industrial, educational, and religious instruction. More reformative ideas were implemented by Eliza Farnham, the chief matron from 1844 to 1847 at Mount Pleasant Female Prison at Ossining, the closest thing to a separate prison for women prior to the Civil War. Though in a detached building, the female unit was on the grounds of Sing Sing prison and still under its authority. Farnham's reforms—which included educating inmates, providing music and flowers, and encouraging outside visitors—enraged some officials at the larger male facility, where the silent system and hard labor prevailed, and eventually led to her ouster. Though brief, Farnham's innovations were models for the reformatory movement to come.

Zebulon Brockway, the most innovative male warden of the late nineteenth century, set aside a "House of Shelter" for women within his institution, the Detroit House of Correction, and put it under the direction of female staff. Brockway hired Emma A. Hall, who served as matron of this facility from 1869 to 1874 and who initiated religious, domestic, and academic training to inculcate her charges with "wholesome womanly virtues." Credit for being America's first entirely separate prison for women goes to the Indiana Reformatory Institution for Women and Girls, opened in 1873 under the leadership of Sarah Smith. Smith was a Quaker minister who had tended Civil War soldiers. She became a prison visitor after the war and thus became involved in the movement advocating completely separate prisons for women. In an unusual role, her husband assisted Superintendent Smith, serving as prison steward while she led this institution through its first decade.

The model of a strong female reform leader becoming superintendent of the new prison for women was repeated throughout the reformatory movement era. Ellen Cheney Johnson, for example, was a leader of the Massachusetts reformatory movement in the 1870s and later became superintendent of the Massachusetts Prison for Women, which opened in Sherborn (later incorporated into

Framingham) in 1877. Jessie D. Hodder, another Massachusetts reformer, became Framingham's superintendent in 1910. Hodder added the word "reformatory" to the prison's name and contributed a number of innovations to the reformatory movement.

Other women who assumed administrative roles in the early women's prisons had unique backgrounds and qualifications compared to most women of the period. Eliza Mosher, who became superintendent at Framingham in 1880, studied medicine at New England Women's Hospital in Boston and the University of Michigan before becoming the Framingham prison physician in 1877 and later the superintendent. Mosher was succeeded in 1882 at Framingham by the already famous Clara Barton, whose nursing work on the battlefields of the Civil War had won her the admiration of the Massachusetts governor. Barton accepted the superintendency reluctantly and stayed less than a year, but her leadership brought visibility to women's able administration of these facilities.

Other women superintendents with extraordinary backgrounds for their day included Florence Monahan, who studied law at Northwestern University and then headed reformatories in Minnesota, Illinois, and California; Elsa Ernst, who studied psychology at Harvard before assuming leadership of the North Carolina reformatory; May Caughey, who received a B.A. in history before becoming the first superintendent at the New Jersey Reformatory for Women at Clinton Farms in 1913, where she pioneered a prisoner self-government system; Edna Mahan, who graduated from Berkeley and did graduate work prior to assuming the superintendency at Clinton Farms in 1928; and Mary Belle Harris, who earned a Ph.D. before becoming superintendent at the Blackwell Island city penitentiary in New York, the Clinton Farms prison in New Jersey, and the Federal Industrial Institution for Women at Alderson, West Virginia, which she opened in 1927.

The most renowned of the early women's prison superintendents was Katharine Bement Davis, who has been described as "perhaps the most influential prison administrator, male or female, of her day" (Rafter 1985b:60). Davis graduated from Vassar and earned a Ph.D. from the University of Chicago in 1900. That same year, a new reformatory for women at Bedford Hills opened and Davis was recommended for the superintendency, which she held until 1913 when she became New York City's commissioner of corrections. Davis's scholarly background led her to study the prisoners scientifically and also to encourage outside researchers. She obtained a grant in 1910 to establish the Laboratory of Social Hygiene at Bedford Hills which, under the leadership of psychologist Mabel Fernald, conducted research and pioneered techniques of prisoner testing and classification which became common in the field. Davis publicized the Bedford research, championed Progressive-era ideals, extended prisoner training to include industrial and other nontraditional work, and strongly influenced both architecture and programming at other women's prisons established in the early twentieth century.

Estelle Freedman has noted that a common theme in all the early women's prisons was the degree to which the superintendent's personality "largely determined correctional treatment" (1981:78). Another recurring theme, however, was the problem of finding adequate female staff, since there were few comparable administrative roles for women in society. As a result, some of the early women superintendents were inadequate or rigid managers, insensitive to both prisoners and their staff, or otherwise devoid of the reform vision. However, it is also true that many of the early superintendents were remarkable women, innovative reformers, and able administrators who championed reformative ideals and pioneered many ideas that ultimately became standard practice in modern corrections. *See also* ALDERSON PRISON; BEDFORD HILLS REFORMATORY; FARNHAM, ELIZA W.; IMPRISONMENT IN THE SOUTH, PRE–CIVIL WAR; MAHAN, EDNA; REFORMATORY MOVEMENT; WOMEN PROFESSIONALS IN THE JUSTICE WORKPLACE; WOMEN'S PRISONS, HISTORY OF.

Further Reading: Freedman 1981, *Their Sisters' Keepers;* Rafter 1990a, *Partial Justice.*

Christine E. Rasche

Women's Prisons, History of

Although the history of women's prisons often parallels that of men's, it also diverges significantly. The first prisons in the United States were built after the Revolutionary War as a humane alternative to corporal and capital punishment. Regardless of offense, age, or sex, prisoners shared rooms, worked irregularly, and mixed freely in large house-like structures. The lack of supervision and discipline allowed corruption and sexual exploitation to flourish. Instead of reducing crime, incarceration in these very early prisons seemed to promote its growth.

In the early nineteenth century, under the influence of rapid industrialization and other wrenching demographic, economic, and political changes, Americans came to believe that crime was the product of social disorder. Thus, Jacksonian era reformers sought to create highly structured environments in which to separate prisoners not only from the disorder in society, but also from the contagion of one another. The 1820 opening of New York's Auburn State Prison was the first step in the creation of the nation's penitentiary system, with its individual cells and rule of silence, lockstep formations, and requirement of hard labor. In their architecture and routines, Auburn and other penitentiaries sought to reinforce order and discipline.

When women were first committed to Auburn in 1825, unlike male inmates, they were neither assigned to individual cells nor subjected to the penitentiary's regimentation. Never having been considered in the original plans, female prisoners were relegated to an attic above the prison's kitchen. The neglect and deprivation they experienced were common in other penitentiaries as well. Women were generally unsupervised, excluded from regular work and exercise, and allowed but limited access to medical and religious personnel. Furthermore, although segregated within predominately male facilities, women were vulnerable to physical and sexual abuse by male guards. Much of the women's ill treatment stemmed from their minority status; administrators refused to allocate funds to provide separate quarters and resources for the small female population. The widely held perception of the female offender as a "fallen" woman, more depraved than her male counterpart, added to her stigma and the disregard in which she was held.

As the number of women sentenced to prison grew, housing developed sporadically and haphazardly. Sometimes a section or wing within the facility was set aside; at other times a separate building, perhaps even off the grounds, was designated for women. Several prisons hired matrons (under a male warden's authority), believing that they could positively influence the female criminal. Likewise, some prisons welcomed "lady visitors" from the community who, through personal relationships, tried to raise prisoners' moral standards. Despite these adjustments, prisons throughout the country remained custodial, making few provisions for their generally poor and immigrant female population. It was not until the late nineteenth century, when women were removed from prisons designed for men and relocated to facilities of their own, that substantive reforms were implemented. The exception to this chronology is the 1839 opening of New York's Mount Pleasant Female Prison, the nation's first women's prison explicitly established by legislation.

Influenced by innovations at Mount Pleasant, the women's reformatory plan that began to evolve in the late 1860s was a distinctive alternative to the penitentiary. The middle-class women who fought to establish and run independent women's reformatories argued that woman's nature was inherently different from that of man and that females' unique needs were best served by other, sympathetic women. While never rejecting the institution of prison, reformers sought to redeem the fallen woman (recast as vulnerable victim) through improved penal treatment and lessons in morality. The reformatories were designed for young, white misdemeanants, who resided in "cottages" on unfenced campuses and were trained for domestic service placements. Few black women were ever sentenced to reformatories, yet they were overly represented in the custodial prisons. Reflecting common racist attitudes, judges often assumed black women to be naturally promiscuous and, thus, unredeemable.

By the early 1900s, a new generation of reformatory administrators, trained in the newly established social sciences, concluded that environmental factors, including poverty, illiteracy, and family dysfunction, affected criminality. They rejected the view of women as innately in need of protection and moral uplift. Thus they promoted women's self-sufficiency through academic and industrial training, developed individualized treatment plans, and provided a variety of social services for female inmates. The work of the reformatories, however, was greatly undermined in the 1920s and 1930s by underfunding, overcrowding and an influx of "difficult" inmates (i.e., women engaged in prostitution, the mentally ill, alcoholics, and drug addicts).

Although reformatories never housed the majority of female offenders, they represent an important departure from the male prison model in physical structure, philosophy, and social conditions. They provided benefits unavailable in custodial prisons, but their rehabilitation efforts institutionalized differential treatment. In an earlier era, "wayward girls" might have served brief sentences in local jails. When sent to a reformatory, however, they received indeterminate sentences that lasted years, often for minor offenses for which men would not have been incarcerated. In the business of "re-forming," the new fa-

cilities often held misdemeanants longer than custodial prisons held felons. Moreover, upon release, a woman's behavior was closely monitored for signs of moral relapse, which could lead to reincarceration. By 1935, enthusiasm for the reformatory movement had ceased and most facilities reverted to the traditional custodial model, holding only felons and gradually relinquishing the ideal of reformation.

Today, despite some accommodations, women's prisons generally replicate the male-based, custodial model. Female prisoners are still far fewer in number than males, and this difference continues to justify fewer facility resources. Condemning these inequities, feminists in the 1970s challenged the century-old model of separate male and female prisons, and a few coed facilities were established. In the 1980s and 1990s, reformers argued instead for parity, the provision of equivalent, though not necessarily identical, care and services based on the unique needs of each sex. Many have also called for community-based alternatives to incarceration, particularly for those charged with nonviolent crimes and drug offenses, currently the fastest growing population of female offenders. *See also* Farnham, Eliza W.; Lekkerkerker, Eugenia; Imprisonment in the South, Pre–Civil War; Reformatory Movement; Women's Prison Administration, Contemporary; Women's Prison Administration, Historical.

Further Reading: Freedman 1996, *Maternal Justice;* Odem 1995, *Delinquent Daughters;* Rafter 1982, "Hard Times"; Rafter 1990a, *Partial Justice.*

Judith Anne Ryder

WORKS CITED

Legal cases and legislation are cited by country, starting on page 343.

Books, Articles, Reports, and Internet Sites

Abel, R. 1989. *American Lawyers*. New York: Oxford.

Abelson, E. S. 1989. "The Invention of Kleptomania." *Signs* 15(1): 123–143.

———. 1990. *When Ladies Go A-Thieving: Middle-Class Shoplifters in the Victorian Department Store*. New York: Oxford University Press.

Acker, J. 1990. "Hierarchies, Jobs and Bodies: A Theory of Gendered Organizations." *Gender and Society* 4: 139–158.

Acoca, L. 1998. "Defusing the Time Bomb: Understanding and Meeting the Growing Health Care Needs of Incarcerated Women in America." *Crime and Delinquency* 44(1): 49–70.

Adelberg, A., and C. Currie, eds. 1987. *Too Few to Count: Canadian Women in Conflict with the Law*. Vancouver, BC: Press Gang Publishers.

———. 1993. *In Conflict with the Law: Women and the Canadian Justice System*. Vancouver, BC: Press Gang Publishers.

Adhikari, R. P., D. Reinhard, and J. M. Johnson. 1993. "The Myth of Protection Orders." In *Studies in Symbolic Interaction*, vol. 15, edited by N. K. Denzin. Greenwich, CT: JAI Press.

Adler, F. 1975. *Sisters in Crime: The Rise of the New Female Criminal*. New York: McGraw-Hill.

———. 1997. "The ASC and Women: One Generation Without, One Generation With." *The Criminologist* 22(3): 1–5.

Agnew, R. 1992. "Foundation for a General Strain Theory of Crime and Delinquency." *Criminology* 30(1): 47–87.

———. 1995. "The Contribution of Social-Psychological Strain Theory to the Explanation of Crime and Delinquency." In *The Legacy of Anomie Theory*, edited by F. Adler and W. S. Laufer. New Brunswick, NJ: Transaction Publishers.

Akers, R. L. 1994. *Criminological Theories*. Los Angeles: Roxbury Publishing Co.

———. 1998. *Social Learning and Social Structure: A General Theory of Crime and Deviance*. Boston: Northeastern University Press.

Albanese, J. 1995. *White Collar Crime in America*. Englewood Cliffs, NJ: Prentice-Hall, Inc.

Albonetti, C. A. 1986. "Criminality, Prosecutorial Screening, and Uncertainty: Toward a Theory of Discretionary Decision-Making in Felony Case Processing." *Criminology* 24(4): 623–644.

———. 1987. "Prosecutorial Discretion: The Effects of Uncertainty." *Law and Society Review* 21(2): 291–313.

———. 1992. "Charge Reduction: An Analysis of Prosecutorial Discretion in Burglary and Robbery Cases." *Journal of Quantitative Criminology* 8(3): 317–333.

———. 1998a. "Direct and Indirect Effects of Case Complexity, Guilty Pleas, and Offender Characteristics on Sentencing for Offenders Convicted of a White-Collar Offense Prior to Sentencing Guidelines." *Journal of Quantitative Criminology* 144: 353–378.

———. 1998b. "The Role of Gender and Departures in the Sentencing of Defendants Convicted of a White-Collar Offense under Federal Sentencing Guidelines." *Sociology of Crime, Law, and Deviance* 1: 3–48.

Albrecht, L. 1996. "Gender-Specific Programming in Juvenile Detention and Corrections." *Journal of Juvenile Justice and Detention Services* 11(2): 55–63.

Alder, C. 1986. "Unemployed Women Have Got It Heaps Worse." *The Australian and New Zealand Journal of Criminology* 19: 210–224.

———. 1995. "Feminist Criminology in Australia." In *International Feminist Perspectives in Criminology: Engendering a Discipline*, edited by N. H. Rafter and F. Heidensohn. Buckingham, England: Open University Press.

———. 1997. "Theories of Female Delinquency." In *Juvenile Crime, Justice and Corrections*, edited by A. Borowski and C. O'Connor. Melbourne, Victoria: Longman.

Alder, C., and J. Baker. 1997. "Maternal Filicide: More Than One Story to Be Told." *Women and Criminal Justice* 9(2): 15–41.

Alder, C., and K. Polk. 1996. "Masculinity and Child Homicide." *British Journal of Criminology* 36: 396–411.

Alder, C., and M. Baines. 1996. *And When She Was Bad? Working with Young Women in Juvenile Justice and Related Areas*. Hobart, Tasmania: National Clearing House for Youth Studies.

Alder, Z. 1987. *Rape on Trial*. London: Routledge and Kegan Paul.

Alexander, R. M. 1995. *The 'Girl Problem': Female Sexual Delinquency in New York, 1900–1930*. Ithaca, NY: Cornell University Press.

Alexander, S. 1983. *Very Much a Lady: The Untold Story of Jean Harris and Dr. Herman Tarnower*. Boston: Little, Brown, and Company.

Allen, H. 1987. *Justice Unbalanced: Gender, Psychiatry and Judicial Decisions*. Milton Keynes, England: Open University Press.

Allison, J. A., and L. S. Wrightsman. 1993. *Rape: The Misunderstood Crime*. Newbury Park, CA: Sage Publications, Inc.

Althouse, A. 1992. "Thelma and Louise and the Law: Do Rape Shield Rules Matter?" *Loyola of Los Angeles Law Review* 25: 757–772.

Altink, S. 1995. *Stolen Lives: Trading Women into Sex and Slavery*. London: Scarlet Press.

American Bar Association, Commission on Women in the Profession. 1995. *Women in the Law: A Look at the Numbers*. Report PC: 4920012. Chicago: The Commission.

American Correctional Association. 1990a. *The Female Offender: What Does the Future Hold?* Washington, DC: St. Mary's Press.

———. 1990b. *Standards for Adult Correctional Facilities*, 3rd ed. Lanham, MD: ACA.

———. 1998. *Facts about the Accreditation of Correctional Facilities*. Lanham, MD: ACA.

American Medical Association. 1981. *Standards for Health Services in Jails*. Chicago: American Medical Association.

Amir, M. 1971. *Patterns of Forcible Rape*. Chicago: University of Chicago Press.

Anderson, G. M. 1994. "Juvenile Justice and the Double Standard." *America* 170(1): 13–15.

Anderson, P. 1994. *Janet Reno: Doing the Right Thing*. New York: J. Wiley.

Anetzberger, G., J. Korbin, and C. Austin. 1994. "Alcoholism and Elder Abuse." *Journal of Interpersonal Violence* 9: 184–193.

Angell, J. E. 1971. "Toward an Alternative to the Classic Police Organizational Arrangement: A Democratic Model." *Criminology* 9: 185–206.

Appier, J. 1998. *Policing Women: The Sexual Politics of Law Enforcement and the LAPD*. Philadelphia: Temple University Press.

Armstrong, G. 1982. "Females under the Law: 'Protected' but Unequal." In *The Criminal Justice System and Women*, edited by B. R. Price and N. J. Sokoloff. New York: Clark Boardman.

Asia Watch and the Women's Rights Project. 1993. *A Modern Form of Slavery: Trafficking of Burmese Women and Girls into Brothels in Thailand*. New York: Human Rights Watch.

Atkinson, D. 1988. *Suffragettes*. London: Museum of London.

Atwood, M. 1996. *Alias Grace*. Toronto: Seal Books, McClelland-Bantam, Inc.

Austin, J., B. Bloom, and T. Donahue. 1992. *Female Offenders in the Community: An Analysis of Innovative Strategies and Programs*. Washington, DC: National Institute of Corrections.

Australian Bureau of Statistics. 1998a. *Prisoners in Australia 1997*. Melbourne, Australia: Commonwealth of Australia.

———. 1998b. *Recorded Crime, Australia, 1997*. Canberra, ACT: Australian Bureau of Statistics, Commonwealth of Australia.

Australian Law Reform Commission. 1994. *ALRC 69 Part I—Equality Before the Law: Justice for Women*. Australian Law Reform Commission 69, Part I and II.

Ayers, E. L. 1984. *Vengeance and Justice. Crime and Punishment in the 19th-Century American South*. New York: Oxford University Press.

Bachman, R. Forthcoming. "Estimates of Violence against Women: A Comparison of the National Crime Victimization Survey and the National Violence against Women Survey." In *Violence against Women* (August 2000).

Bachman, R., and B. M. Taylor. 1994. "The Measurement of Family Violence and Rape by the

Redesigned National Crime Victimization Survey." *Justice Quarterly* 11: 499–512.

Bachman, R., and L. E. Saltzman. 1995. *Violence against Women: A National Crime Victimization Survey Report*. NCJ -145325. Washington, DC: Bureau of Justice Statistics, U.S. Department of Justice.

Bachman, R., and R. Paternoster. 1993. "A Contemporary Look at the Effects of Rape Law Reform: How Far Have We Come?" *Journal of Criminal Law and Criminology* 84(3): 554–575.

Backhouse, C. 1991. *Petticoats and Prejudice: Women and Law in Nineteenth Century Canada*. Toronto: The Osgoode Society.

Bagley, K., and A. V. Merlo. 1995. "Controlling Women's Bodies." In *Women, Law and Social Control*, edited by A. V. Merlo and J. M. Pollock. Needham, MA: Allyn and Bacon.

Bala, N. 1997. *Young Offenders Law*. Concord, Ontario: Irwin Law.

Balkin, J. 1988. "Why Policemen Don't Like Policewomen." *Journal of Police Science and Administration* 16(1): 29–38.

Banks, O. 1981. *Faces of Feminism*. Oxford, England: Martin Robertson.

Bargen, J. 1996. "Kids, Cops, Courts, Conferencing and Children's Rights: A Note on Perspectives." *Australian Journal of Human Rights* 2(2): 209–228.

———. 2000. "Kids, Cops, Courts, Conferencing and Children's Rights: A Note on Perspectives and Update for 1996–98." In *Children on the Agenda: The Rights of Australia's Children*, edited by M. Jones and L. A. B. Marks. Sydney, Australia: Prospect Press.

Barnett, O. W., C. L. Miller-Perrin, and R. D. Perrin. 1997. *Family Violence across the Lifespan*. Thousand Oaks, CA: Sage Publications, Inc.

Bartlett, H. W., and A. Rosenblum. 1977. *Policewoman Effectiveness*. Denver: Civil Service Commission and Denver Police Department.

Bartusch, D. J., and R. Matsueda. 1996. "Gender, Reflected Appraisals, and Labeling: A Cross-Group Test of an Interactionist Theory of Delinquency." *Social Forces* 75(1): 145–177.

Baskin, D., and I. Sommers. 1993. "Females' Initiation into Violent Street Crime." *Justice Quarterly* 10: 559–583.

Baunach, P. J. 1985. *Mothers in Prison*. New Brunswick, NJ: Transaction Books.

Bay Area Sex Workers Advocacy Network. *Prostitutes' Education Network* <http://www.bayswan.org/index.html>, accessed 1 March 2000.

Beattie, J. M. 1975. "The Criminality of Women in Eighteenth Century England." *Journal of Social History* 8: 80–116.

———. 1995. "Crime and Inequality in Eighteenth-Century London." In *Crime and Inequality*, J. Hagan and R. Peterson, editors. Stanford: Stanford University Press.

Becker, H. 1963. *Outsiders: Studies in the Sociology of Deviance*. New York: The Free Press.

Becker, J. 1977. *Hitler's Children: The Story of the Baader-Meinhof Terrorist Gang*. New York: J. B. Lippincott.

Belknap, J. 1991. "Women in Conflict: An Analysis of Women Correctional Officers." *Women and Criminal Justice* 2(2): 89–116.

———. 1996. *The Invisible Woman: Gender, Crime, and Justice*. Belmont, CA: Wadsworth Publishing Company.

Belknap, J., and J. K. Shelley. 1992. "The New Lone Ranger: Police Women on Patrol." *American Journal of Police* 12(2): 47–75.

Belknap, J., and K. Holsinger. 1998. "An Overview of Delinquent Girls: How Theory and Practice Have Failed and the Need for Innovative Changes." In *Female Crime and Delinquency: Critical Perspectives and Effective Interventions*, edited by R. T. Zaplin. Gaithersburg, MD: Aspen Publishing.

Benedict, H. 1992. *Virgin or Vamp: How the Press Covers Sex Crimes*. Oxford: Oxford University Press.

Bennett, E. 1996. "Disclosure of Complainants' Medical and Therapeutic Records." *Canadian Criminal Law Review* 1: 17–30.

Benson, M., M. Evans, and R. Simon. 1982. "Women As Political Terrorists." *Research in Law, Deviance and Social Control* 4: 121–130.

Bergen, R. K. 1996. *Wife Rape: Understanding the Response of Survivors and Service Providers*. Thousand Oaks, CA: Sage Publications, Inc.

Berger, R. J. 1989. "Female Delinquency in the Emancipation Era: A Review of the Literature." *Sex Roles* 21(5/6): 375–399.

Berger, R. J., W. L. Neuman, and P. Searles. 1991. "The Social and Political Context of Rape Law Reform: An Aggregate Analysis." *Social Sciences Quarterly* 72(2): 221–237.

Bergsmann, I. 1994. "Establishing a Foundation: Just the Facts." In *A Time for Change*, National Juvenile Female Offenders Conference, American Correctional Association. Laurel, MD: American Correctional Association.

Bernat, F. P. 1992. "Women in the Legal Profession." In *The Changing Roles of Women in the Crimi-*

nal Justice System, edited by I. Moyer. Prospect Heights, IL: Waveland Press.

Bernat, F. P., W. H. Parsonage, and J. Helfgott. 1994. "Victim Impact Laws and the Parole Process in the United States: Balancing Victim and Inmate Rights and Interests." *International Review of Victimology* 3: 121–140.

Bernstein, I. N., E. Kick, J. T. Leung, and B. Schultz. 1977. "Charge Reduction: An Intermediary Stage in the Process of Labeling Criminal Defendants." *Social Forces* 6(2): 362–384.

Bershad, L. 1985. "Discriminatory Treatment of the Female Offender in the Criminal Justice System." *Boston College Law Review* 26: 389–438.

Bertrand, M. A. 1967. "The Myth of Sexual Equality before the Law." In *Proceedings of the Fifth Research Conference on Delinquency and Criminality*. Montreal: Quebec Society of Criminology.

———. 1969. "Self-Image and Delinquency: A Contribution to the Study of Female Criminality and Women's Image." *Acta Criminologica* 2: 71–144.

———. 1979. *La Femme et le Crime*. Montreal: L'Aurore.

———. 1992. "The Deconstruction of Truth Epistemologies." In *Proceedings of the International Feminist Conference on Women, Law and Social Control, 1991*, edited by M. A. Bertrand, K. Daly, and D. Klein. Vancouver, BC: International Centre for the Reform of Criminal Law and Criminal Justice Policy.

———. 1994. "From '*La Donna Delinquente*' to a Postmodern Deconstruction of the 'Woman Question' in Social Control Theory." *Journal of Human Justice* 5(2): 43–57.

Bertrand, M. A., K. Daly, and D. Klein, eds. 1992. *Proceedings of the International Feminist Conference on Women, Law and Social Control, 1991*. Vancouver, BC: International Centre for the Reform of Criminal Law and Criminal Justice Policy.

Best, J. 1998. *Controlling Vice: Regulating Brothel Prostitution in St. Paul, 1865–1883*. Columbus: Ohio State University Press.

Biddulph, S. 1997. *Raising Boys: Why Boys Are Different—and How to Help Them Become Happy and Well-Balanced Men*. Lane Cove, Sydney, Australia: Finch Publishing Co.

Bienen, L. 1983. "Rape Reform Legislation in the United States: A Look at Some Practical Effects." *Victimology* 8: 139–151.

Binder, A., and J. Meeker. 1992. "Arrest As a Method to Control Spouse Abuse." In *Domestic Violence: The Changing Criminal Justice Response*, edited

by E. S. Buzawa and C. G. Buzawa. Westport, CT: Auburn House.

Birkbeck, C., and G. LaFree. 1993. "The Situational Analysis of Crime and Deviance." *Annual Review of Sociology* 19: 113–137.

Bishop, D. M., and C. E. Frazier. 1984. "The Effects of Gender on Charge Reduction." *The Sociological Quarterly* 25(2): 385–396.

Bjerregaard, B. 1996. "Stalking and the First Amendment: A Constitutional Analysis of State Stalking Laws." *Criminal Law Bulletin* 32: 307–341.

Bjerregaard, B., and C. Smith. 1993. "Gender Differences in Gang Participation, Delinquency, and Substance Use." *Journal of Quantitative Criminology* 9(4): 329–355.

Blackwood, C. 1984. *On the Perimeter*. London: Fontana Paperbacks.

Blagg, H. 1997. "A Just Measure of Shame? Aboriginal Youth and Conferencing in Australia." *British Journal of Criminology* 37(4): 481–501.

Blinn, C. 1997. *Maternal Ties: A Selection of Programs for Female Offenders*. Lanham, MD: American Correctional Association.

Bloch, P. B., and D. Anderson. 1974. *Policewomen on Patrol: Final Report*. Washington, DC: Urban Institute.

Bloom, B. 1996. *Triple Jeopardy: Race, Class, and Gender As Factors in Women's Imprisonment*. Ph.D. dissertation. University of California, Riverside.

Bloom, B., and D. Steinhart. 1993. *Why Punish the Children? A Reappraisal of the Children of Incarcerated Mothers in America*. Washington, DC: National Council on Crime and Delinquency.

Blount, W. R., J. B. Kuhns, and I. J. Silverman. 1993. "Intimate Abuse within an Incarcerated Female Population: Rates, Levels, Criminality, a Continuum, and Some Lessons about Self-Identification." In *Female Criminality: The State of the Art*, edited by C. Culliver. New York: Garland Publishing.

Blum, L. N., N. H. Nielsen, and J. A. Riggs. 1998. "Alcoholism and Alcohol Abuse among Women: Report of the Council on Scientific Affairs." *Journal of Women's Health* 7(7): 861–871.

Bolton, F. G., and S. R. Bolton. 1987. *Working with Violent Families*. Thousand Oaks, CA: Sage Publications, Inc.

Bond, S. 1993. "Psychiatric Evidence of Sexual Assault Victims: The Need for Fundamental Change in the Determination of Relevance." *Dalhousie Law Journal* 16(2): 416–447.

Bonney, R. 1985. *Crimes (Sexual Assault) Amendment Act, 1981: Monitoring and Evaluation*.

Sydney: New South Wales Bureau of Crime Statistics and Research.

Boritch, H., and J. Hagan. 1990. "A Century of Crime in Toronto: Gender, Class and Patterns of Social Control, 1859 to 1955." *Criminology* 28: 567–599.

Bottcher, J. 1995. "Gender As Social Control: A Qualitative Study of Incarcerated Youths and Their Siblings in Greater Sacramento." *Justice Quarterly* 12(1): 33–57.

Bottoms, B. L., and G. S. Goodman. 1994. "Perceptions of Children's Credibility in Sexual Assault Cases." *Journal of Applied Social Psychology* 24(8): 702–732.

Boudouris, J. 1996. *Parents in Prison: Addressing the Needs of Families*. Lanham, MD: American Correctional Association.

Bowker, L. 1978. *Women, Crime and the Criminal Justice System*. Lexington, MA: Heath.

Bowland, A. L. 1994. "Sexual Assault Trials and the Protection of 'Bad Girls': The Battle between the Courts and Parliament." In *Confronting Sexual Assault: A Decade of Social and Legal Change*, edited by J. V. Roberts and R. Mohr. Toronto: University of Toronto Press.

Box, S., and C. Hale. 1983. "Liberation and Female Criminality in England and Wales." *British Journal of Criminology* 23(1): 35–49.

Boyle, C. 1984. *Sexual Assault*. Toronto: Carswell.

Boyle, C., and M. MacCrimmon. 1991. "*R. v. Seaboyer*: A Lost Cause?" *Criminal Reports (4th)* 7: 225–232.

———. 1998/99. "The Constitutionality of Bill C-49: Applying Section 15 As If It Really Mattered." *Criminal Law Quarterly* 41(2): 198–237.

Bradley, A. 1995. "Myra Hindley—A Bad Woman." *Living Marxism* 76 (February). Also: <http://www.informinc.co.uk/lm/LM76/LM76_Ann.html>, accessed 2 March 2000.

Braithwaite, J. 1989. *Crime, Shame and Reintegration*. Cambridge: Cambridge University Press.

———. 1999. "Restorative Justice: Assessing Optimistic and Pessimistic Accounts." In *Crime and Justice: A Review of Research*, vol. 23, edited by M. Tonry, pages 1–127. Chicago: University of Chicago Press.

Braithwaite, J., and K. Daly. 1994. "Masculinities, Violence, and Communitarian Control." In *Just Boys Doing Business? Men, Masculinities and Crime*, edited by T. Newburn and E. A. Stanko. London: Routledge.

Branham, L. S. 1998a. "An Inside Look at Accreditation." In *Corrections Today* 60(5): 92–95.

———. 1998b. *The Law of Sentencing, Corrections, and Prisoners' Rights in a Nutshell*. St. Paul, MN: West Publishing Co.

Brecci, M. 1997. "Female Officers on Patrol: Public Perceptions in the 1990s." *Journal of Crime and Justice* 20(2): 153–165.

Brecher, E. M., and R. Della Penna. 1975. *Health Care in Correctional Institutions*. Washington, DC: National Institute on Law Enforcement and the Administration of Justice.

Brennan, T. 1998. "Institutional Classification of Females: Problems and Some Proposals for Reform." In *Female Offenders: Critical Perspectives and Effective Interventions*, edited by R. T. Zaplin. Gaithersburg, MD: Aspen Publishers.

Brenzel, B. 1975. "Lancaster Industrial School for Girls: A Social Portrait of a 19th-Century Reform School for Girls." *Feminist Studies* 3: 40–53.

———. 1983. *Daughters of the State: A Social Portrait of the First Reform School for Girls in North America, 1856–1905*. Cambridge: Massachusetts Institute of Technology.

Brien, P. M., and C. W. Harlow. 1995. *HIV in Prisons and Jails, 1993*. Office of Justice Programs, Bureau of Justice Statistics. U.S. Department of Justice. Also: <http://www.ojp.usdoj.gov/bjs/abstract/hivip93.htm>, accessed 1 March 2000.

Briere, J. N., and D. M. Elliot. 1994. "Immediate and Long-Term Impacts of Child Sexual Abuse." *The Future of Children* 4: 54–69.

Briere, J. N., L. Berliner, J. A. Bulkley, C. Jenny, and T. Reid, eds. 1996. *The APSAC Handbook on Child Maltreatment*. Thousand Oaks, CA: Sage Publications in cooperation with the American Professional Society on the Abuse of Children.

Brock, R., and S. Thistlewaite. 1996. *Casting Stones: Prostitution and Liberation in Asia and the United States*. Minneapolis, MN: Fortress Press.

Broidy, L., and R. Agnew. 1997. "Gender and Crime: A General Strain Theory Perspective." *Journal of Research in Crime and Delinquency* 34(3): 275–306.

Bronfen, E. 1992. *Over Her Dead Body: Death, Femininity and the Aesthetic*. New York: Routledge.

Brown, A. 1991. *Lizzie Borden: The Legend, the Truth, the Final Chapter*. Nashville, TN: Rutledge Press.

Brown, J. M. 1998. "Aspects of Discriminatory Treatment of Women Police Officers Serving in Forces in England and Wales." *British Journal of Criminology* 38: 265–282.

Brown, J. M., and F. Heidensohn. 2000. *Gender and Policing*. Basingstoke, England: Macmillan.

Works Cited

Browne, A. 1987. *When Battered Women Kill.* New York: The Free Press.

———. 1996. "Violence in Marriage: Until Death Do Us Part?" In *Violence Between Intimate Partners: Patterns, Causes, and Effects*, edited by A. P. Cardarelli. Boston: Allyn and Bacon.

Browne, A., and K. R. Williams. 1993. "Gender, Intimacy, and Lethal Violence: Trends from 1976 through 1987." *Gender and Society* 7: 78–98.

Browne, A., K. R. Williams, and D. G. Dutton. 1998. "Homicide between Intimate Partners: A 20-Year Review." In *Homicide: A Sourcebook of Social Research*, edited by M. D. Smith and M. A. Zahn, pages 149–164. Thousand Oaks, CA: Sage Publications, Inc.

Brownmiller, S. 1975. *Against Our Will: Men, Women and Rape.* New York: Bantam.

Brownstein, H. H., B. J. Spunt, S. Crimmins, and S. C. Langley. 1994. "Changing Patterns of Lethal Violence by Women: A Research Note." *Women and Criminal Justice* 5: 99–118.

Bryant, C. 1990. "Evaluating Contributory Conduct." National Association of Crime Victim Compensation Boards *Report* (November/December): 7–15.

Buchwald, E., P. R. Fletcher, and M. Roth, eds. 1993. *Transforming a Rape Culture.* Minneapolis, MN: Milkweed Editions.

Budnick, K. J., and E. Shields-Fletcher. 1998. *What about Girls?* Office of Juvenile Justice and Delinquency Prevention, Fact Sheet #84. Washington, DC: Office of Justice Programs, U.S. Department of Justice.

Buhrke, R. A. 1996. *A Matter of Justice: Lesbians and Gay Men in Law Enforcement.* New York: Routledge.

Bunge, V. P., and A. Levett. 1998. *Family Violence in Canada: A Statistical Profile.* Ottawa: Canadian Centre for Justice Statistics.

Bureau of Justice Statistics. 1988. *Profile of State Prison Inmates, 1986.* Washington, DC: U.S. Department of Justice.

———. 1994a. *Criminal Victimization in the United States: 1973–92 Trends.* Washington, DC: U.S. Department of Justice.

———. 1994b. *Elderly Crime Victims: National Crime Victimization Survey.* Washington, DC: U.S. Department of Justice, Bureau of Justice Statistics.

———. 1994c. *Women in Prison.* Bureau of Justice Statistics Bulletin No. 145321. Washington, DC: U.S. Department of Justice.

———. 1997a. *Characteristics of Correctional Populations in the United States, 1995.* Washington, DC: U.S. Department of Justice.

———. 1997b. *Criminal Victimization in the United States, 1994.* Washington, DC: U.S. Department of Justice, Bureau of Justice Statistics.

———. 1997c. *HIV in Prisons and Jails, 1995.* Washington, DC: U.S. Department of Justice, Bureau of Justice Statistics.

———. 1997d. *Sourcebook of Criminal Justice Statistics.* Washington, DC: U.S. Department of Justice.

———. 1998a. "Alcohol and Crime: An Analysis of National Data on the Prevalence of Alcohol Involvement in Crime." NCJ 168632. Washington, DC: Office of Justice Statistics, U.S. Department of Justice.

———. 1998b. *Criminal Victimization, 1997: Changes 1996–97 with Trends 1993–97.* Washington, DC: U.S. Department of Justice.

———. 1998c. *Prisoners in 1997.* Washington, DC: U.S. Department of Justice.

———. 1998d. *Sourcebook of Criminal Justice Statistics 1997.* Washington, DC: U.S. Department of Justice.

———. 1999a. *Prison and Jail Inmates at Midyear 1998.* NCJ-173414. Washington, DC: Office of Justice Programs, U.S. Department of Justice.

———. 1999b. *Sourcebook of Criminal Justice Statistics, 1998.* Washington, DC: U.S. Department of Justice, Bureau of Justice Statistics.

———. 1999c. *Women Offenders.* Special report, NCJ-175688. Washington, DC: U.S. Department of Justice, Bureau of Justice Statistics.

Burke, M. E. 1993. *Coming Out of the Blue: British Police Officers Talk about Their Lives in 'the Job' As Lesbians, Gays and Bisexuals.* London: Cassell.

Burnley, J. N., C. Edmunds, M. T. Gaboury, and A. Seymour, eds. 1997. *National Victim Assistance Academy.* Washington, DC: U.S. Department of Justice.

Bursik, R. J. 1988. "Social Disorganization and Theories of Crime and Delinquency: Problems and Prospects." *Criminology* 26(4): 519–551.

Burstyn, V., ed. 1985. *Women against Censorship.* Vancouver, BC: Douglas and McIntyre.

Burton, V., and F. Cullen. 1992. "The Empirical Status of Strain Theory." *Journal of Crime and Justice* 15(1): 1–30.

Bush, D. M. 1992. "Women's Movements and State Policy Reform Aimed at Domestic Violence against Women." *Gender and Society* 6(4): 587–608.

Bush-Baskette, S. R. 1998. "The War on Drugs As a War against Black Women." In *Crime Control and Women: Feminist Implications of Criminal Jus-*

tice Policy, edited by S. L. Miller. Thousand Oaks, CA: Sage.

Butler, A. M. 1985. *Daughters of Joy, Sisters of Misery: Prostitutes in the American West, 1865–90.* Urbana: University of Illinois Press.

———. 1997. *Gendered Justice in the American West: Women Prisoners in Men's Penitentiaries.* Urbana: University of Illinois Press.

Buzawa, E. S., and C. G. Buzawa, eds. 1992. "Introduction." In *Domestic Violence: The Changing Criminal Justice Response,* edited by E. S. Buzawa and C. G. Buzawa. Westport, CT: Auburn House.

———. 1996. *Domestic Violence: The Criminal Justice Response,* 2nd ed. Thousand Oaks, CA: Sage.

Cain, M. 1990. "Realist Philosophy and Standpoint Epistemologies, or Feminist Criminologies As a Successor Science." In *Feminist Perspectives in Criminology,* edited by L. Gelstorpe and A. Morris. Milton Keynes, England: Open University Press.

Calder, J. 1995. "Mafia Women in Non-Fiction: What Secondary Sources Reveal." In *Contemporary Issues in Organized Crime,* edited by J. Albanese. Monsey, NY: Willow Tree.

Cameron, D., and E. Frazer. 1987. *The Lust to Kill: A Feminist Investigation of Sexual Murder.* Cambridge, England: Polity Press.

Camp, J. M., and N. Finkelstein. 1997. "Parenting Training for Women in Residential Substance Abuse Treatment: Results of a Demonstration Project." *Journal of Substance Abuse Treatment* 14: 411–422.

Campbell, A. 1984. *The Girls in the Gang.* Oxford: Basil Blackwell.

———. 1990. "Female Participation in Gangs." In *Gangs in America,* edited by C. R. Huff. Newbury Park, CA: Sage.

———. 1991. *The Girls in the Gang,* 2d ed. Cambridge, MA: Basil Blackwell.

Canada, Commission of Inquiry into Certain Events at the Prison for Women in Kingston. 1996. *Report (The Honourable Louise Arbour, Commissioner).* Ottawa: Public Works and Government Services Canada.

Canada, Department of Justice. 1998. *A Strategy for the Renewal of Youth Justice.* Ottawa: Department of Justice.

Canada, Department of Justice, Committee on Juvenile Delinquency. 1965. *Juvenile Delinquency in Canada.* Ottawa: Queen's Printer.

Canada, Law Reform Commission of Canada. 1989. *Crimes against the Foetus: A Working Paper.* Ottawa: Minister of Supply and Services.

Canada, Royal Commission on Aboriginal Peoples. 1993. *Aboriginal Peoples and the Justice System: Report of the National Round Table on Aboriginal Justice Issues.* Ottawa: The Commission.

Canada, Task Force on Federally Sentenced Women. 1990. *Creating Choices: The Report of the Task Force on Federally Sentenced Women.* Ottawa: Correctional Service of Canada.

Canter, R. J. 1982. "Family Correlates of Male and Female Delinquency." *Criminology* 20: 149–167.

Cappelleri, J. C., J. Eckenrode, and J. L. Powers. 1993. "The Epidemiology of Child Abuse: Findings from the Second National Incidence and Prevalence Study of Child Abuse and Neglect." *American Journal of Public Health* 83: 1622–1624.

Cardarelli, A., ed. 1997. *Violence between Intimate Partners: Patterns, Causes and Effects.* Boston: Allyn and Bacon.

Caringella-MacDonald, S. 1996. "Rape: How Culture, Laws and Practices Reinforce Criminal Sexual Violence." In *Perspectives on Criminal Justice,* edited by C. Calhoun and G. Ritzer. New York: McGraw-Hill.

Carlen, P. 1983. *Women's Imprisonment.* London: Routledge and Kegan Paul.

———. 1988. *Women, Crime and Poverty.* Philadelphia: Open University Press.

———. 1990. *Alternatives to Women's Imprisonment.* Buckingham, England: Open University Press.

———. 1992. "Criminal Women and Criminal Justice." In *Issues in Realist Criminology,* edited by R. Matthews and J. Young. London: Sage Publications.

———. 1998. *Sledgehammer: Women's Imprisonment At the Millennium.* London: Macmillan

Carpenter, M. 1864. *Our Convicts,* 2 vols. London: Longman.

Carrier, J. 1988. *The Campaign for the Employment of Women As Police Officers.* Aldershot, England: Arebury/Gower.

Carrington, K. 1993. *Offending Girls: Sex, Youth and Justice.* St. Leonards, New South Wales: Allen and Unwin.

———. 1998. *Who Killed Leigh Leigh? A Story of Shame and Mateship in an Australian Town.* Sydney: Random House.

Carroll, L. 1988. *Hacks, Blacks and Cons: Race Relations in a Maximum Security Prison.* Prospect Heights, IL: Waveland Press.

Casale, S. 1989. *Women Inside: The Experience of Women Remand Prisoners in Holloway.* London: Civil Liberties Trust.

Cavender, G., and N. C. Jurik. 1998. "Jane Tennison and the Feminist Police Procedural." *Violence against Women* 4: 10–29.

Ceci, S. J., and M. Bruck. 1993. "Suggestibility of the Child Witness: A Historical Review and Synthesis." *Psychological Bulletin* 113(3): 403–439.

Center for Reproductive Law and Policy. 1996. "Punishing Women for Their Behavior during Pregnancy: An Approach That Undermines Women's Health and Children's Interests." *Reproductive Freedom: In Focus* (14 February): 1–10.

Center for Substance Abuse Treatment. 1994. *Practical Approaches in the Treatment of Women Who Abuse Alcohol and Other Drugs.* Rockville, MD: U.S. Department of Health and Human Services.

———. 1997. *Substance Abuse Treatment for Incarcerated Offenders: Guide to Promising Practices.* Rockville, MD: Department of Health and Human Services.

Chambliss, W. J., and R. B. Seidman. 1982. *Law, Order, and Power.* Reading, MA: Addison-Wesley.

Chapkis, W. 1997. *Live Sex Acts: Women Performing Erotic Labor.* New York: Routledge.

Chapman, S. 1999. "Section 276 of the Criminal Code and the Admissibility of 'Sexual Activity' Evidence." *Queen's Law Journal* 25: 121–176.

Chaudhuri, M., and K. Daly. 1992. "Do Restraining Orders Help? Battered Women's Experience with Male Violence and Legal Process." In *Domestic Violence: The Changing Criminal Justice Response*, edited by E. Buzawa and C. Buzawa. Westport, CT: Auburn House.

Chavkin, W. 1990. "Drug Addiction and Pregnancy: Policy Crossroads." *American Journal of Public Health* 80: 483–487.

Cheney, P., and M. Philip. 1998. "Pregnant Crack Dealer Agrees to Jail to Protect Fetus." *The Globe and Mail* (28 November): A1.

Chesney-Lind, M. 1973. "Judicial Enforcement of the Female Sex Role: The Family Court and the Female Delinquent." *Issues in Criminology* 8(2): 51–69.

———. 1977. "Judicial Paternalism and the Female Status Offender: Training Women to Know Their Place." *Crime and Delinquency* 23(2): 121–130.

———. 1978. "Chivalry Re-Examined: Women and the Criminal Justice System." In *Women, Crime, and the Criminal Justice System*, edited by L. H. Bowker. Lexington, MA: Lexington Books.

———. 1986. "Women and Crime: The Female Offender." *Signs* 12(1): 78–96.

———. 1989. "Girls' Crime and Woman's Place: Toward a Feminist Model of Female Delinquency." *Crime and Delinquency* 35: 5–29.

———. 1997. *The Female Offender: Girls, Women, and Crime.* Thousand Oaks, CA: Sage.

———. 1998. "Women in Prison: From Partial Justice to Vengeful Equity." *Corrections Today* 60(7): 67–68, 70, 72–73.

Chesney-Lind, M., and J. M. Hagedorn, eds. 1999. *Female Gangs in America: Essays on Girls, Gangs, and Gender.* Chicago: Lakeview Press.

Chesney-Lind, M., and R. G. Shelden. 1992. *Girls, Delinquency, and Juvenile Justice.* Belmont, CA: Wadsworth.

———. 1998. *Girls, Delinquency, and Juvenile Justice,* 2nd ed. Belmont, CA: West/Wadsworth.

Christenson, R., ed. 1991. *Political Trials in History: From Antiquity to the Present.* New Brunswick, NJ: Transaction Publishers.

Chunn, D. E., and R. Menzies. 1990. "Gender, Madness and Crime: The Reproduction of Patriarchal and Class Relations in a Psychiatric Court Clinic." *Journal of Human Justice* 1(2): 33–54.

———. 1995. "Canadian Criminology and the Woman Question." In *International Feminist Perspectives in Criminology: Engendering a Discipline*, edited by N. H. Rafter and F. Heidensohn. Buckingham, England: Open University Press.

———. 1998. "Out of Mind, Out of Law: The Regulation of 'Criminally Insane' Women inside British Columbia's Public Mental Hospitals, 1888–1973." *Canadian Journal of Women and the Law* 10(3): 1–32.

Chunn, D. E., and S. A. M. Gavigan. 1995. "Women, Crime, and Criminal Justice in Canada." In *Canadian Criminology: Perspectives on Crime and Criminality*, 2nd ed., edited by M. A. Jackson and C. T. Griffiths. Toronto: Harcourt Brace and Co.

Clark, C. 1994. "Crime Victim's Rights: Do Victims Need New Laws and Protections?" *CQ Researcher* (22 July): 625–648.

Clarke, R., P. Ekblom, M. Hough, and P. Mayhew. 1985. "Elderly Victims of Crime and Exposure to Risk." *The Howard Journal* 24: 1–9.

Cloward, R., and L. Ohlin. 1960. *Delinquency and Opportunity.* New York: Free Press.

Cockburn, C. 1991. *In The Way of Women: Men's Resistance to Sex Equality in Organizations.* Ithaca, NY: International Labor Relations Press.

Cohen, A. 1955. *Delinquent Boys: The Culture of the Gang.* New York: Free Press.

Cohen, L. E., and M. Felson. 1979. "Social Change and Crime Rate Trends: A Routine Activity Approach." *American Sociological Review* 44: 588–608.

Coker, D. 1999. "Enhancing Autonomy for Battered Women: Lessons from Navajo Peacemaking."

University of California Law Review 47(1): 1–111.

Coleman, C., and Moynihan, J. 1996. *Understanding Crime Data: Haunted by the Dark Figure*. Buckingham, England: Open University Press.

Coleman, F. L. 1997. "Stalking Behavior and the Cycle of Domestic Violence." *Journal of Interpersonal Violence* 12: 420–432.

Coleman, J. W. 1998. *The Criminal Elite: Understanding White Collar Crime*, 4th ed. New York: St. Martin's Press.

Coleman, V. E. 1990. *Violence between Lesbian Couples: A Between-Groups Comparison*. Ph.D. dissertation. California School of Professional Psychology, Los Angeles. University Microfilms No. 9109022.

———. 1994. "Lesbian Battering: The Relationship between Personality and the Perpetration of Violence." *Violence and Victims* 9: 139–152.

Collins, J. J. 1991. "Drinking and Violation of the Criminal Law." In *Society, Culture, and Drinking Patterns Reexamined*, edited by D. J. Pittman and H. R. White. New Brunswick, NJ: Rutgers Center of Alcohol Studies.

Collins, P. H. 1991. *Black Feminist Thought: Knowledge, Consciousness and the Politics of Empowerment*. New York: Routledge.

Comack, E. 1993. *The Feminist Engagement with the Law: The Legal Recognition of the Battered Woman Syndrome*. Ottawa: Canadian Research Institute for the Advancement of Women.

———. 1996. *Women in Trouble*. Halifax, NS: Fernwood Publishing

Conly, C. 1998. *The Women's Prison Association: Supporting Women Offenders and Their Families*. No. 172858. Washington, DC: National Institute of Justice.

Connell, R. W. 1995. *Masculinities*. St. Leonards, Victoria, Australia: Allen and Unwin.

Cook, A., and G. Kirk. 1983. *Greenham Women Everywhere*. London: Pluto Press.

Cooper, S. 1993. "The Evolution of the Federal Women's Prison." In *In Conflict with the Law: Women and the Canadian Justice System*, edited by E. Adelberg and C. Currie. Vancouver, BC: Press Gang Publishers.

Cowie, J., V. Cowie, and E. Slater. 1968. *Delinquency in Girls*. London: Heinemann.

Cranford, S., and R. Williams. 1998. "Critical Issues in Managing Female Offenders." *Corrections Today* 60(7): 130–134.

Crapsey, E. 1970. "Juvenile Vagrants and Delinquents in New York City, 1872." In *Juvenile Offenders for a Thousand Years*, edited by W. B. Sanders. Chapel Hill: University of North Carolina Press.

Craven, D. 1996. *Female Victims of Violent Crime*. NCJ-162602. Washington, DC: U.S. Department of Justice, Bureau of Justice Statistics.

———. 1997. *Sex Differences in Violent Victimization, 1994*. Special report. Washington, DC: Bureau of Justice Statistics.

Crawford, M., and R. Gartner. 1992. *Woman Killing: Intimate Femicide in Ontario 1974–1990*. Toronto: Government of Ontario, Ministry of Social Services, Women's Directorate.

Crawford, W. 1969. *Report on the Penitentiaries of the United States*. Reprint ed.; orig. pub. 1835. Montclair, NJ: Patterson Smith.

Crew, B. K. 1991. "Sex Differences in Criminal Sentencing: Chivalry or Patriarchy?" *Justice Quarterly* 8(1): 59–83.

Crites, L. 1978. "Women in the Criminal Court." In *Women in the Courts*, edited by W. Hepperle and L. Crites. Williamsburg, VA: National Center of State Courts.

Cromwell, P., J. Olson, and D. Avary. 1991. *Breaking and Entering: An Ethnographic Analysis of Burglary*. Newbury Park, CA: Sage.

Crowley, J. E., and L. M. Adrian. 1992. "Women Misdemeanants in the Allegheny County Jail, 1892–1929." *Journal of Criminal Justice* 20: 311–331.

Culhane, D., and R. Taylor. 2000. "Theory and Practice: Clinical Law and Aboriginal People." In *Law As a Gendering Practice*, edited by D. E. Chunn and D. Lacombe. Toronto: Oxford University Press.

Cunneen, C., and J. Stubbs. 1997. *Gender, "Race" and International Relations: Violence against Filipino Women in Australia*. Sydney: Institute of Criminology.

Cunneen, C., and T. Libesman. 1995. *Indigenous People and the Law in Australia*. Sydney: Butterworths.

Curran, B. A., K. J. Rosich, C. N. Carson, and M. Puccetti. 1985. *The Lawyer Statistical Report: A Statistical Profile of the U.S. Legal Profession in the 1980s*. Chicago: American Bar Association.

Curran, D. J. 1984. "The Myth of the 'New' Female Delinquent." *Crime and Delinquency* 30(3): 386–399.

Curtis, D., A. Graham, L. Kelly, and A. Patterson. 1985. *Kingston Penitentiary: The First Hundred and Fifty Years*. Ottawa: Supply and Services, Canada.

D'Acci, J. 1994. *Defining Women: Television and the Case of Cagney and Lacey*. Chapel Hill: University of North Carolina Press.

Works Cited

Dale, M. J. 1990. "The Female Inmate: An Introduction to Legal Rights and Issues." *American Jails* 4(1): 56–64.

Dalton, K. 1960a. "Menstruation and Accidents." *British Medical Journal* 2: 1425–1426.

———. 1960b. "School Girls' Behavior and Menstruation." *British Medical Journal* 2: 1647–1649.

———. 1961. "Menstruation and Crime." *British Medical Journal* 2: 1752–1753.

Daly, K. 1987. "Structure and Practice of Familial-Based Justice in a Criminal Court." *Law and Society Review* 21(2): 267–290.

———. 1989a. "Neither Conflict nor Labeling nor Paternalism Will Suffice: Intersections of Race, Ethnicity, Gender and Family in Criminal Court Decisions." *Crime and Delinquency* 35: 136–168.

———. 1989b. "Rethinking Judicial Paternalism: Gender, Work-Family Relations, and Sentencing." *Gender and Society* 3: 9–36.

———. 1989c. "Gender and Varieties of White Collar Crime." *Criminology* 27(4): 769–794.

———. 1994. *Gender, Crime, and Punishment*. New Haven: Yale University Press.

———. 1997. "Different Ways of Conceptualizing Sex/Gender in Feminist Theory and Their Implications for Criminology." *Theoretical Criminology* 1(1): 25–51.

———. Forthcoming. "Restorative Justice in Diverse and Unequal Societies." *Law in Context* 17 (June 2000).

Daly, K., and M. Chesney-Lind. 1988. "Feminism and Criminology." *Justice Quarterly* 5(4): 498–538.

Daly, K., and M. Tonry. 1997. "Gender, Race, and Sentencing." In *Crime and Justice: A Review of Research*, edited by M. Tonry. Chicago: University of Chicago Press.

Daly, K., and R. L. Bordt. 1995. "Sex Effects and Sentencing: A Review of the Statistical Literature." *Justice Quarterly* 12(1): 143–177.

Daly, K., M. Venables, M. McKenna, L. Mumford, and J. Christie-Johnson. 1998. *South Australia Juvenile Justice (SAJJ) Research on Conferencing: Research Instruments and Background Notes*. SAJJ Technical Report No. 1. Brisbane: School of Criminology and Criminal Justice, Griffith University. Also: <http://www.aic.gov.au/rjustice/sajj/index.html>.

Daly, M. 1978. *Gyn/Ecology: The Metaethics of Radical Feminism*. Boston: Beacon Press.

Danner, M. J. 1998. "Three Strikes and It's Women Who Are Out: The Hidden Consequences for Women of Criminal Justice Policy Reforms." In *Crime Control and Women: Feminist Implications of Criminal Justice Policy*, edited by S. L. Miller. Thousand Oaks, CA: Sage.

Danner, T., W. R. Blount, I. J. Silverman, and M, Vega. 1995. "The Female Chronic Offender: Exploring Life Contingency and Offense History Dimensions for Incarcerated Female Offenders." *Women and Criminal Justice* 6(2): 45–66.

Datesman, S., and F. Scarpitti. 1980. *Women, Crime and the Criminal Justice System*. New York: Oxford University Press.

Davies, A. 1998. "Youth Gangs, Masculinity and Violence in Late Victorian Manchester and Salford." *Journal of Social History* 32(2): 349–369.

———. 1999. "'These Viragoes Are No Less Cruel Than the Lads': Young Women, Gangs and Violence in Late Victorian Manchester and Salford." *British Journal of Criminology* 39(1): 72–89.

Davis, A. 1967. *Spearheads for Reform: The Social Settlements and the Progressive Movement, 1890–1914*. New York: Oxford University Press.

Davis, A. Y. 1974. *Angela Davis: An Autobiography*. New York: Random House.

———. 1981. *Women, Race and Class*. New York: Random House.

———. 1998. *The Angela Y. Davis Reader*, edited by J. A. James. Cambridge: Blackwell.

Davis, R. C. 1987. "Crime Victims: Learning How to Help Them." *National Institute of Justice Reports* No. 203 (May/June).

Davis, R. C., and M. Henley. 1990. "Victim Service Programs." In *Victims of Crime: Problems, Policies and Programs*, edited by A. Lurigio, W. Skogan, and R. Davis. Beverly Hills, CA: Sage.

Davis, S., S. Haire, and D. R. Songer. 1993. "Voting Behavior and Gender on the U.S. Courts of Appeals." *Judicature* 77: 129–133.

Dawson, T. B. 1998. "First Person Familiar: Judicial Intervention in Pregnancy, Again: *G. (D. F.)*." *Canadian Journal of Women and the Law* 10(1): 213–228.

Decker, S. H., R. Wright, A. Redfern, and D. Smith. 1993. "A Woman's Place Is in the Home: Females and Residential Burglary." *Justice Quarterly* 10(1): 143–162.

DeJong, W., and R. Hingson. 1998. "Strategies to Reduce Driving under the Influence of Alcohol." *Annual Review of Public Health* 19: 359–378.

Delacoste, F., and P. Alexander, eds. 1987. *Sex Work: Writings by Women in the Sex Industry*. Minneapolis: Cleis Press.

Demause, L. 1991. "The Universality of Incest." *Journal of Psychohistory* 19(2): 123–164.

———. 1994. "The History of Child Abuse." *Sexual Addiction Compulsivity* 1(1): 77–91.

Demila, S. 1978. "Homosexuals As Police Officers?" *New York Times* (10 February): 25.

Demos, J. P. 1982. *Entertaining Satan: Witchcraft and the Culture of New England.* Oxford: Oxford University Press.

Denault, L. *Allegiance and Faith in "Paradise Lost."* <http://www.watson.org/rivendell/litengessay1.html>, accessed 1 March 2000.

Deverey, C. 1991. *Disadvantage and Crime in New South Wales.* Sydney: New South Wales Bureau of Crime Statistics and Research.

Devlin, A. 1998. *Invisible Women: What's Wrong with Women's Prisons?* Winchester, England: Waterside Press.

Diana, L. 1985. *The Prostitute and Her Clients: Your Pleasure Is Her Business.* Springfield, IL: Charles C. Thomas.

Dines, G., R. Jensen, and A. Russo. 1998. *Pornography: The Production and Consumption of Inequality.* New York: Routledge.

Dobash, R., and R. E. Dobash. 1979. *Violence against Wives; A Case against Patriarchy.* New York, Free Press.

———. 1988. "Research As Social Action: The Struggle for Battered Women." In *Feminist Perspectives on Wife Abuse,* edited by K. Yllo and M. Boggard, pages 51–74. Newbury Park, CA: Sage Publications.

———. 1992. *Women, Violence and Social Change.* New York: Routledge.

———.1995. *Gender and Crime.* Cardiff, England: University of South Wales.

Dobash, R. P., R. E. Dobash, and S. Gutteridge. 1986. *The Imprisonment of Women.* Oxford, England: Basil Blackwell.

Dobash, R. P., R. E. Dobash, M. Wilson, and M. Daly. 1992. "The Myth of Sexual Symmetry in Marital Violence." *Social Problems* 39(1): 71–91.

Doerner, W. G., and S. P. Lab. 1995. *Victimology.* Cincinnati: Anderson Publishing Co.

Doob, A. N., and J. B. Sprott. 1998. "Is the 'Quality' of Youth Violence Becoming More Serious?" *Canadian Journal of Criminology* 40(2): 185–194.

D'Orban, P., and K. Dalton. 1980. "Violent Crime and the Menstrual Cycle." *Psychological Medicine* 10: 353–359.

Downes, D. M., and P. E. Rock. 1992. *Understanding Deviance,* 3d ed. Oxford: Oxford University Press.

Drachman, V. 1998. *Sisters in Law: Women Lawyers in Modern American History.* Cambridge: Harvard University Press.

Dreifus, C. 1982. "Why Two Women Cops Were Convicted of Cowardice." In *The Criminal Justice System and Women,* edited by B. R. Price and N. J. Sokoloff. New York: Clark Boardman.

Drucker, D. 1979. "The Common Law Does Not Support a Marital Exception for Forcible Rape." *Women's Rights Law Reporter* 5(2–3): 181–200.

Dulaney, W. 1996. *Black Police in America.* Bloomington: Indiana University Press.

Dutton, M. A. 1993. "Understanding Women's Responses to Domestic Violence: A Redefinition of Battered Woman Syndrome." *Hofstra Law Review* 21(4): 1191–1242.

Dworkin, A. 1989. *Pornography: Men Possessing Women.* New York: Plume.

Early, K. E. 1996. *Drug Treatment behind Bars: Prison-Based Strategies for Change.* Westport, CT: Praeger.

Easteal, P. 1992. *The Forgotten Few: Overseas-Born Women in Australian Prisons.* Canberra: Australian Government Publishing Service.

Eaton, M. 1986. *Justice for Women?* Milton Keynes, England: Open University Press.

———. 1993. *Women after Prison,* Buckingham, England: Open University Press.

Edleson, J. L., and M. P. Brygger. 1986. "Gender Differences in Reporting of Battering Incidences." *Family Relations* 35: 377–382.

Edwards, A. 1995a. "Women in Prison." BOCSAR Report B-26. Sydney: NSW Attorney General's Department, NSW Bureau of Crime Statistics and Research. Also: <http://www.lawlink.nsw.gov.au/bocsar1.nsf/page/cjb26link>, accessed 20 June 2000.

———. 1995b. "Women in Prison." *Contemporary Issues in Crime and Justice* 26: 1–7.

Egger, S. A. 1998. *The Killers Among Us: An Examination of Serial Murder and Its Investigation.* Upper Saddle River, NJ: Prentice Hall.

Eich, W. 1986. "Gender Bias in the Courtroom: Some Participants Are More Equal Than Others." *Judicature* 69: 339–343.

Eisenstein, Z. R., ed. 1979. *Capitalist Patriarchy and the Case for Socialist Feminism.* New York: Monthly Review Press.

Elias, R. 1986. *The Politics of Victimization: Victims, Victimology and Human Rights.* New York: Oxford University Press.

———. 1993. *Victims Still: The Political Manipulation of Crime Victims.* Thousand Oaks, CA: Sage Publications, Inc.

Works Cited

Elliott, D. 1994. "Serious Violent Offenders: Onset, Developmental Course, and Termination." *Criminology* 32(1): 1–22.

Elliott, M., ed. 1993. *Female Sexual Abuse of Children.* New York: The Guilford Press.

Ellis, D., and P. Austin. 1971. "Menstruation and Aggressive Behavior in a Correctional Center for Women." *The Journal of Criminal Law, Criminology, and Police Science,* 62(3): 388–395.

Ellison, K. W., and J. Genz. 1983. *Stress and the Police Officer.* Springfield, IL: Thomas.

Emerson, R. M., K. O. Ferris, and C. B. Gardner. 1998. "On Being Stalked." *Social Problems* 45: 289–315.

Empey, L., and M. Stafford. 1991. *American Delinquency: Its Meaning and Construction.* Belmont, CA: Wadsworth.

Emsley, C. 1996. *Crime and Society in England, 1750–1900,* 2nd ed. New York: Longman.

Encyclopaedia Britannica. <http://www.britannica.com/>, "Barker, 'Ma'"; accessed 24 March 2000.

Enos, S. 1997. "Managing Motherhood in Prison: The Impact of Race and Ethnicity on Child Placements." *Women and Therapy* 20: 57–74.

Epps, P. 1962. "Women Shoplifters in Holloway Prison." In *Shoplifting,* edited by T. Gibbens and J. Prince. London: Institute for the Study and Treatment of Delinquency.

Epstein, C. F. 1993. *Women in Law.* Chicago: University of Illinois Press.

Erez, E. 1990. "Victim Participation in Sentencing: Rhetoric and Reality." *Journal of Criminal Justice* 18: 19–31.

———. 1994. "Victim Participation in Sentencing: And the Debate Goes On." *International Review of Victimology* 3(1–2): 17–32.

Estrich, S. 1987. *Real Rape.* Cambridge: Harvard University Press.

Ettorre, E. 1992. *Women and Substance Abuse.* New Brunswick, NJ: Rutgers University Press.

Evans, S., and S. Schaefer. 1987. "Incest and Chemically Dependent Women: Treatment Implications." *Journal of Chemical Dependency Treatment* 1: 141–173.

Factum of the Intervenors, the Aboriginal Women's Council, the Disabled Women's Network of Canada, the Canadian Association of Sexual Assault Centres, and the Women's Legal Education and Action Fund, in *R. V. O'Connor,* LEAF. 1996. *Equality and the Charter: Ten Years of Feminist Advocacy before the Supreme Court of Canada.* Toronto: Edmond Montgomery Publications Ltd.

Fagan, J. 1994. "Women and Drugs Revisited: Female Participation in the Cocaine Economy." *Journal of Drug Issues* 24: 179–225.

Faily, A., and G. Roundtree. 1979. "A Study of Aggression and Rule Violations in a Female Prison Population." *Journal of Offender Counseling, Service and Rehabilitation* 4(1): 81–87.

Faith, K. 1993. *Unruly Women: The Politics of Confinement and Resistance.* Vancouver, BC: Press Gang Publishers.

———. 1995. "Aboriginal Women's Healing Lodge: Challenge to Penal Correctionalism?" *Journal of Human Justice* 6(2): 79–104.

Faiver, K. L. 1997. *Health Care Management Issues in Corrections.* Lanham, MD: American Correctional Association.

Faller, K. 1987. "Women Who Sexually Abuse Children." *Violence and Victims* 2(4): 263–276.

Farnham, E. W. 1846. "Introduction to *Rationale of Crime,* by M. B. Sampson." New York: D. Appleton and Co.

Farnworth, M., and R. H. C. Teske. 1995. "Gender Differences in Felony Court Processing: Three Hypotheses of Disparity." *Women and Criminal Justice* 6(2): 23–44.

Farrell, G. 1995. "Preventing Repeat Victimization." In *Building a Safer Society,* edited by M. Tonry and D. P. Farrington. Chicago: University of Chicago Press.

Fattah, E. A. 1991. *Understanding Criminal Victimization.* Scarborough, Ontario: Prentice Hall.

Federle, K., and M. Chesney-Lind. 1992. "Special Issues in Juvenile Justice: Gender, Race, and Ethnicity." In *Juvenile Justice and Public Policy: Toward a National Agenda,* edited by I. M. Schwartz. Lexington, MA: Lexington Books.

Fedorowycz, O. 1998. "Homicide in Canada, 1997." *Juristat* 18(12): 1–10.

Feeley, M. M., and D. L. Little. 1991. "The Vanishing Female: The Decline of Women in the Criminal Process, 1687–1912." *Law and Society Review* 25(4): 719–757.

Feild, H., and L. Bienen. 1980. *Jurors and Rape.* Lexington, MA: D. C. Heath.

Feinman, C. 1980. *Women in the Criminal Justice System.* New York: Praeger.

———. 1984. "An Historical Overview of the Treatment of Incarcerated Women: Myths and Realities of Rehabilitation." *The Prison Journal* 63(2): 12–26.

———. 1986. *Women in the Criminal Justice System,* 2nd ed. New York: Praeger.

———. 1990. "Justice by Geography: Urban, Suburban, and Rural Variations in Juvenile Justice

Administration." *Journal of Criminal Law and Criminology* 82: 156–210.

———. 1994. *Women in the Criminal Justice System*, 3rd ed. Westport, CT, Praeger.

Felson, M. 1996. "Routine Activity Approach." In *Readings in Contemporary Criminological Theory*, edited by P. Cordella and L. Siegel. Boston: Northeastern University Press.

Felson, M., and L. E. Cohen. 1981. "An Interactionist Approach to Aggression." In *Impression Management Theory and Social Psychological Research*, edited by J. T. Tedeschi. New York: Academic Press.

"Female Offenders." 1998. *Corrections Today Magazine* 60(7): 1–173.

Ferraro, K. J. 1989. "Policing Woman Battering." *Social Problems* 36(1): 61–74.

Ferraro, K. J., and T. Boychuk. 1992. "The Court's Response to Interpersonal Violence: A Comparison of Intimate and Non-Intimate Assault." In *Domestic Violence: The Changing Criminal Justice Response*, edited by E. S. Buzawa and C. G. Buzawa. Westport, CT: Auburn House.

Figueira-McDonough, J. 1985. "Gender Differences in Informal Processing: A Look at Charge Bargaining and Sentence Reduction in Washington, D.C." *Journal of Research in Crime and Delinquency* 22(2): 101–133.

Finkelhor, D. 1984. *Child Sexual Abuse: New Theory and Research*. New York: The Free Press.

———. 1994. "Current Information on the Scope and Nature of Child Sexual Abuse." *The Future of Children* 4: 31–53.

Finkelhor, D., and K. Yllo. 1985. *License to Rape: Sexual Abuse of Wives*. New York: Free Press.

Finley, L. M. 1989. "Breaking Women's Silence in Law: The Dilemma of the Gendered Nature of Legal Reasoning." *Notre Dame Law Review* 64: 886.

Finnane, M. 1997. *Punishment in Australian Society*. Melbourne: Oxford University Press.

Fisher-Giorlando, M. 1995. "Women in the Walls: The Imprisonment of Women at the Baton Rouge Penitentiary, 1835–1862." In *The Wall Is Strong: Corrections in Louisiana*, edited by B. Foster, W. Rideau, and D. Dennis. Lafayette, LA: The Center for Louisiana Studies.

Fitzpatrick, E. 1990. *Endless Crusade: Women Social Scientists and Progressive Reform*. New York: Oxford University Press.

Fletcher, C. 1995. *Breaking and Entering: Women Cops Talk about Life in the Ultimate Men's Club*. New York: HarperCollins.

Flynn, E. E. 1996. "Crime and Age." *Encyclopedia of Gerontology*, vol. 1, edited by J. E. Birren. San Diego: Academic Press.

Fox, J. 1990. "Women in Prison: A Case Study in the Social Reality of Stress." In *The Pains of Imprisonment*, edited by R. Johnson and H. Toch. Newbury Park, CA: Sage.

Fox, J. A., and M. W. Zawitz. 1998. "Homicide Trends in the United States." Washington, DC: Bureau of Justice Statistics. Also: <http://www.ojp.usdoj.gov/bjs/homicide/homtrnd.htm>.

Frank, S. P. 1996. "Narratives within Numbers: Women, Crime and Judicial Statistics in Imperial Russia, 1834–1913". *The Russian Review* 55: 541–566.

Frazier, P. A., and B. Haney. 1996. "Sexual Assault Cases in the Legal System: Police, Prosecutor, and Victim Perspectives." *Law and Human Behavior* 20: 607–628.

Freedman, E. B. 1981. *Their Sisters' Keepers: Women's Prison Reform in America, 1830–1930*. Ann Arbor: University of Michigan Press.

Freedman, E. B. 1996. *Maternal Justice. Miriam Van Waters and the Female Reform Tradition*. Chicago: University of Chicago Press.

Freeman-Davis, B. 1961. *The Desperate and the Damned*. New York: Thomas Y. Crowell Company.

Freud, S. 1933. *New Introductory Lectures on Psycho-Analyses*. Binghamton, NY: Vail-Ballou Press.

Friedrich, W. N., R. L. Beilke, and A. Urquiza. 1987. "Children from Sexually Abusive Families: A Behavioral Comparison." *Journal of Interpersonal Violence* 2: 391–402.

Frohmann, L. 1991. "Discrediting Victims' Allegations of Sexual Assault: Prosecutorial Accounts of Case Rejections." *Social Problems* 38(2): 213–226.

Fromuth, M. E., and V. E. Conn. 1997. "Hidden Perpetrators: Sexual Molestation in a Nonclinical Sample of College Women." *Journal of Interpersonal Violence* 6: 376–394.

Fry, E. 1827. *Observations on the Visiting, Superintendance, and Government of Female Prisoners*. London: Arch.

Fry, M. 1959. "Justice for Victims." *Journal of Public Law* 8: 191–194.

Gabel, K., and D. Johnston, eds. 1995. *Children of Incarcerated Parents*. New York: Lexington Books.

Gagné, P. 1998. *Battered Women's Justice: The Movement for Clemency and the Politics of Self-Defense*. New York: Twayne Publishers.

Works Cited

Gaines, L. K., V. E. Kappeler, and J. B. Vaughn. 1997. *Policing in America*. Cincinnati: Anderson.

Galvin, H. 1986. "Shielding Rape Victims in the State and Federal Courts: A Proposal for a Second Decade." *Minnesota Law Review* 70: 763–916.

Garcia Coll, C., J. L. Surrey, P. Buccio-Notaro, and B. Molla. 1998. "Incarcerated Mothers: Crimes and Punishments." In *Mothering against the Odds: Diverse Voices of Contemporary Mothers*, edited by C. Garcia Coll, J. L. Surrey, and K. Weingarten. New York: Guilford Press.

Garofalo, J., L. Siegel, and J. Laub. 1987. "School-Related Victimization among Adolescents: An Analysis of National Crime Survey (NCS) Narratives." *Journal of Quantitative Criminology* 3: 321–338.

Gartner, R. Forthcoming. "Looking at Violence against Women over Time and across Nations." In *Currents in Criminology: Gender, Crime and Violence*, edited by K. Daly and R. N. Parker. Riverside, CA: The Presley Seminar, Presley Center for Crime and Justice Studies, University of California, Riverside.

Gartner, R., and A. N. Doob. 1994. "Trends in Criminal Victimization, 1988–1993." *Juristat* 14(13): 1–18.

Gartner, R., and B. McCarthy. 1991. "The Social Distribution of Femicide in Urban Canada." *Law and Society Review* 25(2): 287–311.

Gavigan, S. A. M. 1992. "*Morgentaler* and Beyond." In *The Politics of Abortion,* edited by J. Jenson, J. Brodie, and S. A. M. Gavigan. Toronto: Oxford University Press.

Geberth, V. J. 1992. "Stalkers." *Law and Order* 10: 1–6.

Gelsthorpe, L. 1997. "Feminism and Criminology." *The Oxford Handbook of Criminology*, edited by R. Maguire, R. Morgan and R. Reiner. Oxford, England: Oxford University Press.

Gelsthorpe, L., and A. Morris. 1988. "Feminism and Criminology in Britain." *British Journal of Criminology* 28(2): 223–241.

Genty, P. M. 1995. "Termination of Parental Rights among Prisoners." In *Children of Incarcerated Parents*, edited by D. Johnston. New York: Lexington Books.

George, A., and S. Lazarus. 1995. "Private Prisons: The Punished, the Profiteers, and the Grand Prix of State Approval." *Australian Feminist Law Journal* 4: 153–173.

Gerber, J., and S. L. Weeks. 1992. "Women As Victims of Corporate Crime: A Call for Research on a Neglected Topic." *Deviant Behavior* 13: 325–347.

Giallombardo, R. 1966. *Society of Women: A Study of a Women's Prison.* New York: John Wiley and Son.

Gibson, M. 1990. "On the Insensitivity of Women: Science and the 'Woman Question' in Liberal Italy." *Journal of Women's History* 2(2):11–41.

Gidycz, C. A., and M. P. Koss. 1989. "The Impact of Adolescent Sexual Victimization: Standardized Measures of Anxiety, Depression, and Behavioral Deviancy." *Violence and Victims* 4(2), 139–149.

Gilliard, D. K., and A. J. Beck. 1997. *Prison and Jail Inmates at Midyear, 1996.* Bureau of Justice Statistics Bulletin. Office of Justice Programs, U.S. Department of Justice. Washington, DC: Government Printing Office.

Gilligan, C. 1982. *In a Different Voice.* Cambridge: Harvard University Press.

Giordano, P. C. 1978. "Girls, Guys, and Gangs: The Changing Social Context of Female Delinquency." *Journal of Criminal Law and Criminology* 69: 126–132.

Giordano, P. C., and S. A. Cernkovich. 1979. "On Complicating the Relationship between Liberation and Delinquency." *Social Problems* 26(4): 467–481.

Giordano, P. C., S. A. Cernkovich, H. T. Groat, and J. L. Rudolph. 1997. "Gender, Crime and Desistance: Toward a Theory of Cognitive Transformation." Paper presented at the Annual Meeting of the American Sociological Association, Toronto.

Giordano, P. C., S. Kerbel, and S. Dudley. 1981. "The Economics of Female Criminality: An Analysis of Police Blotters, 1890–1975." In *Women and Crime in America*, edited by L. Bowker. New York: Macmillan.

Glaspell, S. 1916. *Trifles.* New York: Frank Shay, The Washington Square Players.

———. 1992. *A Jury of Her Peers.* Reprint ed.; orig. pub. 1917. Mankato, MN: Creative Education.

Glover, N. M., T. P. Janikowski, and J. J. Benshoff. 1995. "The Incidence of Incest Histories among Clients Receiving Substance Abuse Treatment." *Journal of Counseling and Development* 73: 475–480.

Glueck, S., and E. T. Glueck. 1934. *Five Hundred Delinquent Women.* New York: Alfred A. Knopf.

———. 1950. *Unraveling Juvenile Delinquency.* New York: Commonwealth Fund.

———. 1968. *Delinquents and Nondelinquents in Perspective.* Cambridge: Harvard University Press.

Goldfarb, P. 1996. "Describing without Circumscribing: Questioning the Construction of Gender in the Discourse of Intimate Violence." *George Washington Law Review* 64: 582.

Gomez-Preston, C., and J. Trescott. 1995. "Over the Edge: One Police Woman's Story of Emotional and Sexual Harassment." In *The Criminal Justice System and Women: Offenders, Victims, and Workers*, 2nd ed., edited by B. R. Price and N. J. Sokoloff. New York: McGraw-Hill, Inc.

Goodman, G. S., and B. L. Bottoms, eds. 1993. *Child Victims, Child Witnesses: Understanding and Improving Testimony*. New York: Guilford Press.

Goolkasian, G. A., R. W. Geddes, and W. DeJong. 1985. *Coping with Police Stress*. Washington, DC: Government Printing Office.

Gordon, L. 1988. *Heroes of Their Own Lives: The Politics and History of Family Violence, Boston, 1880–1960*. New York: Viking.

Gottfredson, M., and T. Hirschi. 1990. *A General Theory of Crime*. Stanford: Stanford University Press.

Gould, S. J. 1981. *The Mismeasure of Man*. New York: Norton.

Graham, J., and B. Bowling. 1995. *Young People and Crime*. Home Office Research Study, No. 145. London: Her Majesty's Stationary Office.

Grant, I., D. E. Chunn, and C. Boyle. 1994. *The Law of Homicide*. Toronto: Carswell.

Grasmick, H. G., B. S. Blackwell, and R. J. Bursik. 1993. "Changes in the Sex Patterning of Perceived Threats of Sanctions." *Law and Society Review* 27: 679–705.

Grau, J., J. Fagan, and S. Wexler. 1985. "Restraining Orders for Battered Women: Issues of Access and Efficacy." In *Criminal Justice Politics and Women: The Aftermath of Legally Mandated Change*, edited by C. Schweber and C. Feinman. New York: The Haworth Press, Inc.

Gray, T., G. L. Mays, and M. K. Stohr. 1995. "Inmate Needs and Programming in Exclusively Women's Jails." *Prison Journal* 75(2): 186–202.

Greenberg, D. 1974. *Crime and Law Enforcement in the Colony of New York, 1691–1776*. Ithaca, NY: Cornell University Press.

Greenfeld, L. A. 1996. *Child Victimizers: Violent Offenders and Their Victims*. Washington, DC: Bureau of Justice Statistics, U.S. Department of Justice.

———. 1997. *Sex Offenses and Offenders: An Analysis of Data on Rape and Sexual Assault*. Washington, DC: Bureau of Justice Statistics, U.S. Department of Justice.

Greenfeld, L. A., M. R. Rand, D. Craven, P. A. Klaus, C. A. Perkins, C. Ringel, G. Warchol, C. Maston, and J. A. Fox. 1998. *Violence by Intimates: Analysis of Data on Crimes by Current or Former Spouses, Boyfriends, and Girlfriends*. Washington, DC: Bureau of Justice Statistics, U.S. Department of Justice.

Greenspan, J. 1994. "Struggle for Compassion: The Fight for Quality Care for Women with AIDS at Central California Women's Facility." *Yale Journal of Law and Feminism* 6(2): 383–395.

Grennan, S. 1987. "Findings on the Role of Officer Gender in Violent Encounters with Citizens." *Journal of Police Science and Administration* 15(1): 78–85.

Grieve, N., and A. Burns, eds. 1994. *Australian Women: Contemporary Feminist Thought*. Melbourne: Oxford University Press.

Guinier, L., M. Fine, and J. Balin. 1997. *Becoming Gentlemen: Women, Law School, and Institutional Change*. Boston: Beacon Press.

Haarr, R. N. 1997. "Patterns of Interaction in a Police Patrol Bureau: Race and Gender Barriers to Integration." *Justice Quarterly* 14: 53–85.

Haarr, R. N., and M. Morash. 1999. "Gender, Race, and Strategies of Coping with Occupational Stress in Policing." *Justice Quarterly* 16(2): 303–336.

Hagan, J. 1979. "The Sexual Stratification of Social Control: Toward a Gender-Based Perspective on Crime and Delinquency." *British Journal of Sociology* 30: 25–38.

———. 1989. *Structural Criminology*. New Brunswick, NJ: Rutgers University Press.

Hagan, J., A. R. Gillis, and J. Simpson. 1979. "The Sexual Stratification of Social Control." *British Journal of Sociology* 30: 25–38.

———. 1985. "The Class Structure of Gender and Delinquency: Toward a Power-Control Theory of Common Delinquent Behavior." *American Journal of Sociology* 90: 1151–1178.

———. 1987. "Class in the Household: A Power-Control Theory of Gender and Delinquency." *American Journal of Sociology* 92: 788–816.

Hagan, J., and F. Kay. 1990. "Gender and Delinquency in White Collar Families: A Power-Control Perspective." *Crime and Delinquency* 36: 391–407.

———. 1995. *Gender in Practice: A Study of Lawyer's Lives*. New York: Oxford University Press.

Hairston, C. F. 1991. "Mothers in Jail: Parent-Child Separation and Jail Visitation." *Affilia* 6: 9–27.

Hale, D. C., and D. J. Menniti. 1993. "Discrimination and Harassment: Litigation by Women in Policing." In *It's a Crime: Women and Justice*, edited by R. Muraskin and T. Alleman. Englewood Cliffs, NJ: Regents/Prentice Hall.

Works Cited

Haley, K. 1977. "Mothers behind Bars: A Look at the Parental Rights of Incarcerated Women." *New England Journal on Prison Law* 4: 141–155.

Halford, A. 1993. *No Way up the Greasy Pole*. London: Constable.

Halliday, T. C. 1986. "Six Score Years and Ten: Demographic Transitions in the American Legal Profession, 1850–1980." *Law and Society Review* 20(1): 53–78.

Hallwas, J. 1988. "Introduction to *Life in Prairie Land*, by E. W. Farnham." Reprint ed.; orig. pub. 1846. Urbana: University of Illinois Press.

Hamilton, S. L. 1989. *America's Most Wanted, Public Enemy Number One: The Barkers*. Bloomington, MN: Abdo and Daughters.

Hampton, B. 1993. *Prisons and Women*. Sydney: University of New South Wales.

Handler, J. 1990. "Socioeconomic Profile of an American Terrorist: 1960s and 1970s." *Terrorism* 13: 195–213.

Hands, J., V. Herbert, and G. Tennent. 1974. "Menstruation and Behavior in a Special Hospital." *Medicine, Science, and the Law* 14: 32–35.

Hanmer, J., and M. Maynard, eds. 1987. *Women, Violence and Social Control*. London: Macmillan.

Harding, R. W. 1997. *Private Prisons and Public Accountability*. Buckingham, UK: Open University Press.

Harries, K. D. 1997. *Serious Violence: Patterns of Homicide and Assault in America*. Springfield, IL: Charles C. Thomas.

Harris, A. 1977. "Sex and Theories of Deviance." *American Sociological Review* 42(February): 3–16.

Harris, J. 1986. *Strangers in Two Worlds*. New York: Kensington Publishing Corporation.

———. 1988. *They Always Call Us Ladies: Stories from Prison*. New York: Kensington Publishing Corporation.

———. 1991. *Marking Time: Letters from Jean Harris to Shana Alexander*. New York: Kensington Publishing Corporation.

Harris, J., and S. Grace. 1999. *A Question of Evidence? Investigating and Prosecuting Rape in the 1990s*. Research Study 196. London: Home Office.

Harris, M. K. 1998. "Women's Imprisonment in the United States." *Corrections Today* 60(7): 74–76, 78, 80.

Harry, B., and C. M. Balcer. 1987. "Menstruation and Crime: A Critical Review of the Literature from the Clinical Criminology Perspective." *Behavioral Sciences and the Law* 5(3): 307–321.

Hart, B. 1986. "Lesbian Battering: An Examination." In *Naming the Violence*, edited by K. Lobel. Seattle: Seal Press.

Hastie, R., S. D. Penrod, and N. Pennington. 1983. *Inside the Jury*. Cambridge: Harvard University Press.

Hawkes, M. Q. 1991. "Women's Changing Roles in Corrections." In *Change, Challenge and Choices: Women's Role in Modern Corrections*, edited by J. B. Morton. Laurel, MD: American Correctional Association.

———. 1994. *Excellent Effect: The Edna Mahan Story*. Laurel, MD: American Correctional Association.

———. 1998. "Edna Mahan: Sustaining the Reformatory Tradition." *Women and Criminal Justice* 9(3): 1–21.

Hawkesworth, M. 1997. "Confounding Gender." *Signs* 22(3): 649–685.

Hedderman, C., and H. Hough. 1994. "Does the Criminal Justice System Treat Men and Women Differently?" Home Office Research Finding No. 10. London: Her Majesty's Stationary Office.

Heffernan, E. 1972. *Making It in Prison: The Square, the Cool, and the Life*. New York: John Wiley and Son.

———. 1994. "Banners, Brothels, and a 'Ladies' Seminary: Women and Federal Corrections." In *Escaping Prison Myths: Selected Topics in the History of Federal Corrections*, edited by J. Roberts. Washington, DC: American University Press.

Heidensohn, F. M. 1968. "The Deviance of Women: A Critique and an Enquiry." *British Journal of Sociology* 19(2): 160–175.

———. 1987. "Women and Crime: Questions for Criminology." In *Gender, Crime and Justice*, edited by P. Carlen and A. Worrall. Milton Keynes, England: Open University Press.

———. 1992. *Women in Control? The Role of Women in Law Enforcement*. Oxford, England: Clarendon Press.

———. 1995. "Feminist Perspectives and Their Impact on Criminology and Criminal Justice in Britain." In *International Feminist Perspectives in Criminology*, edited by N. Rafter and F. Heidensohn. Buckingham, England: Open University Press.

———. 1996. *Women and Crime*. 2d ed. Basingstoke, England: Macmillan.

———. 1997. "Gender and Crime." In *The Oxford Handbook of Criminology*, 2d ed., edited by M. Maguire, R. Morgan, and R. Reiner. Oxford, England: Clarendon Press.

Heimer, K. 1995. "Gender, Race and the Pathways to Delinquency." In *Crime and Inequality*, edited by J. Hagan and R. Peterson. Stanford: Stanford University Press.

Heising, W. L. 1996. *Detecting Women 2: A Reader's Guide and Checklist for Mystery Series Written by Women.* Dearborn, MI: Purple Moon Press.

Henderson, A. R. 1997. "Prostitution and the City: Review Essay." *Journal of Urban History* 23: 231–239.

Henderson, S. 1998. *Hidden Figures: The Edinburgh Women's Safety Survey.* Edinburgh: The City of Edinburgh Council.

Her Majesty's Inspector of Prisons. 1997. *Women in Prison: A Thematic Review.* London: Home Office.

Herbert, R. 1985. "Note. Women's Prisons: An Equal Protection Evaluation." *Yale Law Journal* 94(5): 1182–1206.

Herman, J. L. 1994. *Trauma and Recovery.* New York: Guildford.

Herrington, N. L. 1997. "Female Cops—1992." In *Critical Issues in Policing,* edited by R. D. Alpert and G. Alpert. Prospect Heights, IL: Waveland Press.

Herrnstein, R. J., and C. Murray. 1994. *The Bell Curve: The Reshaping of American Life by Difference in Intelligence.* New York: Free Press.

Hickey, E. 1997. *Serial Murderers and Their Victims.* Belmont, CA: Wadsworth.

Hilton, N. Z., ed. 1993. *Legal Responses to Wife Assault.* Newbury Park, CA: Sage.

Hindelang, M. J. 1973. "Causes of Delinquency: A Partial Replication and Extension." *Social Problems* 21: 471–487.

Hindelang, M. J., M. R. Gottfredson, and J. Garofalo. 1978. *Victims of Personal Crime: An Empirical Foundation for a Theory of Personal Victimization.* Cambridge, MA: Ballinger.

Hindus, M. S. 1980. *Prison and Plantation: Crime, Justice, and Authority in Massachusetts and South Carolina, 1767–1878.* Chapel Hill: University of North Carolina Press.

Hirschi, T. 1969. *Causes of Delinquency.* Berkeley: University of California Press.

Hobson, B. M. 1987. *Uneasy Virtue: The Politics of Prostitution and the American Reform Tradition.* New York: Basic Books.

Hofford, M., and A. V. Harrell. 1993. *Family Violence: Interventions for Justice Systems.* NCJ 144532. Washington, DC: Bureau of Justice Assistance, U.S. Department of Justice.

Holcombe, B. J., and C. Holcombe. 1992. *The Search for Justice.* Walpole, NH: Meeting House Press.

Holdaway, S., and S. K. Parker. 1998. "Policing Women Police." *British Journal of Criminology* 38: 40–60.

Holland, J., C. Ramazanoglu, and S. Sharpe. 1993. *Wimp or Gladiator: Contradictions in Acquiring Masculine Sexuality.* London: Tufnell Press.

Hollinger, R., and L. Lanza-Kaduce. 1988. "The Process of Criminalization." *Criminology* 26: 101–126.

Holmes, H. J. 1977. "An Analysis of Bill C-46, Production of Records in Sexual Offence Proceedings." *Canadian Criminal Law Review* 2: 71–110.

Holmes, M. D., H. C. Kaudistel, and R. A. Farrell. 1987. "Determinants of Charge Reductions and Final Dispositions in Cases of Burglary and Robbery." *Journal of Research in Crime and Delinquency* 24(2): 233–254.

Holmes, R. M., and S. T. Holmes. 1994. *Murder in America.* Thousand Oaks, CA: Sage.

Holmes, R. M., ed. 1998. *Stalking in America: Types and Methods of Criminal Stalkers.* Thousand Oaks, CA: Sage.

Home Office. 1998a. *Criminal Statistics, England and Wales, 1997.* London: HMSO.

———. 1998b. *Prison Statistics, England and Wales, 1997.* London: HMSO

Horney, J. 1978. "Menstrual Cycles and Criminal Responsibility." *Law and Human Behavior* 2(1): 25–36.

Horney, J., and C. Spohn. 1996. "The Influence of Blame and Believability Factors in the Processing of Simple and Aggravated Rape Cases." *Criminology* 34: 135–162.

Horowitz, R., and A. E. Pottieger. 1991. "Gender Bias in Juvenile Justice Handling of Seriously Crime-Involved Youths." *Journal of Research in Crime and Delinquency* 28: 75–100.

Horton, A. L., K. M. Simonidis, and L. L. Simonidis. 1987. "Legal Remedies for Spousal Abuse: Victims' Characteristics, Expectations, and Satisfaction." *Journal of Family Violence* 2(3): 265–279.

Hoyle, C. 1998. *Negotiating Domestic Violence: Police, Criminal Justice and Victims.* Oxford: Clarendon Press.

Hudson, B. 1998. "Restorative Justice: The Challenge of Sexual and Racial Violence." *Journal of Law and Society* 25(2): 237–256.

Hudson, J., A. Morris, G. Maxwell, and B. Galaway, eds. 1996. *Family Group Conferences: Perspectives on Policy and Practice.* Monsey, NY: Criminal Justice Press.

Hull, N. E. H. 1987. *Female Felons: Women and Serious Crime in Colonial Massachusetts.* Urbana: University of Illinois Press.

Human Rights in China. 1996. "Caught between Tradition and the State: Violations of the Human Rights of Chinese Women." *Women's Rights Law Reporter* 17(3): 285–307.

Human Rights Watch, Women's Rights Project. 1996. *All Too Familiar: Sexual Abuse of Women in U.S. State Prisons*. New York: Human Rights Watch.

Humphries, D., J. Dawson, V. Cronin, P. Keating, C. Wisniewski, J. Eichfeld. 1995. "Mothers and Children, Drugs and Crack: Reactions to Maternal Drug Dependency." In *The Criminal Justice System and Women: Offenders, Victims, and Workers*, edited by B. R. Price and N. J. Sokoloff. New York: McGraw-Hill, Inc.

Hunt, J. C. 1984. "The Development of Rapport through the Negotiation of Gender in Fieldwork among Police." *Human Organization* 43: 283–296.

———. 1990. "The Logic of Sexism among Police." *Women and Criminal Justice* 1: 3–30.

Hunt, J. C., and P. K. Manning. 1991. "The Social Context of Police Lying." *Symbolic Interaction* 14: 51–70.

Hurrell, J. J. 1995. "Police Work, Occupational Stress, and Individual Coping." *Journal of Organizational Behavior* 16: 27–34.

Immarigeon, R. 1995. "What Works?" *Corrections Today* 57: Insert.

Immarigeon, R., and M. Chesney-Lind. 1992. *Women's Prisons: Overcrowded and Overused*. San Francisco: National Council on Crime and Delinquency.

Inciardi, J. A., D. Lockwood, and A. E. Pottieger. 1993. *Women and Crack-Cocaine*. New York: Macmillan Publishing Co.

International Association of Women Police. <http://www.iawp.org/history.htm>, accessed 1 March 2000.

International Coalition Against Sexual Harassment. <http://jan.ucc.nau.edu/~pms/sash.html>, accessed 1 March 2000.

Jackson, K. E. 1998. "The Legitimacy of Cross-Gender Searches and Surveillance in Prisons: Defining an Appropriate and Uniform Review." *Indiana Law Journal* 73: 959.

Jacobs, P. 1987. "How Female Police Officers Cope with a Traditionally Male Position." *Social Science Review* 72: 4–6.

James, M. P., and C. Carcach. 1997. *Homicide in Australia: 1989–96*. Canberra: Australian Institute of Criminology.

Jefferson, T., and P. Carlen, eds. 1996. *Masculinities, Social Relations and Crime*. Special Issue of *British Journal of Criminology* 36(3): 337–444.

Jeffreys, S. 1997. The *Idea of Prostitution*. North Melbourne, Australia: Spinifex Press.

Jenness, V. 1993. *Making It Work: The Prostitutes' Rights Movement in Perspective*. New York: Aldine de Gruyter.

Jennings, K. T. 1993. "Female Child Molesters: A Review of the Literature." In *Female Sexual Abuse of Children*, edited by M. Elliott. New York: The Guilford Press.

Jerin, R. A., and L. J. Moriarty. 1998. *Victims of Crime*. Chicago: Nelson-Hall Publishers.

Johnsen, D. 1989. "From Driving to Drugs: Governmental Regulation of Pregnant Women's Lives after *Webster*." *University of Pennsylvania Law Review* 138: 195–215.

Johnson, H. 1988. *History of Criminal Justice*. Cincinnati: Anderson.

———. 1996. *Dangerous Domains: Violence against Women in Canada*. Scarborough, Ontario: Nelson Canada.

Johnston, D. 1992. "Survey Shows Number of Rapes Far Higher Than Official Figures." *New York Times* (24 April): A14.

———. 1995. "Effects of Parental Incarceration." In *Children of Incarcerated Parents*, edited by K. Gabel and D. Johnston. New York: Lexington Books.

Johnston, E. 1991. *Royal Commission into Aboriginal Deaths in Custody: National Report*. Canberra: Australian Government Publishing Service.

Johnston, L. D., J. G. Bachman, and P. M. O'Malley. 1998. *National Survey Results on Drug Use from the Monitoring the Future Study, 1975–1997*. Washington, DC: U.S. Department of Health and Human Services, National Institute on Drug Abuse.

Johnstone, Q., and M. Wenglinsky. 1985. *Paralegals: Prospects of a Satellite Occupation*. Westport, CT: Greenwood Press.

Jolin, A. 1994. "On the Backs of Working Prostitutes: Feminist Theory and Prostitution Policy." *Crime and Delinquency* 40(1): 69–83.

Jones, A. 1996. *Women Who Kill*, Reprint ed.; orig. pub. 1980. Boston: Beacon Press.

Jones, D. J. V. 1992. *Crime in Nineteenth-Century Wales*. Cardiff: University of Wales Press.

———. 1996. *Crime and Policing in the Twentieth Century: The South Wales Experience*. Cardiff: University of Wales Press.

Jones, L. 1983. "On Common Ground: The Women's Peace Camp at Greenham Common." In *Keeping the Peace*, edited by L. Jones. London: The Women's Press.

Jones, S. 1986. *Policewomen and Equality*. London: Macmillan.

Jouriles, E. N., and K. D. O'Leary. 1985. "Interspousal Reliability of Reports of Marital Violence." *Journal of Consulting and Clinical Psychology* 53: 419–421.

Junor, B. 1997. *Greenham Common Women's Peace Camp: A History of Nonviolent Resistance, 1984–1995*. London: Working Press.

Jurik, N. C. 1988. "Striking a Balance: Female Correctional Officers, Gender Role Stereotypes, and Male Prisons." *Sociological Inquiry* 58: 291–305.

Kampfer, C. J. 1995. "Post-Traumatic Stress Reactions in Children of Imprisoned Mothers." In *Children of Incarcerated Parents*, edited by K. Gabel and D. Johnston. New York: Lexington Books.

Kanter, R. M. 1977. *Men and Women of the Corporation*. New York: Basic Books.

Kantor, E. 1998. "The AIDS Knowledge Base: AIDS and HIV Infection in Prisons," <http://hivinsite.ucsf.edu/akb/1997/01pris/>, accessed 1 March 2000.

Kappeler, V. E., R. D. Sluder, and G. P. Alpert. 1994. *Forces of Deviance: The Dark Side of Policing*. Prospect Heights, IL: Waveland.

Karlsen, C. F. 1987. *The Devil in the Shape of a Woman: Witchcraft in Colonial New England*. New York: W.W. Norton.

Karmen, A. 1984. *Crime Victims: An Introduction to Victimology*. Monterey, CA: Brooks/Cole.

———. 1991. "The Controversy over Shared Responsibility." In *To Be a Victim*, edited by D. Sank and D. Kaplan. New York: Plenum Press.

———. 1996. *Crime Victims: An Introduction to Victimology*. Belmont, CA: Wadsworth Publishers.

Kasinsky, R. G. 1994. "Child Neglect and 'Unfit' Mothers: Child Savers in the Progressive Era and Today." *Women and Criminal Justice* 6(1): 97–129.

Kasl, C. D. 1990. "Female Perpetrators of Sexual Abuse: A Feminist View." In *The Sexually Abused Male*, vol. 1, edited by M. Hunter. Lexington, MA: Lexington Books.

Kaufman Kantor, G., and N. Asidgian. 1996. "When Women Are under the Influence: Does Drinking or Drug Use by Women Provoke Beatings by Men?" In *Recent Developments in Alcoholism*, vol. 13, edited by M. Galanter. New York: Plenum.

Keamy, L. 1998. "Women's Health Care in the Incarcerated Setting." In *Clinical Practice in Correctional Medicine*, edited by M. Puisis. St. Louis, MO: Mosby.

Kelleher, M. D., and C. L. Kelleher. 1998. *Murder Most Rare: The Female Serial Killer*. Westport, CT: Praeger.

Kelling, G., T. Pate, D. Dieckman, and C. E. Brown. 1974. *Kansas City Preventive Patrol Experiment*. Washington, DC: Police Foundation.

Kellor, F. 1901. *Experimental Sociology. Descriptive and Analytical. Delinquents*. New York: Macmillan.

Kelly, D. P., and E. Erez. 1997. "Victim Participation in the Criminal Justice System." In *Victims of Crime*, 2nd ed., edited by R. C. Davis, A. J. Lurigio, and W. G. Skogan. Thousand Oaks, CA: Sage Publications.

Kelly, E. E., and L. Warshafsky. 1987. "Partner Abuse in Gay Male and Lesbian Couples." Paper presented at the Third National Conference for Family Violence Researchers, Durham, NH.

Kelm, M. E. 1992. "'The Only Place Likely to Do Her Any Good': The Admission of Women to British Columbia's Provincial Hospital for the Insane." *British Columbia Studies* 66: 66–89.

Kendall-Tackett, K. A., and A. Simon. 1992. "Comparison of the Abuse Experiences of Male and Female Adults Molested As Children." *Journal of Family Violence* 7: 57–62.

Kendall-Tackett, K. A., and R. Marshall. 1998. "Sexual Victimization of Children: Incest and Child Sexual Abuse." In *Issues in Intimate Violence*, edited by R. Bergen. Thousand Oaks, CA: Sage Publications.

Kendall-Tackett, K. A., L. M. Williams, and D. Finkelhor. 1993. "The Impact of Sexual Abuse on Children: A Review and Synthesis of Recent Empirical Studies." *Psychological Bulletin* 113: 164–180.

Kennedy, L. W., and V. F. Sacco. 1998. *Crime Victims in Context*. Los Angeles: Roxbury Publishing Co.

Kennedy, R. 1997. *Race, Crime, and the Law*. New York: Pantheon.

Kennedy, R. M. 1997. "The Treatment of Women Prisoners after the VMI Decision: Application of a New 'Heightened Scrutiny.'" *American University Journal of Gender and Law* 6: 65–91.

Kerstetter, W. A. 1990a. "Gateway to Justice: Police and Prosecutorial Response to Sexual Assaults against Women." *Journal of Criminal Law and Criminology* 81: 267–313.

———. 1990b. *Justice Pursued: The Legal and Moral Basis of Dispositions in Sexual Assault Cases*. American Bar Foundation Working Paper Series, #9129.

Kerstetter W. A., and B. Van Winkle. 1990. "Who Decides? A Study of the Complainant's Decision to Prosecute in Rape Cases." *Criminal Justice and Behavior* 17: 268–283.

Keve, P. 1991. *Prisons and the American Conscience*. Carbondale: Southern Illinois University Press.

Kinney, J. 2000. *Loosening the Grip: A Handbook of Alcohol Information*, 6th ed. Boston: McGraw-Hill.

Kirby, G. B. 1971. *Years of Experience: An Autobiographical Narrative*. Reprint ed.; orig. pub. 1887. New York: AMS Press.

Klein, D. 1973. "The Etiology of Female Crime: A Review of the Literature." *Issues in Criminology* 8(2): 3–30.

———. 1995. "Crime through Gender's Prism: Feminist Criminology in the United States." In *International Feminist Perspectives in Criminology: Engendering a Discipline* edited by N. H. Rafter and F. Heidensohn. Philadelphia: Open University Press.

Klein, K. G. 1995. *The Woman Detective: Gender and Genre*, 2nd. ed. Champaign: University of Illinois Press.

Kleinig, J. 1990. "Symposium: Criminal Liability for Fetal Endangerment." *Criminal Justice Ethics* (Winter/Spring): 11–51.

Knelman, J. 1997. *Twisting in the Wind: The Murderess and the English Press*. Toronto: University of Toronto Press.

Kohn, S. M. 1991. *American Political Prisoners: Prosecutions under the Espionage and Sedition Acts*. Westport, CT: Praeger Publishers.

Kong, R. 1998. "Canadian Crime Statistics, 1997." *Juristat* 18(11): 1–22.

Konopka, G. 1966. *The Adolescent Girl in Conflict*. Englewood Cliffs, NJ: Prentice Hall.

Koss, M. P. 1988a. "Hidden Rape: Incidence, Prevalence, and Descriptive Characteristics of Sexual Aggression and Victimization in a National Sample of College Students." In *Sexual Assault*, vol. 2, edited by A. W. Burgess. New York: Garland.

———. 1988b. "Criminal Victimization among Women: Impact on Health Status and Medical Services Usage." Paper presented at the Annual Meeting of the American Psychological Association, Atlanta, GA.

———. 1992a. "The Measurement of Rape Victimization in Crime Surveys." *Criminal Justice and Behavior* 23(1): 55–69.

———. 1992b. "The Underdetection of Rape: Methodological Choices Influence Incidence Estimates." *Journal of Social Issues* 48(1): 61–75.

Koss, M. P., and M. R. Harvey. 1991. *The Rape Victim*. Thousand Oaks, CA: Sage Publications.

Koss, M. P., C. A. Gidycz, and N. Wisniewski. 1987. "The Scope of Rape: Incidence and Prevalence of Sexual Aggression and Victimization in a National Sample of Higher Education Students." *Journal of Consulting and Clinical Psychology* 55: 162–170.

Krauss, E., and B. Bonora, eds. 1995. *Jurywork: Systematic Techniques*, 2d ed. New York: Boardman.

Krim, L. 1995. "A Reasonable Women's Version of Cruel and Unusual Punishment: Cross Gender Clothed Body Searches of Women Prisoners." *University of California Women's Law Journal* 6(1): 85–121.

Krohn, M., and J. Massey. 1980. "Social Control and Delinquent Behavior: An Examination of the Elements of Social Bond." *Sociological Quarterly* 21: 529–543.

Kruttschnitt, C. 1983. "Race Relations and the Female Inmate." *Crime and Delinquency* 29(4) 577–592.

Kruttschnitt, C., and D. E. Green. 1984. "The Sex-Sanctioning Issue: Is It History?" *American Sociological Review* 49: 541–551.

Kurz, D. 1992. "Battering and the Criminal Justice System: A Feminist View." In *Domestic Violence: The Changing Criminal Justice Response*, edited by E. S. Buzawa and C. G. Buzawa. Westport, CT: Auburn House.

LaFree, G. D. 1979. "Determinants of Police, Prosecution, and Court Decisions in Forcible Rape Cases." Ph.D. dissertation. Indiana University.

———. 1980. "The Effects of Sexual Stratification by Race on Official Reactions to Rape." *American Sociological Review* 45: 842–854.

———. 1981. "Official Reactions to Social Problems: Police Decisions in Sexual Assault Cases." *Social Problems* 28: 588–594.

———. 1989. *Rape and Criminal Justice: The Social Construction of Sexual Assault*. Belmont, CA: Wadsworth Publishing.

LaFree, G. D., B. F. Reskin, and C. A. Visher. 1985. "Jurors' Responses to Victim's Behavior and Legal Issues in Sexual Assault Trials." *Social Problems* 32: 397–401.

Lane, R. 1979. *Violent Death in the City: Suicide, Accident and Murder in 19th Century Philadelphia*. Cambridge: Harvard University Press.

———. 1986. *Roots of Violence in Black Philadelphia, 1860–1900*. Cambridge: Harvard University Press.

Langan, P. A., and D. P. Farrington. 1998. *Crime and Justice in the United States and in England and Wales, 1981–1996*. Washington, DC: National Institute of Justice.

Lanktree, C., J. Briere, and L. Zaidi. 1991. "Incidence and Impact of Sexual Abuse in a Child Outpatient Sample: The Role of Direct Inquiry." *Child Abuse and Neglect* 15: 447–453.

LaPrairie, C. 1992. "Aboriginal Crime and Justice: Explaining the Present, Exploring the Future." *Canadian Journal of Criminology* 34: 281–297.

———. 1993. "Aboriginal Women and Crime in Canada: Identifying the Issues." In *In Conflict with the Law: Women and the Canadian Justice System*, edited by E. Adelberg and C. Currie. Vancouver, BC: Press Gang Publishers.

Laub, J. H., and J. S. Smith. 1995. "Eleanor Touroff Glueck: An Unsung Pioneer in Criminology." *Women and Criminal Justice* 6(2): 1–22.

Laub, J. H., and R. J. Sampson. 1988. "Unraveling Families and Delinquency: A Reanalysis of the Gluecks' Data." *Criminology* 26: 355–380.

Lawson, A. 1988. *Adultery: An Analysis of Love and Betrayal*. New York: Basic Books.

Leader-Elliot, I. 1993. "Battered but Not Beaten: Women Who Kill in Self Defence." *Sydney Law Review* 15(4): 403–460.

Lees, S. 1997. *Ruling Passions: Sexual Violence, Reputation and the Law*. Buckingham, England: Open University Press.

Lehrman, F. 1996. *Domestic Violence, Practice and Procedure*. Deerfield, IL: Clark, Bordman, and Callahan.

Leinen, S. 1993. *Gay Cops*. New Brunswick, NJ: Rutgers University Press.

Lekkerkerker, E. C. 1931. *Reformatories for Women in the United States*. Batavia, Holland: Bij J. B. Wolter's Uitgevers-Maatschappij.

Lemert, E. 1951. *Social Pathology*. New York: McGraw-Hill.

Leonard, E. 1995. "Theoretical Criminology and Gender." In *The Criminal Justice System and Women*, edited by B. R. Price and N. J. Sokoloff, editors. New York: McGraw-Hill.

Lessing, D. 1985. *The Good Terrorist*. London: Jonathan Cape.

Leventhal, B., and S. E. Lundy, eds. 1999. *Same-Sex Domestic Violence: Strategies for Change*. Thousand Oaks, CA: Sage Publications, Inc.

Lewis, W. D. 1965. *From Newgate to Dannemora: The Rise of the Penitentiary in New York, 1796–1848*. Ithaca, NY: Cornell University Press.

Liddington, J., and J. Norris. 1985. *One Hand Tied Behind Us: The Rise of the Women's Suffrage Movement*. London: Virago Press.

Lie, G., R. Schilit, J. Bush, M. Montagne, and L. Reyes. 1991. "Lesbians in Currently Aggressive Relationships: How Frequently Do They Report Aggressive Past Relationships?" *Violence and Victims* 6: 121–135.

Lieber, M. J., M. Farnworth, K. M. Jamieson, and M. K. Nalla. 1994. "Bridging the Gender Gap in Criminology: Liberation and Gender-Specific Strain Effects on Delinquency." *Sociological Inquiry* 64(1): 56–68.

Lim, L. L. 1998. *The Sex Sector: The Economic and Social Bases of Prostitution in Southeast Asia*. Geneva: International Labour Office.

Littleton, C. 1987. "Reconstructing Sexual Equality." *California Law Review* 75: 1267.

Littrell, W. B. 1979. *Bureaucratic Justice: Police, Prosecutors, and Plea Bargaining*. Beverly Hills, CA: Sage Publications.

Lloyd, A. 1995. *Doubly Deviant, Doubly Damned: Society's Treatment of Violent Women*. Harmondsworth, England: Penguin.

Lobel, K., ed. 1986. *Naming the Violence*. Seattle: Seal Press.

Lock, J. 1979. *The British Policewoman: Her Story*. London: Hale.

Logan, C. H. 1990. *Private Prisons: Cons and Pros*. New York: Oxford University Press.

———. 1991. *Well Kept: Comparing Quality of Confinement in a Public and Private Prison*. Washington, DC: National Institute of Justice.

Lombroso, C., and G. Ferrero. 1893. *La Donna Delinquente: La Prostituta e la Donna Normale*. Torino: Roux.

———. 1894. *Das Weib als Verbrecherin und Prostituierte*. Trans. H. Kurella. Hamburg: Verlagsanstalt and Druckerei, A.G.

Lombroso, C., and W. Ferrero. 1895. *The Female Offender*. Orig. pub. 1893. New York: Appleton Press.

Lombroso-Ferrero, G. 1911. *Lombroso's "Criminal Man."* Reprint ed. 1972. Montclair, NJ: Patterson Smith.

Longrigg, C. 1999. *Mafia Women*. London: Vintage.

Lupton, C., and T. Gillespie, eds. 1994. *Working with Violence*. Basingstoke, England: Macmillan.

Lurigio, A., and W. Skogan. 1994. "Winning the Hearts and Minds of Police Officers." *Crime and Delinquency* 40(3): 315–330.

Lutze, F. 1998. "Do Boot Camp Prisons Possess a More Rehabilitative Environment Than Traditional Prison? A Survey of Inmates." *Justice Quarterly* 15(2): 547–563.

Luxenburg, J., and L. Klein. 1984. "CB Radio Prostitution: Technology and the Displacement of Deviance." In *Gender Issues, Sex Offenses, and Criminal Justice: Current Trends*, edited by S. Chaneles. New York: Haworth Press.

Luxenburg, J., and T. E. Guild. 1993. "Women, AIDS, and the Criminal Justice System." In *It's a Crime: Women and Justice,* edited by R. Muraskin and T. Alleman. Englewood Cliffs, NJ: Regents/Prentice-Hall.

MacDonald, E. 1991. *Shoot the Women First.* New York: Random House.

MacDougall, D. S. 1998. "HIV/AIDS behind Bars: Incarceration Provides a Valuable Opportunity to Implement HIV/AIDS Treatment and Prevention Strategies in a High-Risk Population." *International Association of Physicians in AIDS Care Journal* 4(4): 8–13. Also: <http://thebody.com/iapac/prisons.html>, accessed 1 March 2000.

MacDrimmon, M. T. 1996. "Trial by Ordeal." *Canadian Criminal Law Review* 1: 31–56.

MacDrimmon, M. T., and C. Boyle. 1993. "Equality, Fairness and Relevance: Disclosure of Therapists' Records in Sexual Assault Trials." In *Filtering and Analysing Evidence in an Age of Diversity,* edited by M. T. MacCrimmon and M. Ouellette. Montréal: Canadian Institute for the Administration of Justice.

Mackay, M., and S. Smallacombe. 1996. "Aboriginal Women As Offenders and Victims: The Case of Victoria." *Aboriginal Law Bulletin* 3(80): 17–23.

MacKenzie, D. L., and H. Donaldson. 1996. "Boot Camps for Women Offenders." *Criminal Justice Review* 21: 21–43.

MacKenzie, D. L., J. W. Robinson, and J. W. Campbell. 1995. "Long-Term Incarceration of Female Offenders: Prison Adjustment and Coping." In *Long-Term Imprisonment,* edited by T. J. Flanagan. Thousand Oaks, CA: Sage.

MacKinnon, C. 1978. *The Sexual Harassment of Working Women.* New Haven: Yale University.

————. 1987. *Feminism Unmodified: Discourses on Life and Law.* Cambridge: Harvard University Press.

MacKinnon, C., and A. Dworkin, eds. 1997. *In Harm's Way: The Pornography Civil Rights Hearings.* Cambridge: Harvard University Press.

Madriz, E. 1997. *Nothing Bad Happens to Good Girls: Fear of Crime in Women's Lives.* Berkeley: University of California Press.

Maghan, J., and L. McLeish-Blackwell. 1991. "Black Women in Correctional Employment." In *Change, Challenge and Choices: Women's Role in Modern Corrections,* edited by J. B. Morton. Laurel, MD: American Correctional Association.

Maguigan, H. 1991. "Battered Women and Self Defense: Myths and Misconceptions in Current Reform Proposals." *University of Pennsylvania Law Review* 140(2): 379–486.

Maguin, E., and R. Loeber. 1996. "Academic Performance and Delinquency." In *Crime and Justice: A Review of Research,* vol. 20, edited by M. Tonry. Chicago: University of Chicago Press.

Maguire R., R. Morgan, and R. Reiner, eds. 1994. *The Oxford Handbook of Criminology.* Oxford: Oxford University Press.

————. 1997. *The Oxford Handbook of Criminology,* 2d ed. Oxford: Oxford University Press.

Maguire, K., and A. L. Pastore, eds. 1998. *Sourcebook of Criminal Justice Statistics 1997.* Washington, DC: U.S. Department of Justice, Bureau of Justice Statistics; Government Printing Office.

Maguire, M., and J. Shapland. 1997. "Provision for Victims in an International Context." In *Victims of Crime,* 2nd ed., edited by R. C. Davis, A. J. Lurigio, and W. G. Skogan. Thousand Oaks, CA: Sage.

Mahan, S. 1986. "Doing Time Together." *Corrections Today* 48(6): 134, 136, 138, 140, 164–165.

Maher, L. 1997. *Sexed Work: Gender, Race and Resistance in a Brooklyn Drug Market.* Oxford: Oxford University Press.

Maher, L., and D. Dixon. 1999. "Policing and Public Health: Law Enforcement and Harm Minimization in a Street-Level Drug Market." *British Journal of Criminology* 39(4): 488–512.

Maher, L., and K. Daly. 1996. "Women in the Street-Level Drug Economy: Continuity or Change?" *Criminology* 34(4): 465–491.

Maher, L., T. Nguyen, and T. Le. 1999. "Wall of Silence: Stories of Cabramatta Street Youth." In *Australian Youth Subcultures,* edited by R. White. Hobart: National Clearinghouse for Youth Studies.

Maida, P. D. 1989. *The Mother of Detective Fiction: The Life and Works of Anna Katherine Green.* Bowling Green, OH: Bowling Green State University.

Maier-Katkin, D., and R. Ogle. 1993. "A Rationale for Infanticide Laws." *Criminal Law Review* (December): 903–914.

Mann, C. R. 1984. *Female Crime and Delinquency.* Montgomery: University of Alabama Press.

————. 1995. "Women of Color in the Criminal Justice System." In *The Criminal Justice System and Women,* edited by B. Price and N. Sokoloff. New York: McGraw-Hill.

Mann, C. R., and M. S. Zatz. 1998. *Images of Color, Images of Crime.* Los Angeles: Roxbury.

Manning, T. New Covenant Church of God. *When Eve Failed to Pray and Trust God.* <http://www.nccg.org/132Art-EvePray.html>, accessed 1 March 2000.

March, J., and H. Simon. 1993. *Organizations*. Cambridge, MA: Blackwell.

Martin, B. F. 1990. *Crime and Criminal Justice Under the Third Republic: The Shame of Marianne*. Baton Rouge: Louisiana State University Press.

Martin, D. 1976. *Battered Wives*. New York: Pocket Books.

Martin, E. 1990. "Men and Women on the Bench: Vive la Difference?" *Judicature* 73: 204–208.

Martin, M. 1997. "Connected Mothers: A Follow-up Study of Incarcerated Women and Their Children." *Women and Criminal Justice* 8: 1–23.

Martin, S. E. 1979. "*Police*women and Police*women*: Occupational Role Dilemmas and Choices of Female Officers." *Journal of Police Science and Administration* 7(3): 314–323.

————. 1980. *Breaking and Entering: Policewomen on Patrol*. Berkeley: University of California Press.

————. 1989. *Women on the Move? A Report on the Status of Women in Policing: Police Foundation Report*. Washington, DC: Police Foundation.

————. 1990. *On the Move: The Status of Women in Policing*. Washington, DC: Police Foundation.

————. 1993. "Female Officers on the Move? A Status Report on Women in Policing." In *Critical Issues in Policing: Contemporary Readings*, 2nd ed., edited by R. G. Dunham and G. P. Albert. Prospect Heights, IL: Waveland.

————. 1994. "'Outsider Within' the Station House: The Impact of Race and Gender on Black Women Police." *Social Problems* 41(3): 383–400.

————. 1995. "The Interactive Effects of Race and Sex on Women Police Officers." In *The Criminal Justice System and Women: Offenders, Victims, and Workers*, edited by B. Price and N. Sokoloff. New York: McGraw-Hill.

————. 1997. "Women Officers on the Move: An Update on Women in Policing." In *Critical Issues in Policing: Contemporary Readings*, 3d ed., edited by R. G. Dunham and G. P. Alpert. Prospect Heights, IL: Waveland Press, Inc.

————, ed. 1993. *Alcohol and Interpersonal Violence: Fostering Multidisciplinary Perspectives*. National Institute on Alcohol Abuse and Alcoholism Research Monograph 24, NIH Publication No. 93-3496. Rockville, MD: National Institute on Alcohol Abuse and Alcoholism.

Martin, S. E., and N. C. Jurik. 1996. *Doing Justice, Doing Gender: Women in Criminal Justice Occupations*. Newbury Park, CA: Sage.

Martineau, H. 1838. *Retrospect of Western Travel*. vol. 1. London: Saunders and Otley.

Martinson, D., M. MacCrimmon, I. Grant, and C. Boyle. 1991. "A Forum on *Lavallee v. R.*: Women and Self-Defense." *University of British Columbia Law Review* 25(1): 23–68.

Maruschak, L. 1997. "HIV in Prison and Jails, 1995." U.S. Department of Justice, Office of Justice Programs, Bureau of Justice Statistics Bulletin NCJ-164260. Also: <http://www.ojp.usdoj.gov/bjs/abstract/hivpj95.htm>, accessed 1 March 2000.

Masters, G., and D. Smith. 1998. "Portia and Persephone Revisited: Thinking about Feeling in Criminal Justice." *Theoretical Criminology* 2(1): 5–27.

Mathews, R. J., J. Mathews, and K. Speltz. 1990. "Female Sexual Offenders." In *The Sexually Abused Male*, vol. 1: *Prevalence, Impact, and Treatment*, edited by M. Hunter. Lexington, MA: Lexington Books.

Matoesian, G. M. 1993. *Reproducing Rape: Domination through Talk in the Courtroom*. Cambridge: Polity Press.

Mattix, R. *Bonnie and Clyde in Oklahoma*. <http://www.qns.com/~dcordry/BandC.html>, accessed 1 March 2000.

Maveety, N. 1996. *Justice Sandra Day O'Connor: Strategist on the Supreme Court*. Lanham, MD: Rowman and Littlefield.

Maxson, C., and M. Klein. 1997. *Responding to Troubled Youth*. New York: Oxford University Press.

Maxwell, G., and A. Morris. 1993. *Family, Victims and Culture: Youth Justice in New Zealand*. Social Policy Agency and the Institute of Criminology, Victoria University of Wellington.

McCarthy, B., J. Hagan, and T. S. Woodward. 1999. "In the Company of Women: Structure and Agency in a Revised Power-Control Theory of Gender and Delinquency." *Criminology* 37(4): 761–788.

McClellan, D. S. 1994. "Disparity in the Discipline of Male and Female Offenders in Texas Prisons." *Women and Criminal Justice* 5(2): 71–98.

McDonald, D. C., E. Fournier, M. Russell-Einhorn, and S. Crawford. 1998. *Private Prisons in the United States: An Assessment of Current Practice*. Cambridge, MA: ABT Associates, Inc.

McDonald, D. C., ed. 1990. *Private Prisons and the Public Interest*. New Brunswick, NJ: Rutgers University Press.

McDonald, M. P. 1997. "A Multidimensional Look at the Gender Crisis in the Correctional System." *Law and Inequality Journal* 15: 505–545.

McGibbon, A., L. Cooper, and L. Kelly. 1989. *What Support?* London: Hammersmith and Fulham Council Community Police Domestic Violence Project, Community Safety Unit.

McGregor, H., and A. Hopkins. 1991. *Working for Change: The Movement against Domestic Violence*. North Sydney: Allen and Unwin.

McKean, J., and J. Hendricks. 1997. "The Role of Crisis Intervention in the Police Response to Domestic Disturbances." *Criminal Justice Policy Review* 8(2/3): 269–294.

McLennan, W. 1996. *Women's Safety in Australia: 1996*. Canberra: Australian Bureau of Statistics.

McQuiade, S., and J. Ehrenreich. 1988. "Women in Prison: Approaches to Studying the Lives of a Forgotten Population." *Affilia: Journal of Women and Social Work* 13(2): 233–247.

Meiselman, K. 1978. *Incest: A Psychological Study of Causes and Effects with Treatment Recommendations*. San Francisco: Jossey-Bass.

Meloy, J. R., ed. 1998. *The Psychology of Stalking: Clinical and Forensic Perspectives*. San Diego: Academic Press.

Menkel-Meadow, C. 1985. "Portia in a Different Voice: Speculations on a Women's Lawyering Process." *Berkeley Women's Law Journal* 1(1): 39–63.

———. 1989. "Feminization of the Legal Profession: The Comparative Sociology of Women Lawyers." *Lawyers in Society: Comparative Theories*, edited by R. Abel and P. Lewis. Berkeley: University of California Press.

———. 1994. "Portia Redux: Another Look at Gender, Feminism and Legal Ethics." *Virginia Journal of Law and Social Policy* 2(1): 75–114.

Menzies, R. 1989. *Survival of the Sanest: Order and Disorder in a Pre-Trial Psychiatric Clinic*. Toronto: University of Toronto Press.

Merlo, A., and J. Pollock. 1995. *Women, Law, and Social Control*. Boston: Allyn and Bacon.

Merton, R. 1938. "Social Structure and Anomie." *American Sociological Review* 3(4): 672–682.

———. 1949. *Social Theory and Social Structure*. Glencoe, IL: Free Press.

Messerschmidt, J. W. 1993a. *Masculinities and Crime*. Lanham, MD: Rowman and Littlefield Publishers, Inc.

———. 1993b. "The State and Gender Politics." In *Masculinities and Crime*, by J. Messerschmidt. Lanham, MD: Rowman and Littlefield.

Miethe, T. D. 1987. "Charging and Plea Bargaining Practices under Determinate Sentencing: An Investigation of the Hydraulic Displacement of Discretion." *Journal of Criminal Law and Criminology* 78(1): 155–176.

Miethe, T. D., M. C. Stafford, and J. S. Long. 1987. "Social Differentiation in Criminal Victimization: A Test of Routine Activities/Lifestyle Theories." *American Sociological Review* 52: 184–194.

Mignon, S. I. 1998. "Husband Battering: A Review of the Debate over a Controversial Social Phenomenon." In *Violence in Intimate Relationships: Examining Sociological and Psychological Issues*, edited by N. A. Jackson and G. C. Oates. Boston: Butterworth-Heinemann.

Miller, A. 1984. *Thou Shalt Not Be Aware: Society's Betrayal of the Child*. New York: New American Library.

Miller, B. A., and W. R. Downs. 1995. "Violent Victimization among Women with Alcohol Problems." In *Recent Developments in Alcoholism*, vol. 12: *Alcoholism and Women*, edited by M. Galanter. New York: Plenum Press.

Miller, B. A., W. R. Downs, and M. Testa. 1993. "Interrelationships between Victimization Experiences and Women's Alcohol Use." *Journal of Studies on Alcohol* 11: 109–117.

Miller, J. A. 1996. "Female Gang Involvement in a Midwestern City: Correlates, Nature and Meanings." Ph.D. dissertation. Graduate School, University of Southern California.

Miller, S. L. 1998b. "Rocking the Rank and File: Gender Issues and Community Policing." *Journal of Contemporary Criminal Justice* 14(2): 156–172.

———, ed. 1998a. *Crime Control and Women*. Thousand Oaks, CA: Sage.

Miller, S. L., K. B. Forest, and N. C. Jurik. 1997. "Diversity in Blue: Lesbian and Gay Police Officers in a Masculine Occupation." Paper presented at the annual meeting of the American Association of Criminology, Chicago.

Miller, T., M. Cohen, and B. Wiersema. 1996. *Victim Costs and Consequences: A New Look*. Washington, DC: U.S. Department of Justice.

Milner, E. R. 1996. *The Lives and Times of Bonnie and Clyde*. Carbondale: Southern Illinois University Press.

Milton, C. 1972. *Women in Policing*. Washington, DC: Police Foundation.

Mirrlees-Black, C. 1995. *Estimating the Extent of Domestic Violence: Findings from the 1992 British Crime Survey*. Research Bulletin No. 37. London: Home Office Research and Statistics Directorate.

———. 1999. *Domestic Violence: Findings from a New British Crime Survey Self-Completion Questionnaire*. Research Study 191. London: Home Office.

Mirrlees-Black, C., and C. Byron. 1999. *Domestic Violence: Findings from a New British Crime Sur-*

vey Self-Completion Questionnaire. Home Office Research Findings 86. London: Home Office.

Mirrlees-Black, C., and J. Allen. 1998. *Concern about Crime: Findings from the 1998 British Crime Survey*. Home Office Research, Development and Statistics Directorate, Research Findings No. 83. London: Home Office.

Mirrlees-Black, C., T. Budd, S. Partridge, and P. Mayhew. 1998. "The 1998 British Crime Survey." *Home Office Statistical Bulletin* 21/98.

Moffitt, T. 1993. "Adolescence-Limited and Life-Course Persistent Antisocial Behavior: A Developmental Taxonomy." *Psychological Review* 100: 674–701.

Molina, E. 1997. *Supreme Court Legitimizes Rape of Spouses*. Interpress Third World News Agency (16 June).

Monkkonen, E. H. 1975. *The Dangerous Class: Crime and Poverty in Columbus, Ohio, 1860–1885*. Cambridge: Harvard University Press.

———, ed. 1992. *Crime and Justice in American History. Prostitution, Drugs, Gambling, and Organized Crime*. New York: K. G. Saur.

Monture-Angus, P. 1995. *Thunder in My Soul: A Mohawk Woman Speaks*. Halifax, NS: Fernwood Publishing.

Monture-Okanee, P., and M. E. Turpel. 1992. "Aboriginal Peoples and Canadian Criminal Law: Rethinking Justice." *University of British Columbia Law Review* (special edition): 239–277.

Moone, J. 1993a. *Children in Custody 1991: Private Facilities*. Office of Juvenile Justice and Delinquency Prevention, Fact Sheet #2. Washington, DC: Office of Juvenile Justice and Delinquency Prevention.

———. 1993b. *Children in Custody 1991: Public Juvenile Facilities*. Office of Juvenile Justice and Delinquency Prevention, Fact Sheet #5. Washington, DC: Office of Juvenile Justice and Delinquency Prevention.

Mooney, J. 1994. *The Hidden Figure of Domestic Violence in North London*. London: Islington Council.

Moore, J. 1991. *Going Down to the Barrio: Homeboys and Homegirls in Change*. Philadelphia: Temple University Press.

Morash, M. 1983. "Gangs, Groups, and Delinquency." *British Journal of Criminology* 23: 309–335.

Morash, M., and L. Rucker. 1990. "A Critical Look at the Idea of Boot Camp As a Correctional Reform." *Crime and Delinquency* 36(2): 204–222.

Morash, M., and R. N. Haarr. 1995. "Gender, Workplace Problems, and Stress in Policing." *Justice Quarterly* 12: 113–140.

Morash, M., R. N Haarr, and L. Rucker. 1994. "A Comparison of Programming for Women and Men in U.S. Prisons in the 1980s." *Crime and Delinquency* 40(2): 197–221.

Morash, M., T. S. Bynum, and B. A. Koons. 1995. *Findings from the National Study of Innovative and Promising Programs for Women Offenders*. Rockville, MD: National Criminal Justice Reference Service.

———. 1998. *Women Offenders: Programming Needs and Promising Approaches*. National Institute of Justice Publication No. 171668. Washington, DC: National Institute of Justice.

Morello, K. B. 1986. *The Invisible Bar: The Woman Lawyer in America, 1638 to the Present*. New York: Random House.

Morgan, G. 1986. *Images of Organization*. Newbury Park, CA: Sage.

Morris, A. 1975. "The American Society of Criminology: A History, 1941–1974." *Criminology* 13: 123–165.

Morton, J. B. 1991. "Women Correctional Officers: A Ten Year Update." In *Change, Challenge and Choices: Women's Role in Modern Corrections*, edited by J. B. Morton. Laurel, MD: American Correctional Association.

Morton, J. B. 1998. *Complex Challenges, Collaborative Solutions: Programming for Adult and Juvenile Female Offenders*. Lanham, MD: American Correctional Association.

———, ed. 1991. *Change, Challenge and Choices: Women's Role in Modern Corrections*. Laurel, MD: American Correctional Association.

Moulds, E. F. 1980. "Chivalry and Paternalism: Disparities of Treatment in the Criminal Justice System." In *Women, Crime and Justice*, edited by S. K. Datesman and F. R. Scarpitti. New York: Oxford University Press.

Muir, W. 1977. *Police: Streetcorner Politicians*. Chicago: University of Chicago Press.

Mukherjee, S., B. Cook, and S. Leverett. 1998. *Australian Crime: Facts and Figures 1998*. Canberra: Australian Institute of Criminology.

Mukherjee, S., C. Carcach, and D. McDonald. 1998. *Law and Justice Issues, Indigenous Australians, 1994: Occasional Paper*. Canberra: Australian Institute of Criminology, Australian Bureau of Statistics.

Mullings, J., V. Brewer, and J. Marquart. 1998. "Research in Progress: HIV/AIDS Risk among Women Prisoners." *Corrections Now* 3(1): 4–5.

Muraskin, R., and T. Alleman. 1993. *It's a Crime: Women and Justice*. Englewood Cliffs, NJ: Regents/Prentice Hall.

Murphy, B. S., S. J. Stevens, R. A. McGrath, H. K. Wexler, and D. Reardon. 1998. "Women and Violence: A Different Look." In *Women and Substance Abuse: Gender Transparency,* edited by S. J. Stevens and H. K. Wexler. New York: Haworth Press.

Myers, J. E. B. 1998. *Legal Issues in Child Abuse and Neglect Practice,* 2nd ed. Thousand Oaks, CA: Sage.

Myers, M. A. 1979. "Offended Parties and Official Reactions: Victims and the Sentencing of Criminal Defendants." *Sociological Quarterly* 20: 529–540.

———. 1995. "Gender and Southern Punishment after the Civil War." *Criminology* 33(1): 17–46.

Myers, M. A., and J. Hagan. 1979. "Private and Public Trouble: Prosecutors and the Allocation of Court Resources." *Social Problems* 26(4): 439–451.

Naffine, N. 1987. *Female Crime: The Construction of Women in Criminology.* Sydney, Australia: Allen and Unwin.

Nagel, I., and J. Hagan. 1983. "Gender and Crime: Offense Patterns and Criminal Court Sanctions." In *Crime and Justice,* vol. 4, edited by M. Tonry and N. Morris. Chicago: University of Chicago Press.

Nagel, I., J. Cardascia, and C. Ross. 1980. "Institutional Sexism: The Case in Criminal Court." In *Discrimination in Organizations,* edited by R. Alvarez. San Francisco: Jossey-Bass.

Nagel, S. 1969. *The Legal Process from a Behavioral Perspective.* Homewood, IL: Dorsey Press

Nash, S. D. 1994. *Prostitution in Great Britain, 1485–1901.* Metuchen, NJ: Scarecrow Press.

National Center for Victims of Crime, <http://www.nvc.org/>, accessed 1 March 2000.

National Center for Women and Policing. 1998. *Equality Denied: The Status of Women in Policing, 1997.* Los Angeles: Feminist Majority Foundation Press.

National Center on Child Abuse and Neglect. 1988. *Executive Summary: Study of National Incidence and Prevalence of Child Abuse and Neglect.* Washington, DC: National Center on Child Abuse and Neglect.

National Center on Elder Abuse. 1997. *Types of Elder Abuse; Trends in Elder Abuse; Reporting Elder Abuse,* Elder Abuse Information Series #1, #2, and #3. Washington, DC: National Center on Elder Abuse. Also: <http://www.gwjapan.com/NCEA/basic/index.html>, accessed 1 March 2000.

National Center on Elder Abuse. 1998. *National Elder Abuse Incidence Study.* Washington, DC: National Center on Elder Abuse.

National Clearinghouse for the Defense of Battered Women. 1996. *When Battered Women Are Charged with Crime: A Resource Manual for Defense Attorneys and Expert Witnesses.* Philadelphia: National Clearinghouse for the Defense of Battered Women.

National Clearinghouse on Marital and Date Rape, <http://members.aol.com/ncmdr/index.html<, accessed 1 March 2000.

National Clearinghouse on Marital and Date Rape. 1998. *State Law Chart.* Berkeley, CA: National Clearinghouse on Marital and Date Rape.

National Commission on Correctional Health Care. 1995. *Standards for Health Services in Correctional Facilities.* Chicago: NCCHC.

National Committee on Violence. 1990. *Violence: Directions for Australia.* Canberra: Australian Institute of Criminology.

National Corrective Services Statistics Unit. 1998. *Prisoners in Australia, 1997.* Canberra: Australia Bureau of Statistics.

National Institute of Justice. 1998. *1997 Drug Use Forecasting: Annual Report on Adult and Juvenile Arrestees.* Washington, DC: U.S. Department of Justice.

National Institute on Alcohol Abuse and Alcoholism. 1990. *Alcohol and Women.* Alcohol Alert 10. Rockville, MD: U.S. Government Printing Office.

National Institute on Drug Abuse. 1996. *National Survey Results on Drug Use from the Monitoring the Future Study, 1975–1995.* Rockville, MD: U.S. Department of Health and Human Services.

National Organization for Victim Assistance. 1990. *Victim Rights and Services: A Legislative Directory 1988/1989.* Washington, DC: U.S. Department of Justice.

———. 1993. "A Chronology of the Victims' Rights Movement." *Nova Newsletter* 17: 4.

———. 1998. "Rights Amendment Sent to Senate." *Nova Newsletter* 18: 4.

National Victim Center and Crime Victim Research and Treatment Center. 1992. *Rape in America: A Report to the Nation.* Washington, DC: National Victim Center.

Neto, V., and L. M. Bainer. 1983. "Mother and Wife Locked Up: A Day with the Family." *Prison Journal* 3 (Autumn/Winter): 124–141.

Nettheim, G., H. McRae, and L. Beacroft. 1991. *Aboriginal Legal Issues: Commentary and Materials.* Sydney, Australia: Law Book Co.

Neville, J. F. 1995. *The Press, the Rosenbergs, and the Cold War*. Westport, CT: Praeger.

New York Task Force on Women in the Courts. 1986–87. "Report of the New York Task Force on Women in the Courts." *Fordham Urban Law Journal* 15: 11.

Newburn, T., and E. Stanko, eds. 1994. *Just Boys Doing Business? Men, Masculinities and Crime*. London: Routledge.

Noonan, S. 1993. "Strategies for Survival: Moving beyond the Battered Woman Syndrome." In *In Conflict with the Law: Women and the Canadian Justice System*, edited by E. Adelberg and C. Currie. Vancouver, BC: Press Gang Publishers.

Norland, S., and P. J. Mann. 1984. "Being Troublesome: Women on Probation." *Criminal Justice and Behavior* 2: 115–135.

Northern Ireland Office. 1997. *A Commentary on Northern Ireland Crime Statistics 1997*. Belfast: The Stationary Office.

NSW Bureau of Crime Statistics and Research. 1998. *New South Wales Criminal Courts Statistics 1997*. Sydney: NSW Bureau of Crime Statistics and Research.

Nugent, W. R. 1998 *Participation in Victim-Offender Mediation and Re-Offense: Successful Replications?* Knoxville: College of Social Work, University of Tennessee.

Nye, F. I. 1958. *Family Relationships and Delinquent Behavior*. New York: John Wiley.

O'Brien, D. G. 1996. "*Jeldness v. Pearce*: Will the Requirements of Title IX 'Handcuff' Prison Administrators?" *New England Journal on Criminal and Civil Confinement* 22: 73–112.

O'Brien, P. 1983. "The Kleptomania Diagnosis." *Journal of Social History* 17: 65–77.

O'Brien, R. 1987. "The Interracial Nature of Violent Crimes: A Reexamination." *American Journal of Sociology* 92: 817–835.

———. 1991. "Sex Ratios and Rape Rates: A Power-Control Theory." *Criminology* 29: 99–114.

Odem, M. 1995. *Delinquent Daughters: Protecting and Policing Adolescent Female Sexuality in the United States, 1885–1920*. Chapel Hill: University of North Carolina Press.

Odem, M., and S. Schlossman. 1991. "Guardians of Virtue: The Juvenile Court and Female Delinquency in Early 20th-Century Los Angeles." *Crime and Delinquency* 37(2): 186–203.

Office for Victims of Crime, <http://www.ojp. usdoj.gov/ovc/>, accessed 1 March 2000.

Office for Victims of Crime. 1998. *New Directions from the Field: Victims' Rights and Services for the 21st Century*. Washington, DC: Office of Justice Programs, U.S. Government Printing Office.

Office of Applied Studies. 1997. *Substance Use among Women in the United States*. Rockville, MD: U.S. Department of Health.

Office of Crime Statistics. 1998. *Crime and Justice in South Australia, 1997: Juvenile Justice*. Adelaide, South Australia: Office of Crime Statistics.

Office of Juvenile Justice and Delinquency Prevention. 1998. *Easy Access to Juvenile Court Statistics*. Washington, DC: Office of Juvenile Justice and Delinquency Prevention. Also: <http://www.ojjdp.ncjrs.org/facts/ezaccess.html#JCS>, accessed 8 August 2000.

Ogle, R. S., and S. Jacobs. Forthcoming. *Battered Women Who Kill: A Sociological Framework for Understanding Battering and the Use of Self-Defense*. Westport, CT: Greenwood Press.

O'Malley, P., and K. Carson. 1989. "Contemporary Australian Criminology." *Australian and New Zealand Journal of Sociology* 25: 333–355.

Osborn, D. R., D. Ellingworth, T. Hope, and A. Trickett. 1996. "Are Repeatedly Victimized Households Different?" *Journal of Quantitative Criminology* 12(2): 223–245.

Owen, B. A. 1985. "Race and Gender Relations among Prison Workers." *Crime and Delinquency* 31(1): 147–159.

———. 1998. *In The Mix: Struggle and Survival in a Women's Prison*. Albany: State University of New York Press.

Owen, B. A., and B. Bloom. 1995. "Profiling Women Prisoners: Findings from National Surveys and a California Sample." *Prison Journal* 75(2): 165–185.

Oxley, D. 1996. *Convict Maids: The Forced Migration of Women to Australia*. Melbourne, Australia: Cambridge University Press.

Painter, K., and D. Farrington. 1998. "Marital Violence in Great Britain and Its Relationship to Marital and Non-Marital Rape." *International Review of Victimology* 5(3–4): 257–276.

Paltrow, Lynn M. 1999. "Pregnant Drug Users, Fetal Persons, and the Threat to *Roe v. Wade*." *Albany Law Review* 62: 999–1055.

Parent, D., B. Auerbach, and K. Carlson, eds. 1992. *Compensating Crime Victims*. Washington, DC: U.S. Department of Justice.

Parker, R. N. 1998. "Alcohol, Homicide, and Cultural Context: A Cross-National Analysis of Gender-Specific Homicide Victimization." *Homicide Studies* 2(1): 6–30.

Pate, A., M. A. Wycoff, W. G. Skogan, and L. W. Sherman. 1986. *Reducing Fear of Crime in Hous-*

ton and Newark: A Summary Report. Washington, DC: Police Foundation.

Pear, R. 1987. "Women Reduce Lag in Earnings but Disparities with Men Remain." *New York Times* (4 September).

Pearson, E. 1924. "The Borden Case." In *Studies in Murder*. New York: Macmillan Co.

———. 1937. *Trial of Lizzie Borden: Edited, with a History of the Case*. Garden City, NY: Doubleday, Doran and Co.

Pearson, P. 1997. *When She Was Bad: Violent Women and the Myth of Innocence*. New York: Viking.

Pease, K., and G. Laycock. 1996. *Revictimization: Reducing the Heat on Hot Victims*. Washington, DC: U.S. Department of Justice, National Institute of Justice Research in Action Series.

Pernanen, K. 1991. *Alcohol in Human Violence*. New York: Guilford Press.

Philipson, I. 1993. *Ethel Rosenberg: Beyond the Myths*. New Brunswick, NJ: Rutgers University Press.

Phillips, J. N., and A. L. Gorzell. *Legendary Ladies of Texas—Bonnie Parker: "Tell them I don't smoke cigars."* <http://www.virtualtexan.com/readingroom/books/legend1.htm>, accessed 1 March 2000.

Pierce, J. L. 1995. *Gender Trials: Emotional Lives in Contemporary Law Firms*. Berkeley and Los Angeles: University of California Press.

Pike, D. 1992. "Women in Police Academy Training: Some Aspects of Organizational Response." In *The Changing Roles of Women in the Criminal Justice System*, edited by I. Moyer. Prospect Heights, IL: Waveland.

Pisciotta, A. 1982. "Saving the Children: The Promise and Practice of *Parens Patriae*, 1838–1898." *Crime and Delinquency* 29: 410–425.

Pizzey, E. 1973. *Scream Quietly or the Neighbours Will Hear*. Harmondsworth, England: Penguin.

Platt, A. M. 1969. *The Child Savers and the Invention of Delinquency*. Chicago: University of Chicago Press.

Poe-Yamagata, E., and J. A. Butts. 1996. *Female Offenders in the Juvenile Justice System*. Statistical Summary. Washington, DC: Office of Juvenile Justice and Delinquency Prevention.

Polisar, J., and D. Milgram. 1998. "Strategies That Work." *The Police Chief* (October): 42–54.

Polk, K. 1994. *When Men Kill: Scenarios of Masculine Violence*. Cambridge: Cambridge University Press.

Pollak, O. 1961. *The Criminality of Women*. Reprint ed. New York: A. S. Barnes and Co. Perpetua

Books. Orig. pub. 1950. Philadelphia: University of Pennsylvania Press.

Pollock, J. M. 1986. *Sex and Supervision: Guarding Male and Female Inmates*. New York: Greenwood Press.

———. 1998. *Counseling Women in Prison*. Newbury Park, CA: Sage Publications.

Pollock-Byrne, J. M. 1990. *Women, Prison, and Crime*. Pacific Grove, CA: Brooks/Cole Publishing Company.

Polonsky, S., S. Kerr, B. Harris, J. Gaiter, R. Fichtner, and M. G. Kennedy. 1994. *HIV Prevention in Prisons and Jails: Obstacles and Opportunities*. Washington, DC: U.S. Department of Health. Also: <http://kali.ucsf.edu/social/public_health/2098.2765.html>, accessed 1 March 2000.

Polvi, N., T. Looman, C. Humphries, and K. Pease. 1990. "Repeat Break and Enter Victimization: Time Course and Crime Prevention Opportunity." *Journal of Police Science and Administration* 17: 8–11.

Pope, K., and D. Pope. 1986. "Attitudes of Male Police Officers toward Their Female Counterparts." *The Police Journal* 59: 242–250.

Potter, C. B. 1995. "'I'll Go the Limit and Then Some': Gun Molls, Desire, and Danger in the 1930s." *Feminist Studies* 21(1): 41–66.

Prejean, H. 1993. *Dead Man Walking: An Eyewitness Account of the Death Penalty in the United States*. New York: Random House.

Prentky, R. A., R. A. Knight, and A. F. S. Lee. 1997. *Child Sexual Molestation: Research Issues*. Washington, DC: U.S. Department of Justice, Bureau of Justice Statistics.

President's Task Force on Victims of Crime. 1982. *Final Report*. Washington, DC: U.S. Government Printing Office.

Price, B. R., and N. Sokoloff, eds. 1995. *The Criminal Justice System and Women: Offenders, Victims, and Workers*, 2nd ed. New York: McGraw-Hill.

Price, M. 1997. "Can Mediation Produce Justice? A Restorative Justice Discussion for Mediators." In *ADR [Alternative Dispute Resolution] Report, News and Strategies for Alternative Dispute Resolution Practitioners* 1(13): 6–8.

Puzzanchera, C. 1998. *The Youngest Offenders, 1996*. Office of Juvenile Justice Fact Sheet. Washington, DC: U.S. Department of Justice, Office of Justice Programs.

Radford, J. 1989. "Women Policing: Contradictions Old and New." In *Women, Policing and Male Violence*, edited by J. J. Hanmer, J. Radford, and E. Stanko. London: Routledge.

Radford, J., and D. E. H. Russell. 1992. *Femicide*. Milton Keynes, England: Open University Press.

Radosh, R., and J. Milton. 1997. *The Rosenberg File*. New Haven: Yale University Press.

Raeder, M. 1993. "Gender and Sentencing: Single Moms, Battered Women and Other Sex-Based Anomalies in the Gender-Free World of Federal Sentencing Guidelines." *Pepperdine Law Review* 20(3): 905–990.

Rafter, N. H. 1982. "Hard Times: Custodial Prisons for Women and the Example of the New York State Prison for Women at Auburn, 1893–1933." In *Judge, Lawyer, Victim, Thief: Women, Gender Roles, and Criminal Justice*, edited by N. H. Rafter and E. A. Stanko. Boston: Northeastern University Press.

———. 1985a. "Gender, Prisons, and Prison History." *Social Science History* 9: 233–247.

———. 1985b. *Partial Justice: Women in State Prisons, 1800–1935*. Boston: Northeastern University Press.

———. 1990a. *Partial Justice: Women, Prisons, and Social Control*, 2d ed. New Brunswick: Transaction Publishers.

———. 1990b. "The Social Construction of Crime and Crime Control." *Journal of Research in Crime and Delinquency* 27(4): 376–389.

———. 1997. *Creating Born Criminals*. Urbana: University of Illinois Press.

Rafter, N. H., and E. A. Stanko, eds. 1982. *Judge, Lawyer, Victim, Thief: Women, Gender Roles, and Criminal Justice*. Boston: Northeastern University Press.

Rafter, N. H., and F. Heidensohn. 1995a. *International Feminist Perspectives in Criminology: Engendering a Discipline*. Buckingham, England: Open University Press.

———. 1995b. "Introduction: The Development of Feminist Perspectives on Crime." In *International Feminist Perspectives in Criminology: Engendering a Discipline*. Buckingham, England: Open University Press.

Ramelson, M. 1972. *The Petticoat Rebellion: A Century of Struggle for Women's Rights*. London: Lawrence and Wishart.

Randall, M., and L. Haskell. 1995. "Sexual Violence in Women's Lives: Findings from the Women's Safety Project, a Community-Based Survey." *Violence against Women* 1: 6–31.

Rapaport, E. 1991. "The Death Penalty and Gender Discrimination." *Law and Society Review* 25(2): 367–383.

———. 1996. "Capital Murder, Gender and the Domestic Discount." *Southern Methodist University Law Review* 49: 1507–1548.

Rasche, C. E. 1990. "Early Models for Contemporary Thought on Domestic Violence and Women Who Kill Their Mates: A Review of the Literature from 1895 to 1970." *Women and Criminal Justice* 1: 31–53.

Ratushny, L. 1997. *The Self-Defence Review: Final Report*. Ottawa: Department of Justice and Ministry of the Solicitor General.

Reaves, B. A. 1996. *Local Police Departments*. Washington, DC: Bureau of Justice Statistics.

———. 2000. *Federal Law Enforcement Officers, 1998*. Washington, DC: U.S. Department of Justice, Bureau of Justice Statistics.

Reckless, W. C., and B. A. Kay. 1967. *The Female Offender*. Consultants' Report. Washington, DC: President's Commission on Law Enforcement and Administration of Justice.

Reece, L. E. 1991. "Mothers Who Kill: Postpartum Disorders and Criminal Infanticide." *University of California Los Angeles Law Review* 38(3): 699–757.

Reeves, K. J. 1976. *The Trial of Patty Hearst*. San Francisco: Great Fidelity Press.

Reiss, A. J. 1960. "Sex Offenses: The Marginal Status of the Adolescent." *Law and Contemporary Problems* 25: 309–333.

Reitsma-Street, M. 1991. "A Review of Female Delinquency." In *The Young Offenders Act: A Revolution in Canadian Juvenile Justice*, edited by A. W. Leschied, P. G. Jaffe, and W. Willis. Toronto: University of Toronto Press.

———. 1993. "Canadian Youth Charges and Dispositions for Females before and after Implementation of the *Young Offenders Act*." *Canadian Journal of Criminology* 35(4): 437–548.

———. 1998. "Still Girls Learn to Care: Girls Policed to Care." In *Women's Caring: Feminist Perspectives on Social Welfare in Canada*, rev. ed., edited by C. Baines, P. Evans, and S. Neysmith. Toronto: Oxford University Press.

———. 1999. "Justice for Canadian Girls: A 1990's Update." *Canadian Journal of Criminology* 41(3): 335–363.

Renzetti, C. M. 1992. *Violent Betrayal: Partner Abuse in Lesbian Relationships*. Thousand Oaks, CA: Sage Publications, Inc.

———. 1998. "Connecting the Dots: Women, Public Policy, and Social Control." In *Crime Control and Women: Feminist Implications of Criminal Justice Policy*, edited by S. L. Miller. Thousand Oaks, CA: Sage.

Richardson, S. 1998. "Preferred Care of the Pregnant Inmate." In *Clinical Practice in Correctional Medicine*, edited by M. Puisis. St. Louis, MO: Mosby.

Richter, J. S. 1998. "Infanticide, Child Abandonment, and Abortion in Imperial Germany." *Journal of Interdisciplinary History* 28(4): 511–551.

Riger, S., and M. T. Gordon. 1991. "The Fear of Rape: A Study of Social Control." *Journal of Social Issues* 37: 71–92.

Ritchie, J. 1988. *Myra Hindley: Inside the Mind of a Murderess.* London: Angus Robertson.

Roberg, R. R., and J. Kuykendall. 1997. *Police Management,* 2d ed. Los Angeles: Roxbury Publishing Company.

Roberts, D. 1997. "Representing Race: Unshackling Black Motherhood." *Michigan Law Review* 95: 938–964.

Roberts, T. 1995. *Evaluation of the Victim-Offender Mediation Project. Final Report for the Solicitor General, Canada.* Langley, BC: Community Justice Initiatives Association.

Robinson, D., F. J. Porporino, and W. A. Millson. 1998. "A One-Day Snapshot of Inmates in Canada's Adult Correctional Facilities." *Juristat* 18(8): 1–11.

Rock, P. 1994. "The Social Organization of British Criminology." In *The Oxford Handbook of Criminology,* edited by R. Maguire, R. Morgan, and R. Reiner. Oxford: Oxford University Press.

———. 1996. *Reconstructing a Women's Prison: The Holloway Redevelopment Project, 1968–1988.* Oxford. England: Clarendon Press.

Rodgers, K. 1994. "Wife Assault: The Findings of a National Survey." *Juristat* 14(9): 1–22.

Rodgers, S. 1986. "Fetal Rights and Maternal Rights: Is There a Conflict?" *Canadian Journal of Women and the Law* 1(2): 456–469.

Rose, J. 1980. *Elizabeth Fry.* London: Macmillan.

Rosenbaum, J. 1989. "Family Dysfunction and Female Delinquency." *Crime and Delinquency* 35: 31–44.

Rosenbaum, M., and S. Murphy. 1990. "Women and Addiction: Process, Treatment and Outcome." In *National Institute on Drug Abuse Monograph 98,* pages 120–127. Rockville, MD: U.S. Government Printing Office.

Rosenberg, J., H. Perstadt, and W. R. F. Phillips. 1993. "Now That We Are Here: Discrimination, Disparagement, and Harassment at Work and the Experience of Women Lawyers." *Gender and Society* 7: 415–433.

Roseneil, S. 1995. *Disarming Patriarchy: Feminism and Political Action at Greenham.* Buckingham, England: Open University Press.

Ross, H. L. 1992. *Confronting Drunk Driving: Social Policy for Saving Lives.* New Haven: Yale University Press.

Rowe, G. S. 1985. "Women's Crime and Criminal Administration in Pennsylvania, 1763–1790." *Pennsylvania Magazine of History and Biography* 109(3): 335–368.

Russell, D. E. H. 1986. *The Secret Trauma: Incest in the Lives of Girls and Women.* New York: Basic Books.

———. 1990. *Rape in Marriage.* Bloomington: Indiana University Press.

Russell, M. P. 1994. "Too Little, Too Late, Too Slow: Compassionate Release of Terminally Ill Prisoners—Is the Cure Worse Than the Disease?" *Widener Journal of Public Law* 3(54): 1–57.

Russell, S. 1997. "Private Prisons for Private Profit." *Alternative Law Journal* 22(1): 7–9.

Ryan, W. 1971. *Blaming the Victim.* New York, Random House.

Ryckebusch, J. R., ed. 1993. *Proceedings, Lizzie Borden Conference, Bristol Community College, August 3–5, 1992.* Portland, ME: King Philip Publishing Co.

Ryerson, E. 1978. *The Best-Laid Plans: American's Juvenile Court Experiment.* New York: Hill and Wang.

Rynbrandt, L. J., and R. C. Kramer. 1995. "Hybrid Non-Women and Corporate Violence: The Silicone Breast Implant Case." *Violence against Women* 1: 206–227.

Sacco, V. F. 1990. "Gender, Fear and Victimization: A Preliminary Application of Power-Control Theory." *Sociological Spectrum* 10: 485–506.

Sacco, V. F., and H. Johnson. 1990. *Patterns of Criminal Victimization in Canada.* Ottawa: Minister of Supply and Services Canada.

Salmelainen, P., and C. Coumarelos. 1993. *Adult Sexual Assault in New South Wales.* Crime and Justice Bulletin No. 20. Sydney: New South Wales Bureau of Crime Statistics and Research.

Sampson, R. J., and J. H. Laub. 1992. "Crime and Deviance in the Life Course." *Annual Review of Sociology* 18: 63–84.

———. 1993. *Crime in the Making: Pathways and Turning Points Through Life.* Cambridge: Harvard University Press.

Sangster, J. 1993. "Pardon Tales from Magistrates Court: Women, Crime, and the Court in Peterborough County, 1920–50." *Canadian Historical Review* 74(2): 161–197.

Sarat, A. 1997. "Vengeance, Victims and the Identities of Law." *Social and Legal Studies* 6: 163–189.

Sarnoff, S. K. 1994. *A National Survey of State Crime Victim Compensation Programs: Polices and Ad-*

ministrative Methods. Ann Arbor, MI: University Microfilms International.

———. 1996. *Paying for Crime: The Policies and Possibilities of Crime Victim Reimbursement*. Westport, CT: Praeger Publishers.

Sarri, R. 1983. "Gender Issues in Juvenile Justice." *Crime and Delinquency* 29(3): 381–398.

Scalia, J. 1997. *Prisoner Petitions in the Federal Courts, 1980–1996*. Washington, DC: U.S. Department of Justice, Office of Justice Programs, Bureau of Justice Statistics.

Schafer, S. 1977. *Victimology: The Victim and His Criminal*. Reston, VA: Reston Publishing Company.

Schafran, L. H. 1990. "Overwhelming Evidence: Reports on Gender Bias in the Courts." *Trial* 28 (February).

Schechter, S. 1982. *Women and Male Violence: The Visions and Struggles of the Battered Women's Movement*. Boston: South End Press.

Schilit, R., G. Lie, and M. Montagne. 1990. "Substance Use As a Correlate of Violence in Intimate Lesbian Relationships." *Journal of Homosexuality* 19: 51–65.

Schlossman, S. 1977. *Love and the American Delinquent: The Theory and Practice of "Progressive" Juvenile Justice*. Chicago: University of Chicago Press.

Schlossman, S., and S. Wallach. 1978. "The Crime of Precocious Sexuality: Female Delinquency in the Progressive Era." *Harvard Educational Review* 48: 65–94.

Schmall, L. 1996. "Forgiving Guin Garcia: Women, the Death Penalty and Commutation." *Wisconsin Women's Law Journal* 11: 283–326.

Schmidt, J., and E. H. Steury. 1989. "Prosecutorial Discretion in Filing Charges in Domestic Violence Cases." *Criminology* 27(3): 487–510.

Schott, L. A. 1988. "The Pamela Rae Stewart Case and Fetal Harm: Prosecution or Prevention?" *Harvard Women's Law Journal* 11: 229–245.

Schroedel, J. R., S. Frisch, N. Hallamore, J. Peterson, and N. Vanderhorst. 1996. "The Joint Impact of Race and Gender on Police Department Employment Practices." *Women and Criminal Justice* 8(2): 59–77.

Schulte, R. 1994. *The Village in Court—Arson, Infanticide, and Poaching in the Court Records of Upper Bavaria, 1848–1910*. Cambridge: Harvard University Press.

Schulz, D. M. 1995. *From Social Worker to Crimefighter: Women in United States Municipal Policing*. Westport, CT: Praeger.

Schur, E. 1971. *Labeling Deviant Behavior*. New York: Harper and Row, Publishers.

———. 1984. *Labeling Women Deviant*. New York: McGraw-Hill Publishing Company.

Schweber, C. 1982. "The Government's Unique Experiment in Salvaging Women Criminals: Cooperation and Conflict in the Administration of a Women's Prison—The Case of the Federal Industrial Institution for Women at Alderson." In *Judge, Lawyer, Victim, Thief: Women, Gender Roles and Criminal Justice*, edited by N. H. Rafter and E. A. Stanko. Boston: Northeastern University Press.

———. 1984. "Beauty Marks and Blemishes: The Coed Prison As a Microcosm of Integrated Society." *Prison Journal* 64(1): 3–14.

Scottish Office. 1997. *Recorded Crime in Scotland 1997*. Edinburgh: The Scottish Office.

Scully, D. 1990. *Understanding Sexual Violence: A Study of Convicted Rapists*. Boston: Unwin Hyman Publishers.

Searles, P., and R. J. Berger, eds. 1995. *Rape and Society: Readings and the Problem of Sexual Assault*. Boulder, CO: Westview Press.

Sebba, L. 1996. *Third Parties: Victims and the Criminal Justice System*. Columbus: Ohio State University Press.

Sedlak, A. D., and D. D. Broadhurst. 1996. *Executive Summary of the Third National Incidence Study of Child Abuse and Neglect*. Washington, DC: U.S. Department of Health and Human Services and National Center on Child Abuse and Neglect.

Segal, L. 1990. *Slow Motion: Changing Masculinities, Changing Men*. London: Virago.

Segrave, K. 1992. *Women Serial and Mass Murderers: A Worldwide Reference, 1580 through 1990*. Jefferson, NC: McFarland.

Sereny, G. 1998. *Crimes Unheard*. Basingstoke, England: Macmillan.

Seryak, J. M. 1997. *Dear Teacher: If You Only Knew*. Bath, OH: The Dear Teacher Project.

Shaffer, M. 1997. "The Battered Woman Syndrome Revisited: Some Complicating Thoughts Five Years after *R. v. Lavallee*." *University of Toronto Law Journal* 47(1): 1–33.

Shapiro, A. 1996. *Breaking the Codes: Female Criminality in Fin-de-Siecle Paris*. Stanford: Stanford University Press.

Shaw, M. 1991. *The Release Study: Survey of Federally Sentenced Women in the Community*. Ottawa: Corrections Branch, Ministry of Solicitor General.

Sheehy, E. A. 1991. "Feminist Argumentation before the Supreme Court of Canada in *R. v. Seaboyer; R. v. Gayme.*" *Melbourne University Law Review* 18: 450–468.

———. 1994. "Developments in Canadian Law after *R. v. Lavallee.*" In *Women, Male Violence and the Law*, edited by J. Stubbs, Monograph Series No. 6. Sydney: University of Sydney, Institute of Criminology.

———. 1996. "Legalising Justice for All Women: Canadian Women's Struggle for a Democratic Rape Law Reform." *Australian Feminist Law Journal* 6: 87–113.

———. Forthcoming. "Review of the *Self-Defence Review.*" *Canadian Journal of Women and the Law* 12(1).

Shelden, R. G. 1981. "Sex Discrimination in the Juvenile Justice System: Memphis, Tennessee, 1900–1917." In *Comparing Male and Female Offenders*, M. Q. Warren, editor. Newbury Park, CA: Sage.

Sherman, L. J. 1975. "An Evaluation of Policewomen on Patrol in a Suburban Police Department." *Journal of Police Science and Administration* 3(4): 434–438.

Sherman, L. W. 1992. *Policing Domestic Violence: Experiments and Dilemmas.* New York: Free Press.

Sherman, L. W., and R. A. Berk. 1984. "The Specific Deterrent Effects of Arrest for Domestic Assault." *American Sociological Review* 49: 261–272.

Sherman, L. W., H. Strang, G. Barnes, J. Braithwaite, N. Inkpen, and M. Teh. 1998. *Experiments in Restorative Policing: A Progress Report to the National Police Research Unit.* Canberra, ACT: Law Program, Research School of Social Sciences, Australia National University.

Shichor, D. 1995. *Punishment for Profit: Private Prisons/Public Concerns.* Thousand Oaks, CA: Sage Publications.

Shilts, R. 1980. "Gay Police." *Police Magazine* (January): 32–33.

Shrage, L. 1994. *Moral Dilemmas of Feminism: Prostitution, Adultery, and Abortion.* London: Routledge.

Sikes, G. 1997. *8 Ball Chicks: A Year in the Violent World of Girl Gangsters.* New York: Anchor Books.

Silbert M. H., and A. M. Pines. 1982. "Entrance into Prostitution." *Youth and Society* 13(4): 471–500.

Simon, R. J. 1975. *Women and Crime.* Lexington, MA: D. C. Heath.

Simons, R. L., and L. B. Whitbeck. 1991. "Sexual Abuse As a Precursor to Prostitution and Victimization among Adolescent and Adult Homeless Women." *Journal of Family Issues* 12(3): 361–379.

Simpson, S. 1989. "Feminist Theory, Crime, and Justice." *Criminology* 27: 605–631.

———. 1991. "Caste, Class and Violent Crime: Explaining Differences in Female Offending." *Criminology* 29: 115–135.

Singer, M. I., J. Bussey, L. Y. Song, and L. Lunghofer. 1995. "The Psychosocial Issues of Women Serving Time in Jail." *Social Work* 40(1): 103–114.

Singer, M. I., M. K. Petchers, and D. Hussey. 1989. "The Relationship between Sexual Abuse and Substance Abuse among Psychiatrically Hospitalized Adolescents." *Child Abuse and Neglect* 13: 319–325.

Skolnick, J. H. 1966. *Justice without Trial.* New York: John Wiley and Sons.

Skolnick, J. H., and J. Fyfe. 1994. *Above the Law: Police and the Excessive Use of Force.* New York: Free Press.

Skrapec, C. A. 1993. "Female Serial Murder: An Evolving Criminality." In *Moving Targets*, edited by H. Birch. London: Virago Press.

Smart, C. 1976. *Women, Crime and Criminology.* London: Routledge Kegan Paul.

———. 1990. "Feminist Approaches to Criminology, or Post-Modern Woman Meets Atavistic Man." In *Feminist Perspectives in Criminology*, edited by L. Gelstorpe and A. Morris. Buckingham, England: Open University Press.

Smart, C., and B. Smart, eds. 1978. *Women, Sexuality, and Social Control.* London: Routledge.

Smith, B. L. 1994. *Terrorism in America: Pipe Bombs and Pipe Dreams.* Albany: State University of New York Press.

Smith, M. D., and M. A. Zahn, eds. 1999. *Homicide: A Sourcebook of Social Research.* Thousand Oaks, CA: Sage Publications.

Smykla, J. O. 1979. "Does Coed Prison Work?" *The Prison Journal* 59(1): 61–72.

Snell, T. L., and D. C. Morton. 1994. *Women in Prison.* Special Report. Washington, DC: Bureau of Justice Statistics.

Snyder, H. N., and M. Sickmund. 1999. *Juvenile Offenders and Victims: 1999 National Report.* Washington, DC: Office of Juvenile Justice and Delinquency Prevention, National Center for Juvenile Justice.

Sohn, E. F. 1994. "Antistalking Statutes: Do They Actually Protect Victims?" *Criminal Law Bulletin* 30: 124–136.

South, S. J., and R. B. Felson. 1990. "The Racial Patterning of Rape." *Social Forces* 69: 71–93.

Sparks, R. F. 1981. "Multiple Victimization: Evidence, Theory, and Future Research." In *Victims of Crime: A Review of Research Issues and Methods*. Washington, DC: U.S. Department of Justice, National Institute of Justice.

Spears, J. W., and C. C. Spohn. 1997. "The Effect of Evidence Factors and Victim Characteristics on the Prosecutors' Charging Decision in Sexual Assault Cases." *Justice Quarterly* 14: 501–524.

Spindel, D. J. 1989. *Crime and Society in North Carolina, 1663–1776*. Baton Rouge: Louisiana State University Press.

Spohn, C. 1994. "Crime and the Social Control of Blacks: Offender/Victim Race and the Sentencing of Violent Offenders." In *Inequality, Crime and Social Control*, edited by G. S. Bridges and M. A. Myers. Boulder, CO: Westview Press.

———. 1999. "Gender and Sentencing of Drug Offenders: Is Chivalry Dead?" *Criminal Justice Policy Review* 9: 365–399.

Spohn, C., and J. Horney. 1992. *Rape Law Reform: A Grass Roots Revolution and Its Impact*. New York: Plenum Press.

Spohn, C., J. Gruhl, and S. Welch. 1987. "The Impact of the Ethnicity and Gender of Defendants on the Decision to Reject or Dismiss Felony Charges." *Criminology* 25: 175–191.

Stanko, E. A. 1985. *Intimate Intrusions: Women's Experiences of Male Violence*. London: Routledge.

———. 1990. *Everyday Violence: How Women and Men Experience Sexual and Physical Danger*. London: Virago.

———. 1996. "Warnings to Women: Police Advice and Women's Safety in Britain." *Violence against Women* 2: 5–24.

Stanko, E. A., D. Crisp., C. Hale, and H. Lucraft. 1998. *Counting the Costs: Estimating the Impact of Domestic Violence in the London Borough of Hackney*. Swindon: Crime Concern.

Stanley, D. 1976. *Prisoners among Us*. Washington, DC: The Brookings Institute.

Statistics Canada, Canadian Centre for Justice Statistics. 1998. *Canadian Crime Statistics, 1997.* Ottawa: Ministry of Industry.

———. 1999. *A Graphical Overview of Crime and the Administration of Criminal Justice, Canada, 1997.* Ottawa: Ministry of Industry.

Steffensmeier, D. 1993. "National Trends in Female Arrests, 1960–1990: Assessment and Recommendations for Research." *Journal of Quantitative Criminology* 9(4): 411–441.

Steffensmeier, D., and E. Allan. 1996. "Gender and Crime: Toward a Gendered Theory of Female Offending." *Annual Review of Sociology* 22: 459–487.

Stojkovic, S., and R. Lovell. 1997. *Corrections: An Introduction*, 2nd ed. Cincinnati: Anderson Publishing Co.

Straus, M. A. 1977–78. "Wife Beating: How Common and Why?" *Victimology: An International Journal* 2(3–4): 443–448.

———. 1979. "Measuring Intrafamily Conflict and Violence: The Conflict Tactics (CT) Scale." *Journal of Marriage and the Family* 41: 75–88.

———. 1997. "Physical Assaults by Women Partners: A Major Social Problem." In *Women, Men and Gender: Ongoing Debates*, edited by M. R. Walsh. New Haven: Yale University Press.

Straus, M. A., and R. J. Gelles. 1986. "Societal Changes and Change in Family Violence from 1975 to 1985 as Revealed by Two National Surveys." *Journal of Marriage and the Family* 48: 465–479.

———. 1990. *Physical Violence in American Families: Risk Factors and Adaptations to Violence in 8,145 Families*. New Brunswick, NJ: Transaction.

Streib, V. 1990. "The Death Penalty for Female Offenders." *Cincinnati Law Review* 58(3): 845–880.

Stubbs, J. 1995. "'Communitarian' Conferencing and Violence against Women: A Cautionary Note." In *Wife Assault and the Canadian Criminal Justice System*, edited by M. Valverde, L. Macleod, and K. Johnson. Toronto: Centre of Criminology, University of Toronto.

———, ed. 1994. *Women, Male Violence and the Law*. Sydney: University of Sydney, Institute of Criminology.

Stubbs, J., and J. Tolmie. 1995. "Race, Gender and the Battered Woman Syndrome: An Australian Case Study." *Canadian Journal of Women and Law* 8(1): 122–158.

Sudow, D. 1965. "Normal Crimes: Sociological Features of the Penal Code in a Public Defender Office." *Social Problems* 12(3): 255–276.

Sulton, C., and R. Townsey. 1981. *Women in Policing: A Progress Report*. Washington, DC: Police Foundation.

Summers, A. 1975. *Damned Whores and God's Police: The Colonization of Women in Australia*. Melbourne, Australia: Penguin Books.

Surratt, H. L., and J. A. Inciardi. 1998. "Cocaine, Crack, and the Criminalization of Pregnancy." In *The American Drug Scene: An Anthology*, 2nd ed., edited by J. Inciardi and K. McElrath. Los Angeles: Roxbury Press.

Works Cited

Sutherland, E. H. 1940. "White-Collar Criminality." *American Sociological Review* 5: 1–12.

Swift, W., L. Maher, and S. Sunjic. 1999. "Transitions between Routes of Heroin Administration: A Study of Caucasian and Indo-Chinese Heroin Users in South West Sydney." *Addiction* 94(1): 71–82.

Szinovacz, M. E. 1983. "Using Couple Data As a Methodological Tool: The Case of Marital Violence." *Journal of Marriage and the Family* 45: 633–644.

Tannenbaum, F. 1938. *Crime and the Community.* New York: Ginn and Company.

Tanner, L. 1994. *Intimate Violence: Reading Rape and Torture in Twentieth-Century Fiction.* Bloomington: Indiana University Press.

Tatara, T., and L. Blumerman. 1996. *Summaries of the Statistical Data on Elder Abuse in Domestic Settings: An Exploratory Study of State Statistics for FY 93 and FY 94.* Washington, DC: National Center on Elder Abuse.

Taylor, C. S. 1993. *Girls, Gangs, Women and Drugs.* East Lansing: Michigan State University Press.

Tennenhouse, L. 1989. "Violence Done to Women on the Renaissance Stage." In *The Violence of Representation: Literature and the History of Violence*, edited by N. Armstrong and L. Tennenhouse. New York: Routledge.

Thomas, K. R. 1993. "How to Stop the Stalker: State Anti-Stalking Laws." *Criminal Law Bulletin* 29: 124–136.

Thomas, W. I. 1907. *Sex and Society.* Boston: Little Brown.

———. 1923. *The Unadjusted Girl.* New York: Harper and Row.

Tierney, K. J. 1982. "The Battered Women Movement and the Creation of the Wife Beating Problem." *Social Problems* 29(3): 208–220.

Tjaden, P., and N. Thoennes. 1998a. *Prevalence, Incidence, and Consequences of Violence against Women: Findings from the National Violence against Women Survey.* National Institute of Justice Research in Brief (November). NCJ 172837.

———. 1998b. *Stalking in America: Findings from the National Violence against Women Survey.* Washington, DC: U.S. Department of Justice and the Centers for Disease Control and Prevention.

Tolliver, R. M, L. A. Valle, C. A. Dopke, L. D. Serra, and J. S. Milner. 1998. "Child Physical Abuse." In *Violence in Intimate Relationships: Examining Sociological and Psychological Issues*, edited by N. A. Jackson and G. C. Oates. Boston: Butterworth-Heinemann.

Tolmie, J. 1997. "Pacific-Asian Immigrant and Refugee Women Who Kill Their Batterers: Telling Stories That Illustrate the Significance of Specificity." *Sydney Law Review* 19(4): 472–513.

Tong, R. 1984. *Women, Sex, and the* Law. Totowa, NJ: Rowman and Littlefield.

Tonry, M. H. 1996. *Sentencing Matters.* New York: Oxford University Press.

Tonry, M. H., and J. Q. Wilson, eds. 1990. *Drugs and Crime.* Chicago: University of Chicago Press.

Travisono, A. P., and M. Q. Hawkes, eds. 1995. *Building a Voice: 125 Years of History.* Lanham, MD: American Correctional Association.

Treherne, J. 1984. *The Strange History of Bonnie and Clyde.* New York: Stein and Bay Publishers.

Trilling, D. 1981. *Mrs. Harris: The Death of the Scarsdale Diet Doctor.* New York: Harcourt Brace Jovanovich.

Trojanowicz, R., and B. Bucqueroux. 1990. *Community Policing.* Cincinnati: Anderson.

Turk, A. T. 1982. *Political Criminality: The Defiance and Defense of Authority.* Beverly Hills, CA: Sage Publications.

Uchida, D. C. 1997. "The Development of American Policing: A Historical Overview." In *Critical Issues in Policing*, 3rd ed., edited by R. G. Dunham and G. P. Alpert. Prospect Heights, IL: Waveland Press.

Uggen, C., and C. Kruttschnitt. 1998. "Crime in the Breaking: Gender Differences in Desistance." *Law and Society Review* 32(2): 339–366.

Umbreit, M. S. 1994. *Victim Meets Offender: The Impact of Restorative Justice and Mediation.* Monsey, New York: Criminal Justice Press.

Umbreit, M. S., and R. B. Coates. 1994. *Victim-Offender Mediation: An Analysis of Programs in Four States of the U.S.* St. Paul: Center for Restorative Justice and Mediation, University of Minnesota.

U.S. Attorney General's Task Force against Domestic Violence. 1984. *Final Report.* Washington, DC: U.S. Government Printing Office.

U.S. Census Bureau. 1999. "Historical Poverty Tables—Families." <http://www.census.gov/hhes/poverty/histpov/hstpov13.html>, accessed 1 July 1999.

U.S. Department of Health and Human Services, Substance Abuse and Mental Health Services Administration. 1999. *National Household Survey on Drug Abuse: Main Findings, 1997.* Washington, DC: U.S. Department of Health and Human Services.

———. 1998. *Child Maltreatment 1996: Reports from the States to the National Child Abuse and Neglect Data System.* Washington, DC: U.S. Government Printing Office.

———. 1999. *Child Maltreatment 1997: Reports from the States to the National Child Abuse and Neglect Data System*. Washington, DC: U.S. Government Printing Office.

U.S. Department of Justice. 1997. *Correctional Populations in the United States, 1996*. Washington, DC: U.S. Department of Justice.

———. 1998. *Legal Interventions in Family Violence: Research Findings and Policy Implications*. Washington, DC: U.S. Department of Justice.

———. n.d. *Attorney General Janet Reno*. <http://www.usdoj.gov/ag/jreno.html>, accessed 1 March 2000.

U.S. Department of Justice, Federal Bureau of Investigation. 1981. *Crime in the United States 1980: Uniform Crime Reports*. Washington, DC: U.S. Government Printing Office.

———. 1986. *Crime in the United States 1985: Uniform Crime Reports*. Washington, DC: U.S. Government Printing Office.

———. 1991. *Crime in the United States 1990: Uniform Crime Reports*. Washington, DC: U.S. Government Printing Office.

———. 1994. *Crime in the United States 1993: Uniform Crime Reports*. Washington, DC: U.S. Government Printing Office.

———. 1995. *Crime in the United States 1994: Uniform Crime Reports*. Washington, DC: U.S. Government Printing Office.

———. 1996. *Crime in the United States 1995: Uniform Crime Reports*. Washington, DC: U.S. Government Printing Office.

———. 1997. *Crime in the United States 1996: Uniform Crime Reports*. Washington, DC: U.S. Government Printing Office.

———. 1998. *Crime in the United States 1997: Uniform Crime Reports*. Washington, DC: U.S. Government Printing Office.

———. 1999. *Crime in the United States 1998: Uniform Crime Reports*. Washington, DC: U.S. Government Printing Office.

U.S. Department of Labor. 1997. *National Census of Fatal Occupational Injuries, 1996*. Washington, DC: U.S. Department of Labor.

U.S. General Accounting Office. 1996. *Private and Public Prisons: Studies Comparing Operational Costs and/or Quality of Service*. Washington, DC: U.S. General Accounting Office.

———. 1999. *Women in Prison: Issues and Challenges Confronting U.S. Correctional Systems*. GAO/GGD-00-22. Washington, DC: U.S. General Accounting Office.

U.S. Office of the Inspector General. 1995. *The Tailhook Report*. New York: St. Martin's Press.

U.S. Supreme Court. 1998. *Supreme Court Plus: Sandra Day O'Connor Biographical Information*. <http://www.usscplus.com/info/justices.htm>, accessed 1 March 2000.

Ussher, J. 1991. *Women's Madness: Misogyny or Mental Illness?* Amherst: University of Massachusetts Press.

Van Dyke, J. M. 1977. *Jury Selection Procedures: Our Uncertain Commitment to Representative Panels*. Cambridge: Ballinger.

Van Maanen, J. 1973. "Observations on the Making of Policemen." *Human Organization* 32: 407–418.

Van Ness, D., and K. H. Strong. 1997. *Restoring Justice*. Cincinnati: Anderson Publishing Company.

Van Sickel, R. W. 1998. *Not a Particularly Different Voice: The Jurisprudence of Sandra Day O'Connor*. New York: P. Lang.

Vanburkleo, S. F. 1994. "'To Bee Rooted Out of Her Station': The Ordeal of Anne Hutchinson." In *American Political Trials*, edited by M. R. Belknap. Westport, CT: Praeger Publishers.

Vedder, C. B., and D. B. Sommerville. 1970. *The Delinquent Girl*. Springfield, IL: Charles C. Thomas.

Vetter, H. J., and G. R. Perlstein. 1991. *Perspectives on Terrorism*. Belmont, CA: Wadsworth Publishing Company.

Victims' Rights Sourcebook. <http://www.ncvc.org/law/SBOOK/>, accessed 1 March 2000.

Walker, L. 1984. *The Battered Woman Syndrome*. New York: Springer.

Walker, S. 1977. *A Critical History of Police Reform: The Emergence of Professionalization*. Lexington, MA: Lexington Books.

———. 1985. "Racial Minority and Female Employment in Policing: The Implications of Glacial Change." *Crime and Delinquency* 31(4): 555–571.

Walklate, S. 1995a. "Criminology, Victimology and Feminism." In *Gender and Crime: An Introduction*, edited by S. Walklate, chapter 1. New York: Prentice Hall.

———. 1995b. *Gender and Crime: An Introduction*. London: Prentice Hall/Harvester Wheatsheaf.

———. 1997. "Risk and Criminal Victimization: A Modernist Dilemma?" *British Journal of Criminology* 37(1): 35–45.

Wallace, A. 1986. *Homicide: The Social Reality*. Sydney, Australia: New South Wales Bureau of Crime Statistics and Research.

Wallace, H. 1998. *Victimology: Legal, Psychological, and Social Perspectives*. Boston: Allyn and Bacon.

Wallach, A., and Rubin, L. 1971. "The Premenstrual Syndrome and Criminal Responsibility." *University of California, Los Angeles, Law Review* 19: 209–312.

Waller, P. A., and F. C. Blow. 1995. "Women, Alcohol, and Driving." In *Alcoholism and Women*, edited by M. Galanter; vol. 12 of *Recent Developments in Alcoholism*. New York: Plenum Press.

Walsh, A. 1987. "The Sexual Stratification Hypothesis and Sexual Assault in Light of the Changing Conceptions of Race." *Criminology* 25: 153–173.

Ward, D., M. Jackson, and R. Ward. 1979. "Crimes of Violence by Women." In *The Criminology of Deviant Women*, edited by F. Adler and R. Simon. Boston: Houghton Mifflin.

Warr, M. 1984. "Fear of Victimization: Why Are Women and the Elderly More Afraid?" *Social Science Quarterly* 65: 681–702.

Warshaw, R. 1988. *I Never Called It Rape*. New York: Harper and Row.

Watterson, K. 1995. *Women in Prison: Inside the Concrete Womb*, rev. ed. Boston: Northeastern University Press.

Weaver, J. C. 1995. *Crimes, Constables, and Courts: Order and Transgression in a Canadian City, 1816–1970*. Buffalo: McGill-Queens University Press.

Weidensall, J. 1916. *The Mentality of the Criminal Woman*. Baltimore: Warwick and York.

Weinberg, L., and W. L. Eubank. 1987. "Italian Women Terrorists." *Terrorism: An International Journal* 9(3): 241–262.

Weisburd, D., S. Wheeler, E. Waring, and N. Bode. 1991. *Crimes of the Middle Classes: White Collar Offenders in the Federal Courts*. New Haven: Yale University Press.

Weithorn, L. A. 1988. "Mental Hospitalization of Troublesome Youth: An Analysis of Sky-Rocketing Admission Rates." *Stanford Law Review* 40: 753–838.

Welles, D., G. P. Falkin, and N. Jainchill. 1998. "Current Approaches to Drug Treatment for Women Offenders." *Journal of Substance Abuse Treatment* 15(2): 151–163.

Wellisch, J., M. D. Anglin, and M. Prendergast. 1994. "Treatment Strategies for Drug-Abusing Women Offenders." In *Drug Treatment and the Criminal Justice System*, edited by J. Inciardi. Thousand Oaks, CA: Sage Publications.

Wexler, J. G., and D. D. Logan. 1983. "Sources of Stress among Women Police Officers." *Journal of Police Science and Administration* 11: 46–53.

Whatley, M. A, 1996. "Victim Characteristics Influencing Attributions of Responsibility to Rape Victims: A Meta-Analysis." *Aggression and Violent Behavior* 1(2): 81–95.

Wheeler, K. H. 1997. "Infanticide in Nineteenth-Century Ohio." *Journal of Social History* 31: 407–418.

White, P.; C. Cullen, and Minchin, M. 2000. "Prison Population Brief; England and Wales: February 2000." London: Home Office Research Development and Statistics Directorate. Also: <http://www.homeoffice.gov.uk/rds/areas/prisf.htm>, accessed 20 June 2000.

White, S. E., and K. E. Marino. 1983. "Job Attitudes and Police Stress: An Exploratory Study of Causation." *Journal of Police Science and Administration* 11: 264–274.

Widom, C. S. 1978. "An Empirical Classification of Female Offenders." *Criminal Justice and Behavior* 5(1): 35–52.

———. 1995. *Victims of Childhood Sexual Abuse—Later Criminal Consequences*. Research in Brief Series. Washington, DC: National Institute of Justice, U.S. Department of Justice.

Wiebe, R., and Y. Johnson. 1998. *Stolen Life: The Journey of a Cree Woman*. Toronto: Knopf Canada.

Wilczynski, A. 1997. *Child Homicide*. London: Greenwich Medical Media Ltd.

Wilsnack, S. C., and R. W. Wilsnack. 1995. "Drinking and Problem Drinking in U.S. Women: Patterns and Recent Trends." In *Alcoholism and Women*, edited by M. Galanter; vol. 12 of *Recent Developments in Alcoholism*. New York: Plenum Press.

Wilson, J. Q. 1968. *Varieties of Police Behavior*. Cambridge: Harvard University Press.

Wilson, J. Q., and R. J. Herrnstein. 1985. *Crime and Human Nature*. New York: Simon and Schuster.

Wilson, N. K. 1999. "Taming Women and Nature: The Criminal Justice System and the Creation of Crime in Salem Village." In *It's a Crime: Women and Justice*, edited by R. Muraskin and T. Alleman. Englewood Cliffs, NJ: Prentice-Hall.

Winick, C., and P. M. Kinsie. 1971. *The Lively Commerce: Prostitution in the United States*. Chicago: Quadrangle Books.

Wolfe, D. A. 1985. "Child-Abusive Parents: An Empirical Review and Analysis." *Psychological Bulletin* 97: 462–482.

Wolfgang, M. E. 1958. *Patterns in Criminal Homicide*. New York: John Wiley.

Wolfgang, M. E., and F. Ferracuti. 1967. *The Subculture of Violence*. London: Tavistock.

Wolfgang, M. E., R. Figlio, and T. Sellin. 1972. *Delinquency in a Birth Cohort*. Chicago: University of Chicago Press.

Wooley, S. C. 1993. "Recognition of Sexual Abuse: Progress and Backlash." *Eating Disorders* 1: 298–314.

Worden, A. P. 1993. "The Attitudes of Women and Men in Policing: Testing Conventional and Contemporary Wisdom." *Criminology* 31(2): 203–241.

Worden, R. 1989. "Situational and Attitudinal Explanations of Police Behavior." *Law and Society Review* 26: 667–771.

Wright, J. A., A. G. Burgess, A. W. Burgess, A. T. Laszlo, G. O. McCary, and J. E. Douglas. 1996. "A Typology of Interpersonal Stalking." *Journal of Interpersonal Violence* 11: 487–502.

Wyatt, G. E., D. Guthrie, and C. M. Notgrass. 1992. "Differential Effects of Women's Sexual Abuse and Subsequent Sexual Revictimization." *Journal of Consulting and Clinical Psychology* 60: 167–173.

Wynter, S. 1987. "WHISPER: Women Hurt in Systems of Prostitution Engaged in Revolt." In *Sex Work: Writings by Women in the Sex Industry*, edited by F. Delacoste and P. Alexander. Minneapolis: Cleis Press.

Yllo, K. 1993. "Through a Feminist Lens: Gender, Power, and Violence." In *Current Controversies on Family Violence*, edited by R. Gelles and D. Loseke. Newbury Park, CA: Sage Publications, Inc.

Yllo, K., and M. L. Bograd. 1988. *Feminist Perspectives on Wife Abuse*. Newbury Park, CA: Sage.

Young, L. A. 1996. *Adam and Eve: Who is Guilty, Who Is Innocent?* <http://members.aol.com/wheregod/chapters/adameve.htm>, accessed 25 April 2000.

Young, M. A. 1997. "Victim Rights and Victim Services: A Modern Saga." In *Victims of Crime*, 2d ed., edited by R. C. Davis, A. J. Lurigio, and W. G. Skogan. Thousand Oaks, CA: Sage.

Young, V. 1992. "Fear of Victimization and Victimization Rates among Women: A Paradox." *Justice Quarterly* 9: 419–442.

Zaplin, R. T. 1998. *Female Offenders: Critical Perspectives and Effective Interventions*. Gaithersburg, MD: Aspen Publishers.

Zedner, L. 1991. *Women, Crime and Custody in Victorian England*. Oxford, England: Clarendon Press.

———. 1995. "Wayward Sisters: The Prison for Women." In *The Oxford History of the Prison:*

The Practice of Punishment in Western Society, edited by N. Morris and D. J. Rothman. New York: Oxford University Press.

Zehr, H. 1990. *Changing Lenses: A New Focus for Crime and Justice*. Scottsdale, PA: Herald Press.

Zietz, D. 1981. *Women Who Embezzle or Defraud: A Study of Convicted Felons*. New York: Praeger.

Zimmer, L. E. 1986. *Women Guarding Men*. Chicago: University of Chicago Press.

Zlotnick, C., A. L. Zakriski, M. T. Shea, E. Costello, A. Begin, T. Pearlstein, and E. Simpson. 1996. "The Long-Term Sequelae of Sexual Abuse: Support for a Complex Posttraumatic Stress Disorder." *Journal of Traumatic Stress* 9: 195–205.

Zupan, L. L. 1986. "Gender-Related Differences in Correctional Officers' Perceptions and Attitudes." *Journal of Criminal Justice* 14: 349–361.

———. 1992. "Men Guarding Women: An Analysis of the Employment of Male Correction Officers in Prisons for Women." *Journal of Criminal Justice* 20: 297–309.

Legal Cases and Legislation

Australia

Lane (unreported, N.T. Sup.Ct., May 29, 1980).

R. v. Dennis Narjic (unreported, N.T. Sup. Ct., 1988 at 24–26).

Canada

An Act to Amend the Criminal Code; S.C. 1997, c. C-30.

An Act to Amend the Young Offenders Act, the Criminal Code, the Penitentiary Act and the Prisons and Reformatories Act, R.S.C. 1985 (ed. Supp.), c. 24.

An Act to Amend the Young Offenders Act and the Criminal Code; S.C. 1992, c. 11.

An Act to Amend the Young Offenders Act and the Criminal Code; S.C. 1995, c. 19.

Borowski v. The Queen, 1 S.C.R. 342 (1989); S.C.J. No. 14. (S.C.C.) (1989).

Juvenile Delinquents Act, R.S.C., 1970, c. J-3.

Lavallee v. R. [1990], 55 C.C.C. (3d) 97 (S.C.C.).

Morgentaler v. The Queen, 1 S.C.R. 30 (S.C.C.) (1988).

R. v. Darrach, 38 O.R. (3d) 1 (C.A.) (1998).

R. v. Forsythe, 2 S. C.R. 268 (1980).

R. v. Lavallee, 1 S.C.R. 852 (S.C.C.) (1990).

R. v. O'Connor, 44 C.R. (4th) 1 (S.C.C.) (1995*)*.

R. v. Seaboyer; R. v. Gayme, 2 S.C.R. 577 (1991).

Works Cited

Re A., 28 R.F.L. (3d) 288 (Ont. U.F.C.) (1990).

Re Baby R., 15 R.F.L. (B.C.S.C.) (1988).

Winnipeg Child and Family Services (NorthWest Area) v. G. (D.F.), 3 S.C.R. 925; S.C.J. No. 92 (S.C.C.) (1997).

Young Offenders Act, R.S.C. 1985, c. Y-1.

United States

Bounds v. Smith, 430 U.S. 817 (1977).

Bradwell v. Illinois, 83 U.S. 130, 140 (1873).

Bragdon v. Abbott, 118 Sup. Ct. 2196 (1998).

Buck v. Bell, Superintendent, 274 U.S. 200 (1927).

Canterino v. Wilson, 546 F. Supp. 174 [W.D. Ky. 1982, vacated on other grounds, 869. F. 2d 948 (6th Cir. 1989)].

Carrigan v. Delaware, 957 F. Supp. 1376, 1390 (D. Del. 1997).

Craig v. Boren, 429 U.S. 190 (1976).

Dothard v. Rawlinson, 433 U.S. 321 (1977).

Estelle v. Gamble, 429 U.S. 97 (1976).

Ex Parte Hull, 312 U.S. 546 (1941).

Fisher v. Goord, 981 F. Supp. 140, 174–75 (W.D. N.Y. 1997).

Forts v. Ward, 621 F. 2d 1210 (2d Cir. 1980).

Geduldig v. Aiello, 417 U.S. 484 (1974).

Glover v. Johnson, 478 F. Supp. 1075 (E.D. Mich. 1979). The case continued: *See* Case No. 95-1521:96-1931, United States Court of Appeals for the Sixth Circuit, 2000 U.S. App. LEXIS 2561, February 17, 2000.

Griggs v. Duke Power Co., 401 U.S. 424 (1971).

Gunther v. Iowa State Men's Reformatory, 612 F. 2d 1079 (8th Cir. 1980).

Harris v. Forklift Systems, Inc., 114 Sup. Ct. 367 (1993).

J.E.B. v. Alabama ex Rel. T.B., 511 U.S. 127 (1994).

Jeldness v. Pearce, 30 F. 3d 1220 (9th Cir. 1994).

Johnson v. Avery, 393 U.S. 483 (1969).

Jordan v. Gardner, 986 F. 2d 1521 (9th Cir. 1993).

Klinger v. Department of Corrections, 31 F. 3d 727 (8th Cir. 1994).

Lewis v. Casey, 116 Sup. Ct. 2174 (1996).

Meritor Savings Bank FSB v. Vinson, 106 Sup. Ct. 2399 (1986).

Mitchell v. Untreiner, 421 F. Supp. 886 (N.D. Fla. 1976).

Monmouth County Correctional Institution Inmates v. Lanzaro, 834 F. 2d 326 (3d Cir. 1987).

Niantic West v. Manson, Settlement, No. H83-366 (D. Conn., May 9, 1983).

Pargo v. Elliott, 894 F. Supp. 1243 (S.D. Iowa 1995).

Pennsylvania Department of Corrections v. Yeskey, 118 Sup. Ct. 1952 (1998).

People v. Liberta, Court of Appeals for New York, 64 N.Y. 2d 152, 474 N.E. 2d 567, 485 N.Y.S. 2d 207 (1984).

Planned Parenthood v. Casey, 505 U.S. 833 (1992).

Prison Litigation Reform Act (1995): Public Law 104–134, amending 18 U.S.C. 3626.

Richardson v. McKnight, 117 Sup. Ct. 2100 (1997).

Roe v. Wade, 410 U.S. 113, 93 Sup. Ct. 705, 35 L. ed. 2d 147 (1973).

Sandin v. Conner, 115 Sup. Ct. 305 (1994).

State v. Michaels, 642 A. 2d 1372 (Sup. Ct. of New Jersey, 1994).

Taylor v. Louisiana, 419 U.S. 522 (1975).

United States v. Virginia, 116 Sup. Ct. 2264 (1996).

Victims of Crime Act (1984): Public Law 104–235.

Victims' Rights and Restitution Act of 1990: Public Law 101–647.

Victim Witness Protection Act of 1982: Public Law 97–291.

Webster v. Reproductive Health Services, 429 U.S. 490 (1989).

West v. Virginia Department of Corrections, 847 F. Supp. 402 (W.D. Va. 1994).

Whitner v. South Carolina, 523 U.S. 1145 (1998).

Whitner v. State, 328 Sup. Ct. 1, 429 S.E. 2d 777 (1997).

Women Prisoners of the District of Columbia Dept. of Corrections v. District of Columbia, 93 F. 3d 910 (1996), Certiorari Denied. April 28, 1997, 1997 U.S. App. LEXIS 2686.

INDEX

See also The Alphabetical List of Entries on page xv.

NICOLE HAHN RAFTER is a professor in the Law, Policy, and Society Program at Northeastern University. She also serves on the editorial boards of *Criminology, Punishment and Society,* and *Law and History Review.* Rafter has written and cowritten numerous books on criminological issues, including *Shots in the Mirror: Crime Films and Society (2000); Prisons in America: A Reference Handbook (1999); Creating Born Criminals (1997); International Feminist Perspectives in Criminology: Engendering a Discipline (1995); Partial Justice: Women, Prisons, and Social Control (1990);* and *Judge, Lawyer, Victim, Thief: Women, Gender Roles, and Criminal Justice (1982).* Rafter holds a Ph.D. in criminal justice from the State University of New York, Albany and was recently elected a Fellow of the American Society of Criminology.